CHICAGO PUBLIC LIBRARY
REF .TURE AND LANGUAGE DIVISION
T. ATURE INFORMATION CENTER
400 SOUTH STATE STREET
CHICAGO, ILLINOIS 60605

REF
PA
6281
.S8
C53
1996

HWLCLT

Chicago Public Library

R012920 345

Cicero : pro P. Svlla oratio.

D1293450

CAMBRIDGE CLASSICAL TEXTS AND
COMMENTARIES

EDITORS

J. DIGGLE   E. W. HANDLEY   H. D. JOCELYN
M. D. REEVE   D. N. SEDLEY   R. J. TARRANT

30

CICERO: PRO P. SVLLA ORATIO

CICERO

PRO P. SVLLA ORATIO

EDITED WITH INTRODUCTION
AND COMMENTARY

BY

D. H. BERRY

Lecturer in Classics
University of Leeds

CAMBRIDGE
UNIVERSITY PRESS

Published by the Press Syndicate of the University of Cambridge
The Pitt Building, Trumpington Street, Cambridge CB2 IRP
40 West 20th Street, New York, NY 10011–4211, USA
10 Stamford Road, Oakleigh, Melbourne 3166, Australia

© Cambridge University Press 1996

First published 1996
Printed in Great Britain by Redwood Books, Trowbridge, Wiltshire

A catalogue record for this book is available from the British Library

Library of Congress cataloguing in publication data

Cicero, Marcus Tullius.
Cicero: pro P. Sulla oratio / edited with introduction
and commentary by D. H. Berry.
p.   cm.—(Cambridge classical texts and
commentaries; 30)
Includes index.
ISBN 0 521 48174 0 (hardback)
1. Sulla, Publius Cornelius, d. 45 BC.   2. Rome – History –
Conspiracy of Catiline, 65–62 BC.   3. Speeches, addresses, etc.,
Latin.
I. Berry, D. H.   II. Title.   III. Series.
PA6281.S8C53   1996
875'.01—dc20   95-1196 CIP

ISBN 0 521 48174 0 hardback

TO
R. G. M. NISBET

CHICAGO PUBLIC LIBRARY
LITERATURE AND LANGUAGE DIVISION
LITERATURE INFORMATION CENTER
400 SOUTH STATE STREET
CHICAGO, ILLINOIS 60605

R0129261145

CHICAGO PUBLIC LIBRARY
LITERATURE AND LANGUAGE DIVISION
LITERATURE INFORMATION CENTER
400 SOUTH STATE STREET
CHICAGO, ILLINOIS 60605

CONTENTS

PREFACE

Cicero was the greatest orator of antiquity;[1] and antiquity
was a period in which oratory was held to be of no slight
importance. Yet of the fifty-eight extant speeches of Cicero,
this, the *pro Sulla*, is only the fifth this century to be the
subject of a full-scale scholarly commentary in English: its
distinguished predecessors are R. G. Austin's *pro Caelio*
(Oxford 1933, subsequently revised), R. G. Nisbet's *de Domo
sua* (Oxford 1939), R. G. M. Nisbet's *in Pisonem* (Oxford
1961) and T. E. Kinsey's *pro Quinctio* (Sydney 1971). In languages other than English there have been substantial
modern commentaries on just three speeches: on *pro Archia*
by H. and K. Vretska (Darmstadt 1979), on *pro Murena* by
J. Adamietz (Darmstadt 1989) and on *pro Rabirio Postumo*
by C. Klodt (Stuttgart 1992). Nineteenth-century school
editions are of course ubiquitous, in German as in English, but for the vast majority of the speeches, most
conspicuously the Verrines, Catilinarians, *pro Milone* and
the Philippics, there exists no satisfactory commentary. It
would be wrong to infer, however, that little progress has
been made in Ciceronian studies. Over the past thirty
years important advances have been made in every area,
most obviously perhaps in the field of political history, but
also for example in colometry and textual criticism. There
has been a steady stream of books on Cicero, by no means
all biographies; now in the 1990s this threatens to become a
flood. Some of this work is devoted to specific speeches. W.
Stroh's *Taxis und Taktik* (Stuttgart 1975) and C. J. Classen's
Recht-Rhetorik-Politik (Darmstadt 1985) consist of highly
pertinent studies of individual speeches, most of which

[1] Cf. Quint. *Inst.* 10.1.105–12.

ix

have no adequate commentary, and B. W. Frier's *The Rise of the Roman Jurists* (Princeton 1985) is an original and appropriate treatment of *pro Caecina*, the best commentary on which dates from 1847. Translations, when done well, are also valuable works of scholarship. Special mention should be made of D. R. Shackleton Bailey's translation of the *post reditum* speeches and the Philippics into English, and M. Fuhrmann's of all the speeches into German.

But what scholars now need above all are good, detailed, up-to-date commentaries covering all the relevant fields, history, text and syntax as well as rhetoric and style. There is a danger that without such commentaries to refer to, the quality of the more general interpretative works which are being produced may suffer. The need for commentaries is naturally most pressing for the speeches which have been most neglected, and it is this category to which *pro Sulla* belongs. The speech has received no commentary of note since J. S. Reid's school edition of 1882 (Pitt Press Series), a book which admirably served the purpose for which it was written, and often of use to me in the earlier stages of my work, but precluded by its date, scale and narrow focus from being of more than limited value today. Similarly, there has been no satisfactory edition of the text, since neither A. C. Clark (Oxford Classical Text 1911) nor H. Kasten (Teubner 1933[1], 1949[2], 1966[3]) collated more than two (or possibly three, in the case of Clark) of the manuscripts they cited. There does exist a fairly recent translation by C. Macdonald in the Loeb series (1977), written in an attractive, readable style, but let down by many errors and misunderstandings. The speech was delivered in 62 BC when Cicero was at the height of his political career, with his consulship behind him but his exile still well in the future. It is one of his most lively and, for reasons which I will explain in my introduction, most sensational speeches. My aim has been to provide a comprehensive treatment for the use of scholars and advanced students. For the convenience of readers who will wish only to dip into the book (and at the risk of causing irritation to others), copious cross-references have been provided. Those who miss a translation should use Macdonald's Loeb, which is corrected where necessary in the commentary, where all points of interpretation are in any case fully discussed. To do justice to all aspects of the speech has inevitably been a difficult task. How far I have succeeded, if at all, will be for the reader to decide.

A first version of the introduction and commentary was written as a D. Phil. thesis at the University of Oxford during 1987–91. In the two years which followed my move to the University of Leeds in 1991 the edition was prepared and the introduction and commentary extensively revised; by September 1993 all was complete. For help and guidance over these six years I owe a profound debt of gratitude first to my supervisors, then to my examiners, and finally to the editors of the series. The thesis was supervised by Professor R. G. M. Nisbet and, for one term each, by Dr M. T. Griffin and Dr (now Professor) M. Winterbottom. I have benefited enormously from the learning and kindness of all three, but my debt is greatest to Robin Nisbet, and it gives me great pleasure now to be able to dedicate my book to him. My examiners Professor A. E. Douglas and Dr (now Professor) J. G. F. Powell made a number of helpful suggestions, the latter providing me with substantial written comments which enabled me to make many improvements. The series editors Professor H. D. Jocelyn and Professor M. D. Reeve likewise made extensive comment which was of considerable help in the revision of the book. Comments were received in addition from Professor R. J. Tarrant, who read part of the book during 1993–94. Others to whom I am grateful for help or encouragement include Dr R. W. Brock; Dr D. L. Cairns; Mr R. Cramer, who presented to me an out-of-print copy of Kasten which he found in Germany; the late Mr J. G. Griffith; Dr R. G.

Hawley; Dr M. Heath; my former tutor Dr G. O. Hutchinson, who first suggested Cicero as a suitable subject for research; Dr G. E. Klyve; Dr A. J. W. Laird, who clarified for me some points relating to speech presentation; Dr B. M. Levick; Dr N. J. Richardson, my colleague for three years at Merton College; Professor C. Riedweg; Dr J.-P. Rothschild, who supplemented my list of manuscripts; Dr R. B. Rutherford; Mr T. H. Tarver, III; and Professor W. S. Watt, who sent me some notes he had made on the speech.

I should like to thank the following libraries for supplying microfilms and photographs of manuscripts: the Staatsbibliothek Preussischer Kulturbesitz, Berlin; the Bibliothèque Royale Albert Ier, Brussels; the Biblioteca Medicea Laurenziana, Florence; the Biblioteca Nazionale Centrale, Florence; the Bibliotheek der Rijksuniversiteit, Leiden; the Bayerische Staatsbibliothek, Munich; the Bibliothèque Nationale, Paris; the Biblioteca Apostolica Vaticana, Vatican City; and the Herzog August Bibliothek, Wolfenbüttel. I am also grateful to the President and Fellows of St John's College, Oxford for granting me permission to quote from the unpublished writings of A. E. Housman. Finally, special thanks are due to the three seats of learning at which this book was written: Exeter and Lincoln Colleges, Oxford, and the University of Leeds. All have provided financial support over the years, and in each I have made many friends and learned much.

PREVIOUS EDITIONS AND COMMENTARIES

The following is a select list of editions, commentaries and translations of the speech. With three exceptions, works prior to 1800 are omitted: details of these may be found at J. C. Orelli and J. G. Baiter (edd.), *Onomasticon Tullianum* 1 (Zurich 1836) 197–215, 238–53, 274 (cf. C. J. Classen, *Recht-Rhetorik-Politik* (Darmstadt 1985) 371–3). The commentaries of some of the earlier editors are conveniently amalgamated by C. H. Frotscher, *Doctissimorum Interpretum Commentaria in M. Tullii Ciceronis Orationem pro P. Sulla* (Leipzig 1832).

In the list which follows, where an item belongs within a multi-volume set, the date given is that of the relevant volume. 'E', 'C' and 'T' denote 'edition (or reprinted text)', 'commentary' and 'translation'. Works in this list are cited throughout this book by author's surname only (thus 'Macdonald 302' signifies p. 302 of the 1977 Loeb edition). References to 'Kasten' are to the latest edition (1966), unless otherwise indicated.

F. Sylvius	Paris 1531	E C
C. Minos	Frankfurt 1584	E C
Oxford, Bodl. MS Rawl. D.753	s.xvii	T (by F. Osborn?)
J. A. Ernesti	London 1819	E C
J. C. Orelli	Zurich 1826	E
R. Klotz	Leipzig 1839	E C
K. F. A. Nobbe	Leipzig-London 1850	E

C. D. Yonge (Bohn)	London 1851	T
K. Halm (Orelli[2])	Zurich 1856	E
G. Long	London 1856	E C
C. L. Kayser	Leipzig 1862	E
R. Klotz (Teubner)	Leipzig 1872	E
J. S. Reid (Pitt Press Series)	Cambridge 1882	E C
F. Richter–G. Landgraf[2]	Leipzig 1885	E C
A. Pasdera	Turin 1886	E C
H. Nohl	Vienna-Prague-Leipzig 1889	E
C. F. W. Müller (Teubner)	Leipzig 1892	E
K. Halm–G. Laubmann[5]	Berlin 1893	E C
J. A. Nicklin	Cambridge 1902	T
J. R. King	Oxford 1904	T
A. C. Clark (OCT)	Oxford 1911	E
H. Nohl	Vienna-Leipzig 1920	E C
H. Reumont	Vienna-Leipzig 1920	E C
H. Kasten (Teubner)[1]	Leipzig 1933	E
L. E. Lord (Loeb)	London 1937	E T
A. Boulanger (Budé)	Paris 1943	E T
H. Kasten (Teubner)[2]	Leipzig 1949	E
J. Cochez[4]	Louvain 1952	E
M. M. Peña	Barcelona 1956	E T
J. E. Pabón	Milan 1964	E
H. Kasten (Teubner)[3]	Leipzig 1966	E
G. Vitucci	Florence 1967	E T
M. Zicàri	Turin 1968	E C
C. Macdonald (Loeb)	London 1977	E T
M. Fuhrmann	Zurich-Munich 1978	T

BIBLIOGRAPHICAL LISTS AND SURVEYS

The following are in addition to Marouzeau's *L'Année philologique* (1924–).

W. Allen, 'A Survey of Selected Ciceronian Bibliography, 1939–1953',
  CW 47 (1953–4) 129–39
Bursian's *Jahresbericht* (covering the speeches, 1873–1923):
  I. Müller, 3 (1874–5) 684–91; 10 (1877) 232–52; 14 (1878) 201–22; 22
    (1880) 222–66
  G. Landgraf, 35 (1883) 1–73; 43 (1885) 1–48; 47 (1886) 223–66; 59
    (1889) 186–229; 76 (1893) 1–28; 89 (1896) 63–85; 113 (1902) 74–88
  J. May, 134 (1907) 123–95; 153 (1911) 38–94
  J. K. Schönberger, 167 (1914) 280–356; 183 (1920) 73–123; 204 (1925)
    155–210
N. Criniti, *Bibliografia catilinaria* (Milan 1971); brought up to date by
  Classen 120 n. 1
W. Engelmann rev. E. Preuss, *Bibliotheca Scriptorum Classicorum* II⁸ (Leip-
  zig 1882) 127–227 (covers 1700–1878)
R. Klussmann, *Bibliotheca Scriptorum Classicorum et Graecorum et Latinorum*
  II.1 (Leipzig 1912) 233–330 (covers 1878–96)
S. Lambrino, *Bibliographie de l'antiquité classique 1896–1914* 1 (Paris 1951)
  122–44
J. Marouzeau, *Dix années de bibliographie classique... 1914–1924* 1 (Paris
  1927) 78–92
J. C. Orelli and J. G. Baiter (edd.), *Onomasticon Tullianum* 1 (Zurich 1836)
  274
R. J. Rowland, 'A Survey of Selected Ciceronian Bibliography, 1953–
  1965', *CW* 60 (1966–7) 51–65, 101–15
R. J. Rowland, 'A Survey of Selected Ciceronian Bibliography (1965–
  1974)', *CW* 71 (1977–8) 289–327

BIBLIOGRAPHY AND
ABBREVIATIONS

(See also pp. xiii–xiv above.)

Greek authors are abbreviated as in LSJ, Roman authors as in *OLD* (thus our speech is *Sul.*); if no author is named, then the author is Cicero. Periodicals are abbreviated as in Marouzeau's *L'Année philologique*, with some minor exceptions (e.g. *AJP* not *AJPh*, *CP* not *CPh*). Items in the following bibliography which are mentioned elsewhere in this book are cited by the abbreviation shown (although articles are cited in the normal way, without special abbreviations); works not referred to outside this bibliography have not been assigned an abbreviation. In an attempt to limit the length of this list, all commentaries have been omitted. The list does not, of course, include all works cited.

References to Housman denote pencil marginalia in A. E. Housman's personal copy of J. S. Reid's edition of the speech (Cambridge 1882), now in the possession of St John's College, Oxford.

Achard	G. Achard, *Pratique rhétorique et idéologie politique dans les discours 'optimates' de Cicéron* (*Mnemosyne* Suppl. 68; 1981)
Aili	H. Aili, *The Prose Rhythm of Sallust and Livy* (Studia Latina Stockholmiensia 24; 1979)
	M. v. Albrecht, 'M. Tullius Cicero, Sprache und Stil', *RE* Suppl. XIII.1237.49–1347.9
	M. C. Alexander, *Trials in the Late Roman Republic, 149 BC to 50 BC* (*Phoenix* Suppl. 26; 1990) (*TLRR*)
ALL	*Archiv für lateinische Lexikographie und Grammatik* (Leipzig 1884–1909)
	H. v. Arnim, *Stoicorum Veterum Fragmenta* 3 vols. (Leipzig 1903–5) (*SVF*)
	D. Berger, *Cicero als Erzähler: forensische und literarische Strategien in den Gerichtsreden* (Frankfurt am Main 1978)

D. H. Berry, 'Gulielmius and the Erfurtensis of Cicero: New Readings for *pro Sulla*', *CQ* n.s. 39 (1989) 400–7

G. Boissier, *La Conjuration de Catilina*² (Paris 1908)

Bonnefond-Coudry   M. Bonnefond-Coudry, *Le Sénat de la république romaine* (B.E.F.A.R. 273; 1989)

Bowyer   W. Bowyer (?), *A Dissertation in which the objections of a late Pamphlet... are clearly answered* (London 1746)

T. R. S. Broughton, *The Magistrates of the Roman Republic* I (New York 1951), II (New York 1952), III (Atlanta 1986) (*MRR*)

Brunt   P. A. Brunt, *The Fall of the Roman Republic and Related Essays* (Oxford 1988)

K. Busche, 'Beiträge zum Text ciceronischer Reden', *Hermes* 46 (1911) 57–69

CAH   *The Cambridge Ancient History*

Carcopino   J. Carcopino, *Cicero: the Secrets of his Correspondence*, tr. E. O. Lorimer 2 vols. (London 1951)

Carrington   R. C. Carrington, *Pompeii* (Oxford 1936)

Castner   C. J. Castner, *Prosopography of Roman Epicureans from the Second Century* BC *to the Second Century* AD (Frankfurt am Main etc. 1988)

Castrén   P. Castrén, *Ordo Populusque Pompeianus: Polity and Society in Roman Pompeii* (Rome 1975)

Ciaceri   E. Ciaceri, *Cicerone e i suoi tempi* I² (Milan etc. 1939), II² (Genoa etc. 1941)

CIL   see under *Corpus*

Clark, *Vet. Clun.*   A. C. Clark, *The Vetus Cluniacensis of Poggio* (Anecdota Oxoniensia 10; 1905)

A. C. Clark, 'Zielinski's *Clauselgesetz*', *CR* 19 (1905) 164–72

Clark, *Inv. Ital.*   A. C. Clark, *Inventa Italorum* (Anecdota Oxoniensia 11; 1909)

A. C. Clark, *Fontes Prosae Numerosae* (Oxford 1909)

Clark, *Descent*   A. C. Clark, *The Descent of Manuscripts* (Oxford 1918)

M. L. Clarke, *Rhetoric at Rome: a Historical Survey* (London 1953)

Classen C. J. Classen, *Recht-Rhetorik-Politik: Untersuchungen zu Ciceros rhetorischer Strategie* (Darmstadt 1985)

C. G. Cobet, ''ΑΠΟΜΝΗΜΟΝΕΥΜΑΤΑ W. G. Pluygers', *Mnemosyne* 9 (1881) 136–8

Corpus Inscriptionum Latinarum (*CIL*)

Craig C. P. Craig, *Form as Argument in Cicero's Speeches: a Study of Dilemma* (A.P.A. American Classical Studies 31; 1993)

Crawford J. W. Crawford, *M. Tullius Cicero: the Lost and Unpublished Orations* (*Hypomnemata* 80; 1984)

D'Arms J. H. D'Arms, *Romans on the Bay of Naples* (Cambridge, Mass. 1970)

David J.-M. David, *Le Patronat judiciaire au dernier siècle de la république romaine* (B.E.F.A.R. 277; 1992)

L. Delaruelle, *Études sur le choix des mots dans les discours de Cicéron* (Toulouse 1911)

Desmouliez A. Desmouliez, *Cicéron et son goût* (Brussels 1976)

H. Dessau (ed.), *Inscriptiones Latinae Selectae* 3 vols. (Berlin 1892–1916) (*ILS*)

Diehl H. Diehl, *Sulla und seine Zeit im Urteil Ciceros* (Hildesheim 1988)

W. Dittenberger (ed.), *Sylloge Inscriptionum Graecarum*[3] 4 vols. (Leipzig 1915–24) (*SIG*)

Dorey T. A. Dorey (ed.), *Cicero* (London 1965)

Douglas A. E. Douglas, *Cicero*[2] (Oxford 1979)

Douglas, *Roman Oratory* A. E. Douglas, 'Hellenistic Rhetoric and Roman Oratory' in D. Daiches and A. Thorlby (edd.), *The Classical World* (London 1972) 341–54

H. Drexler (ed.), *Die catilinarische Verschwörung: ein Quellenheft* (Darmstadt 1976)

Drumann–Groebe W. Drumann rev. P. Groebe, *Geschichte Roms*[2] 6 vols. (Berlin/Leipzig 1899–1929)

Entretiens see under Fondation Hardt

Ernout–Thomas A. Ernout and F. Thomas, *Syntaxe latine*[2] (Paris 1953)

Eschebach H. Eschebach, *Pompeji* (Leipzig 1978)

G. E. J. Everts, *Specimen Academicum Inaugurale exhibens Annotationes Selectas in M. Tullii Ciceronis Orationem pro Sulla* (Nijmegen 1835)

Fantham   E. Fantham, *Comparative Studies in Republican Latin Imagery* (*Phoenix* Suppl. 10; 1972)

Fondation Hardt, *Éloquence et rhétorique chez Cicéron* (Entretiens 28; 1982) (Entretiens)

Fraenkel   E. Fraenkel, *Leseproben aus Reden Ciceros und Catos* (Rome 1968)

Frederiksen   M. Frederiksen rev. N. Purcell, *Campania* (Rome 1984)

B. W. Frier, *The Rise of the Roman Jurists* (Princeton 1985)

H. Frisch, 'The First Catilinarian Conspiracy: a Study in Historical Conjecture', *C&M* 9 (1948) 10–36

M. Fuhrmann, *Cicero and the Roman Republic*, tr. W. E. Yuill (Oxford 1992)

M. Gelzer *et al.*, 'M. Tullius Cicero', *RE* VII A.827.31–1274.11, Tullius 29

M. Gelzer, *Cicero: ein biographischer Versuch* (Wiesbaden 1969)

Gelzer   M. Gelzer, *The Roman Nobility*, tr. R. J. Seager (Oxford 1969)

P. G. W. Glare (ed.), *Oxford Latin Dictionary* (Oxford 1982) (*OLD*)

H. C. Gotoff, *Cicero's Elegant Style: an Analysis of the* pro Archia (Urbana etc. 1979)

Grant   M. Grant, *Cities of Vesuvius* (London 1971)

Greenidge   A. H. J. Greenidge, *The Legal Procedure of Cicero's Time* (Oxford 1901)

E. S. Gruen, 'Notes on the "First Catilinarian Conspiracy"', *CP* 64 (1969) 20–24

Gruen   E. S. Gruen, *The Last Generation of the Roman Republic* (London 1974)

Habicht   C. Habicht, *Cicero the Politician* (Baltimore and London 1990)

Habinek   T. N. Habinek, *The Colometry of Latin Prose* (University of California Publications: Classical Studies 25; 1985)

Halm, *Handschriftenkunde*   K. Halm, *Zur Handschriftenkunde der ciceronischen Schriften* (Munich 1850)

N. G. L. Hammond and H. H. Scullard (edd.), *The Oxford Classical Dictionary*² (Oxford 1970) (*OCD*)

Handford   S. A. Handford, *The Latin Subjunctive* (London
                  1947)

Hardy   E. G. Hardy, *The Catilinarian Conspiracy: a Re-
                  study of the Evidence* (Oxford 1924; =*JRS* 7
                  (1917) 153–228)

Haury   A. Haury, *L'Ironie et l'humour chez Cicéron* (Lei-
                  den 1955)

Havet   L. Havet, *Manuel de critique verbale appliquée aux
                  textes latins* (Paris 1911)

Hellegouarc'h   J. Hellegouarc'h, *Le Vocabulaire latin des rela-
                  tions et partis politiques sous la république* (Paris
                  1963)

Hinard   F. Hinard, *Les Proscriptions de la Rome répub-
                  licaine* (C.E.F.R. 83; 1985)

Hofmann   J. B. Hofmann, *Lateinische Umgangssprache*³
                  (Heidelberg 1951)

                  J. B. Hofmann rev. A. Szantyr, *Lateinische
                  Syntax und Stilistik* (Munich 1965) (H.-Sz.)

Holst   H. Holst, *Die Wortspiele in Ciceros Reden* (*Sym-
                  bolae Osloenses* Suppl. 1; 1925)

H.-Sz.   see under Hofmann, J. B.

Humbert   J. Humbert, *Les Plaidoyers écrits et les plaidoiries
                  réelles de Cicéron* (Paris 1925)

ILS   see under Dessau, H.

John   C. John, *Die Entstehungsgeschichte der catilinar-
                  ischen Verschwörung* (*JahrbClPhil* Suppl. 8
                  (1876) 701–819)

                  W. R. Johnson, *Luxuriance and Economy: Cicero
                  and the Alien Style* (University of California
                  Publications: Classical Studies 6; 1971)

Jones   A. H. M. Jones, *The Criminal Courts of the
                  Roman Republic and Principate* (Oxford 1972)

Jongman   W. Jongman, *The Economy and Society of
                  Pompeii* (Amsterdam 1988)

Karsten   H. T. Karsten, *Spicilegium Criticum* (Leiden 1881)

Kennedy   G. A. Kennedy, *The Art of Rhetoric in the Roman
                  World, 300 BC–AD 300* (Princeton 1972)

K.-S.   R. Kühner rev. C. Stegmann, *Ausführliche
                  Grammatik der lateinischen Sprache: Satzlehre*² 2
                  vols. (Hannover 1912–14)

                  E. Laughton, 'Cicero and the Greek Orators',
                  AJP 82 (1961) 27–49

Laughton   E. Laughton, *The Participle in Cicero* (Oxford 1964)

                      L. Laurand, 'Principaux fac-similés des manuscrits de Cicéron', *REL* 10 (1932) 233–7

                      L. Laurand, 'Les Manuscrits de Cicéron', *REL* 11 (1933) 92–128

Laurand   L. Laurand, *Études sur le style des discours de Cicéron*⁴ 3 vols. (Paris 1936–8)

Lausberg   H. Lausberg, *Handbuch der literarischen Rhetorik* 2 vols. (Munich 1960)

Lebreton   J. Lebreton, *Études sur la langue et la grammaire de Cicéron* (Paris 1901)

Leeman   A. D. Leeman, *Orationis Ratio* 2 vols. (Amsterdam 1963)

                      C. A. Lehmann, 'Quaestiones Tullianae', *Hermes* 15 (1880) 348–52, 571–2

                      H. G. Liddell, R. Scott, H. Stuart Jones and R. McKenzie (edd.), *A Greek-English Lexicon*⁹ (Oxford 1968) (LSJ)

Lintott   A. W. Lintott, *Violence in Republican Rome* (Oxford 1968)

LSJ   see under Liddell, H. G.

Madvig, *Adv. Crit.*   J. N. Madvig, *Adversaria Critica* 3 vols. (Copenhagen 1871–84)

Madvig, *Opusc. Acad.* J. N. Madvig, *Opuscula Academica*² (Copenhagen 1887)

Maiuri   A. Maiuri, *Pompeii* (Novara 1960)

                      E. Malcovati (ed.), *Oratorum Romanorum Fragmenta Liberae Rei Publicae* I⁴ (Turin 1976), II (Turin 1979) (*ORF*)

                      E. Manni, *Lucio Sergio Catilina*² (Palermo 1969)

                      D. A. March, 'Cicero and the "Gang of Five"', *CW* 82 (1988–9) 225–34

Martin   J. Martin, *Antike Rhetorik* (Munich 1974)

Martyn   J. R. C. Martyn (ed.), *Cicero and Virgil: Studies in Honour of Harold Hunt* (Amsterdam 1972)

Mau   A. Mau, *Pompeii: its Life and Art*,² tr. F. W. Kelsey (New York 1902)

May   J. M. May, *Trials of Character: the Eloquence of Ciceronian Ethos* (Chapel Hill and London 1988)

                      M. Mello, 'Sallustio e le elezioni consolari del 66 a.C.', *PP* 18 (1963) 36–54

Merguet	H. Merguet, *Lexikon zu den Reden des Cicero* 4 vols. (Jena 1877–84) H. Merguet, *Lexikon zu den philosophischen Schriften des Cicero* 3 vols. (Jena 1887–94)
Michel	A. Michel, *Rhétorique et philosophie chez Cicéron* (Paris 1960)
Michel-Verdière	A. Michel and R. Verdière (edd.), *Ciceroniana: Hommages à Kazimierz Kumaniecki* (Leiden 1975)
Mitchell I	T. N. Mitchell, *Cicero: the Ascending Years* (New Haven and London 1979)
Mitchell II	T. N. Mitchell, *Cicero: the Senior Statesman* (New Haven and London 1991)
Mommsen, *Coll.*	T. Mommsen, *De Collegiis et Sodaliciis Romanorum* (Kiel 1843)
Mommsen, *Staatsrecht*	T. Mommsen, *Römisches Staatsrecht*³ 3 vols. (Leipzig 1887–8)
Mommsen, *Strafrecht*	T. Mommsen, *Römisches Strafrecht* (Leipzig 1899)
MRR	see under Broughton, T. R. S. F. Münzer, 'P. Cornelius Sulla', *RE* IV. 1518.65–1521.37, Cornelius 386
Nägelsbach	K. F. v. Nägelsbach rev. I. Müller, *Lateinische Stilistik*⁹ (Nuremberg 1905)
Nettleship	H. Nettleship, *Contributions to Latin Lexicography* (Oxford 1889)
Neue-Wagener	F. Neue rev. C. Wagener, *Formenlehre der lateinischen Sprache*³ 4 vols. (Leipzig 1892–1905)
Neumeister	C. Neumeister, *Grundsätze der forensischen Rhetorik gezeigt an Gerichtsreden Ciceros* (Munich 1964)
Nicolet	C. Nicolet, *L'Ordre équestre à l'époque républicaine (312–43 av. J.-C.)* 2 vols. (Paris 1966–74)
Nisbet	R. G. M. Nisbet, 'Cola and Clausulae in Cicero's Speeches' in E. M. Craik (ed.), *'Owls to Athens': Essays on Classical Subjects Presented to Sir Kenneth Dover* (Oxford 1990) 349–59
Norden	E. Norden, *Die antike Kunstprosa*² 2 vols. (Leipzig and Berlin 1909)
OCD	see under Hammond, N. G. L.

OLD   see under Glare, P. G. W.

E. Olechowska, *'Pro Cn. Plancio' et 'Pro C. Rabirio Postumo'*: la transmission des textes (Polska Akademia Nauk Archiwum Filologiczne 41; 1984)

Opelt   I. Opelt, *Die lateinischen Schimpfwörter und verwandte sprachliche Erscheinungen* (Heidelberg 1965)

Oppermann   H. Oppermann (ed.), *Römische Wertbegriffe* (Wege der Forschung 34; 1967)

ORF   see under Malcovati, E.

E. Ornato and S. Regnier, 'Classification automatique des manuscrits des discours de Cicéron fondée sur le choix et l'ordre des discours', *RHT* 9 (1979) 329–41

Otto   A. Otto, *Die Sprichwörter und sprichwörtlichen Redensarten der Römer* (Leipzig 1890)

L. Pareti, *La congiura di Catilina* (Catania 1934)

Parzinger   P. Parzinger, *Beiträge zur Kenntnis der Entwicklung des ciceronischen Stils* (Landshut 1910)

Platner–Ashby   S. B. Platner rev. T. Ashby, *A Topographical Dictionary of Ancient Rome* (Oxford 1929)

Pöschl   V. Pöschl, H. Gärtner and W. Heyke, *Bibliographie zur antiken Bildersprache* (Heidelberg 1964)

J. T. Ramsey, 'Cicero, *pro Sulla* 68 and Catiline's Candidacy in 66 BC', *HSCP* 86 (1982) 121–31

Rawson   E. D. Rawson, *Cicero: a Portrait* (London 1975)

RE   see under Wissowa, G.

L. E. Reams, 'The Strange Case of Sulla's Brother', *CJ* 82 (1986–7) 301–5

M. D. Reeve, 'Before and after Poggio: Some Manuscripts of Cicero's Speeches', *RFIC* 112 (1984) 266–84

L. D. Reynolds (ed.), *Texts and Transmission: a Survey of the Latin Classics* (Oxford 1983) (*T.&T.*)

Rice Holmes   T. Rice Holmes, *The Roman Republic* 3 vols. (Oxford 1923)

Richardson, *Pompeii*   L. Richardson, *Pompeii: an Architectural History* (Baltimore and London 1988)

Richardson, *Rome*   L. Richardson, *A New Topographical Dictionary of Ancient Rome* (Baltimore and London 1992)

Riemann   O. Riemann, *Syntaxe latine*[7] (Paris 1940)

S. Rizzo, 'Apparati ciceroniani e congetture del Petrarca', *RFIC* 103 (1975) 5–15

Rizzo, *Tradizione*   S. Rizzo, *La tradizione manoscritta della* pro Cluentio *di Cicerone* (Genoa 1979)

Rizzo, *Catalogo*   S. Rizzo, *Catalogo dei codici della* pro Cluentio *ciceroniana* (Genoa 1983)

Rohde   F. J. A. Rohde, *Cicero, quae de Inventione praecepit, quatenus secutus sit in orationibus generis iudicialis* (Königsberg 1903)

Ross   J. Ross, *A Dissertation in which the Defence of P. Sulla ascribed to M. Tullius Cicero is clearly proved to be spurious after the Manner of Mr. Markland* (London 1745)

Rubenius   P. Rubenius, *Electorum Libri II* (Antwerp 1608)

D. Schmitz, *Zeugen des Prozeßgegners in Gerichtsreden Ciceros* (Frankfurt etc. 1985)

Schoenwitz   W. Schoenwitz, *De re praepositionis usu et notione* .(diss. Marburg 1912)

R. J. Seager, 'The First Catilinarian Conspiracy', *Historia* 13 (1964) 338–47

Seager   R. J. Seager, *Pompey: a Political Biography* (Oxford 1979)

Settle   J. N. Settle, *The Publication of Cicero's Orations* (diss. N. Carolina 1962)

Seyffert   M. L. Seyffert, *Epistola critica ad Carolum Halmium de Ciceronis pro P. Sulla et pro P. Sestio orationibus ab ipso editis* (Brandenburg 1848)

Seyffert, *Schol. Lat.*   M. L. Seyffert, *Scholae Latinae* I[4] (Leipzig 1878), II[3] (Leipzig 1872)

Shackleton Bailey   D. R. Shackleton Bailey, *Cicero* (London 1971)

Shackleton Bailey, *Nomenclature*   D. R. Shackleton Bailey, *Two Studies in Roman Nomenclature*[2] (A.P.A. American Classical Studies 3; 1991)

Shackleton Bailey, *Onomasticon*   D. R. Shackleton Bailey, *Onomasticon to Cicero's Speeches*[2] (Stuttgart and Leipzig 1992)

Shatzman   I. Shatzman, *Senatorial Wealth and Roman Politics* (Brussels 1975)

SIG   see under Dittenberger, W.

St.   T. Stangl (ed.), *Ciceronis Orationum Scholiastae* (Vienna 1912)

Stephanus   H. Stephanus, *In M. T. Ciceronis quam plurimos locos castigationes* (Paris 1557)

C. E. Stevens, 'The "Plotting" of BC 66/65', *Latomus* 22 (1963) 397–435

Stockton   D. L. Stockton, *Cicero: a Political Biography* (Oxford 1971)

Strachan-Davidson J. L. Strachan-Davidson, *Cicero and the Fall of the Roman Republic* (London 1894)

Strachan-Davidson, *Criminal Law*   J. L. Strachan-Davidson, *Problems of the Roman Criminal Law* 2 vols. (Oxford 1912)

K. Strauss, *Die Klauselrhythmen der bobienser Cicero-Scholien* (Landau 1910)

Strenge   J. Strenge, *Einige Bemerkungen zu Ciceros Rede pro Sulla* (Parchim 1898)

Stroh   W. Stroh, *Taxis und Taktik: die advokatische Dispositionskunst in Ciceros Gerichtsreden* (Stuttgart 1975)

G. V. Sumner, 'The Consular Elections of 66 BC', *Phoenix* 19 (1965) 226–31

Sumner   G. V. Sumner, *The Orators in Cicero's* Brutus*: Prosopography and Chronology* (*Phoenix* Suppl. 11; 1973)

SVF   see under Arnim, H. v.

Syme, *RR*   R. Syme, *The Roman Revolution* (Oxford 1939)

Syme, *Sallust*   R. Syme, *Sallust* (Berkeley etc. 1964)

Syme, *AA*   R. Syme, *The Augustan Aristocracy* (Oxford 1986)

Taylor, *PP*   L. R. Taylor, *Party Politics in the Age of Caesar* (Berkeley etc. 1949)

Taylor, *RVA*   L. R. Taylor, *Roman Voting Assemblies* (Ann Arbor 1966)

TLL   *Thesaurus Linguae Latinae* (Leipzig 1900–)

TLRR   see under Alexander, M. C.

T.&T.   see under Reynolds, L. D.

A. Vasaly, *Representations: Images of the World in Ciceronian Oratory* (Berkeley etc. 1993)

Volkmann   R. Volkmann, *Die Rhetorik der Griechen und Römer*² (Leipzig 1885)

Ward   A. M. Ward, *Marcus Crassus and the Late Roman Republic* (Columbia 1977)

Weische   A. Weische, *Ciceros Nachahmung der attischen Redner* (Heidelberg 1972)

Wiesthaler   F. Wiesthaler, *Die Oratio Obliqua als künstlerisches Stilmittel in den Reden Ciceros* (Innsbruck 1956)

Wirszubski   C. Wirszubski, *Libertas as a Political Idea at Rome* (Cambridge 1960)

J. Wisse, *Ethos and Pathos from Aristotle to Cicero* (Amsterdam 1989)

G. Wissowa *et al.* (edd.), *Paulys Real-Encyclopädie der classischen Altertumswissenschaft* (Stuttgart and Munich 1894–1978) (*RE*)

Wölfflin   E. Wölfflin, *Ausgewählte Schriften* (Leipzig 1933)

Wood   N. Wood, *Cicero's Social and Political Thought* (Berkeley etc. 1988)

Woodcock   E. C. Woodcock, *A New Latin Syntax* (London 1959)

Zanker   P. Zanker, *Pompeji: Stadtbilder als Spiegel von Gesellschaft und Herrschaftsform* (Trierer Winckelmannsprogramme 9; 1987)

Zielinski   T. Zielinski, *Das Clauselgesetz in Ciceros Reden* (Leipzig 1904; = *Philologus* Suppl. 9.4 (1904) 589–844)

Zielinski, *Constr. Rhyth.*   T. Zielinski, *Der constructive Rhythmus in Ciceros Reden* (Leipzig 1914; = *Philologus* Suppl. 13.1 (1914) 1–295)

Zinzerling   J. Zinzerling, *Criticorum Iuvenilium Promulsis* (Leiden 1610)

Note: The pamphlet by J. Ross (see above) purports to be an attack on the authenticity of *pro Sulla*, but is in fact a spoof written in parody of J. Markland's *A Dissertation upon Four Orations ascribed to M. Tullius Cicero* (London 1745), which impugned the authenticity of the *post reditum* speeches. Ross' purpose was to expose the flimsiness of Markland's arguments by applying them to a speech of unimpeachable genuineness. The pamphlet was not unreasonably taken at face value by its readership, and W. Bowyer (above), or possibly one of his associates, wrote a sensible rejoinder. Confusingly, copies of Bowyer's pamphlet have the words 'By *John Ross*, the Author of the *Objections*' written on the title page. For the full story of this eccentric mid-eighteenth-century Cambridge dispute see J. Nichols, *Literary Anecdotes of the Eighteenth Century* II (London 1812) 184–8; cf. R. G. Nisbet on *Dom.*, xxx–xxxi; J. Nicholson, *Cicero's Return from Exile* (New York 1992) 5f., 134.

INTRODUCTION

I THE LIFE OF P. CORNELIUS SULLA

P. Cornelius Sulla,[1] as has now been established, was the nephew of L. Sulla the dictator.[2] His father, the dictator's brother, died[3] while Sulla was still a child; his mother remarried and had a son, L. Caecilius Rufus,[4] Sulla's half-brother. One of Sulla's cousins was the dictator's son Faustus,[5] whose twin sister Fausta was married first to C. Memmius,[6] the candidate for the consulship of 53[7] and addressee of Lucretius, and afterwards[8] to T. Annius Milo, Cicero's future client. (For a family tree see Figure 1.)

Sulla first comes to the notice of history during his uncle's proscriptions (82–81) as one of the *sectores* who bought up confiscated property to sell afterwards at a profit. In this way he amassed the fortune which was to play so critical a role in his subsequent career. A generation later his unscrupulous opportunism would again manifest itself: *nec vero umquam bellorum civilium semen et causa deerit, dum homines perditi hastam illam cruentam et meminerint et sperabunt, quam P. Sulla cum vibrasset dictatore propinquo suo, idem sexto tricesimo anno post a sceleratiore hasta non recessit* (*Off.* 2.29). In *pro Sulla* Cicero tries to present Sulla's part in the

---

[1] *RE* iv.1518.65ff. (Cornelius 386); *MRR* ii.82, 138, 157, 281, 290; David 785f.; cf. Drumann–Groebe ii.437–41, 562–4; v.573.
[2] See Appendix 1.
[3] Between 107 and 96: see L. E. Reams, *CJ* 82 (1986–7) 301–5.
[4] 62.7n.; cf. §§ 62–6.
[5] 54.2n.; cf. §§ 54–5.
[6] 55.3n.
[7] All ancient dates are BC unless otherwise indicated.
[8] In 55.

I

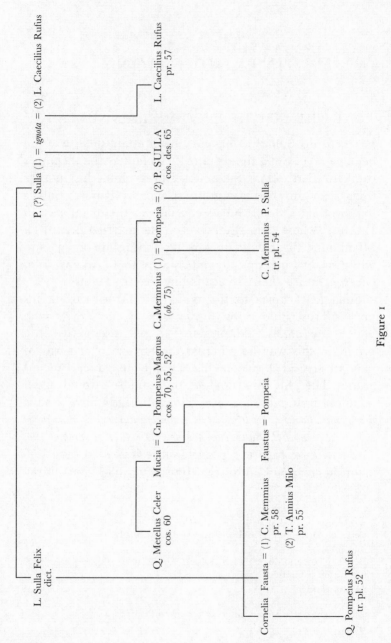

Figure 1

proscriptions in as favourable a light as possible by claiming that he used his influence with the dictator to save
(unspecified) lives (§72); but in the saving of lives, also,
there must have been opportunities for profit.[9] One other
detail is known of Sulla's life during this period: in c.80 he
became one of the *triumviri* appointed to settle a *colonia* of
Sullan veterans at Pompeii, and from then on he acted as a
patronus of the colony.[10]

It is highly probable, although it cannot be said to be certain,[11] that in or shortly after 75 Sulla married the sister of
Pompey, Pompeia,[12] whose previous husband C. Memmius
(a cousin of the Memmius who married Fausta) had been
killed in that year fighting against Sertorius in Spain. Sulla
thus acquired a stepson, Memmius,[13] and later a natural son

[9] See 72.9n.
[10] 60.1n.; cf. §§ 60–62; *MRR* ii.82.
[11] [SULLA AS POMPEY'S BROTHER-IN-LAW.] Orosius (5.23.12) reports that
Pompeia's husband Memmius was killed in 75 (cf. *Balb.* 5; Plut. *Pomp.*
11.2; *id. Sert.* 21.1). That Pompeia subsequently married Sulla is inferred from the existence of a stepson to Sulla, Memmius, at the
time of his prosecution of Gabinius in 54 (*Q. fr.* 3.3.2); cf. F. Münzer,
RE xv.616.41ff.; Syme, *Sallust* 102 n. 88; T. P. Wiseman, *NC* 4 (1964)
157; *id.*, *CQ* n.s. 17 (1967) 167; E. S. Gruen, *Historia* 18 (1969) 76; E.
Fantham, *Historia* 24 (1975) 437. Ward (28f.), however, notes that less
economical hypotheses are not necessarily ruled out: Pompey's
quaestor (and husband of Pompeia) may have been the son of an
unrecorded son of L. Memmius the *praetorius* of 129, and Sulla's
stepson the son of an unrecorded son of C. Memmius the tribune of
111. But this necessitates postulating two unattested Memmii. Ward
opposes the hypothesis that Sulla was Pompey's brother-in-law by
arguing that, had Sulla and his stepson been supporters of Pompey,
they would not have prosecuted his protégé Gabinius; but this overlooks Sulla's overriding desire for rehabilitation. In any case, the
prosecution of Gabinius is entirely in line with the behaviour of other
members of the Sullae and the Memmii towards Pompey at this
date; cf. E. S. Gruen, *Historia* 18 (1969) 105; Gruen 94, 296, 323;
E. Fantham, *Historia* 24 (1975) 437f. Gruen (94, 219, 283, 296, 323) and
J. D. Leach (*Pompey the Great* (London 1978) 104) *inter alios* assume Sulla
to be Pompey's brother-in law without question.
[12] *RE* xxi.2263.37ff. (Pompeius 53).
[13] 89.13n.

was born to him, also named P. Cornelius Sulla.[14] This is the boy whose plight Cicero describes so pathetically at the end of the speech (§§ 88–9).

Sulla held the praetorship not later than 68,[15] and in 66 he was elected *omnibus centuriis* (§ 91) to the consulship for the following year.[16] The other successful candidate was P. Autronius Paetus,[17] who had been at school with Cicero and in 75 had been a colleague of his in the quaestorship (§ 18) before serving as a legate in Greece, probably under M. Antonius Creticus, in 73–2. After the election both men were immediately prosecuted for *ambitus* under the recent *lex Calpurnia*[18] (67), Sulla by the young L. Manlius Torquatus,[19] the homonymous son of one of the unsuccessful candidates,[20] and Autronius by another unsuccessful candidàte, L. Aurelius Cotta.[21] Autronius allegedly made two

[14] 88.14n.

[15] *MRR* ii.138.

[16] The sources for the events of 66–5 are given at *MRR* ii.157.

[17] *RE* ii.2612.20ff. (Autronius 7); *MRR* ii.97, 112, 138, 157.

[18] 17.8n.

[19] See pp. 17–20.

[20] 11.4n.

[21] 11.2n. [SULLA'S PROSECUTOR IN 66.] Asconius (75 C; cf. 88 C) and Dio (36.44.3) give the disappointed rivals Torquatus and Cotta (Asconius inverts the names) as the respective prosecutors of Sulla and Autronius. This is not necessarily contradicted by Cicero's statement at § 50 that it was the younger Torquatus who acquired Sulla's *insignia*: it is possible, as far as we know, that he would have been entitled to them if he was *subscriptor* to his father (cf. M. C. Alexander, *CP* 80 (1985) 21f.). However, the younger Torquatus is clearly shown to have been Sulla's prosecutor by *Fin.* 2.62: *te ipsum . . . voluptasne induxit ut adulescentulus eriperes P. Sullae consulatum? quem cum ad patrem tuum rettulisses, fortissimum virum, qualis ille vel consul vel civis cum semper, tum post consulatum fuit!* The son could hardly be credited with having won the consulship for his father if it had in fact been his father who was the principal prosecutor. The plurals in §§ 49 (*ereptum repetere vos clamitabatis, ut victi in campo in foro vinceretis* etc.) and 90 (*si nihil aliud Sullae nisi consulatum abstulissetis*), therefore, should not be taken in a technical sense as implying that Sulla's prosecution was officially undertaken by both Torquati. See Halm, Introd. § 3; Reid, Introd. § 10 n. 2; Drumann–Groebe ii.437; E. Badian, *Studies in Greek and Roman History*

attempts to halt his trial by violence (§ 15; cf. § 71), but ultimately[22] both men were convicted and deprived of their
prospective consulships. In addition they were expelled
from the senate, permanently debarred from public office
and required to pay a fine.[23] The successful prosecutors, on
the other hand, were rewarded with the *insignia* of the men
whom they had unseated (§ 50).[24]

From the election onwards, Sulla and the Torquati,
father and son, were committed enemies (*inimici*).[25] The
disqualification of Sulla and Autronius necessitated a fresh
election,[26] giving the elder Torquatus and Cotta a further
chance to win the consulship. Sulla's objective now became
to prevent the election of Torquatus.[27] Since it was illegal

---

(Oxford 1964) 248; W. C. McDermott, *Hermes* 97 (1969) 242 n. 2; B. A.
Marshall on Asc. 75.7–8 C. M. Mello (*PP* 18 (1963) 51 n. 59), J. T.
Ramsey (*HSCP* 86 (1982) 129 n. 33) and M. C. Alexander (*CP* 80 (1985)
26 n. 20; cf. *TLRR* no. 201 n. 1) prefer to follow Dio in taking the elder
Torquatus as Sulla's prosecutor, with his son as *subscriptor*. However,
the 'explicit statements of Asconius . . . and Dio' (Alexander) do not
outweigh the evidence of *Fin.* 2.62 (thus Badian), which Mello and
Ramsey have to maintain is slanted. Ramsey asserts that 'it would be
highly unusual for such a prosecution to be entrusted solely to the son
of Sulla's defeated rival', but in fact prosecutors were frequently *adulescentes* (46.4n.). F. Münzer (*RE* xiv.1201.39ff., 1203.46ff.), followed by
E. W. Gray (*Antichthon* 13 (1979) 64), attempts to reconcile Asconius
with Cicero by making Cotta and the younger Torquatus the prosecutors of Sulla, and the elder Torquatus the prosecutor of Autronius.
But it was Torquatus' consulship which Sulla had taken (both were
patricians), and Cotta's which Autronius had taken (both plebeians):
Cotta, therefore, would not have prosecuted Sulla, nor Torquatus
Autronius. In any case, Münzer's scenario runs contrary to the whole
spirit of *pro Sulla*, especially § 49.

[22] The trials were protracted: see J. T. Ramsey, *HSCP* 86 (1982) 128 n.
30.

[23] 17.8n.

[24] 50.4n.

[25] Brunt 370; David 518f.

[26] A formal election would have been necessary even if Torquatus and
Cotta were the only remaining candidates; cf. F. d'Ippolito, *Labeo* 11
(1965) 42–6.

[27] J. T. Ramsey, *HSCP* 86 (1982) 129f.

under the *leges Liciniae Sextiae* (367) for two patricians to hold the consulship together, Sulla therefore sought to block Torquatus' election by giving his support[28] to another patrician, L. Sergius Catilina,[29] who had newly returned from his governorship of Africa. According to the prosecution in 62, violence was used (§ 68). In the event, however, Catiline's candidature was disallowed:[30] he withdrew,[31] and Torquatus and Cotta were duly elected.[32]

The electoral contests of 66 are regarded by some modern scholars as part of a wider struggle between Pompey and the optimates. R. J. Seager, for instance, sees Sulla as 'the candidate of the optimates':[33] in his view, the Pompeians Torquatus and Cotta had to resort to desperate measures in order to overcome their non-Pompeian rivals. What, then, were the political affiliations of the four contenders for the consulships of 65? Sulla, contrary to Seager's assertion, was by no means 'free of the taint of a Pompeian connection': as we have seen, he was almost certainly Pompey's brother-in-law. Moreover, several of those who supported him in 63–2 are known to have had Pompeian ties. Q. Caecilius Metellus Celer,[34] who acted for Sulla in the senate on 1 January 63, was a half-brother of Pompey's wife Mucia, and had served as one of his legates in 66. Sulla's cousin Faustus[35] served under Pompey in 63 and was later to marry his daughter. And of the three men who provided documentary evidence in Sulla's sup-

---

[28] Argued in detail at 68.4n.
[29] *RE* II A.1693.3ff. (Sergius 23); *MRR* II.72, 138, 147, 155; III.192. See 70.3n. (character); 70.7n. (crimes); 81.7n. (*repetundae* trial).
[30] Sal. *Cat.* 18.3; Asc. 89 C; Dio 36.44.3–4; cf. Hardy 6–10; R. J. Seager, *Historia* 13 (1964) 338f.; G. V. Sumner, *Phoenix* 19 (1965) 226–31; B. A. Marshall, *SCI* 3 (1976–7) 130–35; J. T. Ramsey, *HSCP* 86 (1982) 121–31.
[31] Asc. 89 C *Catilina...destitit a petitione.*
[32] *MRR* II.157.
[33] Seager 56.
[34] 65.4n.; cf. Gruen 219f.
[35] 54.2n.

port at his trial in 62 (§ 55) one, C. Memmius, was a partisan of Pompey in the 60s, while another, Q. Pompeius Rufus, is known as a violent follower of his in the next decade.[36] Nevertheless, in spite of these links, Sulla, as A. M. Ward points out,[37] was also solidly supported by Hortensius and the optimates at his trial in 62 (§§ 3–5). He would therefore appear to have been 'a man of many connections',[38] and this may help to explain his striking success in the first election (§ 91). The political affiliations of Autronius, by contrast, are entirely unknown.[39] But Torquatus, like Sulla, had Pompeian links: only the year before he had served as a legate of Pompey in the war against the pirates,[40] and it may be significant also that his wife came from Picenum (§ 25).[41] Finally, Cotta as praetor in 70 had carried the law which brought to an end the senatorial monopoly of the courts;[42] it is by no means clear, however, that this was done at Pompey's behest.[43] So, one pair of antagonists, Sulla and Torquatus, were each connected with Pompey, while the affiliations of the other pair are uncertain. This alone is sufficient to discount the view that the elections of 66 were a struggle between Pompeian and non-Pompeian candidates.[44] Instead, we may conclude that

---

[36] 55.3n.; cf. Gruen 284.

[37] Ward 29.

[38] Ward 29 (cf. 163). There is no evidence, however, to support the statement of Taylor (*PP* 224 n. 23) or the suggestion of Ward (29, 119) that Sulla was aided by Crassus: see E. S. Gruen, *CP* 64 (1969) 22.

[39] Ward (29f., 119) attempts to link him with Pompey and Crassus (cf. Taylor, *PP* 224 n. 23). But there is no evidence for a link with Pompey, and he is unlikely to have been an adherent of Crassus in view of Sal. *Cat.* 48.7; cf. E. S. Gruen, *CP* 64 (1969) 22.

[40] 11.4n.

[41] 25.5n.

[42] *MRR* II.127.

[43] Plut. *Pomp.* 22.3, with P. A. Brunt, *Chiron* 10 (1980) 285f.; cf. G. V. Sumner, *Phoenix* 19 (1965) 230; R. J. Seager in J. Bibauw (ed.), *Hommages à Marcel Renard* (Brussels 1969) II.682–4; Ward 18f.

[44] E. S. Gruen, *CP* 64 (1969) 22 ('That Pompeius Magnus was an issue in the elections of 66 is entirely unattested and rendered unlikely in the

the candidates were simply competing for office on their own behalf, as might in any case have been inferred from Cicero's remarks on the subject in *pro Sulla*: *honoris erat certamen* (§ 49), *honoris enim contentio vos ad causam ... deduxerunt* (§ 90).

The disqualification of Catiline and election of Torquatus was a severe blow to Sulla. At his trial in 62 it was claimed that he and Autronius between them had plotted a desperate last resort: to murder their successful rivals and seize the consulship by force on 1 January 65 (§ 68).[45] This was styled a *prima coniuratio* (§ 81), and the name of Catiline was added.[46] The accusation is preposterous; nevertheless, it is conceivable that Sulla and Autronius had staged some sort of a demonstration in January 65 against the incoming consuls.[47]

Once the new consuls had taken office, Sulla retired to a life of inglorious ease at Naples (§§ 17, 53). Eighteen months later, however, his prospects improved with the election of his half-brother L. Caecilius Rufus[48] to the tribunate. Immediately after assuming office on 10 December 64, Caecilius proposed a bill retrospectively replacing the penalties of the *lex Calpurnia*, under which Sulla had been convicted, with the milder penalties of the *lex Cornelia* (81?) which it had superseded.[49] Sulla's conviction, therefore, would have stood (a point Cicero is at pains to stress in the speech), but he would have been allowed to return to the senate imme-

extreme by the identity of the consuls'); Gruen 132 n. 45, 272; cf. Brunt 473–5 (although the connections between Pompey and the Sullae are underrated at 474f.).

[45] 68.2n.

[46] Since the notorious 'first Catilinarian conspiracy' is now agreed to be a fiction, a detailed account is not appropriate here. A full discussion of the subject may be had, however, by reading the following in order: pp. 150f.; 11.7n.; pp. 265f.; 67.4n.; 67.7n.; 68.2n.; 68.4n.; 81.10n.

[47] 68.2n.

[48] 62.7n.; cf. §§ 62–6.

[49] On these laws see 17.8n.

diately and, once ten years had elapsed from the date of his conviction, to stand again for office.[50] The climate, however, was unfavourable: in response to flagrant bribery in the consular elections of that year a measure still harsher than the *lex Calpurnia* had been proposed in the senate, only to fall victim to a tribunician veto.[51] Autronius resorted to violence, again without success (§ 66); Cicero denies any violence on the part of Sulla or Caecilius, although he does not say that Sulla did not come to Rome to support the bill in person. On 1 January 63, the first day of Cicero's consulship, the opening item of business was the withdrawal of the *rogatio Caecilia* on Sulla's instructions (§ 65). Later in the year Cicero's own *lex Tullia*[52] was carried, adding a ten-year exile to the penalties for bribery: Sulla had in fact been lucky.

Sulla seems to have been in Rome for the consular elections of 63[53] even if, as Cicero argues (§ 52), he did not appear on the Campus Martius. The elections were disrupted by violence: once again we are told that it was Autronius who was responsible (§ 51). Three months later, however, at the time of the notorious meeting at Laeca's house,[54] Sulla was back in Naples, and there he remained throughout the time of the Catilinarian conspiracy (§ 53; cf. § 17).

Thanks to Cicero's careful management of the crisis (which, however, involved the illegal execution of five conspirators),[55] the conspiracy was prevented from breaking out at Rome.[56] Catiline himself was defeated and killed at the beginning of 62,[57] and this was followed by the

[50] Argued at 63.8n.
[51] Asc. 83, 85–6, 88 C.
[52] 17.8n.
[53] Argued at p. 233.
[54] 6.6n.
[55] 21.3n.
[56] For modern accounts of the Catilinarian conspiracy see John; Hardy; Rice Holmes 1.253–82, 455–73.
[57] Liv. *epit.* 103; Dio 37.39.1; cf. *Sest.* 12; Sal. *Cat.* 56–61; Vell. 2.35.5; Flor. 2.12.11–12; App. *BC* 2.7; Dio 37.39.1–37.41.1.

trials[58] of his surviving adherents under the *lex Plautia de vi*[59] over a period of several months (§92). Autronius,[60] L. Vargunteius, Ser. and P. Cornelius Sulla (sons of a Ser. Cornelius Sulla), M. Porcius Laeca and C. Cornelius were among those prosecuted (§§6–7, 18–19), and Cicero's evidence was decisive in securing their convictions (§§10, 21, 48, 83; cf. §71). Finally, Sulla too was accused of having conspired with Catiline, in 66 as well as in 63 (§11). The prosecutor was once again the younger Torquatus, who now had as his *subscriptor* the son of the condemned C. Cornelius. Sulla was defended by Q. Hortensius Hortalus and by Cicero, whose speech *pro Sulla* is that which survives. He was also supported by an impressive array of optimates (§§3–5, 13, 82), among them the two Claudii Marcelli (the praetor of 80 and his son, the consul of 50) and the dictator's brother-in-law M. Valerius Messalla

---

58 *Flac.* 96; *Sest.* 66; *Cael.* 70; [Sal.] *Inv. in Cic.* 3–4; Dio 37.41.2–4; *schol. Bob.* 84 St.; cf. Gruen 282–5.

59 See pp. 14–16.

60 [Autronius in 63 and afterwards.] Autronius' part in the conspiracy is attested in Cicero only in *pro Sulla*, where he is systematically denigrated (see the characterization at §71) in order to justify the inconsistency between Cicero's testifying against him (§10) and defending Sulla (cf. pp. 158f.). His role may therefore have been relatively minor. In Sallust he is present at the fictitious 'first meeting' of the conspirators (*Cat.* 17.3; cf. Flor. 2.12.3). He is put in charge of the storming of the senate-house (accepting Schliack's emendation) at §53, and according to Cicero at §18 (but not elsewhere) he was responsible for sending C. Cornelius to murder Cicero at his home. Although he remained in Rome (17.5n.), he was not arrested on 2–3 December; nevertheless, he was incriminated by Volturcius (Sal. *Cat.* 47.1) and the Allobroges (§§36–8). He was also thought to have been behind L. Tarquinius' incrimination of Crassus (Sal. *Cat.* 48.7). When brought to trial in 62 Autronius begged Cicero, both in person and through his relatives the Marcelli, to undertake his defence, but neither Cicero (§§18–19) nor anyone else (§7) would help him. After his condemnation he went into exile in Epirus (where Cicero had to avoid him in 58: *Att.* 3.2, 3.7.1), and his house was bought by M. Valerius Messalla 'Niger' (*Att.* 1.13.6). He was dead by 46 (*Brut.* 241, 244, 251). On Autronius' oratory see *Brut.* 241. His son became suffect consul in 33, and obtained a triumph (*MRR* III.33).

'Rufus', the future consul of 53 (§ 20). Documentary evidence in Sulla's favour was provided by L. Julius Caesar, the consul of 64, Q. Pompeius Rufus, grandson of the dictator, and C. Memmius, the dictator's son-in-law (§ 55). Two deputations came from Pompeii to show their support (§ 61). Members of Sulla's family attended the trial: his half-brother Caecilius, his young son, and probably also his mother and his stepson Memmius (§§ 62, 88-9). The prosecution tried to gain an advantage by beginning their accusation sooner than the defence expected.[61] It was to no avail: Sulla was acquitted.[62]

After his trial Sulla is next heard of in 57, when his house was used by P. Clodius as a base for organised violence:[63] evidently he no longer felt indebted to Cicero. Later, in 54, he lodged an accusation against A. Gabinius for *ambitus*;[64] his half-brother Caecilius, his son and his stepson Memmius, now tribune,[65] acted as *subscriptores*. Sulla was clearly hoping to regain his former status by a successful prosecution on the same charge as that on which he himself had been convicted.[66] At this time Gabinius, newly returned from his governorship of Syria, was standing

---

[61] 92.4n.

[62] Sulla's acquittal is not directly attested, but may be inferred from his presence in Rome in 54; cf. *Att.* 4.18.3; *Q. fr.* 3.3.2. A guilty verdict would have entailed exile (89.6n.). Acquittal is also implied by (1) Cicero's publication of his defence and (2) the omission of Sulla's name in accounts of the conspiracy of 63 in Sallust and later historians.

[63] *Att.* 4.3.3.

[64] *Q. fr.* 3.3.2; *Att.* 4.18.3.

[65] 89.13n.

[66] Mommsen, *Strafrecht* 509; Taylor, *PP* 114 (note, however, that Sulla was hoping to regain his own former status, not to acquire that of Gabinius: after his *repetundae* conviction Gabinius would not have been of senatorial rank); Gruen 323 n. 59; E. Fantham, *Historia* 24 (1975) 436f.; B. A. Marshall on Asc. 54.12 C; M. C. Alexander, *CP* 80 (1985) 28f. Sulla's action therefore need not be interpreted as an act of hostility towards Pompey; Fantham sees Sulla's associates as aiming to regain their hold over Pompey during this period.

trial for *maiestas*, and was also awaiting prosecution on a *repetundae* charge;[67] for the latter case, a *divinatio* had resulted in the choice of Memmius as official prosecutor. Gabinius was a marked man: it was highly unlikely that he would be acquitted twice, and so stand trial for *ambitus*. However, this suited Sulla perfectly[68] because, if Gabinius were convicted on another charge before the *ambitus* case came to court, it would still be open to him to prosecute Gabinius in his absence.[69] Gabinius would then be condemned by default, and Sulla would be restored to his former position.[70] The younger Torquatus, ever Sulla's enemy, therefore put himself up as a rival prosecutor in an attempt to prevent Sulla's rehabilitation. A further *divinatio* was held, and Sulla secured the right to bring the accusation: he had the greater incentive to see Gabinius convicted. In the event, Gabinius was acquitted of *maiestas*, but fell victim to the *repetundae* charge and went into exile. It is likely that Sulla now brought his case and, winning it by default, returned at last to the senate.[71]

Sulla is generally thought to have served as a legate of Caesar's in 48–7 and to have commanded his right wing at Pharsalia;[72] however, Caesar's legate is more likely to have been Sulla's son,[73] who would by now have been in his mid-twenties.

---

[67] For the sources for these events see *MRR* II.218; cf. Gruen 322–31; E. Fantham, *Historia* 24 (1975) 425–43.

[68] This may be what is implied by *non dubitans quin foris esset* (*Att.* 4.18.3).

[69] Mommsen, *Strafrecht* 333–5; Greenidge 473f.

[70] As shown by D. R. Shackleton Bailey on *Att.* 4.18.1 and 3.

[71] Alternatively, *nam habet damnatos quos pro illo nobis restituat* (*Fam.* 15.19.3) may imply that Sulla was rehabilitated by Caesar. If so, then perhaps Sulla needed two successful prosecutions to secure his rehabilitation (cf. Dio 40.52.3–4).

[72] *MRR* II.281, 290.

[73] As suggested by D. R. Shackleton Bailey on *Att.* 4.3.3 ('In 48 the elder Sulla would have been at least 60, and C.'s account of him at his trial does not suggest military capacities... Caesar liked young commanders'); cf. 88.14n. However, Shackleton Bailey is mistaken in arguing that

The end of Sulla's life mirrors its beginning, with his conspicuous participation in the sales of the confiscated property of the defeated Pompeians (46).[74] It was at this time that Cicero probably considered buying Sulla's house at Naples;[75] perhaps Sulla was realising his capital in order to fund his purchases. But soon afterwards, at the end of 46 (or the beginning of January 45), Sulla died, some said at the hands of bandits, others of overeating.[76] Whether his body was buried in accordance with the family tradition, without first being cremated, is unknown.[77] Cicero expressed no sorrow at the death of his former client,[78] reporting it humorously and receiving a witty reply from Cassius.[79] In particular, he joked that Caesar would now raise less cash at his auctions.[80] Nevertheless, he did concede that in Sulla Rome had lost one of its 'characters': πρόσωπον πόλεως amisimus.[81]

the son could have been '30 or even older' in 48: his parents married no earlier than 75 (89.13n.).

[74] *Fam.* 15.17.2, 15.19.3, 9.10.3; *Off.* 2.29; cf. P. A. Brunt, *Italian Manpower, 225 BC–AD 14*[2] (Oxford 1987) 322.

[75] *Fam.* 9.15.3–5; cf. 17.8n.

[76] His death is reported in January 45: *Fam.* 15.17.2 (to Cassius; his reply, 15.19.3), 9.10.3 (to Dolabella). On the cause: *Fam.* 15.17.2 (cf. 9.10.3).

[77] The dictator Sulla was the first of the Cornelii to break with the custom of his *gens* by being cremated before burial (he did not wish his body to be treated as he had treated Marius'): *Leg.* 2.56–7; Plin. *Nat.* 7.187. Cicero refers to P. Sulla as *combustum* (*Fam.* 15.17.2), but it is not to be supposed that he had troubled to secure accurate information on this point.

[78] Syme goes too far in maintaining that the news 'made Cicero deliriously happy' (*Sallust* 71); cf. his equally unjustified assertion that P. Sittius' death (*Att.* 15.17.1) gave Cicero 'acute pleasure' (*Sallust* 133). On the Romans' alleged indifference towards death see Lintott 44–6 (esp. 46 n. 2).

[79] The play on *iudicium* at *Fam.* 15.19.3 (Cassius' reply) is well appreciated by D. R. Shackleton Bailey.

[80] *Fam.* 15.17.2 (cf. 15.19.3), 9.10.3.

[81] *Fam.* 15.17.2.

II THE TRIAL

(a) Date

It is not possible to fix the date of Sulla's trial as precisely as has usually been thought.[82] Cicero mentions the convictions of the Catilinarians as having occurred *per hos menses* (§ 92); Sulla's trial therefore took place at least several months after Catiline's defeat at the beginning of 62.[83] After the trial Cicero bought a house on the Palatine with money borrowed from Sulla,[84] and in December 62 he told P. Sestius that he had bought this house some time previously.[85] Sulla's trial was therefore held at some point between, perhaps, May[86] and October 62.[87]

On the date of publication of Cicero's speech see pp. 54–9.

(b) The court

Prior to Sulla's trial two laws relating to political violence are attested, a *lex Lutatia* (78?),[88] known only from *Cael.* 70,

---

[82] Reid, Introd. § 24; Macdonald 305f.; contrast Boulanger 92. The arguments for July are based on an unwarranted inference from the mention of a M. Messalla (probably in any case misidentified) at § 20 (20.4n.). That is not to say, of course, that the trial could not have taken place in July.

[83] Liv. *epit.* 103; Dio 37.39.1; cf. *Sest.* 12, with G. V. Sumner, *CP* 58 (1963) 215–19.

[84] Gel. 12.12.2–4.

[85] *Fam.* 5.6.2.

[86] It may be significant that Cicero does not mention his defence of Sulla in his letter to Pompey in April (*Fam.* 5.7).

[87] Cases *de vi* could be heard at any time of the year, even during festivals (*Cael.* 1); cf. Mommsen, *Strafrecht* 363f.; Greenidge 457; R. A. Bauman, *Labeo* 24 (1978) 64f.

[88] Date: Lintott 110f.; Bauman (previous n.) 65f.; cf. *Cael.* 70 *quam legem Q. Catulus armata dissensione civium rei publicae paene extremis temporibus tulit.*

and a *lex Plautia de vi* (70?),[89] which is first mentioned as
the law under which Catiline was charged by L. Aemilius
Paullus in 63.[90] The question of the relationship between
these two laws has been much debated, but now seems
finally to have been settled by L. Labruna.[91] The *lex Lutatia*,
Labruna argues, was an *ad hoc* measure setting up a *quaestio
extraordinaria* to deal with Lepidus' insurrection; later, its
provisions were incorporated into the *lex Plautia*, which established the first permanent *quaestio de vi*.[92] Those ancient
sources which report that Catiline's surviving adherents[93]
and Sulla[94] were tried under the *lex Plautia de vi* are therefore to be believed. Cicero, on the other hand, is strictly
speaking inaccurate when he implies at *Cael.* 70 that the

[89] Date: *MRR* II.128; Lintott III, 122f.; Gruen 227; L. Labruna, *Il console
'sovversivo'* (Naples 1975) 98–106.

[90] Sal. *Cat.* 31.4; Dio 37.31.3; *schol. Bob.* 149 St. (which also mentions
Cethegus) on *Vat.* 25 (*duo...proditores*); cf. *TLRR* no. 223.

[91] Labruna (n. 89) 82–114, 166–74; cf. Bauman (n. 87) 60–74 ('It is to be
hoped that these findings by Labruna will gain general acceptance
and so put an end to a most protracted debate', 69).

[92] [*LEGES DE VI.*] Labruna's hypothesis resembles that of J. N. Hough
(*AJP* 51 (1930) 135–47), although Hough dates the *lex Plautia* to 65–4
(cf. Lintott 114, 123). Mommsen (*Strafrecht* 654 n. 2; cf. *Coll.* 65 n. 17)
took the two laws to be one and the same, arguing that Q. Lutatius
Catulus had had a tribune pass the bill for him; but this is discounted
by *tulit* ('he proposed and carried in his own person') at *Cael.* 70. The
laws must therefore be separate. J. Cousin (*RHD* 22 (1943) 88–94)
regarded both as operating simultaneously, the *lex Lutatia* dealing
with *vis contra rem publicam* and the *lex Plautia* with *vis contra privatos*
(most inappropriately, given that Sulla and the Catilinarians were
tried under the *lex Plautia*; cf. Lintott 114f.). Lintott (107–24) argued
that the *lex Lutatia* aimed to replace the earlier special tribunals by
setting up a permanent *quaestio* to deal with *seditio*, and that the *lex
Plautia* subsequently extended the competence of the court to cases of
violence against private citizens which were held to be *contra rem publicam*; for objections, however, see Gruen 227 n. 70; Bauman (n. 87) 71
n. 36, 73 n. 64. See further Greenidge 424 n. 6; R. G. Austin on *Cael.* 1
and 70; Jones 57; Gruen 224–7 (although cf. Bauman (n. 87) 74 n. 84);
B. A. Marshall on Asc. 55.11 C; A. Cavarzere in *Atti del III seminario
romanistico gardesano 22–25 ottobre 1985* (Milan 1988), 235–50.

[93] [Sal.] *Inv. in Cic.* 3; cf. *Sest.* 66.

[94] *Schol. Bob.* 84 St.

trials of the Catilinarians (and that of Caelius himself) were held under the *lex Lutatia*.[95]

The jury which heard Sulla's case was composed of senators, *equites* and *tribuni aerarii* in equal numbers (§64), as specified by the *lex Aurelia iudiciaria* (70). It is likely that there were twenty-five *iudices* from each category (*decuria*), giving a total of seventy-five.[96] They appear to have been empanelled by the method known as *editio*, according to which the prosecution nominated the *iudices*, their selection then being reduced by means of the defence's *reiectio*.[97] This procedure allowed Cicero to complain that a jury had been empanelled which was potentially biased in the prosecution's favour (§§92-3). The votes were taken by a secret ballot, in accordance with the *lex Cassia tabellaria* (137).[98] Had Sulla been convicted, his punishment would have been *aquae et ignis interdictio*, in effect exile.[99]

Criminal trials were held in the forum[100] (hence 'forensic' oratory), in the open air.[101] The presiding official (usually a praetor, but for trials for murder and violence a *quaesitor*[102]

---

[95] Cf. *Cael.* 70 *quaeque lex sedata illa flamma consulatus mei fumantis reliquias coniurationis exstinxit.* Cicero's aim is to point out the absurdity of Caelius' being tried 'under the same law' (loosely) as the Lepidans and Catilinarians. He was able to treat the two laws as one because the provisions of the *lex Lutatia* were carried over into the *lex Plautia* (Bauman (n. 87) 67; cf. Lintott 121).

[96] *Flac.* 4; *Pis.* 96; *Att.* 4.18.1; *Q. fr.* 3.4.1; Asc. 28 C; cf. Mommsen, *Strafrecht* 217f.; Greenidge 447f.; Jones 69f.; B. A. Marshall on Asc. 28.25 C. 51 *iudices* (out of an initial 81) voted at Milo's trial (Asc. 53 C); but Milo was tried under special procedures.

[97] 92.4n.

[98] *MRR* 1.485; Mommsen, *Strafrecht* 444f.; Greenidge 497.

[99] 89.6n. For standard accounts of the procedure in criminal trials see Mommsen, *Strafrecht* 339-520; Greenidge 456-504; Strachan-Davidson, *Criminal Law* II.112-52 (further bibliography at Kennedy 8 n. 9).

[100] *Ver.* 5.143 and *Flac.* 57 *forum plenum iudiciorum*; *Scaur.* 46-8; *Orat.* 131; Suet. *Aug.* 29.1; cf. N. W. DeWitt, *CP* 21 (1926) 218-24; H. D. Johnson, *The Roman Tribunal* (Baltimore 1927).

[101] Cf. (e.g.) Sen. *Con.* 9.*praef*.4-5.

[102] Lintott 121f.; cf. Mommsen, *Strafrecht* 206f.; Greenidge 417, 495.

of more junior magisterial rank) and the *iudices* occupied a
tribunal at the front of the court. Facing them and seated on
benches (*subsellia*, §5) were the two opposing parties, the
accusatores on one side and the defendant with his advocates
(*patroni*) on the other, each party accompanied by their
advisers (*advocati*), family, friends and witnesses. Behind the
benches a ring (*corona*) of bystanders stood to watch the
performance, allowing the *patronus* when he wished to turn
from the jury to address the public directly. Both Torquatus and Cicero made appeals to the *corona* at Sulla's trial
(§§ 30–1, 33–4), and the crowd which they addressed was a
large one (§ 33).[103]

(c) Prosecution and defence

At a Roman trial the prosecutors' speeches were heard
first, then those of the defence, and only after the end of
the speeches was the evidence taken.[104] Torquatus would
naturally have spoken before his *subscriptor*, and Cicero refers to Hortensius as having already made his speech (§§ 12,
14, 51). The speeches at Sulla's trial were therefore given
in order by Torquatus, Cornelius, Hortensius and finally
Cicero. In speaking last Cicero followed his customary
practice;[105] this was an honour conceded by Hortensius in
acknowledgement of Cicero's greater oratorical ability and
in particular his skill in producing emotional *conclusiones*.[106]

L. Manlius Torquatus,[107] Sulla's *accusator* in 66 and

---

[103] For descriptions of the scene at a trial see *Brut.* 200, 290; Greenidge
458f.; Taylor, *PP* 98–100; Kennedy 16–18; T. P. Wiseman, *Catullus
and his World: a Reappraisal* (Cambridge 1985) 69f.

[104] Greenidge 477–9; Strachan-Davidson, *Criminal Law* II.113f.; Wiseman
(previous n.) 70; cf. 78.1n.

[105] He also spoke last at the trials of Rabirius, Murena, Flaccus, Sestius,
Caelius, Balbus, Plancius, Scaurus and Milo.

[106] *Brut.* 190; *Orat.* 130; cf. p. 304, where both passages are quoted.

[107] *RE* XIV.1203.3ff., Manlius 80; *MRR* II.135, 257, 277, 289, 297f., 445,
485; III.136; *ORF* I.443f.; Sumner 139f. For his villa see D'Arms 189.

again in 62, belonged to a distinguished patrician family
(§§ 23, 25),[108] although the Manlii Torquati had been more
prominent in the third and second centuries than they were
in the first: when his father won the consulship of 65 from
Sulla he became the first of his family to attain that office
since 164. The elder Torquatus[109] (as the consul of 65 will
be referred to throughout) had been a close friend of
Atticus since their school-days together, and his son shared
with Atticus an interest in Epicureanism.[110] Ties between
the Torquati and Cicero were also close: although the
father offended him by not inviting him to join his *consilia*
in 65 (§ 11),[111] he and his son gave him valued support during the Catilinarian conspiracy (§ 34) and afterwards.[112]
The younger Torquatus in particular was a close friend of
Cicero's (§§ 2, 11, 23, 34, 44, 46–50). Although he considered Cicero to have violated their friendship in defending
Sulla (§§ 2, 44, 48, 50), this had no lasting effect on their
good relations: after his death Cicero cast Torquatus as the
advocate of Epicureanism in *de Finibus* 1,[113] which he even
referred to as the *Torquatus*.[114] He also gave him an obitu-
ary notice in the *Brutus*: *L. Torquatus, quem tu non tam cito
rhetorem dixisses, etsi non deerat oratio, quam, ut Graeci dicunt,
πολιτικόν. Erant in eo plurimae litterae nec eae vulgares, sed in-
teriores quaedam et reconditae, divina memoria, summa verborum et
gravitas et elegantia; atque haec omnia vitae decorabat gravitas et
integritas* (265).[115]

---

[108] See J. F. Mitchell, *Historia* 15 (1966) 23–31.
[109] 11.4n.
[110] See Nep. *Att.* 1.4; *Fin.* 1.13–14 etc.; Castner 40–42 (cf. 57–61).'
[111] 11.7n.
[112] *Pis.* 47, 77, 92; *Fin.* 2.62; *Att.* 12.21.1.
[113] Cf. *Att.* 13.19.4.
[114] *Att.* 13.5.1, 13.32.3.
[115] The very different characterisation at Gel. 1.5.3 (*subagresti homo ingenio
et infestivo*) is clearly an inference from the words of Hortensius which
Gellius proceeds to report; cf. L. Holford-Strevens, *Aulus Gellius*
(London 1988) 153 n. 54.

Torquatus held the praetorship in or around 49,[116] which would make him roughly twenty-seven at the time of Sulla's trial (and twenty-three when he secured Sulla's conviction and despoiled him of his *insignia* (§ 50) as an *adulescentulus*[117] in 66). In 62 his political career was just beginning (§§ 24, 30): he probably served as a military tribune in the following year, and had not yet entered the senate.[118] It is virtually certain that Torquatus should be identified with the Manlius Torquatus whose marriage to a Junia Aurunculeia (if that is the correct name)[119] is celebrated in Catullus 61. Friendship with Catullus would be appropriate in view of Torquatus' known interest in both esoteric learning and erotic verse,[120] concerns which were shared by the *poetae novi*; it is therefore reasonable also to identify him with the Manlius[121] of Catullus 68 A, the friend who wrote to Catullus to ask him for *munera... et Musarum... et Veneris* (10). The next definite reference to Torquatus is his attempt to secure the right to prosecute

[116] The date of his praetorship (he is praetor designate at *Fin.* 2.74, but the dramatic date of *Fin.* is otherwise unknown) is traditionally inferred from Caes. *Civ.* 1.24.3 as 49 (*MRR* II.257); however, Shackleton Bailey points out that Cicero does not refer to him as *praetor* at *Att.* 8.11B.1 (cf. *MRR* III.136). The date is therefore uncertain.

[117] *Fin.* 2.62.

[118] 24.3n. For his coins (65) and his membership of the *XVviri s.f.* see 30.3n.

[119] Two *gentilicia* would be unparalleled at this date. For *Junia* R. Syme (in C. L. Neudling, *A Prosopography to Catullus* (Oxford 1955) 185) therefore suggested *Vibia*, an Oscan *praenomen*; if this is correct, Torquatus, like his father (§ 25; cf. 25.5n.), would have married a woman of central Italian origin.

[120] *Brut.* 265; *Fin.* 1.13–14, 1.25, 2.107; Plin. *Ep.* 5.3.5 (where the other Torquatus mentioned is probably the quaestor of 43 and addressee at Hor. *Ep.* 1.5.3 and *Carm.* 4.7.23, Torquatus' brother Aulus; cf. J. F. Mitchell, *Historia* 15 (1966) 26–9).

[121] The MSS give 'Mallius' for 'Manlius', as at Catul. 61.16, 215, where *Torquatus* (209) shows 'Manlius' to be correct. 'Mallius' at *Att.* 1.16.16 is probably also a reference to Torquatus (24.3n.). On this common corruption see T. P. Wiseman, *CR* n.s. 15 (1965) 263; *id.*, *Cinna the Poet* (Leicester 1974) 88f.

Gabinius *de ambitu* in 54; as we have seen,[122] he was probably unsuccessful in preventing Sulla's rehabilitation. In the civil war Torquatus fought on the Pompeian side.[123] He was put in command of Oricum in Epirus, but was forced to surrender to Caesar.[124] At Dyrrachium he broke through Caesar's siege works (48).[125] Finally, escaping with Metellus Scipio after the defeat at Thapsus in 46, he ran into the fleet of P. Sittius[126] at Hippo Regius. The Pompeians' ships were outnumbered and destroyed. Scipio committed suicide.[127] Torquatus was killed[128] – by the forces, coincidentally, of a man who had been attacked in his prosecution of Sulla sixteen years earlier (§§ 56–9).[129]

Of Torquatus' *subscriptor* Cornelius[130] (the *praenomen* is unknown) there is no mention outside Cicero's speech. He was young (*istum puerum*, § 51), the son (§§ 51–2) of C. Cornelius,[131] the Catilinarian conspirator who together with Vargunteius had attempted to murder Cicero at the early morning *salutatio* on 7 November 63. E. S. Gruen[132] suggests that Cornelius may have expected to help his father, who had been condemned (§§ 6, 71), by his prosecution of Sulla. Certainly Torquatus' *subscriptor*, as Gruen remarks, 'added small adornment to the cause'.

The prosecution accused Sulla of conspiracy with Catiline both in 66 and in 63 (§ 11). In 66 Torquatus' father had been consul designate, and in 63 Cornelius' father had

---

122 P. 12.
123 *Att.* 8.11B.1; cf. 7.12.4, 9.8.1.
124 Caes. *Civ.* 3.11.3–4.
125 Luc. 6.285–9, with *schol. Bern.* 199 Usener; Oros. 6.15.19–22.
126 56.1n.
127 *B. Afr.* 96.1–2; Oros. 6.16.4.
128 Oros. 6.16.5 (with incorrect *praenomen*); cf. *B. Afr.* 96.2. He is often erroneously said by modern scholars (e.g. F. Münzer in *RE*) to have committed suicide.
129 *Fam.* 5.17.2.
130 *RE* IV.1250.59ff., Cornelius 7; cf. Nicolet 853.
131 6.6n.
132 284.

been a conspirator: the prosecutors were therefore closely connected with the events which formed the basis of their accusation. The specific charges, which the prosecution threatened to reinforce by torturing Sulla's slaves (§ 78), were as follows: (i) that Sulla took part in the conspiracy of 63 on the evidence of the Allobroges (§§ 36–9), and (ii) that the account of this evidence was falsified by Cicero immediately after the evidence was heard in the senate (§§ 40–45); (iii) that Sulla joined Catiline and Autronius in plotting a massacre at the consular elections of 63 (§§ 51–3); (iv) that Sulla purchased gladiators with a view to committing violence and murder, on the pretext that they were needed by his cousin Faustus (§§ 54–5); (v) that Sulla sent P. Sittius to Further Spain to cause disturbances in Catiline's interest (§§ 56–9); (vi) that Sulla fostered dissension at Pompeii, again in Catiline's interest (§§ 60–62); (vii) that Sulla attempted to force the passage of the *rogatio Caecilia* (§§ 62–6); and (viii) that Sulla took part in the conspiracy of 66 on the evidence of a letter sent to Pompey by Cicero himself (§§ 67–8). Not all of the charges were directly concerned with the Catilinarian conspiracy (and therefore guilt on some counts need not imply Sulla's involvement); nevertheless, they were all pertinent to the *quaestio de vi*.

How the prosecution divided the charges between them is uncertain. (ii) and (viii) above are ascribed in Cicero's speech to Torquatus, and (iii) and (iv) to Cornelius. It is likely that in replying to the bulk of the charges Cicero follows the order in which they were brought up by the prosecution;[133] if this is correct, then it is probable that (iii)–(vii) are all attributable to Cornelius. This would be appropriate given that Cornelius, through his father, was in a better position to know about the conspiracy of 63 than Torquatus. Torquatus' speech, on the other hand, seems to a large extent to have been directed not so much

---

[133] As argued at p. 232.

against Sulla as against those who were defending him. Not even the consulars escaped censure (§§ 81–2), and Cicero in particular was bitterly attacked. Torquatus accused him of inconsistency in defending a Catilinarian conspirator when it was he who had been responsible for the firm measures taken in suppression of the conspiracy (§§ 2–10). He inveighed against him as a foreigner (Cicero was a *municipalis*) who had instituted *regnum* at Rome by his illegal execution of conspirators without trial and by his arbitrary and capricious use of his decisive influence in the trials of 62 (§§ 21–35); in this context Torquatus drew attention to Cicero's starkly contrasting treatment of Autronius and Sulla (§§ 14–20). Cicero, therefore, was Rome's third *rex peregrinus*, in succession to Numa and Tarquinius Priscus (§ 22). Torquatus even accused him of having falsified the record of the senatorial proceedings of 3 December 63 (§§ 40–45). Finally, he protested that Cicero by undertaking Sulla's defence had violated the friendship between them (§§ 48–50). So damaging (§§ 2, 35) was Torquatus' invective that Cicero felt it necessary to devote roughly one-third of his speech to a defence of himself (§§ 2–10, 14–35).

The first speech for the defence, however, was given by Cicero's fellow *patronus* Q. Hortensius Hortalus.[134] Hortensius had been the foremost orator at Rome from c.86[135] until the trial of C. Verres in 70; during this period he opposed Cicero, probably successfully, at the trial of P. Quinctius (81). Upon Verres' conviction the domination of the courts passed to Cicero,[136] and Hortensius' forensic reputation was largely eclipsed. In the five years following his consulship (69), Hortensius allowed his oratorical talents to decline;[137]

---

[134] *RE* VIII.2470.22ff., Hortensius 13; *MRR* II.35, 97, 116, 131, 254, 476; *ORF* I.310–30; Sumner 122f.; David 763–6.

[135] *Brut.* 308.

[136] *Div. Caec.* 24; *Ver.* 35; *Fam.* 9.18.1; Quint. *Inst.* 10.1.112; Dio 36.1a (Xiphil.).

[137] *Brut.* 319–20.

his only known case from this period is a defence, probably unsuccessful,[138] of Vargunteius (§ 6). However, when Cicero himself became consul Hortensius resumed his former activity, and a partnership was begun which continued until the preliminary summons of Milo's slaves (52), their last collaboration before Hortensius' death in 50: *sic duodecim post meum consulatum annos in maximis causis, cum ego mihi illum, sibi me ille anteferret, coniunctissime versati sumus* (*Brut.* 323). The two men are known to have collaborated in the trials of (besides Sulla) Rabirius (63), Murena (63), Flaccus (59), Sestius (56), Plancius (54), Scaurus (54) and Milo (preliminary summons, 52).[139] Nevertheless, forensic jealousy, which Cicero is at pains to deny in the *Brutus*,[140] together with Hortensius' superior social position (he was a *nobilis*),[141] precluded a genuine friendship, and Cicero considered Hortensius to have been a false friend to him at the time of his exile.[142] But Hortensius seems to have been as close to Atticus as Cicero was himself, and Atticus' conciliatory influence enabled the two orators to remain on good terms.[143] In addition they found themselves bound together increasingly by their political views: Hortensius was a staunch optimate, and had no compunction in lauding Cicero's consulship.[144] He was also responsible for introducing Cicero into the College of Augurs in 53 (or 52).[145] Hortensius was honoured by Cicero after his death, especially in the *Brutus*;[146] he was cast as the opponent of

---

[138] 6.1n.

[139] See *TLRR* nos. 221, 224, 247, 271, 293, 295, 306. On Hortensius' involvement in the trial of Plancius see J. Linderski, *PP* 16 (1961) 304–11.

[140] Esp. 1–3.

[141] See D. R. Shackleton Bailey on *Att.* 1.13.2; *id.*, *Onomasticon* 55.

[142] E.g. *Q. fr.* 1.3.8; *Att.* 3.9.2, 4.6.3, 5.17.5.

[143] Nep. *Att.* 5.4.

[144] *Att.* 2.25.1 (quoted at 3.4n.); cf. *Phil.* 2.12.

[145] *Phil.* 2.4; *Brut.* 1; cf. *MRR* II.233; III.209.

[146] See esp. §§ 1–3, 228–30, 301–3, 317–28; cf. *de Orat.* 3.230.

philosophy in the *Hortensius*,[147] and the first edition of the *Academica* (of which the second half survives as the *Lucullus*) was set in his villa at Bauli.[148] Eight years Cicero's senior,[149] Hortensius was fifty-two[150] at the time of Sulla's trial. He was perhaps prevailed upon to defend him, like Cicero (§ 20), by Messalla Rufus: Rufus was Hortensius' nephew.[151]

The prosecution had been able to base their case on their fathers' supposed knowledge of the events concerned, and the defence accordingly divided their reply to the charges so that each *patronus* would be discussing events of which he had had direct personal experience (§ 13). Thus Hortensius replied to the charges relating to the alleged conspiracy of 66, when he had been a prominent member of the elder Torquatus' *consilia*, and Cicero dealt with the charges relating to the *maxima coniuratio* of 63, his consular year (§§ 11–14, 51). In the *partitio defensionis* which Hortensius and Cicero agreed upon, only one detail of the 'first conspiracy' was to be left to Cicero, the question of his letter to Pompey, which the prosecution had cited as evidence in their favour (§§ 67–8). The remaining arguments connecting Sulla with the 'first conspiracy' were answered by Hortensius, whose speech won praise from Cicero: *cum esset copiosissima atque ornatissima oratio, tamen non minus auctoritatis inerat in ea quam facultatis* (§ 12). A clue to Cicero's purpose in making this judgement of Hortensius' speech is provided by an anecdote in Aulus Gellius: *Sed cum L. Torquatus, sub-agresti homo ingenio et infestivo, gravius acerbiusque apud consilium iudicum, cum de causa Sullae quaereretur, non iam histrionem eum esse diceret, sed gesticulariam Dionysiamque eum notissimae salta-*

---

[147] *Fin.* 1.2; cf. *Luc.* 61.
[148] Cf. D'Arms 181.
[149] *Brut.* 230.
[150] Or fifty-one if the trial took place before his birthday (which fell later than early June; cf. Sumner 122f.).
[151] 20.4n.

triculae nomine appellaret, tum voce molli atque demissa Hortensius *'Dionysia'*, inquit, *'Dionysia malo equidem esse quam quod tu, Tor-quate,* ἄμουσος, ἀναφρόδιτος, ἀπροσδιόνυσος' (1.5.3). The oratory practised by Hortensius was of the florid, theatrical variety known as 'Asianist'.[152] His style, according to Cicero, was far removed from ordinary speech (*attuleratque minime vulgare genus dicendi* (*Brut.* 302)), and was reinforced by an exaggerated use of gesture (*motus et gestus etiam plus artis habebat quam erat oratori satis (ibid.* 303)) – as if he were in fact an actor.[153] This type of oratory relied for its effect on being seen in performance (*dicebat melius quam scripsit Hortensius* (*Orat.* 132));[154] unsurprisingly, no more than two words from Hortensius' speeches have survived.[155] The Asianist style had its limitations: as Cicero observes, unless an orator was young, it tended to make him look ridiculous (*haec ... genera dicendi aptiora sunt adulescentibus, in senibus gravitatem non habent* (*Brut.* 326)),[156] and it was in any case less tolerated by the audiences of the 60s than by those of the 80s. Most damagingly, the Asianist style was lacking in *auctoritas*: *genus illud dicendi auctoritatis habebat parum* (*Brut.* 327). This proved increasingly problematic for Hortensius as he became older and more senior: *sed cum iam honores et illa senior auctoritas gravius quiddam requireret, remanebat idem nec decebat idem* (*Brut.* 327). For Torquatus' prosecution, it was essential to undermine the overwhelming consular *auctoritas* of Sulla's two *patroni*. He set out to undermine that of Cicero by criticising his acceptance of the case (§§ 2, 35); he chose to attack Hortensius, on the other hand, by interrupting his speech to mock the lack of *auctoritas* in Hortensius' style

---

[152] *Brut.* 325–7 (cf. 301–3). On Asianism see U. v. Wilamowitz-Möllen-dorff, *Hermes* 35 (1900) 1–52; F. W. Blass, *Die Rhythmen der asianischen und römischen Kunstprosa* (Leipzig 1905), esp. 109–34 on Cicero; Norden 131–52, 218–21; Laurand 343–9; Leeman 91–111.

[153] Gel. 1.5.2.

[154] Cf. Quint. *Inst.* 11.3.8.

[155] *cicatricum mearum* (*orat.* 35, = *ORF* 1.322).

[156] *Brut.* 325–7.

and delivery, comparing him to a well-known dancing-girl, Dionysia. As Gellius relates, Hortensius was able to make a dignified reply, calling Torquatus a stranger to the Muses, to Venus and to Dionysus: his point was that Torquatus, as an Epicurean, was simply a philistine (Epicurus' contempt for education and culture was notorious).[157] The exchange thus reflects the trial of Murena in the previous year: Cato had called Murena a dancer, while Cicero went on to mock Cato's philosophy.[158] But Hortensius' reply was not in fact entirely appropriate. In reality, Torquatus was no stranger to the Muses but, like Hortensius himself,[159] a writer of fashionable erotic verse. Moreover, the point of Catullus' *neque te Venus / neglegit* (61.191–2; cf. 68A.10 *muneraque et Musarum hinc petis et Veneris*) may have been to suggest that the description 'stranger to Venus' was likewise inappropriate.[160] Torquatus' mockery, then, placed Hortensius' *auctoritas* in jeopardy, and it was therefore necessary for Cicero to stress that, although his partner's speech was Asianist in style (*copiosissima atque ornatissima* is the euphemism he uses), it did none the less convey the *auctoritas* which one would expect of a consular.

Once Hortensius had completed his speech (which was probably published afterwards), Cicero delivered the *pro Sulla*.

(d) Cicero's reasons for accepting the case

It is possible to identify the main factors which will have induced Cicero to undertake Sulla's defence, although it

---

[157] S.E. *M.* 1.1–4; D.L. 10.6, 10.120. The Muses, Venus and Dionysus are the themes of Alcaeus at Hor. *Carm.* 1.32.9 (cf. 3.21.21–2).

[158] *Mur.* 13, 60–66.

[159] Var. *L.* 8.14; Ov. *Tr.* 2.441–2; Plin. *Ep.* 5.3.5; Gel. 19.9.7; cf. Catul. 65.2, 65.15, 95.3.

[160] Cf. F. Münzer, *RE* xiv.1205.30ff.; T. P. Wiseman, *Cinna the Poet* (Leicester 1974) 102f. Wiseman suggests that Catullus may in fact have being 'gently malicious' in alluding at 68A.10 to Hortensius' retort.

would of course be rash to attempt to assess the relative importance of these motives. Let us begin, however, by briefly considering Cicero's political position in 62.[161]

Cicero's suppression of the Catilinarian conspiracy at Rome made him the hero of the hour, but his execution of citizens without the trial before the people which had been their legal right left him henceforward open to attack.[162] He was quickly made aware of the insecurity of his position. On 29 December 63, at the end of his term of office, the tribunes Q. Caecilius Metellus Nepos and L. Calpurnius Bestia prevented him from giving the consul's customary retiring speech,[163] Nepos arguing that the man who had punished others without allowing them the right to speak in their own defence ought not to be allowed the right to speak himself.[164] Nepos persisted in his campaign against Cicero and attempted to bring him to trial; Cicero was saved by the senate, which decreed that all who had acted against the conspirators should be immune from prosecution and that anyone who brought such a charge in future should be considered a *hostis*.[165] Nevertheless, a section, at least, of public opinion sided with Nepos,[166] and during the succeeding months Cicero's unpopularity was increased by his role in the trials of Catiline's followers. Every defendant against whom he gave evidence was automatically convicted, and Nepos is said to have remarked that more men had been executed on Cicero's evidence than saved by his eloquence.[167] Roman citizens were being

---

[161] Cf. esp. Mitchell II.65–73.

[162] On the legality of the executions see 21.3n.

[163] 34.2n.

[164] *Fam.* 5.2.8. For the events of this period see Rice Holmes I.282–9, 466f.; C. Meier, *Athenaeum* 40 (1962) 103–25; D. R. Shackleton Bailey on *Fam.* 5.1; Seager 68–71. *Fam.* 5.1 and 5.2 reveal much.

[165] Dio 37.42.1–3.

[166] Support for Nepos: Plut. *Cic.* 23.1; Dio 37.38.1–2, 37.42.1–2; support for Cicero: *Fam.* 5.2.7, 5.7.3; *Pis.* 7; *Rep.* 1.7; Plut. *Cic.* 23.2.

[167] Plut. *Cic.* 26.6; *id. Mor.* 204 e–205 a, 541 f–542 a. For those convicted see p. 10.

condemned, it seemed, on the arbitrary say-so of one man, an impression which compounded the offence given by the executions of December. In *pro Sulla* Cicero devotes much time (§§ 21–35) to a rebuttal of the charge of having instituted *regnum* at Rome, and there is little doubt that in making such an accusation Torquatus was echoing popular feeling:[168] he was able to appeal to the support of the *corona* by deploring the execution of the conspirators (§§ 30, 32), whereas Cicero is found commenting darkly on the dangers which surround him (§§ 27–9). Cicero's position was weakened further by the fact of his being a *novus homo* from outside Rome; by contrast, those whom he had executed included such men as the patrician P. Cornelius Lentulus Sura, consul of 71.

The defence of a man against whom he had made no allegations thus provided Cicero with an opportune means of strengthening his political position in the face of continuing attacks on his consulship and involvement in the trials of the Catilinarians. It enabled him to display his *lenitas* and shake off the image of a *rex peregrinus*, substituting the more congenial picture of himself as the merciful saviour of the Roman state. Moreover, Sulla had influence with the senatorial aristocracy, whose support and protection Cicero would need, and the case allowed him to identify his interests with theirs, sharing with them the credit, and implicitly the responsibility, for the action taken on the Nones of December (§ 9).

Sulla, as observed above,[169] was 'a man of many connections', and these included not just the *boni* at Rome but also his brother-in-law Pompey, shortly to return from the east after his successful termination of the Third Mithridatic War. Cicero had alienated Pompey in the weeks following the suppression of the conspiracy at Rome and was

[168] On *regnum* see 21.1n. For evidence of popular sympathy towards Catiline's memory see *Flac.* 95.
[169] P. 7.

now trying to re-establish friendly relations and, for the reasons just outlined, to secure Pompey's protection.[170] Shortly after the execution of the conspirators Cicero, overwhelmed by the honours which were heaped upon him,[171] had injudiciously sent Pompey a lengthy account of his consulship in which great emphasis was placed on his salvation of the state and especially, it seems, on the fact that this was achieved without recourse to arms (a point which helped to justify the executions).[172] The letter was quoted at Sulla's trial (§67), which indicates that it was simultaneously published at Rome. Pompey, in view of his own remarkable achievements, was affronted, and in his reply he declined to offer Cicero his congratulations.[173] By this time Cicero had further alienated Pompey by his feud with Nepos, who was a half-brother of Pompey's wife Mucia[174] and who was acting in his interests.[175] After his failure to prosecute Cicero, Nepos attempted to have Pompey recalled to take charge of operations against Catiline and also to secure permission for him to stand for the consulship *in absentia*. But the *senatus consultum ultimum* was again passed and Nepos, suspended from his office, fled east to Pompey, threatening revenge.[176] Cicero, now

---

[170] On Cicero's relations with Pompey during 63–2 see B. Rawson, *The Politics of Friendship: Pompey and Cicero* (Sydney 1978) 93–9; Mitchell II.74–83. Neither scholar is aware of the connection between Pompey and Sulla.

[171] 85.3n.; 85.4n.

[172] 67.1n. (cf. 85.4n.).

[173] *Fam.* 5.7.2–3. Pompey's reply may have reached Cicero by the end of March: see D. R. Shackleton Bailey on *Fam.* 5.7.

[174] As was Metellus Celer (65.4n.). For relations between Pompey and the Metelli see E. S. Gruen, *Historia* 18 (1969) 82f.

[175] Although not on his direct instructions: see Stockton 148f.; Seager 68f.; Mitchell II.71f.

[176] Sources at *MRR* II.173f. (the *professio in absentia* proposal is attested only at *schol. Bob.* 134 St. It is not incompatible with the proposal for his recall: the point of allowing Pompey to stand *in absentia* would have been to prevent his having to surrender his *imperium* by crossing the *pomerium*.).

seeing that Pompey might himself have liked the credit for having saved the state, in April sent him a conciliatory letter[177] in which he referred to his disappointment at Pompey's failure to acknowledge his achievements and went on to propose a political partnership and private friendship in which he would take the role of Laelius, with Pompey as a greater Africanus.[178] Not long after this letter was written Cicero was able to give proof of his good intentions towards Pompey by defending his brother-in-law; in return he hoped to gain Pompey's friendship and support.[179]

Besides Pompey, there were other men to whom Cicero was able to pay or repay a favour by undertaking Sulla's defence. Cicero mentions at §65 that as tribune in 63 Sulla's half-brother Caecilius had offered to veto Rullus' agrarian bill, which Cicero strongly opposed; this was a valuable service which could now be repaid. Secondly, Cicero's feud with Nepos required him to show goodwill towards Nepos' brother Metellus Celer,[180] and friendship between Celer and Sulla is suggested by the fact that it was Celer whom Sulla chose to put his wishes before the senate on 1 January 63 (§65). Finally, Cicero may have offended the Claudii Marcelli by refusing their request that he defend Autronius (§19); when they begged him to defend Sulla (§20), it would have been difficult to refuse.

There was also a pecuniary motive: the token of appreciation which Cicero could count on receiving from his grateful client. Now that he was a *consularis*, Cicero was eager to own a house which would reflect his new status (*ad dignitatem aliquam pervenire*, as he put it),[181] and, while Sulla

---

[177] *Fam.* 5.7.

[178] *Fam.* 5.7.3. I do not agree with Habicht (40) that Cicero means that 'Pompey could at best claim to be his equal'.

[179] Cicero's defence of Archias (62) should not be viewed as hostile to Pompey: see Stockton 154.

[180] 65.4n.; cf. *Fam.* 5.1, 5.2.

[181] *Att.* 1.13.6; cf. Carcopino 43f.; J. P. V. D. Balsdon in Dorey, 178; Shatzman 22–4. Cicero's social pretensions in purchasing a house on

was under accusation, the opportunity arose of purchasing from Crassus a house on the Palatine overlooking the forum, *in conspectu prope totius urbis*.[182] Sulla lent Cicero HS 2,000,000 towards the cost of this house, and later in the year, after the trial was over, Cicero purchased it for HS 3,500,000 (a sum nearly sufficient to keep a legion for a year).[183] That Sulla's contribution was a loan, not a gift, is implied by Cicero's jocular remark in December 62 that the purchase had plunged him so deeply into debt that he was ready to join a conspiracy, if anyone would have him.[184] According to an anecdote told by Aulus Gellius,[185] Cicero had to resort to a deception in order to silence public criticism of the deal. News of the transaction and the proposed purchase of the house, Gellius relates, leaked out shortly before Sulla's trial, and Cicero was accused of having received money from a *reus* in contravention of the *lex Cincia*.[186] Cicero responded by denying that he had

the Palatine were mocked by his enemies: *Att.* 1.16.10; [Sal.] *Inv. in Cic.* 2 (cf. [Cic.] *Inv. in Sal.* 14, 20). For Cicero's self-defence on this score see *Off.* 1.138–40; Plut. *Cic.* 8.6; cf. P. A. Brunt, *JRS* 72 (1982) 12f. His Palatine house had previously been occupied by M. Livius Drusus, tr. pl. 91 (Vell. 2.14.3).

[182] *Dom.* 100; cf. *Dom.* 103, 116; Plut. *Cic.* 8.3; Gel. 12.12.2. On Cicero's house see Richardson, *Rome* 123; Platner–Ashby 175; and on its location, M. Royo, *REL* 65 (1987) 89–114; A. Carandini, *Schiavi in Italia* (Rome 1988) 360–73. Richardson, *Rome* 112–41 and Platner–Ashby 154–98 list known residences in Rome: Catiline and Hortensius also lived on the Palatine. M. Caelius moved there too, for similar reasons to Cicero's (*Cael.* 17–18).

[183] For the figures and chronology see *Fam.* 5.6.2 (to P. Sestius in December 62); Gel. 12.12.2. The shortfall seems to have been covered by a loan from C. Antonius: *Fam.* 5.5.2–3; *Att.* 1.12.1 (with D. R. Shackleton Bailey's n.), 1.12.2, 1.13.6, 1.14.7; cf. Carcopino 134–40; D. Lange, *CW* 65 (1971–2) 152–5. T. Frank (*An Economic Survey of Ancient Rome* 1 (Baltimore 1933) 326–8) estimated at HS 4,000,000 the cost of keeping a legion for a year.

[184] *Fam.* 5.6.2. This counts against Carcopino's assertion that 'the loan...was probably a loan in name only' (99).

[185] Gel. 12.12.2–4. The story may be apocryphal; nevertheless, it seems to have the ring of truth (cf. *Att.* 1.16.10).

[186] Cf. pp. 40f.

accepted any money, and claimed to be uninterested in purchasing the house, adding: *'adeo... verum sit accepisse me pecuniam, si domum emero'*. When after the trial Cicero did buy the house, his enemies accused him in the senate of having lied, but he brushed their criticisms aside with a witty rejoinder: 'ἀκοινονόητοι... *homines estis, cum ignoratis prudentis et cauti patrisfamilias esse, quod emere velit, empturum sese negare propter competitores emptionis'*.[187] It would not be surprising if Cicero's deception had indeed been motivated in part by a desire not to arouse the interest of rival purchasers; on 25 January 61 he reported to Atticus that the consul M. Valerius Messalla 'Niger'[188] had recently paid HS 13,400,000 for the house of the exiled Autronius, and that consequently he himself was now reckoned to have made a good buy.[189] The later history of Cicero's house is well known. After his exile in 58 it was demolished by Clodius, who enlarged the adjoining portico of Catulus and erected a shrine to *Libertas* on the site. Upon his return Cicero succeeded in recovering the site, and was awarded HS 2,000,000 for the rebuilding of the house.[190] The morality of Cicero's acceptance of a loan from Sulla will be considered below;[191] for the moment it suffices simply

---

[187] 'A right Roman answer, and well worthy of Cicero and his times' (Long III.156).

[188] 20.4n.

[189] *Att.* 1.13.6. The figure has been questioned, probably wrongly in view of the HS 14,800,000 paid by Clodius (Plin. *Nat.* 36.103): see D. R. Shackleton Bailey *ad loc.*; Ward 202 n. 32. Ward (202) maintains that Crassus let Cicero have the house at well below its market value, but this does not follow: houses might differ greatly in value according to their location, size, antiquity, condition and history. Moreover, *Att.* 1.13.6 implies that at the time Cicero was not thought of especially as having struck a good bargain. Ward also suggests that Crassus helped to arrange the deal between Cicero and Sulla; that is possible, but there is no evidence for it.

[190] *Att.* 4.2.5. See W. Allen, *TAPA* 75 (1944) 1–9; R. G. Nisbet on *Dom.*, *passim* (esp. App. V).

[191] Pp. 39–42.

to observe that the transaction 'added to the orator's enthusiasm'.[192]

There exists one further possible reason for Cicero's defence of Sulla, a reason which Cicero himself gives: that he knew Sulla to be innocent (§§ 14, 20, 92). But this, of course, begs the question of Sulla's guilt, and so it is that to which we should turn next.

(e) Was Sulla guilty?

'Whether or not Sulla was guilty is a question on which posterity will never be able to express any confident opinion, let alone a dogmatic one'.[193] T. A. Dorey's (1964) caution is admirable; nevertheless, the question must still be addressed. The opinion which has generally prevailed, particularly among scholars hostile to Cicero, is that Sulla was indeed a participant in the Catilinarian conspiracy, and was therefore guilty. Thus the description 'Catilinarian' is placed after his name in the indexes to standard works by T. Mommsen (1856) and R. Syme (1939).[194] For F. Münzer (1901), W. Drumann/P. Groebe (1902) and E. G. Hardy (1917), Sulla was almost certainly guilty, and the absence of evidence against him was accounted for by his supposed skill in avoiding self-incrimination.[195] A critical

---

[192] Gruen 284 (cf. Lord 260). Cicero argues at *Off.* 2.71 that money should not be the motive for undertaking a defence, although there is nothing to prevent the orator from defending a rich man if he is also good.

[193] Dorey 30.

[194] T. Mommsen, *Römische Geschichte* III e.g. ed.10 (Berlin 1909) 649; Syme, *RR* 544 (cf. 66). The hostility of Drumann and Mommsen (and, to a lesser extent, Syme) towards Cicero is well known, and their views need no repetition here; for a convenient résumé see Habicht 3–8 (cf. 92–6). See also Dorey 33–44; Douglas 2–13.

[195] F. Münzer, *RE* IV.1520.50ff.; Drumann–Groebe II.443 ('kann man seine Schuld kaum bezweifeln'); Hardy 17 n. 2 ('Cicero's defence of Sulla in 62 is far from convincing; and he was probably in the affair [the 'first conspiracy']').

approach to the question was abandoned altogether by E. Meyer (1919), who asserted that 'Ciceros Rede pro Sulla...ist so durch und durch verlogen..., daß man von seinen Behauptungen immer das Gegenteil als richtig annehmen kann'.[196] A. Boulanger (1943) argued for Sulla's guilt, although placing him among the conspirators of the second rank, while according to J. Carcopino (1947) 'no one doubted Sulla's complicity'.[197] More recently G. A. Kennedy (1972), correctly observing that 'Sulla...has generally been thought to have been guilty', went on to put *pro Sulla* in the same category as *pro Murena* and *pro Flacco*, speeches which 'seem to have been defenses of a client whom Cicero knew to be guilty'.[198]

The question 'was Sulla guilty?' is not quite as straightforward as it appears. For Sulla, guilt has usually been equated with participation in the Catilinarian conspiracy, yet he was put on trial for *vis*, not for Catilinarianism: it is in theory possible that Sulla was guilty of *vis*, but nevertheless had no connection with Catiline. Secondly, it should be remembered that Sulla's guilt is dependent on his actions, not on his possible sympathies or provisional intentions: if he intended to give Catiline his support in the event of the conspiracy's succeeding, that alone would not make him guilty of *vis*. It is necessary, therefore, first to attempt to assess on which charges Sulla may have been

---

[196] E. Meyer, *Caesars Monarchie und das Principat des Pompejus*[2] (Stuttgart and Berlin 1919) 20 n. 3, rightly criticised by P. A. Brunt, *CQ* n.s. 32 (1982) 146 ('Meyer's exaggerated observation betrays an abnegation of critical method. We cannot properly operate on the basis that since Cicero is often untruthful any statement that he makes in a speech can be rejected if it happens not to agree with what we should like to believe'). For Syme's view of Meyer's remark see *Sallust* 90 ('The pronouncement is hasty and unjust. Cicero was much more crafty than that').

[197] Boulanger 94f.; Carcopino 97.

[198] Kennedy 188f. Kennedy seems to have adopted Meyer's principle: Cicero repeatedly states (§§ 14, 20, 85, 92) that he knew Sulla to be innocent.

guilty of *vis*, and then to determine whether participation in the conspiracy is thereby implied. Afterwards, if participation in the conspiracy is not implied, it will be interesting to speculate whether Sulla might have been likely to support Catiline had the conspiracy succeeded, or had it seemed likely to succeed; such speculation would of course be irrelevant to the question of Sulla's guilt.

A detailed assessment of each charge is given in the commentary below; here a brief overview only is required. Cicero has least difficulty in refuting the charge that Sulla sent P. Sittius to Spain to cause disturbances in Catiline's interest: Sittius had his own reasons for going to Spain, and left a year before the conspiracy was formed (§§ 56–9). The charge that Sulla took advantage of Faustus' absence to assemble gladiators in his name without his knowledge also failed to stand up in the light of documentary evidence which proved that the gladiators were purchased on Faustus' orders and for a legitimate purpose (§§ 54–5). Sulla was named in the evidence of the Allobroges: the conspirator Cassius had said that he did not know for certain whether Sulla was with them (§§ 36–9). This may have some bearing on the question of Sulla's sympathies, to which we shall turn below, but it cannot be taken to imply that Sulla had joined the conspiracy, and could on the contrary be taken, as by Cicero, to imply Sulla's innocence. The fact that the prosecution went so far as to accuse Cicero of falsifying the Allobroges' evidence on 3 December 63 is an indication that the evidence did not prove what they wanted it to prove (§§ 40–45). Cicero's letter to Pompey, also used as evidence by the prosecution, patently failed to demonstrate Sulla's guilt (§§ 67–8); for Stevens, it is 'an extraordinarily weak proof'.[199] On other charges, however, Sulla's guilt appears likely. Cicero's reply to the allegation that Sulla fostered dissension at

[199] C. E. Stevens, *Latomus* 22 (1963) 431 (quoted on p. 265).

Pompeii is unconvincing, although the fact that the troubles were long-standing at least indicates that they were not initiated with Catiline in mind (§§ 60–62). The possibility that Sulla may have intended to exploit the situation for Catiline's benefit belongs to the question of Sulla's sympathies, and does not bear upon his guilt: as Cicero points out, Pompeii did not join the conspiracy. The charge that Sulla attempted to force the passage of the *rogatio Caecilia* in 64 is not answered particularly convincingly either: Cicero is unable to deny that violence was used, and can do no better than simply state that the man responsible was Autronius, who also stood to gain from the bill (§§ 62–6). Finally, Sulla was accused of plotting a massacre with Catiline and Autronius at the consular elections of 63, before the inception of the Catilinarian conspiracy (§§ 51–3). It is in fact unclear to what extent this 'massacre' was a figment of Cicero's imagination;[200] nevertheless, Cicero's attempt to imply that Sulla was out of Rome at the time appears suspicious.

It is significant that the charges on which it seems that Sulla is likely to have been guilty are not the charges which relate to the Catilinarian conspiracy. It is quite likely that Sulla made use of the dissension at Pompeii for his own ends, and was in part responsible for the violence at the promulgation of the *rogatio Caecilia* and at the elections of 63. Nevertheless, it does not appear that he took part in the conspiracy. This conclusion is supported by the fact that confessed conspirators did not name him (§ 51), and perhaps also by the fact that throughout the time of the conspiracy he was at Naples (§ 17, 53).[201] D. L. Stockton (1971)

---

[200] 51.7n.

[201] That Sulla is not named as a conspirator by Sallust or later historians is evidence for his acquittal (cf. p. 11), but not (as Halm, Introd. §7) for his innocence: Sallust would have known *pro Sulla*, and perhaps also Hortensius' speech (the source for his account of the 'first conspiracy' (*Cat.* 18–19)?).

and E. D. Rawson (1975) therefore seem justified in re-
marking that 'the prosecution had no really hard proof,
and had to rely on circumstantial evidence and inference'
(Stockton); 'there seems to have been little hard evidence
against Sulla' (Rawson). E. S. Gruen (1974) concludes,
'Sulla's participation in the conspiracy, if there was any
participation, can only have been marginal; the charge
amounted essentially to guilt by association'. Our findings
come nearest to the view of G. Long (1856), who stated: 'It
is not only possible, but it is probable, that Cicero could
truly say that Sulla was not in Catilina's conspiracy; at least
we may believe that there was no evidence against him'.[202]

Some scholars, accepting that the evidence does not
point to Sulla's participation in the conspiracy, have pro-
ceeded to speculate about his sympathies and intentions,
and to guess at whether he would have given Catiline his
support had the conspiracy seemed likely to succeed.
K. Halm (1865), J. S. Reid (1882), D. L. Stockton (1971) and
C. Macdonald (1977) all suggest that, as Stockton puts it,
'probably... Sulla had been sitting on the fence in 63,
possibly giving secret aid or encouragement to Catiline and
Autronius, ready to collect any profit that might accrue,
but far too wily to commit himself'.[203] It is true that Cassius' reply to the Allobroges could bear this interpretation

---

[202] Stockton 157; Rawson 92; Gruen 285; Long III.157. Long has in fact
written more sense than anyone on the question of Sulla's guilt, e.g.
'Cicero says there was no evidence that came before him as consul of
Sulla's being implicated in the second conspiracy... We cannot
contradict Cicero, for we know no more about Sulla than appears in
this oration and in the few other notices in the ancient writers. He
was acquitted too, and though an acquittal is not a proof of innocence, it is a fact on which we cannot found a presumption of
guilt' (on §69); 'it is true that a large part of mankind take the fact of
the charge as a probability on the side of guilt' (on §69). All this in
the year which also saw the publication of Mommsen's influential
attack on Cicero in *Römische Geschichte*!

[203] Halm, Introd. §7; Reid, Introd. §20; Stockton 157; Macdonald 311f.;
cf. the view of Ciaceri (II.13) that Sulla was innocent but had

(§§ 36–9), and it is also possible that Sulla may have considered using his gladiators (§§ 54–5) or his influence at Pompeii (§§ 60–62) in Catiline's interest should Catiline have looked like winning. But on the other hand it is equally possible that Sulla had formed no such schemes. It is not clear whether he would have stood to gain from Catiline's success: he could have recovered his forfeited consulship by supporting Catiline, but on the other hand *novae tabulae* may not have been welcome to a man of his enormous wealth. Long (1856) speculates on how he might have behaved after a victory by Catiline: 'Sulla was, as it seems, a greedy, cunning man, ready to make the most of any opportunity to enrich himself, but too prudent to risk his fortune in a desperate undertaking. If Catilina had succeeded in his designs, Sulla would have bought at his auctions, as he did in his younger days, when the Dictator Sulla offered the property of the proscribed, and as he did again in his old age, when Caesar brought into the market the estates of his enemies.'[204] In any case, whatever Sulla's provisional plans or likely behaviour may have been, these matters, as was said above, have no bearing upon the question of his guilt.

There is one further argument for Sulla's innocence which has been deliberately left out of the reckoning until now, in order not to prejudice the issue: that Cicero would not have undertaken the defence of a conspirator whom he knew to be guilty (§§ 6–7, 19, 83, 85). Is it really credible that any consideration could have induced Cicero, who regarded his suppression of the conspiracy as his greatest achievement, to defend a Catilinarian conspirator? That

maintained friendly relations with the conspirators. J. D. Madden (review, *CW* 71 (1977–8) 276) writes that Macdonald 'is astute enough...to see that the three men defended in this volume by Cicero – Murena, Sulla, Flaccus – are all clearly guilty'; but Macdonald is rightly more cautious than that.
[204] Long III.157.

question is left for each reader of *pro Sulla* to answer for himself.

(f) The morality of Cicero's defence

Cicero's defence has been severely criticised on the supposition that he accepted a bribe to defend a Catilinarian conspirator: *ex coniuratis ... alius domum emebat* ([Sal.] *Inv. in Cic.* 3).[205] J. Carcopino asserted that Cicero 'contented himself with doing a deal with one of the conspirators who, having been detected, flung himself into Cicero's arms. The fiery orator of the Catiline Orations, who without speechifying had promptly put Cethegus, Lentulus and their gang to death, drew on their accomplice Sulla for two million.'[206] T. A. Dorey answers Carcopino by arguing that in defending an adherent of the conspiracy which he himself had suppressed Cicero would have been acting no more improperly than when in the previous year he defended Murena, who was obviously guilty of contravening Cicero's own *lex Tullia de ambitu*.[207] This cannot be correct: Cicero firmly believed that while other crimes are defensible, crimes against the state are not,[208] and in *pro Sulla* he emphasises that to defend a conspirator would be a crime equivalent to joining the conspiracy oneself (§§ 6–7, 19). Nevertheless, Carcopino's criticism is easily rejected: as we have seen, Sulla does not appear to have been a conspirator.

---

[205] It is possible (although I think unlikely: see E. Laughton, *CP* 65 (1970) 3; E. A. Fredericksmeyer, *CP* 68 (1973) 270f.) that Catullus' *optimus omnium patronus* (49.7) may have a second meaning, 'best advocate-of-all', i.e. Cicero is an unprincipled advocate who will defend anyone: see B. Schmidt, *RhM* 69 (1914) 273f. For a balanced discussion of Catul. 49 see now W. J. Tatum, *TAPA* 118 (1988) 179–84.

[206] Carcopino 99. It is difficult to see how 'without speechifying' can be reconciled with the existence of *Cat.* 4.

[207] Dorey 30.

[208] See 6.8n.

If Cicero is to be criticised, then, he must be criticised
on the less sensational grounds of having contravened the
lex Cincia de donis et muneribus, a law of 204 BC which prohibited advocates from accepting fees or gifts in return for
their services.[209] As was mentioned above, Cicero received
a loan of HS 2,000,000 from Sulla, a payment which
attracted hostile criticism both before and after the trial.[210]
These criticisms are reflected in the charge made in the
Invectiva in Ciceronem that Cicero was a *mercennarius patronus*
(5); the invective refers to the transaction by demanding
redde rationem...qua ex pecunia domum paraveris (4; cf. 2).
However, as Dorey has argued, Cicero scarcely deserves to
be criticised on these grounds either.[211] The *lex Cincia* was
an unenforceable law and was regularly broken, not only
by Cicero.[212] Advocates, as Dorey explains, did not provide
their services for nothing. A defence, unless undertaken in
repayment of a favour (as in the cases of Flaccus, Sestius,
Plancius and Milo), would incur an obligation (*officium*)
which the grateful client would be expected to discharge at
a later date, either by giving political support, or more
directly by means of a legacy, loan (low-interest or interest-
free) or gift.[213] The degree to which such favours infringed
the *lex Cincia* varied; Hortensius' well-known receipt of a
valuable ivory sphinx from Verres was perhaps a more

---

[209] Cf. C. G. Bruns, *Fontes Iuris Romani Antiqui*[7] (Tübingen 1909) no. 5;
G. Rotondi, *Leges Publicae Populi Romani* (Milan 1912) 261–3.

[210] Gel. 12.12.2–4; cf. pp. 31f.

[211] Dorey 30f.

[212] That it was passed in 204 indicates that advocates were already receiving payments in the third century; cf. Kennedy 14. Cicero jokes
about the law (*Att.* 1.20.7), which even Carcopino, while nevertheless
criticising Cicero, admits was universally flouted (96f.). For later
controversy over the *lex Cincia* see Tac. *Ann.* 11.5–7, 13.42, 15.20; Plin.
Ep. 5.4, 5.9, 5.13.

[213] Cf. [Sal.] *Inv. in Cic.* 4 *redde rationem...quid tibi litibus accreverit.* Lega-
cies were Cicero's main source of income: see R. J. Smutny, *CW* 45
(1951–2) 49–56; H. C. Boren, *CJ* 57 (1961–2) 17–24; Shatzman 409–
14. On low-interest/interest-free loans see Shatzman 78f., 416–22.

flagrant breach.[214] Although, as we have seen,[215] it was very much in Cicero's interest to undertake Sulla's defence, he was bound to do so by no particular obligation or bond of *amicitia* (in spite of § 48). Moreover, Sulla, excluded from the senate, was not in a position to provide him with any direct political support. Under these circumstances, Dorey argues, 'it is difficult to see how Cicero acted with any great impropriety in taking a loan from Sulla while Sulla was alive rather than waiting for a legacy after Sulla's death'. As M. Gelzer has shown, the use of financial obligation to create a tie between individuals was in fact characteristic of the age.[216] Gellius' account of how Cicero's enemies attempted to embarrass him by mentioning the loan in the senate does not imply that Cicero was considered to have acted dishonestly; on the contrary, the fact that he was able to sidestep the objection with a joke indicates that the matter was not regarded with any great seriousness.[217] Carcopino's criticism of Cicero's acceptance of a loan from Sulla is therefore unwarranted. Whether it was wise of Cicero from a political point of view to buy his Palatine house when he did (it made sense economically)[218] is of course another matter, and not one which it is possible to judge precisely.[219] In any case it is noteworthy that, as far as the *lex Cincia* was concerned, Cicero's moral standards appear to have been significantly higher than those of his contemporaries, to whom, according to Plutarch, his restraint in accepting payments for his services was a cause for surprise.[220]

---

[214] Plut. *Cic.* 7.6. I prefer this version to the earlier one at Plin. *Nat.* 34.48, which seems to have been altered to fit its context.

[215] Pp. 26–33.

[216] Gelzer 110–23.

[217] Cf. G. Boissier, *Cicero and his Friends*,[2] tr. A. D. Jones (London 1897) 84.

[218] *Att.* 1.13.6; cf. Gel. 12.12.4.

[219] Rawson (93) thinks that Cicero had 'probably been foolish' to accept the loan.

[220] Plut. *Cic.* 7.3. On the moral aspect see further *Off.* 2.71; Quint. *Inst.* 12.7.8–12.

So Cicero seems not to deserve the criticism to which he has been subjected for his defence of Sulla. It may be possible to go further and argue that he should even be given a certain amount of credit for defending him. In agreeing to take on Sulla's case Cicero put his own reputation in jeopardy to a far greater extent than he did in the other cases which he undertook: had he been unsuccessful, he would have been regarded as having abandoned his principles by defending a Catilinarian.[221] Yet it is likely that Sulla could have been saved only by Cicero, since all those previously accused on the same charge had been severely punished (§§ 71, 92),[222] and Cicero's refusal to defend him would have been taken as proof of his guilt. If Sulla was indeed innocent of the charges relating to the conspiracy, then Cicero may be regarded as having stepped in, at great personal risk, to save a man who was innocent at least of the main charges on which he was accused, and who otherwise would have been condemned.[223]

III THE SPEECH

(a) Structure

Rhetoricians in antiquity disagreed over the number of parts an 'ideal' speech ought to possess[224] – unsurprisingly, given the unreality and impracticability of such a concept. It came to be appreciated, however, that the various parts would differ in their appropriateness to the particular case in hand, and the structural schemes therefore evolved into

[221] Cf. Stroh 188.
[222] Cf. Humbert 152 n. 2.
[223] A case like Sulla's shows up the inadequacy of the fixed-penalty system of the *quaestiones*: if he was guilty of *vis* on some minor counts but did not join the conspiracy a conviction would be unjust, but an acquittal would seem to let him off too lightly. Under these circumstances the acquittal seems fairer, and this was the verdict chosen by the jury.
[224] For modern accounts see Lausberg 147–9; Martin 52–60.

checklists of parts many but not all of which an orator
might need to employ in any given speech. Aristotle maintained that there are only two essential parts (ἀναγκαῖα
μόρια) of a speech, the statement (πρόθεσις) and the argument (πίστις).[225] These may be added to, he conceded, but
the maximum number of parts (τὰ πλεῖστα μόρια) he set
at four: introduction (προοίμιον), statement (πρόθεσις),
argument (πίστις) and epilogue (ἐπίλογος). The two-part
division was too general to be of much practical use to the
orator, but the four-part scheme came to be accepted as
the most basic standard model and makes frequent appearances in the rhetorical handbooks.[226] Later schemes of
five, six or seven parts were all created by modifying this
four-part formulation. Quintilian states that most authorities preferred the five-part arrangement of *prooemium, narratio, probatio, refutatio* and *peroratio* which he himself advocates,[227] but it is the six-part scheme which we find in the
two handbooks from Cicero's time, Cicero's own *de Inventione* and the *Rhetorica ad Herennium*.[228] Here Aristotle's four
parts have been increased to six by the addition of partition (*partitio, divisio*) following the statement and by subdivision of the argument into proof (of one's own points)
and refutation (of one's opponent's). The technical terms

---

[225] Arist. *Rh.* 3.13. In Aristotle πρόθεσις and διήγησις both describe the
statement of facts (*narratio*), although other rhetoricians use only
διήγησις for *narratio*, and give πρόθεσις a separate meaning, that of
propositio.

[226] *Part.* 4 (*principium, narratio, confirmatio, peroratio*); *Orat.* 122; Aps. *Rh.* 12
(=1.2.297 Spengel–Hammer); D.L. 7.43; Fortunat. *Rh.* 2.12 (=108
Halm; =118 Calboli Montefusco); Victor. *in Cic. Inv.* 1.14 (=194
Halm); Sulp. Vict. *Inst.* 17 (=322 Halm); Isid. *Orig.* 2.7.1.

[227] *Inst.* 3.9.1–5. Quintilian does not regard the *partitio* (see below) as a
proper part, but allows the distinction between *probatio* and *refutatio*;
cf. *de Orat.* 2.307; Phld. *Rh.* 1.202 Sudhaus. A different five-part
scheme, including *propositio* but combining *probatio* and *refutatio*, is
given at Mart. Cap. *Rh.* 44 (=485 Halm; =192 Willis).

[228] *Inv.* 1.19 (cf. Grill. 18, =81 Martin (not in Halm)); *Rhet. Her.* 1.4. The
six-part scheme is also given at *de Orat.* 1.143; Sulp. Vict. *Inst.* 17
(=322 Halm); Cassiod. *Rh.* 9 (=497 Halm; =103 Mynors).

given to each part varied, but according to the terminology of *de Inventione* (which is followed below throughout) these six parts consist of *exordium, narratio, partitio, confirmatio, reprehensio* and *conclusio*.[229] Cicero remarks that Hermagoras added a further part, *digressio*, between *reprehensio* and *conclusio*,[230] but it was never agreed that digressions should occur only and always at this point, and Cicero's own practice is to introduce digressions wherever they serve the interests of his case.[231]

The six-part structure prescribed in *de Inventione* provided the model for many of Cicero's speeches, particularly those delivered early in his career: *pro lege Manilia*, for instance, exhibits perfect six-part partition.[232] After his attainment of the consulship, however, Cicero allowed himself greater freedom in adapting or disregarding the rules laid down by the rhetoricians, most notably in connection with structural arrangement. *Pro Sulla* affords a good illustration of this development. The speech deviates from the prescriptions of *de Inventione* in three important respects. First, the overall structure is distorted by the inclusion at the start of the speech of a long stretch of material (§§ 2–35, with a break at §§ 11–14) in which the matters discussed are strictly speaking irrelevant to the question at issue (viz. whether Sulla infringed the *lex Plautia de vi*). At both the point of departure (§ 2) and the *reditus ad*

---

229 *Rhet. Her.* 1.4 gives *divisio* for *partitio* and *confutatio* for *reprehensio*.

230 *Inv.* 1.97 (cf. *de Orat.* 2.80, 312; Victor. *in Cic. Inv.* 1.51, = 255 Halm). Julius Victor (*Rh.* 1, = 373 Halm; = 2 Giomini–Celentano; 14, = 421 Halm; = 67 Giomini–Celentano) and Martianus Capella (*Rh.* 46, = 487 Halm; = 194 Willis) also have the digression as a fixed part of the speech, but following the *narratio*; this was a practice which originated among the declaimers (Quint. *Inst.* 4.3.1–3).

231 At *de Orat.* 2.312 Antonius states that a digression may come after the *narratio* or before the *conclusio*, or indeed anywhere, if warranted by the case; cf. Quint. *Inst.* 4.3.4. For bibliography on *digressio* in Cicero see p. 133.

232 Laurand gives a bibliography for the structure of Cicero's speeches at 319 n. 1. On the structure of *pro lege Manilia* see Kennedy 173.

propositum (§ 35) Cicero justifies his inclusion of the passage:
Torquatus has attempted to despoil him of his *auctoritas* by
criticising his acceptance of the case, and before turning
to Sulla he is therefore compelled to speak in his own
defence.[233] This justification may be accepted: although
technically irrelevant, the assertion of Cicero's *auctoritas*
was an essential prerequisite for a successful defence.
Whether one labels this passage *digressio* or *praemunitio*, or
chooses some other term, is of little practical importance; I
have opted for *digressio* since it corresponds closely to a
definition of *digressio* given by Quintilian at *Inst.* 4.3.9–11
(cf. 3.9.4).[234]

The second point of departure from the precepts of *de
Inventione* is the omission in *pro Sulla* of a *narratio*.[235] Most
rhetoricians regarded the *narratio* as indispensable, a view
insisted upon by the Apollodoreans.[236] No firm opinion is
given by Aristotle, although he does observe that a defendant who maintains that something has not happened will
naturally have less need of a narration than a prosecutor
who alleges that it has.[237] Quintilian goes further and
argues that there are some circumstances in which a *narratio* is best dispensed with, such as when the facts are not in
dispute and the case turns instead on a point of law, or
when the facts are well known, or when they have been
correctly stated by a previous speaker.[238] However, he
rejects the idea that a simple denial of the charge can

[233] Cf. Stroh 188f.
[234] See pp. 131f.
[235] On omission of the *narratio* see Volkmann 149f.; Rohde 30–32.
[236] Quint. *Inst.* 4.2.4; Sen. *Con.* 2.1.36; Anon. Seguer. 113 (=1.2.372 Spengel–Hammer).
[237] Arist. *Rh.* 3.16 (1417 a 7ff.).
[238] Quint. *Inst.* 4.2.4–9 (cf. 6.5.5). This last reason (the facts correctly stated by a previous speaker) accounts for the omission of a *narratio* in many of Cicero's speeches (*Mur.*, *Flac.*, *Sest.*, *Cael.*, *Balb.*, *Planc.*, *Scaur.*), since it was Cicero's custom to speak last (*Brut.* 190; *Orat.* 130). Rohde, however, points out (31) that it does not apply to our speech because Hortensius had not discussed the events of 63.

render a *narratio* unnecessary. Julius Severianus, on the other hand, agreeing that a *narratio* is superfluous when the facts are well known, argues that it may also be omitted in cases where the defendant simply states that he did not indulge in, for example, *ambitus* or extortion.[239] In this context he draws attention to the absence of a *narratio* in *pro Sulla* and asserts that a statement of facts was not necessary since the defence consisted of a flat denial of Sulla's involvement in the conspiracy: *talis causa Sullae fuit negantis sibi quidquam cum Catilina convenisse contra rem publicam* (*Rh.* 7, = 358 Halm). Cicero's own view is that a *narratio* should be excluded when a separate statement of the facts would cause offence, when the facts have been satisfactorily stated by the opposition, or when they are already known to the audience.[240] The first and third of these reasons are applicable to Sulla's defence: a narration of the course of the Catilinarian conspiracy would not have been to Sulla's advantage, and it was in any case fresh in the minds of the jury. Severianus' point is also valid as an additional reason: since Cicero flatly denied Sulla's involvement in the conspiracy, a *narratio* was not required.

The third structural irregularity is the inversion of *confirmatio* and *reprehensio* which Cicero refers to explicitly at § 69: *iam enim faciam criminibus omnibus fere dissolutis contra atque in ceteris causis fieri solet, ut nunc denique de vita hominis ac de moribus dicam*. Normally, as we have seen, the establishment of one's own arguments preceded the refutation of those of the opposition. *Argumenta ex vita* were traditionally placed first within the *confirmatio*,[241] and so when Cicero explains that he is moving from the *reprehensio* to the arguments *de vita hominis ac de moribus* he is announcing his inversion of

[239] Jul. Sever. *Rh.* 7 (= 358 Halm; = 62 Giomini).
[240] *Inv.* 1.30; cf. *de Orat.* 2.330.
[241] Quint. *Inst.* 7.1.12, 7.2.27. Quintilian states that the *argumenta ex vita* were postponed in *pro Vareno*. See Volkmann 373f.; Humbert 151f.; Stroh 253–5.

the conventional order. The passage continues: *etenim de principio studuit animus occurrere magnitudini criminis, satis facere exspectationi hominum, de me aliquid ipso qui accusatus eram dicere.* This account of Cicero's motivation is not wholly satisfactory;[242] *de me ... dicere* applies to the inclusion of the digressions but has no bearing on the inversion of *confirmatio* and *reprehensio*, while more generally Cicero gives the impression that in deviating from the conventional order he has acted on impulse. A truer explanation is to be found in the practical advantages of the scheme adopted. Broadly speaking, the speech's *confirmatio* and *reprehensio* have been inverted because the contents of the former were likely to prove a more powerful argument for Sulla's acquittal than those of the latter.[243] This is not necessarily to say that Cicero would have considered the arguments of the *reprehensio* unsatisfactory[244] (the order in which he replies to the charges does not reveal any attempt to hide his weaker arguments from sight);[245] but he would have recognised that, taken together, they lacked the force which his own personality and *auctoritas* could give to the *confirmatio*. Therefore, since the defence relied most heavily on Cicero's consular *auctoritas*, this is emphasised immediately before the peroration, while the *reprehensio* is moved back to a less conspicuous point in the speech. Cicero had other reasons, too, for concluding the *argumentatio* with the *confirmatio*. The contents of *confirmatio* II (§§ 80–85) closely

---

[242] *Pace* Humbert 152.

[243] Thus Halm (on § 69). Stroh (254 n. 57) believes that the *argumenta ex vita* have been postponed because of the unimpressiveness of Sulla's life and character; but the place which they occupy (§§ 69–79) does not seem any less prominent than the position in which they would otherwise have been placed, after § 35. In *pro Roscio Amerino* the two parts of the argument are inverted because the content of the *confirmatio* represents a logical progression from that of the *reprehensio*; this is not the case in *pro Sulla*.

[244] Here I disagree with Halm (on § 69).

[245] See p. 232.

resemble those of *digressio* II (§§ 14–20), and it was therefore desirable to keep them widely separated. More generally, §§ 69–85 needed to be clearly differentiated from §§ 2–35, and it was convenient as well as artistically pleasing to achieve this by placing the technical arguments of the *reprehensio* between them. The result is that from § 69 an emotional climax is gradually built up, culminating in the grand *conclusio* of §§ 86–93. This would have been impossible had the order prescribed by the rhetoricians been adopted.

A structural analysis of *pro Sulla* is given below. It is important to stress, however, that Cicero does not in this speech adhere closely to the rules of rhetoric. Individual parts, such as the *partitio* or the *enumeratio* (a subsection of the *conclusio*),[246] do not always fulfil the functions prescribed by the rhetoricians, and transitions are sometimes gradual. It is not intended, therefore, that this analysis should be taken as definitive: it is simply one possible way of illuminating the speech's rhetorical framework.

(a) *First third: on Cicero*
  1   EXORDIVM
  2–10   DIGRESSIO I
  11–14   PARTITIO
  14–20   DIGRESSIO II
  21–35   DIGRESSIO III

(b) *Second third: on the charges*
  36–45   REPREHENSIO I
  46–50   DIGRESSIO IV
  51–68   REPREHENSIO II

(c) *Final third: on Sulla*
  69–79   CONFIRMATIO I
  80–85   CONFIRMATIO II
  86–93   CONCLVSIO

---

[246] See pp. 150, 304f.

(b) Prose rhythm

The history of scholarship on ancient prose rhythm begins with G. Wüst, who wrote a dissertation in 1881 analysing the 'clausulae' (the characteristic rhythms which precede the major pauses within and between sentences) of eighteen selected speeches of Cicero. Since then, the rhythm and colometry of Ciceronian prose have attracted the attention of many scholars.[247] In view of the bewilderingly large number of approaches, and the lack of any strong consensus, it may be as well to recall why prose rhythm itself is a subject of such importance for the reader of Cicero's speeches and other works of artistic prose. First, rhythm is one of the most prominent aspects of prose style – an aspect of which scholars from the end of the renaissance until the late nineteenth century seem to have been entirely unaware. The identification of Cicero's preferred clausulae now allows the reader to recognise or 'hear' the cadences to which Cicero's original audiences are known to have been sensitive;[248] the process is precisely the same as that by which the reader of poetry uses his awareness of metre to respond to the rhythms of verse. Secondly, rhythm is not important only as decoration: by pointing to the pauses within a passage of prose, it acts as a guide

---

[247] Since G. Wüst, *De Clausula Rhetorica* (Strasbourg 1881), there have been the following major contributions: Zielinski (rev. A. C. Clark, *CR* 19 (1905) 164–72); Zielinski, *Constr. Rhyth.* (rev. A. C. Clark, *CR* 30 (1916) 22–6); H. Bornecque, *Les Clausules métriques latines* (Lille 1907); A. W. de Groot, *Der antike Prosarhythmus* (Groningen 1921); *id.*, *La Prose métrique des anciens* (Paris 1926); H. D. Broadhead, *Latin Prose Rhythm* (Cambridge 1922); W. H. Shewring, *CQ* 24 (1930) 164–73; *id.*, *CQ* 25 (1931) 12–22; E. Fraenkel, *NGG* (1933) 319–54 (= *Kleine Beiträge zur klassischen Philologie* (Rome 1964) 1.93–130); Laurand 156–230; W. Schmid, *Hermes Einzelschriften* 12 (1959); L. P. Wilkinson, *Golden Latin Artistry* (Cambridge 1963) 135–64; E. Fraenkel, *SBAW* 1965.2; Fraenkel, *Leseproben* (rev. E. Laughton, *JRS* 60 (1970) 188–94); A. Primmer, *SAWW* 257 (1968); Aili; Habinek; Nisbet.

[248] *Orat.* 168, 213–14.

to the structure of sentences, and thereby to the general movement of thought. This function of rhythm is of particular value in prose of the periodic type favoured by Cicero, where sentences tend to be long and complex. But rhythm would in any case have been useful to Cicero's contemporaries as a reading aid, since punctuation at this time was rudimentary: at best, a text would be marked only with interpuncts between words and an indication of paragraph breaks.[249] Thirdly, knowledge of rhythm is of inestimable value to the textual critic since it provides him with an additional factor to put into the balance when weighing the merits of variant readings.

The scholar particularly associated with the prose rhythm of Cicero's speeches is T. Zielinski, who counted and classified 17,902 of the clausulae (not, unfortunately, the total number) occurring at the major sense-breaks, usually at the end of the sentence, throughout the speeches of Cicero.[250] No scholar since has provided so large a body of statistical information, and Zielinski's figures must therefore remain the basis for any wide-ranging statistical analysis. Recently the clausulae of *pro Sulla* have been counted again by H. Aili, who used this and *pro Murena* as sample speeches for a comparison of the prose rhythm of Cicero with that of Sallust and Livy. But if we wish to compare Cicero's rhythmical practice in *pro Sulla*, not with Sallust and Livy, but with Cicero's other speeches, Zielinski's are the figures which must be used: we shall then be comparing like with like. In any case, Aili provides information for

---

[249] G. B. Townend, *CQ* n.s. 19 (1969) 330–44 is salutary ('we must recognize to what an extent our own dependence upon punctuation in our texts is a measure of our failure to listen to our author's actual words', 344). On Latin punctuation see further R. W. Müller, *Rhetorische und syntaktische Interpunktion* (Tübingen 1964); E. O. Wingo, *Latin Punctuation in the Classical Age* (The Hague 1972); Habinek 42–88; M. B. Parkes, *Pause and Effect* (Aldershot 1992) 9–19.

[250] See Zielinski 7f. (criteria for selection of clausulae), table following p. 253 (statistics).

only the last six syllables of each unit, which is insufficient given that the clausula –⏑– –⏑–⏒, for example, accounts for 18.8 per cent of Zielinski's clausulae.[251] Zielinski's figures are not set out in the most illuminating way, the clausulae being arbitrarily classified as *verae*, *licitae*, *malae*, *selectae* and *pessimae*. But all the information necessary for statistical analysis is present: it needs only to be re-arranged.[252] I have divided Zielinski's clausulae into six new categories, (a) to (f), as follows.

(a) Cretic-spondee/cretic-trochee (–⏑– –⏒), including resolved forms (Zielinski classes resolved forms separately as *licitae* or *malae*).

(b) Double-cretic/molossus-cretic (–⏒– –⏑⏒), including resolved forms and substitution of choriamb (–⏑⏑–)/ epitrite (–⏑– –) for first cretic/molossus.

(c) Cretic-double-trochee/molossus-double-trochee (–⏒– –⏑–⏒), including resolved forms and substitution of choriamb (–⏑⏑–)/epitrite (–⏑– –) for cretic/molossus.

(d) Cretic-hypodochmiac/molossus-hypodochmiac (–⏒– –⏑–⏑⏒), including resolved forms (hypodochmiac = cretic-iambus).

(e) Iambic and trochaic rhythms (–⏑– –⏑–⏑–⏒, –⏑– –⏑–⏑–⏑⏒, –⏑– –⏑–⏑–⏑–⏒, –⏑– –⏑–⏑–⏑–⏑⏒).

(f) Spondaic and dactylic rhythms (– – – –⏒, –⏒– – –⏒, –⏒– – – –⏒, –⏑⏑– –⏒, –⏑– –⏑⏑⏒, –⏑– –⏑⏑–⏒), including resolved forms.

The table below shows the frequency of these categories of clausulae first in *pro Sulla*, then in Cicero's speeches as a whole (the figures indicate percentages).

---

[251] See Aili 51–68, 136 (table A 1). In his text Aili takes account of the last eight syllables of each unit (19), but in his tables he unfortunately confines himself to the last six. He also supposes that *pro Sulla* dates from 63 (45, 51, 52).

[252] See my article in F. Cairns and M. Heath (edd.), *Papers of the Leeds International Latin Seminar* 9 (1996).

	Pro Sulla	All speeches
(a)	35.7	32.4
(b)	21.1	24.4
(c)	34.1	30.1
(d)	1.9	3.6
(e)	1.4	1.6
(f)	5.8	7.9
Total	100	100

These statistics show that there is a close correlation between Cicero's choice of clausulae in *pro Sulla* and in the speeches as a whole. The cretic-spondee/cretic-trochee and the cretic-double-trochee/molossus-double-trochee are favoured slightly more than in the speeches overall, and the double-cretic/molossus-cretic slightly less so. These three types of clausulae, the most frequently occurring, account for 90.9 per cent of the clausulae in *pro Sulla*, but only 86.9 per cent of those in all the speeches together. Consequently, the less frequent types occur more rarely in *pro Sulla* than elsewhere, the cretic-hypodochmiac/molossus-hypodochmiac markedly less so. If we return to Zielinski to look at two rhythms of special interest, the *esse videatur* clausula $(-\cup\cup\cup\ -\underline{\cup})$[253] which Cicero favoured and the 'hexameter ending' rhythm $(-\cup\cup\ -\underline{\cup})$ which he avoided, we find that the figures for these respectively are 7.2 per cent and 0.5 per cent in *pro Sulla*, and 6.4 per cent and 0.6 per cent in the speeches as a whole.

---

[253] The *esse videatur* clausula is a cretic-spondee/cretic-trochee with a resolution of the third syllable. Zielinski's 'Auflösungsgesetz' (34) would not allow two short syllables standing for a long to be divided between words; thus clausulae such as *muneris abesset* (*Sul.* 54) he would not admit to be *esse videatur* (43–55). This law cannot be accepted (W. H. Shewring, *CQ* 24 (1930) 165). Consequently, Zielinski's figures for *esse videatur* clausulae are too low: 5.3 per cent for *pro Sulla* and 4.3 per cent for the speeches as a whole. The percentages I give below include all *esse videatur* clausulae, regardless of word divisions. On the phrase *esse videatur* see 3.9n.

Clausulae, however, do not occur only at the major sense-breaks, such as the ends of sentences, but also within the sentence, at the ends of the shorter units or 'cola'. As E. Fraenkel and R. G. M. Nisbet have shown,[254] colon boundaries may often be identified by one or more of a number of pointers such as the position of unemphatic pronouns, the use of ablative absolutes or vocatives, the presence of hiatus or the occurrence of *atque* before a consonant. The use of *atque* before a consonant is carefully avoided by the Roman elegists, but is freely adopted by Cicero in cases where it provides a more favoured clausula than that which would result from *ac* or *et*.[255] In *pro Sulla*, every case of *atque* before a consonant helps the rhythm, whether at a break within the sentence or at the end. The instances are: §1 *redomiti atque victi*; §1 *vehementem me fuisse atque fortem*; §15 *lapidatione atque concursu*; §17 *dissimilitudinem hominum atque causarum* (with unemphatic *me* following in second position); §18 *flectebar animo atque frangebar*; §19 *cum illorum delubrorum atque templorum*; §33 *quinque hominibus comprensis atque confessis*; §34 *suscepi atque gessi* (with *ille* following in second position); §47 *remissum atque concessum* (end of sentence); §66 *calamitatis socio atque comite* (with hiatus); §79 *spoliatam atque nudatam* (with hiatus); §86 *haec tecta atque templa* (followed by emphatic *me*); §90 *lacrimarum atque maeroris*; §93 *vestri animi atque virtutis*. In cases where the manuscripts are equally divided between *atque* and *ac* or *et* before a consonant, I have therefore assumed that, if *atque* gives the more favoured rhythm, that is what Cicero wrote; hence §15 *verum etiam aspectu atque* (not *et*) *vultu* (with hiatus); §33 *in*

---

[254] See the items by Fraenkel cited above (n.247), esp. *Leseproben* 69–71 on §§4–7; Nisbet. On unemphatic pronouns see also 2.7n.

[255] On the practice of the elegists see M. Platnauer, *Latin Elegiac Verse* (Cambridge 1951) 78–82 (cf. B. Axelson, *Unpoetische Wörter* (Lund 1945) 83–5); on Cicero's practice see J. Wolff, *JahrbClPhil* Suppl. 26 (1901) 637–40. For Quintilian see M. Winterbottom, *CR* n.s. 42 (1992) 449 ('his tendency to employ *atque* before consonants to produce favoured rhythmical units is very striking indeed').

his autem templis atque (not *ac*) *tectis.*[256] If, on the other hand, *atque* brings no special benefit to the rhythm, I have accepted the variant: thus §77 *ac* (not *atque*) *numerum transferetis.*

At the ends of cola, Cicero tends to use the same rhythms as occur at the ends of sentences. Naturally the internal rhythms are not as dependable as the end-of-sentence clausulae; in tricolon, for instance, one often finds a statistically less frequent rhythm at the first or first and second stages. Nevertheless, the use of rhythm within the sentence is remarkably pervasive, and in *pro Sulla* this factor allows many textual questions to be settled which editors have previously had to decide on purely arbitrary grounds. It is essential, however, to determine what is normally the maximum length of a colon. Observation of the colometry of Cicero's speeches has led Nisbet to a tentative figure of sixteen syllables as a normal maximum:[257] units of apparently greater length generally turn out to be divisible into smaller parts. Cola thus tend to be relatively brief, often of ten syllables or so, and this must reflect the physical conditions under which oratory was produced. Cicero addressed large audiences in the open air, without the aid of the microphone. The task of projecting the voice (and the task of listening) would have been made easier by fairly frequent pauses, of greater or lesser emphasis. Before such pauses, within the sentence as at the end, it is natural that Cicero should have preferred to complete what he had to say with words of a euphonious rhythm.

(c) Publication

The political speeches which Cicero delivered as consul are known to have been written up and sent to Atticus in 60, and it is generally assumed that they were then published

---

[256] I also read *perverterim atque perfregerim* at §46, in spite of stronger MS support for *ac*: see 46.8n.

[257] Nisbet 358; cf. C. W. Wooten, *Cicero's* Philippics *and their Demosthenic Model* (Chapel Hill and London 1983) 33f.

III THE SPEECH

as part of a 'propaganda campaign' intended by Cicero as a counterblast to P. Clodius' attacks on his consulship.[258] The pervasive element of apologia in the Catilinarians strongly suggests that those speeches at least were substantially rewritten to take account of the increasing vulnerability of Cicero's position, which had not at the time (as the letter to Pompey makes clear) been fully apparent to him.[259] *Pro Sulla*, like the Catilinarians, contains passages in which Cicero boasts of his suppression of the conspiracy and refers to the dangers to which his heroic actions have exposed him (§§ 27–9, 33–4, 84). These passages, however, are less fervent and much less extensive than the passages on the same theme in the Catilinarians, and they are precisely what would be expected in view of Cicero's political position at the time of Sulla's trial.[260] It seems likely, then,

[258] [PUBLICATION OF *IN CATILINAM*.] See *Att.* 2.1.3 (*ea quae nos scribimus adulescentulorum studiis excitati*; later, *isdem ex libris perspicies et quae gesserim et quae dixerim* etc., implying that Atticus has not seen the speeches before); and on the 'propaganda campaign', Rawson 104 (cf. Settle 127–46; 26.14n.). W. C. McDermott (*Philologus* 116 (1972) 277–84) argues that these speeches were published immediately after delivery in 63, and denies any subsequent revision. Immediate publication is conceivable (the various speeches against Catiline could have been circulated individually after the delivery of each); nevertheless, the collection of four Catilinarians which survives is clearly anachronistic (see below), and so must reflect the version which Cicero produced in 60 rather than any version published in 63. McDermott fails to discuss Cicero's political position in 63 and 60; moreover, his concluding arguments (283f.) are dangerously subjective. On Atticus as Cicero's 'publisher' see Settle 37–46; J. J. Phillips, *CW* 79 (1985–6) 227–37 (esp. 229).

[259] See Madvig, *Opusc. Acad.* 680f.; Laurand 8–10; H. Fuchs, *Hermes* 87 (1959) 463–9; M. Brożek, *Acta Sessionis Ciceronianae diebus 3–5 mensis Decembris a. 1957 Varsoviae habitae* (Warsaw 1960) 63–75; R. G. M. Nisbet in Dorey, 62f.; Kennedy 176–8; C. Helm, *Zur Redaktion der ciceronischen Konsulatsreden* (Göttingen 1979), esp. 247–64; Classen 5f. Cicero's foresight was hardly as miraculous as claimed by Cornelius Nepos (*Att.* 16.4). On the letter to Pompey see 67.1n.

[260] Reid remarks on the difference in tone between *pro Sulla* and the Catilinarians at Introd. § 39. Cicero's political position in 62 is reviewed above at pp. 27f. On the date of the trial see p. 14.

that *pro Sulla* was published soon after Sulla was acquitted, and there is nothing in the speech to imply any later date of publication.[261] Immediate publication of the speech would have been in Cicero's interest in that it would have enabled him to advertise his *lenitas* to a wider audience.[262] It would not have been in his interest, on the other hand, to remind the public at a later date of his defence of Sulla; indeed, Cicero never afterwards refers to the speech, and although he does once mention the trial, he says nothing of his own part in it.[263] A final consideration is that it appears to have been Cicero's usual practice to publish his speeches soon after delivery.[264]

Pro Sulla as published takes roughly an hour and three-quarters to read out aloud, but this information is mean-

---

[261] *Pace* Gruen 285.

[262] See Settle 156–8 ('Cicero's reasons for publishing his *Pro Sulla* at all were reasons to publish as soon as possible', 158).

[263] *Fin.* 2.62. The fact that Sulla became an ally of Clodius (*Att.* 4.3.3) was a further reason for Cicero's silence.

[264] See Laurand 16f.; Settle *passim*; W. C. McDermott, *Philologus* 116 (1972) 278–80. E. Rosenberg argues that certain parallels between *pro Sulla* and *pro Murena* show that both speeches were written up for publication at the same time (*Studien zur Rede Ciceros für Murena* (Hirschberg 1902) 10f.; cf. T. Opperskalski, *De M. Tulli Ciceronis orationum retractatione quaestiones selectae* (Greifswald 1914) 42f.; A. Boulanger, *REA* 42 (1940) 384f.; P. Moreau, *REL* 58 (1980) 231, 237). But this does not necessarily follow (and in any case the precise date of publication of *pro Murena* cannot be ascertained). The echoes of *pro Murena* in Cicero's justification of his defence of Sulla (esp. §§ 2–3) are explained by the fact that in both trials (Sulla's followed Murena's by only a matter of months) Cicero was required to defend the consistency of his actions (cf. pp. 132f.). The anachronistic (before the execution of the conspirators!) references in *pro Murena* to *severitas* and *lenitas* (*Mur.* 3, 6), on the other hand, although resembling passages in *pro Sulla* (e.g. § 8), need not imply that both speeches were published simultaneously: the speech which Cicero published first (whether *pro Murena* or *pro Sulla*) could have been in his mind when he came to write up the other at a later date. Like Laurand (12 n. 4), I therefore regard *pro Murena* as irrelevant to the date of publication of *pro Sulla*.

ingful only if the speech was not revised for publication.[265] Other speeches have been revised in varying degrees: exceptionally, *post reditum in senatu* was read out and therefore survives exactly as delivered, whereas at the other end of the scale *pro Milone* was improved and extended in the light of changed political circumstances.[266] *Pro Sestio*, too, is sometimes thought to have been expanded for publication, its digressions serving no purpose within the context of the trial but providing a political manifesto for the benefit of the wider audience outside the court.[267] The digressive material in *pro Sulla*, however, is not of this type: it is too central to the case, and fits too well into the overall structure.[268] Nevertheless J. Humbert, who advocated revision in the published speeches to a degree which few scholars would now accept,[269] believed that significant changes were made in the published version of *pro Sulla*. His main con-

---

[265] And perhaps not even then: a speech may have taken considerably longer to deliver in the forum than it takes to read aloud to oneself in one's study. My own readings aloud yield similar results to those of J. T. Kirby, *The Rhetoric of Cicero's* Pro Cluentio (Amsterdam 1990) 166.

[266] On *post reditum in senatu* see *Planc.* 74 (cf. *Sest.* 129). On *pro Milone* see Asc. 42 C; Quint. *Inst.* 4.3.17; Dio 40.54.2–4; *schol. Bob.* 112 St.; Laurand 6f., 14; J. N. Settle, *TAPA* 94 (1963) 268–80; Kennedy 232f.; A. W. Lintott, *JRS* 64 (1974) 74; A. M. Stone, *Antichthon* 14 (1980) 88–111; Crawford 210–18; D. H. Berry, *Historia* 42 (1993) 502–4; *id.*, *Omnibus* 25 (1993) 8–10.

[267] I do not myself share this view. See R. G. M. Nisbet in Dorey 66 (cf. W. K. Lacey, *CQ* n.s. 12 (1962) 67–71).

[268] See Douglas 15. On the role of the digressions within the structure of the speech see pp. 44f.

[269] [SPOKEN VS. PUBLISHED VERSIONS.] The question has been much discussed (for the ancient evidence see esp. *Brut.* 91, 328; *Tusc.* 4.55; *Att.* 1.13.5, 2.7.1, 4.2.2, 15.1A.2; *Q. fr.* 3.1.11; Nep. ap. Jer. *Contra Jo. Hier. ad Pamm.* 12 (= *Patr. Lat.* XXIII.365); Quint. *Inst.* 10.7.30, 12.10.49–57; Plin. *Ep.* 1.20.6–10; Dio 46.7.3). Laurand (1–23) argued persuasively for minimal revision (some improvements in style, etc.) before publication, except in special cases. Humbert's thesis (see 142–53 on *pro Sulla*) that the speeches were, to put it crudely, cobbled together from different moments in the trial is, taken as a whole, unconvincing. The weakness of his arguments was seen at the time by A. C. Clark

tention is that Cicero's reply to the charge of falsification (§§ 40–45) must originally have been part of an *altercatio* between Torquatus and Cicero.[270] But there is no reason at all why this, like the other personal attacks on Cicero, should not have been answered in the course of the original speech, when Cicero would have had a better opportunity to put his points across without interruption than in the *altercatio*.[271] Humbert is perhaps on stronger ground when he suggests that Cicero's reply to the rest of the charges (§§ 51–68) may have been somewhat abbreviated.[272] Cicero's arguments certainly seem a little perfunctory as he ticks off the charges one by one, and it is possible that a certain amount of technical detail may have been sacrificed in the published speech (in some speeches Cicero actually cut out his replies to the less important charges, indicating their omission by headings).[273] In general, however, it seems justifiable to take the speech as a close approximation of what was said in court. If Cicero published it immediately, as seems likely, then that would be another argument against any substantial revision for publication.

Pro Sulla therefore seems relatively unproblematic as far as the question of publication is concerned: like most of Cicero's speeches, it was probably published soon after delivery, and with a minimum of alteration. If there has

(*CR* 41 (1927) 74–6), and a full demolition has been undertaken by Stroh (31–54). Other contributions to the debate include M.Schanz rev. C. Hosius, *Geschichte der römischen Literatur* 1⁴ (Munich 1927) 453; Michel 386–8; Settle 60–67; S. F. Bonner in M. Platnauer (ed.), *Fifty Years (and Twelve) of Classical Scholarship* (Oxford 1968), 421–3; Kennedy 276f.; Douglas 14f.; A. D. Leeman, Entretiens 193–200; Classen 3–7; May 197 n. 11; Kirby (n.265) 159–70; R. G. M. Nisbet in A. J. Woodman and J. G. F. Powell (edd.), *Author and Audience in Latin Literature* (Cambridge 1992), 1–17.

[270] Humbert 94, 146f., 149f.; cf. Boulanger 102.
[271] For a full answer to Humbert on this point see Stroh 41.
[272] Humbert 150f.
[273] See *Font.* 20; *Mur.* 57 (cf. Plin. *Ep.* 1.20.7); *Cael.* 19 (doubtful).

been, as Humbert supposed, a certain amount of compression in the reply to the charges, then that would shed an interesting light on Cicero's purpose in publishing the speech: it would suggest that he was not concerned so much to proclaim Sulla's innocence, but rather to show off his own literary and oratorical talents.[274]

(d) Assessment

Opinions as to the merits of *pro Sulla* have differed over the centuries. Fronto, himself an orator of distinction,[275] held the speech in high regard, and appears to have modelled part of one of his own speeches on *digressio* III (§§ 21–35): *in oratione Bithyna . . . multa sunt nova addita, ut arbitror e⟨g⟩o ⟨no⟩n inornate, locus inprimis de acta vita, quem tibi placiturum puto, si legeris quid in simili re M. Tullius pro P. Sylla egregie scriptum reliquit, non ut par pari compares, sed ut aestimes nostrum mediocre ingenium quantum ab illo eximiae eloquentiae viro abfuat (Amic.* 1.14.2 (180 Van den Hout)). The same part of the speech was drawn upon many centuries later by Robespierre. Accused by Louvet of aspiring to 'pouvoir suprême' (i.e. *regnum*), Robespierre retaliated on 5 November 1792 with a speech in which he justified his past conduct with arguments recalling those put forward by Cicero in *pro Sulla*. Robespierre's speech, like Cicero's, was successful, at least in the short term.[276]

In the nineteenth and twentieth centuries, as we have seen,[277] the general assumption was that in his speech

---

[274] Cf. Settle 53f., 156; Kennedy 276; Stroh 52; Crawford 3–7; Classen 5.

[275] Cf. Paneg. 8(5).14.2 *Romanae eloquentiae non secundum sed alterum decus.*

[276] For the text of Robespierre's speech see M. Bouloiseau *et al.* (edd.), *Oeuvres de Maximilien Robespierre* ix (Paris 1958) 79–104. A comparison with *pro Sulla* is made at T. Zielinski, *Cicero im Wandel der Jahrhunderte*[3] (Leipzig and Berlin 1912) 264f.; cf. Strenge 5; Douglas, *Roman Oratory* 344; W. K. Lacey, *Cicero and the End of the Roman Republic* (London 1978) 175. On the Ciceronianism of the period see Wood 3f.

[277] Pp. 33f.

for Sulla Cicero defended a guilty conspirator. Scholars favourable to Cicero therefore chose to ignore the moral implications of the case, and instead presented *pro Sulla* as an ordinary and unremarkable example of Cicero's oratorical art. Most notable among these was J. S. Reid (1882), who wrote that 'the speech, while it cannot be classed with Cicero's highest efforts, is vigorous throughout, and admirable in style ... The speech is ... to be classed with the *pro Plancio*, as offering a thoroughly artistic handling of a somewhat ordinary theme'.[278] J. Strenge (1898) took a broadly similar line.[279] For scholars hostile to Cicero, there was of course no problem: R. Syme (1939), taking Sulla to be a Catilinarian, pointedly described the speech as 'the able defence of an eloquent lawyer to whom he [Sulla] had lent a large sum of money'.[280] Most recently J. M. May (1988), who unlike Syme is generally favourable to Cicero, has not set out to exclude the moral aspect from consideration, and has accordingly produced a highly negative assessment of the speech. 'Despite the neatness of structure and the ultimate success of the plea,' he writes, 'Cicero's speech on behalf of Sulla remains somewhat unsatisfying, at times unconvincing ... the *Pro Sulla* is perhaps too blatant in its appeal to authority for a modern audience; or perhaps one is repelled by the apparent miscarriage of justice. Most likely, however, is the detection by the reader of a bit of laziness, a kind of smug complacency on Cicero's part ...; he seems content to thunder the threat of his authority continually and without much variation. Pragmatically, it was certainly effective, but whether it represents the effort of a Cicero who was at the height of his intellectual and political powers is questionable'.[281] If, however, one could escape from the idea of an 'apparent

---

[278] Introd. § 39.
[279] Strenge esp. 9f., 25.
[280] *RR* 66.
[281] May 78. For my review of this work see *JRS* 80 (1990) 203f.

miscarriage of justice',[282] would Cicero's use of his own *auctoritas* emerge in a more positive light?

I close with a few remarks outlining my own view of the speech, a positive view in that it does not start from the premise that Cicero should never have given the speech at all. First, May is in my opinion right to draw attention to the speech's 'neatness of structure': as I hope has been shown,[283] the ingenuity with which the structure prescribed by the rhetoricians has been adapted to fit the requirements of the case is one of the speech's most distinctive features. Especially successful is the way in which Cicero gradually builds up to the outburst of *indignatio* against Torquatus at the end of the first half of the speech (§§ 46–50) and to the fine peroration at the end of the second (§§ 86–93). On the other hand, May and others are mistaken in viewing the speech as let down by 'unconvincing' arguments:[284] as will be argued in the commentary, in both of the passages traditionally singled out for criticism (§§ 11, 67–8) Cicero's meaning has been seriously misunderstood. There are of course many misleading or false arguments in *pro Sulla*; but they are not such as to vitiate the speech to any greater degree than happens in other speeches. I also take issue with May over the question of Cicero's *auctoritas*: this is deployed with vigour, but great care is nevertheless taken to avoid an impression of arrogance such as would seem to substantiate Torquatus' criticisms. We have already observed the relative absence of the boasting and invective prominent in some of the other speeches;[285] we may

---

[282] The ambiguity at May 77 could mislead: 'Sulla, a defendant generally believed to have been guilty of the charge, had been acquitted largely by the influence of Cicero's consular *auctoritas*'. After his trial Sulla was not (so far as we know) generally believed to have been guilty.

[283] Pp. 42–8.

[284] Cf. Boulanger 99f.; Macdonald 310; May 78. For the others see on §§ 11, 67–8.

[285] P. 55.

note, too, the charm and humour with which Cicero puts
down his young opponent (esp. §§ 23–5, 30–35). The support of the consulars for Sulla is made use of to good effect
(§§ 4–5, 81–2), and the jury is handled with tact and deli-
cacy (§§ 62–6, 92–3). These groups both belong among
the *boni*, about whom we hear much in the course of the
speech.[286] *Pro Sulla* dates from that brief period between
the Catilinarian conspiracy and the 'first triumvirate' when
Cicero's ideal of a *concordia ordinum* came closest to fulfilment, and the speech therefore sheds an interesting light
on his hopes, as well as his fears, for the future. However,
what in my view makes *pro Sulla* of particular interest
is that, as we have seen,[287] Cicero's reputation is here
in jeopardy as in no other speech: it is of the greatest
importance whether or not he did defend a Catilinarian
conspirator. Cato defined an orator as a *vir bonus dicendi
peritus* (*Fil.* 14, = 80.1 Jordan), and it is on *pro Sulla* that
our judgement of Cicero's moral probity must depend. Far
from being, then, a speech concerned with 'a somewhat
ordinary theme' (Reid), *pro Sulla* is one of Cicero's most
sensational speeches. The case was a difficult one for him
not because the evidence against Sulla was particularly
strong (it was not),[288] but because the consequences of los-
ing would have been so momentous. On the other hand,
the risk which Cicero ran in defending Sulla heightened
the glory of his success in obtaining an acquittal. As G. A.
Kennedy has aptly observed, 'to the rhetorician the greater
the challenge which the orator successfully meets, the
greater his speech'.[289]

---

[286] 1.10n.

[287] P. 42.

[288] Pp. 35–7.

[289] Kennedy 181. The same point is made with respect to *pro Sulla* on
p. 191, but I do not agree with the implication that in this case 'the
evidence was strongly against the client'.

IV THE MANUSCRIPTS

(a) The tradition

There are in existence more than two hundred medieval manuscript copies of *pro Sulla*;[290] it has been tentatively suggested by R. H. Rouse and M. D. Reeve that the archetype (ω) from which these all descend may be identifiable with a lost manuscript known to have been in the possession of the abbey of Lorsch in western Germany in the ninth century.[291] The tradition divides into two branches, one consisting of Munich Clm 18787 ('Tegernseensis'; T) and all the *deteriores* (ω), the other of just two manuscripts, Berlin lat. 2°252 ('Erfurtensis'; E) and its sister, Vatican Pal. lat. 1525 (V). A stemma is given in Figure 2.

The earliest manuscript is T, copied in western Germany in the late tenth century.[292] Soon after it was written it appears to have been acquired by the Benedictine abbey of Tegernsee in Bavaria, where it remained until its disappearance some time before the dispersal of the Tegernsee library in 1803. In 1853 it was rediscovered by K. Halm in a Paris bookseller's catalogue, and was duly purchased by his colleague J. G. Baiter; it was said to have come to Paris from Hungary.[293] The omissions and reduplications in T

---

[290] Many of these are listed in Rizzo, *Catalogo*.

[291] See *T.&T.* 82 (cf. 90), with M. D. Reeve in G. Cavallo (ed.), *Le strade del testo* (Bari 1987) 7; cf. Rizzo, *Tradizione* 91f. Rouse and Reeve give an invaluable survey of the tradition at *T.&T.* 78–83.

[292] For a description and bibliography see B. Munk Olsen, *L'Étude des auteurs classiques latins aux XIe et XIIe siècles* I (Paris 1982) 236; cf. K. Halm *et al.*, *Catalogus Codicum Latinorum Bibliothecae Regiae Monacensis* II.3 (Munich 1878) 210. A facsimile of the opening of *pro Sulla* (§§ 1–2) is given at E. Chatelain, *Paléographie des classiques latins* I (Paris 1884–92) pl. XXVII.1. See also C. A. Jordan, *Commentatio de codice Tegernseensi orationis Tullianae pro Caecina* (Leipzig 1848); Halm, *Handschriftenkunde* 6f.; *T.&T.* xxxi, 79f.

[293] See Baiter–Halm, Orelli² II.2 v–vi, 753; Halm's catalogue entry (previous n.); Pabón I.

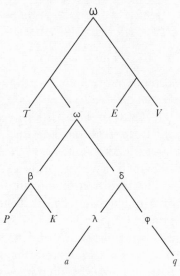

Figure 2

have been studied by A. C. Clark, who concluded that it
was copied from a manuscript very like itself, with a similar
length of line (c.75 letters), and that it may have had another ancestor with shorter lines (19–22 letters).[294]

E, copied in the mid twelfth century, is a large omnibus
edition of Cicero, containing almost half of what was
eventually to survive.[295] It was assembled by Wibald, abbot
of Corvey (in the north of Germany) from 1146 to 1158,
who wrote of his project: 'nec vero ... pati possumus quod

[294] Clark, *Descent* 201, 204–8 (cf. 291f., 306).
[295] For a description and bibliography see Munk Olsen (n.292) 148–50.
See also E. Wunder, *Variae Lectiones* (Leipzig 1827), esp. lxxvii, 93f.
(includes a facsimile of *Planc.* 1–2); W. Freund, *M. Tullii Ciceronis
Oratio pro T. Annio Milone* (Breslau 1838), esp. 43 (includes a complete
facsimile of *Mil.* and a list of abbreviations used in *E*); Seyffert 9–15;
Halm, *Handschriftenkunde* v–vi, 2; A. C. Clark on *Mil.*, xxxviii–xliii; P.
Lehmann, *ABAW* 30.5 (1919) 18f., 35f.; R. G. M. Nisbet on *Pis.*,
xxiii–xxiv; *T.&T.* 58f., 63, 77, 80, 85f., 92f., 96; M. D. Reeve, *Ciceroniana* 6 (1988) 84f.; L. D. Reynolds and N. G. Wilson, *Scribes and
Scholars*[3] (Oxford 1991) 113f.

illud nobile ingenium, illa splendida inventa, illa tanta rerum et verborum ornamenta oblivione et negligentia depereant, sed ipsius opera universa, quantacumque inveniri poterunt, in unum volumen confici volumus'.[296] The manuscript has a splendid frontispiece depicting Wibald himself offering his book to the three patron saints of Corvey, while in the lower half of the picture Cicero sits in his study and displays his writings; behind him are his consular *fasces*, while to one side an assistant, perhaps Tiro, helps him with his scroll.[297] Unfortunately the usefulness of *E* for reconstructing the text of *pro Sulla* is severely limited by the loss at some unknown date between 1610 and 1827 of the folios which contained the end of *pro Caecina* (after § 100 *vincula*) and the greater part of *pro Sulla* (up to § 81 *-tundis Catilinae*). A collation of *E*, including the folios now lost, was made by J. Gulielmius (1555–84) in preparation for an edition which he did not live to produce, and several readings were also published independently by J. Zinzerling in 1610.[298] A selection of Gulielmius' readings (with those of Zinzerling) was reported, but without much precision, by J. Gruter in his edition of 1618,[299] and it is these notes of Gruter's which have formed the basis for the reports of *E* (to § 81) in every subsequent edition. However, in 1974 the copy of Cicero in which Gulielmius made his collation was successfully identified by P. L. Schmidt: this

---

[296] P. Jaffé (ed.), *Bibliotheca Rerum Germanicarum* i *Monumenta Corbeiensia* (Berlin 1864) 327.

[297] The frontispiece is reproduced by A. Boeckler in *Westfälische Studien … Alois Bömer gewidmet* (Leipzig 1928) pl.4 (there is an inferior reproduction in A. Ludorff, *Die Bau- und Kunstdenkmäler von Westfalen: Kreis Höxter* (Münster 1914) pl.45). The prostrate figure with the book (Wibald) is inaccurately labelled as 'abbot' Adelbert (in fact provost, 1147–76) by a later (end of s.xiii: Munk Olsen (n.292) 148) hand: see F. Philippi, *Abhandlungen über corveyer Geschichtsschreibung* (Münster 1906) x–xv; P. Lehmann, *ABAW* 30.5 (1919) 35; R. G. M. Nisbet on *Pis.*, xxiii–xxiv; *T.&T.* 93.

[298] Zinzerling 1–7 (cf. 179f.).

[299] See II.556–8.

was revealed to be the Lambinus edition of 1577–8 now in
the possession of the Bibliotheek der Rijksuniversiteit te
Leiden (shelfmark 762.B.9/10).[300] As a result of Schmidt's
important discovery, and with the aid of high-definition
photographs kindly supplied to me by the authorities at
Leiden, I was able in 1989 to publish a full transcription of
Gulielmius' collation.[301] The present edition of the speech
is therefore the first to be based on reliable reports of E, by
reporting precisely what Gulielmius saw in the folios now
lost.

The sister of E, V, is a classic example of a *recentior non
deterior*, copied at Heidelberg in 1467.[302] This manuscript,
cited by Gruter as 'Pal. ix', belonged to the famous Palatine library, which was plundered in 1622 (when Gruter
was Librarian) and transferred to the Vatican the following
year.[303] V's text of *pro Sulla* unfortunately comes to an
abrupt halt at §43 *meminisse*, after which the scribe wrote
'hic est modicus defectus ut apparet', leaving the rest of the
sheet blank, and beginning *de Senectute* on the verso side of
the page.[304] From §§43 to 81, therefore, the branch of the
tradition represented by EV, with the exception of the reports of Gulielmius and Zinzerling, is unattested. V disagrees with E in two places, but neither disagreement is

---

[300] See P. L. Schmidt, *Die Überlieferung von Ciceros Schrift 'De Legibus' in
Mittelalter und Renaissance* (Munich 1974) 219.

[301] See *CQ* n.s. 39 (1989) 400–7, where I go into greater detail.

[302] For a description and bibliography see E. Pellegrin *et al.*, *Les Manuscrits classiques latins de la Bibliothèque Vaticane* II.2 (Paris 1982) 178–81
(where the suggestion of an Italian origin is unjustified: see M. D.
Reeve in Cavallo (n.291) 5). A facsimile of *Caec.* 1–6 is given at Chatelain (n.292) pl. xxv, and of *Amic.* 1–6 at H. Foerster, *Mittelalterliche
Buch- und Urkundenschriften* (Berne 1946) pl. II. See also K. Halm, *Neue
Jahrb. für Phil. u. Päd.* Suppl. 15.2 (1849) 165–78; Halm, *Handschriftenkunde* 17; K. Busche, *Hermes* 46 (1911) 57–69; *T.&T.* 80, 95.

[303] See J. E. Sandys, *A History of Classical Scholarship* II (Cambridge 1908)
361.

[304] Kasten (vii n. 2) seems to misunderstand the situation; Macdonald
(313) curiously mistranslates Clark's '*desinit* §43'.

significant. At § 37 the reading of the archetype was *afflata fortuna*: *V*, but not *E*, has corrected this to *afflicta fortuna*. At § 42 *E* reads *emisi*, which I accept; the other manuscripts, influenced by *divisi* three words earlier, all give either *divisi* or *dimisi*.[305]

The manuscripts which remain (ω) are the descendants of a lost sister of *T*, and fall into two groups. In one group, only four manuscripts are known: Brussels 14492 ('Parcensis'; *P*), Cambridge, Univ. Dd. 13.2 (*K*), Brussels 9755–63 (*B*) and Wolfenbüttel 338 (= Helmst. 304) (*W*).[306] The other, vast, group consists of all the *Itali*. The four manuscripts of the smaller group are descended from a lost manuscript which I name β; the lost parent of the *Itali* is conventionally known as δ.

I consider first the descendants of β. *P* belonged to the abbey of Parc, near Louvain; it is written in a Netherlandish hand, and probably dates from the first half of the fifteenth century.[307] Its total contents are incorporated in the same order in *K*, a large omnibus edition copied by the Dutch scribe T. Werken in 1444 for William Gray (afterwards bishop of Ely, 1454–78) during his stay at the University of Cologne.[308] *PK* are therefore closely associated in time and place, and Rouse and Reeve have found them to

---

[305] Cf. Clark xii.

[306] Wolfenbüttel 338 has been assigned a siglum purely for the convenience of this discussion. The MS is not cited in the apparatus or commentary.

[307] For a description see P. Thomas, *Catalogue des manuscrits de classiques latins de la Bibliothèque Royale de Bruxelles* (Ghent 1896) 84–6 (dates it to s.xiv); cf. Halm, *Handschriftenkunde* 14f. On the date see R. A. B. Mynors, *Catalogue of the Manuscripts of Balliol College Oxford* (Oxford 1963) 377; *T.&T.* 77, 81.

[308] For a description see *A Catalogue of the Manuscripts preserved in the Library of the University of Cambridge* I (Cambridge 1856) 507–9; cf. J. S. Reid on *Ac.*, pp. 66–8; R. A. B. Mynors, *Trans. Camb. Bibliog. Soc.* I (1949–53) 98 (pl. VII.A reproduces a short extract, *Div.* 2.8–9); Mynors (previous n.) xxix, 377; R. M. Thomson, *Rev. Bén.* 85 (1975) 375f.; *T.&T.* 77, 80f., 95.

be twins.[309] *B* was copied in Flanders or Germany in the second half of the fifteenth century;[310] it was used by Halm, who commented on its similarity to *P* in his edition of 1856.[311] The last known member of the group, *W*, was written in a French hand, also in the second half of the fifteenth century.[312] It is conceivable that further manuscripts, not yet identified, could belong with these four: P. Rubenius (elder brother of the painter Rubens) discovered 'in membranis' various readings belonging to *PKBW*, and it need not have been those manuscripts which he used.[313]

The relation of *BW* to *PK* has not hitherto been established, so this question must now be addressed. I have collated all four manuscripts for §§1–20 of the speech: this proved to be more than enough, given the volume of corruption. The readings which follow are all taken from these sections. (1) *B* and/or *W* agree in error with *P* against *K* in the following places: §2 *necessitudinem*] *consuetudinem PBW*; §4 *per me est*] *est per me est* (*est* alterum om. *B*) *PBW*; §6 *nocentes*] *innocentes PBW*; §7 *plerique*] *plurimique* (*plerunque B*) *PBW*; §9 *nulla est enim*] *nulla est PBW*; *mea causa*] *causa mea*

[309] *T.&T.* 59 n. 23 ('terrible twins'), 81; cf. Reid 158f.; Clark xii n. 2.
[310] For a description see Thomas (n.307) 37; cf. R. J. Tarrant and M. D. Reeve in *T.&T.*, 150, with n.5; P. O. Kristeller, *Iter Italicum* III (London and Leiden 1983) 117 ('perhaps written in Italy').
[311] Orelli² II.2 753; cf. Reid 158; Clark xii n. 2; *T.&T.* 82.
[312] For a description see O. von Heinemann, *Die Handschriften der herzoglichen Bibliothek zu Wolfenbüttel* 1.1 (Wolfenbüttel 1884) 249f.; Rizzo, *Catalogo* no. 164. A collation was published by H. Wrampelmeyer, *Codex Wolfenbuttelanus Nr. 205* [as it was then known], *olim Helmstadiensis Nr. 304* VI (Clausthal 1881) 9–14 (*pro Sulla*), from which Müller noticed its resemblance to *B* (Teubner II.2 xcv); cf. Kasten (1933) xii, (1966) vi n. 1. See also Halm, *Handschriftenkunde* 8f.; Clark, *Vet. Clun.* v–vi, xi–xiii, lxiii, lxvii–lxix; Clark, *Descent* vi, 18–24; S. Rizzo and M. Regoliosi in O. Besomi and M. Regoliosi (edd.), *Lorenzo Valla e l'umanesimo italiano* (Padua 1986) 241–63.
[313] Rubenius 5 (§46 'pertulerim ac perfregerim' = *KW* (*perculerim ac perfregerim P*: *perculerim atque confregerim B*); §48 'an istud tibi' = *PKBW*, but also *TE* (*istud* om. δ)), 12 (§50 'eximiis' = *PKBW*); cf. Clark xii n. 2.

PBW; § 11 *facta esse*] *esse facta PBW*; § 12 *ac dignitatem*] *et dignitatem PBW*; § 14 *mirari*] *imitari PBW*; § 19 *cum vestrorum*] *tum vestrorum PBW*; *cum huius*] *tum huius PBW*; *cum illorum*] *tum illorum PBW*; *cum puerorum*] *tum puerorum PBW*; *cum matronarum*] *tum matronarum PBW*. (2) By contrast, *B* and/or *W* agree in error with *K* against *P* in only two places: § 14 *nullum indicium*] *nullum iudicium KW*; § 16 *in coniuratione*] *coniuratione KB*. Neither agreement is significant. (3) *B* contains the following errors which do not occur in *P*: § 1 *ut p. sulla*] *ait p. sulla B*; *tamen haberet*] *tum haberet B*; *huius*] *huiusmodi B*; *patiar B*; *misericordiamque* om. *B*; *ac victi B*; § 2 *in* om. *B*; *violescet B*; *aliquid de se B*; *locis mihi et data B*; § 3 *a ceteris*] *ceteris B*; *iure secernas*] *secernatis B*; *non reprendatur*] *non comprehendatur B*; *initium B*; § 4 *existimas B*; *salvum*] *salvum eum PKW*: *salvum ei B*; § 5 *an*] *ac PKW*: *at B*; *celsissimam sedem PKW*: *sedem celsissimam B*; *ac magnis*] *magnis B*; *ac periculis PKW*: *atque periculis B*; *defenderam B*; *adesse huic*] *hic adesse B*; § 6 *m.* om. *B*; *quis ad* (ut vid.) *cornelium B*; *quis horum his PKW*: *quis horum B*; *putant*] *putavit B*; *quaedam contagio sceleris*] *quaedam contagio est sceleris PKW*: *contagio quaedam sceleris est B*; *quem obstrictum*] *qui obstrictum B*; § 7 *num collegae B*; *in hac causa*] *in causam B*; § 8 *natura ipsa et voluntas B*; § 9 *omnium bonorum causa PKW*: *omnium causa bonorum B*; *nihil est quod ammirere B*; *in qua*] *qua B*; *tempus*] *causa tempus B*; *mihi fuit magis PK*: *mihi magis fuit B*; *ac timoris B*; *alii esse B*; *praecipuum est consuli B*; § 10 *in antronium quidem testimonium B*; *hoc*] *has igitur B*; *inconstans*] *iudices inconstans B*; *religio* om. *B*; *et moderate ego PKW*: *et ego moderate B*; § 11 *me consule*] *consule B*; *dicis fuisse*] *dicis affuisse B*; *atque optimi viri B*; *tecum summus B*; *esset*] *fuit tecum B*; *expertem temporum illorum PKW*: *expertem illorum temporum B*; *nondum ... nondum*] *numquam B*; § 12 *cum propter*] *tum propter B*; *cum communibus*] *tum communibus PKW*: om. *B*; *est ab eo B*; *tamen*] *cum B*; § 13 *vobis*] *vobiscum B*; *tum* om. *B*; *defenditur B*; *atqui haec B*; § 14 *valere fortasse debet PK*: *fortasse valere debet B*; *defendere*] *defenderim B*; § 15 *sibi ex*] *se ex B*; § 16 *illo* om. *B*; *non modo cum eisdem illis PK*: *non cum eisdem illis B*; § 17 *consolandum B*; *igitur*] *ergo B*; *tantam*] *tam diversam B*; § 18 *enim* om. *B*; *saepius B*; *multa mea*] *multa me B*; *fecerat mihi ipsi B*; *esse* om. *B*; § 19 *atque templorum*] *ac templorum B*; *ac funestae*] *atque funestae B*; § 20 *et feci libenter*] *id est feci libenter PKW*: *libenter id feci B*. (4) *W* contains the following errors which do not occur in *P*: § 1 *everteretur odio W*; § 2 *me defensionis W*; § 5 *et de hoc ... fuisse* om. *W*; § 6 *cum illo*] *cum ullo W*; *cum ille*] *cum illo W*; *putant*] *putavit W*; § 8 *meas res*] *res meas PKB*: *meas W*; *tempus et*] *tempus est W*; § 9 *parte* om. *W*; *mihi fuit magis PK*: *nihil fuit magis W*; § 12 *eximium in re publica PKB*: *in re publica eximium W*; *propulsando in hoc crimine W*; *copiosissimi W*; *prolata*] *probata W*; § 13 *vobis*] *nobis W*; *defenditur W*; § 14 *periculis* om. *W*; *valere fortasse debet PK*: *fortasse debet W*; *magnitudinem W*; *utor*] *utar W*; § 15 *non prodesset*] *prodesset W*; *nihil*] *michi W*; § 16 *illo* om. *W*; *non modo cum eisdem illis PK*: *modo cum eisdem illis W*; *sollicitudinemque W*; § 17 *fuerit*] *fuerat W*; § 18 *praeferebat W*; *uno me*] *uno meo me W*; § 19 *faces*] *fatos W*; § 20 *suscepi causam torquate* om. *W*. (5) By contrast, *P* contains only seven errors which do not occur in *B* and/or *W*: § 9 *impertio*] *impartio PW*; § 10 *sum*] *sim PKW*; § 11 *ad propositum*] *propositum PKW*; § 12 *ad vos*] *ad nos PK*; § 15 *ex*] *e PKW*; § 17 *relictus*] *relictis PK*; § 20 *ego neque*] *neque ego PW*. These readings of *BW* are not significant: they are all corrections, or slips, which a scribe might have made in the course of copying. (6) *BW* thus differ from *P* only in being more corrupt (*B* to a greater degree than *W*). They may therefore be assumed to derive from *P*, and hence may be eliminated. The evidence also confirms that *B* cannot be derived from *W*, nor *W* from *B*. *BW* are therefore twins. (7) *BW* together agree against *P* in these five places: § 6 *putant*] *putavit BW*; § 12 *ad vos*] *ad nos PK*; § 13 *defenditur BW*; § 16 *illo* om. *BW*; § 17 *relictus*] *relictis PK*. These agreements suggest that *BW* were not copied directly from *P*, but from an intermediary. However, since *BW* are to be eliminated, the question is of no practical importance.

It has been demonstrated above that *BW* are twins derived from *P*, perhaps at a remove. Fortunately, then, we need give neither manuscript any further consideration:[314] in order to reconstruct β, it is necessary to take account of *PK* alone.

The lost manuscript β is characterised by the inaccuracy and confusion of its text, a fact which explains why the manuscripts of this group were so seldom copied. There are a large number of astonishingly senseless errors, words have been added or omitted at random and there is carelessness over word order throughout. Rouse and Reeve have pointed out that these errors were made by β, not, as was traditionally assumed, by *P*:[315] *P* cannot be held responsible for errors which it shares with a manuscript (*K*) not derived from it. Indeed, *P* is a reasonably accurate copy of β (*K* is less accurate). The value of β, corrupt as it is, lies in the fact that agreements with *T* against δ will generally show that it is δ rather than *T* which is in error. In seven places I judge that β alone gives a correct reading: §46 *me oblitum* (*oblitum me* δ: *me T*); §48 *coactus sum* (*sum* om. cett.); §48 *et non defendere* (*non* om. cett.); §68 *cogitasset ut* (*ut* om. cett.); §71 *intellegetis* (*intelligitis* cett.); §76 *possit* (*posset* cett.); §79 *vita plurimum* (*vita* om. cett.).[316] H. Kasten in his later editions (1949, 1966) supposed *P* (he took no account of *K*) to be contaminated by readings from the source of *EV* or from *E* itself, but it is not necessary to postulate contamination in order to account for the good readings in β:[317] usually these will simply be cases where *T*δ have made the same error independently. In any case, a scribe who had access to the branch of the tradition represented by *EV* would surely have helped himself more generously to the readings on offer. The eight instances adduced by Kasten in support of his hypothesis are easily disposed of.[318] Two

---

[314] Except for a passing notice at 46.8n.

[315] *T.&T.* 81; contrast Clark xii–xiv; Pabón 6.

[316] Clark (xiv) and Kasten (vi) claim further instances: §39 *se nescire*; §52 *et ut dicitis*. But see apparatus and notes in commentary.

[317] Cf. *T.&T.* 80 n. 154.

[318] Kasten vi.

are misreports: §14 *utor* ω (not *utor* Tδ: *utar* VP); §21 *tum*
TVδ: *tu* β *Schol.* (not *tum* Tδ: *tu* VP *Schol.*). A further two are
inconsequential agreements: §2 *probaro* Tδ: *probavero* Vβ;
§33 *dilectu* Vβ: *delectu* Tδ. The remainder may be explained
as coincidental: §2 *non uterer orationis* Tδ: *orationis non uterer*
Vβ; §22 *hoc tibi* Tδ: *tibi hoc* Vβ; §35 *a me forte* Tδ: *forte a me*
Vβ; §90 *vos contentos* Tδ: *contentos vos* Eβ. Kasten goes on to
give two further lists of places where he suspects contamination. But in seven of these places the reading of
neither *E* nor *V* is known; in one place the reading of *V* is
known, but β does not agree with it; and in the remaining
place *P* is misreported.

Finally I turn from β to the second group of manuscripts
derived from ω, the *Itali*: these manuscripts, some two
hundred in number, are all descended from a single, lost
manuscript, δ, which was lent to Petrarch by his Florentine
friend Lapo da Castiglionchio in 1350.[319] Lapo and Petrarch each made their own copy of δ (λ and φ respectively),
but neither survives. There exists, however, one copy of λ:
Florence, Laur. S. Croce 23 sin. 3 (*a*).[320] This manuscript is
important because, unlike the rest of the *Itali*, which are all
descended from φ, it is free from the conjectures which
Petrarch added to his text: good readings which occur in
the descendants of φ (whether in the margin or in the text
itself), but which are absent from *a*, may be attributed to
Petrarch.[321] *a* is therefore a more honest witness to δ than
the rest of the *Itali*. It ought to be mentioned at this point
that there are five places in which *a* agrees in error with *V*:
§3 *reprehendatur* semel Va; §6 *putant*] *putavit* Va (influenced by

---

[319] See Clark iv–ix; G. Billanovich, *Studi e testi* 124 (1946) 98–100; *id.*,
Petrarca letterato 1 (Rome 1947) 107f.; S. Rizzo, *RFIC* 103 (1975) 6f.;
T.&T. 82, 85f., 94; S.Rizzo (next n.) 10–13.

[320] See A. M. Bandini, *Catalogus Codicum Latinorum Bibliothecae Mediceae
Laurentianae* IV (1777) 170; S. Rizzo in M. Feo (ed.), *Codici latini del
Petrarca nelle biblioteche fiorentine: mostra 19 maggio – 30 giugno 1991*
(Florence 1991), 9–14; cf. previous n.

[321] See S. Rizzo, *RFIC* 103 (1975) 5–15.

putavit earlier); §14 *torquatus*] *torquato V*: *et torquato a* (influenced by *autronio* later); §26 *vacatio*] *vocatio Va*; §43 *in orbe*] *in orbem Va*. These agreements are not significant; like the agreements of β with *VE*, they may be put down to simple coincidence.

Fortunately, it is not necessary for stemmatic purposes to collate and classify all the descendants of φ. Editors have restricted themselves to a small number of manuscripts, chosen somewhat arbitrarily. In particular, attention has centred on Vatican Pal. lat. 1820, Paris, B. N. lat. 14749 (*d*), Florence, Bibl. Naz. Conv. Soppr. J.iv.4 (S. Marco 255) (*b*), Oxford, Bodl. Canon. class. lat. 226 (*c*) and Paris, B. N. lat. 7779 (*k*). J. E. Pabón also took account of a number of *deteriores* in Spanish libraries, supposing them contaminated directly from the archetype, but this manifestly does not follow: as one reviewer remarked, these manuscripts 'do nothing except clutter the apparatus'.[322] I have chosen to avoid cluttering the apparatus myself by using just one manuscript, Vatican Vat. lat. 9305 (which I have named *q*),[323] as representative of φ; other manuscripts, such as *dbck* and Pabón's *deteriores*, are cited only where they are useful as sources of conjectures. The importance of *q* as a witness to φ has been pointed out by S. Rizzo.[324] This manuscript, which dates from the end of the fourteenth century, is one of the earliest descendants of φ, and carefully reproduces in the margin Petrarch's conjectures and annotations: in later manuscripts, these adversaria quickly make their way into the text itself. Kasten considered that the descendants of φ have been contaminated from

---

[322] Pabón 6–8; cf. R. G. M. Nisbet, *CR* n.s. 16 (1966) 118. Pabón's partiality towards 'meos Hispanicos' (6) sometimes leads him astray: see 9.3n.; 65.2n.

[323] For a description see Rizzo, *Catalogo* no. 150.

[324] *RFIC* 103 (1975) 5–15, esp. 7, 15. Rizzo also draws attention to Vatican Pal. lat. 1820 and Vatican Barb. lat. 142 (*G*). I have not found the former to provide anything of use beyond what is given by *q*; I notice the latter six times.

EV.[325] Again, however, there is no reason to postulate contamination: the instances which Kasten adduces show no more than that Italian humanists, faced with the reading of φ, sometimes restored by conjecture what later emerged in manuscripts independent of φ.

Editors of this speech have tended to close their accounts of the manuscript tradition by comparing the merits of *TEV*ω ('inter codices dignitatis contentio fiat'):[326] this allows them, when in doubt, simply to follow the reading of the manuscript they esteem most highly. This is a dangerous procedure, since all manuscripts make mistakes; but it is a procedure which is difficult in practice to avoid entirely. In two places I have found no other considerations to bring to bear, and have had to fall back solely on my impressions of the relative merits of the manuscripts. At §34 the manuscripts are equally divided between *harum omnium rerum* (*T*ω) and *harum rerum omnium* (*V*): both collocations are found in Cicero, and both provide favoured rhythms at the incision before *quas*. Secondly, at §71 there is an equal division between *vita ac natura* (*T*) and *natura ac vita* (ω, inferred); again, both collocations occur in Cicero. In the first instance, I have followed *T*ω simply because *T* is generally speaking more accurate than *V*. In the second place I have followed *T*, believing it more reliable than ω; the reading of *T* is arguably supported by *huius vita et natura* at §73. In all other places I have (I hope) found less haphazard reasons for preferring one reading to another.

Apart from the manuscripts, evidence for the text is provided by the *scholia Bobiensia* (although §§1–9 and 42–90 are lost), and by quotations in Aulus Gellius (§72), Augustine (§25), the rhetoricians Julius Rufinianus (§46) and Grillius (§1), and the grammarian Arusianus Messius (§83).

---

[325] Kasten vii.
[326] See Clark xi–xii; Kasten (1933) xv–xviii, (1949) vi–vii, (1966) vii–viii; Pabón 5f. The quotation is from Clark (xi).

(b) The present apparatus and text

All manuscripts which are cited in the apparatus criticus have been given a siglum. Roman characters represent manuscripts which are extant. The Greek characters ωωβδ denote the agreement of two or more manuscripts (ω = $T(E)(V)$ω, ω = βδ, β = PK, δ = aq), and hence represent manuscripts which are no longer extant, but of which readings may be inferred (thus ω represents the archetype).

The (extant) manuscripts used in the preparation of this edition are of two kinds. First, there are the seven 'principal' manuscripts, which are as follows:

T Munich Clm 18787

E Berlin lat. 2°252 (contains §§ 81 -*tundis Catilinae* –93 only)

V Vatican Pal. lat. 1525 (contains §§ 1–43 *meminisse* only)

P Brussels 14492

K Cambridge, Univ. Dd. 13.2

a Florence, Laur. S. Croce 23 sin. 3

q Vatican Vat. lat. 9305.

Whenever the reading of one or more of these manuscripts is given, the reading of all the others may be inferred. All known readings from the part of E now lost (§ 1–81) have been recorded in full in the apparatus, but readings of E may of course be inferred only for the part of the speech which still survives (§§ 81–93). The sigla which introduce the apparatus on each page make it clear which are the manuscripts about which inferences may be made.

Secondly, there are the following 'supplementary' manuscripts:

B Brussels 9755–63

r Escorial R.1.15

f Florence, Laur. Gadd. 90 sup. 69.2

b Florence, Bibl. Naz. Conv. Soppr. J.IV.4 (S. Marco 255)

m   Madrid 10097
t   Madrid 10119
S   Munich Clm 15734
c   Oxford, Bodl. Canon. class. lat. 226
k   Paris, B. N. lat. 7779
d   Paris, B. N. lat. 14749
G   Vatican Barb. lat. 142.

These manuscripts are cited only occasionally, for the sake of the conjectures which they contain.[327] They are of no value for stemmatic purposes, and no inferences about their contents may be made from the silence of the apparatus.

All the principal manuscripts I have collated myself from microfilms. *TE* I found to have been collated accurately by previous editors. *V* had been collated accurately by J. E. Pabón,[328] but I found a further twenty-two readings which Pabón had presumably felt not worth recording. *PK* had had readings taken from them, but had not been collated. *a* had either received the same treatment as *PK*, or else had been collated extremely carelessly. *q* had never been collated or made use of in any way by editors. Of the 'supplementary' manuscripts, some I have examined myself in microfilm (*BbkdG*) or by autopsy (*c*); for the rest (nine readings in all), I have accepted the reports of K. Halm (*S*), A. C. Clark (*f*) and Pabón (*rmt*).

Without exaggeration, previous editions of the speech contain some hundreds of misreports, either explicitly or by implication. In this edition I have therefore decided to provide a complete account of the evidence. The appara-

---

[327] A number of these conjectures have been reattributed from early editions to the earliest manuscripts in which they appear. For the appropriation of conjectures in manuscripts by the editors of the first printed editions see A. C. Clark, OCT IV (1909) xii–xiii; *id.*, *Inv. Ital.* 27–33.

[328] Cf. Pabón 2. K. Busche at *Hermes* 46 (1911) 57f. published a list of corrections to the Niebuhr–Blum collation – just too late for Clark's OCT (1911), in which the reports of *V* (*e*) are frequently inaccurate.

tus gives complete collations of *TEVaq*. *PK* are so corrupt
that a complete collation would seriously unbalance the
apparatus. In the main I have therefore confined myself to
reporting *PK* in the apparatus only where silence would
allow false inferences to be made. For the sake of com-
pleteness, however, I have provided the rest of my collation of *PK* in Appendix 2. The apparatus and Appendix 2,
taken together, thus represent a complete collation of all
the principal manuscripts on which this edition is based. I
believe there is much to be said in favour of offering a complete account, rather than a selection, of the manuscript
evidence. A selection invariably conveys a false impression
of the relative reliability of manuscripts by excluding a
proportion of their errors. A selection also prevents the
reader from noticing the types of errors to which particular
manuscripts are prone. In a collation, on the other hand,
an apparently trivial error may at some point in the future
be influential in prompting a conjecture, by casting light on
the process of corruption.

As regards the form of the apparatus, I have taken
especial care to ensure that the information on each particular point in the text is presented in exactly the form in
which it may be most quickly and easily understood. Concision has been an aim, although subordinate to clarity. I
have been fairly generous in including conjectures, as I
believe that editors do not cite enough of them (the neglect
of C. Schliack's *curiam* at §53 is a case in point). Nevertheless, not all conjectures discussed in the commentary
have deserved a place in the apparatus; and, of course,
only a fairly small proportion of the conjectures which exist
are mentioned in this book at all. Many of the nineteenth-
century conjectures which I have excluded may be found in
the apparatuses of Halm and C. F. W. Müller.

Moving from the apparatus to the text itself, and to the
question of orthography, I have preferred to retain the
forms with which the reader will be familiar rather than

impose upon the text any sustained attempt at authentic or
period spelling. Where, however, the factor of prose
rhythm implies one spelling rather than another, I have
adopted the spelling dictated by the rhythm. Thus I spell
relicuus not *reliquus* (the spelling of the manuscripts) because
this allows a resolved cretic-spondee at §89 *in malis relicui
fecit* (the same rhythm as at §88 *solacia relicuae vitae*).[329]
Similarly, I spell *recciderunt* not *reciderunt* (the reading of the
manuscripts) at §91: the clausula is a double-trochee (preceded by a cretic).[330] The case of *ac* and *atque* in the clausula has already been discussed.[331] Where contractions are
concerned, prose rhythm can be particularly helpful. Verbs
in -*prehendo* (always given in uncontracted form in the
manuscripts) occur within the clausula in six places, in five
of which it is unambiguously the contracted form which
gives the more favoured rhythm: §32 *nemo reprendit* (double-
trochee) not *nemo reprehendit* (hexameter ending); §32 *rem
publicam reprendis* (double-trochee) not *rem publicam reprendis*
(hexameter ending); §63 *recte reprendis* (double-trochee) not
recte reprehendis (hexameter ending);[332] §63 *iudicium reprendit*
(double-trochee) not *iudicium reprehendit* (hexameter ending);
§81 *adfuerunt reprendantur* (cretic-spondee) not *adfuerunt repre-
hendantur* (hexameter rhythm).[333] The sixth place, §3, is less
clear-cut: *non reprendatur, reprendatur meum* gives a cretic-
spondee capped by a less favoured combination, whereas
non reprehendatur, reprehendatur meum gives a hexameter rhythm
capped by a resolved molossus-cretic. Overall, the evidence of prose rhythm, coupled with the requirement of
consistency, demands that the contracted form of verbs in
-*prehendo* be adopted throughout. Interestingly, this is supported by a corruption at §71, where the manuscripts give

---

[329] Cf. Schoenwitz 63.
[330] See Zielinski 179; Schoenwitz 53–5.
[331] See pp. 53f.
[332] See Zielinski 177; Havet §966; K. Kumaniecki, *Ciceroniana* 1 (1973) 76.
[333] See Zielinski 177; K. Kumaniecki, *Ciceroniana* 1 (1973) 75.

defensionibus, emended by L. Håkanson to *depre(he)nsionibus*. The transmitted reading implies that the word was originally spelt *deprensionibus*.

In punctuating the speech I have followed my own inclinations, taking care not to allow the punctuation to disrupt the colometry any more than is necessary. I have also been at pains to avoid stringing together period after period with the semicolon. This common practice obscures the relationship between Cicero's periods and makes it considerably more difficult for the reader to follow the train of thought.

The chapter (I–XXXIII) and section (1–93) numbers are those which have become traditional. Since these numbers were originally assigned, the chapter numbers by J. Gruter in 1618 and the section numbers by A. Scot in 1588–9,[334] a few of them have become misplaced; but it would not have been helpful to the reader to have returned them to their original positions. Passages in this and other works of Cicero are referred to by section number (§) alone, as is the common practice.

---

[334] See J. Glucker, *GB* II (1984) 103–12; M. D. Reeve's *pro Quinctio* Teubner (Stuttgart and Leipzig 1992) lxi.

TEXT

SIGLA

T   Monacensis 18787
    (Tegernseensis), s. x
E   Berolinensis lat. fol. 252
    (Erfurtensis), s. xii (continet
    §§ 81 -*tundis Catilinae* −93;
    lectiones nonnullas e parte
    codicis hodie deperdita
    excerpserunt J. Gulielmius et
    J. Zinzerlingus, ego publici
    iuris feci *CQ* s.n. 39 (1989)
    400−7)
V   Vaticanus Pal. lat. 1525,
    anno 1467 (continet §§ 1−43
    meminisse)

P   Bruxellensis 14492 (Parcensis),
    s. xv
K   Cantabrigiensis Dd.13.2, anno
    1444

a   Laurentianus S. Crucis 23
    sin.3, s. xiv
q   Vaticanus Vat. lat. 9305, s. xiv

ω   T(E)(V)ω
ω   βδ
β   PK
δ   aq

Hi codices citantur carptim:
B   Bruxellensis 9755−63, s. xv (e
    P derivatus)
r   Scorialensis R. 1. 15, s. xv
f   Laurentianus Gadd. 90
    sup.69.2, s. xv
b   S.Marci 255, Flor. Bibl. Nat.
    Conv. Soppr. J. iv.4, s. xv
m   Matritensis 10097, s. xv
t   Matritensis 10119, s. xv
S   Monacensis 15734
    (Salisburgensis Aulicus 34),
    s. xv
c   Oxoniensis Canon. class. lat.
    226, s. xv
k   Parisinus lat. 7779, anno 1459
d   Parisinus lat. 14749, s. xv
G   Vaticanus Barb. lat. 142,
    s. xiv−xv

Schol. Scholiasta Bobiensis
    (*Ciceronis Orationum Scholiastae*,
    recensuit T. Stangl (Vindo-
    bonae 1912) 77−85), s. iv−v

M. TVLLI CICERONIS
PRO P. SVLLA ORATIO

I 1 Maxime vellem, iudices, ut P. Sulla et antea dignitatis suae
splendorem obtinere et post calamitatem acceptam modes-
tiae fructum aliquem percipere potuisset. sed quoniam ita
tulit casus infestus ut et amplissimo honore cum communi
ambitionis invidia tum singulari Autroni odio everteretur 5
et in his pristinae fortunae reliquiis miseris et adflictis tamen haberet quosdam quorum animos ne supplicio quidem suo satiare posset, quamquam ex huius incommodis
magnam animo molestiam capio, tamen in ceteris malis
facile patior oblatum mihi tempus esse in quo boni viri le- 10
nitatem meam misericordiamque notam quondam omnibus, nunc quasi intermissam agnoscerent, improbi ac perditi cives redomiti atque victi praecipitante re publica
vehementem me fuisse atque fortem, conservata mitem ac
misericordem faterentur. 15

2 Et quoniam L. Torquatus meus familiaris ac necessarius,
iudices, existimavit, si nostram in accusatione sua necessitudinem familiaritatemque violasset, aliquid se de auctoritate meae defensionis posse detrahere, cum huius periculi
propulsatione coniungam defensionem offici mei. quo qui- 5

TVω] **1** 2 obtineret ω: *corr. Naugerius* 3 potuisset (percepisset *a*)
percipere ω 3–5 sed...verteretur *(sic) Grillius (605.27–30 Halm,*
=93.1–4 Martin) 4 ut *om. Grillius* et amplissimo *Grillius*: amplissimo in *Tω*: et in amplissimo *V* 5 Autroni] autronius *scribitur* autronius
vel antronius *vel* antonius *passim in* δ 7 quorum quosdam *a* 10 esse
om. δ 11–12 omnibus quondam ω 12 ac] vero ac β 13 re-
domiti (re domiti *T*) *TVδ*: confusi β: domiti *Clark*: edomiti *Sylvius* **2**
1 L.] A. *a* 2–3 necessitudinem *TVK*: consuetudinem *P*: necessitatem
δ 3 familiaritatemque *Tδ*: familiaritatem *V*: ac familiaritatem
β 5 mei] nostri *a*

dem genere non uterer orationis, iudices, hoc tempore, si mea solum interesset: multis enim mihi locis et data facultas est et saepe dabitur de mea laude dicendi. sed ut ille vidit, quantum de mea auctoritate deripuisset, tantum se de huius praesidiis deminuturum, sic hoc ego sentio, si mei facti rationem vobis constantiamque huius offici ac defensionis probaro, causam quoque me P. Sullae probaturum.

3 Ac primum abs te illud, L. Torquate, quaero, cur me a ceteris clarissimis viris ac principibus civitatis in hoc officio atque in defensionis iure secernas. quid enim est quam ob rem abs te Q̇. Hortensi factum, clarissimi viri atque ornatissimi, non reprendatur, reprendatur meum? nam si est initum a P. Sulla consilium inflammandae huius urbis, exstinguendi imperi, delendae civitatis, mihine maiorem hae res dolorem quam Q. Hortensio, mihi maius odium adferre debent, meum denique gravius esse iudicium qui adiuvandus in his causis, qui oppugnandus, qui defendendus, qui deserendus esse videatur? 'ita,' inquit 'tu enim investi-**II 4** gasti, tu patefecisti coniurationem.' quod cum dicit, non attendit eum qui patefecerit hoc curasse, ut id omnes viderent quod antea fuisset occultum. quare ista coniuratio si patefacta per me est, tam patet Hortensio quam mihi. quem cum videas hoc honore auctoritate virtute consilio praeditum non dubitasse quin innocentiam P. Sullae defenderet, quaero cur qui aditus ad causam Hortensio patuerit mihi interclusus esse debuerit. quaero illud etiam, si

TVω] 6 orationis non uterer *V*β   7 locis mihi et data *T*: l- et d- m-
V   9 vidit] iudices δ   diripuisset *V*β   10 diminuturum
*V*β*q*   hoc *om. V*   11 constantiam *V*   12 probavero *V*β   **3** 1 L.
om. V   4 viri] *bis V*: *post* ornatissimi β*q*   5 reprehendatur *semel*
Va   5–6 initum est consilium a p. sylla *q*   6 huius urbis *Halm*:
huius civitatis *T*: huius urbis huius *V*: civitatis huius ω   7 civitatis]
urbis *Tω*   mihine *Halm*: mihi *Tω*: michi me *V*   10 in hiis *bis*
V   11 deserandus *V*   videtur *V*   **4** 1 cum] tum *V*   5 honore
hoc δ   6 innocentem *Tω*   sille *ex* sillo *ut vid. V*: syllo *T*: sillam
ω   7 adit *T*

me qui defendo reprendendum putas esse, quid tandem de
his existimes summis viris et clarissimis civibus quorum 10
studio et dignitate celebrari hoc iudicium, ornari causam,
defendi huius innocentiam vides. non enim una ratio est
defensionis, ea quae posita est in oratione: omnes qui adsunt, qui laborant, qui salvum volunt, pro sua parte atque
5 auctoritate defendunt. an vero in quibus subselliis haec ornamenta ac lumina rei publicae viderem, in his me appa-
rere nollem, cum ego illum in locum atque in hanc excelsissimam sedem dignitatis et honoris multis meis ac magnis
laboribus et periculis ascendissem? atque ut intellegas, 5
Torquate, quem accuses, si te forte id offendit quod ego,
qui in hoc genere quaestionis defenderim neminem, non
desim P. Sullae, recordare de ceteris quos adesse huic
vides: intelleges et de hoc et de aliis iudicium meum et
6 horum par atque unum fuisse. quis nostrum adfuit Vargunteio? nemo, ne hic quidem Q. Hortensius, praesertim qui
illum solus antea de ambitu defendisset. non enim iam se
ullo officio cum illo coniunctum arbitrabatur, cum ille
tanto scelere commisso omnium officiorum societatem dir- 5
emisset. quis nostrum Ser. Sullam, quis Publium, quis M.
Laecam, quis ⟨C.⟩ Cornelium defendendum putavit? quis
iis nostrum adfuit? nemo. quid ita? quia in ceteris causis
etiam nocentes viri boni, si necessarii sunt, deserendos
esse non putant: in hoc crimine non solum levitatis est 10

*TV*ω] 11 iudicio δ   12 innocentis *q*   est una ratio *V*: una ratione
β: una est ratio δ   14 salvum] salvum eum β   **5** 2–3 appararere
V   3 cum ego *S*: quorum ego ω: quorum ego ope (ope *q mg.*) *Petrarca*: quorum ego auxilio *G mg.* b²*ck*: cur ergo *Madvig*   illum *secl. Pabón*   3–4 celsissimam *T*ω   4 atque honoris *T*ω   ac (hac *K*)] et
T   6 forte *om. T*ω   7 in *om. T*ω   9 intelligeres *T*: et (*om. a*) in-
tellige β*a*   aliis] ceteris ω   **6** 2 Q. *om. V*   3 de *om. V*   ambu-
latu *Ta*   6 vestrum *V*   publicum *T*   7 ⟨C.⟩ *suppl. Manutius*   7–8 quis iis *Garatoni*: quis his *T*δ: quis horum β: quorum *V*   8
nostrum *Ernesti*: horum *TVq*: his β: ipsorum *a*   ceteris in *T*ω   9
deserendos] defendendos *T*ω   10 putavit *Va*   10–11 culpa est *T*:
culpa *V*

culpa verum etiam quaedam contagio sceleris, si defendas eum quem obstrictum esse patriae parricidio suspicere.
7 quid? Autronio nonne sodales, non collegae sui, non veteres amici, quorum ille copia quondam abundarat, non hi omnes qui sunt in re publica principes defuerunt? immo etiam testimonio plerique laeserunt. statuerant tantum illud esse maleficium quod non modo non occultari per se 5
III sed etiam aperiri illustrarique deberet. quam ob rem quid est quod mirere, si cum isdem me in hac causa vides adesse cum quibus in ceteris intellegis afuisse? nisi vero me unum vis ferum praeter ceteros, me asperum, me inhumanum existimari, me·singulari immanitate et crudelitate praeditum. 10
8 hanc mihi si tu propter meas res gestas imponis in omni vita mea, Torquate, personam, vehementer erras. me natura misericordem, patria severum, crudelem nec patria nec natura esse voluit. denique istam ipsam personam vehementem et acrem, quam mihi tum tempus et res publica 5 imposuit, iam voluntas et natura ipsa detraxit. illa enim ad breve tempus severitatem postulavit, haec in omni vita misericordiam lenitatemque desiderat.
9 Quare nihil est quod ex tanto comitatu virorum amplissimorum me unum abstrahas: simplex officium atque una est bonorum omnium causa. nihil erit quod admirere posthac, si in ea parte in qua hos animum adverteris me videbis. nulla est enim in re publica mea causa propria: tempus 5

---

*TV*ω] 11 verum] velut *V*   defendendas *T*   12 eum *om. T*   parricidio *TEV*β*a: om. q*   **7** 1 nonne collegae *V*   3 immo] in uno *V* 4–5 illud tantum *T*   5 non *alterum om. V*   6 aperire *a*   debet *V*   6–7 quid est] quidem *Ta*   8 intelleges *TV*   afuisse *Gb²ct*: affuisse *ω*   9 vis ferum] fers *T*   asperum] asspes *T*   **8** 1 mihi tu si *T*δ: si mihi β   res meas ω   2 mea vita *T*   personam (persona β) torquate ω   3–4 nec natura nec patria *V*   4 persosonam *V*   7 severitatem *om. V*   **9** 2–3 una est (est una *K*) bonorum omnium (omnium bonorum β) ω: u- b- e- o- *T*: u- b- o- *V*   3 erit *T*ω: est *V: secl. Pabón*   amirare *V*   4 in ea] mea *Ta*   animum adverteris *Ta*: animum advertetis *V*: animadvertis β: animadverteris *q*   5 causa mea (in ea *K*) ω

agendi fuit magis mihi proprium quam ceteris, doloris vero
et timoris et periculi fuit illa causa communis. neque enim
ego tunc princeps ad salutem esse potuissem, si esse alii
comites noluissent. quare necesse est, quod mihi consuli
praecipuum fuit praeter alios, id iam privato cum ceteris 10
esse commune. neque ego hoc partiendae invidiae, sed
communicandae laudis causa loquor; oneris mei partem
10 nemini impertio, gloriae bonis omnibus. 'in Autronium testimonium dixisti,' inquit 'Sullam defendis.' hoc totum eius
modi est, iudices, ut si ego sum inconstans ac levis, nec testimonio fidem tribui convenerit nec defensioni auctoritatem; sin est in me ratio rei publicae, religio privati offici, 5
studium retinendae voluntatis bonorum, nihil minus accusator debet dicere quam a me defendi Sullam, testimonio
laesum esse Autronium. videor enim iam non solum studium ad defendendas causas verum etiam opinionis aliquid et auctoritatis adferre; qua ego et moderate utar, iu- 10
dices, et omnino non uterer, si ille me non coegisset.

IV 11   Duae coniurationes abs te, Torquate, constituuntur, una
quae Lepido et Volcacio consulibus patre tuo consule designato facta esse dicitur, altera quae me consule; harum in
utraque Sullam dicis fuisse. patris tui, fortissimi viri atque
optimi consulis, scis me consiliis non interfuisse. scis me, 5
cum mihi summus tecum usus esset, tamen illorum expertem temporum et sermonum fuisse, credo quod nondum
penitus in re publica versabar, quod nondum ad proposi-

TVω] 6 fuit mihi (mihi fuit β) magis *T*β   8 ego *om.* ω   princeps
tunc δ   esse *om.* V   13 impercior *V*: impartio *P*   **10** 1–2
in ... defendis *Schol.*   2 inquit ω *Schol.*: inquod *T*: inquo *V*   2–3 est
eiusmodi β: huiusmodi est *a*   3 sum] sim ω   4 tribuit *a*   convenerit *T*δ: tenuerit *V*: cum venerit β   5 privatio *V*   7 debet] dedit
V   a] ad a *V*   testimonio *fort. delendum esse put. Clark*   8–10
videor ... adferre *Schol.*   8 iam *om.* q   9 etiam *om.* δ   10 et
primum om. V   et moderate ego ω   **11** 1 duae ... constituuntur
Schol.   ab *V*   2–3 designata *V*: designatis β   5 non interfuisse]
interfuisse dicis *V*   7 sermonem *V*   8 versabatur *V*   8–9 prae-
positum *V*

tum mihi finem honoris perveneram, quod me ambitio et
12 forensis labor ab omni illa cogitatione abstrahebat. quis
ergo intererat vestris consiliis? omnes hi quos vides huic
adesse, et in primis Q. Hortensius; qui cum propter honorem ac dignitatem atque animum eximium in rem publicam, tum propter summam familiaritatem summumque 5
amorem in patrem tuum cum communibus tum praecipuis
patris tui periculis commovebatur. ergo istius coniurationis
crimen defensum ab eo est qui interfuit, qui cognovit, qui
particeps et consili vestri fuit et timoris; cuius in hoc crimine propulsando cum esset copiosissima atque ornatissima 10
oratio, tamen non minus auctoritatis inerat in ea quam facultatis. illius igitur coniurationis quae facta contra vos, delata ad vos, a vobis prolata esse dicitur, ego testis esse non
potui: non modo animo nihil comperi, sed vix ad aures
13 meas istius suspicionis fama pervenit. qui vobis in consilio
fuerunt, qui vobiscum illa cognorunt, quibus ipsis periculum tum conflari putabatur, qui Autronio non adfuerunt,
qui in illum testimonia gravia dixerunt, hunc defendunt,
huic adsunt, in huius periculo declarant se non crimine 5
coniurationis ne adessent ceteris, sed hominum maleficio
deterritos esse. mei consulatus autem tempus et crimen
maximae coniurationis a me defendetur. atque haec inter
nos partitio defensionis non est fortuito, iudices, nec temere facta, sed cum videremus eorum criminum nos pa- 10
tronos adhiberi quorum testes esse possemus, uterque nostrum id sibi suscipiendum putavit de quo aliquid scire ipse

TVω] 9 finem] funem *V*   me] mea δ   **12** 3–4 honorem atque
dignitatem ac animum extimumque *V*   6 amorem] honorem
Tω   7–8 ergo…interfuit *Schol.*   10 prosulsando *V*   11 inerat
auctoritatis *Tω*   in ea] mea *V*   12 facta contra vos (nos *K*) *Tω*:
c- v- f- *V*   13 nobis *Ka*   14–15 non…pervenit *Schol.*   14 non
TVPa Schol.: num *K*: nec *q*   modo animo *Tβa Schol.*: animo modo *V*:
modo enim *q*   vix *om. Schol.*   15 famam *Schol.*   **13** 1 vobis *Tβq*:
nobiscum *V*: nobis *a*   2 cognoverunt *Vβ*   3 tum] tuum *T*   5 se]
si *V*   8 haec *Tβ*: hic *V*: *om.* δ   9 defensionis *om.* δ   fortuitu
V   iudices] videlicet *a*   12 sibi] verbi *V*

V 14 atque existimare potuisset. et quoniam de criminibus superioris coniurationis Hortensium diligenter audistis, de hac
coniuratione quae me consule facta est hoc primum attendite.

Multa cum essem consul de summis rei publicae periculis 5
audivi, multa quaesivi, multa cognovi: nullus umquam de
Sulla nuntius ad me, nullum indicium, nullae litterae pervenerunt, nulla suspicio. multum haec vox fortasse valere
deberet eius hominis qui consul insidias rei publicae consilio investigasset, veritate aperuisset, magnitudine animi 10
vindicasset, cum is se nihil audisse de P. Sulla, nihil suspi-
catum esse diceret. sed ego nondum utor hac voce ad hunc
defendendum: ad purgandum me potius utar, ut mirari
Torquatus desinat me qui Autronio non adfuerim Sullam
15 defendere. quae enim Autroni fuit causa, quae Sullae est?
ille ambitus iudicium tollere ac disturbare primum conflato
voluit gladiatorum et fugitivorum tumultu, deinde id quod
vidimus omnes lapidatione atque concursu: Sulla, si sibi
suus pudor ac dignitas non prodesset, nullum auxilium 5
requisivit. ille damnatus ita se gerebat non solum consiliis
et sermonibus verum etiam aspectu atque vultu ut inimicus esse amplissimis ordinibus, infestus bonis omnibus, hostis patriae videretur: hic se ita fractum illa calamitate atque
adflictum putavit ut nihil sibi ex pristina dignitate super- 10
16 esse arbitraretur, nisi quod modestia retinuisset. hac vero
in coniuratione quid tam coniunctum quam ille cum Catilina, cum Lentulo? quae tanta societas ullis inter se rerum

TVω] **14** 5–8 multa... suspicio *Schol.*   7 iudicium *TVK*   8–9
valere fortasse debet β: f- deberet v- *q*   9 qui] que *V*   10
verite *V*   11 is se] ipse ω   audisse *Tδ*: laudis *V*: auditum esse
β   12–13 sed...defendendum *Schol.*   12 hac voce *om.*
Schol.   14 torquato *V*: et torquato *a*   non affuerim *TVβ*: affuerim
a: abfuerim *q*   **15** 1 quae enim...est *Schol.*   autroniis fuit *V*: autronio fuit β: fuit autronii *Schol.*   causam *V*   est] cum *a*   2 tolle
T   conflata *ex* conflato *ut vid. V*   3 gladiorum *T*   et] ac ω   tu-
multu] in multu *V*   4 tibi *V*   6 ille] ita *T*   7 atque] et *V*   9
factum *T*   **16** 1 hac] ac *V*   2 quid] quod *T*   illa *V*

optimarum quanta ei cum illis sceleris libidinis audaciae?
quod flagitium Lentulus non cum Autronio concepit? quod 5
sine eodem illo Catilina facinus admisit? cum interim Sulla
cum eisdem illis non modo noctem solitudinemque non
quaereret sed ne mediocri quidem sermone et congressu
17 coniungeretur. illum Allobroges, maximarum rerum verissimi indices, illum multorum litterae ac nuntii coarguer-
unt: Sullam interea nemo insimulavit, nemo nominavit.
postremo eiecto sive emisso iam ex urbe Catilina ille arma
misit cornua tubas fasces signa legionum, ille relictus intus, 5
exspectatus foris, Lentuli poena compressus convertit se
aliquando ad timorem, numquam ad sanitatem: hic contra
ita quievit ut eo tempore omni Neapoli fuerit, ubi neque
homines fuisse putantur huius adfines suspicionis et locus
est ipse non tam ad inflammandos calamitosorum animos 10
quam ad consolandos accommodatus.

VI Propter hanc igitur tantam dissimilitudinem hominum
18 atque causarum dissimilem me in utroque praebui. veniebat enim ad me et saepe veniebat Autronius multis cum
lacrimis supplex ut se defenderem, et se meum condiscipulum in pueritia, familiarem in adulescentia, collegam in
quaestura commemorabat fuisse; multa mea in se, non- 5
nulla etiam sua in me proferebat officia. quibus ego rebus,
iudices, ita flectebar animo atque frangebar ut iam ex memoria quas mihi ipsi fecerat insidias deponerem, ut iam
immissum esse ab eo C. Cornelium qui me in meis sedibus, in conspectu uxoris ac liberorum meorum trucidaret 10

*TV*ω] 4 illis] vel *a*   7 solicitudinemque *V*   8 equidem *q*   **17**
1–2 illum...indices *Schol.*   2 iudices *V*β*a*   5 tubas] tubes *TV*
falces *T*ω   legionum *Halm*: legiones Ω: legionis *Ant. Augustinus*: legionibus *A. Klotz*   intus] nixus *a*   6 lentu *T*   7–8 hic...fuerit
Schol.   9 putant *V*   suspicionis] scipionis *V*   9–11 et...
accommodatus *Schol.*   10 tam adflammandos calamitates eorum animos *V*   ad *om. q*[1]   13 dissimilemque in utroque *T*   **18** 1–2
veniebat...autronius *Schol.*   3–4 discipulum *V*   6 sua in me etiam
T   7 iam] etiam ω   8 ipsi *V*ω: ipse *ex* ipsi *ut vid. T*: ipse *Gb*   9
ab eo esse *q*   9–10 sedibus meis *T*ω   10 uxoris] uxoris meae ω

obliviscerer. quae si de uno me cogitasset, qua mollitia
sum animi ac lenitate, numquam me hercule illius lacrimis
19 ac precibus restitissem: sed cum mihi patriae, cum vestrorum periculorum, cum huius urbis, cum illorum delubrorum atque templorum, cum puerorum infantium, cum
matronarum ac virginum veniebat in mentem, et cum illae
infestae ac funestae faces universumque totius urbis incen- 5
dium, cum tela, cum caedes, cum civium cruor, cum cinis
patriae versari ante oculos atque animum memoria refricare coeperat, tum denique ei resistebam, neque solum illi
hosti ac parricidae sed his etiam propinquis illius Marcellis
patri et filio, quorum alter apud me parentis gravitatem, 10
alter fili suavitatem obtinebat. neque me arbitrabar sine
summo scelere posse, quod maleficium in aliis vindicas-
20 sem, idem in illorum socio, cum scirem, defendere. atque
idem ego neque P. Sullam supplicem ferre, neque eosdem
Marcellos pro huius periculis lacrimantes aspicere, neque
huius M. Messallae hominis necessarii preces sustinere potui; neque enim est causa adversata naturae, nec homo nec 5
res misericordiae meae repugnavit. nusquam nomen, nusquam vestigium fuerat, nullum crimen, nullum indicium,
nulla suspicio. suscepi causam, Torquate, suscepi et feci
libenter ut me, quem boni constantem, ut spero, semper
existimassent, eundem ne improbi quidem crudelem dicer- 10
ent.
VII 21 Hic ait se ille, iudices, regnum meum ferre non posse.
quod tandem, Torquate, regnum? consulatus credo mei,

$TV\omega$] 12 levitate V **19** 1–2 nostrorum V 5 funestae] venuste
V 6 cum tela *om.* T 6–7 civis pratriae V 8 tum] cum V 11
neque ⟨enim⟩ *Müller*   12 possum V 13 idem nullorum scio V
20 2 eosdem ω: hos T: eorum eodem V 3 marcellis *ex* marcellos *ut
vid.* V pro huius $EV\beta a$: pro T: *om.* q   periculis lacrimantes aspicere TEV: salute orantes β: *om.* δ   3–4 neque huius TVq: neque β: *om. a*
4 necessarie V 5 est *om.* T 5–6 nec res nec homo V 6 misericordiae meae] minime me *a*   7 fastigium ω   nullum crimen $TP\delta$:
nullum nullum crimen V: *om.* K 8 nulla suspicio EV: *om.* $T\omega$ 9 ut *primum*] aut V 10 ne] nunc *a*   **21** 2–3 quod … nihil *Schol.*   2 mei] michi V

in quo ego imperavi nihil et contra patribus conscriptis et
bonis omnibus parui; quo in magistratu non institutum est
a me videlicet regnum, sed repressum. an tum in tanto im- 5
perio, tanta potestate non dicis me fuisse regem, nunc priva-
tum regnare dicis? quo tandem nomine? 'quod, in quos testimonia dixisti,' inquit 'damnati sunt; quem defendis, sperat
se absolutum iri.' hic tibi ego de testimoniis meis hoc respon-
deo, si falsum dixerim, te in eosdem dixisse; sin verum, non 10
esse hoc regnare, cum verum iuratus dicas, probare. de
huius spe tantum dico nullas a me opes P. Sullam, nullam
potentiam, nihil denique praeter fidem defensionis exspec-
22 tare. 'nisi tu' inquit 'causam recepisses, numquam mihi
restitisset, sed indicta causa profugisset.' si iam hoc tibi
concedam, Q. Hortensium, tanta gravitate hominem, si
hos tales viros non suo stare iudicio sed meo, si hoc tibi
dem quod credi non potest, nisi ego huic adessem, hos ad- 5
futuros non fuisse, uter tandem rex est, isne cui innocentes
homines non resistunt, an is qui calamitosos non deserit? at
hic etiam, id quod tibi necesse minime fuit, facetus esse
voluisti, cum Tarquinium et Numam et me tertium peregrinum regem esse dixisti. mitto iam de rege quaerere; il- 10
lud quaero peregrinum cur me esse dixeris. nam si ita
sum, non tam est admirandum regem me esse, quoniam,
ut tu ais, duo iam peregrini reges Romae fuerunt, quam

TVω] 3 et *primum*] sed *b*²   4 parui *om. V*   5 a me iudices *Tω*:
videlicet a me *V*   repressum] promissum *Tω*   5–7 an...dicis
Schol.   5 tum *TVδ*: tu β *Schol.*   6 dices *Schol.*   me *om.* δ   7
dices *Stangl*   quo] quod *V*   quod] quot *V*   8 sperat *bis T*   9
se *om.* q   9–10 respondebo *T*   10–11 si...probare *Schol.*   10 eos
Tω   sin] si *Schol.*   11 iuratus *T Schol.*: iuratis *V*: iuratos ω   12
nullam *q*: vel β: *om. TVa*   13 propter *T*   **22** 2 sed] si *V*   tibi hoc
Vβ   3 gravitate tanta *V*   5 dem *Naugerius*: idem *Tω*: in eo idem
V   6–10 uter...dixisti *Schol.*   8 id...fuit *om. Schol.*   minime
tibi necesse *V*   9 munam *V*   tertium] trinum *V*   11 queror
V   esse me *Tω*   12 quoniam] quam ω   13 ais *T*: agis *V*: vis
ω   duo iam *Müller*: etiam ω   fuerunt] fuisse fuerunt *V*

23 consulem Romae fuisse peregrinum. 'hoc dico,' inquit 'te
esse ex municipio.' fateor et addo etiam ex eo municipio
unde iterum iam salus huic urbi imperioque missa est. sed
scire ex te pervelim quam ob rem qui ex municipiis veniant
peregrini tibi esse videantur. nemo istuc M. illi Catoni seni, 5
cum plurimos haberet inimicos, nemo Ti. Coruncanio,
nemo M'. Curio, nemo huic ipsi nostro C. Mario, cum ei
multi inviderent, obiecit umquam. equidem vehementer
laetor eum esse me in quem tu, cum cuperes, nullam con-
tumeliam iacere potueris quae non ad maximam partem 10
VIII civium conveniret. sed tamen te a me pro magnis causis
nostrae necessitudinis monendum esse etiam atque etiam
puto. non possunt omnes esse patricii – si verum quaeris,
ne curant quidem – nec se aequales tui propter istam cau-
24 sam abs te anteiri putant. ac si tibi nos peregrini videmur,
quorum iam et nomen et honos inveteravit et urbi huic et
hominum famae ac sermonibus, quam tibi illos competitores tuos peregrinos videri necesse erit qui iam ex tota Italia delecti tecum de honore ac de omni dignitate contend- 5
ent! quorum tu cave quemquam peregrinum appelles, ne
peregrinorum suffragiis obruare. qui si attulerint nervos et
industriam, mihi crede, excutient tibi istam verborum iac-
tationem et te ex somno saepe excitabunt, nec patientur se
25 abs te, nisi virtute vincentur, honore superari. ac si, iudices, ceteris patriciis me et vos peregrinos videri opor-
teret, a Torquato tamen hoc vitium sileretur: est enim
ipse a materno genere municipalis, honestissimi ac nobil-

TVω] 14 Romae] *fort.* me   **23** 1–3 hoc…est *Schol.*   1 inquis *V*
2 esse e *Schol.*   eo *om. T*   5–7 nemo…curio *Schol.*   5 nemo] nemo
enim *Tω*   illi *om. Schol.*   6 cum…inimicos *om. Schol.*   Ti. *TVδ Schol.*:
tito β   7 M'. *Manutius:* mario *Schol.: om.* ω   curio *Schol.:* curioni ω
14 curent *T*   **24** 1 videamur *a*   2 et *primum om. V*   huic urbi ω
3 hominum *om. V*   5 ac] et ω   5–6 contendent *TVK*: contenderit *P*:
contendunt δ   6 cave tu *Tω*   7 obruare] obgurgare (*cum* i *sup.* g *primam*) *T*   si] si ita *V*   attulerit *T*   9 ex] e *Kq*   10 supare *V*   **25** 1 ac]
at *V*   2 ceteris *om. V*   peregrini *V*   3 similetur *a*   3–5 est…asculani
Schol.   4 a *om. Schol.*   municipialis *V*   4–5 ac nobilissimi *om. Schol.*

issimi generis, sed tamen Asculani. aut igitur doceat Picen- 5
tis solos non esse peregrinos aut gaudeat suo generi me
meum non anteponere. quare neque tu me peregrinum
posthac dixeris, ne gravius refutere, neque regem, ne derideare. nisi forte regium tibi videtur ita vivere ut non modo
homini nemini sed ne cupiditati quidem ulli servias, con- 10
temnere omnes libidines, non auri, non argenti, non ceter-
arum rerum indigere, in senatu sentire libere, populi utilitati magis consulere quam voluntati, nemini cedere, multis
obsistere. si hoc putas esse regium, me regem esse confiteor; sin te potentia mea, si dominatio, si denique aliquod 15
dictum arrogans aut superbum movet, quin tu id potius
profers quam verbi invidiam contumeliamque maledicti?

IX 26 Ego tantis a me beneficiis in re publica positis si nullum
aliud mihi praemium ab senatu populoque Romano nisi
honestum otium postularem, quis non concederet? sibi
haberent honores, sibi imperia, sibi provincias, sibi triumphos, sibi alia praeclarae laudis insignia; mihi liceret eius 5
urbis quam conservassem conspectu tranquillo animo et
quieto frui. quid si hoc non postulo? si ille labor meus pristinus, si sollicitudo, si officia, si operae, si vigiliae deser-
viunt amicis, praesto sunt omnibus; si neque amici in foro
requirunt studium meum neque res publica in curia; si me 10
non modo non rerum gestarum vacatio sed neque honoris
neque aetatis excusatio vindicat a labore; si voluntas mea,
si industria, si domus, si animus, si aures patent omnibus; si
mihi ne ad ea quidem quae pro salute omnium gessi record-

TVω] 5 esculani *V* 5–6 piceniis *V* 6 solos esse non esse *V*
7 ante non ponere δ tu *om.* ω 8 posthoc (*cum e sup.* o *alteram*) *T*:
postea β ne *alterum*] neque *a* 9 nisi...vivere *Schol.* non
bis a 12–13 populi...voluntati *alludit S. Aurelius Augustinus epist.*
104 (CSEL 34.587.25–6) et 138 (ibid. 44.140.4–5) magis utilitati *V*
14 regium] regnum *V*β regem me *T* 15 sin] si *V* 16 arrogatis
V **26** 1–3 ego...concederet *Schol.* 1 ullum *a* 2 a ω 3
non *om. Schol.* 3–4 si haberent *V*: haberent sibi β: sibi haberent
⟨alii⟩ *Sylvius, cod. H. Stephani*: ⟨ceteri⟩ sibi haberent *Clark* 11 vocatio
Va sed] si *a*

anda et cogitanda quicquam relinquitur temporis: tamen 15
hoc regnum appellabitur, cuius vicarius qui velit esse inve-
27 niri nemo potest? longe abest a me regni suspicio; sin quaeris qui sint Romae regnum occupare conati, ut ne replices
annalium memoriam, ex domesticis imaginibus invenies.
res enim gestae, credo, meae me nimis extulerunt ac mihi
nescio quos spiritus attulerunt. quibus de rebus tam claris, 5
tam immortalibus, iudices, hoc possum dicere, me qui ex
summis periculis eripuerim urbem hanc et vitam omnium
civium satis adeptum fore, si ex hoc tanto in omnis mortalis beneficio nullum in me ipsum periculum redundarit.
28 etenim in qua civitate res tantas gesserim memini, et in qua
urbe verser intellego. plenum forum est eorum hominum
quos ego a vestris cervicibus depuli, iudices, a meis non re-
movi. nisi vero paucos fuisse arbitramini, qui conari aut
sperare possent se tantum imperium posse delere. horum 5
ego faces eripere de manibus et gladios extorquere potui,
sicuti feci, voluntates vero consceleratas ac nefarias nec
sanare potui nec tollere. quare non sum nescius quanto
periculo vivam in tanta multitudine improborum, cum mihi
uni cum omnibus improbis aeternum videam bellum esse 10
X 29 susceptum. quodsi illis meis praesidiis forte invides, et si ea
tibi regia videntur quod omnes boni omnium generum at-
que ordinum suam salutem cum mea coniungunt, conso-
lare te quod omnium mentes improborum mihi uni maxime sunt infensae et adversae; qui me solum non modo 5
idcirco oderunt quod eorum conatus impios et furorem

TVω] **27** 1 a me *EV*: *om. Tω*   sin] si *Tω*   2 replices] explices
Reid   3 ex] et *T*   invenietur *V*   6 hoc] hic *V*   ex] e *q*   7
eripuerim periculis ω   8–9 mortalis] inmortalis *T*   9 ipsum *om.*
Tω   redundarit *TEV*: redundabit ω   **28** 1–4 etenim...removi
Schol.   1 rem tantam *Schol.*   et *om. Schol.*   in qua δ *Schol.*: qua in
TVK: qua *P*   2 verser *TEV Schol.*: versor β: *om.* δ   3 repuli *V*   4
vero] forte β   5 sperari *a*   se] sed *T*   6 faces] faceres *V*   7
sicut ω   10–11 videam bellum (bellum videam β) esse susceptum ω: v-
e- b- s- *T*: v- b- s- e- *V*   **29** 2 regna *T*   5 solum non modo *Busche*:
non modo solum *TV*δ: non solum β: non modo *f*²

consceleratum repressi, sed eo etiam magis quod nihil iam
30 se simile me vivo conari posse arbitrantur. at vero quid ego
mirer si quid ab improbis de me improbe dicitur, cum L.
Torquatus primum ipse his fundamentis adulescentiae iac-
tis, ea spe proposita amplissimae dignitatis, deinde L. Torquati, fortissimi consulis, constantissimi senatoris, semper 5
optimi civis filius, interdum efferatur immoderatione verborum? qui cum suppressa voce de scelere P. Lentuli, de
audacia coniuratorum omnium dixisset tantum modo ut
vos qui ea probatis exaudire possetis, de supplicio [de Len-
31 tulo], de carcere magna et queribunda voce dicebat. in quo
primum illud erat absurdum quod, cum ea quae leviter
dixerat vobis probare volebat, eos autem qui circum iudicium stabant audire nolebat, non intellegebat ea quae
clare diceret ita illos audituros quibus se venditabat ut vos 5
quoque audiretis, qui id non probabatis. deinde alterum
iam oratoris ⟨est⟩ vitium non videre quid quaeque causa
postulet. nihil est enim tam alienum ab eo qui alterum coniurationis accuset quam videri coniuratorum poenam mor-
temque lugere. quod cum is tribunus plebis facit qui unus 10
videtur ex illis ad lugendos coniuratos relictus, nemini mirum est: difficile est enim tacere, cum doleas. te, si quid
eius modi facis, non modo talem adulescentem sed in ea
causa in qua te vindicem coniurationis velis esse, vehemen-
32 ter admiror. sed reprendo tamen illud maxime, quod isto
ingenio et prudentia praeditus causam rei publicae non

---

*TV*ω] 7 magis etiam *V*   iam *om. V*   **30** 1 at] ac *T*   2 miror
ω   3 ipse his fundamentis *T*δ: his fundamentis ipse *V*: hisce fundamentis β   6–7 verberum *a*   7 p. lentuli *T*ω: per lentuli *V*: *secl. Ga-*
ratoni   9–10 de lentulo *TVa*: lentuli β: p. lentuli *q*: *del. Halm*: de vinculis *Jeep*: de laqueo *Reid*: de eculeo *Busche*   10 magna] de magna
V   **31** 2 erat illud *T*   leniter *Sylvius*   3 autem *om. T*   4 in-
tellegebant *V*   6 id *TV*δ: idem β: *secl. Ernesti*   non *om. V*   probabitis
TPa   7 ⟨est⟩ *suppl. Reid*   quid] quod *T*   10–12 quod...doleas
Schol.   10 tribunos *Schol.*   11 nemini *TV Schol.*: vere β: re...
δ   13 facis eius modi *V*   ea] mea *V*   **32**

96

tenes, qui arbitrere plebi Romanae res eas non probari
quas me consule omnes boni pro salute communi gesser-

XI unt. ecquem tu horum qui adsunt, quibus te contra ip- 5
sorum voluntatem venditabas, aut tam sceleratum statuis
fuisse ut haec omnia perire voluerit, aut tam miserum ut
et se perire cuperet et nihil haberet quod salvum esse vellet? an vero clarissimum virum generis vestri ac nominis
nemo reprendit, qui filium suum vita privavit ut in ceteros 10
firmaret imperium; tu rem publicam reprendis, quae domesticos hostis, ne ab iis ipsa necaretur, necavit?

33 Itaque attende, Torquate, quam ego defugiam auctoritatem consulatus mei! maxima voce ut omnes exaudire possint dico semperque dicam. adeste omnes animis qui adestis, quorum ego frequentia magno opere laetor! erigite
mentes auresque vestras et me de invidiosis rebus, ut ille 5
putat, dicentem attendite! ego consul, cum exercitus perditorum civium clandestino scelere conflatus crudelissimum
et luctuosissimum exitium patriae comparasset, cumque
ad occasum interitumque rei publicae Catilina in castris,
in his autem templis atque tectis dux Lentulus esset consti- 10
tutus, meis consiliis, meis laboribus, mei capitis periculis,
sine tumultu, sine dilectu, sine armis, sine exercitu, quinque hominibus comprensis atque confessis incensione urbem, internicione cives, vastitate Italiam, interitu rem publicam liberavi: ego vitam omnium civium, statum orbis 15
terrae, urbem hanc denique, sedem omnium nostrum, ar-

*TV*ω] 3 tenens *a*   orbitrere *V*: arbitrare *K*   4 communi salute
β   5 et quem Ω: *corr. Cratander*   6 sceleratam *V*   7 omni *T*: *om.*
V   9 vestri] nostri *T*   10–11 qui...imperium *Schol.*   10 ceteris
*T*ω   11 rep. *T*   12 iis *k*: his Ω   **33** 1 attende] attende iam
ω   3 adeste] adestote δ   animisque omnes *V*   3–4 qui adestis
Ω: qui adstatis *Reid*: Quirites *Clark*   4 erite *V*   6 putant *V*   ego]
ergo *V*   6–7 perditor *T*   8 cum *T*ω   10 atque] ac *V*   11 periculi *V*   12 delectu *T*δ   13 reprehensis atque confossis *q*   14–15
rep. interitu *T*   15 liberavit *V*

cem regum ac nationum exterarum, lumen gentium, domicilium imperi quinque hominum amentium ac perditorum
34 poena redemi. an me existimasti haec iniuratum in iudicio
non esse dicturum quae iuratus in maxima contione dixis-
XII sem? atque etiam illud addam, ne qui forte incipiat improbus subito te amare, Torquate, et aliquid sperare de te,
atque ut item omnes exaudiant clarissima voce dicam. 5
harum omnium rerum quas ego in consulatu pro salute
rei publicae suscepi atque gessi L. ille Torquatus, cum esset meus contubernalis in consulatu atque etiam in praetura fuisset, auctor adiutor particeps exstitit, cum princeps,
cum ductor, cum signifer esset iuventutis; parens vero eius, 10
homo amantissimus patriae, maximi animi, summi consili,
singularis constantiae, cum esset aeger, tamen omnibus rebus illis interfuit, nusquam est a me digressus, studio consilio auctoritate unus adiuvit plurimum, cum infirmitatem
35 corporis animi virtute superaret. videsne ut eripiam te ex
improborum subita gratia et reconciliem bonis omnibus?
qui te et diligunt et retinent retinebuntque semper nec, si
a me forte desciveris, idcirco te a se et a re publica et a
tua dignitate deficere patientur. sed iam redeo ad causam 5
atque hoc vos, iudices, testor: mihi de memet ipso tam
multa dicendi necessitas quaedam imposita est ab illo.
nam si Torquatus Sullam solum accusasset, ego quoque

TVω] **34** 3–4 atque ... torquate *Schol.*   3 etiam] enim *V*   5 item
Housman: idem ω: id *Reid*   6 rerum omnium *V*   6–7 salute rei
publicae *TEV:* vestra quirites salute β: salute δ   7 atque] et δ   8
meus] ille *T*   consulatu (consalatura *V*)] *verba* pro salute ... consulatu *repetit T, sed hoc loco est* meus contubernalis, *non* ille contubernalis *ut superiore: add.* cum signifer esset cum princeps iuventutis
(cum princeps *om.* δ) ω   9 auctor] actor *Orelli*   9–10 cum ...
iuventutis *om.* β: *post* fuisset *transtul. Clark*   10 ductor *Housman:*
auctor *TVδ*   esse *T*   vero *V:* etiam β: *om. T*δ   11 homo] amo *T*
animi *om. a*   13 numquam ω   a me est *V*   14 adiuvit] adimit *V*
15 virtute animi *V*   **35** 2 et reconciliem] reconciliem *V*   4 forte
a me *V*β   5 tua (*q mg.*) *Petrarca:* sua ω   6 demetipso *V*   7 est
om. V

hoc tempore nihil aliud agerem nisi eum qui accusatus esset defenderem; sed cum ille tota illa oratione in me esset   10
invectus et cum, ut initio dixi, defensionem meam spoliare
auctoritate voluisset, etiam si me meus dolor respondere
non cogeret, tamen ipsa causa hanc a me orationem flagitavisset.

III 36   Ab Allobrogibus nominatum Sullam esse dicis. quis
negat? sed lege indicium et vide quem ad modum nomina-
tus sit. L. Cassium dixerunt commemorasse cum ceteris
Autronium secum facere. quaero num Sullam dixerit Cassius. nusquam. sese aiunt quaesisse de Cassio quid Sulla   5
sentiret. videte diligentiam Gallorum: qui vitam hominum
naturamque non nossent ac tantum audissent eos pari
calamitate esse, quaesiverunt essentne eadem voluntate.
quid tum Cassius? si respondisset idem sentire et secum
facere Sullam, tamen mihi non videretur in hunc id crimi-   10
nosum esse debere. quid ita? quia, qui barbaros homines
ad bellum impelleret, non debebat minuere illorum suspicionem et purgare eos de quibus illi aliquid suspicari vider-
37   entur. non respondit tamen una facere Sullam. etenim
esset absurdum, cum ceteros sua sponte nominasset, mentionem facere Sullae nullam nisi admonitum et interroga-
tum; nisi forte veri simile est P. Sullae nomen in memoria
Cassio non fuisse. si nobilitas hominis, si adflicta fortuna, si   5

TVω] 9 nisi] ni *T*   10 illa ratione *T*: oratione illa *V*   11 ut initio
TV: ut β: initio ut δ   11–12 auctoritate spoliare ω   12 voluissem
V   et si *a*   me meus dolor] dolor meus *Tω*   13 cogerer *V*   rationem *T*   13–14 flagitasset δ   **36** 1–3 ab...sit *Schol.*   1 ab *EV*
Schol.: om. *Tω*   dicis *om.* ω   2 negas *V*   sed lege *TEV Schol.*:
sullae ω   iudicium *EV*   5 nusquam *TEV*β*a*: numquam *q*   7
noscent *V*   audivissent *V*   8 esse quaesiverunt (-ierunt *T*) essentne
eadem *TEV*β: qui fuerunt essent in eadem *a*: qui fuerant esse in eadem
q   9–10 si...sullam *Schol.*   9 si *om. T*   10 videtur *V*   11 bar-
baris *V*   13 purgare] pugnare *T*   13–14 suspicari viderentur *TEV*:
suspicarentur ω   **37** 1 silla *V*   2 absurdum esset *a*   3 sullae facere *T*: facere ω   nullam nisi] sillam ut *a*   4–5 nisi...fuisse
Schol.   5 afflata *TEω*

reliquiae pristinae dignitatis non tam illustres fuissent, tamen Autroni commemoratio memoriam Sullae rettulisset;
etiam, ut arbitror, cum auctoritates principum coniurationis ad incitandos animos Allobrogum colligeret Cassius, et
cum sciret exteras nationes maxime nobilitate moveri, non 10
38 prius Autronium quam Sullam nominavisset. iam vero illud minime probari potest, Gallos Autronio nominato pu-
tasse propter calamitatis similitudinem sibi aliquid de Sulla
esse quaerendum, Cassio, si hic esset in eodem scelere, ne
cum appellasset quidem Autronium, huius in mentem ven- 5
ire potuisse. sed tamen quid respondit de Sulla Cassius? se
nescire certum. 'non purgat' inquit. dixi antea: ne si argueret quidem tum denique, cum esset interrogatus, id
39 mihi criminosum videretur. sed ego in iudiciis et in quaestionibus non hoc quaerendum arbitror, num purgetur aliquis, sed num arguatur. etenim cum se negat scire Cassius, utrum sublevat Sullam an satis probat se nescire?
'sublevat apud Gallos.' quid ita? 'ne indicent.' quid? si 5
periculum esse putasset ne illi umquam indicarent, de se
ipse confessus esset? 'nesciit videlicet.' credo celatum esse
Cassium de Sulla uno, nam de ceteris certe sciebat; etenim
domi eius pleraque conflata esse constabat. qui negare noluit esse in eo numero Sullam quo plus spei Gallis daret, 10
dicere autem falsum non ausus est, nescire dixit. atque
hoc perspicuum est, cum is qui de omnibus scierit de Sulla
se scire negarit, eandem vim esse negationis huius quam si

*TV*ω] 6 reliquae *T*   9–10 Allobrogum...nationes *om. q*[1]   9 Al-
lobrogum] adallobrogum *V*   10 moneri *a*   11 nominasset ω   **38**
2 minime probari (probare *K*) *VK*: probari (probare *P*) minime
*TP*δ   3 aliquod *T*   6 quid] quod *T*   responderit *Ta*   silla de
cassio *V*   9 mihi *om. V*   **39** 1–3 sed...arguatur *Schol.*   1–2 in
iudiciis et quaestionibus ω: in quaestionibus et indiciis *Schol.*   2 ar-
bitrer *T*   2–3 aliqui *Schol.*   3 sed *Schol.*: et ω   negat se δ   5
indicent] iudicentur *V*   quod si *TV*   6 ne] et ne *a*   vindicarent
V   se *om. VP*   7 ipso *V*ω   nescit *T*   videlicet] iudices *q*   8
etenim] et ea *q*   9 negaret *V*   9–10 voluit *T*   10 in eo] meo
V   11 est] se β   13 esse vim *V*

extra coniurationem hunc esse se scire dixisset. nam cuius
scientiam de omnibus constat fuisse, eius ignoratio de ali- 15
quo purgatio debet videri. sed iam non quaero purgetne
Cassius Sullam: illud mihi tantum satis est contra Sullam
nihil esse in indicio.

IV 40   Exclusus hac criminatione Torquatus rursus in me inruit, me accusat: ait me aliter ac dictum sit in tabulas publicas rettulisse. o di immortales! vobis enim tribuam quae
vestra sunt, nec vero possum meo tantum ingenio dare ut
tot res tantas, tam varias, tam repentinas in illa turbulentis- 5
sima tempestate rei publicae mea sponte dispexerim: vos
profecto animum meum tum conservandae patriae cupiditate incendistis, vos me ab omnibus ceteris cogitationibus
ad unam salutem rei publicae convertistis, vos denique in
tantis tenebris erroris et inscientiae clarissimum lumen 10
41 menti meae praetulistis. vidi ego hoc, iudices, nisi recenti
memoria senatus auctoritatem huius indici monumentis
publicis testatus essem, fore ut aliquando non Torquatus
neque Torquati quispiam similis – nam id me multum fe-
fellit – sed ut aliquis patrimoni naufragus, inimicus oti, bo- 5
norum hostis aliter indicata haec esse diceret, quo facilius
vento aliquo in optimum quemque excitato posset in malis
rei publicae portum aliquem suorum malorum invenire.
itaque introductis in senatum indicibus institui senatores
qui omnia indicum dicta interrogata responsa perscriber- 10

*TV*ω] 14 sciri *T*   16 deberet *a*   non *om. T*   purgetne *T*δ: quid
purgetne *V*: purgare nec β   17 est] esse *V*   18 iudicio *V*ω   **40** 1–
3 exclusus...immortales *Schol.*   2 me accusat *secl.* Pluygers   sit *TV*
Schol.: est ω   3 enim tribuam (tribuo *T*) *TV*β*a*: tribuam enim *q*   5
in] tam in *a*   6 tempestate] potestate *V*   rep. *T*   dispexerim δ:
despexerim *TV*: disposuerim β   9 convertistis *TV*β: contensus *a*:
contulistis *q*   11 menti mei praetulistis *V*: praetulistis menti meae
ω   **41** 1 iudices *q*: vidi *T*β*a*: *om. V*   2 iudiciis *V*   4 nam id me *bis*
a   5 patrimonio ω   6 iudicata haec *V*: haec indicata β   7 quem-
que] quemtib *V*   8 aliquem suorum maiorum *TV*: suorum malorum
aliquem ω   9 iudicibus *V*: indictionibus β   9–42.4 institui...posse
Schol.   constitui ω   10 iudicum *V Schol.*   10–11 proscriberent *a*

42 ent. at quos viros! non solum summa virtute et fide, cuius
generis erat in senatu facultas maxima, sed etiam quos scie-
bam memoria scientia consuetudine et celeritate scribendi
facillime quae dicerentur persequi posse, C. Cosconium,
qui tum erat praetor, M. Messallam, qui tum praeturam 5
petebat, P. Nigidium, App. Claudium. credo esse neminem qui his hominibus ad vere referendum aut fidem pu-
XV tet aut ingenium defuisse. quid deinde? quid feci? cum
scirem ita esse indicium relatum in tabulas publicas ut
illae tabulae privata tamen custodia more maiorum conti- 10
nerentur, non occultavi, non continui domi, sed statim describi ab omnibus librariis, dividi passim et pervulgari atque edi populo Romano imperavi. divisi toti Italiae, emisi
in omnes provincias: eius indici, ex quo oblata salus
43 esset omnibus, expertem esse neminem volui. itaque dico
locum in orbe terrarum esse nullum, quo in loco populi
Romani nomen sit, quin eodem perscriptum hoc indicium
pervenerit. in quo ego tam subito et exiguo et turbido tempore multa divinitus, ita ut dixi, non mea sponte providi, 5
primum ne qui posset tantum aut de rei publicae aut de
alicuius periculo meminisse quantum vellet; deinde ne cui
liceret umquam reprendere illud indicium aut temere creditum criminari; postremo ne quid iam a me, ne quid ex
meis commentariis quaereretur, ne aut oblivio mea aut me- 10
moria nimia videretur, ne denique aut neglegentia tur-

TV (usque ad 43.7 meminisse) ω] **42** 1 at] ad *TV Schol.*   virtute et *om.*
Schol.   1–2 cuius . . . maxima *om. Schol.*   2 erat *om.* δ   3 memoria *om. V*
consuetudine et *om. Schol.*   sceleritate *VP*   4 prosequi *V*   5 messali *a*:
mesalline *q*   6–7 neminem] memorem δ   7 qui *om. V*   homini-
bus] omnibus δ   ad *TEV*: aut ω   vere referendum *TV*: facundiam
β: vere referendis δ   fidem *om.* δ   9 esse *om.* ω   iudicium *V*   relatum *om. q*   10 pravata *T*   tamen] tum *VK*   more *om. T*   11–
12 describi statim ab omnibus β: d- ab o- s- δ   12 passim] possim
V   13 emisi *E*: dimisi *T*β: divisi *V*δ   14 iudicii *V*   ex *T*: et *V*: e
ω   salus oblata ω   **43** 2 orbem *Va*   2–3 populi Romani] r. p.
δ   3 iudicium *V*   4 tam *Gck*: tum ω   6 qui] quis *a*   de rep.
TV   11 nimia diceretur β: videretur nimia δ

44 pis aut diligentia crudelis putaretur. sed tamen abs te, Torquate, quaero: cum indicatus tuus esset inimicus et esset
eius rei frequens senatus et recens memoria testis, ⟨et⟩ tibi
meo familiari et contubernali prius etiam edituri indicium
fuerint scribae mei, si voluisses, quam in codicem rettulis- 5
sent, cur cum videres aliter referri tacuisti, passus es, non
mecum aut ⟨ut⟩ cum familiari tuo questus es aut, quoniam
tam facile inveheris in amicos, iracundius aut vehementius
expostulasti? tu, cum tua vox numquam sit audita, cum indicio lecto descripto divulgato quieveris tacueris, repente 10
tantam rem ementiare et in eum locum te deducas ut,
ante quam me commutati indici coargueris, te summae ne-
VI 45 glegentiae tuo iudicio convictum esse fateare? mihi cuiusquam salus tanti fuisset ut meam neglegerem? per me ego
veritatem patefactam contaminarem aliquo mendacio?
quemquam denique ego iuvarem, a quo et tam crudelis
insidias rei publicae factas et me potissimum consule con- 5
stitutas putarem? quodsi iam essem oblitus severitatis et
constantiae meae, tamne amens eram ut, cum litterae posteritatis causa repertae sint, quae subsidio oblivioni esse
possent, ego recentem putarem memoriam cuncti senatus
commentario meo posse superari? 10

46 Fero ego te, Torquate, iam dudum fero, et nonnumquam animum incitatum ad ulciscendam orationem tuam
revoco ipse et reflecto, permitto aliquid iracundiae tuae,
do adulescentiae, cedo amicitiae, tribuo parenti. sed nisi

Tω] **44** 2 inimicus esset δ   3 ⟨et⟩ tibi *Halm*: tibi ω: tibi⟨que⟩
Meerdervoort: ⟨cumque⟩ tibi *Huldrich*   5 codicem] eo dicere *q*   6
cur *hoc loco Nohl*: ante tacuisti β: *om. T*δ   referri *Orelli*: ferri *T*: fieri
ω   7 aut ⟨ut⟩ *Clark*: aut ω: ut *Oehler*   familiari tuo *Richter*: familiari (familiare β) meo ω: familiarissimo *Eberhard*: familiari ideo *Oehler*:
familiari *Pluygers*   quoniam aut *a*   8 inveheres *a*   aut] et
P   11 enuntiare δ   13 indicio *q*   coniunctum *T*   esse *om.*
β*a*   **45** 2 meam] mea *a*   4 et tam *Garatoni*: etiam *Ta*: et *q*: *om.*
β   5 rei publicae] in rem publicam *q*   me] in me *q*   consulem
β*q*   5–6 constitutas *E*: *om. Tω*   8 esse *om. a*   9 possint β   **46**
1 fero…fero *Iulius Rufinianus (42.4 Halm)*   4 caedo *T*   nisi] non *a*

tibi aliquem modum tute constitueris, coges me oblitum 5
nostrae amicitiae habere rationem meae dignitatis. nemo
umquam me tenuissima suspicione perstrinxit quem non
perverterim atque perfregerim. sed mihi hoc credas velim:
non iis libentissime soleo respondere quos mihi videor fa-
47 cillime posse superare. tu quoniam minime ignoras consuetudinem dicendi meam, noli hac nova lenitate abuti mea,
noli aculeos orationis meae, qui reconditi sunt, excussos arbitrari, noli id omnino a me putare esse amissum, si quid
est tibi remissum atque concessum. cum illae valent apud 5
me excusationes iniuriae tuae, iratus animus tuus, aetas,
amicitia nostra, tum nondum statuo te virium satis habere
ut ego tecum luctari et congredi debeam. quodsi esses usu
atque aetate robustior, essem idem qui soleo cum sum la-
cessitus; nunc tecum sic agam tulisse ut potius iniuriam 10
XVII 48 quam rettulisse gratiam videar. neque vero quid mihi iras-
care intellegere possum. si quod eum defendo quem tu accusas, cur tibi ego non suscenseo quod accusas eum quem
ego defendo? 'inimicum ego' inquis 'accuso meum.' et amicum ego defendo meum. 'non debes tu quemquam in con- 5
iurationis quaestione defendere.' immo nemo magis eum
de quo nihil est umquam suspicatus quam is qui de aliis
multa cognovit. 'cur dixisti testimonium in alios?' quia
coactus sum. 'cur damnati sunt?' quia creditum est. 'regnum est dicere in quem velis, et defendere quem velis.' 10
immo servitus est non dicere in quem velis, et non defend-

*T*ω] 5 tute *TE*β: vitae δ   oblitum me δ: me *T*   7 novissima
a   perstrinxerit *T*   8 perverterim *Ta*: perculerim *P*: pertulerim *K*:
praeverterim *q*   atque perfregerim *B*: aut perfregerim *T*: ac perfregerim *E*β: *om.* δ   9 iis] his ω   **47** 2 nova lenitate (levitate β*a*) ω:
lenitate nova *T*   3 rationis *T*   4 putare omnino a me ω   a-
missum *TE*β*a*: obmissum *q*   8 usu *om.* *T*   **48** 3 ego] quoque ipse
ω   quod] qui δ   accuses *q*   4 ego *alterum om.* ω   4–5 ami-
cum] inimicum *T*   5 tu] tamen δ   in *om.* *T*β*a*   7 est umquam
*E*β: umquam est *T*: est δ   qui *om.* *a*   8 cognovit] cogitavit
*T*β*q*   9 sum *om.* *T*δ   10 et *T*: ac sic etiam β: ac si *a*: ac *q*   11 non
alterum om. *T*δ

ere quem velis. ac si considerare coeperis utrum magis
mihi hoc necesse fuerit facere an istud tibi, intelleges hon-
estius te inimicitiarum modum statuere potuisse quam me
49 humanitatis. at vero cum honos agebatur familiae vestrae
amplissimus, hoc est consulatus parentis tui, sapientissimus vir familiarissimis suis non suscensuit [pater tuus],
cum Sullam et defenderent et laudarent: intellegebat hanc
nobis a maioribus esse traditam disciplinam ut nullius ami- 5
citia ad pericula propulsanda impediremur. et erat huic iudicio longe dissimilis illa contentio. tum adflicto P. Sulla
consulatus vobis pariebatur, sicuti partus est; honoris erat
certamen; ereptum repetere vos clamitabatis, ut victi in
campo in foro vinceretis. tum qui contra vos pro huius sal- 10
ute pugnabant, amicissimi vestri, quibus non irascebamini,
consulatum vobis eripiebant, honori vestro repugnabant et
tamen id inviolata vestra amicitia, integro officio, vetere
VIII 50 exemplo atque instituto optimi cuiusque faciebant. ego vero
quibus ornamentis adversor tuis aut cui dignitati vestrae
repugno? quid est quod iam ab hoc expetas? honos ad patrem, insignia honoris ad te delata sunt. tu ornatus exuviis
venis ad eum lacerandum quem interemisti: ego iacentem 5
et spoliatum defendo et protego. atque hic tu et reprendis
me quia defendam et irasceris. ego autem non modo tibi
non irascor sed ne reprendo quidem factum tuum. te enim
existimo tibi statuisse quid faciendum putares et satis idoneum offici tui iudicem ipsum esse. 10
51 At accusat ⟨C.⟩ Corneli filius et id aeque valere debet ac

---

Tω] 13 istud *TE*β: *om.* δ   **49** 1 at *S*: aut *T*: an ω   1–2 amplissimus familiae vestrae ω   3 pater tuus ⟨U⟩: *del. Rinkes*   6 ad
propulsanda pericula ω   et erat *q*: aderat *Ta*: erat β: at erat
Halm   8 si certi δ   11 *post* non *litteram* g *add. T*   13 id *om.*
β*q*¹   veterem *a*: veteri *q*   **50** 3 honos] honor ω   4 ornatus] ornatus huius *G mg. c²k*   exuviis *TE*: eximiis β: et vivus *a*: erumpnis
q   8 ne] neque ω   9 quid] quod *T*   10 tui *TE*: *om.* ω   ipsum
esse *Madvig*: potuisse *T*: posuisse ω: ⟨esse⟩ potuisse *Halm*   **51** 1 ⟨C.⟩
suppl. ed. Veneta (a. 1471)   et id aeque *T*β: et idemque *a*: idemque *q*

si pater indicaret. o patrem [Cornelium] sapientem qui,
quod praemi solet esse in indicio, reliquerit, quod turpitudinis in confessione, id per accusationem fili susceperit! sed
quid est tandem quod indicat per istum puerum Cornelius? 5
si vetera, mihi ignota, cum Hortensio communicata, respondit Hortensius; sin, ut ais, illum conatum Autroni et
Catilinae, cum in campo consularibus comitiis quae a me
habita sunt caedem facere voluerunt, Autronium tum in
campo vidimus. sed quid dixi vidisse nos? ego vidi: vos 10
enim tum, iudices, nihil laborabatis neque suspicabamini,
ego tectus praesidio firmo amicorum Catilinae tum et Au-
52 troni copias et conatum repressi. num quis est igitur qui
tum dicat in campum aspirasse Sullam? atqui si tum se
cum Catilina societate sceleris coniunxerat, cur ab eo dis-
cedebat, cur cum Autronio non erat, cur in pari causa
non paria signa criminis reperiuntur? sed quoniam Corne- 5
lius ipse etiam nunc de indicando dubitat, ut dicitis, informat ad hoc adumbratum indicium filium, quid tandem de
illa nocte dicit, cum inter falcarios ad M. Laecam nocte ea
quae consecuta est posterum diem nonarum Novembrium
me consule Catilinae denuntiatione convenit? quae nox 10
omnium temporum coniurationis acerrima fuit atque acerbissima. tum Catilinae dies exeundi, tum ceteris manendi
condicio, tum discriptio totam per urbem caedis atque incendiorum constituta est; tum tuus pater, Corneli, id quod
tandem aliquando confitetur, illam sibi officiosam provin- 15
ciam depoposcit ut, cum prima luce consulem salutatum

---

*T*ω] 2 Cornelium Ⲱ: *del. Cobet*   3 iudicio β*a*   4 id *exp. ut vid.*
T   5 quid] quod *T*   indicet *T*β*a*   6 si vetera *T*: sin ea β: su-
escam *a*: si est causa *q*   6–7 respondeat β: respondet δ   7 con-
atum] comitatum ω   8 in *om. a*   10 sed *Madvig*: et Ⲱ   quid]
quod *T*   12 tum et β*a*: tum *T*: tunc et *q*   **52** 2–3 secum *T*β*a*   3
catilinam *T*   4 ire pari causa *T*: in re pari *Clark*   6 nunc] nos
a   ut dicitis] et ut diximus β   6–7 et informat *Winterbottom*   7
filii ω   de *om. T*   9 nonarum Novembrium *Tq*: nonarum no-
vembris β: non novit *a*   13 descriptio Ⲱ: *corr. Bücheler*   14 tum]
tunc *q*   16 cum] eum *T*

veniret, intromissus et meo more et iure amicitiae me in
IX 53 meo lectulo trucidaret. hoc tempore cum arderet acerrime
coniuratio, cum Catilina egrederetur ad exercitum, Lentulus in urbe relinqueretur, Cassius incendiis, Cethegus caedi
praeponeretur, Autronio ut occuparet curiam praescriber-
etur, cum omnia ornarentur instruerentur pararentur, ubi 5
fuit Sulla, Corneli? num Romae? immo longe afuit. num in
iis regionibus quo se Catilina inferebat? multo etiam longius. num in agro Camerti Piceno Gallico, quas in oras maxime quasi morbus quidam illius furoris pervaserat? nihil
vero minus. fuit enim, ut iam ante dixi, Neapoli, fuit in ea 10
parte Italiae quae maxime ista suspicione caruit.

54   Quid ergo indicat aut quid adfert aut ipse Cornelius aut
vos qui haec ab illo mandata defertis? gladiatores emptos
esse Fausti simulatione ad caedem ac tumultum? 'ita prorsus: interpositi sunt gladiatores.' quos testamento patris
deberi videmus. 'adrepta est familia; quae si esset praeter- 5
missa, posset alia familia Fausti munus praebere.' utinam
quidem haec ipsa non modo iniquorum invidiae sed aequo-
rum exspectationi satis facere posset! 'properatum vehementer est, cum longe tempus muneris abesset.' quasi
vero tempus dandi muneris non valde appropinquaret. 10
'nec opinante Fausto, cum is neque sciret neque vellet,
55 familia est comparata.' at litterae sunt Fausti, per quas ille
precibus a P. Sulla petit ut emat gladiatores et ut hos ipsos
emat, neque solum ad Sullam missae sed ad L. Caesarem,
Q. Pompeium, C. Memmium, quorum de sententia tota
res gesta est. 'at praefuit familiae Cornelius.' iam si in par- 5

Tω] 18 lecto δ   **53** 4 curiam *Schliack*: etruriam ω   5 ornarentur *Landgraf*: ordinarentur ω   instituerentur δ   6 affuit
Ta   in *om. T*   7 his legionibus ω   8 in oras *T*: oras β: in has *a*:
horas *q*   11 ista] ea ω   **54** 2 haec ab illo *T*: ab eo haec (hic *K*) β*q*:
ab eo *a*   5 videmus] debemus *q*   si] se *q*¹   6 munus] minus
T   7 quidquid *a*   invidiae sed *r*: invidia (invida *a*) esset ω   8
properatum] praeparant δ   9 est *om.* ω   **55** 5 Cornelius ⟨libertus⟩
Boulanger

anda familia nulla suspicio est, quis praefuerit nihil ad rem
pertinet. sed tamen munere servili obtulit se ad ferramenta
prospicienda: praefuit vero numquam, eaque res omni
tempore per Balbum Fausti libertum administrata est.

XX 56   At enim Sittius est ab hoc in ulteriorem Hispaniam mis-
sus ut eam provinciam perturbaret. primum Sittius, iudices, L. Iulio C. Figulo consulibus profectus est aliquanto
ante furorem Catilinae et suspicionem huius coniurationis.
deinde est profectus non tum primum, sed cum in isdem 5
locis aliquanto ante eadem de causa aliquot annos fuisset,
ac profectus est non modo ob causam sed etiam ob neces-
sariam causam magna ratione cum Mauretaniae rege contracta. tum autem illo profecto Sulla procurante eius rem
et gerente plurimis et pulcherrimis P. Sitti praediis vendi- 10
tis aes alienum eiusdem ⟨est⟩ dissolutum ut, quae causa
ceteros ad facinus impulit, cupiditas retinendae possessio-
57 nis, ea Sittio non fuerit praediis deminutis. iam vero illud
quam incredibile, quam absurdum, qui Romae caedem facere, qui hanc urbem inflammare vellet, eum familiarissimum suum dimittere ab se et amandare in ultimas terras!
utrum quo facilius Romae ea quae conabatur efficeret, si 5
in Hispania turbatum esset? at haec ipsa per se sine ulla
coniunctione agebantur. an in tantis rebus, tam novis consiliis, tam periculosis, tam turbulentis hominem amantissimum sui, familiarissimum, coniunctissimum officiis usu
consuetudine dimittendum esse arbitrabatur? veri simile 10
non est ut, quem in secundis rebus, quem in otio secum
semper habuisset, hunc in adversis et in eo tumultu quem

Tω] 6 quis *Ta*: quid β: quod *q*   praefuerit *T*: refert β: profert
δ   rem] pertem *a*   7 sed] is *Clark*   tamen] tantum *Orelli*   8–9
omni tempore *post* libertum ω   9 balbum *E*: bellum *Tω*   **56** 1 si-
cius β*a*: cincius *q*   4 ante] autem *T*   5 cum] eum *T*   7 ob *alterum
om.* ω   11 ⟨est⟩ dissolutum *Halm*: dissolutum ⟨est⟩ *Angelius*   **57** 4
mandare ω   5 utrum] virum *q*   6 in hispaniam turbatum isset
d   at] ad *T*   9–10 consuetudine usu *T*   10 arbitratur *a*: arbitraretur *q*   11–12 semper secum habuisset *TK*: sem- h- sec- *a*

58 ipse comparabat ab se dimitteret. ipse autem Sittius – non
enim mihi deserenda est causa amici veteris atque hospitis
– is homo est aut ea familia ac disciplina ut hoc credi possit, eum bellum populo Romano facere voluisse? ut cuius
pater, cum ceteri deficerent finitimi ac vicini, singulari ex- 5
stiterit in rem publicam nostram officio et fide, is sibi nefarium bellum contra patriam suscipiendum putaret? cuius
aes alienum videmus, iudices, non libidine sed negoti ger-
endi studio esse contractum; qui ita Romae debuit ut in
provinciis et in regnis maximae ei pecuniae deberentur, 10
quas cum peteret non commisit ut sui procuratores quicquam oneris absente se sustinerent: venire omnis suas possessiones et patrimonio se ornatissimo spoliari maluit quam
59 ullam moram cuiquam fieri creditorum suorum. a quo quidem genere, iudices, ego numquam timui, cum in illa rei
publicae tempestate versarer. illud erat hominum genus
horribile et pertimescendum, qui tanto amore suas possessiones amplexi tenebant ut ab iis membra citius divelli ac 5
distrahi posse diceres. Sittius numquam sibi cognationem
cum praediis esse existimavit suis. itaque se non modo ex
suspicione tanti sceleris verum etiam ex omni hominum
sermone non armis sed patrimonio suo vindicavit.

XI 60 Iam vero quod obiecit Pompeianos esse a Sulla impulsos
ut ad istam coniurationem atque ad hoc nefarium facinus
accederent, id cuius modi sit intellegere non possum. an
tibi Pompeiani coniurasse videntur? quis hoc dixit umquam, aut quae fuiṭ istius rei vel minima suspicio? 'diiun- 5
xit' inquit 'eos a colonis ut hoc discidio ac dissensione
facta oppidum in sua potestate posset per Pompeianos hab-

*T*ω] **58** 2 deseranda *T*   4–6 populo…exstiterit *om.* β   4 populo r. *T*: r. p. *a*: rei. p. *q*   5 cum ceteri *bis a*   10 ei maximae
T   12–13 positiones *T*   14 creditorum] hereditorum *T*   **59** 3
genus hominum ω   4–5 amplexi (complexi β) suas possessiones
β*a*   5 iis *k*: his ω   divelli citius ω   **60** 1 obicit *q*   2 atque] ac
q   4–5 umquam dixit δ   5–6 disiunxit ω   6 inquit eos *T*: eos
inquit β: inquam eos δ   ut] non *a*   7 per] et ω   7–8 habentem *a*

ere.' primum omnis Pompeianorum colonorumque dissensio delata ad patronos est, cum iam inveterasset ac multos
annos esset agitata; deinde ita a patronis res cognita est ut 10
nulla in re a ceterorum sententiis Sulla dissenserit; postremo coloni ipsi sic intellegunt non Pompeianos a Sulla
61 magis quam sese esse defensos. atque hoc, iudices, ex hac
frequentia colonorum, honestissimorum hominum, intellegere potestis, qui adsunt laborant, hunc patronum defensorem custodem illius coloniae si in omni fortuna atque
omni honore incolumem habere non potuerunt, in hoc ta- 5
men casu in quo adflictus iacet per vos iuvari conservarique cupiunt. adsunt pari studio Pompeiani, qui ab illis
etiam in crimen vocantur; qui ita de ambulatione ac de suffragiis suis cum colonis dissenserunt ut idem de communi
62 salute sentirent. ac ne haec quidem P. Sullae mihi videtur
silentio praetereunda esse virtus, quod, cum ab hoc illa colonia deducta sit, et cum commoda colonorum a fortunis
Pompeianorum rei publicae fortuna diiunxerit, ita carus
utrisque est atque iucundus ut non alteros demovisse sed 5
utrosque constituisse videatur.
XXII   At enim et gladiatores et omnis ista vis rogationis Caeciliae causa comparabatur. atque hoc loco in L. Caecilium,
pudentissimum atque ornatissimum virum, vehementer invectus est. cuius ego de virtute et constantia, iudices, tan- 10
tum dico, talem hunc in ista rogatione quam promulgarat
non de tollenda, sed de levanda calamitate fratris sui fuisse
ut consulere voluerit fratri, cum re publica pugnare noluerit: promulgarit impulsus amore fraterno, destiterit frat-

Tω] 10 esse *q*   exagitata β: excogitata δ   12 pompeiano *T*   **61**
3 et laborant β   4–5 atque in omni *bck*   6 in *om.* δ   quo *om.*
a   iuvari *TE*: tutari ω   7 illis] his *T*   8 ambitione β   ac] et
ω   9 communi] omni *q*   **62** 2 hac *a*   2–3 coloniae *T*   4 rei
publicae *TEω*: populi Romani *Angelius*   diiunxerit *Gruter*: disiunxerit
E: divixerit *T*: diviserit ω   5 est *om. T*   7 omnes *a*   7–8 caeliae
T   9 prudentissimum β*q*   13 consulere *T*β: consulem *a*: consul
esse *q*

63 ris auctoritate deductus. atque in ea re per L. Caecilium
Sulla accusatur in qua re est uterque laudandus. primum
Caecilius, qui id promulgavit in quo res iudicatas videbatur voluisse rescindere, ut restitueretur Sulla. recte reprendis. status enim rei publicae maxime iudicatis rebus con- 5
tinetur, neque ego tantum fraterno amori dandum arbitror
ut quisquam, dum saluti suorum consulat, communem relinquat. ⟨at⟩ nihil de iudicio ferebat, sed poenam ambitus
eam referebat quae fuerat nuper superioribus legibus constituta. itaque hac rogatione non iudicum sententia, sed 10
legis vitium corrigebatur. nemo iudicium reprendit, cum
de poena queritur, sed legem. damnatio est enim iudicum,
64 quae manebat, poena legis, quae levabatur. noli igitur animos eorum ordinum qui praesunt iudiciis summa cum
gravitate et dignitate alienare a causa. nemo labefactare
iudicium est conatus, nihil est eius modi promulgatum:
semper Caecilius in calamitate fratris sui iudicum potesta- 5
tem perpetuandam, legis acerbitatem mitigandam putavit.
XXIII sed quid ego de hoc plura disputem? dicerem fortasse, et
facile et libenter dicerem, si paulo etiam longius quam
finis cotidiani offici postulat L. Caecilium pietas et frater-
nus amor propulisset. implorarem sensus vestros, unius 10
cuiusque indulgentiam in suos testarer, peterem veniam errato L. Caecili ex intimis vestris cogitationibus atque ex
65 humanitate communi. lex dies fuit proposita paucos, ferri
coepta numquam, deposita est in senatu. kalendis Ianuar-

$T\omega$] **63** 1 re per] re publica ω 3 qui id ω: qui si id *Halm*: – quid?
'id (. . . 4 Sulla') *Clark*   promulgarit β: promulgare δ ·   3–4 videatur
Garatoni   4 restitueretur *m*: stitueretur *T*: statueretur ω 4–5 reprehendit δ   6 dandum] neque dandum *T*   7 dum saluti] cum (*om.*
δ) de salute ω 8 ⟨at⟩ *suppl. Orelli*   de *om.* ω 9 ferebat
δ   fuerat] fecerat *T*   10 hanc rogationem β*a*   sententiam
q   11 corrigebat ω 12 enim est ω **64** 3 aliena *a*   5 iudicium
T   6 perpetiundam *TP*: per pecuniam *a*: *om.* *K*   8 dicem *T*   9
L. Caecilium *post* amor ω 10 propulisset *TE*β: protulisset δ   nostros *a*   10–11 unicuiusque *T*   11–12 errato veniam δ   **65** 2 deposita *E*: posita *T*ω 2–3 kalendis ianuariis *TE*β: r. lateri δ

iis cum in Capitolium nos senatum convocassemus, nihil
est actum prius, et id mandatu Sullae Q. Metellus praetor
se loqui dixit, Sullam illam rogationem de se nolle ferri. ex 5
illo tempore L. Caecilius egit de re publica multa: agrariae
legi, quae tota a me reprensa et abiecta est, intercessorem
se fore professus est, improbis largitionibus restitit, senatus
auctoritatem numquam impedivit, ita se gessit in tribunatu
ut onere deposito domestici offici nihil postea nisi de rei 10
66 publicae commodis cogitarit. atque in ipsa rogatione ne
per vim quid ageretur, quis tum nostrum Sullam aut Caecilium verebatur? nonne omnis ille terror, omnis seditionis
timor atque opinio ex Autroni improbitate pendebat? eius
voces, eius minae ferebantur, eius aspectus concursatio 5
stipatio greges hominum perditorum metum nobis seditionis ⟨caedis⟩que adferebant. itaque P. Sulla hoc importu-
nissimo cum honoris tum etiam calamitatis socio atque
comite et secundas fortunas amittere coactus est et in adversis sine ullo remedio atque adlevamento permanere. 10
XXIV 67 Hic tu epistulam meam saepe recitas quam ego ad Cn.
Pompeium de meis rebus gestis et de summa re publica
misi, et ex ea crimen aliquod in P. Sullam quaeris et, si
furorem incredibilem biennio ante conceptum erupisse in
meo consulatu scripsi, me hoc demonstrasse dicis, Sullam 5
in illa fuisse superiore coniuratione. scilicet ego is sum qui
existimem Cn. Pisonem et Catilinam et Vargunteium et
Autronium nihil scelerate, nihil audacter ipsos per sese
68 sine P. Sulla facere potuisse. de quo etiam si quis dubitasset

---

*T*ω] 4 mandato ω   praetor *q*: p. r. *T*a: populo romano β   5
cognationem δ   6 multa de re publica egit ω   7–8 intercessorem
se *E*β: se i- *T*: i- δ   8 professus] perpessus δ   10–11 de rep.
T   **66** 2 tum *TE*β: tamen δ   3 error *a*   4 pendebat *om. a*   5
eius in me deferebantur *a*   6–7 seditionis ⟨caedis⟩que *Shackleton Bailey*: seditionesque ω: ⟨caedis⟩ seditionisque *Madvig*: seditionis ⟨suspi-
ciones⟩que *vel* suspicionesque *Lehmann*   8 cum] tum ω   **67** 2 rei
publicae (r. p. *a*) ω   4 et rupisse *T*   6 superiorem *T*   scilicet *om.*
a   ego is sum *T*: is e- s- *E*: is s- β*q*: ipsum *a*   **68**

antea num id quod tu arguis cogitasset, ut interfecto patre
tuo consul descenderet kalendis Ianuariis cum lictoribus,
sustulisti hanc suspicionem cum dixisti hunc, ut Catilinam
consulem efficeret, contra patrem tuum operas et manum 5
comparasse. quod si tibi ego confitear, tu mihi concedas
necesse est hunc, cum Catilinae suffragaretur, nihil de suo
consulatu quem iudicio amiserat per vim recuperando cog-
itavisse. neque enim istorum facinorum tantorum tam
atrocium crimen, iudices, P. Sullae persona suscipit.   10

69 Iam enim faciam criminibus omnibus fere dissolutis contra atque in ceteris causis fieri solet, ut nunc denique de
vita hominis ac de moribus dicam. etenim de principio studuit animus occurrere magnitudini criminis, satis facere
exspectationi hominum, de me aliquid ipso qui accusatus 5
eram dicere: nunc iam revocandi estis eo quo vos ipsa
causa etiam tacente me cogit animos mentesque convertere.

XXV Omnibus in rebus, iudices, quae graviores maioresque
sunt, quid quisque voluerit cogitarit admiserit non ex crimine, sed ex moribus eius qui arguitur est ponderandum. 10
neque enim potest quisquam nostrum subito fingi neque
70 cuiusquam repente vita mutari aut natura converti. circumspicite paulisper mentibus vestris, ut alia omittamus,
hosce ipsos homines qui huic adfines sceleri fuerunt. Catilina contra rem publicam coniuravit. cuius aures umquam
hoc respuerunt conatum esse audacter hominem a pueritia 5
non solum intemperantia et scelere sed etiam consuetudine
et studio in omni flagitio stupro caede versatum? quis eum

Tω] 2 num] an *Eberhard*   ut *om. T*δ   3 consule ω: *corr. O. Müller* descendere *q*   4 sustuli *T*   dixi *Ta*   6 confiteor δ   7 suo] meo
T   9 istorum] horum *a*   **69** 5 ipso *T Eβ*: de ipso δ   6 eram
T Eβa: erat *q*   7 etiam *om. T*   animos *E*: animus *Ta*: animis *q*: *om.* β
7–8 mentesque convertere *E*: *om. Tω*   9 iudices β*q*: videlicet *a*: *om. T*
10 noluerit *q*   12 fringi *T*   **70** 2 mittamus *T*   3–4 catilinam δ   4–5
umquam hoc δ: umquam haec *T*: hoc umquam (numquam *P*) β   5
audacter *om.* ω   6 et *om. q*   7 versatum] grassatum *E*

contra patriam pugnantem perisse miratur quem semper
omnes ad civile latrocinium natum putaverunt? quis Lentuli societates cum indicibus, quis insaniam libidinum, 10
quis perversam atque impiam religionem recordatur qui
illum aut nefarie cogitasse aut stulte sperasse miretur?
quis de C. Cethego atque eius in Hispaniam profectione
ac de vulnere Q. Metelli Pii cogitat cui non ad illius poe-
71 nam carcer aedificatus esse videatur? omitto ceteros, ne
sit infinitum. tantum a vobis peto ut taciti de omnibus
quos coniurasse cognitum est cogitetis: intellegetis unum
quemque eorum prius ab sua vita quam vestra suspicione
esse damnatum. ipsum illum Autronium, quoniam eius no- 5
men finitimum maxime est huius periculo et crimini, non
sua vita ac natura convicit? semper audax petulans libidi-
nosus, quem in stuprorum deprensionibus non solum verbis uti improbissimis solitum esse scimus verum etiam pugnis et calcibus, quem exturbare homines ex possessionibus, 10
caedem facere vicinorum, spoliare fana sociorum, vi [con-
atum] et armis disturbare iudicia, in bonis rebus omnis
contemnere, in malis pugnare contra bonos, non rei publicae cedere, non fortunae ipsi succumbere. huius si causa
non manifestissimis rebus teneretur, tamen eum mores ip- 15
sius ac vita convinceret.

XXVI 72   Agedum, conferte nunc cum illius vita vitam P. Sullae,
vobis populoque Romano notissimam, iudices, et eam
ante oculos vestros proponite. ecquod est huius factum aut
commissum non dicam audacius, sed quod cuiquam paulo

Tω] 9 latrocinium] patrocinium (ni *s.s.*) *T*   notum *T*   12 cogitasse aut stulte sperasse *E*: cogitasse (*om.* ω) aut stulte cogitasse
Tω   **71** 3 intelligitis *T*δ   4 ab] a ω   vestra *T*: a vestra β: nostra
δ   7 natura (*om.* δ) ac vita ω   convincit ω   8 stuprum *T*β   deprensionibus *Håkanson*: defensionibus ω   10 ex *T*β: et *a*: e *q*   11 vi]
vi et (et *deletum*) *T*   11–12 conatum (ornatum *K*)] *hoc loco T*δ: *post* armis β: *del. Lambinus*: conari *Pabón*: comitum *Winterbottom*: *fort.* comitia (*cf.*
§*51*)   12 indicia *a*   13 contemnerem *T*   **72** 1 conferre *a*   illis
ck   vita vitam *Angelius*: vita *T*: vitam ω   3 nostros *Ka*   et quod
ω: *corr. ed. Mediolanensis (a. 1498)*   est *om.* q

minus consideratum videretur? factum quaero? verbum ec- 5
quod umquam ex ore huius excidit in quo quisquam posset
offendi? at vero in illa gravi L. Sullae turbulentaque victoria quis P. Sulla mitior, quis misericordior inventus est?
quam multorum hic vitam est a L. Sulla deprecatus! quam
multi sunt summi homines et ornatissimi et nostri et 10
equestris ordinis quorum pro salute se hic Sullae obliga-
vit! quos ego nominarem – neque enim ipsi nolunt et huic
animo gratissimo adsunt –, sed quia maius est beneficium
quam posse debet civis civi dare, ideo a vobis peto ut
73 quod potuit, tempori tribuatis, quod fecit, ipsi. quid relicuam constantiam vitae commemorem, dignitatem, liberalitatem, moderationem in privatis rebus, splendorem in
publicis? quae ita deformata sunt a fortuna ut tamen a natura incohata compareant. quae domus, quae celebratio co- 5
tidiana, quae familiarium dignitas, quae studia amicorum,
quae ex quoque ordine multitudo! haec diu multumque et
multo labore quaesita una eripuit hora. accepit P. Sulla,
iudices, vulnus vehemens et mortiferum, verum tamen
eius modi quod videretur huius vita et natura accipere po- 10
tuisse. honestatis enim et dignitatis habuisse nimis magnam
iudicatus est cupiditatem, quam si nemo alius habuit in
consulatu petendo, cupidior iudicatus est hic fuisse quam
ceteri; sin etiam in aliis nonnullis fuit iste consulatus
amor, fortuna in hoc fuit fortasse gravior quam in ceteris. 15
74 postea vero quis P. Sullam nisi maerentem demissum adflictumque vidit, quis umquam est suspicatus hunc magis

Tω] 5 verbum] *post* umquam β: verbis *a*   5–6 ecquod *d*: et quod
ω   6 huius] eius β*a*   quo *om. q*   7 in illa] nulla *a*   7–8 victoria turbulentaque ω   8 quis m-...est *E*: *om. Tω*   9
quam...deprecatus *Gellius 7.16.6*   quam *primum Gellius*: *om.* ω   est
a L.] sit a *Gellius*   12 volunt *a*   15–73.1 quod potuit...quid *om.*
β   **73** 1–2 relicuae *Richter*   2–3 libertatem *T*   4 a fortuna deformata sunt ω   5 inchoata *T*β*q*   quae *alterum secl. Jordan*   6
familiaris δ   7 multumque *TE*β: multum δ   9 iudices] videlicet
a   11 enim *om.* δ   15 fortasse fuit *q*   **74**

odio quam pudore hominum aspectum lucemque vitare?
qui cum multa haberet invitamenta urbis et fori propter
summa studia amicorum, quae tamen ei sola in malis resti- 5
terunt, afuit ab oculis vestris et, cum lege retineretur, ipse
XXVII se exsilio paene multavit. in hoc vos pudore, iudices, et in
hac vita tanto sceleri locum fuisse creditis? aspicite ipsum,
contuemini os, conferte crimen cum vita, vitam ab initio
usque ad hoc tempus explicatam cum crimine recogno- 10
75 scite. mitto rem publicam, quae fuit semper Sullae caris-
sima: hosne amicos, tales viros, tam cupidos sui, per quos
res eius secundae quondam erant ornatae, nunc sublevan-
tur adversae, crudelissime perire voluit, ut cum Lentulo et
Catilina et Cethego foedissimam vitam ac miserrimam tur- 5
pissima morte proposita degeret? non, inquam, cadit in hos
mores, non in hunc pudorem, non in hanc vitam, non in
hunc hominem ista suspicio.

Nova quaedam illa immanitas exorta est, incredibilis fuit
ac singularis furor; ex multis ab adulescentia collectis per- 10
ditorum hominum vitiis repente ista tanta importunitas in-
76 auditi sceleris exarsit. nolite, iudices, arbitrari hominum illum impetum et conatum fuisse: neque enim ulla gens tam
barbara aut tam immanis umquam fuit in qua non modo
tot, sed unus tam crudelis hostis patriae sit inventus. beluae quaedam illae ex portentis immanes ac ferae forma 5
hominum indutae exstiterunt. perspicite etiam atque etiam,
iudices, – nihil enim est quod in hac causa dici possit vehementius – penitus introspicite Catilinae Autroni Cethegi
Lentuli ceterorumque mentes: quas vos in his libidines,
quae flagitia, quas turpitudines, quantas audacias, quam 10

Tω] 5 tamen] tantum β: *post* afuit *transpos. Sauppe*   6 affuit *Ta*
7 iudices *E*: iudicii *Tω*   8 credatis *Zielinski*   9 os] hos *T*   conferre *T*   vitam *TE*: *om.* ω   9–10 ab initio usque *Tβa*: ab initio *E*:
usque *q*   10 explicatam *TE*: explicata ω   **75** 3 ornatae *b²ck*: ordinatae *ω*   **76** 1 arbitrare *T*   5 et portenta *Shackleton Bailey*   6
perspicue β: prospicite *a*   7 iudices] videte β   posset *Tδ*

incredibiles furores, quas notas facinorum, quae indicia
parricidiorum, quantos acervos scelerum reperietis! ex
magnis et diuturnis et iam desperatis rei publicae morbis
ista repente vis erupit, ut ea collecta et eiecta convalescere
aliquando et sanari civitas posset; neque enim est quis-   15
quam qui arbitretur illis inclusis in re publica pestibus diutius haec stare potuisse. itaque eos non ad perficiendum
scelus, sed ad luendas rei publicae poenas Furiae quaedam
incitaverunt.

XVIII 77   In hunc igitur gregem vos nunc P. Sullam, iudices, ex his
qui cum hoc vivunt atque vixerunt honestissimorum homi-
num gregibus reicietis, ex hoc amicorum numero, ex hac
familiarium dignitate in impiorum partem atque in parricidarum sedem ac numerum transferetis? ubi erit igitur illud 5
firmissimum praesidium pudoris, quo in loco nobis vita
ante acta proderit, quod ad tempus existimationis partae
fructus reservabitur, si in extremo discrimine ac dimicatione fortunae deseret, si non aderit, si nihil adiuvabit?

78   Quaestiones nobis servorum accusator et tormenta minitatur. in quibus quamquam nihil periculi suspicamur, tamen illa tormenta gubernat dolor, moderatur natura cuiusque cum animi tum corporis, regit quaesitor, flectit libido,
corrumpit spes, infirmat metus, ut in tot rerum angustiis 5
nihil veritati loci relinquatur. vita P. Sullae torqueatur, ex
ea quaeratur num quae occultetur libido, num quod lateat

*T*ω] 11 facinorum] scelerum ω   12 scelerum] facinorum ω   14
collecta *scripsi*: confecta ω   15 et sanari aliquando *a*   posset *k*:
possit ω   18 sed abluendas *a*   **77** 1 P.] per *a*   his] iis *ck*   2
atque δ: aut *T*: ac β   honestissimorum *bis a*   2–3 hominum] amicorum *T*   3 amicorum *R. Klotz*: hominum ω   4 familiari δ   5
sedem] cedem δ   ac] atque *T*   6 fortissimum ω   7 acta ante
a   parta *T*   8 in ω: non *T*: nos in *Richter*   9 deseret *k*: deserit ω:
deseruerit (*q mg.*) *Petrarca*   si *primum*] nsi (*sic*) *T*   si *alterum om.*
T   **78** 1 accusator et tormenta] ac t- a- ω   2 in...suspicamur *om.*
β   nihil *om. T*   4 cum *Tq*: tum *deletum a: om.* β   regit quaestor δ:
om. β   6 veritati loci *Tq*: l- v- β: v- loci loci *a*   torquatur *a*: torquate *q*   7 num...num] non...non *a*

facinus, num quae crudelitas, num quae audacia. nihil erroris erit in causa nec obscuritatis, iudices, si a vobis vitae
perpetuae vox, ea quae verissima et gravissima debet 10
79 esse, audietur. nullum in hac causa testem timemus, nihil
quemquam scire, nihil vidisse, nihil audisse arbitramur. sed
tamen si nihil vos P. Sullae fortuna movet, iudices, vestra
moveat. vestra enim, qui cum summa elegantia atque in-
tegritate vixistis, hoc maxime interest, non ex libidine aut 5
simultate aut levitate testium causas honestorum hominum ponderari, sed in magnis disquisitionibus repentinisque periculis vitam unius cuiusque esse testem. quam
vos, iudices, nolite armis suis spoliatam atque nudatam
obicere invidiae, dedere suspicioni: munite communem ar- 10
cem bonorum, obstruite perfugia improborum! valeat ad
poenam et ad salutem vita plurimum, quam solam videtis
ipsam ex sua natura facillime perspici, subito flecti fingique non posse.

XXIX 80 Quid vero? haec auctoritas – semper enim est de ea
dicendum, quamquam a me timide modiceque dicetur –
quid? inquam, haec auctoritas nostra, qui a ceteris coniurationis causis abstinuimus, P. Sullam defendimus, nihil
hunc tandem iuvabit? grave est hoc dictu fortasse, iudices, 5
grave, si appetimus aliquid: si, cum ceteri de nobis silent,
non etiam nosmet ipsi tacemus, grave. sed si laedimur, si
accusamur, si in invidiam vocamur, profecto conceditis, iudices, ut nobis libertatem retinere liceat, si minus liceat
81 dignitatem. accusati sunt uno nomine consulares, ut iam

Tω] 9 iudices] videlicet *a*   10 gravissima et verissima *Pa*: gravissima *Kq*   10–11 esse debet *q*   11 audiretur *a*   **79** 3–4 monet
videlicet nostra moneat *a*   4 qui] qua *T*   5 non *Tq*: ne β: *om.*
a   9 nos *a*   10 dedere *q*: delere *T*: livori β: debere *a*   suspica-
tioni *T*   12 vita *om. T*δ   13 ipse *T*   sua natura *T*: natura sua et
in β: vi sua naturaque δ   **80** 1 auctoritas *om. q*   semper *Tω*: semper iam *E*: saepe *Spengel*   est] *hoc loco T*: *post* ea β: *post* dicendum
δ   2 modice δ   3 vestra *a*   5 grave … iudices *E*: *om. Tω*   dictum *E*: *corr. Madvig*   8 invidia *q*   8–9 iudices] videlicet *a*   **81** 1
⟨omnes⟩ consulares *Clark*

videatur honoris amplissimi nomen plus invidiae quam dignitatis adferre. 'adfuerunt' inquit 'Catilinae illumque laudarunt.' nulla tum patebat, nulla erat cognita coniuratio:
defendebant amicum, aderant supplici, vitae eius turpitu- 5
dinem in summis eius periculis non insequebantur. quin
etiam parens tuus, Torquate, consul reo de pecuniis repetundis Catilinae fuit advocatus, improbo homini, at supplici, fortasse audaci, at aliquando amico. cui cum adfuit
post delatam ad eum primam illam coniurationem, indica- 10
vit se audisse aliquid, non credidisse. 'at idem non adfuit
alio in iudicio, cum adessent ceteri.' si postea cognorat
ipse aliquid quod in consulatu ignorasset, ignoscendum est
iis qui postea nihil audierunt; sin illa res prima valuit, num
inveterata quam recens debuit esse gravior? sed si tuus pa- 15
rens etiam in ipsa suspicione periculi sui tamen humanitate
adductus advocationem hominis improbissimi sella curuli
atque ornamentis et suis et consulatus honestavit, quid est
quam ob rem consulares qui Catilinae adfuerunt repre-
82 ndantur? 'at idem iis qui ante hunc causam de coniuratione dixerunt non adfuerunt.' tanto scelere astrictis hominibus statuerunt nihil a se adiumenti, nihil opis, nihil auxili
ferri oportere. atque ut de eorum constantia atque animo
in rem publicam dicam quorum tacita gravitas et fides de 5
uno quoque loquitur neque cuiusquam ornamenta orationis desiderat, potest quisquam dicere umquam meliores
fortiores constantiores consulares fuisse quàm his temporibus et periculis quibus paene oppressa est res publica? quis
non de communi salute optime, quis non fortissime, quis 10
non constantissime sensit? neque ego praecipue de consu-

TE (*inde a* 81.8 -tundis) ω] 3 inquid *T*   4 tum] tamen δ   6 non
om. a   10 deletam *E*: delatum *P*   10–11 iudicavit *TE*   11 at] ad
E   12 si (*q mg.*) *Petrarca*: sed ω   14 iis *r*: his ω   num] non
ω   16 ipsa] illa ω   18 quid est] quidem *a*   **82** 1 iis *b²*: his *TE*β:
is δ   hanc *T*   2–3 non ... statuerunt *om. q*   3 a *om. a*   4 ferre
TE: fieri β   de *om. a*   7 dicere quisquam *E*   10 optime *Spengel*:
apertissime ω

laribus disputo: nam haec et hominum ornatissimorum
qui praetores fuerunt et universi senatus communis est
laus ut constet post hominum memoriam numquam in illo
ordine plus virtutis, plus amoris in rem publicam, plus 15
gravitatis fuisse. sed quia sunt descripti consulares, de his
tantum mihi dicendum putavi quod satis esset ad testa-
ndam omnium memoriam, neminem esse ex illo honoris
gradu qui non omni studio virtute auctoritate incubuerit
ad rem publicam conservandam. 20

XXX 83   Sed quid ego? qui Catilinam non laudavi, qui reo Catilinae consul non adfui, qui testimonium de coniuratione dixi
in alios, adeone vobis alienus a sanitate, adeo oblitus constantiae meae, adeo immemor rerum a me gestarum esse
videor ut, cum consul bellum gesserim cum coniuratis, 5
nunc eorum ducem servare cupiam et in animum inducam, cuius nuper ferrum rettuderim flammamque restinxerim, eiusdem nunc causam vitamque defendere? si me
dius fidius, iudices, non me ipsa res publica meis laboribus
et periculis conservata ad gravitatem animi et constantiam 10
sua dignitate revocaret, tamen hoc natura est insitum ut
quem timueris, quicum de vita fortunisque contenderis,
cuius ex insidiis evaseris, hunc semper oderis. sed cum agatur honos meus amplissimus, gloria rerum gestarum singularis, cum, quotiens quisque est in hoc scelere convictus, 15
totiens renovetur memoria per me inventae salutis, ego
sim tam demens, ego committam ut ea quae pro salute omnium gessi casu magis et felicitate a me quam virtute
84 et consilio gesta esse videantur? 'quid ergo? hoc tibi sumis'
dicet fortasse quispiam 'ut, quia tu defendis, innocens iudi-

TEω] 13 senatus] sentit *a*   14 post] primo *ut vid. a*   15 in rep.
T   17–18 ad testandum *T*: attestante β: attestantem δ   18 memoriam (memoria β) omnium (hominum *a*) ω   **83** 1 qui *primum om.*
q   3 et avi⟨us⟩ a sanitate *Arusianus Messius* (*7.458.1 Keil,* =*78 della*
Casa)   6 in *secl. Reid*   8 nunc] non *a*   9 iudices] videlicet *a*   rep.
T   13 ex] et *a*   15–16 cum...salutis *om. E*   15 quisquam δ   17 sim
om. T   **84** 2 defenderis δ   2–3 iudicetur] videtur iudicetur *T*

cetur?' ego vero, iudices, non modo mihi nihil adsumo in
quo quispiam repugnet sed etiam, si quid ab omnibus con-
ceditur, id reddo ac remitto. non in ea re publica versor, 5
non iis temporibus caput meum obtuli pro patria periculis
omnibus, non aut ita sunt exstincti quos vici aut ita grati
quos servavi, ut ego mihi plus appetere coner quam quan-
85 tum omnes inimici invidique patiantur. grave esse videtur
eum qui investigarit coniurationem, qui patefecerit, qui
oppresserit, cui senatus singularibus verbis gratias egerit,
cui uni togato supplicationem decreverit, dicere in iudicio:
'non defenderem, si coniurasset.' non dico id quod grave 5
est, dico illud quod in his causis coniurationis non auctoritati adsumam, sed pudori meo: 'ego ille coniurationis investigator atque ultor certe non defenderem Sullam, si coniurasse arbitrarer.' ego, iudices, de tantis omnium periculis
cum quaererem omnia, multa audirem, crederem non om- 10
nia, caverem omnia, dico hoc quod initio dixi, nullius indicio, nullius nuntio, nullius suspicione, nullius litteris de P.
Sulla rem ullam ad me esse delatam.

XXI 86   Quam ob rem vos, di patrii ac penates, qui huic urbi atque huic rei publicae praesidetis, qui hoc imperium, qui
hanc libertatem, qui populum Romanum, qui haec tecta
atque templa me consule vestro numine auxilioque servas-
tis, testor integro me animo ac libero P. Sullae causam de- 5
fendere, nullum a me sciente facinus occultari, nullum scelus susceptum contra salutem omnium defendi ac tegi. nihil

*TE*ω] 5 id] hic *q*   6 iis] his ω   meum caput *E*   patriae ω:
corr. Cratander   7–9 non...omnes *om.* β   8 ego] eo *T*δ   8–9
quamquam tum *TEa*   **85** 1 esse *fort. delendum esse put. Clark*   2 eum]
post grave β: *post* esse δ   4 uno *T*   9 iudices] videri *a*   10–11
multa...caverem omnia *om. T*   non crederem omnia ω   11 initio
*E*δ: in initio *T*: in iudicio β   12 nullius nuntio *om. T*ω   suspitionis
a   nullis litteris δ   12–13 de re p. sullae rem δ   **86** 1 patri
T   2 rei publicae] imperio *q*   praesidens *a*   3 qui populum
Romanum *TEa*: populi (populo *K*) Romani β: populumque Romanum
q   4 nomine *T*: munimime *P*: munimine *Ka*   auxilio *a*   6 scien-
tem facilius *a*

de hoc consul comperi, nihil suspicatus sum, nihil audivi.
87 itaque idem ego ille qui vehemens in alios, qui inexorabilis
in ceteros esse visus sum, persolvi patriae quod debui: relicua iam a me meae perpetuae consuetudini naturaeque de-
bentur. tam sum misericors, iudices, quam vos, tam mitis
quam qui lenissimus. in quo vehemens fui vobiscum nihil 5
feci nisi coactus, rei publicae praecipitanti subveni, patriam demersam extuli: misericordia civium adducti tum
fuimus tam vehementes quam necesse fuit. salus esset
amissa omnium una nocte, nisi esset severitas illa sus-
cepta. sed ut ad sceleratorum poenam amore rei publicae 10
sum adductus, sic ad salutem innocentium voluntate deducor.
88 Nihil video esse in hoc P. Sulla, iudices, odio dignum,
mïsericordia digna multa. neque enim nunc propulsandae
calamitatis suae causa supplex ad vos, iudices, confugit,
sed ne qua generi ac nomini suo nota nefariae turpitudinis
inuratur. nam ipse quidem, si erit vestro iudicio liberatus, 5
quae habebit ornamenta, quae solacia relicuae vitae quibus laetari ac perfrui possit? domus erit, credo, exornata,
aperientur maiorum imagines, ipse ornatum ac vestitum
pristinum recuperabit. omnia, iudices, haec amissa sunt,
omnia generis nominis honoris insignia atque ornamenta 10
unius iudici calamitate occiderunt. sed ne exstinctor patriae, ne proditor, ne hostis appelletur, ne hanc labem tanti
sceleris in familia relinquat, id laborat, id metuit, ne denique hic miser coniurati et conscelerati et proditoris filius
nominetur. huic puero qui est ei vita sua multo carior me- 15
tuit, cui honoris integros fructus non sit traditurus, ne ae-
89 ternam memoriam dedecoris relinquat. hic vos orat, iudi-

TEω] **87** 1 ego idem *q*   4 quas vos *T*   7 tum] tunc ω   9 omnium amissa ω   11 sic] si *T*   **88** 4 ne qua *Tq*: qua *E*: neque
β*a*   6 habebit *Pluygers*: habet ω   reliqua *E*   7 ac] et δ   9
pristinum *om. Tω*   recuperavit *T*   12 ne hostis] ut hostis *T*   ap-
pelleretur δ   13 sceleris] generis ω   13–16 ne…metuit *om.*
ω   16 honores *q*   **89** 1 hoc *T*

ces, parvus, ut se aliquando si non integra fortuna, at ut
adflicta patri suo gratulari sinatis. huic misero notiora sunt
itinera iudiciorum et fori quam campi et disciplinarum.
non iam de vita P. Sullae, iudices, sed de sepultura conten- 5
ditur: vita erepta est superiore iudicio, nunc ne corpus eiciatur laboramus. quid enim est huic relicui quod eum in
hac vita teneat, aut quid est quam ob rem haec cuiquam
XXII vita videatur? nuper is homo fuit in civitate P. Sulla ut
nemo ei se neque honore neque gratia neque fortunis ante- 10
ferret: nunc spoliatus omni dignitate quae erepta sunt non
repetit. quod fortuna in malis relicui fecit, ut cum parente,
cum liberis, cum fratre, cum his necessariis lugere suam
calamitatem liceat, id sibi ne eripiatis vos, iudices, obtestatur. 15

90 Te ipsum iam, Torquate, expletum huius miseriis esse
par erat et, si nihil aliud Sullae nisi consulatum abstulissetis, tamen eo vos contentos esse oportebat; honoris enim
contentio vos ad causam, non inimicitiae deduxerunt. sed
cum huic omnia cum honore detracta sint, cum in hac for- 5
tuna miserrima ac luctuosissima destitutus sit, quid est quod
expetas amplius? lucisne hanc usuram eripere vis plenam
lacrimarum atque maeroris, in qua cum maximo cruciatu
ac dolore retinetur? libenter reddiderit adempta ignominia foedissimi criminis. an vero inimicum ut expellas? 10
cuius ex miseriis, si esses crudelissimus, videndo fructum
caperes maiorem quam audiendo.

91 O miserum et infelicem illum diem quo consul omnibus
centuriis P. Sulla renuntiatus est, o falsam spem, o volu-

*TE*ω] 2 parvus] patruus δ   at *om.* δ   3 afflicto *E*   4 iudiciorum itinera ω   campi et *E*: et *T*: *om.* ω   8 vita hac δ   teneatur
Ka   est *om. a*   13 lugere] iungere *q*   **90** 1 esse *om. q*   2 par
erat] pateat δ   3 contentos vos *E*β   esse *om. a*   5 omnia *om.*
a   sunt *T*β   6 misera ω   sit] est *E*   7 expectas *T*δ: expectes
β   9 ac] atque (et *P*) ω   12 maiorem caperes *E*   **91** 1 0...diem
Schol.   et *om. Schol.*

crem fortunam, o caecam cupiditatem, o praeposteram
gratulationem! quam cito illa omnia ex laetitia et voluptate
ad luctum et lacrimas recciderunt, ut qui paulo ante consul 5
designatus fuisset repente nullum vestigium retineret pristinae dignitatis! quid enim erat mali quod huic spoliato fama
honore fortunis deesse videretur? aut cui novae calamitati
locus ullus relictus [esset]? urget eadem fortuna quae coepit,
repperit novum maerorem, non patitur hominem calamito- 10
sum uno malo adflictum uno in luctu perire.

XXXIII 92   Sed iam impedior egomet, iudices, dolore animi ne de
huius miseria plura dicam. vestrae sunt iam partes, iudices, in vestra mansuetudine atque humanitate causam totam repono. vos reiectione interposita nihil suspicantibus
nobis repentini in nos iudices consedistis, ab accusatoribus 5
delecti ad spem acerbitatis, a fortuna nobis ad praesidium
innocentiae constituti. ut ego quid de me populus Romanus existimaret, quia severus in improbos fueram, labo-
ravi, et quae prima innocentis mihi defensio est oblata suscepi, sic vos severitatem iudiciorum, quae per hos menses 10
in homines audacissimos facta sunt, lenitate ac misericor-
93 dia mitigate. hoc cum a vobis impetrare causa ipsa debet,
tum est vestri animi atque virtutis declarare non esse eos
vos ad quos potissimum interposita reiectione devenire convenerit. in quo ego vos, iudices, quantum meus in vos amor
postulat, tantum hortor ut communi studio, quoniam in re 5
publica coniuncti sumus, mansuetudine et misericordia vestra falsam a nobis crudelitatis famam repellamus.

TEω] 4 illa *Eq*: sylla *T*: illi β*a*   et] ex *T*β   5–6 ante eos desig-
natos *a*   6 retineret repente (repente *om. a*) nullum vestigium δ:
retineret nullum repente suffragium β   7–8 honore fama δ   9 esset
ω: est *b*¹: *del. Clark*: esse *cod. H. Stephani*   ceperat β: ceperit *a*   10
reoperit *T*   memorem *a*   11 malo] modo δ   **92** 2 iam sunt
δ   4 reperio ω   4–6 vos…acerbitatis *Schol.*   4 vos *Schol.*: vos ex
TE: vos et ω   6 dilecti *q*   7 destituti *E*   11 sunt] est ω   **93** 1
impetrare a vobis ipsa causa ω   4 qua *q*   iudices (video *a*) vos ω
amor in vos (nos *K*) ω   6–7 vestra] nostra *Gdk*

COMMENTARY

§1 EXORDIVM

Cicero laments Sulla's cruel fate in being deprived of the consulship in 66 and now, despite subsequent good behaviour, in having to face the spite of his jealous rivals a second time. However, he is pleased at having an opportunity to demonstrate his own natural compassion in place of the firmness which was required of him when the state was in danger.

At *de Orat.* 2.318 it is recommended that the *exordium* be drawn *ex ipsis visceribus causae*, and this *exordium* accordingly provides a quick review of virtually all the main themes of the speech: Sulla's humility after his conviction in 66, Autronius' criminality, the persistent persecution of Sulla by his jealous enemies, Cicero's merciful nature, the contrast of *boni* with *improbi* and the recent deliverance of the state from danger. The comprehensiveness of the *exordium* might suggest that this was the last part of the speech to be written prior to delivery. At *de Orat.* 2.315 the speaker Antonius is made to recommend that the *exordium* be written last, and this may have been Cicero's normal procedure; it was a practice which was later to incur Quintilian's disapproval (*Inst.* 3.9.8–9).

Cicero at *Inv.* 1.20–21 distinguishes five different *genera causarum* and outlines the *exordium* appropriate to each. *Pro Sulla* most nearly matches the *admirabile* (παράδοξον) or 'strange' case (*Rhet. Her.* 1.5 (*turpe*); Quint. *Inst.* 4.1.40–41), one where the sympathies of the audience have been alienated, leaving a prejudice which the orator is required to overcome: the case was *admirabile* in that it was 'strange' that anyone (particularly Cicero) should defend a suspected Catilinarian. In 'strange' cases two types of *exordium* are possible, the *principium* (προοίμιον) or the more cautious *insinuatio* (ἔφοδος). For *pro Sulla*, Cicero chooses the *principium*, which is permissible in 'strange' cases where the jury is not totally hostile (*Inv.* 1.21). The aim of the *principium*, as of other types of *exordium*, is to render the jury *benevoli*, *attenti* and *dociles* (*Inv.* 1.20; *Rhet. Her.* 1.6; Quint. *Inst.* 4.1.5). Attentiveness and receptiveness are achieved here by the attention which Cicero draws to Sulla's former standing and spectacular

125

downfall (cf. *Inv.* 1.23; *Rhet. Her.* 1.7; *Part.* 28–30). *Benevolentia*, on the other hand, may be won from four quarters: from one's own side, from the opposition, from the jury and from the case itself (*Inv.* 1.22; *Rhet. Her.* 1.8; *de Orat.* 2.321). In this *exordium* Cicero draws on the first two of these sources by evoking pity for Sulla's tragic fate, by referring to his own feelings and character, and by criticising obliquely the motives and methods of the opposition.

Thus in this *exordium* Cicero follows rhetorical precept where content is concerned. As regards style, his recommendation is that the *exordium* should contain *splendoris et festivitatis et concinnitudinis minimum* (*Inv.* 1.25; cf. *Rhet. Her.* 1.11; Quint. *Inst.* 4.1.54–60). Stylistic brilliance in the *exordium* was to be avoided because it gave the impression of studied preparation: as Neumeister has emphasised (130–55), it was prudent for the forensic orator to conceal his rhetorical virtuosity. The *exordium* of *pro Sulla* does indeed avoid *splendor* and *festivitas*, but its careful balance and complex subordination are signs of *concinnitudo*. The *exordia* of some of Cicero's other speeches of the period, however, defy rhetorical precept more conspicuously. *Pro Rabirio* (63) and *pro Murena* (63), for example, both open with passionate invocations of the gods (in the latter case in imitation of Demosthenes, *de Corona*), while the *exordium* of *pro Archia* (62) is arranged in an antithetical pattern of an intricacy unparalleled in Cicero's speeches.

A shortening of the *exordium* is evident in the speeches of these years, and may be a consequence of Cicero's rise to fame. The rhetorical handbooks are unenlightening on the question of length, merely stating that the *exordium* should not be over-long, but in proportion to the rest of the speech (*Inv.* 1.26; *Rhet. Her.* 1.11; *de Orat.* 2.320; Quint. *Inst.* 4.1.35, 4.1.62; brevity is not regarded as a fault). In Cicero's earliest speeches, such as *pro Roscio Amerino* (80), the *exordium* tends to be lengthy. The *exordium* of *pro Sulla*, on the other hand, consists of only one section (as Minos first pointed out: §2 is a link passage, introducing the digression which follows it), and thus is even shorter than that of *pro Murena*, which strictly speaking comprises only the first one and a half sections of that speech. Presumably in 63–62, at the height of his fame and *auctoritas*, Cicero had less need to render his audiences *attenti* and *dociles* with lengthy *exordia*: they would automatically be attentive and receptive simply because he was Cicero.

On the *exordium* in an ancient speech see Arist. *Rh.* 3.14; [Arist.] *Rh. Al.* 36 (1443 b 23ff.), with 29, 36 (1441 b 30ff.); *Inv.* 1.20–26; *Rhet. Her.* 1.4, 1.5–11; *de Orat.* 2.315–25; *Part.* 28–30; *Orat.* 50, 122, 124; Quint. *Inst.* 3.9.8–9, 4.1.1–79, 10.7.30. For modern accounts see Lausberg 150–63; Martin 60–75; Rohde 9–26; Laurand 319–23; and on Cicero's *exordia*, P.

Prill, *Rhetorica* 4 (1986) 93–109. Douglas discusses the opening sections of *pro Sulla* at *Roman Oratory* 348–50.

I 1.1 Maxime vellem, iudices 'I should have wished...' is one of the standard openings of ancient oratory, and is illustrated as such by Demosthenes at *prooem.* 16, 32 (cf. 14, 33, 45). It is used most notably at Is. 10.1; Antiph. 5.1; Antisth. *Aj.* 1; Lucil. 26–7; D.H. 7.48.1; *id. Is.* 8, 10; *id. Dem.* 3; Cic. *Phil.* 9.1; Sal. *Hist.* 1.77.1; *B. Afr.* 54.2–3 (modelled on our passage?); Fro. *Ant.* 3.1 (162 Van den Hout); cf. F. Marx on Lucil. 26; Weische 75, 147, 155, 168f. In Cicero's time the opening had become somewhat hackneyed, as is implied by his mockery of Q. Caecilius Niger for supposing that the expression *'vellem, si fieri potuisset, iudices'* will alone be sufficient to prepare him for Verres' prosecution (*Div.Caec.* 43).

P. Sulla as a general rule, Sulla is referred to by *praenomen* and *cognomen* in passages where his importance and standing are especially felt; elsewhere, such as in passages of argumentation, or where the name is frequently repeated, the *cognomen* alone is used. Autronius and Catiline are nowhere in the speech dignified by the addition of the *praenomen*. On naming conventions see *RE* xvi.1648.35ff.; H. L. Axtell, *CP* 10 (1915) 386–404; J. N. Adams, *CQ* n.s. 28 (1978) 145–66; Syme, *AA* 391; Shackleton Bailey, *Onomasticon* 3–8.

dignitatis...splendorem *dignitas* denotes the standing conferred by office, and, by extension, the office itself (*TLL* v.1.1138.38ff.). The office forfeited by Sulla was the consulship of 65: as a result of his *ambitus* conviction in 66, he was permanently debarred from the senate and from public office, and was required to pay a fine (17.8n.). *splendor* denotes 'spotlessness', as at *Clu.* 46; *Planc.* 30; *Rep.* 2.69; cf. Nettleship 588. Contrast §73, where the meaning is 'magnificence'.

1.2 obtinere *obtineret* (ω) has been caused by the expectation of a subjunctive after *ut*. For other places where the MSS read the imperfect subjunctive for the infinitive see *Quinct.* 31, 82, 83.

et...potuisset cf. *Arch.* 9 *Gabini, quam diu incolumis fuit, levitas, post damnationem calamitas.* W. G. Pluygers (anticipated by Sylvius) conjectured *aut...aut* for *et...et* on the grounds that it would have been impossible, logically speaking, for Sulla both to have kept his office and to have reaped the fruits of modesty after his conviction (*Mnemosyne* 9 (1881) 136). But this is over-literal. Cicero is aiming to arouse pity for his client: *et...et* serves to give an impression of an accumulation of misfortunes. Sulla's behaviour after his conviction is described in words with agricultural associations (*calamitatem* ('blight'), *fructum...percipere* ('reap'); cf. *Arch.* 23 *gloriae fructum...percipi*), contrasting with *dignitatis suae splendorem* above. These imply arbitrary misfortune (*calamitatem*), lowliness (hence *modestia*), remote seclusion (absence from Rome and the forum: Sulla retired to Naples, §§ 17, 53) etc. The primary meaning of *calamitas* is a 'disaster to crops' (*TLL* III.118.61ff.), but the word is regularly used, like the Greek συμφορά, of ruin in the courts (cf. W. Y. Fausset on *Clu.*, p. 275): *calamitas* occurs eleven times in *pro Sulla*, in all but one instance (§ 91) referring to Sulla's conviction in 66 (see also *Corn.* ap. Asc. 75 C). On Latin words of agricultural origin see J. Marouzeau, *Quelques aspects de la formation du latin littéraire* (Paris 1949) 7–25 (also *id.*, *Récréations latines* (Toulouse and Paris 1940) 87–91); L. R. Palmer, *The Latin Language* (London 1954) 69–72. Despite Clark and Kasten, the reading of *E* at *percipere potuisset* is unknown; see my note at *CQ* n.s. 39 (1989) 402.

1.3 sed quoniam *sed... everteretur* is quoted by Grillius (22, = 605 Halm; = 93 Martin) as an example of Cicero's recommendation at *Inv.* 1.22 that *benevolentia* be secured through reference to misfortunes suffered.

1.4 tulit casus infestus Sulla's downfall is attributed not to his own malpractices but to chance (73.4n.). For *ferre* used after fortune etc. see *TLL* III.579.30ff.; *OLD* s.v. 30b.

et amplissimo honore '(Sulla) both (was turned out of) the highest office...'. For the omission of *et* (provided by *V Grillius*) in *Tω* cf. *Har.* 2 *et (om.* Brussels 5345 and *E) ex consurrectione... et ex comitatu...* The MSS add *in* before (*V*) or after (*Tω*) *amplissimo*, but the resulting construction (*in amplissimo honore... everteretur*) is too awkward. The text quoted by Grillius presents no difficulty (an ablative, without *ex*, is normal after *evertere*: see *TLL* v.2.1028.59ff.). *in* perhaps entered the MSS through the influence of *et in his... reliquiis* below.

cum... odio two charitable reasons for Sulla's downfall in 66; Cicero succeeds in avoiding mention of Sulla's crime while nevertheless commenting unfavourably on Autronius. *ambitio* in Cicero is virtually always neutral, indicating simply 'political competition', with no pejorative nuance (*Sul.* 11; *de Orat.* 1.1; *Phil.* 5.47; cf. Hellegouarc'h 209f.). Cicero implies that the *ambitiosus* regularly attracts *invidia* from those who are less successful, but that this is one of the hazards of a political career (cf. § 73 *accepit... vulnus... eius modi quod videretur huius vita et natura accipere potuisse*). The second reason for Sulla's downfall, the unpopularity of Autronius (*tum... odio*), is given greater weight than the first. Here, as often in Cicero (e.g. §§ 12, 47, 66, 78, 93), '*cum* introduces the general statement and *tum* the particular application, on which the main stress is laid' (R. G. Nisbet on *Dom.* 1); cf. H.-Sz.625f.

1.7 supplicio *supplicium* denotes a severe penalty, most often execution: see Nettleship 592f.; Greenidge 298f. At *Mil.* 5 it is used of exile. Used here of Sulla's comparatively mild penalty (1.1n.), it is clearly an exaggeration intended to suggest that Sulla has already been punished enough.

1.8 huius i.e. Sulla.

1.9 magnam...capio for a different reaction to Sulla's conviction cf. *Corn.* ap. Asc. 75 C *ut spectaculum illud re et tempore salubre ac
necessarium, genere ⟨et⟩ exemplo miserum ac funestum videremus.* On the meaning of *molestia* ('(mental) distress') see T. E. Kinsey on *Quinct.* 44. For
animo capere cf. *Planc.* 1 *capiebam animo non mediocrem voluptatem.*

in ceteris malis viz. the unpopularity which induced Cicero to accept the case (and also, perhaps, privately, his failure to arrange a
friendship with Pompey); cf. pp. 28–30.

1.10 facile...esse cf. *Att.* 16.16c.1 *numquam putavi fore ut supplex ad
te venirem; sed hercule facile patior datum tempus in quo amorem experirer tuum.*
For *tempus* as 'opportunity' see *OLD* s.v. 9a.

boni viri in a political sense, the antithesis of *improbi ac perditi cives*
below (1.12n.). (The order *bonus vir* is much less common than *vir bonus*,
but not unusual.) The *boni* (*omnes boni, consensus omnium bonorum*) have
been defined as 'the supporters and defenders of what Cicero regarded
or interpreted as *populi Romani libertas, senatus auctoritas, hic rei publicae
status, cum dignitate otium* and the like' (C. Wirzubski, *JRS* 51 (1961) 13f.).
For Cicero in 62 the factor which in practical terms determined whether
a man was a *bonus* or its opposite (*improbus, perditus, audax*) was his attitude towards the Catilinarian conspiracy and the actions by which it was
suppressed. The frequency with which the *boni* are referred to in *pro Sulla*
reflects the uncertainty of Cicero's position in the aftermath of the
conspiracy, and his need to retain public support for his actions (cf. pp.
27f). Cicero's political outlook is expounded at length at *Sest.* 96–143.
There the *boni* of every class are seen as *optimates* who aspire to *cum dignitate otium,* i.e. domestic peace and tranquillity with appropriate individual and communal honour, the traditional form of republican senatorial government. See H. Strasburger, *Concordia Ordinum* (Borna-
Leipzig 1931); C. Wirzubski, *JRS* 44 (1954) 1–13; J. P. V. D. Balsdon,
CQ n.s. 10 (1960) 43–50; M. Fuhrmann, *Gymnasium* 67 (1960) 481–500; C.
Wirzubski, *JRS* 51 (1961) 12–22; W. K. Lacey, *CQ* n.s. 12 (1962) 67–71;
id., *G&R* 17 (1970) 3–16; G. Achard, *LEC* 41 (1973) 207–21; Achard, esp.
72–142; J. Christes, *Gymnasium* 95 (1988) 303–15; Mitchell 11.9–62.

lenitatem meam misericordiamque another theme of the speech
(cf. §§8, 18, 20, 47, 87, 92–3), used to account for Cicero's defence of
Sulla, and to counteract allegations of *crudelitas* (7.10n.) and *regnum*
(21.1n.) in his execution of the conspirators. Cicero's merciful disposition
is regularly referred to in related speeches (e.g. *Cat.* 1.16, 2.6, 2.27–8,
4.11–13; *Mur.* 6 (quoted at 8.4n.), 9), and the theme is picked up at *Dom.*

94, where Cicero claims that he is now seen *non ut crudelem tyrannum, sed ut mitissimum parentem*. Later in 44 he remarked to Antony that severity had never been part of his nature except in so far as the national interest demanded it (*Att.* 14.13B.3). Plutarch makes much of Cicero's mild disposition: ἐπιείκεια is central to his portrait (esp. *Cic.* 19.4–5). See further H. Pétré, *REL* 12 (1934) 376–89; Desmouliez 104f.; May 70f.; below, p. 305.

1.12   intermissam cf. *Fam.* 3.1.1 *intermissa nostra consuetudine.* Cicero's *lenitas* has been interrupted because of the execution of the conspirators in December 63, and the trials of 62 in which he gave decisive evidence for the prosecution.

agnoscerent *agnoscant* (and *fateantur* for *faterentur* below) would be expected after *patior*, but the tenses have been determined instead by *oblatum... esse*, which, although a true perfect rather than an aorist, may sometimes take historic sequence; cf. K.-S.II.179.

improbi... cives balancing *boni viri* above (the link is made by adversative asyndeton; β interpolates *vero* after *improbi*). *improbi* and *perditi* (like *audaces*, 16.4n.) were the political opponents of the *boni*, extreme radicals and demagogues (in the eyes of Cicero and those who shared his outlook), reckless men who disregarded law and favoured revolution: the terms do not primarily refer to moral character. For bibliography see 1.10n.

1.13   redomiti the word has been objected to on two counts: it occurs nowhere else in Latin, and the prefix *re-* has no apparent meaning (the meaning 'again', 'a second time', i.e. since the 'first conspiracy' of 66, is not appropriate). Garatoni (followed by Seyffert 39f.) advocated *re domiti* (the reading of *T*); this eliminates the *hapax legomenon*, but the expression is meaningless. Halm's *perdomiti* is no improvement either: the word does not appear in Cicero. Sylvius' *edomiti* looks at first sight more plausible (cf. *Fat.* 10 *vitiosam enim naturam ab eo sic edomitam... esse doctrina*), but *edomare* is elsewhere used of people only at Cato *orig.* 95 Peter, and there the text is doubtful. Clark simply deleted *re-* (which might have insinuated itself from *re publica* below); cf. *Rep.* 1.5 *Miltiadem victorem domitoremque Persarum*; Asc. 76 C (perhaps reflecting Cicero's wording) *plebem ex Maniliana offensione victam et domitam esse dicit.* The objections to *redomiti*, however, do not justify emendation. Cicero has many words which are *hapax legomena* at least in classical Latin, two of them occurring in this speech (*immoderatio* (§ 30), *adlevamentum* (§ 66); cf. *propulsatio* (§ 2), *incensio* (§ 33)): for a list see F. Ellendt on *de Orat.* 2.94. Moreover, *re-* frequently occurs in poetry without semantic force for the sake of the metre (see Schoenwitz 45–51); in the heightened style of the present context *redomiti* instead of the more prosaic *domiti* might not be out of place. *redomiti* is additionally supported by usages such as *redeo*, 'turn' (35.5n.); cf. H. D. Jocelyn, *YCS* 21 (1969) 117 n. 102.

victi Reid 'corrects' *victi* to *revicti* (as *b²*; *revincere* is attested elsewhere in Cicero only at *Arch.* 11) on grounds of rhythm. But the change in fact creates a hexameter ending (11.1n.); moreover, Cicero's practice is to write *atque* before a consonant only where it provides a more favoured rhythm (pp. 53f.).

praecipitante re publica cf. *Sul.* 87 *rei publicae praecipitanti subveni*; *Sest.* 25 *praecipitanti patriae non subvenirent. praecipitante* is intransitive (= *ruente*), 'rushing headlong to destruction' when Catiline was at large; cf. *TLL* x.2.465.49ff.

§§2–10 DIGRESSIO I

Torquatus has attempted to undermine Cicero's auctoritas by criticising his acceptance of the case; Cicero will therefore defend Sulla by defending himself. Torquatus is wrong, he argues, to make a distinction between Cicero's position and that of Hortensius and the consulars: the consulars and he together rightly refused to support those who had conspired against the state. Torquatus should not be surprised to find Cicero on the side of the consulars: he is not, after all, any more cruel than they. Cicero, the consulars and all boni *share a common cause, and if Cicero's behaviour is consistent with theirs, then he is wrongly accused of inconsistency in the present trial. Torquatus has compelled him to bring his* auctoritas *to bear, but he will use it sparingly.*

On the place of the digressions within the structure of the speech see pp. 44f.

'In *Pro Caelio* and *Pro Sulla* much is gained, by digression and return' (Douglas 15). Digressions in Cicero are common, and can occur anywhere within the speech (*de Orat.* 2.312); here he digresses immediately after the *exordium*, as also in *in Verrem* 2 (2–10, praise of the Sicilians), *pro Murena* (2–10, justification of Cicero's acceptance of the case), *de Domo sua* (3–31, a defence of Cicero's political actions) and *pro Milone* (7–22, *praeiudicia*; cf. Quint. *Inst.* 4.3.17, 6.5.10). The early digression in *pro Sulla* is necessitated by the need for Cicero to defend himself against the charge of inconsistency before advancing any other arguments: his *auctoritas* had been called into question, and needed to be reasserted at once (§§ 2, 35). The first third of the speech (§§ 2–35, excluding the *partitio*) is therefore devoted to a rebuttal of Torquatus' criticisms. This was crucial to the defence: without it Sulla might conceivably have been convicted.

The rhetoricians have relatively little to say about the *digressio* and do not class it as one of the fixed and necessary parts of the speech: *nobis autem non placuit hanc partem in numerum reponi (Inv.* 1.97). Where they do discuss *digressio,* they generally have in mind passages of amplification or literary embellishment such as the account of the rape of Proserpine at *Ver.* 4.106–8, the description of Syracuse at *Ver.* 4.117–9 or the encomium of civil law at *Caec.* 70–75. This type of *digressio* was an opportunity for the orator to show off his talents, and came to be favoured especially in declamation (cf. Quint. *Inst.* 4.3.2). Digressions of the type found in *pro Sulla* and regularly throughout Cicero's speeches (for example in *pro Sestio*) attract less attention, for two reasons. First, rules cannot be given for their use, since these digressions generally spring from the particular circumstances of each case, which cannot be predicted. Secondly, the Romans had a wider view of what was relevant in a court of law than we do, and therefore would not have regarded digression as such a prominent feature of their forensic oratory. However, Quintilian shows an awareness of a type of digression distinct from literary embellishment when he describes the digression as an *utilis ante quaestionem praeparatio* to be used when one's case initially appears unfavourable *(Inst.* 4.3.9–11); this is exactly the situation in *pro Sulla.* Elsewhere he describes the digression *in causa* as an *adiutorium vel ornamentum* of the passage from which digression is made *(Inst.* 3.9.4); here again he seems to recognise a second type of digression distinct from the *ornamentum* and more directly linked to the requirements of the case. Quintilian, therefore, does allow that there may be digressions which are not of the ornamental kind, but which consist of passages which, although 'irrelevant' to the charge, nevertheless usefully serve the orator's interests. Moreover, Cicero himself evidently regarded *Sul.* 2–35 (excluding the *partitio*) as digressive since at both the beginning and the end of this passage (§§ 2, 35) he provides a justification for its inclusion.

The charge of inconsistency was one faced by Cicero only the previous year in his defence of Murena: Cicero had himself been the author of the *lex Tullia de ambitu,* under which Murena was indicted. It is not surprising, therefore, to discover a closely similar approach being adopted in both speeches, especially as regards digression. Cicero begins his defence of Murena, like that of Sulla, with a brief *exordium* followed immediately by a digressive justification of his acceptance of the case and an open admission that he intends this justification to enable him to speak *maiore auctoritate (Mur.* 2). Moreover, in both speeches Cicero uses the same technique to effect the transition from *exordium* to *digressio*: a link passage (the second half of *Mur.* 2, the whole of *Sul.* 2) beginning in both cases *Et quoniam* announces the digression and its necessity, and shortly afterwards the argumentation begins with *Et primum (Mur.)* / *Ac primum (Sul.).* Both of these link passages conclude with general statements of Cicero's aim, giving an air of finality which obscures the fact that Cicero has already entered upon his digression. I have chosen (perhaps somewhat arbitrarily) to class these link passages as digression. Although their style may resemble the longer periods of the *exordia*, their content and function place them firmly within what follows, while they would not of course be required at all were it not for the digressions which they introduce.

For the rhetorical writers on digression see *Inv.* 1.97; *de Orat.* 2.80, 2.311–2; *Part.* 128; *Brut.* 82; Quint. *Inst.* 3.9.1, 3.9.4, 4.3.1–17. Greek theory on the removal of prejudice is also instructive: Arist. *Rh.* 3.15; [Arist.] *Rh. Al.* 36 (1442 a 21ff.). For modern accounts of *digressio* see Lausberg 187f.; Martin 89–91; M. Heath, *Unity in Greek Poetics* (Oxford 1989) 90–101; and on digression in Cicero, H. V. Canter, *AJP* 52 (1931) 351–61 (provides a list); J. C. Davies, *Latomus* 27 (1968) 894–903 (republished under altered title at *RhM* 131 (1988) 305–15); Michel 400–3.

2.1 Et quoniam continues from *sed quoniam* above. The subtle entry into digression is typical; cf. H. V. Canter, *AJP* 52 (1931) 360f. §2 is programmatic, explaining the relevance of the digression to come.

meus…necessarius *meus* is emphatic (2.7n.). *Familiaritas* and *necessitudo* are both types of *amicitia* (48.4n.) implying a quasi-familial relationship. The terms *familiaris* and *necessarius* are often paired (as at *Rab. Post.* 32; *Phil.* 2.3, 11.32; *Fam.* 13.12.1, 13.15.1, 13.26.2), but they are not quite identical in meaning: with *familiaris* the emphasis is on proximity and the frequency and regularity of social relations, but the idea behind *necessarius* is that of the bonds of obligation towards family, friends and colleagues (highly appropriate in this context). See Hellegouarc'h 68–76; R. J. Rowland, *CJ* 65 (1969–70) 193–8; David 195–211. Torquatus had accused Cicero of violating their friendship in defending Sulla; Cicero here acknowledges the intimacy and ties between Torquatus and himself, but will reserve a full answer to Torquatus' complaint until §§48–50. It was not unusual for Cicero to appear for the defence when a friend was prosecuting: Brunt (375 n. 80) cites eleven instances (cf. Rohde 19). On the techniques which could be used in such circumstances see C. P. Craig, *TAPA* 111 (1981) 31–7.

2.2 necessitudinem familiaritatemque cf. *Mur.* 7 *me familiaritatis necessitudinisque oblitum causam L. Murenae contra se defendere*; *Deiot.* 39; *Fam.* 13.31.2, 13.44, 13.70, 13.74. The order *familiaris ac necessarius… necessitudinem familiaritatemque* is not a rhetorical figure but the natural order. Leeman (22) has pointed out that in Greek and Latin it is the order A B A B which is artificial and rhetorical: the order A B B A was not thought worthy of comment until the second century AD at the earliest ([Hermog.] *Inv.* 4.3; Sch. Isoc. 12.47), when it was termed 'chiasmus'.

2.3 violasset Torquatus of course maintained that it was Cicero who had violated their friendship, not himself (§48).

auctoritate meae defensionis *auctoritas* (the word is derived from *auctor*) was the influence which belonged to the senate and its most prominent members (*principes*): the possession of *auctoritas* ensured that the opinions of the possessor would carry weight and win acceptance (cf. Tac. *Germ.* 11.2, on German chiefs at assemblies, seen through Roman eyes: *prout aetas cuique, prout nobilitas, prout decus bellorum, prout facundia est, audiuntur auctoritate suadendi magis quam iubendi potestate*). *Auctoritas* was obviously invaluable in oratory: cf. for instance *Brut.* 111 *in Scauri oratione . . . gravitas summa et naturalis quaedam inerat auctoritas, non ut causam, sed ut testimonium dicere putares, cum pro reo diceret*; Quint. *Inst.* 5.13.52; *id. Inst.* 10.1.111 *tanta auctoritas inest ut dissentire pudeat, nec advocati studium sed testis aut iudicis adferat fidem* (the last two passages both refer to Cicero). Sulla's defence relied above all on the *auctoritas* of Cicero, who had a unique knowledge of the Catilinarian conspiracy; Torquatus had attempted to undermine this *auctoritas*, so Cicero will now assert it by justifying his actions (the point is repeated at §35). On the role of *auctoritas* in Sulla's trial see further A. Thierfelder, *Gymnasium* 72 (1965) 395f.; Kennedy 188f.; May 69–79; below, pp. 293f.

2.4 huius periculi 'of the danger to him'. *periculum* often denotes the danger incurred in criminal trials (*OLD* s.v. 3).

2.5 propulsatione 'the action of warding off or repelling' (*OLD* s.v.). Many words in *-io* (*immoderatio* (§30); *incensio* (§33)) appear first or exclusively in Cicero, and may be coinages; Nägelsbach 235–9 gives a list. *propulsatio* is found elsewhere only at Gel. 6.3.15 (*propulsare* and *propellere* are of course common). See 1.13n. on *hapax legomena*.

offici mei Cicero's 'duty' to bring aid to Sulla in satisfaction of the claims of *amicitia*, a thoroughly Roman concept; cf. E. Bernert, *De vi atque usu vocabuli officii* (Breslau 1930); Hellegouarc'h 152–63.

quo . . . orationis echoing Demosthenes' justification of digression at 18.9 (cf. 35.8n., where passage quoted); for similar apologies see *Clu.* 10; *Rab. Perd.* 1; *Sest.* 31; *Planc.* 3. *T*δ give *non uterer orationis*, and *V*β *orationis non uterer*. Pabón argues (8) that *ñuterer* might have been omitted and later re-inserted, in which case its omission would be more understandable after *genere* than after *orationis*. Or, on the other hand, *V*β may each have altered the word order to avoid hyperbaton. Both these explanations would suggest that *non uterer orationis* was the original reading.

2.7 multis . . . dabitur cf. *Clu.* 10 *tamen multae mihi ad satis faciendum reliquo tempore facultates dabuntur*. *TV*ω each put *mihi* in a different position:

presumably the word was mistakenly omitted and subsequently added in the margin, remaining in the margin in the exemplar of *Tω*. The orders of ω (*enim mihi*) and *V* (*data mihi*) are each preferable to that of *T* (*locis mihi*) given that in Latin, as in other languages of Indo-European origin, unstressed pronouns, and enclitics in general, tend to occupy the second place in their clause; cf. J. Wackernagel, *IF* 1 (1892) 333–436 (= *Kleine Schriften* 1 (Göttingen 1953) 1–104); E. Fraenkel, *NGG* (1933) 319–54 (= *Kleine Beiträge zur klassischen Philologie* (Rome 1964) 1.93–130). The omission of *mihi* is most easily explained if the word was originally placed after *enim*, with both words abbreviated (thus Kasten viii); my choice is therefore *multis enim mihi locis* (ω). For *locis* as 'occasions' see *OLD* s.v. 21a (cf. §77).

2.8 laude 'laudable achievements'; cf. Hellegouarc'h 365–9.

ut ille vidit *ut* looks forward to *sic* (and *ille* back to *L. Torquatus* above). δ substitutes *iudices* for *vidit*, a common error caused by the similarity of the abbreviations *uid* and *iud*; some descendants of φ then interpolate *speravit, putavit* or *putat* after *deminuturum* to complete the sense. Similar corruptions have occurred below at §§13, 73, 78, 79, 80, 83 (in each case *iudices*] *videlicet a*); 21 (*videlicet*] *iudices Tω*); 39 (*videlicet*] *iudices q*); 41 (*iudices q: vidi Tβa*: om. *V*); 69 (*iudices βq: videlicet a*: om. *T*); 76 (*iudices*] *videte* β); 85 (*iudices*] *videri a*); and 93 (*iudices*] *video a*).

2.9 de mea auctoritate deripuisset cf. *de auctoritate...detrahere* above; *Fin.* 1.43 *terroribus cupiditatibusque detractis et omnium falsarum opinionum temeritate derepta*. *deripere* is a stronger word than *detrahere*, and carries the idea of stripping a garment from a person (downwards); for the metaphorical use of these terms see Nägelsbach 584.

2.10 sic hoc ego sentio *sic* responds to *ut* above; *hoc* (omitted in *V*) serves to indicate that *sic* is not to be taken with *ego sentio*. The antithetical structure of the end of this section resembles the structure of the ending of §1.

2.11 mei facti...defensionis Cicero's theme during the first third of the speech (§§1–35). The phrase *mei facti rationem* shows Cicero's defence to have been an *officium*: cf. *Fin.* 3.58 *est autem officium quod ita factum est ut eius facti probabilis ratio reddi possit*; *Off.* 1.8 *medium autem officium...quod cur factum sit ratio probabilis reddi possit*.

2.12 probaro...probaturum cf. *Sest.* 87 *existimo, si Milonis causam...probaro, vos in hoc crimine parem Sesti causam existimaturos*. *probaro* (*Tδ*) is read in preference to *probavero* (*Vβ*) because it provides a double-trochee (preceded by a cretic) rather than a cretic-iambus.

3.1 Ac primum completing the transition begun at *Et quoniam*, §2; cf. *Et quoniam...Et primum* at *Mur.* 2–3, where a similar transition is made.

abs te Cicero writes *abs* only before *te* (except *Fam.* 10.34A.1 *abs tua voluntate*), and came increasingly to prefer *a te* (*abs te* does not appear at all in Cicero after 54 BC, except in the letters). See *TLL* 1.3.12ff.; Wölfflin 108; Neue–Wagener II.828–30; Parzinger 133–6.

L. Torquate Cicero turns from the jury to address Torquatus directly. Apostrophe was banned from the *exordium* by some rhetoricians (Quint. *Inst.* 4.1.63). Here it is used immediately after the *exordium*.

3.2 clarissimis...civitatis the adjective *clarissimus* is generally reserved for prominent senators, just as leading *equites* were conventionally referred to as *splendidi* (these terms were not yet the formal titles they were to become in late antiquity); cf. *TLL* III.1275.8ff.; G. Landgraf on *S. Rosc.* 140; Nicolet 213–24; R. G. M. Nisbet and M. Hubbard on Hor. *Carm.* 1.20.5; D. R. Shackleton Bailey, *Profile of Horace* (London 1982) 90. (On *splendor* see 73.3n.) Gelzer provides complete lists of all those described by Cicero as *clarissimi* (40–43) and *principes civitatis* (44f.). Cicero also sees himself as a *princeps civitatis* at *Fam.* 12.24.2 and *ad Brut.* 2.1.2.

3.3 defensionis iure cf. Quint. *Inst.* 3.6.73 *habeo ius actionis*.

secernas in the *post reditum* speeches Cicero was to use the same technique as Torquatus when he singled out Piso and Gabinius for criticism, but did not venture to attack Caesar and Pompey.

3.4 clarissimi...ornatissimi Hortensius is again spoken of with approval at §§ 4 and 12 (and is *clarissimus* (3.2n.) elsewhere at *Man.* 51, 66; *Mur.* 10; *Sest.* 3). No doubt Cicero was likewise spoken of in flattering terms by Hortensius. After the trial of Flaccus, whom Cicero and Hortensius defended in 59, Cicero told Atticus of his delight at the account Hortensius had given of his suppression of the Catilinarian conspiracy: *quam plena manu, quam ingenue, quam ornate nostras laudes in astra sustulit, cum de Flacci praetura et de illo tempore Allobrogum diceret! sic habeto, nec amantius nec honorificentius nec copiosius potuisse dici* (*Att.* 2.25.1).

3.5 non reprendatur, reprendatur meum? the repetition is unavoidable in Latin when the negative statement precedes the positive; cf. § 21 *an tum...non dicis me fuisse regem, nunc...regnare dicis?*; § 85 *non dico id quod grave est, dico illud*... See Rohde 89.

nam si est initum cf. *Mur.* 80 *inita sunt...consilia...urbis delendae, civium trucidandorum, nominis Romani exstinguendi.*

3.6 inflammandae...civitatis cf. *Sul.* 57 *qui hanc urbem inflammare vellet*; *Har.* 18 *hanc recentem urbis inflammandae delendique imperi coniurationem.* Tω invert *urbis* and *civitatis*, as L. Spengel first realised (*Philologus* 2 (1847) 297); this order must be incorrect since, although setting fire to a *civitas* metaphorically is just possible (Pabón 8 n. 1; cf. *Dom.* 129), it upsets the escalation of horror in the three cola (4.13n.). *delendae urbis* would also spoil the molossus-double-trochee rhythm at the incision before *mihine*.

The inversion was presumably caused by the similarity of *inflammandae* and *delendae*, which may have been a line apart in the exemplar of *Tω*; cf. Kasten's 1933 preface xviii; Pabón 8f., who compares §§ 76, 77. The MSS also disagree as to the position of *huius*. Given that *V*, which puts *urbis . . . civitatis* in the correct order, reads *huius urbis huius*, and that confusion over the position of *huius* is also present in *Tω*, it seems likely that the exemplar of *Tω* read *huius civitatis huius*, and that *Tω* each made a different choice as to which *huius* to omit. The archetype, then, would also have contained the double *huius*. Since the MSS cannot show whether Cicero wrote *huius urbis* or *urbis huius* (Kasten's reasoning in his 1933 preface (xviii) is unsound), the best course is simply to adopt the more usual position of the demonstrative, preceding its noun. *huius urbis* is also supported by § 19 *mihi . . . cum huius urbis . . . veniebat in mentem*.

Cicero repeatedly accuses the Catilinarians of planning fires (here the grandiose *inflammandae* and the use of imagery heighten the effect; on fire imagery see Pöschl 474f.; Fantham 7–11, 130). With flooding, fire was the greatest natural danger at Rome (cf. Z. Yavetz, *Latomus* 17 (1958) 510–17), and allegations of arson were therefore an effective means of removing popular sympathy for Catiline's cause. It is unlikely that Catiline had actually intended to burn down Rome, although he may have planned small-scale fires to cause confusion.

3.7 mihine the MSS offer *mihi* (*Tω*) or *michi me* (*V*); Halm's *mihine* is an easy change. The question is not of a type in which the interrogative particle is customarily omitted: see K.-S.II.501–3. Kasten's *mihi ⟨non⟩ne* is demonstrably wrong: it would imply that Cicero considered that Rome's fate mattered more to him than to Hortensius, a possibility rejected in the following argument (4.1n.). The position of the pronoun in this and the following clauses is emphatic (2.7n.).

3.9 gravius 'more severe' (*TLL* VI.2.2297.44ff.). Cicero would not have a more severe judgement than Hortensius of the Catilinarians' crimes.

qui adiuvandus . . . esse videatur? *qui* is sometimes written for *quis* in Cicero, e.g. *Inv.* 1.93, 97; *S. Rosc.* 2; *Clu.* 105; *Sul.* 43; *Off.* 1.144. See E. Löfstedt, *Syntactica* (Lund 1956) II.79–96. The indirect questions are dependent on *iudicium*; cf. *Clu.* 75; *Fin.* 4.13; *Tusc.* 4.57; *Off.* 1.3 *nos autem quantum in utroque profecerimus, aliorum sit iudicium*.

Cicero's partiality for the rhythmical phrase *esse videatur* was commented on in antiquity (and the expression was avoided by Sallust, Livy, Seneca and Tacitus): see Quint. *Inst.* 9.4.73 *'esse videatur', iam nimis frequens*; id. *Inst.* 10.2.18 *noveram quosdam qui se pulchre expressisse genus illud caelestis huius in dicendo viri sibi viderentur si in clausula posuissent 'esse videatur'*; Tac. *Dial.* 23.1 *'nolo inridere "rotam Fortunae" et "ius verrinum" et illud tertio*

quoque sensu in omnibus orationibus pro sententia positum "esse videatur"'. The
$- \cup \cup \cup \ - \cup$ clausula occurs in this speech with a slightly above-average
frequency: see p. 52. See further Laurand 187f.; Aili 60–62.

3.11 'ita,' inquit the first instance in *pro Sulla* of ascribed *oratio
recta*, generally used as an alternative to *oratio obliqua* to provide a stark
summary of the opposition's argument which can then be knocked down
with great effectiveness. Such a summary is often given at the *end* of a
passage of argumentation. Sometimes remarks attributed to the prosecutor can be used to form a type of *altercatio* (21.1n.) in which Cicero can
display his cleverness and frame the opposition's case in a manner allowing easy refutation. The opposition's arguments are given in *oratio
obliqua*, on the other hand, when an instantaneous refutation is for the
moment impossible (e.g. § 36). Wiesthaler (71–3) analyses the stylistic effects of *oratio obliqua* in *pro Sulla*. Cf. D. M. MacDowell on Dem. 21, p. 34.

'tu enim ... coniurationem' cf. § 85 *qui investigarit coniurationem, qui
patefecerit.*

II 4.1 quod cum dicit Cicero points out an apparent flaw in the
prosecution's reasoning: the danger to Rome did not affect him more
than Hortensius because when consul he had immediately published all
the information relating to the conspiracy (cf. §§ 40–45).

4.3 quare ista coniuratio the colometry from here until the end
of § 7 is articulated by Fraenkel (69–71).

4.5 honore ... consilio Reid distinguishes between *honore auctoritate* (public position) and *virtute consilio* (personal character); this distinction is confirmed by the break (double-trochee) after *auctoritate* (cf.
Nisbet 358).

4.6 non dubitasse quin the argument runs: 'we both have an
equal knowledge of the conspiracy; why then, when you see a man of
Hortensius' stature not hesitating to defend Sulla, do you criticise me
for defending him?' For other instances of *non dubito quin* used to mean
'I do not hesitate to' (instead of 'I do not doubt that', the more usual
meaning) cf. *Man.* 68; *Agr.* 2.69; *Mil.* 63. See K.-S.11.263–5; J. S. Reid on
Senect. 16.

innocentiam P. Sullae this, the reading of *V*, is clearly correct, especially in view of *defendi huius innocentiam* below; cf. C. A. Lehmann,
Hermes 15 (1880) 348f. *innocentem p. sillam* (ω) is probably a conjecture intended to correct an archetype reading containing *sillo* (perhaps caused
by *consilio*).

4.8 mihi interclusus *mihi* is emphatic (2.7n.). Cicero twice refers
to the *aditus* to a person being *interclusus*: *S. Rosc.* 110 (access to Sulla), *Ver.*
1.136 (to Verres); here the image is more metaphorical, as at *Fin.* 2.118
and twice at *Tusc.* 5.27.

4.9 qui H. Kraffert proposed *quia* (*Beiträge zur Kritik und Erklärung lateinischer Autoren* (Aurich 1881–3) III.117), but the indicative is permissible; cf. *Senect*. 46 *habeoque senectuti magnam gratiam, quae mihi sermonis aviditatem auxit, potionis et cibi sustulit. qui* and *quia* are easily interchanged in MSS, but nineteenth-century editors were too ready to alter either word to the other. *quia* is proposed for *qui* at §§ 39 (Madvig), 47 (Pluygers) and 69 (Reid), and *qui* for *quia* at § 50 (Ernesti); at § 47 the change actually impairs the sense.

quid...existimes Cicero knows very well what Torquatus thinks of the consulars who are supporting Sulla (§§ 81–2). Cicero's first argument was that the prosecution are inconsistent in criticising him but not Hortensius; now he begins his second argument (*quaero illud etiam...*), that the prosecution are similarly inconsistent in criticising him but not the consulars. This argument has two parts: (i) the consulars and he are defending Sulla equally, and (ii) it would have been improper of him not to have joined with the consulars. The conclusion, reached at the end of § 5, is that the position of Cicero and the consulars is identical (*par atque unum*).

4.10 summis...civibus cf. *Cat*. 1.29; *Cael*. 43, 73. Cicero is thinking of those who have attained high office; on *clarissimi* see 3.2n.

4.12 non...defensionis Cicero answers a possible objection, that his active defence of Sulla goes further than the consulars' passive defence. The MSS present three variations of word order, with *est* placed after *non enim* (V), *una* (δ) and *ratio* (T). β, however, reads *una ratione*; this is probably a corruption of the order *una ratio est* (T), so the order of δ, preferred by Fraenkel (70 n. 7) for its hyperbaton, is unlikely to be the reading of the archetype. *una* requires emphasis, which reduces the attractiveness of the order of V, *est una ratio* (Kasten's textual argument (viii) is unpersuasive). The order of T is therefore adopted.

4.13 omnes...volunt cf. *Quinct*. 75 *omnes...adsunt, defendunt... laborant*; *Sul*. 61 *qui adsunt laborant*. In tricolon there is often an increase in scale from the first to the second and from the second to the third unit (as here), or alternatively there is an increase only from the second to the third. The later units, particularly the third, are also more likely to contain the more favoured rhythms. See E. Lindholm, *Stilistische Studien* (Lund 1931) 157–73.

5.1 an vero the question takes the form of an enthymeme *ex pugnantibus* (32.9n.).

subselliis the benches on which the two opposing parties sat facing the *tribunal*: see p. 17.

ornamenta...rei publicae cf. *Caec*. 28; *Cat*. 3.24; *Prov*. 22 *haec lumina atque ornamenta rei publicae*; *Planc*. 23; *Mil*. 37 *lumen et ornamentum rei* *publicae* [sc. *Hortensius*]; *Deiot.* 15; *Phil.* 2.37, 2.51, 11.24. Cicero aims to impress the jury with the consulars' *auctoritas*.

5.3 cum ego illum the reading of the archetype, *quorum ego illum*, has given rise to numerous conjectures. One approach has been to insert an ablative after *ego*, whether *ope* (*q mg.*, Petrarch; cf. S. Rizzo, *RFIC* 103 (1975) 9), or *auxilio* (*G mg. b²ck*), or *exemplo* (A. Klotz). However, *ope* and *auxilio* are inappropriate since Cicero is stressing that he attained the consulship without any help or advantages (cf. *Planc.* 67), while *exemplo* is impossible because the other consulars were not *novi homines*. In any case *in his* must surely refer to *in quibus subselliis*, not *haec ornamenta ac lumina*, an objection which also rules out Pabón's *quorum e coetu ego* (9 n. 2). R. Sydow's *luminum* for *illum* (*RhM* 92 (1944) 185f.) avoids this difficulty but produces a contorted arrangement of clauses. It is certainly true that the point of *illum . . . hanc* is not immediately clear; probably the words should be taken to mean 'that eminent position of *consularis*, this exalted place which I now occupy', *illum* referring to Cicero's position as a consular in the hypothetical context of the argument, *hanc* transposing this to real life, the position the speaker holds. But Pabón (9) goes too far in deleting *illum*. The central problem lies not with *illum* but with *quorum*. Madvig's *nollem? cur ergo* (from *quor ergo: Adv. Crit.* III.133) has merit: Cicero would be arguing that there would have been no point in his attaining the consulship if he were not going to sit alongside the consulars once his efforts had paid off. Nevertheless *cum* (*S*) for *quorum* (corrupted from *quom*) is still neater, allowing *ego* to remain as transmitted and providing a link between *nollem* and *ego . . . ascendissem*. For the corruption of *quom* to *quorum* cf. *Mur.* 89, where *quom* has been corrupted to *quod*. The spelling *cum* began to replace *quom* in Cicero's lifetime (see W. M. Lindsay, *The Latin Language* (Oxford 1894) 581; F. Sommer rev. R. Pfister, *Handbuch der lateinischen Laut- und Formenlehre*⁴ I (Heidelberg 1977) 126; H.-Sz.618f.). *cum*, then, seems a certain correction, even if doubts remain over *illum*.

excelsissimam sedem *Tω* give *celsissimam sedem*; *celsus*, however, appears only four times in Cicero's prose (*de Orat.* 1.184; *Orat.* 59; *Tusc.* 5.42; *N.D.* 2.140), and on each occasion is accompanied by *erectus*. *sedem*, literally speaking, is the *sella curulis* (81.17n.); cf. *Cat.* 4.2 *haec sedes honoris* (after which the MSS interpolate *sella curulis*).

5.4 et honoris I adopt this reading rather than *atque honoris* (*Tω*) because it avoids four consecutive trochees (cf. 39.13n.; 48.7n.; (74.8n.); 78.10n.; 91.9n.); the sense and the position of *meis* (2.7n.) both indicate a slight incision after *honoris*. Cicero normally avoids extended iambic and trochaic rhythms: they account for only 1.6 per cent of the end-of-sentence clausulae in the speeches overall, and 1.4 per cent in this speech (see pp. 51f.). But for an exception see R. G. M. Nisbet on *Pis.* 25, *purpurissataeque*.

multis...laboribus *labor* was regarded as a virtue by the Romans: see D. Lau, *Der lateinische Begriff* Labor (Munich 1975); E. Burck, *Vom Menschenbild in der römischen Literatur* II (Heidelberg 1981) 49–56. Cicero makes frequent reference during the speech to his own *labor* (*meis laboribus et periculis* recurs below at §83), and refers once (§73) to that of Sulla: Cicero's *labor* enabled him to become the first member of his family to attain the consulship, an office usually monopolised by the *nobiles* (cf. *Mur.* 17 *cum vero ego tanto intervallo claustra ista nobilitatis refregissem*; *Planc.* 67).

5.7 in hoc genere quaestionis cf. §48 *in coniurationis quaestione*. Like the others suspected of Catilinarian involvement, Sulla was tried under the *lex Plautia* in the *quaestio de vi*: *Sest.* 66; [Sal.] *Inv. in Cic.* 3; *schol. Bob.* 84 St.; cf. pp. 14–16.

defenderim neminem a claim repeated at §92.

5.9 intelleges for the parataxis cf. *Ver.* 2.57; *Cat.* 1.8; *Sul.* 71; *Phil.* 2.115; *Tusc.* 1.29, 5.100. Cicero now completes his second argument by concluding that his own position is identical to that of the consulars; Torquatus is therefore wrong to single him out for criticism.

de aliis the reading of ω is a repetition of *de ceteris* above.

6.1 Vargunteio none of the consulars supported L. Vargunteius (*RE* VIII A.377.37ff., Vargunteius 3; *MRR* III.215), not even Hortensius, who had previously defended him on an *ambitus* charge. The occasion of the *ambitus* trial is unknown, although it is usually (without good reason) inferred from the reference to Vargunteius in connection with the 'first conspiracy' at §67 that it took place in 66. A conviction in 67 or later would have resulted in expulsion from the senate (17.8n.). This would neatly account for the uncertainty whether he was an *eques* (*Cat.* 1.9) or a senator (Sal. *Cat.* 17.3, 28.1) in 63 when with C. Cornelius (6.6n.) he attempted to murder Cicero at the *salutatio* on 7 November, the morning after the meeting at Laeca's house; cf. J. Linderski, *Historia* 12 (1963) 511f. (questioned by Nicolet 1060f.); *TLRR* no. 202. Plutarch (*Cic.* 16.2) and Appian (*BC* 2.3) wrongly identify both would-be assassins (cf. R. P. Robinson, *CW* 40 (1947) 138–43, who argues for M. Ceparius in place of Vargunteius). It was doubtless his expulsion from the senate and the ruin of his political career which prompted Vargunteius to join Catiline; afterwards he was incriminated by T. Volturcius (Sal. *Cat.* 47.1) and condemned in 62.

6.2 praesertim qui concessive, 'and he moreover a man who...'; cf. *Fam.* 15.21.2 *cum tribuno plebis quaestor non paruisti, cui tuus praesertim collega pareret*. See *TLL* x.2.865.41ff.; J. N. Madvig on *Fin.* 2.25.

6.3 non...diremisset Hortensius was right to refuse to defend Vargunteius in 62; for the idea that crimes against the state break the normal bond of obligations see *Off.* 3.19, 3.32. Cicero now moves on to a more general justification (§§ 6–7 *illustrarique deberet*) of the consulars' policy, which has been identical to his own. The argument is repeated with greater force at § 82.

6.6 quis nostrum...putavit? *nostrum* (*Tω*), not *vestrum* (*V*), must be correct, because of the parallelism with *quis nostrum..?* above. The only Catilinarians known to have been prosecuted after the suppression of the conspiracy are those named here, together with Autronius and Vargunteius; cf. *TLRR* nos. 228–33. It appears from § 71 that all were condemned (cf. Dio 37.41.4).

Ser. Cornelius Sulla (*RE* iv.1521.53ff., Cornelius 389) and P. Cornelius Sulla (*RE* iv.1518.40ff., Cornelius 385) were brothers, sons of Ser. Cornelius Sulla (Sal. *Cat.* 17.3); their names, Fraenkel suggests (71 n. 11), are bound together by a molossus-cretic rhythm, unless there is a break after *Ser. Sullam*. Both men were senators who supposedly attended the 'first meeting' of the conspirators (Sal. *Cat.* 17.3; Flor. 2.12.3); Ser. Sulla, like Vargunteius, was later incriminated by T. Volturcius (Sal. *Cat.* 47.1). Klotz, Long, Halm, Reid (Introd. § 21) and Macdonald (305) are mistaken in supposing that Ser. and P. Sulla were nephews of the dictator (see Appendix 1): they were at most only his second cousins (cf. L. E. Reams, *CJ* 82 (1986–7) 304, with n. 11).

M. Porcius Laeca (*RE* xxii.213.28ff., Porcius 18; *MRR* ii.495) was a senator (Sal. *Cat.* 17.3; Flor. 2.12.3), and is chiefly remembered as having been the owner of the house *inter falcarios* where the celebrated nocturnal meeting of 6–7 November took place (*Cat.* 1.1, 1.8–9, 2.6, 2.13; *Sul.* 52; Sal. *Cat.* 27.3; for the dating see 52.9n.).

C. Cornelius (*RE* iv.1255.4ff., Cornelius 19; cf. Nicolet 852f.) was an *eques* belonging to the plebeian branch of the *gens Cornelia*; his *praenomen* has been omitted by haplography, as at § 51. Cornelius too is described by Sallust as having attended the 'first meeting' of the conspirators (Sal. *Cat.* 17.4), and he was also present at the meeting at Laeca's house on 6 November, attempting with Vargunteius (6.1n.) to murder Cicero the following morning (cf. *Cat.* 1.9–10; *Mur.* 79; *Sul.* 18, 52; Sal. *Cat.* 28.1–3; Plut. *Cic.* 16.1–2; App. *BC* 2.3; Dio 37.32.4). It is this man's son (§§ 51–2) who is prosecuting Sulla.

On *defendendum* Lebreton (20f.) notes that two or more personal subjects generally take a plural verb, but not when anaphora emphasises their singularity.

6.7 quis iis nostrum these words are garbled in the MSS. Garatoni's *iis* for *his*, which would be over-emphatic, is an easy change:

the two words are very frequently interchanged in MSS (on the un-emphatic second position see 2.7n.). Ernesti's *nostrum* gives a better sense than *horum*, and follows on from *quis nostrum...?* (twice) above.

6.8   nemo rhetorical questions in Cicero are sometimes answered, but more usually not; here *nemo* is included partly to echo and reinforce *nemo* above and lead on to *quid ita?*, and partly to complete the (cretic-spondee) clausula (cf. Fraenkel 71 n. 12, with 213).

quia in ceteris causis some would consider *ceteris in causis* (*T*ω) a more elegant order, but I have opted for the cretic-spondee rhythm of the reading of *V*; cf. *Man.* 15 *nam in ceteris rebus*... The phrase is proleptic, looking forward to *in hoc crimine*, and Fraenkel is probably right to infer from this an incision after *causis* (71 nn. 13, 14; he reads *ceteris in causis*, but on grounds not justified by the stemma (n. 13; cf. 70 n. 7)).

Cicero now argues that the defence of friends, even if guilty, is the normal *officium* (the wording *deserendos esse non putant* makes defending a guilty man seem respectable); in a case such as this, however, where the interests of the state break the normal bond of obligations, defence of the guilty would be tantamount to participating in the crime oneself (the point is repeated with reference to Autronius at §19). By implication, therefore, Sulla is innocent. These views are consistent with Cicero's own practice and with his prescriptions in the *philosophica*. He was happy to consider defending Catiline on a *repetundae* charge in 65 (*Att.* 1.2.1; cf. 81.7n.), despite believing him guilty (*Att.* 1.1.1); for admissions of the dubiousness of some of the cases which Cicero did undertake see *Fin.* 4.1; Quint. *Inst.* 2.17.21. The *philosophica* present the view that one has a duty towards guilty friends, but only up to a point. Rules on the mor-ality of defence are given at *Off.* 2.51, where Cicero argues that it is permissible to defend a guilty man provided that he is not *nefarium im-piumque*: for *vult hoc multitudo, patitur consuetudo, fert etiam humanitas* (com-passion was always regarded as a proper motive for defence; cf. *Div. Caec.* 4–5; *Clu.* 157; *Sul.* 81; *Vat.* 5; *de Orat.* 1.169, 1.202; *Off.* 2.62). He does, however, hesitate (*praesertim cum de philosophia scriberem*) in accepting the view of Panaetius that it is the business of the judge to discover the truth and of the *patronus* to twist the facts (*Off.* 2.51). At *Amic.* 36–7 Cicero ridicules the idea that obligation to friends should still hold when it comes into conflict with duty to the state; at *Amic.* 61 he argues that one may defend guilty friends whose life and reputation are at stake, but only as long as extreme disgrace does not ensue. See further W. L. Grant, *CJ* 38 (1942–3) 472–8; Michel 503–12; cf. 19.11n. (Cicero's refusal to defend Autronius); 49.4n. (the conflict between *amicitiae* and defence); 81.5n. (the consulars' support for Catiline).

6.9   necessarii see 2.1n.

6.10   est culpa *est* (which is necessary) is omitted in *V* and misplaced in either *T* or ω; but the cretic-trochee rhythm immediately decides in favour of ω. Kasten (viii) compares §9 *una est bonorum*, and argues that in each case *est* in the margin of the archetype has been correctly restored to its place in ω, incorrectly restored in *T* and simply passed over in *V* (9.2n.).

6.11   contagio sceleris *contagio* ('infection', 'pollution') is often used metaphorically; cf. *Mur.* 78 *latius patet illius sceleris contagio quam quisquam putat.* Spartacus' uprising is a *contagio* at *Ver.* 5.6–7. Pliny, writing to Trajan about the Christians, refers to *superstitionis istius contagio* (*Ep.* 10.96.9). On metaphors of sickness and healing see 76.12n.

defendas the subjunctive is employed because of the indefinite use of the second person: see Lebreton 351–3.

6.12   patriae parricidio in a technical sense *parricidium* denoted the murder initially of a free man (Fest. p. 221 M) and later, more specifically, of close relations, especially parents (Isid. *Orig.* 5.26.16). But the word is also commonly used with *patriae* in the sense of 'destruction', 'betrayal': see *TLL* x.1.447.69ff. (cf. 442.23ff.); Opelt 131f., 200f. On legal aspects of *parricidium* see *RE* xviii.4.1472.44ff.; A. Pagliaro, *Studi in onore di L. Castiglioni* (Florence 1960) 669–731; W. Kunkel, *Untersuchungen zur Entwicklung des römischen Kriminalverfahrens in vorsullanischer Zeit* (Munich 1962) 37–45; J. D. Cloud, *ZRG* 88 (1971) 1–66.

suspicere even suspicion of involvement in such a crime makes defence reprehensible.

7.1   nonne...amici groups of people who would normally have been under an obligation to give Autronius their support (on the claims of *amicitia* see 48.4n.); that they did not do so is intended by Cicero as an indication of the seriousness of his crimes. Note, however, that Autronius was not deserted by his *propinqui*, the Marcelli (§ 19). The *sodalitates* were religious associations of ancient origin; some were responsible for the organisation of particular rites and festivals, while others functioned principally as dining societies and burial clubs for the poor (*sodalicia* were their illegal counterparts). The *collegia* were essentially groups of people with the same occupation or trade; like the *sodalitates*, they usually had a religious and a social dimension (the four great priestly 'colleges' presided over Rome's religious affairs and held lavish dinners). Importantly, members of *sodalitates* and *collegia* (it is not known to which ones Autronius belonged) were bound by social obligations which extended to political support: see *CIL* i².583.10, 20, 22; *Mur.* 56; *Cael.* 26; *de Orat.* 2.200; *Brut.* 1 (for the closeness of the tie), 166; Q. Cic. (?) *Pet.* 16. See further *RE* iv.380.14ff.; Mommsen, *Coll.*; Lintott 77–83; F.

M. Ausbüttel, *Untersuchungen zu den Vereinen im Westen des römischen Reiches* (Kallmünz 1982).

sui ('his very own'; cf. Lebreton 134) and *veteres* emphasise the closeness of the relationship between Autronius and his *collegae* and friends. *V* reads *nonne collegae*, but in Latin the usual wording is *nonne...non... non...*: see K.-S.II.516; H.-Sz.462.

7.4 laeserunt for *laedere* used of witnesses and their evidence (also at §10) see *TLL* VII.2.869.13ff.

statuerant...maleficium cf. §82 *tanto scelere astrictis hominibus statuerunt nihil a se adiumenti, nihil opis, nihil auxili ferri oportere.*

7.5 quod non modo non for the relative used instead of *ut* (conjectured by Lambinus) after *tantus* see K.-S.II.298f. *V* omits the second *non*, but the negative is in this case indispensable since there is no negative in the *sed etiam* clause; cf. K.-S.II.61; H.-Sz.519; G. Long on Cicero's speeches, 1.645–9; Seyffert 19–21. See §§16, 25, 26 and 50 for similar constructions.

occultari cf. §86 *testor...nullum a me sciente facinus occultari.*

per se 'with their connivance' (Housman), i.e. similar to *a se*, but implying less deliberate action.

III 7.6 quam ob rem Cicero now finishes the argument of §§3–8 by disposing of an objection, that his situation is different from that of the consulars because he is crueller than they are.

7.7 adesse...afuisse cf. *Mil.* 97; *Amic.* 23; *Phil.* 2.95, 10.8. For play on different compounds of the same root see Holst 63–70. The archetype read *affuisse* for *afuisse*, but some later MSS (*Gb²ct*) have the required emendation; for similar confusions see §§14, 53 and 74. *abesse* is to 'fail to help' someone in a court of law: see *TLL* I.209.5ff.; *OLD* s.v. 2b.

7.8 nisi vero like *nisi forte* (25.9n.), *nisi vero* (with the indicative) very frequently carries an ironic implication (as at §28); cf. Haury 81; K.-S. II.416. On irony and humour in Cicero see, besides Haury's exhaustive study (in bibliography), Laurand 248–55; H. V. Canter, *AJP* 57 (1936) 457–64. The early commentators (e.g. Minos) are often alive to irony where their successors fail to notice it.

7.10 immanitate et crudelitate cf. *Ver.* 5.153 *immanitatis et inauditae crudelitatis; Cat.* 4.11 *quae potest esse in tanti sceleris immanitate punienda crudelitas? Immanitas* implies both size and savagery; it is a characteristic attributed to the Catilinarians at §§75–6. Cicero's emphasis on his *lenitas* and *misericordia* (1.10n.) is intended to counter accusations of *crudelitas* in his execution of the conspirators (cf. Plut. *Cic.* 19.4–5). Significantly, *crudelitas* was closely identified with *regnum* (21.1n.); cf. J. R. Dunkle, *TAPA* 98 (1967) 151–71. After 62 *crudelitas* continued to be alleged against Cicero: see *Red. Sen.* 17; *Dom.* 75, 93–4; *Pis.* 14, 17; [*Sal.*] *Inv. in Cic.* 5.

8.1 hanc mihi si tu the extreme hyperbaton *hanc...personam* has the effect of emphasising *hanc*; cf. E. Fraenkel, *Iktus und Akzent* (Berlin 1928) 164, 321 n. 3. (See 82.12n. for a similar case.) *mihi* then follows in second position (2.7n.). *T*δ give *tu si*, but this overemphasises *tu*.

imponis...personam the image is taken from the theatre (cf. F. W. Wright, *Cicero and the Theater* (Smith Coll. Class. Stud. 11; 1931) 100–3; Pöschl 569); *imponere* may mean 'to put garments etc. on a person' (*TLL* VII.1.654.77ff.; *OLD* s.v. 6a). The primary meaning of *persona* is an actor's mask representing a particular type of character; by extension the word comes to mean a character in a play, and then a man's character or personality (cf. §68). Later it indicated, in legal contexts, the person involved in a case, and finally an individual person in the modern sense (cf. *Leg.* 2.48). See M. Nédoncelle, *RSR* (1948) 277–99; W. Y. Fausset on *Clu.*, p. 280; cf. the use of πρόσωπον, which, from its primary meaning of 'face', regularly indicates a mask or a dramatic part.

8.2 vehementer erras a favourite expression; cf. Merguet II.211, IV.834.

me...esse voluit Cicero's nature is fundamentally merciful (1.10n.), but when he was consul the national interest required him to adopt severity; the argument of §8 is repeated at §87. *V* inverts *patria* and *natura*, upsetting the natural order (2.2n.); *crudelem* is strongly emphasised. The inversion in *V* has evidently been caused by the double *nec*; the same type of error is found in *V* at §20 *nec homo nec res*.

8.4 denique...detraxit the theatrical imagery (8.1n.) continues, enabling Cicero to account for the apparent contradiction between his execution of the conspirators and his defence of Sulla: his recent severity amounts to no more than a change of dress. The notion that this severity was a mask forcibly imposed but voluntarily removed recurs at *Mur.* 6, where the imagery of the stage is developed further: *ego autem has partis lenitatis et misericordiae quas me natura ipsa docuit semper egi libenter, illam vero gravitatis severitatisque personam non appetivi, sed ab re publica mihi impositam sustinui* (cf. Michel 505). A comparison with actors is explicitly made at *Off.* 1.114 where Cicero talks of *necessitas* compelling one to act out of character. Here (*Sul.* 8) Cicero insists that despite possible appearances to the contrary his character has not changed; later (§§69, 79), when Sulla's character is being discussed, he will go a step further by declaring character to be not suddenly alterable (69.12n.).

8.6 illa...haec refer to the second and more powerful word in each pair above, *res publica...natura*.

9.1 nihil est quod 'there is no reason why' (K.-S.II.278). By arguing that his nature is compassionate rather than cruel, Cicero has rejected the last possible ground for the prosecution's differentiation between him and the other consulars; during the course of the argument he has also justified the consulars' conduct. Now in §§ 9–10 he concludes with a passionate summing-up of his position, based on his own political philosophy, in which he lays claim to the moral support and *auctoritas* of the consulars and *omnes boni*.

9.2 simplex . . . causa 'the duty of all good patriots is single and their cause one' (Douglas, *Roman Oratory* 351), and so Cicero should not be treated separately. The identification of Cicero's conduct with the wishes and actions of the *boni* (1.10n.) is a prominent theme of the speech. *est* is necessary but, as at § 6 *levitatis est culpa*, has been misplaced in either *T* or ω, and omitted altogether in *V*. At § 6 the position offered by ω was judged the more attractive (6.10n.); here ω is probably again to be preferred, this time because it provides a more natural order, with the verb separating the two units, and *bonorum omnium* remaining together.

9.3 erit *V* reads *est*, a mistake probably caused by *nihil est* above. Kasten thought the word interpolated for the parallelism with *nihil est quod* and was tempted to delete (1933 preface xv); Pabón actually does delete, but for the strange reason that his MSS in Spain, with one exception, have *est* (9f.). Deletion is certainly unwarranted.

9.4 in ea parte i.e. on the side of the consulars. *pars* (or *partes*) denotes one of two opposing sides in political, legal or military situations. In political contexts, Cicero more often uses the word to indicate a group surrounding a prominent politician than, as here, the leaders of the senate in general. See Taylor, *PP passim* (definition at 10f.); Hellegouarc'h 110–15; Brunt 443–502.

9.5 nulla . . . propria Cicero's own political interests cannot be regarded as separate from those of the consulars and *omnes boni*. *causa* is emphatic and contrasted with *tempus agendi*.

9.6 doloris . . . communis 'but in the shock, the fear and the peril we had a common cause': therefore, although Cicero crushed the conspiracy, all *boni* should share the praise.

9.8 tunc *tunc* is much less common than *tum* before the early empire, after which it overtakes (in spite of resistance from Quintilian and Tacitus) and eventually replaces its rival: see H.-Sz.519f. Medieval scribes may often be detected altering *tum* to *tunc*, as at §§ 51, 52, 87; but here the tradition is unanimous in favour of *tunc*. The order of δ, *princeps tunc ad salutem*, is in all probability a simple miscopying, although it may represent a deliberate avoidance of *tunc* + consonant, a combination apparently disliked by the Augustan poets (except Manilius: see A. E. Housman on Man. 5, pp. 115f.). Cicero, however, seems to have had no such objection (contrary to Reid's belief, App. A): he places *tunc* twenty-four times before a consonant, and only eleven times before a vowel.

princeps ad salutem cf. *Phil.* 10.24 *principem...ad conatum exercitus comparandi*; *Fam.* 10.17.2 *ad omnia pericula princeps esse non recusavit.* Cicero in many places boasts of his own pre-eminent part in the suppression of the Catilinarian conspiracy, but when it suits his purpose he is also generous in acknowledging help received from friends (such as the Torquati!, §34) or in attributing his success to the gods (40.3n.).

9.9 comites predicate, 'if others had been unwilling to be my helpers'.

9.10 praecipuum 'peculiar to me' (like *proprium* above). *praecipuus* is contrasted with *communis* again at §12.

praeter alios 'to a greater degree than others', 'beyond others' (K.-S. 1.558f.); cf. §7 *praeter ceteros. alii* is sometimes found with the sense of *ceteri* meaning 'the others', but (*pace* Lebreton 110; K.-S. 1.650f.) this does not seem to be the situation here (cf. §§19, 48). *cum ceteris* refers to the *boni* mentioned at the end of the section. For the opposition *praeter alios...cum ceteris* cf. §87 *ille qui vehemens in alios, qui inexorabilis in ceteros esse visus sum.*

9.11 partiendae...communicandae cf. *Mur.* 20 *L. Lucullus tantum laudis impertiit quantum neque ambitiosus imperator neque invidus tribuere alteri in communicanda gloria debuit. communicare* is slightly preferred by Cicero to *partire* (*-iri*), particularly when referring to *gloria* and related ideas; cf. *Ver.* 5.5, 5.125; *Pis.* 79; *Marc.* 6; *Luc.* 3; *Tusc.* 5.56; *Fam.* 12.2.1.

9.13 bonis omnibus see 1.10n.

10.1 'in Autronium...defendis' here ascribed *oratio recta* is used at the end of a passage of argumentation to sum up the opposition's view (3.11n.). Cicero has been arguing that he has acted in the same way as the consulars, and was right to do so. A more specific justification for his defending Sulla after having given evidence against Autronius will follow after the *partitio*.

10.3 si...levis as the scholiast remarks, the argument is neatly summed up in the form of a *complexio* (διλήμματον), i.e. 'the offering to the opponent...of two choices such that he must choose one or the other, and either choice hurts him' (Craig 25); cf. *Inv.* 1.44–5; *Rhet. Her.* 2.38–9, 4.52; Quint. *Inst.* 5.10.69–70; [Hermog.] *Inv.* 4.6; Serv. *A.* 2.675, 10.449; Seyffert, *Schol. Lat.* 1.138f.; Rohde 70–76; R. R. Dyer, *JRS* 80 (1990) 23f.; Craig (discusses *pro Sulla* at 89–103). The figure is usually used to express an argument tightly and succinctly, with an impression of invincibility (cf. §§21, 25, 25, 39, 51, 73, 81). Craig explains: 'Part of that apparent invincibility is the impression that a dilemma is exhaustive. The dilemma seems to cover every possibility, so the possibilities that it does not treat seem to disappear' (101). Alternatively, the *complexio* structure may be used to raise the emotional pitch (§ 90). A famous example of this latter use occurs at C. Gracchus, *orat.* 61 (= *ORF* 1.196); cf. M. Bonnet, *REA* 8 (1906) 40–46. In our dilemma, which is of the first type, Cicero presents two extremes, and their apparently exhaustive character prevents the jury from forming an ambivalent view of Cicero's actions and motives (Craig 93). Cicero's raising the possibility that he is *inconstans ac levis* (even though it is not seriously entertained) also allows him to present himself as an impartial judge of the case; he justifies this aspect of his defence at §§ 84–5 (cf. pp. 293 f.; 85.5n.). The same technique is used at § 14 (and often, e.g. *Clu.* 18); in that passage Cicero assumes in addition the role of principal witness (14.5n.).

10.4 auctoritatem see 2.3n. *conveniat* has to be understood; cf. K.-S.II.558.

10.5 sin the double conditional is the most usual means of structuring a *complexio* (§§ 21, 25, 51, 73, 81); cf. Craig 214, 216; H.-Sz.669f.

ratio...bonorum rising tricolon (4.13n.). *religio* indicates a passionate concern; *ratio* and *studium* are regularly used with genitives in this way, but the construction with *religio*, sandwiched between the two, is less common (although cf. *Ver.* 3.2, 5.35; *Sest.* 8). For *boni* see 1.10n.

10.6 nihil minus...quam i.e. Torquatus ought to say least of all that... Logically the second conditional (*sin est in me...*) follows *hoc totum eius modi est...ut*, but grammatically it does not. W. G. Pluygers would therefore read *debeat* for *debet* (*Mnemosyne* 9 (1881) 136), but this is pressing logic too far (as at § 1: see 1.2n.): *sin est in me* looks like a clean break from what has come before, and at this point in the sentence *hoc totum eius modi est...ut* has evidently been forgotten.

10.7 testimonio...Autronium adversative asyndeton. Cicero means that Torquatus should not say that Sulla is defended and Autronius harmed by him, and point to the two actions as inconsistent. Clark suggests deletion of *testimonio*. The fact that we have just been told that Cicero gave evidence against Autronius might not have prevented some scribe from providing the information in a pedantic gloss, while deletion of *testimonio* would perhaps make the Latin neater and more pointed. However, Cicero might not wish to say that Autronius was harmed *a me*: he did not harm Autronius, he merely gave evidence which was accepted. For *laedere* used of evidence see 7.4n.

10.8 videor...adferre understatement (*videor...aliquid*); Cicero rather ostentatiously avoids giving an impression of arrogance. *opinionis* is used in a passive sense ('(good) reputation'; cf. *TLL* IX.2.720.72ff.), as sometimes are other substantives in *-io*: see Nägelsbach 243–6.

§§ 11–14 PARTITIO

Sulla is accused of complicity in the 'first conspiracy' of 66 and in the conspiracy of 63. As consul in 65 Torquatus' father did not invite Cicero to join his deliberations, and so Cicero is not qualified to deal with the earlier conspiracy. Hortensius, however, did take part in these deliberations, and has used this experience to rebut those charges which relate to the conspiracy of 66. It now remains for Sulla to be defended on the charge of conspiracy in 63: this will be done by Cicero, who as consul had first-hand knowledge of the events concerned.

Pro Sulla does not contain a *narratio*, and so it is the *partitio* which begins at this point. For Cicero's reasons for omitting the *narratio* see pp. 45f.

According to the rhetoricians, the *partitio* of a speech should consist of either a statement of where the speaker agrees and where he disagrees with his opponents, or alternatively a listing of the heads under which he will treat what is to follow, or both of these (cf. *Inv.* 1.31; *Rhet. Her.* 1.4, 1.17; *de Orat.* 1.143; Quint. *Inst.* 4.5.1). Few of Cicero's speeches (only *Quinct., S. Rosc., Ver.* 2, *Man., Clu., Mur., Phil.* 7) contain *partitiones* which satisfy these requirements, and *pro Sulla* dates from just the period when Cicero is abandoning the *partitio* as a formal part of the speech. In the passage which follows he does not divide up what he is going to say, but instead he explains how and why the two *patroni* have divided up their reply to the charges (cf. *Mur.* 54; *Cael.* 23; *Balb.* 17). This passage is not, therefore, a *partitio* in the strictest sense, but an interesting variation from it, representing a transitional phase in Cicero's oratorical development. Cicero's reasons for rejecting a conventional *partitio* in this instance are not difficult to surmise: since so much of what was to follow was going to be digressive, he wished to avoid a *partitio* such as would concentrate the attention of the jury on the real points at issue. On the other hand a *partitio* of the type found here performs a valuable function in emphasising that each *patronus* was dealing exclusively with those charges of which he had first-hand knowledge as a witness: the fact that Cicero possesses this unique knowledge adds considerably to the *auctoritas* which he is able to bring to bear.

In accounting for the way in which he and Hortensius have divided their reply to the charges between them, Cicero places great emphasis on the contrast between Hortensius' personal knowledge of the 'first conspiracy' and his own ignorance of it (§ 12 *vix ad aures meas istius suspicionis fama pervenit*). This professed ignorance has rightly been suspected, since Cicero had not on previous occasions considered himself unqualified to speak on the matter (cf. *Tog. Cand.* ap. Asc. 92 C; *Cat.* 1.15; *Mur.* 81; the letter to Pompey (67.1n.)). Modern scholars, however, have failed to discern Cicero's purpose in pretending ignorance of the 'first conspiracy', and consequently this passage has been severely criticised: for Stevens it is 'as near to nonsense as Cicero could possibly risk' (*Latomus* 22 (1963) 402), while Stockton condemns it as 'fraudulent and disingenuous' (155). These criticisms are undeserved because there is a straightforward reason for Cicero's insistence on his lack of knowledge of the 'first conspiracy': this is his resentment at having been excluded, in spite of his political prominence, from the *consilia* of the elder Torquatus in 65. The younger Torquatus had accused Cicero in his speech of violating their friendship by defending Sulla (§§ 48–50); Cicero therefore seizes this opportunity to remind the Torquati of an occasion on which they had failed to fulfil the duties of friendship towards himself. This motive is sufficient to explain the ignorance which Cicero so emphatically, if implausibly, proclaims. The true reason why this part of the defence was undertaken by Hortensius is probably more prosaic than the one given by Cicero: it will be simply that Cicero had to leave some part of the case for his fellow *patronus* to answer. If Cicero were to speak last, as was his customary practice (cf. *Brut.* 190; *Orat.* 130), and if he were in addition to deal himself with the conspiracy which took place during his consulship, then that left only the charges relating to the earlier period to be answered by Hortensius. Of course it is possible that, as is usually suggested, Cicero agreed to leave the 'first conspiracy' to Hortensius partly because in speaking of it he would have had to contradict his earlier references to that conspiracy. Nevertheless, it is by no means clear that any such contradiction would have been required. In his earlier references Cicero (as far as we can tell) exaggerated the 'conspiracy', incriminated Catiline and said nothing of any involvement on Sulla's part. In the little that he does say in *pro Sulla* about the 'first conspiracy' he takes precisely the same line (cf. pp. 265f.).

On the *partitio* in an ancient speech see *Inv.* 1.31–3; *Rhet. Her.* 1.4, 1.17; Quint. *Inst.* 3.9.1–3, 4.5.1–28. The *partitio* is not regarded by Quintilian as one of the fixed parts of a speech. For modern accounts see Martin 91–5; Rohde 35–40; Michel 403–7.

IV 11.1 Duae ... constituuntur viz. the 'first conspiracy' of 66 (cf. 68.2n.; 68.4n.) and the conspiracy of Catiline in 63. On *abs te* see 3.1n. *constituuntur* is 'established', 'put in position', so 'posited' (*TLL* IV.521.20ff.). The hexameter ending is rare but possible: see p. 52. Clausulae of this type are least undesirable when the final word consists of four or five syllables, and most avoided when it consists of two or three; cf. F. W. Shipley, *CP* 6 (1911) 410–18; Fraenkel 198–200; Aili 63–5. On Cicero's use of *oratio obliqua* see 3.11n.

11.2 Lepido et Volcacio consulibus i.e. 66 BC (*MRR* II.151). M'.
Aemilius Lepidus (*RE* I.550.61ff., Aemilius 62; *MRR* II.526; III.6) and L.
Volcacius Tullus (*RE* IX A.754.65ff., Volcacius 8; *MRR* II.635; III.223)
were men of little political importance, although it was Volcacius who
formed a *consilium publicum* and on its advice disallowed Catiline's candidature at the supplementary election held (in October–December) as
a consequence of the convictions of Sulla and Autronius (Asc. 89 C,
with Sal. *Cat.* 18.3; B. A. Marshall on Asc. *ad loc.*; G. V. Sumner, *Phoenix*
19 (1965) 226–31; J. T. Ramsey, *HSCP* 86 (1982) 124f.; that it was (as
stated by Sallust) the supplementary election at which Catiline attempted to stand is argued at 68.4n.). Both men are listed among the
consulars who supported Cicero's actions in 63 (*Phil.* 2.12) and among
those who spoke in the debate on 5 December (*Att.* 12.21.1). In March 49
both decided to attend Caesar's senate (*Att.* 8.15.2); Volcacius is afterwards found toadying to Caesar in 45 by opposing Marcellus' pardon
(*Att.* 4.4.4).

patre ... designato this gives a more specific dating than *Lepido ... consulibus* for the 'first conspiracy' alleged by Torquatus: it is not
seen as having been formed until after the supplementary election, when
the elder Torquatus (11.4n.) and L. Aurelius Cotta (*RE* II.2485.59ff.,
Aurelius 102; *MRR* II.127, 157, 161, 333) were elected. For the significance
of this see 68.4n., with J. T. Ramsey, *HSCP* 86 (1982) 127f.

11.3 facta esse dicitur vague language is used because Cicero is
about to insist that he personally knew nothing of the 'first conspiracy'.

11.4 fortissimi ... consulis the double-cretic rhythm and the
unemphatic *me* (2.7n.) mark an incision after *consulis*.

The compliments given to the elder L. Manlius Torquatus (*RE*
XIV.1199.48ff., Manlius 79; *MRR* II.61 etc., 138, 146, 149, 157, 163, 169;
III.136; Sumner 128f.) are conventional; when the phrase *optimus consul*
was used of Cicero himself, he considered it faint praise (*Att.* 12.21.1). *vir
fortis(simus)* is commonly applied to men with a military reputation;
Torquatus is again so described at *Sul.* 30, *Pis.* 78 and *Fin.* 2.62. Torquatus had been proquaestor under L. Sulla in the east and in Italy
during 84–1, and had taken part in the battle at the Colline Gate (Plut.
Sull. 29.4); this service may have been rewarded with a military decoration (81.17n.). His praetorship may tentatively be dated to 68 (the
latest date possible under the Cornelian law), in which case his colleagues would have included Catiline, and probably also Sulla and Autronius. Torquatus assumed the proconsulship of Asia during the course
of 67, but Broughton has convincingly suggested that he spent the
earlier part of that year as a legate of Pompey in the war against the
pirates (*MRR* II.151 n. 16, with 142 n. 9; cf. Seager 36; 25.5n. below).

After his return to Rome in 66 Torquatus was elected consul at the supplementary election occasioned by the convictions of Sulla and Autronius; during his consulship, which marked the year of Horace's birth (*Carm.* 3.21.1 *o nata mecum consule Manlio*; cf. *Epod.* 13.6), he appeared in support of Catiline at his *repetundae* trial (81.7n.), a fact which disproves Cicero's subsequent allegations of conspiracy (81.10n.). Torquatus afterwards governed Macedonia (64–3) and on Cicero's motion was voted the title Imperator (*Pis.* 44). He arrived back in Rome in time to advise Cicero during the Catilinarian crisis (*Sul.* 34; *Fin.* 2.62; *Att.* 12.21.1; cf. *Phil.* 2.12, with D. R. Shackleton Bailey, *HSCP* 83 (1979) 281f.), and his support is attested again in 58 (*Pis.* 77) and in 55 (*Pis.* 47, 92). He was also, like Cicero, a friend of Atticus (Nep. *Att.* 1.4). Cicero frequently praises Torquatus in the highest terms (e.g. §§ 30, 34, 49); he judged him *elegans in dicendo, in existimando admodum prudens, toto genere perurbanus* (*Brut.* 239). For his wife see 25.5n.

11.5 consiliis non interfuisse in spite of the friendship between them, the elder Torquatus did not invite Cicero to join his *consilia* in 65. The tone of the remarks Cicero will go on to make indicates that he felt slighted, and the reference at *Fin.* 2.62 to Torquatus' excellence *cum semper, tum* (= 'and more especially': 1.4n.) *post consulatum* suggests that the slight was never forgotten. Cicero must have felt especially aggrieved given that, as an inscription from Oropus reveals, he had been a member of a consular *consilium* as early as 73; cf. R. K. Sherk, *Roman Documents from the Greek East* (Baltimore 1969) no. 23 (= *SIG* 747) 11–12 (with *N.D.* 3.49). On a consul's use of unofficial advisory *consilia* see *Tog. Cand.* ap. Asc. 89 C; *Pis.* 80; *Rep.* 3.28; *Att.* 16.16c.11; *RE* iv.919.5ff.; J. A. Crook, *Consilium Principis* (Cambridge 1955) 4–7.

scis me ... fuisse Cicero pointedly repeats what he has just said, emphasising the friendship which Torquatus violated in unexpectedly shutting him out (*tamen* in first position highlights the inconsistency of Torquatus' behaviour).

11.7 credo in recent years this passage has been seriously misunderstood, with unfortunate consequences for the estimation of the speech as a whole (although Reid (Introd. §§ 23, 31) hints at the correct interpretation). Cicero is ostensibly being generous to Torquatus by suggesting possible excuses for the latter's failure to invite him to join his *consilia*. But *credo* is nicely ironic (as often (e.g. §§ 21, 27, 39, 88), especially when used in parenthesis): by expressing hesitation and doubt, the word allows Cicero's real feelings to show through, revealing that he does not believe the charitable reasons he is about to give for Torquatus' behaviour. This impression is reinforced by the reasons themselves, which are intentionally made to sound inadequate: it is plainly nonsense to claim that Cicero in 65 was not yet at the heart of political life. Cicero's real purpose, then, far from being to offer a charitable motivation for Torquatus' treatment of him, is to underline the fact that Torquatus had no adequate grounds for excluding him from his *consilia*.

Stevens (*Latomus* 22 (1963) 401f., 432f.), Syme (*Sallust* 90), Stockton (155f.), Boulanger (97), Macdonald (310f.) and Craig (93) all take *credo* as a sincere statement, and so understand Cicero to be providing a strangely feeble explanation of his inability to discuss the 'first conspiracy'. Stevens, Stockton and Macdonald are then forced to construct elaborate theories to explain why Cicero should argue what is transparently false, that he had not yet had experience of high office. But an ironic reading makes it unnecessary to search for a sinister purpose behind Cicero's proclaimed ignorance of the events of 66–5; in particular, it considerably weakens the force of Stevens' hypothesis that the 'first conspiracy' was directed against Pompey's supposedly imminent return. Stevens imagines that Cicero is concealing the real reason for his lack of knowledge, namely that as a supporter of Pompey he, unlike Hortensius, had not been let into the secret of an optimate conspiracy against the Pompeian Torquatus. The improbability of Stevens' speculation is most conspicuous when he states that on his interpretation our passage 'does not really make sense' (432). It is also significant that in his summary of the passage (402) the word *credo* is omitted.

On ironic *credo* see further Seyffert, *Schol. Lat.* 1.131f.; R. G. Austin on *Cael.* 36; Haury 76; H.-Sz.837. For an analogous case (*Cat.* 1.5) where the ironic tone of parenthetic *credo* was previously overlooked see G.Stégen, *Latomus* 23 (1964) 828f.

11.9 finem honoris 'the goal of high office', viz. the consulship of 63. *honos* often signifies 'high political office', while retaining its basic connotations of 'honour' (*TLL* VI.3.2926.27ff.); cf. H. Drexler in Oppermann, 446–67 (esp. 460).

ambitio . . . labor in fact Cicero's *forensis labor* in 65 was not overwhelming: he is known to have defended C. Cornelius (*TLRR* no. 209) and C. Orchivius (*TLRR* no. 211; Crawford 73f.), and perhaps some others (*TLRR* nos. 207, 210, 213; Crawford 75f.). *ambitio* (referring to Cicero's campaign for the consulship) has of course no derogatory overtones (1.4n.).

12.2 vestris i.e. of both the elder Torquatus and his son.

12.3 cum propter honorem the contents of the first *cum* clause are general (Hortensius' public distinction) and relate to those of the second (*communibus . . .*); likewise the contents of the first *tum* clause are specific (Hortensius' private friendship with the elder Torquatus) and relate to those of the second *tum* clause (*praecipuis . . .*). In each case the main emphasis is put on the *tum* clause, as is usual in the *cum…tum* correlation (1.4n.). *V* inverts *ac* and *atque*; but *ac* is not used before vowels, and Cicero's practice is to write *atque* before a consonant only where it provides a more favoured rhythm (pp. 53f.).

12.6 amorem in patrem tuum by stressing Hortensius' relationship with the elder Torquatus and by talking at this point of *patrem tuum*, Cicero maybe hints that the young Torquatus has overstepped the mark in opposing his father's friends. Cicero also underlined his own familiarity with the elder Torquatus (§ 11).

cum…praecipuis the same contrast was used at § 9.

12.7 periculis it may have been believed that Sulla and Autronius might resort to force in order to regain their lost consulships (68.2n.). Dio mentions that a bodyguard was voted to the consuls by the senate (36.44.4); the occasion for which this protection was intended is likely to have been Manilius' trial, which the consuls were directed to attend (Asc. 60 C). See B. A. Marshall, *CP* 72 (1977) 318–20.

12.8 qui interfuit… et timoris rising tricolon (4.13n.). As the scholiast points out, Hortensius is presented not simply as a *patronus* but as a witness: emphasis on their personal acquaintance with the events on which the charges are based is one way in which Cicero and Hortensius aim to counteract Torquatus' and Cornelius' appeal to their fathers' first-hand knowledge. *cognovit* (cf. §§ 13, 14) means 'investigated', 'looked into', in a general sense: see *TLL* III.1506.27ff. The postponement of *et timoris* makes more pointed the contrast with *et consili* (a more common formulation: Merguet III.543) besides aiding the rhythm.

12.10 copiosissima… oratio relying on his reputation as a great orator, Cicero often pronounces upon the literary merits of his partner's speech (Hortensius is also complimented at *Rab. Perd.* 18; *Mur.* 48; *Flac.* 41; *Sest.* 3, 14; *Planc.* 37), just as below he draws on his critical faculties to expose the defects in the speech of his opponent (31.6n.). Sometimes he also profits from a patronising approbation of the opposition's oratorical attempts (e.g. *Cael.* 8; *Planc.* 58). Here the praise of Hortensius' speech, which Cicero maintains was an accomplished piece of Asianist oratory but nevertheless a dignified performance, is intended to minimise the damage done by Torquatus' mockery (Gel. 1.5.3): see pp. 24–6. The terms *copiosus* and *ornatus* are also used in Cicero's enthusiastic assessment of the content of Hortensius' *pro Flacco* at *Att.* 2.25.1 (quoted at 3.4n.).

12.11 auctoritatis inerat this order (*V*) is preferable to *inerat auctoritatis* (*Tω*): the important words, *auctoritatis* and *facultatis*, are placed first and last, with *inerat in ea* together between them.

12.12 facta contra vos in view of the parallelism between *facta* and *delata*, I have adopted this order in preference to *contra vos facta* (*V*). *facta contra vos* (*Tω*) also gives the more favoured rhythm (cretic-spondee).

delata...prolata cf. *Ver.* 2.179 *causam non a me prolatam, sed a me delatam.* For play on different compounds of the same root see Holst 63–70.

12.14 animo nihil comperi Cicero laughs at how little he knew in 66–5 of the 'first conspiracy' (in order to belittle that knowledge): 'not only did I discover nothing with my mind (i.e. by investigation), but the breath of suspicion scarcely got as far as my ears!' He is fond of playing in this way with the contrast between *animus* and *aures*; cf. *Q. Rosc.* 19; *Ver.* 1.28, 3.131, 4.105; *Agr.* 3.3; *Sul.* 26, 33; *Arch.* 12; *Har.* 20; *Balb.* 4; *Phil.* 8.28; *de Orat.* 2.355; *Orat.* 9; *Fam.* 16.21.2. *comperire*, to 'find out facts by investigation', 'discover', is commonly used of conspiracies etc. (see J. S. Reid on *Luc.* 62). We know that the word was used against Cicero by his colleague Antonius (*Fam.* 5.5.2, December 62), by Clodius (*Att.* 1.14.5, February 61) and possibly by Caesar at Clodius' trial in 61 (Suet. *Jul.* 74.2, with W. C. McDermott, *Latomus* 6 (1947) 173–5). These opponents attributed the word *comperire* to Cicero in order to criticise the action taken against men incriminated on his evidence alone: the reference must be to the Catilinarians convicted in 62 (as in fact shown by [Sal.] *Inv. in Cic.* 3), and not to those executed in 63, since the latter were punished on independent evidence. Cicero afterwards denied that he had used the word (*Fam.* 5.5.2), but since it occurs here and at §86 it would not be surprising if he had also used it in other trials. Its occurrence here suggests that Cicero's enemies had not yet begun to taunt him with the word when our speech was published. For this situation in reverse, Cicero's mockery of an expression favoured by Catiline (*Quo usque tandem* (*Cat.* 1.1)), see D. A. Malcolm, *CQ* n.s. 29 (1979) 219f.

vix omitted by the scholia. *vix* disappeared in later Latin and consequently was often corrupted or omitted by scribes (despite the damage thus done to the sense): see T. Stangl, *RhM* 65 (1910) 436 n. 1.

12.15 pervenit for the expression *ad aures pervenire* cf. *Ver.* 3.132, 4.64; *Cat.* 4.14; *Phil.* 10.6 (*OLD* s.v. *pervenio* 4a).

13.2 cognorunt 'investigated', 'looked into' (12.8n.). The contracted form (*Tδ*) gives the more favoured rhythm (cretic-spondee).

13.3 conflari *conflare* (also with *periculum* at *Clu.* 18) is often used figuratively to describe bringing about undesirable consequences (*OLD* s.v. 3a); cf. §15 *conflato...tumultu*; §39 *pleraque conflata esse*. The imagery of kindling fire or of metal-working and the element of orchestration implicit in *con-* are both applicable; cf. Fantham 47.

qui Autronio non adfuerunt not quite true (7.1n.).

13.4 **hunc defendunt** strictly speaking, Hortensius and Cicero alone are the ones defending Sulla; however, *non enim una ratio est defensionis, ea quae posita est in oratione: omnes qui adsunt... defendunt* (§4). The structure of the sentence starts to turn back on itself at this point: *hunc defendunt* (speak for Sulla) balances *qui in illum testimonia gravia dixerunt* (speak against Autronius), *huic adsunt* reflects *qui Autronio non adfuerunt*, and *in huius periculo declarant* (Sulla's peril) matches *quibus ipsis periculum tum conflari putabatur* (the consulars' peril). For the polyptoton *hunc... huic... huius* cf. *Sest.* 144 *hunc hoc anno in hac toga*.

13.7 **mei** strongly stressed (2.7n.).

13.8 **maximae** 'very great'.

13.9 **non... temere facta** i.e. with appropriate thought and care (for the pairing cf. *Orat.* 186; *Tusc.* 1.118; *Off.* 1.103). On litotes in Cicero see Parzinger 13–17; F. Porstner-Rösel, *WS* 49 (1931) 76–82; more generally, M. E. Hoffmann, *Negatio Contrarii: a Study of Latin Litotes* (Assen and Maastricht 1987).

13.10 **criminum... patronos** *criminum... testes* is a normal expression (cf. *Cael.* 50), but *criminum... patronos* is not; thus this is an instance of syllepsis (33.4n.). In fact the use of *patronus* + gen. to mean 'protector against' seems to be unique. It may have been created by analogy from *defensor* + gen., 'repeller of', i.e. 'defender against'; cf. *Div. Caec.* 11 *defensorem calamitatum*; *Ver.* 4.143 *defensor periculorum*; *Mur.* 3 *defensor... periculi*; *Mil.* 58 *defensores necis*.

V 14.2 **hac** 'the latter', 'the recent', as at §56 *suspicionem huius coniurationis*; cf. *TLL* VI.3.2722.20ff.

14.3 **hoc primum attendite** in fact Cicero will not begin discussing the charges relating to the conspiracy of 63 until §36.

§§14–20 DIGRESSIO II

In the course of his investigations into the conspiracy Cicero heard no mention of Sulla. This fact could be used to argue Sulla's innocence, but for the moment Cicero will use it merely to explain why he is defending Sulla after refusing to help Autronius. The actions of the two men are compared. After their convictions in 66 Autronius' reaction was to resort to violence, but Sulla chose instead to yield to the law. Autronius' central part in the plotting of 63 was confirmed by the Allobroges; Sulla on the other hand hid himself away at Naples during this period. These differences account for Cicero's differing treatment of the two men. Contrary to his natural disposition and despite the pleas of the Marcelli, he resisted the entreaties of the guilty Autronius: to have defended him would have been criminal. But when he was approached by the blameless Sulla, together with the Marcelli and M. Messalla, he gladly seized the opportunity of ridding himself of a reputation for cruelty.

On the place of the digressions within the structure of the speech see pp. 44f.

In *digressio* I Cicero justified his defence of Sulla on the grounds that his actions were and had always been in accord with those of Hortensius, the consulars and *omnes boni*. Now, after the brief pause provided by the *partitio*, he continues his denial that he has been inconsistent or arbitrary by justifying his decision to defend Sulla after having given decisive evidence against Autronius. This passage follows on neatly from the *partitio* as well as from the earlier digression: Cicero will henceforward confine himself to 'his' conspiracy, and say no more about the events of 66.

In accounting for his differing treatment of Autronius and Sulla, Cicero makes use of the main argument upon which his defence is based, that he, whose knowledge of the conspiracy is unrivalled, knows Autronius to be guilty and Sulla to be innocent. Cicero makes the most of this argument by deploying it twice over, in slightly different forms and at opposite ends of the speech: it is used here (§ 14) to justify his defence, and it will be used again at the end of the *confirmatio* (§ 85) to affirm Sulla's innocence. Thus for the moment the central argument of the speech is ostensibly employed merely to demonstrate Cicero's honesty, while taking Sulla's innocence for granted; later in the speech Cicero's integrity will be taken as proven, and Sulla's innocence will be inferred as a consequence.

Cicero's claim that he is not inconsistent because as consul he knew Autronius to be guilty and Sulla to be innocent is stated at § 14 and reinforced in §§ 15–20 by a comparison between the two men. The σύγ-κρισις (*comparatio*) is used in oratory to bring out similarities or differences which are favourable to one's own side and unfavourable to the opposition. Comparisons involving similarity occur at *Ver.* 1.70, where Verres is likened to a wicked governor of Africa (Verres was more criminal, but had better luck), and at *Pis.* 15 (Piso and Gabinius resemble Catiline, but are in the end worse). But more often comparisons stress difference. For instance, Aeschines' career is compared unfavourably with that of Demosthenes (Dem. 18.257–69), and Ser. Sulpicius Rufus' with that of Murena (*Mur.* 15–53). Similarly, Piso's return to Rome is, to his disadvantage, set beside that of Cicero (*Pis.* 51–5), and Clodius' acts of violence are contrasted with Milo's abstention from such methods (*Mil.* 36–43, a close parallel to the present passage). Here in *pro Sulla*, Cicero is concerned to make Autronius and Sulla appear as unalike as possible. Since their simultaneous election and condemnation in 66, the two had generally been thought of as a pair (cf. § 37 *Autroni commemoratio memoriam Sullae rettulisset*; § 71 *eius nomen* [sc. *Autroni*] *finitimum maxime est huius periculo et crimini*), and it was important for Cicero to counteract this impression (cf. *Cael.* 10–14, where Cicero dissociates Caelius from Catiline). He therefore constructs an extended comparison which sharply distinguishes the guilt of Autronius from the innocence of Sulla. The conduct of the two men in 66 is contrasted in § 15, then their behaviour in 63 in §§ 16–17: this provides an appropriate setting for a description of Cicero's differing reactions to their appeals for his aid in §§ 18–20. Cicero's need for self-justification and his defence of Sulla both require him to blacken Autronius' character throughout the speech (cf. Stroh 189f.), and Autronius' role in the conspiracy is therefore greatly exaggerated: he becomes a leading conspirator, frequently mentioned in the same breath as Catiline. It is interesting to observe by contrast the paucity of references to Autronius in other accounts, and particularly the absence of any mention of him in the Catilinarian speeches. This example well illustrates how rhetoric may be used to distort and falsify historical truth. On σύγκρισις see further Quint. *Inst.* 9.2.100–1, 9.3.32–3; F. Leo, *Die griechisch-römische Biographie nach ihrer literarischen Form* (Leipzig 1901) 149–52; F. Focke, *Hermes* 58 (1923) 327–68; H. Erbse, *Hermes* 84 (1956) 398–424; Lausberg 393–5.

Despite the fact that this passage is intended to convey a strong impression of Sulla's innocence, it is still technically digression since Cicero is (at least on the surface) defending his own actions rather than those of his client. The neatness of the way in which § 14 follows on from § 10 also tells against our treating this section, with Reid, as *confirmatio*; on the contrary, it is best regarded as a phase within the larger digression of §§ 2–10 and 14–35. *Digressio* II is the part of this digression most relevant to the case, and indirectly it does Sulla as well as Cicero much good.

14.5 Multa Cicero ostensibly begins his reply to the charges relating to the conspiracy of 63; this opening sentence, which introduces the strongest argument of his defence, is repeated in closely similar language at the end of § 85. It was noticed above (10.3n.) how Cicero tries to dominate the case by presenting himself as impartial judge as well as advocate; in this passage he assumes in addition the role of principal witness (a point made by the scholiast, 77–8 St.). For the technique cf. the description of Scaurus' oratory at *Brut.* 111 (quoted at 2.3n.); Quint. *Inst.* 4.1.7 *sic enim continget ut non studium advocati videatur adferre, sed paene testis fidem*; *id. Inst.* 10.1.111 (referring to Cicero, also quoted at 2.3n.). By adopting this stance Cicero is able to provide a seemingly impartial (cf. *fortasse* below) yet vigorously argued presentation of his case by making the jury feel that his *auctoritas*, testimony and opinions are decisive in

Sulla's favour. The use of rhetorical devices in this passage – tricolon, tetracolon, anaphora, homoeoteleuton and polyptoton – is striking.

14.6 multa cognovi *cognovi* again means 'investigate', 'look into' (12.8n.), not, as Halm and Reid take it, 'find out (facts)': it is rhetorically neater if *audivi, quaesivi* and *cognovi* are all taken to describe Cicero's investigations, and *nullus umquam... suspicio* the consequences of those investigations. *multa quaesivi* and *multa cognovi* are balanced by rhythm (cretic-spondee) as well as by anaphora: see Zielinski, *Constr. Rhyth.* 148–50; Fraenkel 131f. *multa cognovi* vouches for *multa cognovit* at §48.

14.7 litterae no letter incriminating Sulla came to light during Cicero's consulship; by contrast, *multorum litterae ac nuntii* prove Autronius' guilt at §17. It was the letters intercepted at the Mulvian Bridge which provided proof of the guilt of Lentulus and the other Catilinarian leaders (*Cat.* 3.4–7; Sal. *Cat.* 44, 46–7); at *Cat.* 3.10–13 Cicero describes the scene in the senate as the conspirators were made to acknowledge their seals and handwriting. Evidence was also provided by the anonymous letters sent to Crassus and delivered by him to Cicero (Plut. *Cic.* 15.2–3; *Crass.* 13.3), the letter sent to L. Saenius from Faesulae, Manlius' letter to Q. Marcius Rex, and the letters of Catiline to Q. Lutatius Catulus and several other consulars (Sal. *Cat.* 30–35).

14.8 nulla suspicio the postponement of *nulla suspicio* allows the sentence to end with a double-cretic clausula, and throws emphasis on the lack of suspicion attaching to Sulla; there is no justification for either Mommsen's deletion of the words or Karsten's (27) relocation of them after *indicium*. Nägelsbach (716–19) analyses the different ways in which tetracola are split up and classes this as a 'Form 3 + 1'. Cicero uses similar language when he repeats this argument at the end of this *digressio, nullum crimen, nullum indicium, nulla suspicio* (§20), and again immediately before the *conclusio, dico hoc quod initio dixi, nullius indicio, nullius nuntio, nullius suspicione, nullius litteris de P. Sulla rem ullam ad me esse delatam* (§85).

haec vox *vox* often denotes the words or facts which the voice expresses (*OLD* s.v. 7a); cf. *hac voce* below.

fortasse valere deberet 'might perhaps be expected to count for much'; for *fortasse* + potential see *TLL* VI.1.1141.53ff. On the choice of a past tense instead of a present to refer to what has been spoken immediately before cf. the use of the dramatic aorist in Greek (see H. W. Smyth, *Greek Grammar* (Cambridge, Mass. 1956) § 1937); *diceret* (below) is similarly put into a past tense. *fortasse* adds a touch of modesty (helping to dispel the impression of arrogance; cf. pp. 293f.) and gives Cicero an air of impartiality, as if he were above the issue and could pronounce upon it with statesmanlike neutrality. The third-person form of reference in the rest of the sentence (which is otherwise a repetition of the previous sentence) contributes to this effect: it is as if Cicero were describing the actions of someone else. The subjunctives (influenced by *deberet*) help to distance Cicero from the events he describes by making the sentence more vague and general.

14.9 rei publicae objective genitive after *insidias* (*TLL* VII.1.1892. 59ff.), not dependent on *consilio* (as Reid and Macdonald take it); cf. §45 *insidias rei publicae*. The rhythm implies a pause after *rei publicae* (double-cretic), not after *consilio*; and to take *rei publicae consilio* together would upset the increasing tricolon (4.13n.).

14.10 veritate aperuisset *veritas* implies openness, honesty and correct behaviour. Cicero's *veritas* in making known all the facts of the conspiracy is exemplified by his immediate publication of full details (§§41–3).

magnitudine animi the expression *magnitudo animi*, which is often applied to *nobiles*, is very frequently used by Cicero in connection with the virtues of *fortitudo*, *constantia* and *clementia*; cf. U. Knoche, *Philologus* Suppl. 27.3 (1935); Hellegouarc'h 290–4. At *Fam.* 5.7.3 (April 62) Cicero informs Pompey of his *animi magnitudo* in dealing with the conspiracy.

14.12 sed ego nondum utor Cicero has stated twice over that as consul he knew nothing incriminating Sulla. Now he says that he is not yet going to draw from this the obvious inference, that Sulla is innocent (that can wait until a more prominent point in the speech, *confirmatio* II, §§80–85): instead he will use this argument to clear himself of the charge of inconsistency. Cicero's seemingly magnanimous renunciation of an argument which he has, by mentioning it, already made use of is an example of *praeteritio*, a device by which emphasis is given to what is ostensibly being dismissed: see Seyffert, *Schol. Lat.* 1.86–91; Lausberg 436f.; Martin 289f. The technique resembles *reticentia* (22.10n.) and *occultatio* (73.1n.). Further examples occur below at §39 (an exactly parallel instance: 39.16n.) and §64.

14.13 ad purgandum me it is only now that we see that Cicero has begun a digression, and does not yet intend to fulfil the promise made at the end of the *partitio*.

14.14 Autronio non adfuerim δ omits *non*; *a* then repeats the mistake, while *q* emends *affuerim* to *abfuerim*. For similar confusions see §§7, 53 and 74.

15.1 Autroni fuit causa the scholia read *fuit Autronii causa*, normalising the hyperbaton; this gives a Ciceronian rhythm only if the un-Ciceronian form *Autronii* is allowed.

15.2 ambitus iudicium when, after his election to the consulship of 65, Autronius was prosecuted under the *lex Calpurnia* (17.8n.) by L. Aurelius Cotta.

disturbare the usual word for breaking up courts; cf. *Corn.* ap. Asc. 66 C; *Sul.* 71; *Sest.* 135; *Vat.* 34. Autronius' attempts to halt his trial by violence are referred to again at §71, *vi [conatum] et armis disturbare iudicia*. Cicero also attributes to Autronius the violence over the *rogatio Caecilia* in 64 (§66).

conflato ... tumultu literally, the gladiators and runaways, rather than the *tumultus*, were *conflati* (cf. §33 *exercitus perditorum civium... conflatus*); but Cicero often uses *conflare* figuratively (see 13.3n.) and alteration of the text is certainly unwarranted (Landgraf proposed *conflata...multitudine*; Eussner argued for the inversion of *tumultu* and *concursu*, spoiling both rhythms).

The use of gladiators for organised violence, well documented in the 50s BC (Lintott 83–5), is also attested in the 60s: the tribune Metellus Nepos used them in his bid to have Pompey recalled in January 62 (Plut. *Cat. Mi.* 27.1; cf. p. 29). Gladiators were kept at training schools (*ludi*) and were hired out or sold by their trainers (*lanistae*) to those who wished to make use of them, whether for shows (see §§54–5, esp. 54.4n.) or for personal protection. *Fugitivi* were also a factor in the 60s (*Tog. Cand.* ap. Asc. 87 C; Sal. *Cat.* 56.5; Suet. *Aug.* 3.1); but the word is used here, as often, in a rhetorical, not a technical, sense (on this use cf. *Luc.* 144). Sallust gives a vivid picture of the freedmen of Lentulus and Cethegus scouring the streets in search of artisans, slaves and professional gang-leaders to be used in a rescue bid (Sal. *Cat.* 50.1–2; cf. 52.14). On gladiators see R. Auguet, *Cruelty and Civilization: the Roman Games* (London 1972); G. Ville, *La Gladiature en occident des origines à la mort de Domitien* (B.E.F.A.R. 245; 1981); T. Wiedemann, *Emperors and Gladiators* (London 1992). On the political violence of the period see A. N. Sherwin-White, *JRS* 46 (1956) 1–9; P. A. Brunt, *Past and Present* 35 (Dec. 1966) 3–27; Lintott, esp. 209–16 (list of incidents).

15.3 quod vidimus omnes many of those present at Sulla's trial must have attended that of Autronius in 66. Reid notes the hexameter ending. The pause after *omnes* is comparatively minor, however; the main breaks occur after *disturbare* (not a characteristic rhythm), *tumultu* (double-trochee) and *concursu* (cretic-spondee).

15.4 lapidatione atque concursu men were brought in from the streets to throw stones and disrupt the proceedings; cf. *Dom.* 12–14, 67; *Sest.* 34, 77; *Pis.* 23; *Mil.* 41. *Lapidatio* and *concursus* both have military associations (*lapides* were used as missiles in war): Cicero emphasises the violence of Autronius' lawless behaviour. On *lapidatio* as a feature of demonstrations see Lintott 6–8. Reid's 'correction' (App. A) of *concursu* to *concursatione* is not justified: Cicero's practice is to write *atque* before a consonant only where it provides a more favoured rhythm (pp. 53f.).

Sulla... prodesset adversative asyndeton. Despite their grammatical position *sibi suus* refer of course to Sulla, not to *pudor ac dignitas*; the subjunctive *prodesset*, bringing out Sulla's own line of thought, helps to justify this use of the reflexive (cf. K.-S.i.607f.).

15.5 nullum auxilium requisivit unlike Autronius, Sulla preferred to rely solely on good behaviour after his conviction; Cicero does not yet mention his alleged use of violence in support of Catiline's candidature at the supplementary election in 66 (§68; cf. 68.4n.) or the failed *rogatio Caecilia* of 64–3 (§§62–6). *auxilium* continues the military language used above in connection with Autronius: Sulla declined to call in reinforcements. The reversion to the indicative at *requisivit* stresses the important fact that Sulla did not seek aid. At §68 Cicero will again underline Sulla's rejection of violence in 66.

15.7 aspectu atque vultu the ancients regarded the face as revealing thoughts, intentions and character, and considered *vultus* to be derived from *velle* and *voluntas* (cf. R. Maltby, *A Lexicon of Ancient Latin Etymologies* (Leeds 1991) 657). See M. Seyffert and C. F. W. Müller[2] on *Amic.* 65 (pp. 421f.); Otto 147; R. G. M. Nisbet on *Pis.* 1; E. C. Evans, *Physiognomics in the Ancient World*, *TAPS* 59.5 (1969) 39–46, 92f. We hear more of Autronius' *aspectus* at §66, while at §74 Cicero argues that Sulla's *os* reveals his innocence.

inimicus... infestus... hostis a tricolon which increases in force at each stage (4.13n.). The *amplissimi ordines* are the senators and *equites* (and *tribuni aerarii*), from whom the jury was selected; the *boni* comprise a wider category (1.10n.). Unlike Catiline and Manlius (Sal. *Cat.* 36.2; at *ibid.* 31.8 Catiline is not yet technically a *hostis*), Autronius was never officially declared a *hostis*; but this does not prevent Cicero from treating him as one. On *hostes* see P. Jal, *REA* 65 (1963) 53–79 (with 74 n. 7 on *hostis patriae*); Opelt 130f.; Habicht 37f. For *domestici hostes* see 32.11n.

15.9 calamitate see 1.2n. *modestia* (below) also echoes the sentiments of the opening words of the speech.

16.1 hac 'the recent' (14.2n.). Cicero in his comparison moves now from 66 to 63.

16.2 cum Catilina not a hexameter ending (11.11n.) since the rhythm runs on into *cum Lentulo* to become a molossus-cretic.

16.3 cum Lentulo P. Cornelius Lentulus Sura (*RE* iv.1399.45ff., Cornelius 240; *MRR* ii.76, 102, 121, 166; Sumner 127) was the most prominent of the five men executed on 5 December 63 (30.7n.). He had been quaestor in 81 (70.10n.), praetor in charge of the *quaestio de repetundis* in 74 (where he presided over the trial of Terentius Varro, acquitted by a bribed senatorial jury) and consul in 71; in the following year he was expelled from the senate by the censors. In 63, re-entering the senate, he was again praetor; further advancement being unlikely, however, he joined Catiline as one of the leaders of the conspiracy, believing himself destined to become the third of the Cornelii (after Cinna and Sulla) to rule Rome (*Cat.* 3.9, 3.11, 4.2, 4.12; *Sul.* 70; Sal. *Cat.* 47.2; Flor. 2.12.8; Quint. *Inst.* 5.10.30; Plut. *Cic.* 17.4; App. *BC* 2.4). His guilt was proved by the pledge given to the Allobroges and by the letter in which he urged Catiline to recruit slaves (*Cat.* 3.4, 3.6, 3.9–12; Sal. *Cat.* 44). Lentulus is characterised in Cicero by idleness (*Cat.* 3.6; *Cat.* 3.16 *P. Lentuli somnum*; cf. Sal. *Cat.* 58.4; Dio 37.32.3), and his pitiful end is vividly described by Sallust (*Cat.* 55), who portrays him as a typical example of the moral bankruptcy of the contemporary aristocracy. Plutarch gives a similar picture (*Cic.* 17). For Cicero on Lentulus' oratory see *Cat.* 3.11; *Brut.* 235.

societas *societas* is often pejorative, as at §52 *societate sceleris*. See Achard 107f.

16.4 sceleris libidinis audaciae stock terms of Ciceronian invective (cf. *Ver.* 3.5, 5.189); *libido* and *audacia* are especially frequently found together (e.g. §§71, 76, 78). *Libido* is often used in political contexts to denote reckless pursuit of one's own self-interest; when appropriate, sexual misconduct may also be implied. On *audaces* see C. Wirszubski, *JRS* 51 (1961) 12–22 ('*audaces*, as the opposite of *boni* in a political sense, is used to describe those who, in the judgement of their opponents, are so reckless as to have the audacity to endanger or even to overthrow what the *boni* regard as the established order', 14). See further M. Seyffert and C. F. W. Müller² on *Amic.* 19 (pp. 116f.); 1.12n. on *improbi*.

16.6 admisit 'perpetrate' (*TLL* 1.752.68ff.), as at §69.

cum interim continuative, denoting attendant circumstances; cf. K.-S.11.342, 345f. The sentence is only loosely attached to the preceding questions (cf. *Pis.* 22).

16.7 noctem solitudinemque Cicero refers principally to the meeting at Laeca's house on 6–7 November 63 described at §52. For the pairing cf. *Clu.* 193; *Agr.* 2.12; *Pis.* 53; *Mil.* 50.

16.8 ne mediocri...congressu Reid offered the 'correction' *mediocriter*, 'not even slightly'; but *mediocri*, 'ordinary', 'normal', makes good sense (cf. *TLL* VIII.561.59ff.). Nägelsbach (230f.) discusses pairs of words with endings in *-us* and *-io*; *congressio* is virtually synonymous with *congressus*, but is less common. *sermo* and *congressus* are paired at *Clu.* 41; *Sest.* 111; *Luc.* 6; *Att.* 9.12.1; *Fam.* 6.4.5.

17.1 Allobroges...verissimi indices see esp. *Cat.* 3.4–14, 4.5; Sal. *Cat.* 40–42, 44–5, 50.1. The Allobroges were a Gallic tribe con-

quered in 121, whose territory extended south-west from Geneva to the
Rhône. In 63 their representatives came to Rome to seek relief from
exploitation and debt (ill-treatment is suggested by Cicero's description
of C. Calpurnius Piso as *pacificatorem Allobrogum* (*Att.* 1.13.2) and by L.
Licinius Murena's success in collecting old debts (*Mur.* 42)). Rebuffed by
the senate, they were approached by the Catilinarians through P. Umbrenus, but reported the conspiracy to their patron, Q. Fabius Sanga,
who informed Cicero. Under Cicero's direction the Allobroges played
an important part in the Mulvian Bridge ambush and in the acquisition
of evidence needed to convict Autronius and his associates in 62. Cicero
describes them as *verissimi indices* to suit his immediate purpose; at §§ 36–
9, when he has to explain the naming of Sulla in the Allobroges' evidence, he plays down the authority of their testimony. Earlier in *pro
Fonteio*, he had made much of the untrustworthiness of the Gauls (cf.
Font. 26 *vos Volcarum atque Allobrogum testimoniis non credere timetis?*), and at
Cat. 4.12 he pictures the Allobroges settling on the ashes of Rome. *in-
fidelis Allobrox* receives a mention in Horace (*Epod.* 16.6). See further *RE*
1.1587.38ff.; C. L. Jullian, *Histoire de la Gaule* (Paris 1908–26) III.119–24,
VI.330–35.

17.2 multorum...nuntii see 14.7n.; cf. § 85 *nullius nuntio...nullius
litteris.*

17.3 Sullam...nominavit this is directly contradicted at § 36,
where we are told that Sulla was named in the evidence of the Allobroges. Cicero shows great ingenuity in making use of the Allobroges'
incrimination of Autronius while disregarding their incrimination of
Sulla: *multorum...nuntii* serves to deflect the listener's attention from the
Allobroges for a moment in order to make the untruthfulness of
nemo...nominavit less apparent. *insimulavit* gives a hexameter ending, but
the word is of five syllables (11.1n.) and occurs at a very minor break.
nemo nominavit (and other combinations of *nemo* and *nominare*) is a favourite Ciceronian jingle: see Merguet III.328f.

17.4 eiecto sive emisso Cicero expresses a doubt as to which
term better describes Catiline's departure from Rome (cf. *Cat.* 2.1 *vel
eiecimus vel emisimus*). At *Cat.* 2.12–16 he defends himself at length against
the charge of having driven out Catiline, but at *Cat.* 3.2 (also to the
people) he asserts *eiciebam* and at *Cat.* 3.16 *pellebam*. The reason for the
ambiguity is that Cicero was criticised by some for driving Catiline to a
course he would not otherwise have adopted but by others for allowing
him to escape. The omission of the first *sive* is quite rare in Cicero, as
Reid notes, although common in Tacitus (e.g. *Ann.* 6.12); cf. Nägelsbach
361. For *sive* as 'or, one might say, ...' see Ernout–Thomas 446f.;
K.-S.II.438.

arma . . . signa legionum Autronius is credited with the prepara-
tions attributed to Catiline at *Cat.* 2.13 *cum arma, cum securis, cum fascis,
cum tubas, cum signa militaria, cum aquilam illam argenteam . . . scirem esse prae-
missam*; cf. *Cat.* 1.24; Sal. *Cat.* 24.2, 30.2, 36.1.

The archetype reading *tubes*, corrected to *tubas* in ω, requires explanation. Kasten daringly brings in *secures* from *Cat.* 2.13 to read *tub⟨as,
secur⟩es*, but it is easier to suppose that *tubes* has simply been influenced
by *fasces*; Pabón (10) cites parallels from *V* for this kind of error. For *falces*
(for *fasces*) in *Tω* cf. the similar corruption at *Mil.* 91. *legiones* (ω) presents
a more difficult problem: Cicero could hardly have claimed that Autronius sent out legions from Rome. Elsewhere he stresses how few men
joined Catiline from Rome and how many were left behind (*Cat.* 2.4;
Mur. 78), and according to Sallust (*Cat.* 56.1–2) Catiline's eventual forces
comprised only two legions (= Catiline's original 2,000 men + Manlius'
army + *quisque voluntarius aut ex sociis in castra venerat*; in Appian (*BC* 2.7)
and Plutarch (*Cic.* 16.4) the total force has become 20,000 men. Plutarch
(*loc. cit.*) states that Catiline took 300 men with him out of Rome.). F. C.
Wolff (followed by W. G. Pluygers, *Mnemosyne* 9 (1881) 137) deleted
legiones as a corruption of *legionis*, regarding this as a gloss on *signa*.
Deletion, however, would spoil the rhythm, while Kasten's 1933 conjecture *ad legiones* may also be discounted since it gives a hexameter
ending (cf. R. G. M. Nisbet, *CR* n.s. 8 (1958) 285). Pabón (10) explains
legiones in the same way as *tubes*, arguing that the scribe had the ending
-es, from *fasces*, fixed in his mind, but it is more likely that *legiones* was
simply miscopied as an accusative to match the long sequence of accu-
satives which precedes it. In either event, it is a different case that is
needed. A. Klotz (*PhW* 54 (1934) 572) suggested the dative *legionibus*,
'standards for legions', but the genitives *legionis* (Ant. Augustinus) and
legionum (considered by Halm and, subsequently, Clark) are more obvious possibilities. Seyffert (17) favours *legionis*, while Halm (in his apparatus to Orelli²) argues that Cicero would have preferred the expression
signa legionum or *signa legionaria* to *signa legionis* (cf. *signa militaria* at *Cat.*
2.13). The corruption would be more easily explained by *legionis* (a scribe
may have thought the word accusative plural), but on the other hand the
genitive plural ('legionary standards') is, as Halm says, the more natural
expression. At the only other place in Cicero where the two words are
put together we find *signa legionum* (*Sest.* 42), and I therefore read the
same here. The rhythm is *esse videatur* followed by hiatus.

17.5 relictus . . . foris cf. *Cat.* 2.11 *intus insidiae sunt, intus inclusum
periculum est, intus est hostis*; *Mur.* 78 *intus, intus, inquam, est equus Troianus.*
Autronius did not join Catiline in Etruria, but was in Rome until after
the execution of the conspirators (Sal. *Cat.* 48.3–7 also implies that Au-

tronius was in Rome during this period). The worst that Cicero can say against him, therefore, is that he was 'awaited' by Catiline. Laughton (133) infers from the antithesis between *intus* and *foris* that the 'essential colon-division' is after *foris*. This break in sense coincides with a molossus-cretic clausula, but there is also a slight incision, marked by a double-trochee rhythm, after *intus*. The rhythm need not deteriorate at *compressus* if the third unit (itself dividing into three, with *compressus* as a weaker first articulus) is taken as running on to *ad sanitatem* (4.13n.).

17.6 Lentuli poena see 16.3n. *poena* is a mild word for Lentulus' punishment: execution is more normally *supplicium* (1.7n.).

17.7 aliquando Reid rightly takes *aliquando* as 'at last', rather than 'sometimes' (*contra*, *TLL* 1.1600.61f.; *OLD* s.v. 4a); cf. *Phil.* 2.118 *respice, quaeso, aliquando rem publicam, M. Antoni*. Frustrated by Lentulus' execution, Autronius turned at last to fear, but never to reason.

17.8 eo tempore omni Neapoli fuerit Sulla was not of course in exile, and he may have returned to Rome on occasion, e.g. to support the *rogatio Caecilia* in 64 (§§ 62–6), and to be present at the elections of 63 (§§ 51–3). Naples ceased to be a possible place of exile upon acceptance of the citizenship under the *lex Iulia* (90); cf. Plb. 6.14.8; *Balb.* 21–2; *Fam.* 13.30.1; D'Arms 155. Cicero attributes Sulla's retirement to his feelings of modesty and shame (§§ 15, 74). His social disgrace and exclusion from the senate would have been less conspicuous in Naples than in Rome, and he no doubt found congenial the life of ease which the region traditionally offered (the Bay of Naples is described as *cratera illum delicatum* at *Att.* 2.8.2). He may have acquired his Naples villa during the Sullan proscriptions (under which he profited; cf. *Off.* 2.29), perhaps as a result of the massacre of the population of Naples in 82 by L. Sulla's troops (App. *BC* 1.89). Cicero in 46 considered purchasing a *domum Sullanam* at Naples (*Fam.* 9.15.3–5), probably the residence of his former client (cf. D'Arms 35, 178). Shackleton Bailey (on *Fam.* 9.15.5) suggests that this house may have been Faustus'; but Faustus' villa was at Cumae (*Att.* 4.10.1; cf. D'Arms 177). On Naples see *RE* xvi.2112.53ff.; M. A. Napoli (*sic*), *Napoli greco-romana* (Naples 1959); D'Arms, esp. 177f. on Sulla; Frederiksen 360. See also §§ 60–62 below on the Sullan colony at Pompeii.

Sulla's *ambitus* conviction in 66 is put into perspective at this point by the scholia in a brief excursus on *leges de ambitu* (cf. Mommsen, *Strafrecht* 865–75; A. W. Lintott, *JRS* 80 (1990) 1–16); B. A. Marshall (on Asc., p. 12) believes that the source may be a lost commentary by Asconius on *pro Sulla*. To clarify, the laws are as follows: (i) the (presumably Sullan) *lex Cornelia* (81?), which prohibited candidates found guilty of electoral corruption from resuming their candidature within a period of ten years (our scholiast is the sole source; cf. Greenidge 423f., 508; Gruen 212); (ii) the *lex Calpurnia* (67), which imposed expulsion from the senate, permanent disqualification from public office and payment of a fine; this was the law under which Sulla and Autronius were convicted (*Mur.* 46, 67; *Sul.* 88 (with 88.8n.); Asc. 69, 75–6, 88 C; Dio 36.38.1, 37.25.3; cf. Greenidge 425, 508, 521f.; C. Nicolet, *RHD* 36 (1958) 262–6; Gruen 213–16); (iii) Cicero's own *lex Tullia* (63), responding to calls for even stricter provisions, a law which regulated electoral practices (see 54.4n.), defined malpractices more specifically and added to the penalties of the *lex Calpurnia* exile for ten years (*Mur.* 3, 5, 45–7, 67, 89; *Sest.* 133; *Vat.* 37; *Planc.* 83; Dio 37.29.1; *schol. Bob.* 140.5–9 St.; cf. Greenidge 425, 474, 508f.; Nicolet, *op. cit.* 266–9; Gruen 222f.).

ubi … suspicionis cf. §53 *in ea parte Italiae quae maxime ista suspicione caruit.* Nearby Capua, however, important for its gladiatorial school and strategic position, was in danger of falling to the rebels (*Sest.* 9–11); a slave revolt took place there, and troops were sent there in October 63 (Sal. *Cat.* 30). *adfinis* may take a genitive or a dative: see *TLL* 1.1218.70ff. G. Landgraf on *S. Rosc.* 18 takes the genitive to be used when the sense is of 'participating in' and the dative when it is of 'connected with'; but this distinction is artificial, and does not suit §70 *huic adfines sceleri.*

17.10 calamitosorum see 1.2n.

17.11 ad consolandos Naples was popular as a retreat for the aged and infirm (D'Arms 143, 183f.), but Cicero is referring, euphemistically and wittily, to its notoriety as a place of luxury and pleasure-seeking. Without going so far as to accuse his client of loose living, he nicely makes the point that conspirators do not pass their time at *Naples*.

VI 17.12 igitur *igitur* announces that Cicero has now completed his answer to the question, *quae enim Autroni fuit causa, quae Sullae est?* (§15). To conclude his demonstration that ·he was justified in treating Autronius and Sulla differently, Cicero now proceeds to describe the circumstances of his refusal to defend Autronius (§§18–19) and his decision to speak for Sulla (§20).

18.1 veniebat … saepe veniebat for the repetition (which suggests Autronius coming again and again to plead with Cicero) Reid compares *Quinct.* 40; *Ver.* 3.152; *Ver.* 5.121 *errabas, Verres, et vehementer errabas; Sul.* 55, 64. The fact that not even the most persistent appeals could induce Cicero to defend a guilty conspirator is intended to suggest that Cicero's defence of Sulla implies the latter's innocence.

18.3 supplex ut *veniebat … supplex ut* has to be understood as *supplicabat ut.* Autronius, who was weeping (*multis cum lacrimis*), would literally have thrown himself at Cicero's feet. In 54 the tribune C. Memmius (89.13n.) kicked Gabinius' suppliant son from his feet, and in 52

P. Plautius Hypsaeus was rejected by Pompey after he had thrown himself at his feet (V. Max. 8.1 abs.3, 9.5.3). Such rejections were unusual and shocking (David 77f.).

condiscipulum *V* reads *discipulum*; but Autronius was not Cicero's pupil. The idea of pursuing life together, often with military comradeship included, is a topos in ancient literature; cf. (e.g.) Aristoph. *Vesp.* 236–9; Hor. *Carm.* 1.7.30–1, 1.36.7–8, 2.7.1–16; Sen.(?) *Her. O.* 586–99; Luc. 1.299–300.

18.5 quaestura Autronius' quaestorship is thus dated to 75 (*MRR* II.97). Cicero spent the year serving under Sex. Peducaeus in Western Sicily (*MRR* II.98).

18.6 officia on *officium* (implying *amicitia*) see 2.5n. Cicero claims that Autronius could set no more than a few services that he had paid to Cicero against the many that Cicero had paid to him: ingratitude is neatly added to Autronius' crimes. Cf. *Cael.* 7 *tecum, Atratine, agam lenius, quod . . . meum erga te parentemque tuum beneficium tueri debeo.*

18.7 flectebar . . . frangebar for the play on words see Wölfflin 260.

18.9 immissum . . . C. Cornelium *immittere* is often used with reference to assassins and the like: see *TLL* VII.1.470.75ff. Cornelius, together with Vargunteius (6.1n.), attempted to murder Cicero on 7 November 63, the morning after the meeting at Laeca's house (6.6n.). Autronius is not elsewhere credited with having instigated the attempt; at §52, when the younger Cornelius is being addressed, we are allowed to suppose that the plan was Cornelius' own, and at *Cat.* 1.9–10 it is more naturally Catiline who was to blame. Cicero thus attributes responsibility to whomsoever he pleases at any given moment. Similarly, Vargunteius is not mentioned here (or at §52) because Cicero wishes to focus attention on Cornelius, thus arousing greater *odium* against the prosecution.

in meis sedibus *Tω* read *in sedibus meis*, but the order *in meis sedibus* (*V*) gives *meis* greater emotional force and provides a more favoured rhythm (double-cretic). Lambinus' *aedibus* for *sedibus*, although palaeographically neat (*aedes* and *sedes* are often confused in MSS after *s*: see Müller's apparatus), is not necessary: *sedes* may be used in the plural to refer to a single home (*OLD* s.v. 4a), and Cicero grandly refers to his house (although a different house by this time) as his *sedes* (pl.) again at *Dom.* 143, 145, 147; *Har.* 15.

18.10 uxoris ac liberorum Cicero's wife Terentia (*RE* V A.710.29ff., Terentius 95) bore him two children, on whom he doted. The elder, Tullia (*RE* VII A.1329.24ff., Tullius 60), born in c.79, had married C. Calpurnius Piso Frugi by 63, while the younger M. Tullius Cicero

(*RE* VII A.1281.1ff., Tullius 30) was born in 65 and so was still an infant. The family is pictured again at *Cat.* 4.3: *neque meam mentem non domum saepe revocat exanimata uxor et abiecta metu filia et parvolus filius, quem mihi videtur amplecti res publica tamquam obsidem consulatus mei, neque ille qui exspectans huius exitum diei stat in conspectu meo gener.*

18.11 qua mollitia sum the relative has the effect of *tantus* in constructions of this kind. Cicero is again concerned to stress his mild nature (1.10n.): he is naturally sympathetic towards the innocent, and severe towards the guilty only when the public interest is involved.

18.12 me hercule Cicero preferred *me hercule* to *me hercules* (*Orat.* 157; see J. E. Sandys' note *ad loc.*); he used the phrase less frequently after 63 than before. See Neue–Wagener II.988–92.

19.1 sed cum the protasis is divided into two halves, *sed cum...* and *et cum...* In the first of these Cicero for the most part lists things held dear (the *patria*, temples, children etc.), and in the second he describes what might have happened to them. The anaphora of *cum* raises the emotional pitch without appearing as overblown as it would in English; for parallels see *Ver.* 1.28; *Rab. Perd.* 21; *Cat.* 2.13; *Sul.* 34; *Flac.* 5; *Red. Pop.* 13; *Dom.* 131; *Har.* 39 (cf. 26.7n. on anaphora of *si*). Sallust makes Caesar characterise the previous speeches made at the debate of 5 December: *rapi virgines pueros, divelli liberos a parentum conplexu, matres familiarum pati quae victoribus conlubuissent, fana atque domos spoliari, caedem incendia fieri, postremo armis cadaveribus, cruore atque luctu omnia conpleri* (*Cat.* 51.9). Our passage is very much the type of oratory to which Caesar refers.

19.2 illorum...templorum *delubra* and *templa* are commonly paired and, whatever their original meanings (cf. Prob. *app. gramm.* 4.202 Keil; Isid. *diff.* 1.407), were by Cicero's time synonymous. See H. Jordan, *Hermes* 14 (1879) 567–83. *illorum* is deictic: Cicero points to the temples in the forum.

19.3 puerorum *puer* may refer to girls too when used in the plural (*OLD* s.v. 4a).

19.4 veniebat in mentem for the impersonal construction *sibi in mentem venire* + genitive see *TLL* VIII.723.52ff.; K.-S.I.472 (cf. §38). Petrarch conjectured insertion of *imago* towards the beginning of the section to account for the genitive (*q mg.*).

19.5 infestae ac funestae faces the rhyme is commented upon and many parallels are given at H.-Sz.704–6.

19.6 cum caedes...patriae for the pairing of *caedes* and *cruor* see Wölfflin 255. *cinis patriae* is a striking metaphor suggesting both arson and the funeral pyre; cf. *Rhet. Her.* 4.12 (illustrating the grand style) *patriae...cinerem*; *Cat.* 2.19 *cinere urbis*; *Cat.* 4.12 *cinere...imperi*; Virg. *A.* 10.59 *cineres patriae.*

19.7   animum...refricare *versari...coeperat* balances *veniebat in mentem. refricare* is used of rubbing wounds and making them raw again. It is in Cicero that it is first attested in the metaphorical sense of re-awakening unpleasant feelings or 'reopening old wounds' (*OLD* s.v. 2).

19.8   tum denique 'then at last' (cf. §38), when all these memories had passed across his mind.

19.9   hosti ac parricidae cf. *Phil.* 4.5, 14.4. Autronius was seen as a *hostis patriae* at §15 (15.7n.); in Sallust (*Cat.* 31.8) Catiline is branded a *hostem atque parricidam* in the senate after the delivery of *Cat.* 1. The Catilinarians are regularly *parricidae* (6.12n.) in Cicero (*Cat.* 1.29, 2.7, 2.22; *Sul.* 77; *Planc.* 90), as in Sallust (*Cat.* 14.3, 51.25, 52.32).

Marcellis patri et filio these Marcelli, both called C. Claudius Marcellus and descendants of the Marcellus who captured Syracuse in 211, had pleaded with Cicero on Autronius' behalf (the relationship referred to is unknown), and were now supporting Sulla (*his* implies their presence in court; cf. §20 *huius M. Messallae*; §62 *hunc* [sc. *Caecilium*]). The father (*RE* III.2733.1ff., Claudius 214; *MRR* II.84, 545f.) was praetor in 80, proconsul in Sicily the following year and in 70 a member of the jury which tried Verres; he was later augur with Cicero. The son (*RE* III.2734.8ff., Claudius 216; *MRR* II.208, 228, 247; III.54), probably the candidate for the aedileship of 56 mentioned at *Att.* 4.3.5, was praetor by 53 and became the Pompeian consul of 50, although neutral during the civil war. He married Caesar's grand-niece Octavia; their son Marcellus was the nephew and intended successor of Augustus, and their elder daughter Marcella was married to Agrippa in c.28. Cicero remained on excellent terms with the Marcelli and letters of his to them survive (*Fam.* 15.7–11, 51–50 BC); in *pro Marcello* (46 BC) he expressed gratitude for the restoration of their respective nephew and cousin. A. Riedenauer (*Eos* 2 (1866) 622) regarded *patri et filio* as a gloss; but these words allow the colon to end with a double-cretic instead of a series of eight long syllables.

19.11   sine summo scelere the essence of the prosecution's criticism of Cicero's defence of Sulla. Torquatus alleged that in defending a conspirator Cicero was himself committing a serious crime. Cicero therefore now, as earlier at §6, turns this argument to his own advantage: stressing his agreement that defence of a traitor whom one knows to be guilty is tantamount to participating in the crime oneself, he uses this to justify in the strongest terms his refusal to help Autronius (in spite of the pleas of the Marcelli) and his decision to speak for Sulla. By arguing in this way he is also showing that his actions were determined by a responsible consideration of right and wrong, and not by other factors. On the Roman view of the morality of defence see 6.8n.

19.12 in aliis Lebreton (109) rightly takes this as simply 'in others', not 'in the others', as M. Vaccaro does (cf. §§ 9, 48).

20.1 atque idem ego 'and yet I (this same man)...'. *idem* draws attention to an inconsistency between two ideas, as at *Sul.* 87 *idem ego...persolvi patriae quod debui*; *Arch.* 15 *atque idem ego hoc contendo*; cf. *TLL* VII.1.192.73ff.

20.3 lacrimantes *lacrimare* was more high-flown than *flere*, and in Cicero is about half as common. See *TLL* VII.2.844.38ff.

20.4 huius M. Messallae probably M. Valerius Messalla 'Rufus', the consul of 53 and brother-in-law of L. Sulla, i.e. the same man as is mentioned below at §42 (*M. Messallam, qui tum praeturam petebat*; cf. 42.5n.); cf. *RE* VIII A.166.61ff., Valerius 268; *MRR* II.173, 227f., 255, 282 etc.; III.214; F. Münzer, *De Gente Valeria* (Oppeln 1891) 53 (no. 60); R. Syme, *JRS* 45 (1955) 155–60. Alternatively, the commentators (each repeating his predecessor in a sequence which began with Sylvius in 1531; see Appendix 1 for a similar case) and others (e.g. Gruen 130 n. 35, 284) take Cicero to be referring not to Rufus but to his cousin M. Valerius Messalla 'Niger', the optimate consul of 61 and subsequent supporter of Pompey (*RE* VIII A. 162.48ff., Valerius 266); the lack of unanimity on the question is such that even the two men's respective *RE* biographers are in disagreement (Niger: F. Münzer, col. 164.17ff.; Rufus: R. Hanslik, col. 167, 19f.). A clue seems to be provided by the description *hominis necessarii*; which Messalla was a personal friend of Cicero? Those who support Niger cite Cicero's view of him at the start of his consulship in 61 (within a year of *pro Sulla*): *Att.* 1.13.2 *eius autem collega et in me perhonorificus*; *Att.* 1.14.6 *Messalla consul est egregius; fortis, constans, diligens, nostri laudator, amator, imitator*. Thus for E. Badian it is Niger who was 'a friend and ally of Cicero' (*OCD* s.v. *Messal(l)a (2)*). However, Cicero indicates that he is surprised by the consul's goodwill (*Att.* 1.14.6 *quod non speraram*); these letters, then, may even suggest that Cicero and Niger had not been on friendly terms in 62. Shackleton Bailey, who previously (on *Att.* 1.13.2) backed Niger, now takes the opposite view: 'Both references in the *Pro Sulla* are to Rufus. *hominis necessarii* in the former suits his known friendly relations with Cicero in the fifties. No such relationship with Niger is recorded, though Cicero approved of his conduct as consul' (*Onomasticon* 96). The 'known friendly relations' with Rufus are established primarily by four references in the letters to Rufus as *Messalla noster* (all 54 BC: *Att.* 4.17.3; *Q. fr.* 3.3.2, 3.6(8).3, 3.7(9).3; Cicero is delighted by the acquittal of a 'Valerius' at *Att.* 2.3.1 (60 BC), but there is no certainty that Rufus is meant). There are two further, and perhaps stronger, arguments in Rufus' favour. First, Rufus was chosen by Cicero to record the proceedings of the senate on 3 December 63 (§42): this probably implies good relations with Cicero. Secondly, Rufus was L. Sulla's brother-in-law (and clearly also one of his augurs; cf. Syme, *AA* 5, 228): he would therefore have been a natural choice as someone to plead with Cicero on Sulla's behalf. Moreover, Syme (*Sallust* 71 n. 50) argues for Rufus on the grounds that Sulla and Rufus are found together in 47 (*Att.* 11.22.2); this Sulla is probably our Sulla's son (88.14n.), but even so this could still point to a friendship with the family. The arguments for Rufus, therefore, heavily outweigh those for Niger. Consequently, Reid (Introd. § 24), Macdonald (306) and M. C. Alexander (*TLRR* no. 234 n. 1) are not justified in taking the present passage as an indication of the date of the speech (see p. 14). But even if we were dealing with Niger, it is hard to see how Cicero mentions him 'in such a way as to indicate that the consular elections of 62 had not yet been held' (Macdonald).

Rufus held the praetorship in (or after) 61 (42.5n.); after his consulship he was successfully defended on an *ambitus* charge by his uncle Hortensius in 51, but then convicted *de sodaliciis* (*Brut.* 328; V. Max. 5.9.2; cf. *ORF* 1.329). He was an augur for fifty-five years (Macr. 1.9.14), and served as a legate of Caesar during the civil war; rehabilitated by Caesar, he lived on until 26. His presence at Sulla's trial is indicated by *huius* (cf. 19.9n.).

20.5 neque ... naturae *naturae* refers to Cicero's nature, not (as at § 8) to nature in general. The possessive adjective may be omitted in cases where it is not in doubt to whom reference is made, and where no contrast is intended: see Nägelsbach 385; T. E. Kinsey on *Quinct.* 57; D. R. Shackleton Bailey on *Att.* 4.18.2. Madvig's *causae ... natura* (*Adv. Crit.* III.133f.) is unattractive because it breaks the parallelism with the next clause (*causa* is parallel with *res*, *naturae* with *misericordiae meae*).

nec homo nec res this order is preferable to *nec res nec homo* (*V*) because it puts the man, Sulla, first. The inversion has evidently been caused by the double *nec* (Kasten 1933 preface xvi; 1949, vi); the same type of error is found in *V* at § 8 *nec patria nec natura*. *res* ('situation') has been quite unnecessarily questioned by some scholars: Pluygers read *nec reus*, which necessitated deletion of *nec homo*, while Campe retained *nec homo* but deleted *nec res*. In cases where the *res* was disgraceful, the orator was advised to concentrate on the *homo*: see *Rhet. Her.* 1.9.

20.8 nulla suspicio Cicero ends *digressio* II with forceful language similar to that with which he began it (14.8n.). Two parallel clauses, then tricolon are used to build up an emphatic climax. *nulla suspicio* is omitted by *Tω*, but it is more likely to have dropped out than to have been interpolated; it is supported by § 14; and its omission would spoil the double-cretic clausula.

suscepi ... suscepi this type of gemination, found below at §§ 46 and 80, is known as *regressio* (ἐπάνοδος): see Lausberg 393–5; H.-Sz.809f. For repetition of *suscepi* cf. *Ver.* 2.1 *suscepi enim causam totius ordinis, suscepi causam rei publicae.*

20.9 boni...improbi echoing the thought of the *exordium*, § 1 (on Cicero's use of these terms see 1.10n.; 1.12n.). As a result of his defence of Sulla not even *improbi*, Cicero hopes, will call him *crudelis* (7.10n.): he will have thrown off the mask of severity to reveal his merciful nature once more, and will no longer be subject to criticism for his treatment of the Catilinarians.

§§21–35 DIGRESSIO III

Torquatus has accused Cicero of regnum in his consulship and in his participation in the Catilinarian trials. But when consul Cicero obeyed the senate and actually suppressed a tyranny, while in the trials he simply told the truth about those who were condemned, and is now protecting an innocent man from the tyranny of the prosecutor. Torquatus, however, calls him not only a rex but a rex peregrinus. Cicero replies that a municipal origin is no cause for shame, and if Torquatus thinks so he had better look out: his snobbery will cost him votes at the elections. Cicero's services to the state do not constitute tyranny, and he will be happy to receive no reward for them if only he can escape the dangers which threaten him. Torquatus accuses Sulla of conspiracy, but inconsistently denounces Cicero for his severity in punishing conspirators; he has also misjudged the support of the Roman people for Cicero's measures. Cicero sees no reason to try to excuse his consulship, but instead he glories in it, and ends by announcing that Torquatus, despite his present stance, in fact played a significant part himself in the suppression of the conspiracy.

On the place of the digressions within the structure of the speech see pp. 44f.

Having finished his reply to the charge of inconsistency, Cicero now turns to some of the other criticisms relating to himself. In particular, Torquatus had portrayed him as Rome's third *rex peregrinus*, an outsider whose power over the lives of 'native' Romans was insupportable. The representation of Cicero as a *peregrinus* was an appeal to upper-class Roman prejudice which did not concern his actions and could therefore be repudiated without much ado. The *regnum* accusation, on the other hand, was based on controversial or offensive deeds which he had done, his execution of the conspirators in 63 and his testifying for the prosecution in the Catilinarian trials of 62. If Cicero were viewed as a holder of autocratic power, his attempt to use his *auctoritas* to secure Sulla's acquittal would be undermined. It was therefore necessary for him to justify his past actions before beginning his reply to the charges against

Sulla. As he claims at §35 (repeating §2), Torquatus has set out to rob him of his *auctoritas* (partly by accusing him of inconsistency, partly by calling him a tyrant), and Sulla's interests therefore demand that he defend his own conduct: *etiam si me meus dolor respondere non cogeret, tamen ipsa causa hanc a me orationem flagitavisset*. Thus although *digressio* III is on the surface the least relevant of the digressions in the speech – Sulla is scarcely mentioned – it is nevertheless, as Cicero maintains, central to the case.

Torquatus' speech had been intended to alienate Cicero from all sources of support or sympathy by portraying him as arbitrary and cruel, un-Roman, and out of line with Hortensius and the other consulars: in sum, a foreign tyrant. In his reply Cicero also aims to alienate his opponent, representing him as out of tune with the opinions not only of Cicero, but of Hortensius, the consulars, the jury, the *boni* and the entire Roman people. Thus when replying to the accusation of *peregrinitas*, Cicero identifies himself with some of the great names of Roman history, and proceeds to alienate Torquatus by turning an insult which had been directed solely at himself into an attack on all those not born into a patrician family. With great ingenuity he even suggests that it is Torquatus who is a foreigner (§25) and a tyrant (§§22, 27). Condescension is a further tactic used by Cicero in this part of the speech. In view of Torquatus' comments on the execution of the Catilinarians (§§30–2), he might have felt justified in treating him as a treacherous *improbus* and revolutionary. It would not have been to his advantage, however, to be seen to bully an opponent so much younger than himself, and in any case he no doubt wished to avoid damaging his friendship with the Torquati any more than was necessary. Instead, therefore, he chooses to treat Torquatus as a *bonus* whose youthful inexperience has led him to undertake an injudicious prosecution, but who will in time learn how to behave. The patronising tone must have infuriated Torquatus, and entertained the jury.

It is this digression which contains the most conspicuous passages of Ciceronian self-praise in the speech. Fourth-century orators were not averse to singing their own praises on occasion (cf. Dem. 5.4), and the Asianist style of the Hellenistic period was noted for its bombastic and boastful character. At Rome, the Asianist oratory of speakers such as Hortensius likewise featured an element of bombast, while the Roman concern for *dignitas* and *gloria* also made a certain degree of boastfulness tolerable to, and even expected by, Roman audiences. Nevertheless, Cicero's immodesty in his constant references to his consulship was criticised in antiquity, and therefore must have seemed to some of his contemporaries to have exceeded the bounds of propriety (cf. *Dom.* 92–

3; *Har.* 17; *ad Brut.* 1.17.1; [Sal.] *Inv. in Cic.* 3; Sen. *Dial.* 10.5.1; Plut. *Cic.* 24.1–2, 51 (= *Compar.* 2); *id. Mor.* 540 f-541 a; Dio 37.38.2). Cicero's apparent obsession with the achievements of his consulship increased as his political importance diminished. A publicity campaign (consisting of accounts of his consulship and publication of his consular speeches) was required in 60 when it seemed that the question of the execution of the conspirators might be re-opened, and the references to the Nones of December become more frequent after the disgrace of his exile (58–7). But self-praise may be objected to only if it is irrelevant to the point at issue and introduced for frivolous reasons, such as vanity or self-importance. Cicero himself argued that in his case, when he spoke boastfully, he was compelled to do so for reasons of self-defence (*Dom.* 93, 95; *Har.* 17; for Plutarch (*Mor.* 540 c–541 a, *de Laude ipsius*), self-praise is justifiable if the speaker is required to defend his reputation). Although psychological influences such as the insecurity and self-doubt of the *novus homo* may well have been an underlying factor, Cicero's justification nevertheless remains broadly speaking valid. As Quintilian observes in his excellent discussion of the question (*Inst.* 11.1.17–24), Cicero generally had a reason for speaking as he did, and his praises of his consulship were as a rule required by the interests of the cases which he was undertaking (cf. 11.1.18 *et plerumque illud quoque non sine aliqua ratione fecit . . . ut illorum quae egerat in consulatu frequens commemoratio possit videri non gloriae magis quam defensioni data*; 11.1.23 *plerumque contra inimicos atque obtrectatores plus vindicat sibi: erant enim illa tuenda cum obicerentur*). This explanation accounts for most of the self-praise which we find in *pro Sulla*. Here Cicero's boastfulness is best seen not as the result of an obsessive vanity but as the most effective means of deploying his full *auctoritas* in Sulla's favour. Cicero would have been unwise in his defence of Sulla not to have made use of his primary role in the events of 63, and the best way to argue against Torquatus that his consulship needed no justification was for him to glory unashamedly in what he had achieved. On the problem of Cicero's supposed vanity see further Strachan-Davidson 192–6; W. Allen, *TAPA* 85 (1954) 121–44; Douglas 24–6; Rawson 90f.

VII 21.1   Hic ait *Hic* is 'in this context', sc. of Cicero's alleged cruelty towards the Catilinarians and his alleged autocratic and inconsistent behaviour (cf. §§ 22, 50, 67). *Hic ait . . . iudices* abruptly takes the digression off in a new direction as Cicero eschews the subtle transitions used earlier (§§ 2, 14): the effect of this is that we are suddenly confronted with Torquatus' charge of *regnum* (Torquatus' criticisms are taken in ascending order of seriousness, with the allegation of falsification left until last

(§§ 46–50); cf. Douglas, *Roman Oratory* 351f.). Cicero's answer to this part of Torquatus' invective is arranged in three parts. He begins and ends with the more damaging *regnum* charge, and in between provides a witty refutation of the *peregrinitas* gibe (§ 22 *at hic etiam* (*hic* is again used for the transition) to § 25 *ne gravius refutere*). The second part of the treatment of *regnum* (§§ 25–35) is concerned with its most sensitive aspect, Cicero's actions as consul. Here (§§ 21–2), however, Cicero remarks that he has been accused of *regnum* on two counts and then, for the moment passing over the criticisms of his consulship, he turns first to Torquatus' complaint that his inconsistent and arbitrary behaviour in the trials of 62 amounts to *regnum*. This argument begins with a passage which resembles an *altercatio* (cf. *Att.* 1.16.10; Quint. *Inst.* 6.4.1–22; Martin 137f.) in which Cicero provides the accusations as well as the triumphant responses in quick, pointed, cut-and-thrust fashion; the technique is used again below at §§ 38–9, 48, 54–5, 81–2. On Cicero's use of *oratio obliqua* see 3.11n.

regnum *rex, regnum* and related terms which implied excessive or absolute power were part of the stock-in-trade of political invective in the last century of the republic. Such words called to mind the Hellenistic kings against whom Rome had fought for two centuries (Mithridates was vanquished only in 63) and, less immediately, the kings of early Rome (§ 22). Allegations of *regnum* and *dominatio* were directed against Ti. Gracchus, Saturninus, Cinna, L. Sulla, Rullus, Catiline, Clodius, Gabinius, Piso, Pompey, Caesar and Antony; Cicero, after his execution of the conspirators, was regularly accused by his enemies of aiming at or implementing *regnum* (cf. Plut. *Cic.* 23.2 τὴν Κικέρωνος δυναστείαν). With this in mind, he defends himself at *Cat.* 1.30 and 2.14 against those who would consider him *non diligentissimum consulem sed crudelissimum tyrannum* (2.14) if he were to take firm action against Catiline. He is called a *rex* by Clodius in the famous *altercatio* at *Att.* 1.16.10 (61 BC), and when he had been driven into exile in 58 Clodius pointedly dedicated a shrine to *Libertas* (to *Licentia*, it is claimed at *Leg.* 2.42) on the site of his house (cf. W. Allen, *TAPA* 75 (1944) 1–9). Cicero still found it necessary to counter such accusations after his return: see *Dom.* 75, 94; *Sest.* 109; *Vat.* 23, 29; *Mil.* 12; *Phil.* 14.15; cf. [Sal.] *Inv. in Cic.* 3, 5. The allegations of *regnum* were closely linked in his case to a reputation for *crudelitas* (7.10n.), which accounts for the emphasis in the speech on Cicero's *lenitas* and *misericordia* (1.10n.). *Regnum* also seemed to be implied by Cicero's domination of the courts, exemplified by his decisive influence in the Catilinarian trials: '*regnum est dicere in quem velis, et defendere quem velis*' (§ 48). In 70 Cicero had criticised Hortensius' *dominatio regnumque iudiciorum* (*Ver.* 35; cf. *Div. Caec.* 24; *Ver.* 1.58, 2.77); by 62 he was himself said *regnare* in *iudiciis* (Quint. *Inst.* 10.1.112; cf. *Fam.* 7.24.1, 9.18.1). On *regnum* see J. Béranger, *REL* 13 (1935) 85–94; W. Allen, *TAPA* 84 (1953) 227–36; Wirszubski, esp. 62–4; Hellegouarc'h 560–65; J. R. Dunkle, *TAPA* 98 (1967) 151–71; *id.*, *CW* 65 (1971–2) 12–20; E. Rawson, *JRS* 65 (1975) 148–59; Diehl 184–8; K. M. Coleman on Stat. *Silv.* 4.1.46; A. Erskine, *CQ* n.s. 41 (1991) 106–20.

21.2 credo ironic (11.7n.). Cicero begins a brief *reductio ad absurdum*: his *regnum* could not have been during his consulship, when he actually suppressed a *regnum*. And it would be absurd to say that it occurred when he no longer had consular power, if it did not take place when he had it.

21.3 in quo ... parui Reid observes that Cicero often uses the relative to tack a brief refutation onto his opponent's charge, as at §§ 31 and 54.

As in other passages of self-justification, Cicero disclaims all personal responsibility for the execution of the five captured Catilinarian conspirators on 5 December 63. The line he takes is that the responsibility lay with the senate, while he, although approving of the decision, merely obeyed their orders; cf. *Sest.* 145 *quid tanto opere deliqui illo die ... cum parui vobis?*; *Pis.* 14 *senatui parui; nam relatio illa salutaris et diligens fuerat consulis, animadversio quidem et iudicium senatus*; *Phil.* 2.18 *comprensio sontium mea, animadversio senatus fuit.* Cicero's private view was that the conspirators by their actions (and irrespective of any senatorial decree – only Catiline and Manlius had been formally declared *hostes*; cf. Sal. *Cat.* 36.2) had abdicated all claim to be treated as citizens: see Lintott 171. The execution of the conspirators was of questionable legality because it had never been satisfactorily established that either the passing of the S.C.U. (*Cat.* 1.3–4; Sal. *Cat.* 29.2–3; Asc. 6 C; Plut. *Cic.* 15.4; Dio 37.31.2) or the senate's decree that the men had acted *contra rem publicam* (Sal. *Cat.* 50.3) was sufficient to deprive a citizen of his right under the *lex Sempronia* (*Cat.* 4.10; cf. *Rab. Perd.* 12) to a trial before the people. Technically speaking, the responsibility for the executions did lie with Cicero: the consul held the *imperium*, and consulted the senate as his *consilium* (as implied at *Pis.* 7; *Phil.* 2.11). Cicero acted merely on the advice of the senate, not on their instructions: he was in theory free to reject their recommendation, although in practice this would have been difficult. On the issues raised by the executions see esp. Strachan-Davidson 151–6; *id.*, *Criminal Law* 1.240–45; Greenidge 403f.; Rice Holmes 1.278–82; H. Last, *JRS* 33 (1943) 93–6; Lintott 149–74; T. N. Mitchell, *Historia* 20 (1971) 47–61; Habicht 35–8, 114 n. 9.

b² conjectures *sed* for *et* before *contra*; however, *et* (and, more rarely, *ac*, *atque* and *-que*; cf. § 36 *ac tantum audissent*) may be used in an adversative sense, especially after a negative clause (see K.-S.II.28). On *boni* see 1.10n.

21.5 a me videlicet regnum the order of *Tω* provides a cretic-spondee, which is preferable to the spondaic rhythm of *videlicet a me regnum* (*V*). In *Tω*, however, *videlicet* has been miscopied as *iudices*. For this common corruption see 2.8n.

an tum...potestate *an* is often ironic in Cicero; cf. Haury 318; 7.8n. above. *tum* (*TVδ*), strongly emphatic and in contrast with *nunc*, must be correct, not *tu* (β *Schol.*); the *-m* was perhaps omitted because of *in* following. *Imperium* and *potestas* are both technical (cf. *RE* IX.1201.1ff., XXII.1040.66ff.): *imperium* refers to Cicero's power as consul to command an army, and *potestas* (of which the *fasces* were a symbol) to the non-military powers associated with his office. The terms also cover the emergency powers voted to the consuls of 63 by the senate through the S.C.U.; cf. Sal. *Cat.* 29.3 *ea potestas per senatum more Romano magistratui maxuma permittitur: exercitum parare, bellum gerere, coercere omnibus modis socios atque civis, domi militiaeque imperium atque iudicium summum habere.* Cicero had these supreme powers available to him, he argues, but did not use them to institute *regnum* (cf. 33.12n.).

tanta potestate is the reading of the MSS and is correct (Kasten, through three editions, Boulanger and Pabón all state that they do not know the reading of the MSS at this point). Asyndeton between two nouns is natural in Cicero where the nouns have adjectives, especially in anaphora (T. Stangl cites examples of such asyndeton with *tantus* at *RhM* 65 (1910) 438 n. 1); thus Mai's *tantaque* is unnecessary. On such *asyndeton bimembre* see S. Preuss, *De bimembris dissoluti apud scriptores Romanos usu sollemni* (Edenkoben 1881), esp. 11.

21.6 non dicis...dicis the strong contrast *tum...non dicis... nunc...dicis* is intended to bring out the inconsistency of Torquatus' position, although the repetition of the verb is of course unavoidable when the negative clause precedes the positive (3.5n.). The first *dicis* is given by the scholia as *dices*; Stangl elects to read *dices* in both places.

21.7 quo tandem nomine? 'on what grounds?' *nomen* often contains the idea of a head or account (in a list or ledger); cf. §81 *accusati sunt uno nomine consulares.* Here the word indicates 'a ground of accusation or complaint' (*OLD* s.v. 25). *tandem* indicates impatience and exasperation, as at *Cat.* 1.1.

'quod, in quos...absolutum iri' cf. §48 *'cur dixisti testimonium in alios?' quia coactus sum*; §83 *qui testimonium de coniuratione dixi in alios.* Torquatus' vigorous accusation is deliberately lamely expressed. Editors object to the slight ellipses, but they are natural in the colloquial Latin in which Cicero is expressing Torquatus' grievance. W. G. Pluygers wanted to tidy up the sentence by reading *defendis ⟨is⟩ sperat* (*Mnemosyne* 9

(1881) 137), unnecessarily. On ascribed *oratio recta* see 3.11n.; a type of *altercatio* has now begun (21.1n.).

21.10 si...probare a neat *complexio*, with each of the two possible alternatives effectively rebutting the opposition's argument (10.3n.). For the 'indirect' *si falsum dixerim* see Ernout-Thomas 421f. *Tω* have *eos* for *eosdem*, but the scholia confirm the reading of *V*. However, the scholia give *si* for *sin*, an easy and common mistake made also at §§25 and 27 below. *probare* is 'to prove your case'; Graevius thought the word unnecessary, but it completes the sense besides providing a molossus-double-trochee clausula instead of a series of eight long syllables.

21.12 tantum '*only* so much', and no more (*OLD* s.v. 2a). The restrictive use is common in Cicero (cf. §§36, 39, 43, 62, 71, 82).

opes...potentiam for the pairing cf. (e.g.) *Sest.* 134; *de Orat.* 2.335; *Phil.* 1.29; *Off.* 1.9, 1.86, 2.24. Both words are commonly used as characteristics of *regnum*: see H. Drexler, *RhM* 102 (1959) 50–95; Hellegouarc'h 237–42 ('le mot *potentia*...a souvent revêtu un sens péjoratif et désigne alors l'autorité brutale des tyrans', 242); Diehl 73–6.

21.13 fidem defensionis cf. *Clu.* 10, 118.

22.2 profugisset except in cases of emergency defendants were not imprisoned before or during the trial, and voluntary exile was therefore commonly resorted to (e.g. by Verres and Milo) as a means of avoiding condemnation; cf. Greenidge 467.

si...concedam *iam* is 'for the moment', 'for the sake of argument'; cf. J. N. Madvig on *Fin.* 4.66; H. A. J. Munro on Lucr. 1.968. I read *hoc tibi* (*Tδ*), not *tibi hoc* (*Vβ*), because of the parallel phrase *si hoc tibi dem* below; cf. *Ver.* 4.8 *si id quod vis tibi ego concedam*.

22.4 suo stare iudicio 'rely on their own judgement'; cf. *Pis.* 77 *ut illi plane suo stare iudicio non liceret* (with R. G. M. Nisbet's note).

si hoc tibi dem balancing *si iam· hoc tibi concedam* above, with *dem* meaning the same as *concedam*, i.e. 'grant', 'concede' (cf. §63 *tantum fraterno amori dandum*).

22.6 uter tandem rex est Cicero succeeds in turning the argument round (*retorsio argumenti*) to make Torquatus the *rex*, the man from whom innocent victims flee into exile *indicta causa*; at §27 he will even produce a tyrant from Torquatus' own family-tree. It is a noteworthy feature of Cicero's method of argument that he aims, where possible, not only to clear himself of the accusations made against him, but to prove the prosecution themselves guilty of what they allege. We see this again at §25 where Cicero, in reply to the charge of being a *peregrinus*, shows Torquatus himself to be of 'foreign' descent. Similarly, remembering the accusations of *crudelitas* and *regnum*, Cicero suggests at §90 that Torquatus may be something of a sadist in his continued persecution of Sulla. The technique may be used with any argument which is *commune* (*Inv.* 1.90; Quint. *Inst.* 5.13.29) to both parties; cf. Rohde 128f.

22.7 calamitosos see 1.2n.

at hic etiam *hic* is again 'in this context' (cf. §§ 21, 50, 67). Having completed his initial remarks on the *regnum* charge, Cicero now makes a transition to the less damaging part of Torquatus' invective, the allegation that he is a *peregrinus*. When this is completed he will revert (§ 25) to the *regnum* accusation to justify his actions as consul. The transition from *regnum* to *peregrinitas* is made in two stages. In this sentence the element of *peregrinitas* is added to Torquatus' *regnum* charge; in the next the *regnum* element is removed, leaving the *peregrinitas* to be accounted for.

22.8 id...fuit Cicero makes a patronising criticism of the younger orator's judgement (31.6n.): Torquatus has not learned to appreciate when joking is misplaced (cf. *de Orat.* 2.244, 2.247). Antony is similarly faulted: *at etiam quodam loco facetus esse voluisti. Quam id te, di boni, non decebat!* (*Phil.* 2.20). At the trial of Murena, on the other hand, Cato deemed Cicero's joking inappropriate for a Roman consul (Plut. *Cat. Mi.* 21.5). On Cicero's use of humour see Laurand 234–55; Haury *passim.* I place *minime* after *necesse* (as *Tω*) rather than after *quod* (*V*): the dislocation of the word is more easily explained if it originally followed *necesse* (thus Pabón 10). See also K. Busche, *Hermes* 46 (1911) 60.

22.9 Tarquinium et Numam the two most conspicuously 'foreign' kings of Rome, the fifth and the second (one can only guess at why Cicero inverts their chronological order). The scholia give the traditional version of their origins, that Numa Pompilius (*RE* XVII.1242.44ff., Numa 1) came from Sabine Cures, and that (L.) Tarquinius 'Priscus' (*RE* IV A.2369.27ff., Tarquinius 6) was the son of a Demaratus of Corinth *qui fugiens dominationem Cypseli in Italiam se Tarquinios contulerat ibique liberos procrearat*; cf. Polyb. 6.11a.7; Cic. *Rep.* 2.25, 2.34; *Tusc.* 5.109; Virg. *A.* 6.811; Dion. Hal. 2.58.3, 3.46.3–5; Liv. 1.18.1, 1.34.2; Strab. 5.2.2, 8.6.20; V. Max. 3.4.2; *CIL* XIII.1668 (=*ILS* 212) col. 1; Plin. *Nat.* 35.16, 35.152; Plut. *Num.* 3.3–4, *Rom.* 16.8, *Publ.* 14.1. Numa may have been Sabine, although his names appear Etruscan (cf. R. M. Ogilvie on Liv. 1–5, p. 88). The Demaratus story is consistent with the archaeological evidence (Corinthian pottery predominates in seventh-century Etruria) and seems credible, although the tale of Demaratus' migration to Etruria should be separated from the stories of Tarquinius' migration to Rome and accession; cf. A. Blakeway, *JRS* 25 (1935) 129–49; Ogilvie, *op. cit.* 141f., 145. Tarquinius 'Superbus' was also Etruscan; but since he was not the first Etruscan king his *peregrinitas* was less conspicuous, and thus the position of third foreign king could be reserved for Cicero. With

Cicero's designation as third foreign king cf. Lentulus' boast that he was destined to be the third of the Cornelii to rule Rome (16.3n.).

me … dixisti i.e. *cum Tarquinium et Numam peregrinos reges fuisse et me tertium (esse) dixisti* (Putsche). To remove the ellipse, Müller suggested deletion of *Tarquinium et Numam et* as a gloss. K. Busche felt an interpolator would not have put the kings in the wrong order, and conjectured instead *Tarquinium et Numam ante, me tertium*, comparing Sal. *Cat.* 47.2 *Cinnam atque Sullam antea, se tertium esse* (*Hermes* 46 (1911) 61f.). Both proposals weaken the force of Cicero's words.

Cicero now introduces the *peregrinitas* which will occupy him until § 25 *ne gravius refutere*. *peregrinus* applied to Cicero is of course an overstatement since *cives* were not *peregrini*; nevertheless Cicero, achieving the political success normally granted only to members of the most aristocratic Roman families (cf. Sal. *Cat.* 23.6), was frequently sneered at on account of his *origo municipalis* (23.2n.; for Cicero's views on Roman snobbery see *Fam.* 3.7.5). He was taunted by Catiline (like Torquatus, a patrician) as an *inquilinus civis urbis Romae* (Sal. *Cat.* 31.7; cf. App. *BC* 2.2) and mocked by Metellus Nepos (Plut. *Cic.* 26.6) and by Clodius (*Att.* 1.16.10 *'quid', inquit, 'homini Arpinati cum aquis calidis?'*). According to the scholia (in a note thought by B. A. Marshall (on Asc., pp. 12f.) to be perhaps derived from a lost commentary by Asconius on *pro Sulla*), Cicero's consular colleague Antonius ridiculed his origin in a similar fashion (Asc. 93–4 C; Quint. *Inst.* 9.3.94). Further gibes are found at *Har.* 17, and in [Sal.] *Inv. in Cic.*, 1 *reperticius, accitus ac paulo ante insitus huic urbi civis*, 4 *homo novus Arpinas* and 7 *Romule Arpinas* (cf. Quint. *Inst.* 9.3.89). A more favourable picture of *hic novus Arpinas, ignobilis et modo Romae / municipalis eques* (237–8) is given at Juv. 8.236–44. There was also a tradition that Cicero was descended from a Volscian king who waged war on Rome (Plut. *Cic.* 1.1). See further T. Zielinski, *Cicero im Wandel der Jahrhunderte*[3] (Leipzig and Berlin 1912) 280–88; G. B. Lavery, *CB* 49 (1972–3) 86–9; Desmouliez 116–18. Imputations of ξενία are a stock feature of Greek invective: see W. Süss, *Ethos* (Leipzig and Berlin 1910) 248.

22.10 mitto iam Cicero says that he is not for the time being (*iam*, until § 25) going to answer the charge that he is a tyrant. This is an example of *reticentia*, a device by which the orator passes over something (and truly passes over it), leaving the audience with the impression that there were additional points which he could have used; cf. S. Usher, *AJP* 86 (1965) 175–92 (lists Ciceronian instances). The technique thus resembles *praeteritio* (14.12n.) and *occultatio* (73.1n.). This example of *reticentia* is not quite typical since Cicero later will argue his points; but he still gives the impression here of forgoing useful arguments. Further examples (often introduced by *mitto* or *omitto*) occur below at §§ 70, 71, 72 and 92. The term *reticentia* is also used to translate ἀποσιώπησις, a sudden breaking-off of speech. *mittere* + infinitive is colloquial; the construction is found elsewhere in the speeches only at *Quint.* 85 and *S. Rosc.* 53 (quoted in next note). See G. Landgraf on *S. Rosc.* 53.

illud quaero adversative asyndeton; cf. *Quint.* 85 *mitto illud dicere... illud dico; S. Rosc.* 53 *mitto quaerere qua de causa; quaero qui scias; S. Rosc.* 76 *verum haec missa facio; illud quaero...; Flac.* 79 *mitto* (six times)*...; illud quaero; Luc.* 95 *sed hoc omitto, illud quaero.*

22.11 peregrinum emphatic by position. Cicero indicates that this is the part of the accusation to which he now turns.

ita i.e. a *peregrinus* (on *ita* used for the adjective *talis* see K.-S.I.9f.). Cicero ridicules Torquatus' gibe: 'if I really am a foreigner, it is less extraordinary that I should be a king – for, as you have shown, there are precedents for foreign kings at Rome – than it is that a consul at Rome should have been a foreigner'. Torquatus called Cicero a foreign king, but Rome is used to them: a foreign consul (a constitutional impossibility) would be more surprising.

22.12 me esse *Tω* read *esse me*, but I prefer the more natural order found above (*peregrinum cur me esse dixeris*).

22.13 duo iam the MSS have *etiam*, which gives the wrong sense. *duo iam* (from *II iam*) is Müller's (not Clark's) brilliant solution; he also offered, less persuasively, *iam* and *iam ante*.

22.14 Romae the word seems superfluous. *me* would fit the argument better: *non tam est admirandum regem me esse... quam consulem me fuisse peregrinum*; the corrupt *Romae* (spelt in the MSS *rome*) would have been remembered from *Romae* above. But I refrain from printing my own conjecture in this instance.

23.2 ex municipio *municipia* (the term denotes the obligation to provide troops, *munus*) were originally (i.e. from 338) Italian communities which had accepted Roman *civitas sine suffragio*; they were autonomous in everything except foreign policy. Arpinum became a *municipium* in 305–3 and progressed to full citizenship as a *municipium civium Romanorum* in 188; a century later (90–89) the *suffragium* was extended to all remaining Latin and allied states. After the political unification of Italy the distinction between those of urban and municipal origin came to be forgotten, but this was a slow process in aristocratic circles: the adjective *municipalis* is used disparagingly as late as Tacitus (of Sejanus: *Ann.* 4.3 *municipali adultero*). Cicero's defiant pride in his *municipium* is in part a reaction against this prejudice (22.9n.): he enjoyed comparing himself with his famous Arpinate predecessor Marius (23.3n.) and he made a point of speaking out for the municipal men of Italy (at e.g. *Planc.* 20, mentioning Cato, Coruncanius and Marius; *Leg.* 2.6; *Phil.* 3.15) on whose support, especially during his exile, he depended (cf. R. Syme, *PBSR* 14 (1938) 5f.; E. T. Salmon in Martyn, 75–86). The irony of the *municipalis* who saved Rome from the aristocrats who sought to destroy it was later elaborated by Juvenal at 8.231–44. On *municipia* see *RE* xvi.570.25ff.; H. Rudolph, *Stadt und Staat im römischen Italien* (Leipzig 1935); A. N. Sherwin-White, *The Roman Citizenship*[2] (Oxford 1973), esp. 165–73; M. Humbert, *Municipium et civitas sine suffragio* (C.E.F.R. 36; 1978).

fateor et addo etiam an example of *concessio*, where an unfavourable point is conceded as an expression of confidence; cf. Lausberg 425f.

23.3   unde iterum iam salus Arpinum was also the birthplace (c. 157 BC) of C. Marius, the seven-times consul who reorganised the army and saved Rome from the Teutoni and Cimbri in 102–1; cf. *RE* Suppl. vi.1363.41ff., Marius 14; T. F. Carney, *A Biography of C. Marius* (*Proc. Afr. Cl. Ass.* Suppl. 1; 1961); J. Van Ooteghem, *Caius Marius* (Brussels 1964). Cicero and Marius had a certain amount in common (they were distantly related, and both were *novi homines*); nevertheless Marius' salvation of Rome, a favourite point of comparison (*Red. Pop.* 9; *Sest.* 50; *Leg.* 2.6), was of a different order to that of Cicero. On Cicero's view of Marius and use of him as an *exemplum* see T. F. Carney, *WS* 73 (1960) 83–122; Diehl 122–5. Juvenal follows his passage on Cicero with a similar treatment of Marius (8.245–53), and a comparison is also made by Valerius Maximus, *conspicuae felicitatis Arpinas municipium, sive litterarum gloriosissimum contemptorem sive abundantissimum fontem intueri velis* (2.2.3). On Marius' origins see *Planc.* 20; *schol. Bob.* 89.4–7 St.; V. Max. 6.9.14; Plin. *Nat.* 33.150; Fro. *Pr. Hist.* 8 (207 Van den Hout); Sidon. *Carm.* 2.230, 9.258.

23.4   pervelim the only forms of 'pervolo' to occur in Cicero (and in extant Latin, with the exception of *pervelle* once in Livy, 39.43.3) are *pervelim* and *pervellem*.

23.5   esse videantur see 3.9n.

nemo…seni *Tω*, but not *V Schol.*, add *enim* after *nemo* (the two words are palaeographically similar): it is conceivable that *enim* is genuine, since the scholia provide only an abbreviated version of this sentence. Cicero now proceeds to cite some of his favourite *exempla* (who often appear with C. Fabricius, a native Roman therefore not appropriate here); cf. *Mur.* 17; *Planc.* 20; *Brut.* 55; *Parad.* 12; *N.D.* 2.165; *Senect.* 15, 43; *Amic.* 18, 39. On the use of such *exempla* by Cicero and others see H. W. Litchfield, *HSCP* 25 (1914) 1–71; T. P. Wiseman, *New Men in the Roman Senate, 139 BC–AD 14* (Oxford 1971) 107–16.

M. Porcius Cato 'Censorius' (*RE* xxii.108.8ff., Porcius 9; *MRR* 1.339,

374f.; III.170; Sumner 33), consul in 195 and censor of notorious severity in 184, was a *novus homo* born in 234 at Tusculum, a *municipium* which in 381 had been the first Latin state to obtain Roman *civitas*. See A. E. Astin, *Cato the Censor* (Oxford 1978); D. Kienast, *Cato der Zensor*[2] (Darmstadt 1979). *seni* indicates 'of old' (*OLD* 1c); Cicero often describes Cato thus, to differentiate him from his famous great-grandson (tr.pl. 62). In this sense, *senex* does not necessarily imply longevity (cf. Stat. *Silv.* 1.2.252–3 *Philitas / Callimachusque senex*); but Cato did in fact live to be eighty-five, dying in 149.

23.6 inimicos cf. *Ver.* 5.180 (*M. Cato*) *hominum potentissimorum suscepit inimicitias*. Cato's active opposition to the corruption and philhellenism of the aristocracy earned him many enemies; his censorship also claimed prominent victims (L. Flamininus, L. Scipio). He was prosecuted many times but never convicted: see Liv. 39.40.8–9; Plin. *Nat.* 7.100; Plut. *Cat. Ma.* 29.4 (= *Compar.* 2.4); [Victor] *de vir. ill.* 47.7.

Ti. Coruncanio Ti. Coruncanius (*RE* IV.1663.47ff., Coruncanius 3; *MRR* I.190f., 210, 216) came from outside Rome, whether, like Cato, from Tusculum (the standard late republican view; cf. *Planc.* 20; *schol. Bob.* on this passage) or from Camerium (Tac. *Ann.* 11.24). The latter ascription will derive from the emperor Claudius' researches; cf. R. Syme, *Tacitus* (Oxford 1958) 710 n. 4. The two statements need not be incompatible: F. Münzer suggests that the family originated in Camerium and later settled at Tusculum (*RE* IV.1663.1ff.). Coruncanius was an early jurist, consul in 280, dictator in 246 and the first plebeian *pontifex maximus*, 254–43.

23.7 M'. Curio M'. Curius Dentatus (*RE* IV.1841.9ff., Curius 9; *MRR* I.183f., 195f., 198; III.78f.; Sumner 28f.) appealed to Cicero (cf. *Mur.* 17) as a *novus homo* from outside Rome and a plebeian hero whose achievements were comparable with those of Marius. He was consul in 290, 275 and 274, and censor in 272; he completed the Third Samnite War in 290 and the war against Pyrrhus in 275. His place of origin is uncertain. *Sabinis oriundus videtur*, the scholiast's guess, is a false inference from *Rep.* 3.40 and *Senect.* 55, where Cato's Sabine farm is said not to be far from Curius' abode (in the territory he captured, not where he was born): see G. Forni, *Athenaeum* 31 (1953) 183–93. The anecdote referred to by the scholiast, how Curius declined the Samnites' gold, is told at *Senect.* 56 and elsewhere (see J. G. F. Powell on *Senect.* 55). The praenomen, omitted by the MSS, is added by Manutius; the scholiast gives it as *Mario* (from *C. Mario* ahead) in the lemma, but reports it correctly in the accompanying note.

huic ... C. Mario *huic* indicates a leap forward in time; *nostro* is 'my fellow Arpinate'. For Marius see 23.3n.

23.8 inviderent cf. *Prov.* 19 *quis plenior inimicorum fuit C. Mario?*, where Cicero cites as enemies L. Crassus, M. Aemilius Scaurus and the Metelli. Marius made many enemies: his patron Metellus Numidicus, whom he supplanted in Africa (Sal. *Jug.* 64; Plut. *Mar.* 8; cf. *Off.* 3.79); the optimates, through his association with Saturninus; and L. Sulla. Marius was also hated for his massacre at Rome in 87.

23.10 iacere potueris as in English, insults may be 'hurled': see *OLD* s.v. 7; H. A. Holden on *Planc.* 30. There is a hint here of further condescending criticism of Torquatus' oratorical attempt (31.6n.).

VIII 23.11 a me *a/ab* with the ablative after the gerundive is used here instead of the more usual dative (found at e.g. §82) to express the agent. This usage, relatively rare in Latin outside Cicero's speeches and letters, is employed most often when the object is personal, either to give emphasis or to avoid ambiguity; cf. E. Audouin, *RPh* 11 (1887) 69–74; J. N. Madvig on *Fin.* 2.30; K.-S.1.730. J. G. Griffith (*CR* n.s. 10 (1960) 189–92) remarks that this construction often occurs in legal or religious contexts and so may have been formal.

causis...necessitudinis for *causis* as 'ties' of friendship see *TLL* III.688.4ff.; Merguet III.276. The expression *causa...necessitudinis* is quite common in Cicero.

23.12 monendum...atque etiam Cicero now applies the condescension which is a characteristic feature of his attitude towards Torquatus, advising him how to conduct himself, criticising his oratorical efforts (§§ 22, 25, 30–32) and later, with seeming generosity, making allowances for his youth and temper (§§ 46–7). Cornelius on the other hand is simply dismissed as a *puer* (§ 51).

The tactic is widely used in other speeches, especially where Cicero's opponent is young (cf. Quint. *Inst.* 11.1.68). Caecilius has to face a long lecture on the qualifications of a prosecutor, filled with supposedly well-meant advice which in fact demolishes every pretension of his to speak in public (*Div. Caec.* 27–47). In *pro Murena* Sulpicius is gently (as if he were Cicero's own brother, 10) told that his birth and legal expertise count for nothing (15–30), while Cato, Cicero opines, will become calmer and more mellow when he grows older (60–66). Cicero patronisingly compliments the youthful Atratinus on the obvious reluctance with which he attacked Caelius' morals (*Cael.* 8) and at *Lig.* 8 he looks favourably on Tubero, his *adulescentis propinqui* who, he says, shows considerable promise.

23.13 patricii patricians were the privileged non-plebeian class of citizens; the origin of the patriciate has been much disputed, but identification with the *patres* (senators) of the early republic is generally agreed. In Cicero's time patricians retained much of their social prestige but the patriciate was by now of diminished political importance: patricians alone enjoyed the *patrum auctoritas* and could become *interrex* and perhaps *princeps senatus*, but (as from 367) only one consulship in each year was open to them. By 55 the number of patrician *gentes* represented in the senate had dropped to fourteen: Caesar and Octavian found it necessary to create more patrician families to enable the patriciate to fulfil its traditional duties (the greater *flamines* and half the *pontifices* were still required to be patrician). Torquatus had attacked Cicero's origins (Sulla's, of course, were impeccable), but it would be surprising if, like Ser. Sulpicius Rufus the previous year (*Mur.* 15–16), he had made much of his own patrician status. By replying as if he had, Cicero aims to arouse against him *invidia* on the part of the jury, few if any of whom are likely to have been patrician. On patricians see further *RE* xviii.4.2222.65ff.; A. Momigliano, *JRS* 53 (1963) 117f.; J. Heurgon, *The Rise of Rome to 264 BC* (London 1973) 110–12; A. Momigliano, *CAH²* vii.2.101–6.

23.14 curant the subject, 'those who are not *patricii*', is understood: see Lebreton 151.

aequales tui 'men of your age', condescending again. *tui* is genitive (see K.-S.1.448).

23.15 abs te anteiri i.e. 'are inferior to you'. On *abs te* see 3.1n.

24.2 et nomen et honos the first *et* is omitted in *V*, but omission seems more likely than interpolation.

inveteravit intransitive, 'have become familiar' (singular after the nearer subject); cf. §81 *num inveterata quam recens debuit esse gravior?*

24.3 competitores tuos Torquatus must have been facing an election in the near future, but the office is uncertain. If he was standing for the quaestorship, the delay before he reached the praetorship in c. 49 (see p. 19) would seem unaccountably long, given his family and connections; Sumner (139f.) therefore suggests that he was standing for either the military tribunate (six military tribunes for each of the four *legiones urbanae* were elected by the people) or the vigintisexvirate. The former is more likely in view of T. P. Wiseman's plausible identification of the Mallius of *Att.* 1.16.16 (taking a letter of Cicero's to Macedonia in the spring of 61) with Torquatus, who might therefore have been setting out on a military tribunate (*CR* n.s. 15 (1965) 263; cf. L. R. Taylor, *The Voting Districts of the Roman Republic* (Rome 1960) 228; Shackleton Bailey, *Nomenclature* 31).

24.4 iam 'now', in the forthcoming election.

ex tota Italia delecti i.e. the most talented men from every Italian *municipium* (23.2n.). Technically, Italy still terminated at the Rubicon, despite the extension of the citizenship in 89 to all communities south of the Po; Cisalpine Gaul was incorporated within Italy by Augustus. Cicero often talks of *tota Italia* (Merguet IV.757); on his affection for Italy see E. T. Salmon in Martyn, 75–86. R. Syme (*PBSR* 14 (1938) 5f.) remarks that the senate included many municipal men at this date, but that there were still peoples which had not yet sent a senator to Rome.

24.5 honore ... dignitate 'office ... position' (1.1n.).

24.6 tu cave the choice between *tu cave* ('you take care...') and *cave tu* (presumably 'take care that you...', with *appelles*) is difficult. Both would be possible: see G. Lodge, *Lexicon Plautinum* (Leipzig 1901–33) 1.243f. Perhaps *tu cave* (*V*) is more appropriate, stressing *cave* rather than *appelles*; cf. *Att.* 1.19.10 *hic tu cave dicas*.

24.7 peregrinorum suffragiis ironic: real *peregrini* could not vote.

nervos commonly used figuratively for 'energy', 'determination' or perhaps 'muscle'; cf. *Ver.* 35; *Flac.* 13; *Fam.* 6.1.3. The *municipales* are lean, sleek competitors. *nervi* often feature in discussions of rhetorical style: see A. E. Douglas on *Brut.* 121.

24.8 excutient *excutere* is used for 'shaking' some undesirable characteristic or opinion out of someone; cf. *Mur.* 30; *Cael.* 67; *Tusc.* 1.111; *N.D.* 3.7. The colloquialism and vigour of the word suit it well to comedy: see Fantham 53; R. O. A. M. Lyne, *Further Voices in Vergil's* Aeneid (Oxford 1987) 52, 58f.

24.9 ex somno ... excitabunt another metaphor; *somnum* often describes a lack of awareness or alertness (e.g. *Cat.* 3.16 *P. Lentuli somnum*). One is reminded of Marcellus the candidate (probably the *filius* of § 19) snoring the night before the elections (*Att.* 4.3.5).

24.10 abs te see 3.1n.

virtute *virtus* was a quality open to all *viri*, and in Cicero's eyes peculiarly appropriate to *novi homines*, whose *virtus* enabled them to overcome the disadvantage of their equestrian origin: see Hellegouarc'h 476–83; Mitchell II.33, 50.

25.1 ac si *ac* and *at* are very easily confused in MSS. *at si* (*V*) would certainly be possible (cf. K.-S.II.83f.; *TLL* II.1002.28), but *quod si* or *sin* would be more usual. *ac si* at the start of § 24 is another argument for reading *ac si* here.

25.2 patriciis see 23.13n.

et vos Cicero casually implies that Torquatus had also accused the jury of being *peregrini*.

25.3 hoc vitium sileretur 'this defect should have been passed over in silence'. The subjunctive is best taken as jussive, despite Reid's objections; cf. J. B. Mayor on *N.D.* 3.76; J. N. Madvig on *Fin.* 2.35; Handford 6of.; Nägelsbach 421f.; K.-S.I.187. On the transitive use of *silere* cf. *Flac.* 6; *Red. Sen.* 30; *Tusc.* 3.57; *Phil.* 9.10 (K.-S.1.264). Cicero again slips in a patronising criticism of Torquatus' oratorical prudence (31.6n.). He has already argued that it is Torquatus, not he, who is the tyrant (§ 22): now similarly it is Torquatus who is the *peregrinus* (*retorsio argumenti*). Cicero is highly ingenious in making fun of Torquatus as both a patrician and a foreigner. Gulielmius (and, later, Rubenius (4)) proposed *convicium* for *vitium* on the grounds that *peregrinitas* is not a fault, but this misses Cicero's irony.

25.4 a materno genere this is an extension of the use of *a* in *a matre*, 'on the mother's side' (the scholia omit the preposition); cf. *TLL* VIII.468.21ff.

municipalis see 23.2n.

nobilissimi generis see 37.5n.

25.5 sed tamen Asculani this more than negates the approbation just given. It was a massacre of Roman citizens at Asculum (in Picenum, north-east of Rome) which in 91 sparked off the Social War; the town surrendered after a two-year siege and was severely punished (Liv. *epit.* 72, 76; Vell. 2.21.1; Fron. *Str.* 3.17.8; App. *BC* 1.38, 1.47–8; Flor. 2.6.9– 14; Oros. 5.18; cf. *RE* II.1527.37ff.). The pointed emphasis on *Asculani* ensures that the reference will not be missed: Cicero is implying that Torquatus sprang from stock hostile to Rome. Criticism of parents' origins was a regular feature of ancient invective (cf. *Phil.* 3.15 *ignobilitatem obicit C. Caesaris filio . . . 'Aricina mater'. Trallianam aut Ephesiam putes dicere*): see R. G. M. Nisbet on *Pis.*, p. 194 (cf. 22.9n.). C. E. Stevens (*Latomus* 22 (1963) 413), G. V. Sumner (*Phoenix* 19 (1965) 230), R. J. Seager (J. Bibauw (ed.), *Hommages à Marcel Renard* (Brussels 1969) II.684) and Stockton (78) all point out that a Picentine wife would link the elder Torquatus with Pompey's *clientela*. This is plausible in view of Torquatus' having served as a legate of Pompey in 67 before going out to Asia (11.4n.).

aut igitur the start of a *complexio* (10.3n.).

25.7 non anteponere to have been born at Arpinum was obviously better than to have had one's origins at Asculum. *ante non ponere* (δ) gives a more favoured rhythm (double-cretic) than *non anteponere*, as Clark observes; for the division of *anteponere* cf. *Off.* 3.71 *ponit ante*; Hor. *S.* 1.3.92 *positum ante*. But *non anteponere* (cretic-iambus) is not in itself objectionable.

neque . . . dixeris on the use of the perfect subjunctive in prohibitions see Lebreton 300; and on the negatives *neque . . . neque* instead of *neve . . . neve* in this construction see K.-S.1.194.

25.8 neque regem, ne derideare Cicero began *digressio* III with a defence of his alleged *regnum* in the courts before moving on to his reply to the *peregrinitas* gibe. Now he effects the transition to the potentially more damaging part of the *regnum* charge, that relating to his conduct during his consulship (briefly touched upon in § 21).

25.9 nisi forte regium on one level this sentence can be understood, as it is by the scholiast, without reference to Stoicism, simply as an ironic comment that if by *regnum* Torquatus means the exact opposite of how tyrants normally behave, then Cicero is happy to declare himself a tyrant, i.e. for Cicero to be called a tyrant, normal definitions have to be reversed (*nisi forte* frequently introduces irony, as at § 37; cf. Seyffert, *Schol. Lat.* 1.131f.; Haury 81; 7.8n. above). The passage thus makes sense without prior philosophical knowledge. Those members of Cicero's public acquainted with Stoicism, on the other hand, would have appreciated his meaning to the full. It was a commonplace of Stoic teaching that the wise man, having attained virtue, was a βασιλεύς (besides being free, rich, happy, beautiful etc., doctrines later treated in Cicero's *Paradoxa Stoicorum* (46)); cf. *SVF* 1.53.10; 111.81.31, 150.17, 158.24, 158.35, 159.1, 159:15, 159.23, 242.1; *Fin.* 3.75 *rectius enim appellabitur rex quam Tarquinius*; Hor. *Ep.* 1.1.59–60 *'rex eris' aiunt, / 'si recte facies'*. So there is one respect only in which Cicero is a *rex*: his exemplary behaviour corresponds to that of the enlightened Stoic βασιλεύς, the antithesis of the τύραννος he is accused of being. On *rex* as a term of approbation see M. T. Griffin, *Seneca, a Philosopher in Politics* (Oxford 1976) 141–7; K. M. Coleman on Stat. *Silv.* 4.1.46. On Cicero and Stoic ethics see M. Valente, *L'Éthique stoïcienne chez Cicéron* (Paris 1956); G. B. Kerferd in Martyn, 60–74.

25.10 homini nemini *nemo homo* originated in early Latin as an intensification of *nemo*; here, however, *homini* is required in order to contrast with *cupiditati*. It is generally stated that in Cicero the words are always found separated except here and at *Fam.* 13.55.1, but to these exceptions add *N.D.* 1.78 and *Fam.* 3.5.1; cf. *TLL* VI.3.2884.42ff.; H.-Sz.56, 205; Hofmann 92 (cf. 196). The Stoics did not approve, naturally, of being enslaved to another person (cf. *Parad.* 5 (*omnem stultum servum*, = 33–41), esp. 41), although they did consider influencing an autocrat to be a valid means of effecting political change; cf. *SVF* 111.173f.

cupiditati . . . ulli the Stoic βασιλεύς has overcome greed; cf. Hor. *Carm.* 2.2.9–10 *latius regnes avidum domando / spiritum.*

contemnere . . . libidines the wise man subdues his passions; cf. *SVF* 1.50ff., 129f.; 111.108ff. The Stoics aimed to eradicate violent passion (πάθος), but not emotion: see F. H. Sandbach, *The Stoics*[2] (Bristol 1989) 59–68.

25.11 non auri . . . indigere the wise man alone is rich; cf. *Parad.* 6 (= 42–52); *SVF* 111.154ff.

25.12 in senatu sentire libere *sentire = sententiam dicere* (*OLD* s.v.

7a); cf. §82 *quis non constantissime sensit?* Cicero now moves to teachings which are less central to the doctrine but more relevant to his own position: *sentire libere* is to give one's own independent view regardless of the consequences to oneself. The concept is contained in the Stoic paradox that the wise man alone is free (cf. *SVF* III.154ff.), treated by Cicero as *Parad.* 5 (=33–41; cf. 34 *quis igitur vivit ut vult nisi... qui nihil dicit... nisi libenter ac libere..?*). On freedom of speech (παρρησία, ἐλευθερία; cf. 80.9n.) see Wirszubski 18, 21, 89.

populi...voluntati freedom of policy, which distinguishes the statesman from the demagogue; cf. *Cat.* 4.9 *intellectum est quid interesset inter levitatem contionatorum et animum vere popularem saluti populi consulentem; Amic.* 93. The contrast occurs later in a passage quoted by Aquila Romanus: *tam diu Ti. Gracchus populo gratus fuit, quam diu leges ad voluntatem eius, non ad utilitatem rei publicae compositas ferebat* (34, =33 Halm); and also in Augustine: *et ubi est quod et vestrae litterae illum laudant patriae rectorem, qui populi utilitati magis consulat quam voluntati? (epist.* 104 in A. Goldbacher (ed.), *Corp. Script. Eccl. Lat.* XXXIV (Vienna etc. 1895) 587), *quorum potius utilitati consulendum est quam voluntati (epist.* 138 in *op. cit.* XLIV (1904) 140).

25.13 nemini...obsistere the balance is aided by similar rhythms; cf. Zielinski, *Constr. Rhyth.* 155.

25.14 si...confiteor the argument is again in the form of a *complexio* (10.3n.). *regium* (*T*δ) is greatly preferable to *regnum* (*V*β) on grounds of sense. *me regem* (*V*ω), with *me* emphatic (2.7n.), appears to be the reading of the archetype, although one can sympathise with the preference of Clark and K. Busche (*Hermes* 46 (1911) 60f.) for *regem me* (*T*).

25.15 sin te potentia mea *V* has *si* for *sin*, a common mistake made also at §§21 and 27. For *potentia* (here virtually = *regnum*) see 21.12n. In this tricolon the third unit is extended, and ends in a more favoured rhythm than the first two (4.13n.).

dominatio τυραννίς (21.1n.).

25.17 verbi invidiam the *verbum* is *regnum*. Cicero talks of *verbi invidia* elsewhere at *Cat.* 3.3, *Planc.* 75 and *Fin.* 1.43, always referring to a specific word.

IX 26.1 Ego having completed the more closely argued part of his reply to Torquatus' attack on his *regnum*, Cicero now moves to the offensive, justifying his actions by giving an assertive account of the nature of his services to the state and expressing pride in his achievement. Once this is completed, he will be in a position to examine the charges against Sulla at §§36ff.

positis *ponere* may be used of expending money, trouble etc. on (*in*) a specified object; cf. *Tul.* 15; *Mur.* 45; *Att.* 1.13.1.

26.3 honestum otium retirement from public life which is honourable, i.e. not marked by idleness and dissipation. This type of *otium* differs from *cum dignitate otium* (1.10n.): *honestum otium* involves separation from affairs of state, while *cum dignitate otium*, with reference to an individual, refers to leisure within an active political career (C. Wirszubski, *JRS* 44 (1954) 12f.; cf. M. Kretschmar, *Otium: Studia Litterarum* (Leipzig 1938); J.-M.André, *L'Otium dans la vie morale et intellectuelle romaine* (Paris 1966) 279–334; W. A. Laidlaw, *G&R* 15 (1968) 42–52). Cicero's argument is as follows: no one could object if he declined the usual rewards of political success, and instead asked only for an honourable retirement; but since he does not ask even for that, but continues to labour for the benefit of others, how can he be called a tyrant? The scholiast quotes a passage of C. Gracchus which Cicero may have had in mind, *si vellem aput vos verba facere et a vobis postulare* (since my family has suffered so much because of you etc.) *ut pateremini hoc tempore me quiescere...haud ⟨scio⟩ an lubentibus a vobis impetrassem* (*orat.* 47, = *ORF* 1.190f.); cf. Norden 178. See also Liv. ap. Plin. *Nat. praef.* 16.

sibi haberent honores cf. *Cat.* 3.26 *quibus pro tantis rebus, Quirites, nullum ego a vobis praemium virtutis, nullum insigne honoris, nullum monumentum laudis postulabo praeterquam huius diei memoriam sempiternam. In animis ego vestris omnis triumphos meos, omnia ornamenta honoris, monumenta gloriae, laudis insignia condi et conlocari volo; Cat.* 4.23 *pro imperio, pro exercitu, pro provincia quam neglexi, pro triumpho ceterisque laudis insignibus quae sunt a me propter urbis vestraeque salutis custodiam repudiata, pro clientelis hospitiisque provincialibus... nihil a vobis nisi huius temporis totiusque mei consulatus memoriam postulo.* Cicero's rejection of worldly honours continues the philosophical presentation of his behaviour introduced in § 25. The subjunctive is parallel with *liceret* below and must be potential: 'they would keep their honours...', i.e. 'if I were to ask for *otium*, I would not be asking the others to give up their honours...'. *haberent* has no expressed subject, and in view of the antithesis of *mihi liceret* some editors have supplied ⟨*alii*⟩ or ⟨*ceteri*⟩. But since it is far from clear which word should be added and in which position, I have left the subject (viz. 'the other consulars') to be understood; possibly the lack of an expressed subject helps Cicero to avoid causing offence to the consulars who are present. For the anaphora of *sibi* with *habere* cf. *Flac.* 104 *sibi habeant potentiam, sibi honores, sibi ceterorum commodorum summas facultates; liceat eis qui haec salva esse voluerunt ipsis esse salvis; Senect.* 58 (see J. G. F. Powell *ad loc.*). G. Monaco (*Studi classici in onore di Quintino Cataudella* (Catania 1972) III.21–6) believes that Cicero has modelled both these passages and our passage on Plaut. *Curc.* 178–9 *sibi sua habeant regna reges, sibi divitias divites, / sibi honores, sibi virtutes, sibi pugnas, sibi proelia.*

   26.4   imperia military commands (21.5n.).

provincias Cicero was proud of his ostensible unselfishness in declining to take a province; cf. *Agr.* 1.25–6 (1.25 *ut neque provinciam neque honorem neque ornamentum aliquod aut commodum... appetiturus sim*); *Pis.* 5; *Att.* 2.1.3; *Fam.* 5.2.3; Sal. *Cat.* 26.4; Plut. *Cic.* 12.4; Dio 37.33.4. Macedonia and Cisalpine Gaul had been assigned as the consular provinces for 62. Cicero first allowed his colleague Antonius to take the more lucrative Macedonia and later (in May or June) renounced Cisalpine Gaul, which was then allotted to the praetor Metellus Celer (65.4n.). See Rice Holmes 1.457f.; W. Allen, *TAPA* 83 (1952) 233–41; Crawford 82–4.

26.5 alia...insignia cf. §50 *insignia honoris ad te delata sunt* (with 50.4n.); §88 *honoris insignia atque ornamenta. alia* denotes distinctions other than those just mentioned. In a technical sense, *insignia* indicates most importantly the *toga praetexta* (the mark of curule status), the *sella curulis* (81.17n.), the *fasces* and triumphal and priestly robes (for *ornamenta* see 50.2n.); cf. *Sest.* 17 *illis fascibus ceterisque insignibus summi honoris atque imperi.* See Mommsen, *Staatsrecht* 1.372–467. *Insignia* could have regal connotations (*TLL* vii.1.1899.54ff.), and Cicero's renunciation of them therefore underlines the inappropriateness of the accusations of *regnum.* Reid plausibly suggests that Cicero has in mind Pompey as the person most conspicuous for the *honores* granted to him: in 63 he had been voted the right to wear triumphal *insignia* at the games (cf. Vell. 2.40.4; Dio 37.21.3–4). Pompey was never far from Cicero's thoughts, especially during 63–62 (*Fam.* 5.7; *Cons.* fr. 6 Soubiran).

mihi strongly emphatic (2.7n.).

26.6 tranquillo...quieto cf. *Mur.* 55 *cum...fortunatos eos homines iudicarem qui remoti a studiis ambitionis otium ac tranquillitatem vitae secuti sunt*; *Rep.* 1.1 [sc. Cato] *in his undis et tempestatibus ad summam senectutem maluit iactari quam in illa tranquillitate atque otio iucundissime vivere.* The philosophical outlook continues, but without being (as in §25) specifically Stoic: the ideal of *tranquillitas* was common to all philosophers (cf. Sen. *Dial.* 9, *de Tranquillitate Animi*).

26.7 quid...postulo? Nägelsbach's analysis of this passage reveals the elegance and order of its structure (723f.). The clauses are arranged as follows: (a) *quid si hoc non postulo?*; (b) *si* × 5... *omnibus*; (c) *si neque...neque...*; (d) *si me non modo non...sed neque...neque...*; (e) *si* × 5...*omnibus*; (f) *si mihi ne ad ea quidem...* The arrangement follows a natural order (2.2n.), with (e) matching (b) and (d) matching (c). Cicero also uses extensive anaphora of *si* at *Dom.* 147; *Prov.* 35; *Balb.* 64; *Mil.* 67; *Phil.* 13.29 (cf. 19.1n. on anaphora of *cum*).

labor meus pristinus on *labor* see 5.4n. *pristinus* is 'long-standing' (*OLD* s.v. 4).

26.8 officia the aid Cicero has brought to individuals (2.5n.).

26.9 si...in curia cf. *Senect.* 32 *non curia vires meas desiderat, non rostra, non amici, non clientes, non hospites.*

26.11 rerum gestarum vacatio the genitive expresses the reason for the exemption, 'because of what I have achieved' (Nägelsbach 433); cf. *Cael.* 30 *vacationem adulescentiae; Leg.* 1.10 *aetatis... vacationi;* Nep. *Att.* 7.1 *aetatis vacatione.*

26.12 aetatis excusatio cf. *Sest.* 112 *nec valetudinis excusationem nec senectutis; Pis.* 36 *vel aetatis excusatione vel honoris; Deiot.* 9 *aetatis excusatione.* Cicero was forty-four in 62. The *morbi excusatio* was a means of avoiding court appearances: see Greenidge 474.

26.13 industria one of the qualities brought to bear by the *municipales* at § 24.

si animus, si aures on Cicero's fondness for play on *animus* and *aures* see 12.14n.

26.14 quae...gessi cf. § 34 *quas... pro salute rei publicae suscepi atque gessi;* § 83 *quae pro salute omnium gessi.*

recordanda et cogitanda Cicero finally found time for such reflection in 60, when he completed a prose account of his consulship in Greek and contemplated a Latin version (cf. *Att.* 1.19.10, 1.20.6, 2.1.1; Dio 46.21.3). Soon afterwards he wrote a poem *de Consulatu suo,* parts of which survive (frr. ed. J. Soubiran 1972). See F. Bömer, *Hermes* 81 (1953) 236–41; M. Laffranque, *RPhilos* 152 (1962) 351–8; O. Lendle, *Hermes* 95 (1967) 90–109.

26.16 regnum see 21.1n.

vicarius 'successor'; cf. *Mur.* 80 *in exitu iam est meus consulatus; nolite mihi subtrahere vicarium meae diligentiae.*

27.1 a me omitted by *Tω*; the words prepare for the *retorsio argumenti* to follow.

sin *Tω* have *si* for *sin,* a common error made also at §§ 21 and 25.

27.2 ut ne...memoriam the clause is 'stipulative', with jussive subjunctive, meaning 'without your doing so and so'; cf. Handford 52; R. G. Austin on *Cael.* 8; G. Landgraf on *S. Rosc.* 55; J. S. Reid on *Fin.* 2.24. *replicare* is to 'unroll' a book (as at *Corn.* 1 fr. 44 Puccioni); the word is used figuratively again at *Leg.* 3.31 *si velis replicare memoriam temporum.* Reid questioned *replices,* proposing *explices,* which has the same meaning but is more common. *memoriam* is (written) history; cf. *TLL* VIII.675.59ff.

27.3 ex domesticis imaginibus wax masks of ancestors who had held curule office were kept in cupboards (*armaria*) within the *atria* of the houses of the *nobiles,* and were displayed and adorned on special occasions and paraded at funerals. The masks were labelled (with *tituli*) and arranged in the form of a family-tree, while nearby rooms contained archives relating to the careers of the men represented; cf. Plin. *Nat.*

35.6–8; Polyb. 6.53 (with F. W. Walbank's notes); *RE* IX.1097.27ff.; E. Bethe, *Ahnenbild und Familiengeschichte bei Römern und Griechen* (Munich 1935); H. T. Rowell, *MAAR* 17 (1940) 131–43; E. Courtney on Juv. 8.1–9. On the *ius imaginum* see 88.8n. The would-be tyrant to whom Cicero alludes is M. Manlius Capitolinus (*RE* XIV.1167.59ff., Manlius 51; *MRR* 1.92, 99), the consul of 392, who in 387 saved the Capitol from the Gauls after being awoken by the sacred geese (cf. R. M. Ogilvie on Liv. 1–5, pp. 694, 734): in 384 he was charged with aiming at tyranny and thrown from the Tarpeian rock (Liv. 6.20; Diod. 15.35.3; cf. *Dom.* 101; *Rep.* 2.49; *Phil.* 1.32, 2.87, 2.114). Manlius Capitolinus was the great-uncle of T. Manlius Imperiosus Torquatus, the ancestor of Torquatus who is referred to at § 32. In alluding to Manlius Capitolinus, Cicero neatly turns the charge of *regnum* back on Torquatus; the same technique was used earlier (§ 22) when Cicero argued that it is Torquatus, not he, who is the *rex*.

27.4 credo ironic (11.7n.).

extulerunt . . . attulerunt for play on different compounds of the same root see Holst 63–70. For *spiritus* as 'arrogance' see *OLD* s.v. 7d.

27.6 qui . . . adeptum fore Cicero expresses his achievement in similar words at § 33 *ego vitam omnium civium . . . urbem hanc denique. eripuerim periculis* (ω) has some claim to consideration as providing the less obvious order; *TV* might each have normalised the hyperbaton independently. On the use of *fore* + perfect participle to express the moment at which an action will be completed see Neue-Wagener III.152f.; K.-S.I.165; Riemann 270.

27.8 in omnis mortalis Landgraf (on *S. Rosc.* 11, followed by Reid; cf. Nägelsbach 126) states that Cicero writes *mortales* for *homines* only in conjunction with *multi*, *omnes* or *cuncti*, although *mortalis nemo* is found at *Amic.* 18. See, however, *Har.* 32; *Div.* 2.30, 2.127. Used in this sense the word has a poetic flavour (cf. *N.D.* 2.110).

27.9 nullum . . . redundarit cf. *Cat.* 1.29 *certe verendum mihi non erat ne quid hoc parricida civium interfecto invidiae mihi in posteritatem redundaret*; *Dom.* 69 *sed prospexistis ne quae popularis in nos aliquando invidia redundaret*; *de Orat.* 1.3 *hoc tempus omne post consulatum obiecimus iis fluctibus qui per nos a communi peste depulsi in nosmet ipsos redundarent*. The scholiast (on § 28) regards the present passage as exhibiting remarkable foresight, but to Cicero in 62 the dangers which he faced were obvious enough: see pp. 27f. In 60, when the Catilinarians were published (*Att.* 2.1.3), they were greater still (pp. 54f.).

28.1 res tantas referring loosely to § 27 *res enim gestae* and *quibus de rebus tam claris, tam immortalibus*. Seyffert (8) prefers *rem tantam* (*Schol.*), referring to *beneficio*, but this seems less appropriate.

in qua urbe I prefer the reading of the scholia to the probable reading of the archetype, *qua in urbe*, because of the strict parallelism in the rest of this sentence.

28.3 a vestris cervicibus depuli danger is regularly placed on or removed from the *cervices*; cf. *Cat.* 3.17 *non facile hanc tantam molem mali a cervicibus vestris depulissem*; *Dom.* 63 *hanc ego vim, pontifices, hoc scelus, hunc furorem... ab omnium bonorum cervicibus depuli, omnemque impetum discordiarum... excepi meo corpore*; *Phil.* 3.8. *V* offers *repuli* (i.e. *reppuli*), which may be correct (cf. *Mil.* 77 *'P. Clodium... a cervicibus vestris reppuli'*); *depuli* is preferred merely because the three instances given above of *depellere a cervicibus* outnumber the single case of *repellere*, and because the context of *Cat.* 3.17 and *Dom.* 63 is similar to that here.

a meis adversative asyndeton.

28.4 nisi vero ironic (7.8n.).

28.6 faces... extorquere Cicero regularly describes his suppression of the conspiracy in such language, e.g. *Cat.* 2.2 *ei ferrum e manibus extorsimus*; *Cat.* 3.2 *ignis... restinximus, idemque gladios in rem publicam destrictos rettudimus mucronesque eorum a iugulis vestris deiecimus*; *Sul.* 83 *cuius nuper ferrum rettuderim flammamque restinxerim*; *Flac.* 97 *P. Lentulo ferrum et flammam de manibus extorsimus*; *Planc.* 98 *impium ferrum ignisque pestiferos meus ille consulatus e manibus extorserat* (cf. *Att.* 1.14.3 *totum hunc locum quem ego varie meis orationibus... soleo pingere, de flamma, de ferro (nosti illas* ληκύθους*)...*). At *Off.* 1.77, however, we are told that the weapons fell to the ground of their own accord: *ita consiliis diligentiaque nostra celeriter de manibus audacissimorum civium delapsa arma ipsa ceciderunt*.

28.7 nec sanare... tollere on metaphors of sickness and healing see 76.12n. *nec tollere* is postponed for the sake of the rhythm.

28.8 quanto periculo vivam Cicero again hints at the dangers which threaten him.

28.9 in... improborum cf. *Sest.* 47 *in tanta improborum multitudine*. On the political terminology of this passage see 1.10n.; 1.12n.

mihi uni cf. §9 *oneris mei partem nemini impertio, gloriae bonis omnibus*.

28.10 aeternum... susceptum cf. *Cat.* 4.22 *qua re mihi cum perditis civibus aeternum bellum susceptum esse video*. The MSS offer three different positions for *esse*, but only the reading of ω gives a satisfactory clausula (cretic-spondee); cf. Zielinski 204.

X 29.2 omnes boni... ordinum variations of the phrase *omnes omnium generum aetatum ordinum* are common in Cicero; cf. *Cat.* 4.14; *Sest.* 25; *Pis.* 41, 52, 96; *Off.* 2.84; *Att.* 2.19.2.

29.5 solum non modo the archetype read *non modo solum*, and some later MSS, followed by most editors, have accordingly deleted either *modo* or *solum. non modo* is more likely to be correct than *non solum*:

the abbreviation *nõ mõ* might have caused the confusion (Clark, in apparatus), and *non solum* is undesirable because it increases an already lengthy succession of long syllables. Moreover, *non modo* is found in the strikingly similar construction at *S. Rosc.* 94, *quae non modo idcirco praetereo quod te ipsum non libenter accuso verum eo magis etiam quod...* However, K. Busche's *solum non modo* (*Hermes* 46 (1911) 62) saves *solum* from deletion and gives perfect sense, continuing the argument from *mihi uni* above (§§ 28, 29). It is easy to see how *me solum* would have become mixed up with *non modo* following.

29.7 etiam magis *V* gives *magis etiam*; but *etiam magis* is nearly three times as frequent in Cicero.

30.1 at vero Cicero now moves away from the personal dangers he faces for having saved the state, and on to the disapproval voiced by Torquatus of his suppression of the conspiracy. He will show that Torquatus' supposed disapproval is muddle-headed, and that in fact the Torquati gave him their full support at the time.

30.2 ab improbis...improbe see 1.12n.

30.3 primum ipse the contrast with *deinde...filius* is more pointed if *ipse* is read in this position (*T*δ), rather than after *fundamentis* (*V*), and there is no reason why *ipse* should appear within the ablative absolute. The two Torquati are compared in terms flattering to each, but the effect is undone at *interdum...verborum*, where we discover that the son has not inherited all his father's virtues. The same technique is used against Flaccus' prosecutor: *numquam tamen existimavi, iudices, D. Laelium, optimi viri filium, optima ipsum spe praeditum summae dignitatis, eam suscepturum accusationem quae sceleratorum civium potius odio et furori quam ipsius virtuti atque institutae adulescentiae conveniret* (*Flac.* 2).

fundamentis adulescentiae his greatest achievement to date had been his successful prosecution of Sulla for *ambitus* in 66, which enabled his father to become consul (*Fin.* 2.62). He had also been a moneyer during his father's consulship, and was a member of the priestly college of *XVviri sacris faciundis* (*MRR* III.136; cf. II.135, 445, 485). The metaphor *fundamenta adulescentiae* recurs at *Senect.* 62.

30.4 amplissimae dignitatis referring to an expectation (never realised) of the consulship (1.1n.), not to his more immediate electoral aims (24.3n.).

30.5 fortissimi...filius tricolon. *fortissimi consulis* points to the elder Torquatus' military reputation; cf. § 11 *fortissimi viri atque optimi consulis* (11.4n.). The compliments are conventional (the adjectives recur twice at § 82); *optimi civis* is especially common (Merguet 1.420).

30.6 immoderatione verborum *immoderatio* (*TLL* VII.1.483.12ff.) is not elsewhere found in classical Latin; see 1.13n. on *hapax legomena* (and

2.5n. on words in *-io*). *moderatio verborum* is a quality which comes with age, and which Torquatus has not yet acquired, but no doubt will in time. Cicero was once prone himself to exaggerated language (in *pro Roscio Amerino*; cf. *Orat.* 107). *interdum* implies that Torquatus' failing was habitual.

30.7 suppressa voce Torquatus had apparently spoken quietly of the conspirators' wickedness, so that only the jury could hear, but had deplored their punishment at the top of his voice, in order to win the approval of the *corona*. His behaviour illustrates how orators were concerned to persuade the general public as well as the jury at a trial; it also reveals that, in spite of Cicero's assertions at § 32, public opinion no longer supported the measures by which the conspiracy had been suppressed (cf. pp. 27f.). For the technique of speaking softly so that only the jury may hear cf. *Flac.* 66.

de scelere P. Lentuli Garatoni's deletion of *P. Lentuli* leaves *de scelere* rather feeble; *omnium*, however, does not necessarily imply the existence of a name after *scelere*, as Halm maintained. For Lentulus see 16.3n.; it is he who is mentioned here because, as a praetor and ex-consul, it was his *scelus* which was the most shocking. He was the most prominent of the five who were executed: Caesar talks of *P. Lentuli et ceterorum scelus* at Sal. *Cat.* 51.7, and Cato of *P. Lentulo ceterisque* at *ibid.* 52.17.

30.8 audacia see 16.4n.

30.9 exaudire when *exaudire* differs from *audire*, it differs in referring simply to the physical act of hearing, or of being able to hear ('to catch a sound'), as at *Att.* 4.8A.1 *dic, oro te, clarius; vix enim mihi exaudisse videor*; cf. *TLL* v.2.1189.67ff. The definitions 'to be able to hear in spite of a hindrance' (Halm; A. S. Wilkins on *Cat.* 1.22) and thus 'to hear only just, and no more' (Long) are over-precise. The word is used of physical hearing again at §§ 33 and 34.

[de Lentulo] *de Lentulo* seems oddly inappropriate between the much more general *de supplicio* and *de carcere*, and βq therefore make the obvious change to ⟨P.⟩ *Lentuli* on analogy with *de scelere P. Lentuli* above. *de Lentulo* looks suspiciously like a gloss on *supplicio* (cf. the interpolation of *Lentulum* after *Publium* by *ck* at § 6), and I have therefore accepted Halm's deletion; the gloss would have been conditioned by *P. Lentuli* above. The possibility that the words could be a misreading has given rise to some imaginative conjectures, viz. *de vinculis* (Jeep), *de laqueo* (Reid: the five executed on 5 December were strangled), *de eculeo* (an instrument of torture (*TLL* v.2.730.54ff.): K. Busche, *Hermes* 46 (1911) 62f.). Sydow's ⟨*sumpto*⟩ *de Lentulo* (*Philologus* 46 (1937–8) 227) persuades Kasten but strikes me as clumsy.

30.10 de carcere the *carcer* ('carcer Mamertinus' from the medieval period) was the state prison of Rome, situated at the foot of the Capitol. It consisted of two chambers, one above the other. Executions were carried out in the lower, subterranean, chamber, known as the Tullianum and graphically described by Sallust (*Cat.* 55.3–6). See *RE* VII A.794.28ff.; Richardson, *Rome* 71; Platner–Ashby 99f.; E. Nash, *Pictorial Dictionary of Ancient Rome*² (London 1968) 1.206–8. Dio makes Q. Fufius Calenus play on the verbal similarity between the Tullianum and Cicero's *nomen* (46.20.5).

queribunda the word occurs elsewhere only at V. Fl. 7.126; Sil. 13.583; Calp. *Ecl.* 5.65. On adjectives in *-bundus* see E. Pianezzola, *Gli aggettivi verbali in -bundus* (Florence 1965), esp. 122f.; Nägelsbach 501.

31.1 in quo...absurdum Cicero has three criticisms to make. The first concerns Torquatus' lack of common sense. Correctly realising that talking quietly about the Catilinarians' wickedness would allow the jury but not the bystanders to hear, Torquatus however failed to appreciate that a vociferous condemnation of Cicero's measures would cause the jury to doubt the sincerity of his earlier words. For *in quo* used to append a refutation see 21.3n. On the structure of this period see J. Marouzeau, *Traité de stylistique latine*² (Paris 1946) 239; Nägelsbach 645; H.-Sz.734.

31.2 leviter *leviter* is 'quietly', contrasting with *clare* below just as *suppressa voce* above contrasted with *magna et queribunda voce* (cf. Catul. 84.8; Var. *L.* 6.67). Scribes and editors have sometimes altered the word to *leniter* when it occurs with this meaning, without justification: see *TLL* VII.2.1217.71ff.; Seyffert 44.

31.3 qui...stabant the *corona*; cf. p. 17.

31.6 qui id non probabatis 'who did not approve it (Torquatus' criticism of Cicero's measures)'. *ea* (above) referred to Torquatus' specific comments, but Cicero has now switched to the singular (*id*) to refer more generally to the line taken by Torquatus. The change of number is natural (cf. J. N. Madvig on *Fin.* 2.22, 2.61): *id* should be retained. Orators were advised to avoid expressing opinions with which the jury would not agree: see *Inv.* 1.92; *Rhet. Her.* 2.43; *de Orat.* 2.304–5.

deinde...postulet Torquatus' second fault is not so much a failure of common sense as a lack of rhetorical judgement: the inconsistency in his position results in an argument which rhetoricians would fault as *inconstans* (*Inv.* 1.93). Criticism of the oratorical attempts of his opponents is a favourite Ciceronian ploy used at e.g. *S. Rosc.* 53, 72 and 82 (Erucius' failure to give motives, his declamatory recitation of stock charges), *Mur.* 11 (the attack on Murena's private life a feeble effort), *Cael.* 7 (Atratinus' sense of propriety inhibited him from making his slander sound convincing) and *Planc.* 62 (L. Cassius even himself aware of his oratorical limitations; cf. 66). At *Brut.* 277–8 Cicero recounts how he criticised M. Calidius' speech in his defence of Q. Gallius. Cicero has earlier criticised Torquatus' effort at §§ 22 (*id quod tibi necesse minime fuit*), 23 (*iacere potueris*) and 25 (*hoc vitium sileretur*).

The MSS omit *est*, but the ellipse would be awkward and insertion of the word is supported by the rhythm (resolved cretic-spondee); *est* often drops out in MSS (Reid, App. A).

31.8 alienum ab eo loosely, 'inappropriate in someone'; for the idiom see *TLL* 1.1575.84ff.

31.10 is tribunus plebis as the scholiast notes (possibly drawing on a lost commentary by Asconius on *pro Sulla*: see B. A. Marshall on Asc., pp. 7, 13), the tribune Cicero has in mind will be one of the two who prevented him from giving his speech on leaving office (34.2n.), Q. Caecilius Metellus Nepos or L. Calpurnius Bestia (cf. *RE* III.1216.44ff., Caecilius 96; *RE* III.1367.13ff., Calpurnius 24; *MRR* II.174). *ex illis* indicates that the man was a conspirator, so Bestia must be the tribune meant: according to Sallust he was a member of the conspiracy (*Cat.* 17.3) and was given the task of signalling the start of operations by denouncing Cicero at a *contio* (*Cat.* 43.1; cf. App. *BC* 2.3). This Bestia is probably not to be identified with the man of the same name whom Cicero was shortly to defend six times (*pace* R. G. Austin on *Cael.*, pp. 154–7; R. Syme, *CP* 50 (1955) 134; *MRR* III.46): see E. S. Gruen, *Athenaeum* 49 (1971) 67–9; Crawford 143f.

31.12 difficile...doleas this refers primarily of course to Bestia, but also, by implication, to Torquatus, since he has been criticised for his outspokenness (§ 30); the definite (and emphatic) *te*, following the indefinite *cum doleas* ('when one is grieving'), makes the reference more pointed (the subjunctive is not 'iterative' (Reid): see A. M. Cook, *CR* 2 (1888) 39f.). Torquatus is thus ironically turned into a Catilinarian sympathiser. *Sententiae* such as this are rare in Cicero (as the scholiast remarks), although Quintilian (*Inst.* 4.2.121) cites *Mil.* 29 and *Clu.* 14; on Cicero's restraint in using them see M. Winterbottom, Entretiens 26of.

31.13 eius modi facis a decision between this (*Tω*) and *facis eius modi* (*V*) is difficult. I am inclined to think that *eius modi facis* rather than the alternative is the order which has been normalised.

31.14 vindicem coniurationis Cicero uses the same phrase of himself at *Fam.* 5.6.2.

vehementer admiror balancing *nemini mirum est*.

32.1 sed reprendo...maxime Cicero's third and most severe criticism is that Torquatus has apparently failed to appreciate that the *plebs* approves of the measures taken against the conspirators. In fact,

Cicero misrepresents the situation, and it was Torquatus who was more in tune with popular feeling: see pp. 27f.

32.3 tenes 'understand', 'grasp' (*OLD* s.v. 23a). For *causam... tenere* cf. *Tusc.* 1.29 *rationes et causas rerum non tenebant*; *Div.* 1.127 *qui... teneat causas rerum futurarum, idem necesse est omnia teneat quae futura sint.*

32.4 omnes boni... gesserunt Cicero again aligns the *boni* (1.10n.) with his own position in an attempt to isolate Torquatus. On the responsibility of *omnes boni* for the action taken see §§ 9 and 21 (21.3n.). *communi salute* (β) gives a cretic-spondee in place of a series of long syllables; but I accept the reading of the archetype.

XI 32.7 ut... voluerit cf. *Att.* 15.6.3 *noli sinere haec omnia perire. haec* is commonly used to mean 'Rome and her empire', as at e.g. § 76 *diutius haec stare potuisse* (where *c²* glosses *hoc imperium*). For further examples see *TLL* VI.3.2706.57ff.; Nägelsbach 213f. To avoid the repetition of *perire*, Campe proposed *perdere*; cf. *Att.* 1.16.5 *iudices... perire maluerint quam perdere omnia*; *Att.* 2.21.1; Catul. 29.24; Liv. *praef.* 12 *desiderium... pereundi perdendique omnia.* However, Cicero is not asking Torquatus whether he thinks any of the bystanders are conspirators (as would be implied by *perdere*), but simply whether any of them wished for Rome's destruction, i.e. failed to approve the measures which were taken (Macdonald's translation assumes *perdere*, but his text has *perire*; Lord is more accurate). Clark considered adding ⟨*se salvo*⟩ after *perire* for the sake of the rhythm; but the clausula is probably best regarded as a resolved cretic-iambus.

32.8 cuperet... haberet the balance between the two *ut* clauses is made less precise by a change of tense: see Riemann 374f.; Lebreton 230f.; H.-Sz.815f.

32.9 an vero Cicero's second question takes the form of an enthymeme *ex pugnantibus* or *argumentum ex contrario* (cf. *Rhet. Her.* 4.25–6; *Top.* 55; Quint. *Inst.* 5.10.1–3, 5.14.1–26; Martin 102f.; Rohde 102–6): a double question is set up in which the answer expected by the second question conflicts with that expected by the first, leaving an inference to be drawn. In Cicero the first part often begins with *an* or *an vero*, the second with adversative asyndeton, and neither part is subordinated to the other (parataxis): see e.g. *Font.* 26; *Rab. Perd.* 16; *Cat.* 1.3; *Dom.* 8 (with R. G. Nisbet *ad loc.*), 79; *Planc.* 26, 41 (with H. A. Holden on 41); also Seyffert, *Schol. Lat.* 1.128f. § 5 begins with the figure (*an vero...*), although the first part is subordinated. See 52.2n. for the enthymeme *ex consequentibus*.

clarissimum virum T. Manlius Imperiosus Torquatus (*RE* XIV. 1179.51ff., Manlius 57; *MRR* 1.135f.), the leader of the Romans against the Latins who, while consul for a third time (340), executed his son for disobeying his orders in leaving the line and fighting a (glorious) single combat; cf. Liv. 8.7; *Fin.* 1.23, 1.35, 2.60; *Off.* 3.112; Virg. *A.* 6.824–5. Later generations looked back uneasily on Torquatus as a model of antique severity and patriotism, and he became a common subject for rhetorical *exempla* (Quint. *Inst.* 5.11.10; cf. Sen. *Con.* 9.12.19, 10.3.8). Sallust makes Cato refer to him in an enthymeme reminiscent of our passage: *Torquatus...filium suom...necari iussit...: vos de crudelissumis parricidis quid statuatis cunctamini? (Cat.* 52.30–2). Cicero could have said, but does not, that the prosecutor shares with his unfortunate ancestor a youthful over-enthusiasm for attacking his enemies. *clarissimus* is conventionally applied to distinguished senators (3.2n.).

32.11 imperium Torquatus' son had been *oblitus imperii patrii consulumque edicti* (Liv. 8.7.8), had respected *neque imperium consulare neque maiestatem patriam* (Liv. 8.7.15) and *contra imperium in hostem pugnaverat* (Sal. *Cat.* 52.30). Our Torquatus at *Fin.* 1.35 is made to conjecture whether the father's motive had been *ut dolore suo sanciret militaris imperi disciplinam.* Orders of excessive cruelty came to be known proverbially as *imperia Manliana (Fin.* 2.105; Liv. 4.29.6, 8.7.22, 8.34.2; Gel. 1.13.7, 9.13.20); cf. R. G. M. Nisbet, *CQ* n.s. 9 (1959) 73f.

tu...reprendis it was of course Cicero, not the *res publica,* whom Torquatus had criticised.

domesticos hostis for the expression see P. Jal, *REA* 65 (1963) 72 n. 5; Habicht 35f. The conspirators arrested at Rome were not *hostes* (15.7n.) in any conventional sense, but Cicero describes them as such so as to hide the illegality of their execution (21.3n.).

32.12 necaretur, necavit *necare* is commonly used of most forms of execution, including strangulation (the fate of the conspirators): see J. N. Adams, *Glotta* 68 (1990) 230–55 (esp. 244f.), 69 (1991) 94–123. For the play with active and passive forms of the same verb see Holst 60f. The juxtaposition helps to give a sense of the logical necessity for the killings.

33.1 Itaque...consulatus mei! Cicero's arguments against the charge of *regnum* now lead to a climax in which he vigorously proclaims the greatness of his achievement in terms intended to impress his audience and to convey a strong impression of the *auctoritas* which his defence ought to carry; after this he will go on to testify to Torquatus' contribution towards that achievement, thus complimenting his friend while at the same time exposing the hypocrisy of his criticisms. *quam ego defugiam* is best taken ironically as 'how much I evade'; cf. Nägelsbach 262, 371. *auctoritatem* is 'responsibility' (Nettleship 365f.); for *auctoritatem defugere* cf. Pl. *Poen.* 147; Ter. *Eun.* 390.

33.2 exaudire Torquatus had spoken *suppressa voce* about the punishment of the conspirators, so that only the jury could hear (§30);

Cicero by contrast speaks *maxima voce* on the subject, *ut omnes exaudire possint*. For *exaudire* see 30.9n.

33.3 dico semperque dicam cf. §35 *retinent retinebuntque semper*. The construction is common (especially in the form 'present tense + *semper* perfect tense'): see e.g. *Planc.* 94; *Amic.* 102.

adeste . . . qui adestis lit., 'be present, everyone, with your minds, you who are present', i.e., 'pay attention, all you who are here today'. *V* reads *adeste animisque omnes qui adestis*. This may indicate that a word has dropped out, and Nohl and Landgraf accordingly proposed *animis* ⟨*mentibus*⟩*que* and ⟨*oculis*⟩ *animisque* respectively; alternatively, K. Busche explained the additional -*que* by postulating *Quirites qui adestis* (*Hermes* 46 (1911) 63). But the reading can be more simply accounted for: the scribe, after writing *adeste*, mistook *animis qui* for *animisque* and normalised the position of *omnes* before continuing with *qui...* The repetition *adeste... adestis* has also aroused suspicion: for *qui adestis* Reid printed *qui adstatis* (spoiling the double-trochee) and Clark *Quirites* (comparing *Phil.* 4.1). But these changes too are unwarranted: as S. Rizzo observes (*RFIC* 103 (1975) 14; cf. S. G. Owen, *CR* 26 (1912) 23), Cicero is enjoying 'un gioco di parole' by contrasting *adeste* in the mental sense with *adestis* in the physical sense, 'be present with your minds, you who are present (with your bodies)'. The point, she argues, was appreciated by Petrarch, who noted *corporibus* (*q mg.*) in his text. For the expression *adeste animis* cf. *Mil.* 4; *Rep.* 6.10; the play resembles *circumspicite... mentibus* at §70.

33.4 quorum ego . . . laetor a large and amenable *corona* was indispensable to an orator; cf. *Mil.* 1; *Deiot.* 5; *Brut.* 192 *si a corona relictus sim, non queam dicere*, 290. Flaccus' prosecutor D. Laelius also turned from the jury to address the bystanders (*Flac.* 69); sometimes the bystanders would interrupt (*Caec.* 28; *de Orat.* 3.101; *Orat.* 236; Catul. 53).

erigite . . . vestras 'prick up your minds and ears'; cf. *Ver.* 1.28 *quo tempore igitur auris iudex erigeret animumque attenderet?* (*TLL* v.2.778.38ff.). The construction by which a verb or noun governs two objects and in doing so produces a common expression (*erigite... aures*) in parallel with a less common or pointed one (*erigite mentes*) is known as syllepsis (*conceptio*); cf. e.g. Tac. *Ann.* 2.29 *manus ac supplices voces ad Tiberium tendens*. See Martin 300f. For Cicero's fondness for play on 'mind' and 'ears' (here *animis... mentes auresque*) see 12.14n.; cf. Catul. 62.15.

33.6 exercitus . . . conflatus Catiline's followers were, paradoxically, a hostile army of *cives* (cf. *Cat.* 2.15 *L. Catilinam ducere exercitum hostium*): see P. Jal, *REA* 65 (1963) 76f. On *perditi* see 1.12n. For *conflare* used of armies etc. see *TLL* iv.241.33ff.

33.7 crudelissimum . . . exitium '*exitium* does not often have an epithet, especially a strong one, at all, before a late period', R. O. A. M. Lyne, *CQ* n.s. 21 (1971) 250. The language of this passage is strikingly hyperbolic.

33.8 cumque *cumque* (*V*) was more likely to have been mistaken for *cum* (*Tω*) than *vice versa*.

33.10 his templis atque tectis cf. §86 *haec tecta atque templa*. The phrase is common in Cicero: Wölfflin (276) gives some instances. Cicero no doubt gestures towards the temples in the forum, as at §19.

Lentulus esset constitutus for Lentulus see 16.3n. Two or more personal subjects generally take a plural verb, but here *Catilina* and *Lentulus* are considered as acting in isolation grammatically: see Lebreton 19f.

33.11 meis consiliis...periculis much use is made of anaphora, tricolon and tetracolon in the excited passage which follows. The groupings are: Cicero's exertions; the measures he did not resort to; five men arrested; the dangers from which he saved the state; the things which he saved, by the punishment of five men. On *labor* see 5.4n.

33.12 sine tumultu...sine exercitu cf. *Cat.* 3.23 *erepti sine caede, sine sanguine, sine exercitu, sine dimicatione*. A *tumultus* was technically a war caused by an uprising in Italy or incursion of Gauls: once such a 'state of emergency' had been declared, the normal exemptions from military service were suspended (*Phil.* 8.2–4). Strictly speaking, Cicero is in error: a ταραχή (*tumultus*) was declared at the passing of the S.C.U. (Dio 37.31.1), and Sallust refers to *cohortis veteranas, quas tumulti causa conscripserat* (*Cat.* 59.5). Nevertheless, Cicero boasts that his suppression of the conspiracy at Rome involved no *tumultus*: *Cat.* 1.11 *nullo tumultu publice concitato*; *Cat.* 2.26 *sine vestro metu ac sine ullo tumultu*; *Cat.* 2.28 *nullo tumultu*. Similarly, a *dilectus* was indeed held: Sal. *Cat.* 30.5 *praetores...exercitum conpararent*; *ibid.* 36.3 *decernit uti consules dilectum habeant*; but Cicero did not himself make use of it. Cicero's assertions have to be understood strictly from his own point of view: a *tumultus*, *dilectus*, arms and an army were expedients resorted to only by those who dealt with the Catilinarians in the field, not by Cicero. Cicero regarded his own victory against Catiline as superior to theirs because he had achieved it as a *togatus* (85.4n.), without the use of military force. It was in his view the most glorious type of victory possible. The self-centredness of Cicero's psychology as revealed by this passage is remarkable.

33.13 confessis 'having confessed' (not *ad confessionem adactis*, Halm). Deponent participles in absolute construction are rare in Cicero, and always used intransitively; cf. Laughton 110f.; K.-S.1.783f. Mention of the five captured conspirators' confession of their guilt (*Cat.* 3.10–13, 4.5; Sal. *Cat.* 47, 52.36) is entirely appropriate because it suggests that they were justly punished (although in law a man's confession did not in fact justify his punishment without trial; cf. J. A. Crook, *PCPS* n.s. 33 (1987) 38–52). **confectis** (attributed to Baiter, but already suggested by Bowyer (21–3)) should therefore be rejected, as should deletion of *atque confessis* (W. G. Pluygers, *Mnemosyne* 9 (1881) 137): see K. Busche, *Hermes* 46 (1911) 64. *confossis* (*q*) is impossible because the conspirators were strangled (Sal. *Cat.* 55.5).

incensione . . . liberavi a paraphrase of the wording of the official *supplicatio* decreed in Cicero's honour on 3 December, but in much grander language; cf. *Cat.* 3.15 '*quod urbem incendiis, caede civis, Italiam bello liberassem*' (context quoted at 85.4n.). For *incendiis*, Cicero has written *incensione*, a word found elsewhere in classical Latin only at *Cat.* 3.9 (*TLL* VII.1.871.64ff.; cf. 2.5n. on words in *-io*), for *caede* he has substituted *internicione*, a stronger and less common term, and for *bello* he has put *vastitate*. A slightly more modest paraphrase occurs at *Fam.* 5.2.8: *eum qui curiam caede, urbem incendiis, Italiam bello liberasset*.

33.15 ego . . . civium cf. §27 *eripuerim urbem hanc et vitam omnium civium*.

statum orbis terrae for *status* as '(good) condition' and so 'stability' here and at §63 cf. *Agr.* 1.26; *Flac.* 3; *Sest.* 1; *Cael.* 70; *Har.* 41. The expression *orbis terrarum* is almost four times as frequent in Cicero as *orbis terrae*. For other authors' preferences see *TLL* IX.2.914.68ff.

33.16 sedem omnium nostrum the laudatory nature of the following lines appealed to excerptors: *sedem . . . imperi* is (mis)quoted in a Bodleian anthology of c. 1500, MS Lat. misc. c. 62, fol. 39ʳ. Minos compares Mart. 12.8.1–2 *terrarum dea gentiumque Roma, / cui par est nihil et nihil secundum. omnium nostrum* is not (*pace* Reid) 'of all of us' (an English idiom), but 'of us all': see R. G. Nisbet on *Dom.* 128; Riemann 119; K.-S.1.246.

arcem . . . exterarum cf. *Ver.* 5.184 *ista arce omnium nationum*; *Agr.* 1.18 *sedem urbis atque imperi . . . hanc arcem omnium gentium*; *Cat.* 4.11 *videor enim mihi videre hanc urbem, lucem orbis terrarum atque arcem omnium gentium, subito uno incendio concidentem.* arx is regularly used figuratively (e.g. §79 *munite communem arcem bonorum*); cf. Nägelsbach 36. There is an increase in scale from *regum ac nationum* to *gentium* to *imperi*, then a diminution with *quinque hominum*. Cicero bought so much at so small a cost (*pretio redimere* is the usual phrase).

33.17 lumen . . . imperi Caesar is *omnium gentium atque omnis memoriae clarissimum lumen* at *Deiot.* 15. *lumen* is more common than *lux* in metaphors: see J. S. Reid on *Luc.* 26. For *domicilium imperi* cf. *Cat.* 3.1, 3.26; *Prov.* 34; *de Orat.* 1.105. *domicilium* is frequently metaphorical in Cicero: see *TLL* V.1.1876.12ff.

34.1 iniuratum ... iuratus the contrast emphasises the illogicality of Torquatus' supposed thinking. This play on words is one of Cicero's favourites; cf. *Q. Rosc.* 45, 47; *Ver.* 32; *Font.* 24; *Caec.* 3; *Off.* 3.108 (translation of Eur. *Hipp.* 612). For the type see Holst 70–76. Oaths were taken by the *iudices*, prosecution and witnesses, but not by the defence.

34.2 in maxima contione on 29 December 63 the tribunes Nepos and Bestia (31.10n.) forbade Cicero to give the customary retiring speech, allowing him only to swear the oath that he had obeyed the laws during his period of office (cf. Mommsen, *Staatsrecht* 1.625). Cicero forwent the speech, but altered the oath to a claim that he had saved the state: *Pis.* 6 *iuravi rem publicam atque hanc urbem mea unius opera esse salvam.* See *Fam.* 5.1.1, 5.2.7 (Nepos; cf. J. Van Ooteghem, *LEC* 25 (1957) 168–72); *Dom.* 94; *Sest.* 11 (*schol. Bob.* 127 St. supplies both names); *Pis.* 6–7 (Asc. 6 C names Nepos); *Rep.* 1.7; *Att.* 6.1.22; *ad Brut.* 1.17.1 (Bestia); Plut. *Cic.* 23.1–2 (both named); Dio 37.38.2 (Nepos).

XII 34.3 atque ... addam Torquatus' remarks might imply Catilinarian sympathies, but Cicero can assure his audience that Torquatus does not support revolution: in fact he and his father gave Cicero generous help in suppressing the conspiracy. The apparently well-meaning compliments expose Torquatus' hypocrisy and invalidate his criticisms (the scholiast comments on Cicero's *insidiosa quadam benignitate*).

improbus ... amare both words are used in a political sense. See 1.12n. (*improbus*); Hellegouarc'h 142f. (*amare*).

34.5 ut item omnes exaudiant the MSS give *idem*, which, as Spengel was the first to point out, would be nominative plural, referring back to §33 *ut omnes exaudire possint.* But the reference seems pointless. Reid contemplated *id*, but *item*, which Housman first considered, is the neatest solution. *ut item* is reasonably common, especially when one *ut* clause is linked to another (*Orat.* 202; *Fin.* 5.82; *N.D.* 1.96; cf. *Ver.* 2.54; *Cat.* 3.10). For *exaudire* see 30.9n.

34.6 harum omnium rerum on this reading see p. 74.

ego *ego* here is not enclitic, but emphatic in antithesis to *L. ille Torquatus.*

pro salute ... gessi cf. §§ 26 and 83 *quae pro salute omnium gessi.*

34.7 cum esset ... fuisset Cicero emphasises the closeness of the relationship between Torquatus and himself (cf. § 44 *meo familiari et contubernali*). A *contubernalis* is a 'sharer of the same tent' (in the army), hence a 'close friend'; but the word may also indicate attendance on a senior in e.g. military or educational contexts. The situation here is paralleled by the relationship between L. Gellius and the consul C. Papirius Carbo in 120: *Brut.* 105 *L. Gellius ... se illi contubernalem in consulatu fuisse narrabat.*

The MSS are confused. *V* gives what is clearly the correct reading (except for the slip *in consalatura*, influenced by *in praetura*: see Pabón 10). The descendants of ω interpolate words which occur below. *T* repeats *pro salute . . . in consalatu*, giving *ille contubernalis* (from *L. ille Torquatus*) first time round but avoiding this mistake in the second copying. The most obvious cause of the dittography is the double *in consalatu*, but an additional factor is noticed by Clark (*Descent* 207): the lines in the exemplar of *T* appear to have been of the same length as the repeated passage, so the scribe may have copied one line twice over. Clark observes (*Descent* vi) that ὁμοιότης and line division frequently operate together as causes of dittography and omission. For an example of ὁμοιότης causing omission see 58.4n.

34.9 auctor . . . iuventutis there are two clauses, each with rising tricolon (4.13n.). Clark inverts them, in order to link *cum princeps . . . iuventutis* to the earlier *cum* clause, but there are reasons for leaving the text as it is: being more general in meaning, *cum princeps . . . iuventutis* is not exactly parallel to *cum esset . . . fuisset*, and *cum princeps . . . iuventutis* is more weighty than *auctor . . . exstitit* and so better placed at the end of the sentence. The repetition of *auctor* in the MSS (*auctor adiutor . . . cum princeps, cum auctor . . .*) is a more serious difficulty: it seems likely that in one of the two places *auctor* is corrupt. Orelli and Clark replaced the first *auctor* with *actor* ('agent'), Orelli arguing that the young Torquatus could not be described as having been the 'originator' of Cicero's plans (cf. *Sest.* 61 *dux auctor actor rerum illarum fuit*; Nep. *Att.* 3.2). This objection is not strong, however, since *auctor* would most naturally mean not 'originator' but 'advisor', 'supporter' (i.e. *TLL* II.1198.38ff. (not 1201.32); Nägelsbach (262) prefers 'Vertreter', which is also possible). Moreover, the play *auctor adiutor* is common in Cicero: see *Agr.* 2.12, 2.14; *Red. Pop.* 9; *Dom.* 30, 66; *Sest.* 40; *Har.* 47; *Phil.* 10.18; *Off.* 3.116; *Att.* 5.5.2. It is the second *auctor* in fact which is unacceptable: *auctor . . . iuventutis* is an implausible expression, and I have therefore adopted Housman's easy change *ductor*. *ductor* removes the repetition, gives good sense, and results in an appropriate escalation *princeps . . . ductor . . . signifer* (*signifer* is often metaphorical). The word is found once elsewhere in Cicero, at *Tusc.* 1.89 *non modo ductores nostri, sed universi etiam exercitus.*

princeps iuventutis (also found at *Ver.* 1.139, *Vat.* 24 and *Fam.* 3.11.3, and used eight times in Livy) is non-technical under the republic, indicating a young nobleman of outstanding qualities, a prominent member of the *iuventus*; under the empire the term became an honorific title for young members of the imperial family. *iuventus* in a technical sense refers to the *equites equo publico* alone. See *RE* XXII.2297.20ff.; M. della Corte, *Iuventus* (Arpino 1924).

34.10   parens vero eius the elder Torquatus is described in highly flattering if conventional terms, the implication being that his son would do well to follow his example (on the terms used cf. e.g. *Font.* 41 *summi consili et maximi animi*). Torquatus (11.4n.) arrived back in Rome from Macedonia by the autumn of 63, and so was able to be of help to Cicero in the suppression of the conspiracy (*Fin.* 2.62) and to speak in the debate on 5 December (*Att.* 12.21.1).

34.13   nusquam... digressus *V* reads *a me est*, but *est a me* is preferable on account of the hyperbaton (which was liable to normalisation). Cicero of course exaggerates in saying that the elder Torquatus never left his side; for similar hyperbole see Xenoph. *Mem.* 4.2.40; *Balb.* 5; *Phil.* 1.1; Liv. 37.53.18.

studio... plurimum further praise; cf. *Fin.* 2.62 *quo quidem auctore nos ipsi ea gessimus*, referring to Torquatus' help in 63. *unus* is 'above all others' (*OLD* s.v. 8a).

34.14   cum... superaret *animi virtute* (*Tω*) is conspicuously preferable to *virtute animi* (*V*), providing an *esse videatur* clausula instead of a hexameter ending; cf. Zielinski 204; K. Busche, *Hermes* 46 (1911) 61. It also juxtaposes *corporis animi*. Torquatus' Stoic mastery of the body by the power of his mind is thoroughly admirable; cf. *Phil.* 7.12; *Phil.* 14.4 *A. Hirtius, cuius imbecillitatem valetudinis animi virtus et spes victoriae confirmavit.*

35.1   ut... bonis omnibus Cicero pretends that he has exploded a generally-held belief that Torquatus sympathises with traitors. The thought is: by opposing Cicero Torquatus has endeared himself to the *improbi*; but he is and will always be a loyal *bonus*; his prosecution of Sulla is therefore (like Cicero's *severitas*, § 8) out of character (cf. *subita*), a youthful error of judgement. In Cicero's eyes prosecution of Sulla (and indeed opposition to Cicero) is incompatible with loyalty to the state. On the political terminology see 1.10n.; 1.12n. *V* omits *et* before *reconciliem*; although the omission is defended by C. A. Lehmann (*Hermes* 15 (1880) 349), *et* seems better retained.

35.3   retinent retinebuntque semper cf. § 33 *dico semperque dicam* (33.3n.).

si... desciveris I read *si a me forte* (*Tδ*) in preference to *si forte a me* (*Vβ*) because *si* and *forte* are more usually separate than together in Cicero (see Merguet 11.365; Pabón 10f.); this also gives *a me* suitable emphasis. *desciveris* carries the idea of Torquatus throwing off his allegiance to Cicero like a soldier deserting his general: see *TLL* v.1.654.75ff.

35.4   idcirco... patientur rising tricolon (4.13n.). *idcirco* is 'for that reason', i.e. for deserting Cicero (cf. T. E. Kinsey on *Quinct.* 87; K.-S.11.387). The archetype had *a sua dignitate*; *tua* (*q mg.*) is Petrarch's correction (cf. S. Rizzo, *RFIC* 103 (1975) 9).

35.5 redeo ad causam for *redeo* as 'turn', 'come duly' (not 're-turn') cf. Cato *Agr. praef.* 4 *nunc ut ad rem redeam*; *Cael.* 37 *redeo nunc ad te*; *Att.* 5.11.6 *nunc redeo ad ea*; *Att.* 13.21.3 *nunc ad rem ut redeam*; *Fam.* 11.14.2 *ut ad rem redeam*; Sal. *Jug.* 4.9 *nunc ad inceptum redeo*; Hor. *S.* 1.10.[8] *ut redeam illuc*; Hor. *Ep.* 2.1.48 *redit ad fastos*; Gel. 16.8.4 *redimus... ad Graecos libros.* See J. K. Schönberger, *Tulliana* (Augsburg 1911) 22f. (On the prefix *re-* used without semantic force see 1.13n.) Cicero admits that he is turning only now to the *causa*, but argues that the digressions have been necessary because of Torquatus' attempt to rob him of his *auctoritas*. The points made at § 2 are now repeated. The figure by which digression is concluded is known as *reditus ad propositum* or ἄφοδος (Quint. *Inst.* 9.3.87). Seyffert lists Ciceronian instances at *Schol. Lat.* 1.84–6; cf. C. J. Classen, Entretiens 150f.

35.6 mihi emphatic (2.7n.).

35.8 nam si... accusasset Cicero closes his digression with a justification recalling Demosthenes' similar justifications for digression in *de Corona*, (i) εἰ μὲν οὖν περὶ ὧν ἐδίωκε μόνον κατηγόρησεν Αἰσχίνης, κἀγὼ περὶ αὐτοῦ τοῦ προβουλεύματος εὐθὺς ἂν ἀπελογούμην· ἐπειδὴ δ' οὐκ ἐλάττω λόγον τἆλλα διεξιὼν ἀνήλωκε καὶ τὰ πλεῖστα κατεψεύσατό μου, ἀναγκαῖον εἶναι νομίζω καὶ δίκαιον ἅμα βραχέ', ὦ ἄνδρες Ἀθηναῖοι, περὶ τούτων εἰπεῖν πρῶτον (18.9; the line of thought is similar to that of *Sul.* 2), and (ii) ἀξιῶ δ', ὦ ἄνδρες Ἀθηναῖοι, καὶ δέομαι τοῦτο μεμνῆσθαι παρ' ὅλον τὸν ἀγῶνα, ὅτι μὴ κατηγορήσαντος Αἰσχίνου μηδὲν ἔξω τῆς γραφῆς οὐδ' ἂν ἐγὼ λόγον οὐδέν' ἐποιούμην ἕτερον· πάσαις δ' αἰτίαις καὶ βλασφημίαις ἅμα τούτου κεχρημένου ἀνάγκη κἀμοὶ πρὸς ἕκαστα τῶν κατηγορημένων μίκρ' ἀποκρίνασθαι (18.34). See M. A. Muretus, *Variarum Lectionum Libri* (various edns.) II.xviii; Weische 75f., 147, 155. Cicero need not be consciously imitating Demosthenes: see H. Wankel on Dem. 18.9.

35.9 agerem Ernesti's needless deletion of this word was supported by W. G. Pluygers (*Mnemosyne* 9 (1881) 137). Cicero sometimes uses ellipse in this construction, but more usually gives the full expression: see G. Landgraf on *S. Rosc.* 108; K.-S.II.564.

35.10 tota illa oratione looks forward to *hanc... orationem* below. *illa oratione* (exemplar of *Tω*) is therefore preferable to *oratione illa* (*V*). The dislocation of *illa* in *V* may have been caused by the similarity of the adjacent words *tota* and *illa*. Garatoni needlessly proposed deletion of *illa* or alteration to *sua*.

35.11 cum... voluisset *ut initio dixi* refers to § 2. Cicero returns to the theme of *auctoritas* (2.3n.), this time expressing Torquatus' aim more forthrightly (cf. § 2 *existimavit... aliquid se de auctoritate meae defensionis posse detrahere). spoliare* suggests military combat; military imagery was also used at *desciveris* above.

35.12   me meus dolor cf. *Cael.* 32 *me mea fides et causa ipsa coget.* Tω read *dolor meus*, but *me* is clearly required, and its omission is most understandable if it originally stood before *meus*, as in *V* (cf. K. Busche, *Hermes* 46 (1911) 58). Orelli proposed *dolor me meus*, but the separation of *dolor* and *meus* is undesirable. *dolor* in this context means something like 'feeling of injury': Cicero feels hurt because he has been attacked by a friend.

35.13   flagitavisset *postulare* is usual after *causa*, while *flagitare* is much stronger; cf. *Quinct.* 13 *tametsi causa postulat, tamen quia postulat, non flagitat, praeteribo.*

§§36–45 REPREHENSIO I

The *confirmatio* would normally be expected to follow at this point; for Cicero's inversion of the recommended order see pp. 46–8.

The *reprehensio*, to which Cicero now turns, is the part of the speech in which the orator replies to his opponent's *confirmatio* (*Inv.* 1.78). It is the very essence of a defence, and could not be prepared in advance to the same extent as the other parts: the orator had to wait to hear the prosecution's arguments before he could formulate his own. The *reprehensio*, then, called for improvisation, and required far greater skill than the *confirmatio* of the prosecution; as Quintilian observes, *tanto est accusare quam defendere quanto facere quam sanare vulnera facilius* (*Inst.* 5.13.3).

In this *reprehensio* Cicero follows his own recommended procedure by answering his opponents' arguments one by one (*accidere autem oportet singula: sic universa frangentur* (*Part.* 44). The testimony of the Allobroges, which had proved fatal to others, was on the surface the strongest argument for Sulla's guilt, and so it is this with which Cicero begins; the point needed to be answered before further progress could be made. The charge of falsification which Torquatus had made against Cicero also needed to be dealt with at the outset since this, the most sensational of the charges, bore directly on Cicero's credibility and *auctoritas*. Emotional appeals were to be avoided in the *reprehensio* (Quint. *Inst.* 5.13.2), and Cicero's response to Torquatus' accusation is impressively calm and measured. Only when he has finished arguing his case does he digress to give vent to his feelings of outrage and indignation (§§46–50). Once he has completed this digression he will turn his attention back to the remaining charges, and so complete the *reprehensio* (§§51–68).

On the *reprehensio* in an ancient speech see Arist. *Rh.* 2.26, 3.17 (1418 b 4ff.); [Arist.] *Rh. Al.* 7 (1428 b 33ff.); *Inv.* 1.78–96; *Rhet. Her.* 1.4, 2.3–12; *de Orat.* 2.331; *Part.* 44–51; *Orat.* 122; Quint. *Inst.* 3.9.5, 5.13.1–60. Aristotle does not favour a distinction between proof and refutation, and these two parts of the argumentation are often taken together by the rhetoricians. For modern accounts see Martin 124–33; Rohde 121–31.

(i) The evidence of the Allobroges (§§ 36–39)

Sulla is named in the Allobroges' evidence, but only because Cassius had encouraged the Allobroges to infer that Sulla as well as Autronius was involved. When they had asked him whether Sulla was in the plot, Cassius, thinking it dangerous to say what he knew to be untrue, had replied that he did not know for certain. This strongly implies Sulla's innocence.

Cicero begins his refutation by explaining how Sulla's name came to be included in the evidence of the Allobroges. There are, however, not one but two reasons why Cassius might have replied to the Allobroges *se nescire certum*. In saying that he did not know whether Sulla was involved Cassius may indeed have been trying to impress the Allobroges by implying what he nevertheless knew to be false. But *se nescire certum* could also indicate that Sulla had been approached, but had not committed himself: Cassius and the other conspirators hoped, perhaps, that Sulla was with them, but did not know for sure. Cicero, naturally, does not explore this latter possibility, but instead confines himself to the first explanation, which he presents with great psychological plausibility.

XIII 36.1 Ab Allobrogibus *ab* dropped out easily before *Allobrogibus* in *Tω*; cf. the addition of *ad* before *Allobrogum* in *V* at §37 below. The Allobroges (17.1n.) had given their *indicium* in the form of a written statement (Sal. *Cat.* 52.36); for its contents see Hardy 79. On the use of *oratio obliqua* here see 3.11n.; Cicero's argument will not be strong enough for him to use ascribed *oratio recta* until §38.

quis negat? sed lege indicium Cicero frequently responds to a charge with *quis negat?* (*Ver.* 3.183; *Font.* 38; *Cael.* 10; *Planc.* 63; *Rab. Post.* 5, 42). Gulielmius, accurately I believe, reported *E* as having read, inaccurately, *iudicium*: see my note at *CQ* n.s. 39 (1989) 403.

36.3 L. Cassium L. Cassius Longinus (*RE* III.1738.54ff., Cassius 64; *MRR* II.152; III.51) was one of the leading conspirators, and was involved in the negotiations with the Allobroges (cf. *Cat.* 3.9; Sal. *Cat.* 44); he was also to have supervised the arson (*Cat.* 3.14, 4.13; *Sul.* 53). He seems to have realised that the Allobroges were not to be trusted: he avoided giving them his oath and left Rome immediately, thus escaping arrest. The sentence passed against Lentulus and the others was also to apply to Cassius in the event of his capture (Sal. *Cat.* 50.4). Cassius had been praetor (in charge of the *maiestas* court) with Cicero in 66, but had been unsuccessful in the consular elections for 63 (Q. Cic. (?) *Pet.* 7; Asc. 82 C). His corpulence (*L. Cassi adipes*) is ridiculed at *Cat.* 3.16 (cf. Asc. 82 C *Cassius quamvis stolidus tum magis quam improbus videretur*).

36.5   nusquam 'nowhere', sc. in the *indicium* which Cicero has just directed the prosecution to read.

36.6   qui...non nossent the Allobroges did not know that Sulla's *vita* and *natura* were exemplary. Zinzerling reports *E* as having read *naturamque hominum*, but he appears to have miscopied: see my note at *CQ* n.s. 39 (1989) 403.

36.7   ac tantum...esse for *ac* with an adversative sense after a negative see 21.3n. *tantum* is restrictive (21.12n.). I read *audissent* (*Tω*) rather than *audivissent* (*V*) partly because *nossent* is contracted, and partly because *V* appears to have a tendency to expand contracted forms (cf. § 2 *probavero*; § 13 *cognoverunt*). *pari calamitate* refers to Sulla and Autronius' conviction for *ambitus* in 66 (1.2n.).

36.9   quid tum Cassius? the answer is withheld until §38 *se nescire certum.* Seyffert (*Schol. Lat.* 1.98) punctuates *quid tum? Cassius...,* which is much weaker. In any case, as Niebuhr pointed out, the scholiast's lemma begins *si respondisset.*

36.11   quia...viderentur in contrast to §17, where the Allobroges were described as *verissimi indices,* Cicero is now concerned to play down the authority of their testimony, and therefore talks of *barbaros homines* and (below, §37) *exteras nationes.* He says that Cassius would not have allayed their suspicions: it is implied that he would have tried to increase them. According to Sallust, the Allobroges were supplied with false names by Umbrenus: *coniurationem aperit, nominat socios, praeterea multos quoiusque generis innoxios, quo legatis animus amplior esset* (*Cat.* 40.6). For the corruption *suspicarentur* (ω) for *suspicari viderentur* (*TEV*) Reid compares *facerent* for *facere dicerent* at *Luc.* 70.

37.2   mentionem facere Sullae the omission of *Sullae* in ω probably implies that *V* (*mentionem facere Sullae*) rather than *T* (*mentionem Sullae facere*) preserves the original order: *Sullae* would have been relegated to the margin in the exemplar of *Tω.* Cicero's tendency, moreover, is to keep *mentionem* and *facere* unseparated: see Merguet II.306.

37.4   nisi forte...non fuisse *nisi forte* introduces irony (25.9n.). On *veri simile est* see 57.10n. For the construction *in memoria esse* with a dative see *TLL* VIII.669.69ff. Reid considered *adfuisse* for *fuisse*; this would weaken the clausula (cretic-double-trochee).

37.5   nobilitas hominis the precise signification of *nobilitas* has been disputed. Gelzer (27–40) lists all those called *nobiles* by Cicero and concludes that the qualification for *nobilitas* was a consul in one's ancestry (cf. *Phil.* 3.15). P. A. Brunt (*JRS* 72 (1982) 1–17), however, has reaffirmed the wider definition of Mommsen (*Staatsrecht* III.462f.), which included all who were descended from curule magistrates. But recent scholarship has favoured a return to Gelzer's definition: see D. R. Shackleton Bailey, *AJP* 107 (1986) 255–60; E. Badian, *Chiron* 20 (1990) 371–413. Other discussions of *nobilitas* include A. Afzelius, *C&M* 1 (1938) 40–94, 7 (1945) 150–200; H. Drexler, *Romanitas* 3 (1961) 158–88.

adflicta fortuna *afflicta* is the reading of *V*; *TEω* give *afflata*, which was therefore the reading of the archetype. *adflata* is not appropriate: *adflare* occurs only three times in Cicero (*Ver.* 1.35; *Senect.* 59; *Att.* 16.5.1), always with the meaning 'waft'. But Sulla's *fortuna* is *adflicta* at §89 (cf. §1 *pristinae fortunae reliquiis... adflictis*), and he himself is *adflictus* at §§15, 49, 61, 74 and 91. On *fortuna* see 73.4n.

37.6   pristinae dignitatis a reference to the consulship (1.1n.). Cicero's words here are reminiscent of the *exordium* (§1).

37.7   Autroni... Sullae the pair were commonly thought of as partners; cf. §71 *eius nomen* [sc. *Autroni*] *finitimum maxime est huius periculo et crimini*. See pp. 158f.

37.8   auctoritates *auctoritates*, rarely found in the plural, here indicates the individual *auctoritas* ('impressiveness') of each of the leaders of the conspiracy (*TLL* II.1225.36ff.); cf. *Ver.* 52 *circumstant te summae auctoritates*. The word cannot be rendered precisely by a plural noun in English (a point emphasised by Long). Mommsen's 'Anträge' ('proposals') for *auctoritates* here and at Tac. *Ann.* 2.32, *quorum auctoritates adulationesque rettuli* (better 'gewichtige Namen', Nipperdey), is not persuasive (*Staatsrecht* III.978). Conceivably, *principum* should be deleted, as suggested to me by Professor H. D. Jocelyn.

37.10   cum sciret... nominavisset the Allobroges are represented as aliens, *exteras nationes*, and are contrasted with the Roman *nobilis* Sulla. Cicero alludes to the fact that Autronius' birth was less exalted than that of Sulla: the Autronii were a relatively obscure plebeian *gens*, and were not *nobiles* (although see *CIL* xiv.4192, which may imply a consul).

38.1   illud... potest K. Busche (*Hermes* 46 (1911) 61) prefers the order of *Tδ*, *illud probari minime potest*, because it puts *minime* next to the verb it qualifies, but *V* gives the more natural order (cf. Merguet III.545), and also the better rhythm (double-cretic) if an incision is taken after *potest*.

38.3   calamitatis again, the conviction for *ambitus* in 66 (1.2n.).

38.4   Cassio... potuisse adversative asyndeton, followed by the impersonal construction after *in mentem venire* (19.4n.); lit., '(when at the same time) Sulla (*huius*) could not occur to Cassius even once he had named Autronius...', i.e. it is impossible that Cassius' mention of Autronius should have prompted the Allobroges to ask about Sulla, but have failed to remind Cassius of him.

38.6 se nescire certum the answer to *quid tum Cassius?* (§ 36).

38.7 'non purgat' inquit having presented his arguments, Cicero is now in a position to refute Torquatus more decisively by using ascribed *oratio recta* (3.11n.). He reduces Torquatus' position to absurdity by setting up his arguments in the manner of an *altercatio* (21.1n.).

dixi antea at § 36 *si respondisset idem sentire ... suspicari viderentur.*

38.8 tum denique 'then in the end' (cf. § 19), when the Allobroges happened to ask Cassius specifically about Sulla.

39.1 sed ego ... in quaestionibus for a list of similar observations in Cicero see C. J. Classen, Entretiens 164 n. 5. The reading of the scholia is inferior to that of the archetype: the sense demands *iudiciis* not *indiciis*, and the order of the scholia spoils the cretic-hypodochmiac before *non hoc*. The similarity of words has also caused the omission of *in* before *indiciis* in the scholia. The terms *iudicium publicum* and *quaestio* were in Cicero's time synonymous: see Jones 45. On pleonasm see E. Löfstedt, *Syntactica* (Lund 1956) 11.173–232; H.-Sz.784–808.

39.2 num ... arguatur *aliquis* (ω) is the more normal pronoun, not *aliqui* (*Schol.*). After this, an adversative (*sed, Schol.*) is obviously required (the MSS have *et*). Cicero's point responds to *'non purgat'*: the onus is not on him to show Sulla innocent, but on the prosecution to show him guilty. Nevertheless he will go on to argue that Cassius' reply proves Sulla to be innocent.

39.4 utrum ... se nescire? the argument takes the form of a *complexio* (10.3n.). Cassius said he did not know whether Sulla was involved. The prosecution could argue that Cassius knew Sulla to be involved, but this is impossible because there would be no reason for him to conceal the fact. Or they could argue that Cassius really did not know, but this too is impossible. Cassius must therefore have known Sulla not to be involved in the conspiracy.

39.5 quid? si *TV* have *quod si*, but *T*, as Halm points out (in Orelli[2]), frequently confuses *quid* and *quod*, so we are left in effect with a free choice. *quod si* would follow on awkwardly after *'ne indicent'*, and editors therefore prefer *quid? si*, picking up *quid ita?*

39.7 ipse *Vω* agree in giving *ipso* as against *ipse* in *T*, but it is likely that *ipse* was changed after *de* (*V*) / *de se* (ω) to *ipso* in both MSS independently. The meaning in both cases amounts to the same; *ipse*, however, represents Cicero's normal usage (K.-S.1.632). Pabón (11) is mistaken in thinking *ipse* the *lectio difficilior.*

credo ... de Sulla uno Cicero is on weaker ground here when he argues that Cassius must have known whether Sulla was involved. Irony is used for the scornful dismissal of a genuine possibility (see 11.7n. on *credo*). For the passive of *celare* as 'to be kept in the dark (about something)' see K.-S.1.302.

39.9 domi eius...conflata esse there is no other evidence for anything having happened at Cassius' house. On *conflata* see 13.3n.

qui...dixit *qui* is 'he who...'. There is no need for Madvig's *quia* (*Adv. Crit.* III.134); cf. 4.9n. Cassius is seen as implying Sulla's involvement in order to impress the Allobroges, despite knowing him not to be involved; according to Sallust, the Allobroges were deliberately supplied with false names (*Cat.* 40.6, quoted at 36.11n.). However, Cassius did not dare *dicere...falsum*, i.e. to state unequivocally that Sulla was in the · plot. Cicero is not quite assuming what he has to prove (Reid, Macdonald) because he has already 'proved' that Cassius must have known Sulla not to be involved (otherwise Cassius would have given a definite affirmative answer).

β gives *se* for *est* after *ausus*. Clark therefore inserts *se* before *nescire* (keeping *ausus est*), supposing *se* to be a survival from the archetype (xiv); but for *se* to have been in the archetype it would have to have been omitted independently from all of *TVδ*. A better place for *se* would be in the unemphatic position (2.7n.) before *dixit* (thus Lambinus). But in fact *se* is not required at all. As Reid has shown (on *Ac.* 1.18), ellipse of the pronominal subject before the infinitive is well attested in Cicero and other authors. The zeal of editors such as Müller who have interpolated the supposedly missing *se* into numerous passages is therefore misplaced. See Lebreton 376–8.

39.12 perspicuum est this phrase, rare outside Cicero, is thought by T. E. Kinsey to have been a piece of philosophical jargon (= ἐναργές ὅτι?) popular during Cicero's youth: see J. Bibauw (ed.), *Hommages à Marcel Renard* (Brussels 1969) 1.501–5. It might equally have been advocates' jargon.

39.13 eandem vim esse the MSS offer a straight choice between *vim esse* (*Tω*) and *esse vim* (*V*). *esse vim* has the hyperbaton in its favour, but entails a markedly trochaic rhythm (however *huius* is scanned) such as Cicero would normally be at pains to avoid (5.4n.).

39.14 extra coniurationem as at Sal. *Cat.* 39.5; for this use of *extra* see K.-S.1.548; *TLL* v.2.2056.15ff.

nam...videri the same could be said of Cicero's own knowledge. For the play *ignoratio...purgatio* see Nägelsbach 247f.

39.16 sed iam...Sullam yet Cicero has just been arguing precisely that Cassius' ignorance does clear Sulla. This *praeteritio* exactly resembles that at §14 (14.12n.): a hypothetical argument with *debere*, followed by an ostentatious and seemingly magnanimous renunciation of such an argument. *purgetne* is the reading of the exemplar of *Tω* (β has *purgare nec* before continuing *Cassium nec Sillam*). Kasten and Lehmann tried to make use of *quid* before *purgetne* in *V* (Kasten's 1933 preface xv, *id purgetne*; C. A. Lehmann, *Hermes* 15 (1880) 572, quid ⟨*purget aut*⟩ *purgetne*); but *quid* is most likely an interpolation influenced by *quaero*.

39.17 tantum restrictive (21.12n.). *tantum* is clearly to be taken with *illud*, not (as by J. N. Madvig on *Fin.* 1.30) with *satis*. One would expect *mihi* to separate *illud tantum*: see 2.7n.

(ii) Cicero's alleged falsification of records (§§ 40–45)

Torquatus accuses Cicero of having falsified the record of the senatorial proceedings of 3 December 63. Cicero realised that the accuracy of this account might later be challenged: he therefore ensured that a true and complete record was taken, and immediately had it copied and distributed throughout the empire. Torquatus made no protest at the time, and falsification is in any case most improbable.

Torquatus accused Cicero of having falsified the account he had had made of the interrogation of Volturcius and the Allobroges in the senate on 3 December (cf. *Cat.* 3.8–10; Sal. *Cat.* 47). Cicero admits that Sulla was named by the Allobroges (§ 36), and Torquatus therefore presumably alleged that Cicero had altered the passages relating to Sulla but had not removed them altogether.

It would certainly have been possible for Cicero in his *commentarius* to have misrepresented the evidence given: falsification could have taken place when the accounts of the four senators were being amalgamated into one version for multiple copying (cf. E. Gabba, *SCO* 10 (1961) 89–96, who suggests that Torquatus' collaboration with Cicero during the conspiracy might have given him knowledge of underhand dealings). However, any such falsification would surely have been detected by the senators who had attended the meeting (§ 45), and it is noteworthy that an attempt to bribe Cicero to induce the Allobroges to incriminate Caesar was unsuccessful (Sal. *Cat.* 49.1). In any case a deal between Cicero and Sulla as early as 3 December 63 is virtually inconceivable.

Falsification was a live issue in 62: the consuls of the year carried a *lex Iunia et Licinia* ruling *ne clam aerario legem inferri liceret* (*schol. Bob.* 140 St.). Cicero was later to be accused by Clodius of forging the decree which authorised the execution of the conspirators (*Dom.* 50; cf. Rice Holmes 1.482) and by Appian of modifying the ultimatum to Antony in January 43 (*BC* 3.61; cf. Gabba, *loc. cit.*). For the forgery of senatorial decrees see further *Phil.* 5.11–12, 12.12; *Att.* 4.17.2, 15.26.1; *Fam.* 9.15.4, 12.1.1, 12.29.2; Plut. *Cat. Mi.* 17.3.

Cicero's refutation of this charge leads on well to the outburst of *indignatio* against Torquatus at §§ 46ff.

XIV 40.1 Exclusus... me accusat the imagery of *exclusus* and *inruit* is suggestive of hunting (of boars). W. G. Pluygers (*Mnemosyne* 9 (1881) 137) thought *me accusat* feeble and proposed deletion. The rhythm is admittedly weak, but the sense is appropriate: Torquatus is meant to be accusing Sulla, not Cicero. Moreover, the words are supported by the scholia.

40.2 ait me... rettulisse *oratio obliqua* is used when beginning a refutation (3.11n.). The issue to be treated is simply whether falsification occurred, a *coniectura incidens*, as the scholiast remarks, i.e. *status coniecturae* (cf. Quint. *Inst.* 3.6.5; Lausberg 70f., 89–94; Martin 30–32). But the scholiast (followed by Peña) is mistaken in asserting that the question is *an P. Syllae nomen subtraxerit Cicero*: see above (p. 216). For the expression *in tabulas publicas referre* see R. G. Nisbet on *Dom.* 50; cf. *Ver.* 1.158 *referendo in tabulas et privatas et publicas quod gestum non esset, tollendo quod esset, et semper aliquid demendo, mutando, interpolando*; *Ver.* 4.134; *Balb.* 11. A semi-official private record (*commentarius*) of senatorial proceedings could be taken by the presiding consul; on 3 December, to avoid any suspicion of falsification, Cicero appointed four senators to make his *commentarius* for him. Such *commentarii* were treated as *tabulae publicae*, but were nevertheless deposited in the magistrate's own house (42.10n.), not in the *aerarium*. Cicero had his *commentarius* published rather than kept at home, again as a precaution against the charge of falsification. See Mommsen, *Staatsrecht* III.1015–17 (but note that Cicero's precautions are exceptional); *id.*, *Strafrecht* 512–20; *RE* Suppl. vi.718.35ff.; Settle 288–93. Regular senatorial minutes were not instituted until 59 (Suet. *Jul.* 20.1).

40.3 o di immortales... sunt indignation at the preposterousness of Torquatus' allegation causes Cicero to break off suddenly with an address to the gods. Cicero often attributes his achievement to divine providence rather than to his own *ingenium*: *Cat.* 2.29, 3.1, 3.18–23; *Sul.* 86; *Att.* 1.16.6; cf. [Sal.] *Inv. in Cic.* 3, 7; Quint. *Inst.* 5.11.42, 11.1.23. Here the gods are responsible for prompting him to take the precautions which would enable him to refute a charge such as this (§ 43). Müller and Clark read *tribuo* (*T*), but *tribuam* (*Vω*) is likely to be the reading of the archetype.

40.5 in... rei publicae cf. § 59 *in illa rei publicae tempestate*; *Ver.* 5.26; *de Orat.* 1.2 *qui locus... in eo maximae moles molestiarum et turbulentissimae tempestates exstiterunt. potestate* (*V*) is an obvious misreading; there is no need to conjecture ⟨*meae*⟩ *potestatis tempestate* (Pabón, comparing *Mur.* 81).

40.7 cupiditate incendistis the imagery is commonplace; cf. *TLL* VII.1.868.51ff.

40.9 in tantis tenebris...praetulistis the *error* and *inscientia* (cf. *Fin.* 1.46), the general uncertainty over what was happening and what should be done, persisted until the gods enlightened Cicero. For the imagery *in tantis tenebris...clarissimum lumen* cf. Lucr. 3.1 *o tenebris tantis tam clarum extollere lumen*; *Agr.* 1.24 *vox et auctoritas consulis repente in tantis tenebris inluxerit*; *Sest.* 60; *Planc.* 42; *Deiot.* 30; *Tusc.* 1.74; *N.D.* 2.96; *Phil.* 2.76. For *lumen...praetulistis* cf. [Cic.] *Exil.* 9; V. Max. 3.2.2; Sen. *Ep.* 88.45; Plin. *Ep.* 5.17.4.

41.1 iudices *vidi* (*T*β*a*) is more likely than *iudices* (*q*) to have been the reading of the archetype (*V* omits either word). Nevertheless, the careful, explanatory tone of *iudices* is much more appropriate than an impassioned repetition of *vidi*. The two words are very frequently interchanged in MSS: see 2.8n.

41.3 non Torquatus...similis drawing attention to Torquatus; the tone is similar to that of §31. *quispiam* gives a more favoured rhythm than *aliquis*, and prevents repetition below.

41.5 patrimoni...hostis on the order see 2.2n. *naufragus* often refers to the loss of property (see 58.13n. on the disgrace of selling one's *patrimonium*); for *patrimoni naufragium* cf. *S. Rosc.* 147; *Phil.* 12.19. The Catilinarians are *naufragi* ('castaways') at *Cat.* 1.30 and 2.24. Nautical imagery (continued below) is common in Cicero: see Fantham 23f. (for bibliography see Pöschl 546f.). Cicero is thinking of the *concordia ordinum* at this point (1.10n.); cf. *Sest.* 15, 17; *Phil.* 11.36 on the terms used.

41.8 portum...invenire by stirring up a wind against all patriots the traitor who is unlike Torquatus might have been able to find a haven from his own troubles. For this use of *portus* + gen. cf. *Caec.* 100 *perfugium portusque supplici*; see *TLL* x.2.62.76ff.

41.9 institui *institui* (*Schol.*) and *constitui* (Ω) may both mean 'appoint', but the former is more common in this sense. *constitui* may have been written by a scribe wishing to avoid the repeated *in* (*introductis in...indicibus institui*). See Seyffert 7.

42.1 at quos viros! the reliability of the four senators is irrelevant: it was Cicero himself whom Torquatus had accused of falsification. For the exclamation cf. Ter. *Ph.* 367; *Font.* 39; *Flac.* 90; *Brut.* 65; *Fam.* 9.20.1 (*TLL* II.995.71ff.; Merguet 1.304).

cuius...maxima Cicero flatters the senators on the jury (cf. §82). Reid compares *Amic.* 62 *sunt...constantes* [sc. *amici*] *eligendi, cuius generis est magna penuria.*

42.3 memoria...celeritate scribendi the senators' talents are articulated in three units, (i) *memoria*, bound together by rhythm with (ii) *scientia*, then (iii) *consuetudine... scribendi*; the final syllable of *celeritate* is kept short before *scribendi* (cf. R. G. M. Nisbet on *Pis.* 70), giving a cretic-spondee rhythm at the incision before *facillime*. The commentators take Cicero as referring to the use of shorthand. This does not seem likely (nor is it a detail we should expect Cicero to supply); nevertheless, it is possible that the senatorial proceedings of 3 December were taken down using a form of shorthand notation. According to Plutarch (*Cat. Mi.* 23.3), Cato's speech in the senate on 5 December was transcribed by τοὺς διαφέροντας ὀξύτητι τῶν γραφέων whom Cicero had previously instructed in the use of shorthand, this being the first time that shorthand was used at Rome. These 'exceptionally rapid writers' are perhaps to be identified with our four senators (cf. *celeritate scribendi*), in which case Cicero will have used the same men on both occasions, having taught them shorthand for the purpose. See *RE* XI.2217.1ff.; R. J. A. Talbert, *The Senate of Imperial Rome* (Princeton 1984) 316; B. Bischoff, *Latin Palaeography: Antiquity and the Middle Ages*, tr. D. Ó Cróinín and D. Ganz (Cambridge 1990) 80–82; D. R. Shackleton Bailey on *Att.* 13.32.3. *consuetudine et* was deleted by editors from Halm (Orelli²) to Clark on account of its supposed omission in *V Schol.* K. Busche (*Hermes* 46 (1911) 58), however, saw that the words do in fact occur in *V*; omission in *Schol.* is not significant since the scholia provide only a very abbreviated version of this sentence.

42.4 persequi 'to keep up with', when taking notes, as at *Att.* 13.25.3 (*OLD* s.v. 6).

C. Cosconium after his praetorship C. Cosconius (*RE* IV.1668.40ff., Cosconius 4; *MRR* II.166, 176, 192) had gone out to Further Spain as proconsul in 62 (*Vat.* 12). He died in 59 while serving as one of the *vigintiviri* appointed to implement Caesar's agrarian legislation; Cicero declined to take his place (*Att.* 2.19.4).

42.5 M. Messallam i.e. 'Rufus', who is probably also the man referred to at §20 (20.4n.). He is here described as having been a candidate for the praetorship in December 63; since the elections took place late in July, he would not have become praetor, if successful (and he may not have been, given that he had to wait until 53 for the consulship), until 61, when his cousin was consul (*MRR* mistakenly dates his praetorship to 62). *qui tum praeturam petebat* does not necessarily indicate that he is no longer standing for the praetorship; the wording (chosen to match *qui tum erat praetor*) simply expresses his standing at the time when Cicero called upon his services. The passage can therefore provide no clue to whether Sulla's trial occurred before or after the election at which Rufus was a candidate. On the date of the trial see p. 14.

42.6 P. Nigidium P. Nigidius Figulus (*RE* XVII.200.53ff., Nigidius

3; *MRR* II.190, 194, 245; III.147), a friend of Cicero (*Fam.* 4.13 is addressed to him and he is given a part in *Timaeus*), was praetor in 58 and a legate in Asia in 52–1; he supported Pompey during the civil war and died in exile in 45. He was a Pythagorean, and wrote treatises on theology, grammar, divination and other mystical and pseudo-scientific subjects (frr. ed. A. Swoboda 1889). He was supposed at Octavian's birth to have prophesied his future greatness (Suet. *Aug.* 94.5; Dio 45.1), and his astrological predictions feature in Lucan (1.639–72). His learning, but not his influence, was comparable to that of Varro (Gel. 19.14.1–3; cf. Serv. *A.* 10.175). For Nigidius' help to Cicero in 63 see *Fam.* 4.13.2; Plut. *Cic.* 20.2; Plut. *Mor.* 797 d. See further A. della Casa, *Nigidio Figulo* (Rome 1962).

App. Claudium App. Claudius Pulcher (*RE* III.2849.56ff., Claudius 297; Suppl. 1.320.41f.; *MRR* II.200, 221, 229, 247f.; III.57) was the eldest brother of P. Clodius, and Cicero's rapacious predecessor in the governorship of Cilicia (53–1). As praetor in 57 he refused to support Cicero's recall. The governorship of Sardinia followed in 56, then the consulship of 54, and, after Cilicia (and trials for *maiestas* and *ambitus*), the censorship of 50, during which he expelled Sallust among others from the senate for immorality. He was also augur (dedicating a book on augury to Cicero), and he shared some of Nigidius' esoteric interests (e.g. necromancy; cf. *Tusc.* 1.37; *Div.* 1.132). He died early in 48, while in command of Greece under Pompey. Cicero got on with Appius as best he could; the letters in *Fam.* 3 are all addressed to him.

42.7 qui...referendum *ad* is known to have been read in *E*, but the reading of *E* at *referendum* is uncertain and at *hominibus* unknown: see my note at *CQ* n.s. 39 (1989) 403f.

XV 42.8 quid deinde? quid feci? *quid deinde?* (sometimes followed by a further question) is found at *Q. Rosc.* 49, *Ver.* 5.10, *Agr.* 3.11, *Sest.* 43, *Deiot.* 26, *N.D.* 3.48. The alternative punctuation, *quid? deinde quid feci?*, adopted by some editors, gives rise to an unusual word order in the second unit.

42.9 relatum in tabulas publicas see 40.2n.

42.10 privata tamen custodia...continerentur cf. *Dom.* 11; *Scaur.* 48; *Phil.* 11.24. Official state documents, most importantly *leges* and *senatus consulta*, were lodged in the *aerarium* (from 78 the adjacent *tabularium* was also used), but *commentarii* were retained by the magistrates who had made them. *more maiorum* implies that even if Cicero had kept his *commentarius* at home this would have been in no way irregular.

42.11 statim describi...imperavi Cicero does use an infinitive after *imperare*, but only a passive or deponent: see K.-S.II.231. The *librarii* were the *scribae librarii* or public copyists whom Cicero refers to at §44 as *scribae mei*, presumably because they were allocated to him as consul; cf. Mommsen, *Staatsrecht* 1.346–55; A. H. M. Jones, *JRS* 39 (1949) 38–55.

42.13   toti Italiae Madvig objected to the dative and proposed *tota Italia*, 'throughout the whole of Italy' (*Adv. Crit.* II.209); *tota Italia* might have been corrupted to *tota Italiae* before *emisi* and then 'corrected' to *toti Italiae* (Madvig postulated an intermediate stage to account for the supposed reading *totae* in *V*). However, *dividere* as 'distribute' with a dative is permissible: see *TLL* v.1.1597.33ff.

emisi *dimisi* (*Tβ*) and *divisi* (*Vδ*) must be corruptions influenced by *divisi* above; cf. *Flac.* 41, where all MSS but one alter *emisso* to *demisso* or *dimisso*.

42.14   ex quo ... esset *et* in *V* is more likely to be a misreading of *ex* (*T*) than of *e* (ω), therefore *ex* is read. J. S. Van Veen pointed out that *salutem offerre* is not otherwise found with *offerre* meaning 'provide', and proposed *adlata* (*Hermes* 23 (1888) 316). Nevertheless, *offerre* does occur as 'provide' with other words; cf. *Ver.* 4.107 (*auxilium*); *Man.* 49 (*bonum*); *Phil.* 13.18 (*praesidium*).

43.1   dico locum ... loco *dico nullum* for *nego ullum* is infrequent (cf. K.-S.I.819f.). The repetition *locum ... loco* is necessary to avoid ambiguity after *in orbe terrarum*. See F. Ellendt on *de Orat.* 1.174; K.-S.II.283f.; H.-Sz.563f.

43.4   exiguo 'brief'; the word is not unusual in this sense with *tempus* (*TLL* v.2.1472.65ff.).

43.5   ita ut dixi at § 40.

43.6   ne qui posset tantum Cicero sometimes writes *qui* for *quis* (3.9n.); *quis* (a) is therefore unnecessary. *tantum* is restrictive (21.12n.).

43.7   meminisse quantum vellet Zielinski (204) proposed *recordari* for *meminisse* because of the rhythm, but the incision comes after the (unrhythmical) *quantum vellet*, and so the hexametrical *meminisse* may stand. *meminisse de* cannot be objected to: see K.-S.I.472. After *meminisse V* comes to an abrupt halt.

43.8   creditum impersonal, with *ei* understood (Reid); cf. Lebreton 173; K.-S.I.102.

43.9   ex meis commentariis see 40.2n. Unlike the version kept at Cicero's house, the published account could not be subsequently altered.

43.11   neglegentia ... diligentia cf. *Flac.* 87; *Att.* 8.11.6. For this type of play on words see Holst 63–70.

43.12   crudelis see 7.10n.

44.1   abs te ... quaero on *abs te* see 3.1n. Cicero now completes his reply to Torquatus' allegation with a series of rhetorical questions highlighting its improbability (§§ 44–5).

44.3 frequens...memoria i.e. *frequentis senatus recens memoria*, which Karsten would prefer to read (29, comparing §41 *recenti memoria senatus*; §45 *recentem...memoriam cuncti senatus*). On *frequens senatus* ('a crowded house') see J. Stroux, *Philologus* 93 (1938) 85–101; J. P. V. D. Balsdon, *JRS* 47 (1957) 19f.; Bonnefond-Coudry 425–35.

⟨**et**⟩ **tibi meo...contubernali** asyndeton between subordinated clauses is possible in Latin (cf. F. Leo, *Plautinische Forschungen*² (Berlin 1912) 272 n. 4), but on the other hand a scribe waiting for the subordination to end may well have omitted a conjunction. I incline towards the latter possibility, and adopt Halm's ⟨*et*⟩ *tibi*. This complex period is corrupt in several places, and *et* would very easily have been omitted before *tibi*. Halm later preferred Meerdervoort's *tibi*⟨*que*⟩, which is also attractive. Huldrich's ⟨*cumque*⟩ *tibi* is possible, but *tibi* ⟨*autem*⟩ (W. G. Pluygers, *Mnemosyne* 9 (1881) 137) and *tibi* ⟨*vero*⟩ (Eberhard) seem less plausible. For Torquatus as Cicero's *contubernalis* see 34.7n.

44.4 edituri...fuerint this form is used as a substitute for the pluperfect subjunctive of an unreal apodosis (here *edidissent*) in subordinate clauses in which the subjunctive would in any case have to be used; cf. Handford 159f.; Lebreton 238; Madvig, *Opusc. Acad.* 583–6; K.-S.ii.409f.

44.5 scribae mei see 42.11n.

44.6 cur...tacuisti *cur* is omitted by *T*δ; its inclusion in β before *tacuisti* will be conjectural, unless *T*δ omitted the word independently. I adopt Nohl's *cur cum* (*cur* would easily have dropped out from this position): this makes the structure clearer by separating *cum...referri* from the previous clauses governed by *cum*, and it also helps the tricolon *tacuisti, passus es, non mecum aut...questus es aut...expostulasti?* by making it clear that *cur* is not to be taken with *tacuisti* alone (Karsten (29) resorts to adding *cur* before all three cola). *referri* is Orelli's easy change from *ferri* (*T*); *fieri* in ω is perhaps a rationalisation of *ferri*.

44.7 aut ⟨**ut**⟩ **cum familiari tuo** the reading of the MSS *aut cum familiari meo* is nonsense. The sense required is: 'with me you did not either (a), as one (you) would normally do with a (your) friend, complain, or (b), seeing that you do not behave to me like a friend, angrily protest'. *aut* has to be parallel with *aut* below, rather than providing an alternative to *mecum*. In choosing a solution, we have first to consider whether to retain *aut* and insert ⟨*ut*⟩ (with Clark) or simply to alter *aut* to *ut* (with F. Oehler, *Philologus* 13 (1858) 682). I prefer to keep *aut*: it is, after all, given by the MSS (*ut* would easily have disappeared after *aut*, as *et* before *tibi* and *cur* before *cum* above), and the logical balance of *aut...aut* reinforces the sense. Secondly, *familiari meo* must be emended to give the overall sense '(either as) with a friend (of yours)'. Various possibilities have been suggested: *familiari* (W. G. Pluygers, *Mnemosyne* 9 (1881) 137), *familiari tuo* (Richter), *familiarissimo* (Eberhard) and *familiari ideo* (Oehler). It seems desirable to account for *meo* rather than simply to ignore it (as Pluygers does). Oehler's *ideo* is neat but redundant; more attractive is Eberhard's *familiarissimo*, which also gives the more favoured rhythm (double-cretic before *aut*). But the best explanation seems to me to be offered by Richter's *tuo* (*meo* would be an error of association caused by *meo familiari* above); this also gives a double-cretic rhythm. I have therefore opted for *aut ⟨ut⟩ cum familiari tuo*, not previously formulated but essentially the solution of Richter.

44.10 quieveris tacueris on *asyndeton bimembre* see 21.5n.; cf. J. Marouzeau, *Traité de stylistique latine*[2] (Paris 1946) 247f.; Nägelsbach 704f.

44.12 commutati indici cf. *Ver.* 3.83 *an audacius tabulas publicas commutavit?*

XVI 45.1 mihi Cicero turns finally to *argumenta a persona*; cf. Lausberg 204–6.

45.2 fuisset the use of the pluperfect subjunctive in repudiating deliberative questions is rare, and first found in Cicero; cf. Woodcock 131f.; Riemann 297; H.-Sz.338.

45.5 rei publicae objective genitive, as at § 14 (14.9n.).

45.7 tamne Reid prints *tamenne tam* for *tamne* on the grounds that *tamne* 'is rarely met with in Cic. if at all' (App. A). *tamne* occurs elsewhere three times (at *Tusc.* 3.26 and twice at *Att.* 7.12.3; *tamenne* occurs nineteen times), but rarity does not justify alteration of the text in this instance.

cum litterae ... possent the sense is obscure; the point must lie partly in the contrast *posteritatis ... recentem*. I attempt a paraphrase: 'Written accounts are intended for future generations which have no recollection of the events recorded; would I then have been so stupid as to use an account of this kind to misrepresent a recent meeting which the entire senate had attended and could remember?' Cicero has a good point (that he could never have hoped to get away with falsification), but he is padding it out. For *subsidio oblivioni*, an 'aid against forgetfulness', Halm compares Caes. *Gal.* 2.20.3 *his difficultatibus duae res erant subsidio.*

45.10 commentario meo see 40.2n.

§§46–50 DIGRESSIO IV

Cicero has made allowances for Torquatus' behaviour, and has refrained from answering him as he deserves. He is unable to grasp Torquatus' grounds for considering

that he has violated their friendship by defending Sulla: he was compelled by amicitia *and* humanitas *alike to speak in Sulla's defence. Torquatus' conduct is
strikingly at variance with that of his father, who in 66 recognised that his friends
had a duty to support Sulla and so oppose his own consulship. Moreover, in this trial
Torquatus has nothing to gain: he has already defeated his enemy. These are the
circumstances in which Torquatus censures Cicero; nevertheless Cicero for his part
would not presume to judge Torquatus' decisions.*

On the place of the digressions within the structure of the speech see
pp. 44f.

Cicero has answered Torquatus' criticisms relating to the public aspects of his acceptance of the case (§§ 2–35): now it remains for him to
reply to a private aspect, Torquatus' complaint that he has violated the
amicitia between them by defending Sulla. Cicero could have chosen to
include this passage after § 35; instead he gives the impression at § 35
that he has finished with Torquatus, and then presents this passage as a
spontaneous outburst of *indignatio* prompted by the charge of falsification (§§ 40–45). Thus he makes it seem as if he had originally decided to
confine himself to the question of his suitability for the defence, but
later found himself unexpectedly driven to speak out by the unfairness
of Torquatus' accusations.

In spite of its apparent spontaneity, however, this passage has been
carefully prepared for in advance. The order in which Torquatus' criticisms are answered is arranged so as to give the impression that
Torquatus has become progressively more outspoken until finally he
oversteps the mark, and has to be brought into line. This structural
progression enables Cicero to exploit Torquatus' youth and inexperience by presenting him as an impulsive young man who has not yet
acquired his father's qualities of moderation and good judgement, while
at the same time Cicero is able to make allowance for these failings with
his now familiar mock-generosity. This in turn allows him to represent
himself as wrongfully abused: his patience has been tried to the limit,
and he has difficulty in holding himself back. But the fact that in the end
he does so, pointedly observing that he at least is not so rude as to
criticise his opponent's judgements (§ 50), enlists our sympathy for his
side. His final reply to Torquatus is a *tour de force*, and a splendid climax
to the first half of the speech.

46.1 Fero...fero as at § 21, Cicero begins his digression not with a
gradual shifting of position but with a sudden change in tone. These
words are quoted (with Enn. *scen.* 203 Jocelyn and Virg. *E.* 3.25–6)
by Julius Rufinianus (41–2 Halm) as an example of *indignatio* (ἀγα-

νάκτησις); cf. Lausberg 239; Martin 155f. The term *indignatio* also denotes a part of the *conclusio* (90.1n.). The repeated *fero* is an example of *regressio* (20.8n.); cf. *Ver.* 5.175 *tulit haec civitas quoad potuit... tulit.*

46.3 reflecto cf. *de Orat.* 1.53 *quae nisi qui naturas hominum vimque omnem humanitatis causasque eas quibus mentes aut incitantur aut reflectuntur penitus perspexerit, dicendo quod volet perficere non poterit.* The metaphors are from driving horses (cf. Fantham 66). Cicero has had to rein in his sense of outrage.

permitto cf. *Cael.* 7 *tecum, Atratine, agam lenius, quod et pudor tuus moderatur orationi meae et meum erga te parentemque tuum beneficium tueri debeo*; further examples of this type of irony are given by H. V. Canter at *AJP* 57 (1936) 462. As Reid remarks, four verbs (with *aliquid* understood after the last three) express the same idea, an example of the figure *distributio* (Lausberg 340f.); cf. *Flac.* 9 *tribuo illis litteras, do multarum artium disciplinam, non adimo sermonis leporem... si qua sibi alia sumunt, non repugno.*

46.4 adulescentiae prosecutors were frequently *adulescentes*, who had less to lose and more to gain (50.4n.) than their seniors; cf. *Div. Caec.* 24, 70; *Cael.* 73; *Pis.* 82; *Off.* 2.49; Quint. *Inst.* 12.6.1; Tac. *Dial.* 34.7; Plut. *Luc.* 1.1–2; Gelzer 83–5.

cedo amicitiae cf. *Div. Caec.* 23 *da mihi hoc; concede quod facile est*; *Ver.* 1.32 *date hoc et concedite pudori meo*; *Ver.* 3.16, 3.218; *de Orat.* 1.57. Ernesti proposed *concedo* in order to avoid *cedo* with an accusative (*aliquid*), but neuter pronouns and adjectives are allowable after *cedere* (e.g. *Off.* 2.64 *multa... cedentem*). On *amicitia* see 48.4n.

parenti see 11.4n.

46.5 me oblitum *oblitum* is omitted in *T*, and βδ disagree as to its position. However, the order *me oblitum*, with *me* in second place within its clause, is clearly to be preferred (2.7n.).

46.7 perstrinxit 'grazed', figuratively (*OLD* s.v. 2b).

46.8 perverterim the reading of *E* is not known; see my note at *CQ* n.s. 39 (1989) 404.

atque perfregerim *ac* (*E*β) before *perfregerim* appears to be the reading of the archetype; *T* gives *aut* and δ omits. *atque* (conjectured by Clark, but already given by *B*), however, provides the better clausula, a double-cretic (and therefore allowable before the consonant: see pp. 53f.). In view of the fact that *T* writes *aut* for *atque* at §77 (77.2n.), I am emboldened to adopt *atque* here, in spite of the stronger MS support for *ac*.

mihi... velim cf. *Fam.* 2.16.3 *credas hoc mihi velim*; *Fam.* 13.29.4 *hoc mihi ut testi velim credas*; *Fam.* 13.29.7 *hoc mihi velim credas.*

47.1 minime ignoras for the litotes see 13.9n.

47.2 noli... abuti mea the rising tricolon is emphasised by anaphora of *noli* (4.13n.). I prefer the order of ω, *nova lenitate*, to *lenitate nova*

(*T*): the mind grasps *hac nova lenitate*...*mea* more readily than *hac lenitate nova*...*mea*, while elision of *lenitate* before *abuti* is more attractive than elision of the iambic *nova* with a following short vowel (avoided in the poets). *abuti* is to 'take advantage of' (*OLD* s.v. 3); Reid well compares *Cat.* 1.1. On Cicero's newly-displayed *lenitas* see 1.10n.

47.3 noli aculeos...excussos arbitrari lit., 'do not suppose that the barbs (*OLD* s.v. *aculeus* 3a; *TLL* 1.457.79ff.) of my oratory, which have been put back in their place (*OLD* s.v. *recondo* 2b), have been shaken off (*TLL* v.2.1309.22ff.; cf. 24.8n.)'; i.e. 'do not imagine that you have shaken off the barbs of my oratory: I have not deployed them'. *quia* for *qui* (Pluygers, Reid) impairs the sense (cf. 4.9n.). The image is one of sharp arrows, which Cicero is refraining from shooting at his opponent; it does not concern swords, and translations such as 'sheathed' (Nicklin, King, Lord, Macdonald), 'rinfoderati' (Vitucci, Zicàri), 'émoussés' (Boulanger) and 'embotados' (Peña) miss the point. The metaphor is usually interpreted in terms of bees and their stings (e.g. by Halm, Long, Reid, Zicàri and Macdonald), but this is not appropriate, especially in view of the fact that 'bees always leave their stings behind...and so die' (Reid). Sylvius (comparing Plin. *Nat.* 8.125) even goes so far as to see an allusion to porcupines and their quills; this is accepted by Long and many others. Figurative use of *aculeus* is common in Cicero: see *TLL* 1.457.77ff. On imagery involving arrows see Pöschl 534.

47.4 noli...concessum ω places *putare* after *id*, but this results in a slightly clumsy sequence of long syllables *omnino a me esse amissum*. For the play in *amissum*...*remissum* on different compounds of the same root see Holst 63–70.

47.5 cum...amicitia nostra the considerations which lead Cicero to deal gently with Torquatus are repeated from *permitto aliquid ...parenti* (§46): Cicero is in fact emphasising to the jury Torquatus' hot-headedness, his youthful inexperience and his disloyalty. *excusationes* wittily assumes that an attempt has been made by Torquatus to excuse or explain away his attack on Cicero.

47.7 tum...debeam the *tum* clause gives Cicero's more specific reason, as would be expected in the *cum*...*tum* correlation (1.4n.). The metaphor this time concerns a different form of combat, wrestling (oratorical strength is compared to physical strength); cf. e.g. Pi. *N.* 93–4; Ar. *Eq.* 841; *id. Nu.* 126, 551; Pl. *Lg.* 682 e; *id. Phdr.* 236 b; *id. R.* 544 b; *Clu.* 52 *sed ut quidquid ego apprenderam, statim accusator extorquebat e manibus.*

47.8 usu...robustior cf. *Cael.* 7 *vellem aliquis ex vobis robustioribus hunc male dicendi locum suscepisset; aliquanto liberius et fortius et magis more nostro refutaremus istam male dicendi licentiam. Tecum, Atratine, agam lenius...* On *usus* and *aetas* cf. *Div. Caec.* 47 *L. Appuleium esse video proximum subscriptorem,* *hominem non aetate sed usu forensi atque exercitatione tironem*; *Ver.* 4.138; *Mur.* 65; *de Orat.* 1.5, 2.117; *Deiot.* 1.

47.10 tecum sic agam Cicero often tells his opponents how he is going to deal with them, e.g. at *S. Rosc* 73; *Ver.* 5.164; *Mur.* 10; *Cael.* 7 (quoted in previous n. and at 46.3n.), 33, 36; *Phil.* 2.34.

tulisse ... videar for the play *tulisse ... rettulisse* see Holst 70–76; cf. § 63 *ferebat ... referebat*; § 66 *ferebantur ... adferebant. rettulisse gratiam* ('to have returned the favour') is ironic (cf. *TLL* VI.2.2219.29ff.); *gratiam* balances *iniuriam* and its deletion (Pluygers) is unwarranted (deletion would also impair the rhythm; cf. Zielinski 204).

XVII 48.1 neque vero ... possum a transition. Cicero has been discussing his self-restraint in his treatment of Torquatus. Now he moves on to recapitulate some of his earlier points (§ 48) and to rebut Torquatus' complaint that he has violated their *amicitia* (§§ 49–50).

48.2 si quod 'if it is because ...'. Cicero is now in a position to provide quick answers to objections he has already discussed in detail, and so remind the jury of his arguments. The method used is that of the *altercatio* (21.1n.), in which Torquatus' objections are formulated in short snatches of *oratio recta* and then capped with equal concision. Again, ascribed *oratio recta* occurs at the *end* of a section of argumentation (3.11n.). The stylistic difference between these pointed contrasts and what has preceded is marked: the new style expresses Cicero's self-confidence. See Wiesthaler 30.

48.3 cur ... defendo? evidently when Cicero agreed to undertake Sulla's defence he did not know that Torquatus was to be the prosecutor. *quoque ipse* for *ego* (before *non suscenseo*) in ω looks like a gloss which has ousted *ego*.

48.4 et amicum ... meum *et* brings out the correspondence with the previous statement; for parallels see K.-S.II.5f. Each orator believes that it is the other who has misjudged the claims of *amicitia*. Torquatus feels justified in attacking his *inimicus*, and considers that Cicero by intervening has violated their *amicitia*; Cicero regards Torquatus as having pursued his *inimicitiae* too far, thus bringing him into conflict with himself. The term *amicitia* can denote relationships of various kinds, *necessitudo* (2.1n.) at one extreme, formal politeness and no more at the other. Sulla was an *amicus* of Cicero (cf. *Att.* 1.13.6 *amicorum facultatibus*), but there was not the affection between the two that existed between Cicero and the Torquati. This is the nub of Torquatus' complaint: Torquatus was Cicero's *familiaris ac necessarius* (§ 2), Sulla his *amicus* merely for form's sake. Nevertheless, the claims of an *amicus* who was a *reus* outweighed all others, irrespective of the relative degrees of intimacy (§ 49). For studies of *amicitia* see J. Steinberger, *Begriff und Wesen der Freundschaft bei Aristoteles* *und Cicero* (Erlangen 1955); Gelzer 101–10; Brunt 351–81; David 171–226. On the importance of *amicitia* in the trial see Douglas, *Roman Oratory* 352f. See also D. F. Epstein, *Personal Enmity in Roman Politics, 218–43 BC* (London etc. 1987), esp. 121f.

48.5 in...quaestione cf. §5 *in hoc genere quaestionis defenderim neminem* (5.7n.).

48.7 de aliis multa cognovit Lebreton (109) rightly takes *de aliis* as simply 'about others', not 'about the others', as M. Vaccaro does (cf. §§ 9, 19). *cognovit* (*a*, probably a conjecture) is preferable to *cogitavit*: Cicero is repeating the argument used at §14, where he wrote *multa cognovi. multa cognovit* gives a cretic-spondee clausula, which is more attractive than the trochaic *multa cogitavit* (cf. 5.4n.; Zielinski 204).

48.8 'cur...in alios?' cf. §21 *'quod, in quos testimonia dixisti,' inquit 'damnati sunt...'*; §83 *qui testimonium de coniuratione dixi in alios.*

quia coactus sum cf. *Ver.* 3.89 *cur fecit? coactus est. quis hoc dicit? tota civitas*; *Sul.* 87 *nihil feci nisi coactus. sum* occurs only in β; either, therefore, the word was omitted by *T*δ independently (thus Clark xiv), or else it was added in β as a conjecture (Kasten, 1933 preface xii; later (1949 v; 1966 vi) he viewed the reading as resulting from contamination, but see pp. 71f.). In either case, the word seems necessary: ellipse of *sum* is much less common than ellipse of *est*, and the word is required to balance *quia creditum est* below. *sum* would easily have dropped out before *cur*. For *coactus* as 'compelled (by the exigencies of a situation)' cf. *Mur.* 6; *Sul.* 87; *Flac.* 14; *Dom.* 93; *Rab. Post.* 5; *Off.* 1.83; Hor. *Carm.* 1.16.14.

48.9 creditum est impersonal, with *mihi* understood (43.8n.).

regnum...servitus Torquatus had accused Cicero of *regnum* (21.1n.), a charge answered at §§ 21–35. *servitus*, like *regnum*, has political overtones: see Hellegouarc'h 559. *et defendere (T)*, not *ac defendere*, is correct, because of the parallelism with *et non defendere* below.

48.11 et non defendere all MSS except β give *et defendere*, which has clearly been influenced by *et defendere* above. ω, however, gave *ac defendere* (with variations) above: the omission of *non*, therefore, cannot have been made independently in *T*δ, but must go back to the archetype. Consequently, *et non defendere* in β must be conjectural. Kasten (vi) attributes the reading of *P* to contamination, but see pp. 71f.

48.13 intelleges...humanitatis this is certainly critical of Torquatus, in spite of Cicero's claim at the end of §50. *Humanitas* in this instance is the impulse to come to the aid of one's fellow (cf. *Off.* 2.51, quoted at 6.8n.): the word brings to mind Cicero's merciful nature (1.10n.). Cicero feels that his motives for defending Sulla are of a higher order than Torquatus' for prosecuting him (cf. Douglas 12).

49.1 at vero...amplissimus cf. §83 *sed cum agatur honos meus am-*

plissimus. Cicero now contrasts the present case with Sulla's trial for *ambitus* in 66, which, unlike this prosecution, was undertaken for a justifiable reason (the point is repeated at § 90, *honoris enim contentio vos ad causam, non inimicitiae deduxerunt*). At the same time Torquatus' poor judgement is contrasted with his father's wisdom: the father did not criticise his friends for supporting Sulla, even though this might have cost him his consulship.

at vero (*S*) is an easy change from *aut vero* (*T*); ω gives *an vero*, but the sentence is not a question (49.2n.). ω places *amplissimus* after *agebatur*, normalising the hyperbaton.

49.2 hoc...parentis tui of 65 BC. J. C. G. Boot (on *Att.*² p. 601) proposed deletion of this clause, without justification (it ends in a double-cretic).

sapientissimus vir...non suscensuit the *vir* is Torquatus' *parens* (11.4n.). *non* indicates that this sentence is not to be taken as a question. *an vero* in ω (above) led to the removal of *non* in Stephanus' MS (Stephanus 88f.); Madvig argued for retention of the word (*Adv. Crit.* II.209 n. 1).

49.3 [pater tuus] the position of these words is very awkward (the clause naturally comes to an end at *non suscensuit*, molossus-cretic), and I have accepted Rinkes' deletion. *pater tuus* is exactly the sort of information a scribe might be expected to provide (cf. § 51 [*Cornelium*]).

49.4 laudarent in the technical sense of providing *laudationes*, sworn testimonials to the defendant's character; cf. § 81 '*adfuerunt*' inquit '*Catilinae illumque laudarunt*'. At *Ver.* 5.57 Cicero claims that to have fewer than ten looked bad. See Greenidge 490f.

intellegebat hanc...impediremur *hanc* is given emphasis by hyperbaton (8.1n.). Roman custom, as Torquatus' father recognised, had always regarded defence as overriding all duties of *amicitia* (the point is repeated at the end of the section). This is well illustrated by *Mur.* 7–10, where Cicero answers Sulpicius' complaint that by defending Murena he has broken the ties of friendship between them: *atque hoc non modo non laudari sed ne concedi quidem potest ut amicis nostris accusantibus non etiam alienissimos defendamus* (8); cf. *omnes enim ad pericula propulsanda concurrimus et qui non aperte inimici sumus etiam alienissimis in capitis periculis amicissimorum officia et studia praestamus* (*Mur.* 45). The younger Torquatus, then, is presented as being at variance with both his own father and the *mos maiorum*. On the moral rules of defence see 6.8n.

ω gives *ad propulsanda pericula*: it is perhaps more likely that this was written for *ad pericula propulsanda* (*T*) than *vice versa*. C. A. Lehmann argued that *amici* or *amicorum* should be added before or after *ad* (*Hermes* 15 (1880) 571f.), but this is misconceived: defence overrides *amicitia* not only when *amici* are on trial. For *impedire ad faciendum aliquid* cf. *TLL* VII.1.534.42ff.; K.-S.1.749f.; Nägelsbach 523f.

49.6 et erat *Ta* read *aderat*, which is unacceptable. What is needed before *erat*: *et* (*q*), *at* (Halm), *atque* (later suggested by Halm) or nothing (β)? In spite of the palaeographic neatness of *at erat*, an adversative is not required: the sense is rather, 'your father appreciated that the claims of the defence outweighed those of the prosecution in 66 – and how much stronger were the claims of the prosecution then than now!' I therefore opt for *et erat* (*q*), the reading preferred by Halm in his later editions.

49.8 honoris erat certamen cf. § 90 *honoris enim contentio; Off.* 1.38 *aliter contendimus si est inimicus, aliter si competitor (cum altero certamen honoris et dignitatis est, cum altero capitis et famae).*

49.9 ut victi...vinceretis for the play with active and passive forms of the same verb see Holst 60f. *in campo in foro* means both 'in the Campus Martius...in the forum' (places) and, metonymically, 'in the elections...in the courts'.

49.11 quibus non irascebamini Cicero is reiterating what he said in the first part of this section. Campe objected to these words on the grounds that they interrupt the line of thought. They do interrupt it – intentionally, to give the point strong emphasis.

49.13 inviolata...faciebant this repeats *intellegebat...impediremur* above, appealing strongly to Roman tradition. Incisions occur after *amicitia* (hiatus), *officio, instituto* (hiatus) and *faciebant*. On *officium* see 2.5n.

XVIII 50.2 ornamentis i.e. the *insignia honoris* (50.4n.); cf. § 81 *sella curuli atque ornamentis;* § 88 *quae habebit ornamenta..?* A senator's *ornamenta* in a wider sense consisted of *locus, auctoritas, domi splendor, apud exteras nationes nomen et gratia, toga praetexta, sella curulis, insignia, fasces, exercitus, imperia, provinciae (Clu.* 154). See Mommsen, *Staatsrecht* 1.455–67.

dignitati 'office' (1.1n.).

50.3 quid...expetas? cf. § 90 *quid est quod expetas amplius?*

50.4 insignia...delata sunt cf. *Sul.* 26 *praeclarae laudis insignia; Sul.* 88 *honoris insignia atque ornamenta; Phil.* 8.32 *nostri honoris insignia.* Taylor has argued that a successful prosecutor, if a senator, acceded to his victim's rank of seniority in the senate; thus after Verres' trial Cicero himself, although only just elected aedile, would have been entitled to wear the *toga praetexta* (26.5n.) and would have been treated as a *praetorius* in the senatorial hierarchy when called upon to give his *sententia (PP* 112–16; see, however, the qualifications made by M. C. Alexander, *CP* 80 (1985) 20–32). Here Cicero states that in 66 Sulla's consulship (*honos*) passed to the elder Torquatus (11.4n.), while the younger Torquatus (as prosecutor) acquired the '*insignia* of office' (i.e. the *toga praetexta*).

Alexander (*op. cit.* 26f.) interprets these *insignia* as the consular *insignia* of
the elder Torquatus, which the younger Torquatus could expect to
possess, and display in the *atrium* of his house, upon his father's death.
But this interpretation is discounted by the perfect *delata sunt*; also, *ornatus exuviis* etc. seems to imply that Torquatus is actually wearing his
spoils (see next n.). Taylor's view is therefore to be preferred (*PP* 114):
Torquatus acquired Sulla's *insignia* and rank directly. Alexander is correct, however, in observing that, on Taylor's interpretation, it is not
clear whether the *insignia* acquired by Torquatus would have been
praetorian or consular: Sulla had only become consul-designate, not
consul (nevertheless he was *creatus*, as David points out (519 n. 81)). A
further complication is that Torquatus was unlikely to have been a
member of the senate at this date (24.3n.); presumably, therefore, 'even
a man not yet in the senate could secure senatorial *ornamenta* from such
an accusation' (Taylor, *PP* 220 n. 53).

ornatus exuviis Torquatus was evidently wearing in court the *toga
praetexta* which he had won from Sulla; Cicero draws attention to an
invidious honour (cf. *S. Rosc.* 83; *Balb.* 57). Comparison of the *insignia*
to *exuviae* (the word occurs elsewhere in Cicero only at *Man.* 55) enables
Cicero to introduce an image drawn from battle in which Torquatus is
presented as a merciless attacker who, not content with killing and de-
spoiling his adversary, is fighting to mutilate his corpse (related imagery
is used at §§ 79, 89, 91). Cicero represents himself, on the other hand, as
a man motivated by compassion to rescue the body of his fallen com-
rade. Editors from Gruter onwards wrongly report *E* as having read
huius after *exuviis*: see my note at *CQ* n.s. 39 (1989) 404. *huius* does not
occur in *Tω*, but in *G mg. c²k*, where it is placed after *ornatus*. The word
is a conjecture, not I think necessary to the sense (the rhythm is
unaffected).

50.6 hic 'in this context' (cf. §§ 21, 22, 67).

50.7 quia Ernesti preferred *qui* (cf. 4.9n.).

ego ... factum tuum the structure *reprendis ... irasceris ... non irascor
... ne reprendo quidem* helps to bring out Cicero's point that his behaviour
will be the very reverse of that of Torquatus. In spite of his sudden refusal to criticise his opponent he has in fact been making implied criticisms throughout §§ 48–50, and will criticise Torquatus openly at § 90
below.

50.10 offici ... esse Cicero ends his reply to Torquatus on a note
of quiet irony, claiming that he (unlike Torquatus) would not presume
to judge his opponent's assessment of his *officia* (2.5n.). Neither *potuisse*
(*T*) nor *posuisse* (ω) makes adequate sense, and both give hexameter
ending rhythms. *posuisse* is accepted by Kasten because he believes that

to be the reading of *E* (as well as of ω), and therefore of the archetype. But the reading of *E* is not recorded, and Kasten's argument (v) is unsound: see my note at *CQ* n.s. 39 (1989) 404f. Pabón (11) has been misled by Kasten into thinking a conjecture involving *potuisse* to be stemmatically impossible. I formerly (*op. cit.*) expressed a preference for Halm's easy change ⟨*esse*⟩ *potuisse*, which provides an *esse videatur* clausula (Reid's *potuisse* ⟨*esse*⟩ is unrhythmical: see Zielinski 204). But *potuisse* seems superfluous after *idoneum*. I therefore now accept Madvig's *ipsum esse* (*Adv. Crit.* III.134), which neatly accounts for *posuisse* in ω. The clausula is a cretic-trochee.

§§51–68 REPREHENSIO II

Cicero has already dealt with the prosecution's two most serious allegations (§§36–45); now he returns to the *reprehensio* to answer those charges which remain. In the arrangement of arguments the recommended procedure was to begin and conclude with one's strongest points, and hide away the weaker ones in between (*Orat.* 50; cf. *de Orat.* 2.314). This policy does not seem to have been followed here. The first refutation (iii, plotting at the elections of 63) makes a powerful appeal to Cicero's *auctoritas*, but the argument is nevertheless weak. The second passage (iv, purchase of gladiators) is stronger: here the prosecution manifestly fail to prove their case. This is followed by the most convincing refutation of all (v, Sittius), in which Cicero is entirely successful in demonstrating that Sulla's friend cannot have had any connection with the conspiracy. After this Cicero is evidently on weaker ground (vi, machinations at Pompeii; vii, *vis* at the promulgation of the *rogatio Caecilia*). Finally, the treatment of the 'first conspiracy' (viii, letter to Pompey) is flawed, although on this charge the prosecution's main argument was very feeble indeed. The overall impression, then, is that the order chosen by Cicero is not strategic: the weaker arguments are not hidden from sight, nor is the strongest refutation (v, Sittius) put in a position of prominence. Instead, therefore, it is likely that Cicero has simply followed the order in which the charges were raised by the prosecution, starting here with Cornelius' points (iii and iv, probably also v–vii) and then returning to a point of Torquatus' (viii). The charges also seem to have been answered roughly in order of decreasing importance, and it may be that this was an arrangement which suited both prosecution and defence.

(iii) Sulla's alleged plotting at the elections of 63 (§§51–53)

The son of the conspirator C. Cornelius is accusing Sulla. His charges which relate to the events of 66–65 have already been answered by Hortensius; but he also links

Sulla with Autronius' and Catiline's intended massacre at the consular elections of 63, over which Cicero presided. However, it was Autronius who was seen there, not Sulla, and he was seen by Cicero, who himself suppressed the attempt. No one believes that Sulla attended the election. But what does the elder Cornelius have to say of the meeting at Laeca's house, at which he volunteered to kill Cicero? While this and other events were taking place, Sulla was not at Rome but far away at Naples.

This passage concerns one incident, the consular elections of July 63, at which, the prosecution and defence agree, Autronius and Catiline intended to perpetrate a massacre. Cicero's aim is to show not only that Sulla was not party to their plans, but that he was not even present on the occasion. His argument is based on his assertion that he himself was in the best position to know what happened: he was presiding, he was the only person who was aware of the danger, and it was he by whose efforts the massacre was prevented from taking place. So, he implies, when he says that he saw Autronius but not Sulla on the Campus Martius, it can be assumed that Sulla was absent. At this point Cicero unexpectedly digresses to talk of the meeting at Laeca's house more than three months afterwards, when Cornelius and Vargunteius had plotted Cicero's murder. On the surface Cicero's intention is simply to arouse *odium* against the prosecution, by enlarging on the most shocking incident in which Cornelius was known to have been involved. But behind this there lies a more subtle motive. When discussing the events on the *campus*, Cicero does not state outright whether or not Sulla was in Rome: he merely says that he himself saw Autronius (!). He then casually moves on to the events of three to four months later, and concludes by announcing that during this period Sulla was at Naples: in this way he encourages his audience to infer that Sulla was actually at Naples at the time of the elections. Cicero's deviousness on this point strongly suggests that Sulla did indeed visit Rome for the elections of 63.

51.1   At accusat ⟨C.⟩ Corneli filius this sentence, expressing the prosecution's position, is virtually ascribed *oratio recta* (3.11n.). On Torquatus' *subscriptor* Cornelius, the son of the Catilinarian C. Cornelius (6.6n.), see p. 20. The father's *praenomen* has been omitted by haplography, as at §6.

51.2   o ... susceperit! Torquatus' father was described as *sapientissimus vir* at §49; now Cornelius' father is, ironically, *patrem sapientem*. The elder Cornelius would have been stupid not to take advantage of the rewards offered to informers, and yet admit his own guilt by claiming to know of Sulla's involvement: the implication is that he did not know Sulla to be involved. The *praemium* referred to is the customary (*quod...solet*) reward available to informers under the *lex Plautia de vi* (cf. M. C. Alexander, *CP* 80 (1985) 30f.). Other rewards were also available: early in November the senate had offered specific *praemia* for informers, *impunitas* with 200,000 sesterces or, for slaves, manumission with 100,000 sesterces (Sal. *Cat.* 30.6, 36.5), and after the capture of the conspirators *praemia* were voted to Volturcius and the Allobroges (*Cat.* 4.5, 4.10; Sal. *Cat.* 50.1). In addition, *impunitas* was offered to certain informers whose testimony was self-incriminating (*Cat.* 3.8; Sal. *Cat.* 47.1, 48.3–9; Dio 37.41.2).

I accept Cobet's deletion of *Cornelium* as a gloss. The name intrudes awkwardly, especially since it has just been given above, and this is exactly the sort of information a scribe might be expected to provide (cf. §49 [*pater tuus*]). Deletion of *Cornelium* does not affect the rhythm (a hexameter ending; but such rhythms are least undesirable when the final word consists of four or five syllables: 11.1n.).

51.5 indicat cf. §54 *Quid ergo indicat..?* The archetype had the subjunctive *indicet*, which is defended by Pabón (11). But the sense is not, 'what is there which he might allege?' (this would imply 'nothing'), but 'what is there which he does allege?' For the distinction see Lebreton 317f.

istum puerum contemptuous; for *iste* see 61.7n. On the youth of prosecutors see 46.4n.

51.6 si...Hortensius the start of a *complexio* (10.3 n.). *vetera* refers to the events of 66–5 which, as Cicero stressed in the *partitio* (§§11–14), he knows nothing about, Torquatus' father not having had the courtesy to invite him to his *consilia*. These events were discussed (*communicata*) at the time with Hortensius (§12), who has already answered the charges which relate to them.

51.7 illum conatum Cicero describes an intended massacre by Autronius and Catiline in the Campus Martius at the consular elections of July 63, over which he as consul presided (Reid and McGushin (on Sal. *Cat.*, p. 298) strangely take this as referring to the 'first conspiracy'). The attempt, we are told below, was suppressed by Cicero *tectus praesidio firmo amicorum*. Further versions of the incident are given in *Mur.* and *Cat.* 1: at *Mur.* 52 Cicero, realising that Catiline is leading an armed band of conspirators to the Campus Martius, alerts the Roman people to the danger by appearing with a bodyguard and wearing a cuirass; at *Cat.* 1.11 Catiline attempts to murder his fellow-candidates together with Cicero but is thwarted by Cicero's private bodyguard. Neither version mentions Autronius, who has presumably been introduced by the prosecution because of his association with Sulla. Moreover, the absence of murder plans at *Mur.* 52 makes it likely that these have been invented by

234

Cicero (Catiline being dead) here and at (the rewritten) *Cat.* 1.11. See further Sal. *Cat.* 26.5; Plut. *Cic.* 14.2–5; Dio 37.29.2–5.

51.9 Autronium we are expected to infer that if Autronius had been seen, Sulla could not have been seen. Autronius' presence at the elections had clearly been noticed, whether or not he had had criminal intentions.

51.10 sed...nos? this is the type of *correctio* usually known in Greek as ἐπιδιόρθωσις or μετάνοια; cf. Lausberg 387; Martin 279f. *sed* is invariably the conjunction used, so editors adopt Madvig's *sed* (*Opusc. Acad.* 152) for *et* (ω). Seyffert (41) defends *et* by citing *Ver.* 4.6 *nuper homines nobilis eius modi, iudices, – et* (codd.: *sed* Halm, edd.) *quid dico 'nuper'? immo vero modo ac plane paulo ante vidimus*; but clearly the same error has occurred there as in our passage. The point of the *correctio* is to emphasise Cicero's personal knowledge of the events in question (14.5n.).

51.11 nihil...suspicabamini the senate was slow to wake up to the danger. Cicero had had the elections postponed for one day to allow discussion of Catiline's pre-election speech, but the senate did not believe Cicero's allegations and no action was taken (*Mur.* 51 *congemuit senatus frequens neque tamen satis severe pro rei indignitate decrevit; nam partim ideo fortes in decernendo non erant, quia nihil timebant, partim, quia omnia*; cf. Plut. *Cic.* 14.3–4; Dio 37.29.3). The elections then went ahead without further delay.

51.12 tectus...amicorum cf. *Cat.* 1.6 *vives...multis meis et firmis praesidiis obsessus*; *Cat.* 1.11 *compressi conatus tuos nefarios amicorum praesidio et copiis*; *Mur.* 52 *cum firmissimo praesidio fortissimorum virorum.* Perhaps a bodyguard was one of the things which Cicero had asked for, but failed to obtain (Dio 37.29.3).

Catilinae tum et Autroni this is one unit (cretic-spondee rhythms at *amicorum* and *Autroni*), with *tum* in second position (2.7n.). *T* omits *et*, while in *q tum* has been altered to *tunc* (9.8n.).

52.2 aspirasse lit. 'breathed towards', hence 'approached', 'went near' (*TLL* II.841.8off.); cf. *Ver.* 2.76 *quando...homo tantae luxuriae...nisi Februario mense aspirabit in curiam?*; *Paneg.* 12(9).14.4 *non ille aspirare in campum.* In Cicero the word is used only in negative or near-negative sentences: see Nägelsbach 580.

atqui the argument is well stated by Reid: 'Sulla did not appear in the *campus*; but if he had been in league with Catiline he would have appeared there; therefore he was not in league with Catiline'. The form is that of a syllogism, known variously as an enthymeme *ex consequentibus* or epicheirema (cf. *Top.* 55; Quint. *Inst.* 5.10.1–3, 5.14.1–26; Martin 102–6; Rohde 100–2). *atqui* often introduces the minor premise of a syllogism; cf. *TLL* II.1089.42ff. See 32.9n. for the enthymeme *ex pugnantibus*.

52.3 societate sceleris cf. *Sul.* 16 *societas...sceleris* (with 16.4n.); *Clu.* 35 *sceleris societate coniunctae.*

52.4 in pari causa i.e. if Sulla's case really is identical to that of Autronius; Cicero argued against this in *digressio* II (§§ 14–20). *T* gives *ire* for *in*, so Clark suggested *in re pari* (without *causa*).

52.6 ipse Cicero exploits the fact that the conspirator Cornelius was not in a position to appear in person.

ut dicitis β gives *et ut diximus* (*diximus* is a miscopying). *et* cannot be correct in this position: *Cornelius...dubitat* rather than *informat... filium* approximates to the position of the prosecutors. *et* before *ut dicitis* would also spoil the resolved double-cretic before *informat* by giving rise to an incision after *dubitat*, where there is no characteristic rhythm. *et* could be placed instead after *dicitis* (as suggested to me by Professor M. Winterbottom). But the word is unnecessary in view of the antithesis (*ipse...filium*); *informat* may be taken simply as adversative asyndeton.

informat...filium *aliquem informare* is to 'mould someone by instruction' (the metaphor is derived from moulding metals, wax etc.); cf. *Arch.* 4 *eis artibus quibus aetas puerilis ad humanitatem informari solet. adumbrare* is a metaphor from drawing, meaning to 'sketch in outline' (σκια-γραφεῖν), without adding any detail; cf. *Cael.* 12 *habuit enim ille* [sc. Catilina] *...permulta maximarum non expressa signa sed adumbrata virtutum.* Both metaphors are commonplace, and suggest the unreliability of young Cornelius' allegations.

52.7 quid...dicit Cicero now moves to the offensive, and at the same time moves forward from the events of July 63 to those of 6 November, when the conspirators met at Laeca's house and decided that Cornelius and Vargunteius should murder Cicero at the *salutatio* early the following morning (6.6n.): the prosecution have naturally omitted to mention this incident. Nocturnal meetings were characteristic of conspiracies, and were therefore banned by the XII Tables (8.26); cf. W. Nippel, *JRS* 74 (1984) 24.

52.8 inter falcarios i.e. the scythe-makers' quarter, mentioned elsewhere only at *Cat.* 1.8, *dico te priore nocte venisse inter falcarios.* Its location is not known (Richardson, *Rome* 211). It may be speculated that the conspirators obtained their weapons from the scythe-makers.

52.9 quae...nonarum Novembrium the night 'which followed the day after the nones (5th) of November', i.e. the night of 6–7 November. For the genitive cf. *Tusc.* 1.114 *post eius diei diem tertium*; *Att.* 3.7.1 *post diem tertium eius diei*; *Q. fr.* 3.2.1 *postridie autem eius diei*; Tac. *Hist.* 1.26 *postero iduum die* (see H.-Sz.64). It is from this fixed point that *Cat.* 1 is dated to 8 or, as now seems more plausible, 7 November: cf. *Cat.* 1.1 *quid proxima, quid superiore nocte egeris* (pleonastic, = 'last night'); *Cat.* 1.8

noctem illam superiorem ... priore nocte; *Cat.* 2.6 *omnia superioris noctis consilia*; *Cat.* 2.12 *hesterno die, cum domi meae paene interfectus essem.* On the respective dating of the meeting at Laeca's house and *Cat.* 1 see T. Mommsen, *Hermes* 1 (1866) 431–7; R. A. Lange, *Römische Alterthümer* (Berlin 1871) III.249; John 777–88; C. John, *Philologus* 46 (1888) 650–65; A. S. Wilkins[2] (Halm) on *Cat.* 1–4, xxiv n. 55; Rice Holmes 1.461–5; M. Gelzer, *RE* II A.1706.23ff., VII A.877.30ff.; W. Steidle, *Historia* Einzelschriften 3 (1958) 93f.; K. Vretska, *Ciceroniana* 1 (1959) 185–96; Syme, *Sallust* 78f.; T. Crane, *CJ* 61 (1965–6) 264–7; Stockton 338f.; J. D. Madden, *CW* 71 (1977–8) 276–8. H. C. Nutting believes that *nocte ea ... Novembrium* may be a quotation from the Allobroges' evidence taken in the senate on 3 December (*AJP* 29 (1908) 316–21; cf. *TAPA* 38 (1907) xxxix).

52.11 acerrima ... acerbissima the next sentence explains why. For the alliteration see Wölfflin 253.

52.12 tum ... exeundi Cicero gives another account of the arrangements at *Cat.* 1.9: *distribuisti partis Italiae, statuisti quo quemque proficisci placeret, delegisti quos Romae relinqueres, quos tecum educeres, discripsisti urbis partis ad incendia, confirmasti te ipsum iam esse exiturum, dixisti paulum tibi esse etiam nunc morae, quod ego viverem.* See also Sal. *Cat.* 27.4.

ceteris manendi condicio 'the provision under which the rest were to stay behind', i.e. those who were to remain in Rome were given their instructions. *condicio*, like *denuntiatione* ('summons') above, has a legal ring.

52.13 discriptio ... incendiorum Bücheler rightly changed *descriptio* (ω) to *discriptio*: the prefix is *di* – when the meaning is of dividing and distributing. Reid remarks on *Ac.* 1.17, 'since Bücheler set the fashion, many editors have run to excess in changing *descriptio* into *discriptio*'. Cicero regularly pairs *caedes* and *incendia* (e.g. §53): Wölfflin (255) gives some instances.

52.14 tum tuus pater for the attempt see 6.6n. In *q tum* has been altered to *tunc*: see 9.8n.

52.15 tandem aliquando pleonasm (39.1n.), 'at long last'; cf. *Quinct.* 94; *Agr.* 2.13; *Cat.* 1.18, 1.25, 2.1; *Mur.* 33; *Phil.* 2.75; *Fam.* 11.27.5, 16.9.2.

confitetur i.e. only now does he admit his guilt, by claiming to know of Sulla's involvement (cf. §51 *quod turpitudinis in confessione, id per accusationem fili susceperit*).

sibi ... depoposcit this conflicts with other versions: see 18.9n. For the metaphorical use of *provincia* cf. *Cael.* 63; *Att.* 12.26.2.

52.17 iure amicitiae nothing is known of any *amicitia* (48.4n.) between Cicero and the conspirator Cornelius. *ut ... trucidaret* narrates what Cornelius said when volunteering to murder Cicero: a reference to *ius amicitiae* in this context emphasises that Cornelius deliberately set out to abuse Cicero's trust.

in meo lectulo cf. *Cat.* 1.9 *se... paulo ante lucem me in meo lecto interfecturos esse pollicerentur*; *Cat.* 4.2 *ille consul... cui... non lectus ad quietem datus.*

XIX 53.1 hoc tempore cum arderet 'at this time, a time when (i.e. such that)...'. It seems that the subjunctives ('descriptive') do not merely state the time, but characterise it; cf. T. E. Kinsey on *Quinct.* 53; Woodcock 191.

53.2 egrederetur 'was on the point of leaving'. He left Rome the following evening, 7 November.

Lentulus see 16.3n.

53.3 Cassius... praeponeretur cf. *Cat.* 4.13 *attribuit nos trucidandos Cethego et... urbem inflammandam Cassio.* For Cassius and his supervision of the arson see 36.3n. C. Cornelius Cethegus (*RE* IV.1278.12ff., Cornelius 89; *MRR* II.489), a young senator in 63 (Sal. *Cat.* 17.3, 52.33) and previously the would-be assassin of Metellus Pius (70.13n.), was a leading conspirator and one of the five men executed on 5 December (Sal. *Cat.* 55.6); his own brother voted for his execution (Amp. 19.12). He negotiated with the Allobroges (*Cat.* 3.9–10; Sal. *Cat.* 44.1), and was to have undertaken Cicero's murder (*Cat.* 4.13; Sal. *Cat.* 43.2); his house served as the conspirators' arsenal (*Cat.* 3.10; Plut. *Cic.* 18.2, 19.2). According to Sallust *natura ferox, vehemens, manu promptus erat* (*Cat.* 43.4), and Cicero refers to his *furiosam temeritatem* (*Cat.* 3.16; cf. 4.11); Cethegus objected to the hesitation and indecision shown by the other conspirators (*Cat.* 3.10; Sal. *Cat.* 43.3). See also Luc. 2.543, 6.794. For the play *incendiis... caedi* see 52.13n.; and on the singular *praeponeretur*, 33.10n. *incendium* and *caedes* denote fire and killing on a grand scale.

53.4 curiam this is C. Schliack's brilliant and almost universally ignored conjecture for *Etruriam* (ω): see *Proben* (Cottbus 1888) 10f. We were told at §17 that after Catiline's flight Autronius stayed in Rome until after the execution of the conspirators (17.5n.); later, at §52, we learned that upon Catiline's departure the rest were to remain in Rome. But here, according to the MSS, it is being arranged that Autronius should seize Etruria. The contradiction would not, perhaps, be impossible for Cicero, but the instruction itself, to seize Etruria, is inexplicable: Etruria has already been held for some time by Manlius (*Cat.* 1.5, 1.7, 2.6; Sal. *Cat.* 27.1, 28.4, 30.1), and in any case we have just been told that Catiline himself is going *ad exercitum*. The error may be neatly explained by dittography of *et*. The seizure of the senate-house would be an obvious objective for the conspirators (*Cat.* 4.2; Sal. *Cat.* 43.3), and that the task should be allotted to Autronius accords well with Cicero's hostile picture of Autronius elsewhere in the speech (e.g. §71).

53.5   ornarentur *ornare* and *ordinare* are often confused in MSS. At §75 below *Tω* have *ordinatae*, while *b²ck* offer *ornatae*; there the meaning 'adorned', 'honoured' shows that only *ornatae* can be correct. Here at §53 the MSS give *ordinarentur*. *ordinare* occurs elsewhere only twice in Cicero (becoming common later), at *Inv.* 1.19 ('put into an order') and *N.D.* 2.101 ('prescribe', i.e. 'put into an order in advance'); in each case the idea is specific, almost numerical. Here, therefore, since *omnia* indicates that the sense is general, I adopt Landgraf's *ornarentur*, 'when everything was being made ready'.

ubi fuit Sulla this question-and-answer sequence in which the orator progressively closes off the possibilities open to the opposition is known technically as *subiectio* (ὑποφορά); cf. *Rhet. Her.* 4.33–4; Quint. *Inst.* 9.2.15; Lausberg 381–3; Martin 285f. The technique is similar to that in which arguments are given in the form of an *altercatio* (21.1n.).

53.6   afuit *Ta* give *affuit*; for similar confusions see §§7, 14 and 74.

53.7   regionibus sc. of Italy; although Italy was not formally divided into eleven *regiones* until Augustus. See R. Thomsen, *The Italic Regions from Augustus to the Lombard Invasion* (Copenhagen 1947) 11f.

quo = *in quas*, not unusually; see Nägelsbach's parallels, 363f.

53.8   in agro ... Gallico i.e. in the territory of Camerinum (adj., *Camers*) or Picenum, or in the *ager Gallicus*. Camerinum was a town in Umbria, east of Perusia; the *ager Gallicus* (taken from the Senones (Gauls) in 284) was to the east of Umbria, on the Adriatic seaboard north of Picenum. Picenum and the *ager Gallicus*, with Etruria and Apulia, were the chief centres of unrest (*Cat.* 2.6; Sal. *Cat.* 27.1, 42.1); Camerinum was the home of one Septimius who Sallust alleges was sent by Catiline to Picenum (*Cat.* 27.1). It was from Picenum and the *ager Gallicus* that the praetor Metellus Celer (65.4n.) raised his army (*Cat.* 2.5, 2.26; Sal. *Cat.* 30.5, 57.2). It is perhaps significant that Apulia, in spite of disturbances there (*Cat.* 2.6, 3.14; Sal. *Cat.* 27.1, 30.2–3, 42.1, 46.3), is not mentioned at this point (e.g. instead of Camerinum). Possibly Cicero wishes to refer only to areas north of Rome: Apulia was relatively close to Naples.

53.9   quasi morbus ... pervaserat for *pervadere* used of epidemics cf. Apul. *Apol.* 50; (in image) Liv. 42.5.7 *contagione, velut tabes, in Perrhaebiam quoque id pervaserat malum*; (of poison) Tac. *Ann.* 13.16.2. On metaphors of sickness and healing see 76.12n.

53.10   ut iam ante dixi at §17.

53.11   quae maxime ... caruit cf. §17 *ubi neque homines fuisse putantur huius adfines suspicionis*. Capua, however, was suspected: see 17.8n.

(iv) Sulla's purchase of gladiators (§§ 54–55)

Cornelius claims that Sulla purchased gladiators with a view to committing violence and murder. But the gladiators were obtained at Faustus' request for games stipulated by his father's will. This is proved by letters which Faustus sent to Sulla and others. Sulla's freedman Cornelius did procure the weapons, but overall charge lay in the hands of Faustus' freedman.

In § 53 Cicero moved the focus of our attention from Rome to Naples, and accordingly the next charge concerns Sulla's activities during his residence there. Naples was conveniently placed for the purchase and training of gladiators: Campania was famous for its gladiatorial schools, particularly that at Capua, and the games are thought to have originated in this area (see G. Ville, *La Gladiature en occident des origines à la mort de Domitien* (B.E.F.A.R. 245; 1981) 1–8).

Cornelius accused Sulla of having acquired gladiators *ad caedem ac tumultum* (§ 54), presumably with a view to aiding Catiline. He was aware that the dictator's will obliged Faustus to put on games, and that this was the reason Sulla gave for buying gladiators (cf. § 54 *Fausti simulatione*); he was also careful to stress that Faustus had had no part in Sulla's activities (§ 54 '*nec opinante Fausto, cum is neque sciret neque vellet, familia est comparata*'). Cornelius, then, argued that Sulla took advantage of Faustus' absence to assemble gladiators for Catiline on the pretext that the gladiators would be needed by Faustus on his return to Italy.

Cicero is able to disprove this line of argument by conveniently producing letters from Faustus to Sulla and three other men which show that Faustus did know of the purchase of gladiators, and indeed had authorised it. So unless Faustus himself had had treacherous motives, an implication Cornelius was anxious to avoid, there was nothing in itself suspicious about Sulla's hasty purchase of gladiators. That is not to say, of course, that Sulla could not have intended to use the gladiators to further his own interests or even those of Catiline. However, there is no evidence to show that the reason given by Sulla for his purchase of gladiators is not legitimate, and the prosecution therefore fail to prove their case.

As it turned out, Campania played no part in the conspiracy, and only in passages of Ciceronian hyperbole (*Cat.* 2.7, 2.9) is it claimed that gladiators were involved. Faustus' games did take place, although not until 60; since the gladiators were acquired on the command of Faustus, this fact does not throw suspicion on Sulla.

54.1 Quid ergo indicat referring back to § 51 *sed quid est tandem quod* *indicat per istum puerum Cornelius?* Two or more personal subjects generally take a plural verb; but when the verb precedes, it is usually put in agreement with the subject which is nearest: see Lebreton 17f.

54.2 qui...defertis for the play *adfert...defertis* cf. *Vat.* 12; *de Orat.* 3.227 (see 12.12n.). ω, normalising the hyperbaton, read *qui ab eo haec mandata defertis.*

gladiatores...tumultum? on the use of gladiators for personal protection and political violence see 15.2n.

Faustus Cornelius Sulla 'Felix' (*RE* iv.1515.35ff., Cornelius 377; *MRR* ii.170, 207, 223, 261, 297; iii.73), born in the second half of 86 or in 85 (cf. J. P. V. D. Balsdon, *JRS* 41 (1951) 3f.; Sumner 88), was the son of the dictator and hence P. Sulla's cousin; when he came of age he would have taken over from P. Sulla as the dictator's political heir (L. E. Reams, *CJ* 82 (1986–7) 303 n. 8). His inheritance of his father's wealth, later squandered (Plut. *Cic.* 27.3), led to a prosecution *de peculatu* in 66, but thanks in part to Cicero the case was rejected (cf. E. S. Gruen, *Athenaeum* 49 (1971) 56–8; Crawford 61–3; *TLRR* no. 196); his wealth also attracted the attentions of Rullus (*Agr.* 1.12). In 63 Faustus served in the east as a military tribune under Pompey, whose daughter, Pompeia, he later married (in 54 or 53; cf. B. A. Marshall, *AncSoc* 18 (1987) 91–101); at Jerusalem he was rewarded for being first over the walls of the Temple. His absence from Rome during this period explains why the arrangements for the games in the dictator's honour were left in the hands of Sulla (and the others mentioned in §55). The games were eventually held, with great magnificence, in 60 (*Vat.* 32; Dio 37.51.4), and it was perhaps these gladiators which came to be known as *Faustini* (Var. *L.* 9.71). Faustus became augur by 57 and quaestor in 54; in 52 he supported Milo (his twin sister Fausta's then husband) and restored the *curia*, burnt after Clodius' death. He fought for Pompey in the civil war, and was killed in Mauretania by P. Sittius' troops after Thapsus in 46 (56.1n.). For his villa at Cumae, probably once the dictator's, see D'Arms 31f., 177 (cf. 17.8n.). The punctuation of §54 has caused difficulties for editors (see Karsten 30f.); I follow Lord.

54.3 'ita prorsus...gladiatores' *ita prorsus* is not ironic (cf. *Brut.* 156, 161; *Fin.* 5.27; *Tusc.* 2.67 etc.); *ita prorsus...gladiatores* must therefore represent the prosecution's position, hence the quotation marks. *interpositi* implies deception and fraud (*TLL* vii.1.2247.53ff.), i.e. gladiators were brought in under false pretences; again, this suits the prosecution's point of view. Cicero once more sets up his argument in the manner of an *altercatio* (21.1n.).

54.4 quos...videmus Cicero's reply; on the use of the relative to introduce a brief refutation see 21.3n. As Halm remarks, *populo* must be understood after *deberi* (with *testamento* as ablative). *videmus* perhaps indicates that the dictator's will was produced in evidence. Gladiatorial games were in origin funeral rites (hence *bustuarii*, gladiators) performed as a service (*munus*; cf. Nettleship 53of.) to the dead man: see Tert. *Sp.* 12.1–3. Games were given by individuals, often by aspiring magistrates, and until Caesar's games in 46 they were always, at least ostensibly, held in honour of a deceased relative. It was common for games to have been specified in wills: Cicero's *lex Tullia de ambitu* of 63 (17.8n.) forbade the giving of games within two years prior to candidature for office, *nisi ex testamento praestituta die* (*Vat.* 37; cf. *Sest.* 133–5). It was not unusual for games to take place many years after the death of the man being honoured (cf. B. A. Marshall and R. J. Baker, *Historia* 24 (1975) 227 n. 31); in the present case the delay was occasioned by Faustus' youth. See further E. J. Jory, *CQ* n.s. 36 (1986) 537–9.

54.5 'adrepta...praebere' the prosecution's next point; Clark misunderstands it, putting only *adrepta est familia* in quotation marks. *adrepta* is 'seized', i.e. 'acquired in a(n unnecessary) hurry' (*at empta*, from Stephanus' MS (Stephanus 89), misses the point); Sulla's haste is taken to imply his guilt. A *familia* is a company of gladiators (*TLL* VI.1.239.34ff.).

54.6 utinam...posset! Cicero's reply. Macdonald explains, 'the company was not up to a successful performance as gladiators, let alone to fighting in a revolution as the prosecution alleged was its purpose'. *haec ipsa* is the *familia* purchased by Sulla. Lambinus' emendation *invidiae sed* was anticipated by *r* (cf. Pabón 6).

54.8 properatum vehementer est this repeats *adrepta est familia* above, but introduces a different point. The games did not take place until 60 (54.2n.).

54.12 est comparata for *comparare* used of gladiators etc. cf. *Sest.* 127; Suet. *Jul.* 10.2; Apul. *Met.* 10.18. W. H. Kirk (*CP* 21 (1926) 79) remarks that '*parare* and *comparare* are often used with the expression or implication of a price and so are virtually equivalent to *emere*'. *emere* and *parare* are used below for the sake of variation (§ 55).

55.1 litterae from Faustus in Palestine.

55.2 precibus...petit cf. *Lig.* 13 *quodne nos petimus precibus ac lacrimis..?*

ut emat...et ut...emat emphatic; cf. 18.1n.

55.3 L. Caesarem, Q. Pompeium, C. Memmium L. Caesar and Q. Pompeius are both likely to have owned property in Campania (see D'Arms 183f., 194) and so, like Sulla, would have been in a good position to obtain gladiators for Faustus. L. Julius Caesar (*RE* x.468.6off., Julius 143; *MRR* II.89, 161, 171, 238; III.110) was the consul of 64; his sister Julia was married first to M. Antonius Creticus, to whom she bore the triumvir Antony, and then to the Catilinarian Lentulus (16.3n.). L. Caesar was appointed, with his more famous relative C. Caesar, as *duumvir perduellionis* for Rabirius' trial in 63; he served with Caesar in Gaul (52–49), but did not participate in the civil war. Later he opposed Antony and was proscribed, but was saved by Julia's intercession. At the debate on 5 December 63 he gave a memorable speech recommending the death penalty for his brother-in-law Lentulus and the other conspirators (*Cat.* 4.13, with *schol. Gronov.* 290 St.; *Phil.* 2.14, 8.1; *Att.* 12.21.1): his testimony at Sulla's trial would have carried weight.

Q. Pompeius and C. Memmius were both relatives of Faustus with inglorious later careers. Q. Pompeius Rufus (*RE* XXI.2252.20ff., Pompeius 41; *MRR* II.236; III.166) was a son of the dictator's daughter Cornelia, and hence Faustus' nephew. As tribune in 52 he was prominent in the scenes following Clodius' death; on leaving office he was successfully prosecuted (probably in January 51) by Caelius on a charge of burning the *curia* (afterwards restored by Faustus) and retired, presumably illegally, to Bauli in Campania (Cael. *Fam.* 8.1.4). C. Memmius (*RE* XV.609.61ff., Memmius 8; *MRR* II.153, 194, 203; Sumner 88, 134; cf. 89.13n.) was the first husband of Fausta, Faustus' twin sister (the second being T. Annius Milo, whom she married in 55). He was a strong supporter of Pompey in the 60s, attacking the Luculli when tribune in 66 (or 65); as praetor in 58 he opposed Caesar's *acta* before going out to Bithynia and Pontus as governor in 57, taking with him Catullus and Cinna (like Hortensius and the Torquati, he was a writer of erotic verse: Plin. *Ep.* 5.3.5). He stood for the consulship of 53, with Caesar's support, but on conviction *de ambitu* went into exile at Athens (see Cicero's letter to him, *Fam.* 13.1), possibly not permanently. He was to become most famous for being Lucretius' addressee (on his doubtful Epicureanism see Castner 99–104). For Cicero on Memmius' oratory see *Brut.* 247.

55.5 'at ... Cornelius' this is the reading of the MSS (giving a resolved molossus-cretic clausula). Early editors assumed that the man in charge must be Sulla, and therefore accepted Manutius' deletion of *Cornelius*. However, the man allegedly in charge, Cicero goes on to explain, was under the control of Faustus' freedman, and this naturally rules out Sulla: as Orelli first saw, the name Cornelius must indicate one of Sulla's freedmen. Orelli suggested that some *notae* may have dropped out of the text and accordingly proposed ⟨*Publi libertus*⟩ (i.e. *P.L.*), an implausible expression and unrhythmical. Clark then printed the influential ⟨*libertus eius*⟩ (double-trochee), reduced by Boulanger to the more satisfactory if unrhythmical ⟨*libertus*⟩. But supplements such as these sound unconvincing and laboured within a short, summary interjection put into the mouth of the prosecutor. Since Cicero is recapitulating the

prosecution's argument, it is likely that the jury had already been introduced to the freedman Cornelius and so were aware of his identity;
readers of the published speech, on the other hand, would doubtless
have appreciated that a Cornelius mentioned in connection with over-
seeing Sulla's business would have been one of his freedmen. There is
therefore no reason to alter the text.

55.7 sed tamen... administrata est 'hoc omnino corruptum'
(Orelli); it is also possible that this passage, and the rest of §55, was
hastily composed. Critical attention has centred on *munere servili*, which is
left hanging on its own, 'in a servile task': the position of *se* (2.7n.) reveals an incision (with hiatus) after *servili* which separates *munere servili*
from *obtulit... prospicienda*. The attention devoted to *munere servili* has in
part been prompted by the fact that the words are an impossibility for
those editors who delete *Cornelius* above (making the passage refer to
Sulla). Thus various conjectures have been proposed: *munere Servili*
(Madvig, *Adv. Crit.* 1.127f.), with its refinements *munere Servi* (Clark, referring to Ser. Sulla (!), §6) and *munere Servi ille* (Kasten, 1949); *ut muneri
serviret* (Landgraf); and *muneri inserviens* (Kornitzer). The first point to
emphasise, therefore, is that Cicero is referring (still) to Sulla's freedman
Cornelius, and not to Sulla himself: lit., 'but he did, it is true, in a servile
task, offer his services for looking out weapons, although he was never
in charge...'. Secondly, it is not impossible, I think, that a freedman
should be described as having undertaken a servile task, given that
Cicero's aim is to demonstrate that Sulla's freedman took no initiative
in the matter, but was under orders from Faustus' freedman throughout.
Thus the argument runs, 'it does not matter who was in charge; but in
any case he was not in charge, he was merely doing (freedman though
he was) the job of a slave'. The only valid objection to *munere servili*, then,
is the awkwardness of 'in a servile task' (Halm read *in munere servili*,
which is not an improvement); but it is hard to see how this could be
avoided. Again, therefore, it seems best to accept the reading of the
MSS.

The remaining textual points may be dealt with more briefly. The
proximity of the adversatives *sed tamen* and *vero* has caused disquiet.
Halm considered moving *praefuit vero numquam* after *pertinet*, but this
necessitated altering *eaque* to *ea quidem* or *ea quoque* (cf. Seyffert 52f.).
Clark more simply proposed *is* for *sed*, and to clarify the sense Orelli
advocated *tantum* for *tamen*; however, the construction of the sentence,
even if contorted, seems plausible. *prospicienda* has also aroused suspicion, Lambinus offering *perspicienda* and W. G. Pluygers *inspicienda*
(*Mnemosyne* 9 (1881) 137; cf. Suet. *Tit.* 9.2 *gladiatorum spectaculo... ferramenta
pugnantium inspicienda porrexit*). But *prospicienda*, 'to look out for (with a

view to acquiring)' (cf. *OLD* s.v. 4b; K.-S.1.337; Lebreton 179), is exactly right in this context, since in both *ferramenta* (usually = 'tools') and *prospicienda* Cicero is using euphemistic vocabulary to soften the fact that Sulla's freedman did assemble arms (it is this phrasing which shows that *sed tamen...prospicienda* should not be put in quotation marks and given to the prosecution); cf. Cethegus' use of the innocent-sounding *ferramentorum* at *Cat.* 3.10. The final texual point concerns the name of Faustus' freedman (*balbum E: bellum Tω*). For reasons which I give at *CQ* n.s. 39 (1989) 405, I prefer to call him Balbus, following *E*.

(v) Sulla's connection with P. Sittius (§§ 56–59)

P. Sittius, it is claimed, was sent by Sulla to cause disturbances in Further Spain. But Sittius left for Spain in 64, and he had had long-standing business interests in those parts. He did have debts at Rome, but these were paid off through Sulla's agency by the sale of Sittius' property. It is highly improbable, moreover, that Sittius had any connection with the conspiracy, given the circumstances and in view of Sittius' own character. Cicero repeats that Sittius paid his debts by selling his inheritance: by contrast, it was the debtors who clung to their possessions who gave Cicero cause to fear, not men such as Sittius.

Cicero's purpose in this passage is to free Sulla from any suspicion which might arise from his connection with P. Sittius. Sulla was undeniably a friend of his, and so Cicero's method is not to deny the link between the two men but instead to argue Sittius' own innocence. Sittius, as it happened, was also on close terms with Cicero himself, and the defence which follows is therefore intended as much for Sittius' benefit as for Sulla's: *non enim mihi deserenda est causa amici veteris atque hospitis* (§ 58). Sittius' debts and his departure for Spain, which recalled that of Piso and ultimately evoked memories of Sertorius, allowed the prosecution to allege his involvement in the conspiracy, and thus to argue Sulla's complicity. But in spite of the reference to Sittius in Sallust (*Cat.* 21.3), a connection between Sittius and Catiline nevertheless seems highly implausible, and Cicero has no difficulty in refuting it: Sittius left for Spain in 64, before the conspiracy had been planned.

Cicero was afterwards in a letter to Sittius to refer to the service he performed here in speaking out in Sittius' defence: *cum in tui familiarissimi iudicio ac periculo tuum crimen coniungeretur, ut potui accuratissime te tuamque causam tutatus sum* (*Fam.* 5.17.2). For a modern opinion on the passage the judgement of J. Heurgon is worth quoting: 'il n'existe pas, à notre connaissance, d'autre discours de Cicéron où un ami de l'accusé, non accusé lui-même, et dont seule la réputation était en jeu, lui ait inspiré une digression si éloquente' (*Latomus* 9 (1950) 372).

XX 56.1   At enim Sittius ... perturbaret this sentence, expressing the prosecution's position, is virtually ascribed *oratio recta* (3.11n.); cf. Wiesthaler 40f. P. Sittius (*RE* III A.409.45ff., Sittius 3; for a portrait see J. M. C. Toynbee, *Roman Historical Portraits* (London 1978) 68), in Stockton's phrase 'a colourful and shady adventurer' (156), was an *eques* from Nuceria in Campania (Sal. *Cat.* 21.3) and a friend of Cicero (*Fam.* 5.17 is addressed to Sittius; cf. J. Heurgon, *Latomus* 9 (1950) 369–77) as well as of Sulla; Cicero had already given him his support on a previous occasion (*Fam.* 5.17.2). We learn here that Sittius left on business for Further Spain and Mauretania in 64, leaving behind him large debts which were then paid off by the sale of some of his estates, through Sulla's agency. Sittius' purpose was to call in loans which he had made some time earlier to the Spanish provincials and to the king of Mauretania (§58). Sittius is next heard of in 57 when he was condemned, unjustly, according to Cicero, on an unknown charge connected in some way with the grain shortage (*Fam.* 5.17.2). Leaving his son behind (*Fam.* 5.17.4), he went into exile to become a military adventurer in Africa, supporting one king against another with his army of Italian and Spanish troops known as *Sittiani* (App. *BC* 4.54; Dio 43.3.1–2). The date at which these exploits began is disputed, Shackleton Bailey (on *Fam.* 5.17) apparently favouring 64 and Syme (*Sallust* 101) the 40s, but Appian and Dio state that the military operations began at the time when Sittius went into exile, i.e., presumably, 57; moreover, one may infer from *Fam.* 5.17.4, on Sittius' separation from his son, that both were previously together in Italy. So Sittius made several business trips, one of which began in 64, prior to the trial in 57; when condemned, he naturally chose the area of his business interests as his place of exile, and there built up a military following. These operations continued until 46, when Sittius was able to serve Caesar by joining Bocchus II of Mauretania in opposing Juba and defeating the surviving Pompeians after Thapsus; these included Faustus (54.2n.), who was captured alive but killed by the troops (his wife Pompeia and their children being spared by Caesar), and, as it happened, Torquatus, killed at Hippo Regius (cf. p. 20). Sittius was rewarded with the territory around Cirta which had belonged to Massinissa; he settled the region with his followers, but was killed by Arabio, son of Massinissa and ally of Juba, shortly after Caesar's murder in 44 (cf. *B. Afr.* 25, 36, 95–6; App. *BC* 4.54; Dio 43.3.1–4, 43.12.2; Cicero on Sittius' death, *Att.* 15.17.1 *Arabioni de Sittio nihil irascor*). A link between Sittius and Catiline is given by Sallust at *Cat.* 21.3, where

Catiline, attempting to encourage his followers (therefore not necessarily telling the truth; cf. *Cat.* 40.6), claims that Sittius is in Mauretania with an army and is party to the conspiracy. But as Syme rightly argues (*Sallust* 100f., 133), Sallust must be in error since Sittius did not have an army in 64: the reference has clearly been conditioned by Sittius' later career.

56.2 primum Sittius, iudices this first objection is decisive in Sittius' favour; all the later points are subsidiary.

56.3 L. Iulio C. Figulo consulibus i.e. 64 BC (*MRR* II.161). For L. Julius Caesar see 55.3n. His colleague C. Marcius Figulus (*RE* XIV.1559.57ff., Marcius 63; *MRR* II.143; III.138) supported Cicero in 63 (*Phil.* 2.12) and spoke in the debate on 5 December (*Att.* 12.21.1); he is last heard of as having had an expensive tomb (*Leg.* 2.62). He is almost certainly (*pace* E. W. Gray, *Antichthon* 13 (1979) 56–63) to be identified with the Thermus (i.e. *RE* XV.1965.49ff., Minucius 60) mentioned at *Att.* 1.1.2 as a candidate for the consulship of 64 (he would have become 'C. Marcius Figulus Thermus' on adoption, or simply 'Thermus' (as at *Att.* 1.1.2) in ordinary usage): see D. R. Shackleton Bailey on *Att.* 1.1.2; id., *Nomenclature* 78; id., *Onomasticon* 66.

56.4 huius 'the recent' (14.2n.).

56.8 ratione ... contracta for *rationem contrahere* ('to enter into a business arrangement') cf. *Clu.* 41 *cum illo nemo iam rationem ... contrahebat*; *Off.* 1.15, 1.53, 2.64, 3.61. Sittius had gone to call in loans which he had made on his earlier visit (§58).

56.9 illo profecto deponent participles in absolute construction are rare in Cicero, and always used intransitively; cf. Laughton 110f. (with 136, on the structure); K.-S.1.783f.

procurante ... et gerente 'under the Republic procurator was a term of private law, meaning the personal agent or bailiff of an individual ... and it always remained so except when applied to the emperor's procurators', A. H. M. Jones, *Studies in Roman Government and Law* (Oxford 1960) 117. See also A. N. Sherwin-White, *PBSR* 15 (1939) 11–26. *et gerente* is postponed for the sake of the rhythm.

56.10 praediis these had been inherited (§§58–9).

56.11 ⟨est⟩ dissolutum 'was paid off' (*TLL* V.1.1500.72ff.); cf. *Off.* 2.84 (referring to 63 BC) *numquam nec maius aes alienum fuit nec melius nec facilius dissolutum est; fraudandi enim spe sublata vendendi necessitas consecuta est.* Halm notes that *est* is more likely to have dropped out after *eiusdem* than after *dissolutum*.

quae causa ... possessionis as Cicero recognised (*Cat.* 2.4, 2.8, 2.18–21; *Fam.* 5.6.2), debt was a major cause of the conspiracy (cf. Sal. *Cat.* 14.2, 16.4, 20.13, 21.2, 24.3, 33.1–2); a bill for the cancellation of debts had been unsuccessfully promulgated at the start of his year of office (*Off.* 2.84; Dio 37.25.4). Of the six categories of conspirators defined at *Cat.* 2.18–23, the first four consist of debtors. *cupiditas retinendae possessionis* characterises the first category, men who could have paid off their debts by selling their estates, but were not prepared to do so: *qui magno in aere alieno maiores etiam possessiones habent quarum amore adducti dissolvi nullo modo possunt* (*Cat.* 2.18; cf. *Sul.* 59). Sittius is not to be classed with these men, Cicero argues, because he sold a large part of his property to pay off his debts; Catiline, likewise, insisted that he was capable of paying off his debts from his own resources (Sal. *Cat.* 35.3; he had done well out of the proscriptions (70.7n.)). On debt see M. W. Frederiksen, *JRS* 56 (1966) 128–41.

56.13 praediis deminutis *deminuere* may denote diminution in size or number; presumably diminution in number is meant here. W. G. Pluygers (*Mnemosyne* 9 (1881) 138) and Karsten (31), noticing the inconsistency with *omnis suas possessiones* (§58), proposed deletion of these two words. But at §58 Cicero exaggerates; and, as Zielinski pointed out (204), *praediis deminutis* gives an impeccable cretic-double-trochee rhythm, which deletion would spoil.

57.1 iam vero illud having stated the facts, Cicero now goes on to give a series of *argumenta a re* based on probabilities; cf. Lausberg 206–8. To deny that one's opponent's argument is credible is a means of refutation cited at *Inv.* 1.79–80 (cf. Rohde 124f.).

57.3 hanc urbem inflammare cf. §3 *consilium inflammandae huius urbis.*

57.4 amandare for the corruption *mandare* (ω) cf. *Quint.* 49; *S. Rosc.* 44.

57.6 haec at Rome. The conspiracy at Rome did not require any such contact with Spain; it is only at *Cat.* 4.6 that Cicero visualises the conspiracy as having spread into the provinces.

57.7 an in tantis rebus answering *utrum* ... For the ironic *an* see 21.5n.

57.9 coniunctissimum ... consuetudine this is the extended third unit of the tricolon which begins at *amantissimum sui* (4.13n.). *T* reads *consuetudine usu* for *usu consuetudine* (ω); I have opted for the latter because *usus* and *consuetudo* are paired in that order at *S. Rosc.* 15 and *Phil.* 7.6. On *officium* see 2.5n.

57.10 veri simile ... dimitteret as Halm points out, when the sense is negative (i.e. 'it is not likely'), *veri simile* is regularly followed by *ut* with the subjunctive instead of the accusative and infinitive (found e.g. at §37); cf. *S. Rosc.* 121; *Ver.* 4.11 *veri simile non est ut ... religioni suae ... pecuniam anteponeret*; *Sest.* 78 (see K.-S.II.242–4). Lambinus' deletion of *veri simile non est* is therefore unwarranted. The construction had its origin in repudiating questions; hence the imperfect *dimitteret*, the natural tense in the repudiating question from which the *ut* clause has developed (see Handford 38, 75). This imperfect, then, is not to be explained in terms of the potential (Halm; K.-S.II.185) or of incompleted action (Reid) or of attraction (Lebreton 249f.). The MSS disagree at *secum semper habuisset*: here the error in *a* may be ignored (*secum* was missed before *semper* and added after *habuisset*) and the *esse videatur* rhythm of *secum semper habuisset* (*Pq*) preferred to the hexametrical *semper secum habuisset* (*TK*).

58.1 ipse autem Sittius Cicero now turns from *argumenta a re* to *argumenta a persona* (45.1n.).

58.2 amici...hospitis Cicero stresses that he is a man who fulfils his obligations, to Sittius as to Sulla. For his friendship with Sittius see *Fam.* 5.17; and on *amicitia*, 48.4n.

58.4 populo Romano cf. *Cat.* 2.11 and 3.22 *bellum populo Romano facere.* δ gives *rei publicae*: *p.r.* and *r.p.* are very often interchanged in MSS. Abbreviation has also caused β to jump from *rei publicae* (in its exemplar) here to *in rem publicam* below, thus omitting *populo Romano...exstiterit.* For ὁμοιότης as a cause of dittography and omission see 34.7n.

cuius pater an argument from Sittius' *cognatio*, family (*Inv.* 1.35); cf. Rohde 49. Cicero must be referring to the Social War: Sittius' father (*RE* III A.409.31ff., Sittius 2), also named P. Sittius (*Fam.* 5.17, heading), remained loyal to Rome when *finitimi ac vicini* went over to the Italians (*deficerent*). It is not immediately clear whether Sittius remained loyal together with his fellow Nucerians (Halm) or in contrast to them (Reid). Appian (*BC* 1.42) tells of the Italian general C. Papius burning the country around Nuceria and winning over the nearby towns, while Florus (2.6.11) reports the devastation of Nuceria by the allies. Presumably, therefore, Nuceria, unlike its neighbours (notably Pompeii and Stabiae: 60.1n.), did not go over to the Italians: Cicero gives Sittius the credit for this.

58.5 singulari given emphasis by the hyperbaton (8.1n.).

58.7 putaret as at *dimitteret* above, the tense is determined by the repudiating question which underlies the construction. Huldrich's *putarit* is therefore unnecessary.

58.8 libidine i.e. living according to one's own pleasure.

58.9 ut...deberentur *in provinciis et in regnis* seems to be an exaggeration since we have only been told of one *provincia* (Further Spain) and one *regnum* (Mauretania). After *regnis* there is an incision marked by a cretic-spondee rhythm, after which the MSS disagree, offering a choice between *ei maximae pecuniae* (*T*) and *maximae ei pecuniae* (ω). I prefer the latter because it puts *maximae*, not *ei*, in the position of emphasis (2.7n.); the placing of *maximae* next to its noun in *T* would be an obvious normalisation.

58.11 commisit 'allow' (*TLL* III.1912.45ff.).

procuratores see 56.9n.

58.12 omnis suas possessiones a further exaggeration, since we were told at §56 that only some of Sittius' estates were sold (*plurimis . . . praediis venditis*; later, *praediis deminutis*). The reason for the exaggeration is the antithesis *omnis . . . ullam.*

58.13 patrimonio selling off one's *patrimonium* would normally incur strong disapproval (*Clu.* 141; *de Orat.* 2.224); cf. §41 *patrimoni naufragus.* C. Antonius Hybrida had been expelled from the senate in 70 *quod propter aeris alieni magnitudinem praedia manciparit bonaque sua in potestate non habeat* (Asc. 84 C). Here Cicero presents Sittius' sale of his inheritance in a favourable light: debt was the greater disgrace.

58.14 moram for *mora* as a term used in connection with the repayment of debts see *TLL* VIII.1468.14ff.

59.1 a quo . . . timui for *timere ab aliquo* see K.-S.1.339, 493. Cicero again emphasises his personal acquaintance with the events of his consulship (14.5n.).

59.3 tempestate cf. §40 *in illa turbulentissima tempestate rei publicae.*

hominum genus . . . pertimescendum the Catilinarians are contrasted with Sittius. This passage resembles *Cat.* 2.18 (quoted at 56.11n.), the first category of conspirators. Ross (72f.) notes the contradiction between *pertimescendum* and Cicero's view at *Cat.* 2.18, *sed hosce homines minime puto pertimescendos.* ω has *genus hominum*: this order, in which the nominative is placed first, is perhaps the more likely to be corrupt.

59.5 divelli ac distrahi cf. *Planc.* 102 *qui a me mei servatorem capitis divellat ac distrahat*; *Fin.* 1.50. ω places *citius* after *divelli*, but *divelli* and *distrahi* are best kept closely together (as in the passages cited).

59.6 cognationem 'blood-relationship'. Estates, even if inherited, are not linked to their owners in the same way as limbs, or blood-relations. Sylvius compares *Balb.* 56, where Cicero again has to play down the importance of properties staying within the family. Cicero is wisely being quite brief on the subject of Sittius' sale of his estates.

(vi) Sulla's part in the dissension at Pompeii (§§ 60–62)

The accusation that Sulla drove the Pompeians to join the conspiracy is refuted a fortiori by the fact that they took no part in it. The charge is restated: Sulla, it is claimed, fostered dissension at Pompeii between the original inhabitants and the

Sullan colonists, in order to win control of the town with the help of the former.
However, the quarrel, which was long-standing, was reported to Sulla and the other
patroni *only at a late stage, and has now been settled by the unanimous agreement*
of the patroni *and to the complete satisfaction of the colonists. Witness the depu-*
tations from the colonists and the native Pompeians: both parties are here to express
their equal support for Sulla. Observe also the conspicuous gratitude in which Sulla
is held for having restored harmony at Pompeii.

Cicero's answer to this charge is perhaps his least persuasive. The prosecution alleged that Sulla fostered dissension at Pompeii in order to win
the support of the indigenous population for his own schemes and, further, that these schemes were connected with the conspiracy. The latter
point is brushed aside with two rhetorical questions in which Cicero
points out that Pompeii did not go over to Catiline. After this, Cicero
confines himself to the troubles. He shows that these were long-standing, which at least indicates that they were not initiated with Catiline in
mind, or, in all probability, by Sulla. Granted this, however, Cicero
does nothing to refute the possibility that Sulla attempted to turn the
situation to his own advantage, perhaps with a view to aiding Catiline
should the need arise. Instead, his method is to play down the dissension
and, by pointing to the support of the native Pompeians and the perhaps more questionable support of the colonists, to underline Sulla's
achievement in restoring harmony at Pompeii. We are invited to infer
that if Sulla has reconciled the two parties, he cannot have set them at
odds. The inference is not valid, but Cicero can provide no stronger
arguments with which to support his conclusion.

In fairness to Cicero, the weakness of this passage may be due to the
possibility that the prosecution had failed to substantiate their case,
giving him only unsupported insinuations against which to argue.
Moreover, as we shall see below, Sulla appears to have done a great deal
of good in righting the wrongs at Pompeii. Thus Cicero's argument that
Sulla not only did not foster the dissension but actually resolved it is one
which, when combined with the *laudationes* from both of the parties involved, would at the time have carried considerable weight.

XXI 60.1 Pompeianos Pompeii, a prosperous town on the Bay of
Naples at the mouth of the Sarnus, took the side of the allies in the
Social War (App. *BC* 1.39) and was besieged in 89 by L. Sulla (Vell.
2.16.2; App. *BC* 1.50; Oros. 5.18.22; cf. *CIL* IV.5385). As a punishment for
its resistance a colony of veterans was settled there in c.80, possibly,
R. C. Carrington suggests (*JRS* 21 (1931) 114f., although the argument

is weak), in the former territory of Stabiae, destroyed by Sulla in 89 (Plin. *Nat.* 3.70); the colony was known officially as *colonia Cornelia Veneria Pompeianorum* (*CIL* x.787; = *ILS* 5915). P. Sulla, in spite of his youth, became a founder (§ 62) and *patronus* (§ 61) of the new *colonia*; his title, one assumes, was *triumvir coloniis deducendis*, and the *triumviri*, according to normal practice, would have become the first (hereditary) *patroni* (cf. *CIL* I².594 (= *ILS* 6087) xcvii (*lex col. Gen.*); *MRR* II.82; Mommsen, *Staatsrecht* II.737 n. 4; E. Badian, *Foreign Clientelae* (Oxford 1958) 162; H.-J. Gehrke, *Hermes* III (1983) 475; L. E. Reams, *CJ* 82 (1986–7) 303). As at other Sullan colonies (e.g. Praeneste, Faesulae), relations between the newcomers and the indigenous population seem to have been strained. Tension between the two groups, whom Cicero refers to as *Pompeiani* and *coloni* (implying that the original inhabitants were not classed as *coloni*), persisted for many years and centred around the rights and privileges enjoyed by the colonists (61.8n.). The *patroni* were eventually appealed to as arbiters (cf. Mommsen, *Staatsrecht* III.1203 n. 1), presumably by the aggrieved party, the indigenous Pompeians, and a settlement was reached; it appears that the issue was decided in the Pompeians' favour (60.11n.). But in spite of their differences, Cicero adds, the two factions were unanimous in their support for Sulla; it may be significant, however, that they sent separate deputations (as it appears) to his trial. The literature on Pompeii is large, but see esp. *RE* xxi.1999.26ff.; Mau; M. L. Gordon, *JRS* 17 (1927) 165–83; Carrington; G. O. Onorato, *RAAN* 26 (1951) 115–56; Maiuri; Grant; C. Gatti, *CSDIR* 6 (1974–5) 165–78; Castrén; V. Weber, *Klio* 57 (1975) 179–206; Eschebach; J. Andreau, *REA* 82 (1980) 183–99; H.-J. Gehrke, *op. cit.* 471–90; Frederiksen; Zanker; Jongman; Richardson, *Pompeii.* On the Sullan colonies see E. T. Salmon in Martyn, 76f.; E. Gabba, *Republican Rome, the Army and the Allies* (Oxford 1976) 44–7; P. A. Brunt, *Italian Manpower, 225 BC–AD 14*² (Oxford 1987) 300–12. Cicero had previously had first-hand acquaintance with the problems caused by Sulla's colonising schemes when he defended the citizen rights of a woman from Arretium in 79 or 78 (*Caec.* 97; cf. Crawford 33f.; *TLRR* no. 132).

60.5 'diiunxit' inquit the accusation is perhaps put into ascribed *oratio recta* because Cicero has to hand three apparently strong (although in reality inconclusive) arguments with which to answer it (3.11n.).

60.6 discidio ac dissensione cf. *Att.* 1.17.7 *ut, quod una non estis, non dissensione ac discidio vestro sed voluntate ac iudicio tuo factum esse videatur.* Karsten (31f.) thought *ac* an interpolation.

60.8 primum Cicero has dismissed the idea of a connection between the events at Pompeii and the conspiracy. In what follows he does not have the conspiracy in mind: he argues simply that Sulla was in no way responsible for the dissension. His first point is that Sulla became (officially) involved only at a late stage.

60.9   patronos among them Sulla (§ 61). On patronage of colonies see *TLL* iii.1702.11ff. (for epigraphic evidence); A. v. Premerstein, *Vom Werden und Wesen des Prinzipats* (*ABAW* n.f. Heft 15 (1937)); L. Harmand, *Le Patronat sur les collectivités publiques* (Paris 1957); E. Badian, *Foreign Clientelae* (Oxford 1958) 160–67; Gelzer 86–101; J. Nicols, *Hermes* 108 (1980) 365–85.

60.10   esset agitata ω must have had *esset exagitata* (β), which replaces an *esse videatur* clausula with a hexameter ending.

cognita est i.e. a formal enquiry was undertaken (*TLL* iii.1506.44ff.).

60.11   dissenserit the perfect puts greater emphasis than the imperfect on the event's actually happening (here, not happening); cf. Riemann 372; K.-S.ii.188. The prosecution clearly did not incriminate Sulla's fellow *patroni*.

postremo ... defensos Cicero feels it necessary to refute the suggestion that Sulla had been partial towards the *Pompeiani*; evidently, then, the dispute was settled in their favour. This inference is supported by the reappearance of Sabellians in the *ordo* of Pompeii by 55 (Castrén 55, 122); see 61.8n. J. Andreau notes that the rapidity with which certain families re-emerge once the *dissensio de suffragiis* has been resolved would suggest that not all of the property of the indigenous Pompeians had been confiscated (*REA* 82 (1980) 194).

61.1   hac the two factions had each sent a deputation to give a *laudatio* (49.4n.) at the trial.

61.3   qui adsunt laborant cf. § 4 *omnes qui adsunt, qui laborant, qui salvum volunt ... defendunt*. For the *asyndeton bimembre* (21.5n.) cf. e.g. *Div. Caec.* 11 *adsunt queruntur Siculi universi*.

patronum ... custodem *defensor* occurs under the empire as a term applied to patrons of colonies; cf. O. Hirschfeld, *Die kaiserlichen Verwaltungsbeamten bis auf Diocletian*[3] (Berlin 1963) 132. For the association of *custos* with *patronus* see W. Neuhauser, *Patronus und Orator* (Innsbruck 1958) 42.

61.4   si ... non potuerunt a pathetic reminder of Sulla's election to the consulship and subsequent conviction in 66 (cf. § 1). On *fortuna* see 73.4n. **incolumem** signifies 'undamaged in position', i.e. not having suffered a *calamitas* (cf. *Arch.* 9, quoted at 1.2n.); like *calamitas*, *incolumis* is probably agricultural in origin.

61.6   iuvari conservarique cf. *Tusc.* 1.32 *quae est melior igitur in hominum genere natura quam eorum, qui se natos ad homines iuvandos tutandos conservandos arbitrantur?*; *Off.* 3.25.

61.7   ab illis i.e. the prosecutors, who have indirectly accused the

Pompeians of conspiracy. The MSS are divided between *ab his* (*T*) and *ab illis* (ω); editors (except Zicàri), however, adopt instead R. Klotz's *ab istis*, on the grounds that a pejorative tone is required to make it clear that Cicero is not referring to the *coloni* (cf. Ernout-Thomas 188). This is mistaken because, as is noted at *TLL* VII.1.344.23f., Cicero declines elsewhere in the speech to refer to his friend Torquatus as *iste* (although he has no compunction in calling Cornelius *istum puerum* at §51). *ab illis* should therefore be read; *ille* is regularly used of adversaries by orators (cf. *TLL* VII.1.344.18ff.), and so any ambiguity is minimal.

61.8 de ambulatione ac de suffragiis suis Cicero alludes to the grievances of the native Pompeians which lay at the root of the dissension between the two factions. The meaning of *de ambulatione* is fairly certain, but its significance is less clear. The word *ambulatio* may denote '(the act of) walking' or, by extension, 'a place where walking is done'. Commentators interpret the word here in the latter sense as an open or a covered walk (thus 'promenade' or 'portico'), citing *Dom.* 116, 121; Catul. 55.6 *in Magni simul ambulatione*; Ulp. *dig.* 8.5.8 *porticus ambulatoriae* (see *TLL* 1.1869.77ff.). Three alternative explanations of the meaning of the word have been proposed in order to escape the apparent oddity of a dispute about a 'promenade' or 'portico', but none of these may be accepted. R. Garrucci (*Questioni Pompeiane* (Naples 1853) 31–3) thought *ambulatio* a synonym for *ambitio* (β indeed reads *ambitione*), but, as has often been pointed out, *ambulatio* is not elsewhere used in this sense. Castrén supposes that 'somewhat limited rights of movement inside the town walls were imposed on the local inhabitants by the colonists' (55; cf. 92); however, *de ambulatione* on its own will not support the meaning 'about the right of movement'. Thirdly, F. Coarelli suggested privately to Castrén (55 n. 1) that the *pontes* used for voting by each tribe may have been alternatively known as *ambulationes*; this interpretation is ruled out by the fact that Cicero here uses the word in the singular (cf. T. P. Wiseman, *LCM* 2 (1977) 21).

So it seems that *ambulatione* has to be taken as 'a promenade' or 'a portico'. What, then, was the nature of the dispute 'about a promenade / portico'? C. Gatti (*CSDIR* 6 (1974–5) 175f.) argues that a solution must be found which relates closely to the Pompeians' second grievance, *de suffragiis suis*; cf. E. Gabba, *Athenaeum* 37 (1959) 318 n. 21. This may make for a more elegant expression, but it nevertheless seems a questionable requirement. Cicero is trying hard to play down the troubles at Pompeii, and it does not seem likely that he would in effect state the main cause of grievance twice over (if *de ambulatione* were also concerned with voting at elections, Cicero would surely have contented himself simply with *de suffragiis suis* on its own); furthermore, the repeated *de* probably suggests a different, not related, reason. This, incidentally, is a point which reduces the attractiveness of β's conjecture (or miscopying; *Ta* have a similar error at §6) *de ambitione*. Gatti, observing that the *porticus Minucia frumentaria* at Rome may have been used as a place of assembly for the tribes when voting in the *comitia tributa* (cf. Taylor, *RVA* 69), argues that there may also have been a portico at Pompeii where the colonists assembled for voting in elections: this explanation would tie in with the mention of *suffragia*. It is not certain, however, that the *porticus Minucia* was used for the purpose stated, and, even if it was, the fact that the tribes at Rome met in a portico at election time does not necessarily mean that those at Pompeii did so too. Gatti, then, is right to base her argument on an interpretation of *ambulatio* as 'portico'; but the solution she advocates has nothing to recommend it.

A more satisfactory hypothesis is offered by T. P. Wiseman (*op. cit.* 21f.), who also provides a plausible identification of the portico in question. Vitruvius (5.9.1) states that *porticus et ambulationes* were regularly built adjoining theatres: they proved useful as a store for stage machinery and as a place of refuge for the audience when it rained. At Pompeii there was (and is) a large *quadriporticus* sited immediately behind the original theatre (of c.200 BC) and the smaller adjoining *theatrum tectum* (or *odeum*) on the south side of the town (for a plan see *CIL* IV Suppl.2 (1909), at end; Mau, plan III; Carrington 42; Eschebach 295; Zanker 11; or Richardson, *Pompeii* 406). Wiseman cites two inscriptions (*CIL* x.844, 852; = *ILS* 5636, 5627) which reveal that the *theatrum tectum* as well as a substantial part of the amphitheatre was built by two Sullan *duoviri quinquennales* named C. Quinctius Valgus (the father-in-law of Rullus (*Agr.* 3.3): see *RE* xxiv.1103f.; R. G. M. Nisbet and M. Hubbard on Hor. *Carm.* 2, pp. 167f.) and M. Porcius. These men, in the case of the amphitheatre, seem to have intended their benefaction strictly for the use of the colonists alone: *et coloneis locum in perpetuom deder*[*unt*], *CIL* x.852 (= *ILS* 5627). (One need not suppose that the Pompeians were kept out of the amphitheatre altogether: it is more likely that only a certain area, that paid for by Valgus and Porcius, was reserved for the colonists.) The *quadriporticus* seems to have been built rather earlier than the *theatrum tectum* (Richardson, *Pompeii* 85), and so is not likely to have been given by Valgus and Porcius; nevertheless this was probably a new building in the early days of the Sullan colony, and it is quite possible that its use was restricted to the new colonists in much the same way as the amphitheatre was. Wiseman therefore suggests that this was the cause of the *dissensio de ambulatione* and concludes, 'the dispute was not about "public walks" in general, but over the use of one particular *ambulatio*, a new and conspicuously attractive amenity of the town..., to which the indigenous *Pompeiani* were evidently denied access'. Perhaps the *quadriporticus* had been put up shortly before the foundation of the colony and was then appropriated by the arriving colonists; this would explain the strength of feeling among the indigenous Pompeians.

Wiseman's explanation of the *dissensio de ambulatione* cannot be said to be irrefutable and a political solution should not be ruled out altogether; the argument for discrimination would be weakened, for instance, if (as seems to me unlikely: see 60.1n.) Valgus and Porcius meant by *coloneis* the entire population of Pompeii (the view of H.-J. Gehrke, *Hermes* III (1983) 489). But at the very least this interpretation seems to lack the drawbacks inherent in the other hypotheses; the obscurity of the reference would not be an objection since the matter had presumably been brought up earlier in the trial (cf. the case of Sulla's freedman: 55.5n.). For further details of the *quadriporticus* (later converted into gladiators' barracks) see Mau 157–64; Eschebach 296; Richardson, *Pompeii* 83–7. Illustrations may be found at Mau, pl. IV; Maiuri 55; Grant 75; Eschebach, pls. 61, 79 and 81.

The *dissensio de suffragiis suis* is fortunately less problematic: the suffrage of the *Pompeiani* had evidently been in some way restricted (Gabba, *op. cit.* 318). Sabellian names virtually disappear among the magistrates for the first two or three decades of the colony (60.11n.) and so it is possible that the native Pompeians had been debarred from voting or standing for office, at least for the more important magistracies (Gatti, *op. cit.* 174f.). A less drastic possibility is suggested by Gehrke (*op. cit.* 486f.): if the voters were divided into *curiae*, as at Rome, the newcomers may simply have had a majority over the native Pompeians (in which case the settlement made by the *patroni* might have consisted of a ruling that a man's *curia* should thenceforth be decided by place of occupation). The fact that the electoral propaganda dating from this period is directed exclusively towards the colonists (Castrén 54, 86f., 92, 122) would only be significant if, as one would infer from Cicero, the native Pompeians were not judged to be *coloni* (60.1n.). But in any case the Pompeians' grievances seem to have been considerable. If not actually disenfranchised, they were at least disadvantaged electorally and deprived of their share in municipal administration. Moreover, their access to certain public amenities, notably the amphitheatre and the *quadriporticus*, may well have been restricted. As a result the Pompeians may have felt that they had been relegated to the status of second-class citizens. If Sulla was indeed responsible for righting these wrongs, as Cicero claims below, the *Pompeiani* would have had good reason for supporting him with enthusiasm at his trial.

61.9 ut idem ... sentirent Reid (App. A) takes *idem* as nominative plural (cf. 34.5n.), and so proposes the less rhythmical *consentirent*; but *idem* would more naturally be understood as accusative singular.

62.3 cum commoda...diiunxerit a delicate euphemism, elegantly put (cf. *Pis.* 35). For the play on the different senses of *fortuna* cf. *Fortunam ipsam anteibo fortunis meis*, Trab. *com.* 5 (ap. *Tusc.* 4.67); *Rhet. Her.* 4.24. This is a favourite Ciceronian technique (Holst 56–8).

62.5 est *est* is omitted in *T*; Kasten (vii n. 4), thinking the word omitted in the archetype and wrongly placed in ω, proposed *carus est utrisque*, noting the improved rhythm (in fact cretic-iambus, not as stated) before *atque iucundus*. There is no reason, however, to take an incision at this point.

alteros demovisse the Pompeians. Although Sulla founded the colony and although this led to dissension (the colony and the dissension were both to the Pompeians' disadvantage), nevertheless Sulla was not thought to have dispossessed the Pompeians (because he went on to decide in their favour); cf. J. Andreau, *REA* 82 (1980) 184.

62.6 utrosque constituisse i.e. the colonists by his foundation of the colony, and the Pompeians by his settlement of their grievances.

(vii) Sulla and the *rogatio Caecilia* (§§ 62–66)

The prosecution have accused Sulla of attempting to force Caecilius' bill, and have also made an unwarranted attack on Caecilius himself. Cicero explains that in proposing his bill Caecilius did not seek to overturn judicial decisions – that would indeed have been reprehensible – but simply to rectify a defect in the law, and so mitigate his brother's punishment. If Caecilius went too far, it was brotherly love that motivated him; but in fact he did not, for the bill was very soon withdrawn on Sulla's request. The remainder of Caecilius' tribunate was exemplary. When the bill was proposed, no one feared violence from Sulla or Caecilius, only from Autronius; the failure of the bill compelled Sulla to linger on in adversity.

This charge is concerned with *vis*, but has no connection with the Catilinarian conspiracy. Sulla is alleged to have used *vis* in an unsuccessful attempt to force the passage of the *rogatio Caecilia* (December 64), which proposed retrospective amendments to the *lex Calpurnia de ambitu* (67), under which Sulla had been convicted. The bill, if successful, would have mitigated the penalties paid by Sulla and Autronius as a result of their convictions in 66, allowing their immediate return to the senate. Cicero, while not denying that violence was used, predictably attributes it exclusively to Autronius. He might have reinforced his contention by reiterating that Sulla was at Naples during this period (cf. §§ 17, 53); that he does not do so strongly suggests that Sulla had come to Rome to support Caecilius' bill in person.

257

The greater part of Cicero's reply, however, is concerned not with the alleged *vis* but with the intentions and implications of Caecilius' proposal, a question strictly speaking irrelevant to the matter in hand. No doubt Cicero was concerned partly to defend Caecilius' reputation (cf. the passage on Sittius, §§ 56–9). But the real point at issue is whether Sulla is a man who shows a proper respect for juries. The prosecution seem to have interpreted Caecilius' bill as an attack on the principle of the irreversibility of *res iudicatae* (§ 63), and they doubtless argued that Sulla held all juries in contempt and considered himself to be above the law. Cicero's primary aim in this section, therefore, is to counter such a picture by arguing that Caecilius considered the law, and not the jury, to be at fault, and that Sulla had not intended to question the wisdom of the jury which had convicted him in 66. In comparison, the actual charge of *vis* at the time of the promulgation of the bill is treated as of little importance, and is simply brushed aside.

XXII 62.7 At enim this sentence, expressing the prosecution's position, is virtually ascribed *oratio recta* (3.11n.).

et gladiatores . . . vis this looks back to §§ 54–5, not to the charge just answered.

rogationis Caeciliae causa L. Caecilius Rufus (*RE* iii.1232.3ff., Caecilius 110; *MRR* ii.167, 200, 210) was a half-brother (*frater*) of Sulla through their mother. Immediately upon entering his tribunate on 10 December 64, he proposed a *rogatio* to replace the penalties of the *lex Calpurnia* (67), under which Sulla and Autronius had been convicted, with those set by the *lex Cornelia* (81?), the earlier *ambitus* law which the *lex Calpurnia* had superseded (17.8n.). The bill was to apply retrospectively, and the penalties paid by Sulla and Autronius would therefore have been mitigated to a simple ten-year suspension of the right to stand for public office; they would presumably have been allowed to return to the senate immediately (63.8n.). However, flagrant bribery in the elections of 64 (cf. Asc. 83 C) had recently led the senate to attempt to replace the *lex Calpurnia* with a still harsher law (an objective which was shortly to find fulfilment in the *lex Tullia*): the reaction to Caecilius' proposal was therefore unfavourable, and after violence had been resorted to without success (§ 66) the bill was withdrawn on Sulla's request at the opening of business on 1 January 63. See Dio 37.25.3; Greenidge 521; Gruen 219f. Later in his tribunate Caecilius helped Cicero by offering to veto Rullus' agrarian bill (§ 65). As *praetor urbanus* in 57 he initiated measures for Cicero's recall and offered him financial support (*Red. Sen.* 22); his house was attacked by Clodius during the food shortage of that year (*Mil.* 38; Asc. 48 C). Caecilius went on to be proconsul, probably of Sicily, in 56, and in 54 he joined Sulla in his prosecution of Gabinius (*Q. fr.* 3.3.2; cf. 89.13n.). He is last heard of as having been spared by Caesar after the siege of Corfinium in 49 (Caes. *Civ.* 23.2). For his *elogium* see *CIL* 1².761 (= xiv.2464; *ILS* 880).

62.9 pudentissimum commonly so used in expressing approbation. *prudentissimum* (βq) is an obvious corruption and much less appropriate.

62.10 tantum dico restrictive (21.12n.).

62.11 hunc indicating Caecilius' presence in court (cf. 19.9n.).

62.12 calamitate see 1.2n.

63.2 primum Caecilius sc. *accusatur* (not *laudandus est*). Cicero does not proceed to *deinde Sulla* below. Anacolouthon is rare in the speeches, although more common in the *philosophica*; cf. K.-S.ii.585f.

63.3 qui id promulgavit the text may be corrupt. Nineteenth-century editors adopt Halm's *qui si id*, but it is very doubtful whether *qui* may thus stand for *quem* (governed by *reprendis*), and in any case the sense would be unsatisfactory seeing that Caecilius did indeed promulgate a bill in which he seemed (*videbatur*) to wish to overturn *res iudicatae*. Clark, on the other hand, takes *id...Sulla* as representing the prosecution's point of view, and so reads – *quid? 'id...Sulla'*. But the – *quid?* seems pointless, and the prosecution would not claim that Sulla appeared to wish to overturn judicial decisions, they would claim that he did wish to: *qui...Sulla* suits Cicero's view, not that of the prosecution. Awkward though it may be, then, the text is not improved by such alteration (although *ut restitueretur Sulla* could possibly be deleted). Translate, 'First Caecilius (is accused), who proposed a bill in which he apparently wished to overturn judicial decisions, so as to restore Sulla (to his former position). You are right to censure this (viz. the overturning of judicial decisions). The stability of the constitution...'. For further attempts to give sense to the passage see Stephanus 90f.; Seyffert 24–6; C. Schliack, *Proben* (Cottbus 1888) 11f. (deletes *in quo...rescindere*).

res iudicatas the plural is used because the bill would have affected Autronius' case as well as that of Sulla. Caecilius seemed to want to overturn the two guilty verdicts, but Cicero will explain below that the bill would not have had this effect.

63.4 restitueretur Pantagathus' emendation was anticipated by *m* (cf. Pabón 6). *restitutio* denotes the 'reinstatement (of an exile or other disgraced person) in his former position or dignity' (*OLD* s.v. 2).

recte reprendis Reid (App. A) considered *recte reprehenditur*, which would ease the syntax if *qui si id* is read above.

63.5 status...continetur cf. *Ver.* 5.12 *perditae civitates desperatis iam omnibus rebus hos solent exitus exitialis habere, ut damnati in integrum restituantur,* *vincti solvantur, exsules reducantur, res iudicatae rescindantur*; *Clu.* 57; *Agr.* 2.8; *Agr.* 2.10 *iudiciorum perturbationes, rerum iudicatarum infirmationes, restitutio damnatorum, qui civitatum adflictarum perditis iam rebus extremi exitiorum solent esse exitus.* 'Restitution (*in integrum restitutio*) or the reversal of the sentence of a court with its effects is an idea that has never appealed strongly to the legal mind. The sanctity of the *res iudicata* was peculiarly great at Rome, and the stability of the constitution was thought to be shaken by spasmodic exercises of the power of pardon... But in a city where the criminal courts had always been used as political weapons, such procedure was inevitable', Greenidge 519f. For *status* as 'stability' see 33.15n. (cf. Nägelsbach 203).

63.6 dandum i.e. *concedendum* (22.4n.). *neque dandum* in *T* led Mommsen to conjecture *concessum esse neque dandum*. Cicero's opinion stated here conforms with his views on the morality of defence (6.8n.).

63.8 ⟨at⟩ nihil...constituta Cicero now explains that Caecilius' bill would not have overturned judicial decisions; had the bill been passed, Sulla and Autronius would still have been deemed guilty. ⟨*at*⟩ is Orelli's necessary supplement, which must have dropped out of the text by haplography after *relinquat*. The subject of the sentence I take to be *Caecilius* (from *primum Caecilius* above), not 'sa proposition' (Boulanger), 'his proposal' (Macdonald): *at* [sc. *haec rogatio*] *nihil de iudicio ferebat* would be much less normal than *at* [sc. *Caecilius*] *nihil de iudicio ferebat*. A (literal) translation, then, would be, 'but Caecilius was (for) carrying no measure affecting the judgement, he was instead (for) bringing back that penalty for *ambitus* which had previously been operative (i.e. until superseded in 67 by the *lex Calpurnia*) under earlier laws (viz. the *lex Cornelia* (81?))'. *poenam ambitus... referebat* denotes 'bringing back' the earlier penalty, not 'referring to' it (Macdonald mistranslates, 'it only raised the question of the penalty for bribery'). *quae fuerat... constituta* means, literally, 'which had been having-been-established', i.e. 'which had been operative'. The relatively unusual form of the pluperfect passive describes a past state or condition (cf. R. G. Nisbet on *Dom.* 95), and is not equivalent to *erat constituta* (again Macdonald mistranslates: 'which had recently been introduced in earlier legislation'). For *nuper* as 'previously' (not 're-cently') see 89.9n.

Properly understood, this sentence gives us our best evidence for the provisions of the *rogatio Caecilia*: the bill evidently did not set out to repeal the *lex Calpurnia* but simply to emasculate it by revoking its penalties (by the process known as *derogatio*) and substituting the milder penalties of the *lex Cornelia* which the *lex Calpurnia* had superseded (the *lex Calpurnia* had been the subject of derogation once already by 65: see *Corn.* ap. Asc. 69, with B. A. Marshall *ad loc.*; Lintott 132f.). This would have allowed Sulla and Autronius back into the senate immediately, with the chance of a second attempt at the consulship once ten years had elapsed from the date of their convictions. For further details of these laws and their penalties see 17.8n. For the play *ferebat...referebat* see Holst 70–76; cf. §47 *tulisse...rettulisse*; §66 *ferebantur...adferebant*.

63.12　est enim iudicum this gives a better rhythm than *enim est iudicum* (ω); the reading of *T* also offers the *lectio difficilior* in placing *enim* in third place (permissible when *est* precedes: see W. S. Watt, *CQ* n.s. 30 (1980) 120–23, with 80.1n. below). After *damnatio*, every syllable in this sentence forms part of a clausula: double-cretic, double-trochee, double-trochee, cretic-spondee.

64.2　eorum ordinum since the *lex Aurelia iudiciaria* (70), juries had been drawn equally from senators, *equites* and *tribuni aerarii*. See *MRR* ii.127; Jones 56. Cicero is flattering the jury.

64.3　labefactare more common in Cicero than *labefacere* (which appears five times).

64.5　calamitate see 1.2n.

64.6　perpetuandam a hexameter ending rhythm; but these are least undesirable when the final word consists of four or five syllables (11.1n.), and in any case the incision is not strongly felt. *perpetuare* is rare; the word occurs elsewhere in Cicero only at *de Orat.* 3.181.

XXIII 64.7　dicerem...dicerem emphatic; cf. 18.1n. *plura* has to be supplied. This sentence is an example of *praeteritio* (14.12n.): had Caecilius gone too far (not that he did), Cicero would now speak as follows.

64.9　pietas...amor laudable impulses. ω, it seems, has normalised the word order in placing *L. Caecilium* after *amor*.

65.1　lex...paucos the perfect passive formulation *fuit proposita* describes a past state or condition (cf. 63.8n.), i.e. the law was proposed only for a few days and then no longer. The hyperbaton *dies...paucos* (8.1n.) and the strong pause after *paucos* emphasise how brief this period was. The bill cannot have survived until the expiry of its *trinundinum* (twenty-four days) if it was withdrawn on 1 January (Caecilius entered office on 10 December).

65.2　deposita est 'it was abandoned' (*OLD* s.v. 8b; cf. *TLL* v.1.579.15) in the senate, and so never reached the assembly. For the play in *proposita...deposita* on different compounds of the same root see Holst 63–70.

kalendis Ianuariis *kalendis Ianuariis* has been corrupted in δ to *r. lateri*. This has become *relaturi* in one of Pabón's *deteriores* (*t*), and Pabón (9 n. 1, also in apparatus) actually considers introducing this word into his text before *convocassemus*.

65.3 in Capitolium at the beginning of each new year the senate met in the Temple of Jupiter on the Capitol. Political matters were discussed only when the religious ceremonies had been completed. See Mommsen, *Staatsrecht* 1.616f.; Bonnefond-Coudry 65–80 (esp. 70).

65.4 Q. Metellus praetor i.e. Q. Caecilius Metellus Celer (*RE* iii.1208.66ff., Suppl. 1.267.57ff., Caecilius 86; *MRR* ii.156, 166, 176, 182f.; iii.37; Sumner 132f.; Shackleton Bailey, *Nomenclature* 69). That Metellus Celer was chosen to put Sulla's wish before the senate has been taken to imply that he was the *praetor urbanus* mentioned at V. Max. 7.7.7, but a more convincing candidate for this has now been put forward by R. J. Seager (Metellus Creticus, probably in 73; cf. *CR* n.s. 20 (1970) 11), and in any case *Flac.* 6 and 100 suggest that it was L. Valerius Flaccus who was the urban praetor in 63 (*MRR* iii.37). Celer, then, will have been chosen instead 'because of some private tie' (Seager): this tie must have consisted of the fact that he was a half-brother of Pompey's wife Mucia, and hence a relation by marriage of Sulla. Celer was tribune in 68 and served as a legate of Pompey in 66 (Dio 36.54.2–4; and perhaps also in 67: cf. *Man.* 58 with R. Syme, *JRS* 53 (1963) 58; T. P. Wiseman, *CQ* n.s. 14 (1964) 122f.; Sumner 132; Gruen 182 n. 72). As praetor in 63 he terminated the trial of Rabirius and at the end of October was put in charge of the forces against Catiline (Plut. *Cic.* 16.1), raising troops in Picenum and the *ager Gallicus* (53.8n., unlikely had he been urban praetor). He was appointed to the proconsulship of Cisalpine Gaul (for 62) which Cicero had relinquished (26.4n.), and his operations against Catiline enabled him to reach his province by December 63 (cf. G. V. Sumner, *CP* 58 (1963) 215–9); thus he will not have been present at Sulla's trial. In the dispute (34.2n.) between Cicero and the tribune Nepos, Celer supported his brother (*Fam.* 5.1, 5.2; cf. J. Van Ooteghem, *LEC* 25 (1957) 168–72). He became consul in 60 (cf. Hor. *Carm.* 2.1.1), and opposed both Pompey (who had divorced Mucia on returning to Rome) and Clodius, the brother of his wife Clodia. Celer died early in 59, of poisoning it was suspected (*Sest.* 131, with *schol. Bob.* 139.8–10 St.; *Vat.* 19; *Cael.* 59–60; cf. T. R. S. Broughton, *TAPA* 79 (1948) 73–6). For Cicero on his oratory see *Brut.* 247.

65.6 agrariae legi Caecilius' fellow-tribune P. Servilius Rullus had proposed a far-reaching agrarian bill to provide land for the poor and for Pompey's veterans by empowering *decemviri* to divide up the *ager Campanus* and other *ager publicus* and to purchase lands with war booty and public funds. The bill was unsuccessful in the face of Cicero's opposition (cf. Plin. *Nat.* 7.117) and Caecilius' threatened veto. Three out of four speeches of Cicero *de lege agraria* survive (although part of the first speech is lost); on the fourth see Crawford 79–81. The demand for land was eventually to be met by Caesar's agrarian legislation in 59. On Rullus' bill see *MRR* II.168; E. G. Hardy, *Some Problems in Roman History* (Oxford 1924) 68–98; A. Afzelius, *C&M* 3 (1940) 214–35; E. Gabba in R. Chevallier (ed.), *Mélanges d'archéologie et d'histoire offerts à André Piganiol* (Paris 1966) 769–75; G. V. Sumner, *TAPA* 97 (1966) 569–82; A. M. Ward, *Historia* 21 (1972) 250–58; Gruen 389–96; Mitchell I.184–205.

Reid is tempted to read *legis* for *legi* since Livy regularly writes *intercessor* with a genitive (e.g. 2.41.7 *intercessor legis agrariae*; cf. 4.53.4). In such constructions, however, Cicero prefers the case normally taken by the verb (here *intercedere*) from which the substantive derives: see H. A. Holden on *Planc.* 1 *eius honori viderem esse fautores* (i.e. *favere*).

65.7 intercessorem se *se* is placed before *intercessorem* in *T* and omitted in δ. But *E* (unknown to editors) and β (misreported by editors) both give *intercessorem se*, which was therefore the reading of the archetype. *se* in the unemphatic second position is wholly appropriate (2.7n.). See my note at *CQ* n.s. 39 (1989) 405f.

65.8 improbis largitionibus i.e. the free distribution of land. Cicero was opposed on principle to agrarian reform of this type (cf. *Att.* 1.19.4, 2.16.1–2) and saw it as *largitio* ('doles', even 'bribes'): see *Agr.* 1.4, 1.21, 2.10, 2.12, 2.16, 2.76; *Mur.* 24; *Pis.* 4.

senatus auctoritatem in a technical sense, *senatus auctoritas* denoted an expressed opinion of the senate which had been rendered ineffective either because of a tribune's veto or for some procedural reason (Dio 55.3.4; cf. *Fam.* 1.7.4, 8.8.6–8; *Att.* 5.2.3). Cicero means that Caecilius did not ever use his power of veto to block a senatorial decree or oppose the senate's wishes.

65.11 cogitarit the perfect puts greater emphasis than the imperfect would on the event's actually happening; cf. Riemann 372; K.-S.II.188.

66.1 atque in ipsa rogatione '[and] over the bill itself' (Macdonald), not 'and even at the voting' (Reid), since the bill did not come to a vote (65.1n.). Cicero finally returns to the actual charge of *vis* (cf. §62).

66.4 ex Autroni improbitate Cicero's technique is the same as that used in the σύγκρισις at §§ 15–20; cf. in particular §15, where Autronius' use of *vis* at his trial in 66 is contrasted with Sulla's submissiveness. On *improbitas* see 1.12n.

eius made emphatic by the position (2.7n.) and the anaphora, 'his (were the) shouts (which)...'.

66.5 ferebantur for the play *ferebantur... adferebant* see Holst 70–76; cf. §47 *tulisse... rettulisse*; §63 *ferebat... referebat*.

aspectus at §15 Autronius' *aspectus* (after his conviction in 66) revealed him to be an enemy of the state (15.7n.).

66.6 stipatio only here in Cicero. The word describes Autronius' followers crowding round him; cf. Var. *L.* 7.52. See *OLD* s.v. 1b; Lebreton 53.

greges ... perditorum for *grex* used pejoratively see 77.1n.

metum ... adferebant the reading of the MSS, *metum nobis seditionesque adferebant*, requires emendation: Autronius' activities indeed brought fear upon Cicero and others, but hardly *seditiones*. There are three possible approaches: one could replace *seditionesque* with a different accusative; one could read *seditionis* and add another accusative (with -*que*) to accompany *metum*; or one could read *seditionis* and add a genitive of related meaning (with -*que* following the later word). C. A. Lehmann (*Hermes* 15 (1880) 349) tried the first two lines of approach. His *suspicionesque* has in its favour the frequency with which *metus* and *suspicio* ('apprehension') are paired in Cicero (e.g. *S. Rosc.* 6; *Ver.* 5.70; *Caec.* 43; *Sest.* 35; cf. Sis. *hist.* 45); in such pairings, however, *suspicio* is usually in the singular, and here one is left wondering '*suspiciones* of what?' Lehmann's preferred alternative was *seditionis* ⟨*suspiciones*⟩*que*, but this seems too close a repetition of *omnis seditionis timor atque opinio* above. The third approach is more promising in that it entails placing emphasis on the criminality of Autronius instead of the timidity of Cicero and the others. Madvig plausibly suggested that the missing word might be *caedis* and accordingly proposed ⟨*caedis*⟩ *seditionisque* (*Adv. Crit.* iii.134f.); the expression *metum caedis* finds parallels at *Red. Sen.* 33, *Har.* 48 and *Prov.* 43. On the other hand one would ideally prefer *caedis* following *seditionis* in order to provide an escalation of horror (cf. 3.6n.); this is perhaps why D. R. Shackleton Bailey writes that Madvig's conjecture 'should be adopted in the form *seditionis* ⟨*caedis*⟩*que*' (*HSCP* 83 (1979) 260). I have chosen to adopt Madvig's proposal as formulated by Shackleton Bailey, although this can be no more than an intelligent guess; all that is clear is that the reading of the MSS is unacceptable.

66.8 cum ... calamitatis the *cum ... tum* correlation (1.4n.) puts greater emphasis on Sulla and Autronius' *ambitus* convictions in 66 (*calamitatis*) than on their designated consulships (*honoris*). Cicero is introducing a note of pathos with which to end this passage.

66.9 secundas fortunas more usually either *secundam fortunam* or *secundas res*; see however *Part.* 96.

66.10 sine ... adlevamento i.e. without the mitigation of his punishment which the *rogatio Caecilia* would have brought. *adlevamentum* (from *adlevare*) is not elsewhere found in classical Latin; cf. *TLL* 1.1673.42ff.; J. Perrot, *Les Dérivés latins en* -men *et* -mentum (Paris 1961) 67. See 1.13n. on *hapax legomena*. The pairing of the word with the commonplace *remedium* assists comprehension.

(viii) Cicero's letter to Pompey (§§ 67–68)

Torquatus cites Cicero's letter to Pompey detailing the events of his consulship. In this letter Cicero had stated that the madness conceived two years previously had broken out in 63: Torquatus infers from this that Cicero thought Sulla involved in the earlier conspiracy. But of course Cicero did not think Sulla involved! In any case, had Sulla really plotted to make Catiline consul, he could not have intended to use force to recover the consulship for himself.

Cicero announced in the *partitio* (§§ 11–14) that he did not have first-hand knowledge of the 'first conspiracy', and that this part of the defence had therefore been left to Hortensius. There was, however, one aspect of the question of Sulla's complicity in the 'first conspiracy' with which Cicero was inescapably connected, and a reply to this therefore had to come from him. Torquatus had produced as evidence a letter in which Cicero himself had implied a direct connection between the conspiracy of 63 and the plotting of 'two years previously'. This alleged link had been used by Torquatus to argue that Sulla's involvement in one conspiracy implied his involvement in the other: thus from Sulla's supposed participation in the conspiracy of 63 he inferred that Sulla had also played a part in the earlier 'conspiracy'. He might have chosen to put his argument the other way round and argue forwards from 66 to 63, but he evidently judged it a better tactic to argue from the stronger case to the weaker: he wished to prove Sulla's participation in both conspiracies, and he must have felt that his participation had been more plausibly demonstrated in the conspiracy of 63 than in the 'first conspiracy'. Torquatus' argument, then, was that on Cicero's own evidence Sulla's involvement in 66 could be inferred from his involvement in 63; as for Cicero, having refuted to his satisfaction the charges relating to 63, this is the natural point at which to turn to deal with such an argument. ˙

Torquatus' argument from Cicero's letter 'is an extraordinarily weak proof, and one can wonder whether he was not short of arguments against an innocent man' (C. E. Stevens, *Latomus* 22 (1963) 431). The first weakness in Torquatus' argument lies in the premise that Sulla was involved in the conspiracy of 63: if, as Cicero has argued, Sulla had no part in the main conspiracy, then it cannot be inferred from the letter that he had been involved in a conspiracy at an earlier date. Secondly, the date of the 'conspiracy' alluded to in the letter does not tally with the date of the 'conspiracy' in which Torquatus alleged that Sulla took part: Torquatus' 'first conspiracy' was allegedly formed in 66 (§ 11), whereas the letter, written at the end of 63, mentioned *furorem incredibilem biennio ante conceptum* (§ 67). Cicero, then, could have answered Torquatus first by emphasising that he had shown that Sulla had had no part in the conspiracy of 63, and then by going on to point out that, in any case, 'two years previously' takes one back as far as Catiline in 65, but not to the events of 66 alleged by Torquatus. He rejects this line of defence, however, and instead replies to Torquatus with a scornful dismissal of the idea that he could have thought Sulla's participation necessary to the 'first conspiracy' followed by an argument intended to show that, if Sulla had indeed plotted to make Catiline consul, as Torquatus claims, he could not have had similar ambitions for himself. No doubt Cicero felt that a reply to Torquatus on the lines suggested above would not have provided a sufficiently forceful rejection of the alleged 'first conspiracy' of 66. But why did Cicero not at least point out the discrepancy between the date of the 'conspiracy' alleged by Torquatus and that of the 'conspiracy' alluded to in the letter? His failure to do so does not appear to be accidental. When replying to Torquatus he ridicules the idea that Piso, Catiline, Vargunteius and Autronius should have been incapable of committing crimes without Sulla's help (§ 67). The names are significant. Piso and Catiline were the men whom Cicero had on several occasions accused of planning massacres for 29 December 66 (*Cat.* 1.15) and 5 February 65 (*Tog. Cand.* ap. Asc. 92 C; *Mur.* 81), i.e. the men to whom he was alluding in his letter. Autronius, on the other hand, would have been included in Torquatus' allegation of a plot to murder his father and L. Aurelius Cotta and seize their consulships on 1 January 65: he belongs to Torquatus' 'conspiracy', and not with those previously accused of conspiracy by Cicero. Cicero, therefore, has not only failed to point out that the two 'conspiracies' are separate, but he has deliberately set out to merge them into one – the 'first Catilinarian conspiracy', believed in by ancient and, until recently, by modern historians. It would therefore seem that Cicero's aim is to throw the responsibility for all of Torquatus' allegations which could not otherwise be disproved onto Piso, Catiline, Vargunteius and Autronius. The crimes which Sulla is alleged to have committed in 66, Cicero is happy to concede, were in fact the work of the men to whom he had alluded in his letter. This argument was as useful to Cicero as it was to Sulla: while it absolved Sulla of responsibility for Torquatus' 'conspiracy' of 66 by providing convenient scapegoats, it also served Cicero's general political interests by allowing further denigration of the Catilinarians. Cicero thus found himself in a paradoxical situation where his aims could be more effectively served by accepting Torquatus' misrepresentation of his letter to Pompey than by refuting it.

XXIV 67.1 **Hic** 'in this context', sc. of Sulla's attempts to regain his forfeited consulship (cf. §§ 21, 22, 50).

tu Torquatus, as the references to his father in §68 make clear.

epistulam meam a famous letter, now lost, sent to Pompey in Asia and containing a detailed record of the events of Cicero's consulship; Torquatus' quotation from it implies that it was simultaneously published at Rome. According to the Bobbio scholiast, the letter was *non mediocrem ad instar voluminis scribtam . . . aliquanto, ut videbatur, insolentius scribtam*, and its boastful tone succeeded only in irritating the great general, *quod quadam superbiore iactantia omnibus se gloriosis ducibus anteponeret* (*schol. Bob.* 167.22–30 St.). The letter must have been written soon after the execution of the conspirators, before the weakness of Cicero's position became apparent. The pointed absence of congratulation in Pompey's reply was a public affront to Cicero, who had quickly found himself in need of Pompey's support (cf. *Fam.* 5.7, written to Pompey in April 62). Pompey apparently compensated for the affront on his return to Rome at the end of the year (*Phil.* 2.12; *Off.* 1.78), but the harm done to Cicero by the letter was remembered at Plancius' trial (*Planc.* 85). See F. Bömer, *Hermes* 81 (1953) 236f.; W. Allen, *TAPA* 85 (1954) 134f.; M. Laffranque, *RPhilos* 152 (1962) 351–8.

saepe recitas 'the prosecutor irritatingly persisted in reading out extracts . . . to prove his case from Cicero's own pen' (Stockton 146). Cicero's words do not, however, betray any embarrassment: they merely suggest the futility of Torquatus' incessant quotation from the letter.

67.2 de summa re publica 'the supreme interest of the state', 'matters of the highest national importance'. The expression is common in Cicero (ten occurrences in this form). See S. P. Oakley, *CR* n.s. 33 (1983) 217.

67.4 biennio ante conceptum i.e. in December 65, reckoning strictly chronologically, or at any point during 65, if Cicero was thinking in consular years. In either case this would invalidate Torquatus' interpretation of Cicero's remark as a reference to a 'first conspiracy' in 66 (§11). R. J. Seager therefore suggests that Cicero's remark was instead intended to refer to the beginning of Catiline's election campaign (*Historia* 13 (1964) 340). But this would be a very obscure allusion. Surely the point Cicero was making in his letter was that the conspiracy of 63 showed the alarmist allegations (81.10n.) which he had previously made against Catiline to have been well justified. He would therefore have been alluding in his letter to his version of the 'first conspiracy' as given at *Tog. Cand.* ap. Asc. 92 C and subsequently at *Mur.* 81, viz. a *caedes optimatum* planned by Catiline and Piso for 5 February 65 (the historical basis of this allegation seems to consist of a demonstration made in connection with the trial of Manilius; cf. Asc. 66 C, with R. J. Seager, *Historia* 13 (1964) 345; E. S. Gruen, *CP* 64 (1969) 22–4; E. J. Phillips,

Latomus 29 (1970) 601, 606; B. A. Marshall, *CP* 72 (1977) 318–20). Reckoning by consular years would allow this 'conspiracy' to be described as *biennio ante conceptum* the writing of Cicero's letter.

erupisse *erumpere* is commonly used of the breaking out of conspiracies and sedition; cf. *Cat.* 1.31 *nescio quo pacto omnium scelerum ac veteris furoris et audaciae maturitas in nostri consulat·is tempus erupit*; *Mur.* 81 *omnia quae per hoc triennium agitata sunt ... in hoc tempus erumpunt*; *Sul.* 76; *Q. fr.* 2.15(14).2. In such passages it is not possible to identify the metaphor underlying *erumpere* unless the metaphor is extended. At §76 we are clearly to think of disease. Here *conceptum* suggests that the metaphor relates to the engendering and birth of monsters (see R. G. M. Nisbet and M. Hubbard on Hor. *Carm.* 2.13.9); this is supported by similar metaphors in §§75–6.

in meo consulatu ... me *meo* (before its noun) and *me* (in first place: 2.7n.) are strongly emphatic, and set the tone for the next sentence.

67.6 scilicet ego is sum an ironic denial that Cicero, of all people, could have thought Sulla's participation necessary to the 'first conspiracy' (not, as R. J. Seager takes it, a denial that his letter alluded to a 'first conspiracy' in 66: see *Historia* 13 (1964) 340). *E* read *scilicet is ego sum*, but *scilicet ego is sum* (*T*) gives *ego* greater emphasis and is therefore more appropriate; see my note at *CQ* n.s. 39 (1989) 406.

67.7 Cn. Pisonem Cicero implies that Cn. Calpurnius Piso (*RE* III.1379.67ff., Calpurnius 69; *MRR* II.159, 163) and the others listed here were implicated in the 'first conspiracy'. Piso was sent to Hispania Citerior as *quaestor pro praetore* in 65 by decree of the senate (*CIL* I².749; = *ILS* 875), perhaps because of a shortage of governors (in which case Sallust's *duas Hispanias* (*Cat.* 18.5) may be correct); this is said to have been arranged by Crassus, who would have hoped to undermine Pompey's influence there (Sal. *Cat.* 19.1; but his sources may have been vitiated). The following year Piso was murdered by the Spaniards under his command, allegedly at Pompey's instigation (Sal. *Cat.* 19.3–5; Asc. 92–3 C; Dio 36.44.5). Once dead, Piso became a convenient target for slander: in Cicero what was perhaps a demonstration with Catiline at Manilius' trial becomes blown up into a projected *caedes optimatum* (67.4n.), and thus Piso, and in Sallust his mission to Spain, came to be associated with the 'first conspiracy' (cf. Sal. *Cat.* 18.4–8; Asc. 92 C; Dio 36.44.4–5; Suetonius (*Jul.* 9.3), however, does not regard Piso as involved). Sallust even makes Catiline claim that the sending of Piso to Spain was preparatory to the conspiracy of 63 (*Cat.* 21.3). See J. P. V. D. Balsdon, *JRS* 52 (1962) 134f.; Syme, *Sallust* 88–91; R. J. Seager, *Historia* 13 (1964) 346.

Vargunteium this is the only source to name Vargunteius among those involved in the 'first conspiracy'. Cicero may simply have thrown in his name for good measure; the allegation would have sounded plausible in view of Vargunteius' *ambitus* conviction (6.1n.).

67.8 audacter see 16.4n.

67.9 P. Sulla the inclusion of the *praenomen* increases Sulla's stature and helps to dissociate him from the men just mentioned (1.1n.).

68.2 num 'whether not perhaps', inclining to an affirmation. Cicero usually expresses this sense by writing *dubito an*: Clark and others therefore adopt Eberhard's *an* (supported by Madvig, *Adv. Crit.* II.209f.). But cf. *Fam.* 7.32.1 *addubitavi num a Volumnio senatore esset* ('I was inclined to wonder whether it might not be from . . .') – where Madvig also substitutes *an* for *num*. D. R. Shackleton Bailey *ad loc.* (and at *HSCP* 83 (1979) 260) suggests that there is 'a semantic difference between *num* and *an*, the former ('whether by any chance') implying that the possibility in mind is unlikely or unwelcome'. *num*, then, is exactly right in our passage. For *dubito num* see *TLL* v.1.2093.22ff.; K.-S.II.266.

ut only in β. Either the word is a conjecture, or it occurred in the archetype but was omitted by Tδ independently (thus Clark xiv). Kasten in his 1933 edition (xii) hesitantly attributed *ut* to conjecture, but later implausibly viewed the reading as resulting from contamination (1949, v; 1966, vi): see pp. 71f. But whatever its status (and I am inclined to agree with Clark), *ut* is certainly required.

interfecto patre tuo . . . lictoribus in § 68 Cicero argues that two allegations made by Torquatus respecting Sulla's supposed complicity in the 'first conspiracy' of 66 are mutually incompatible; as will appear, Cicero's refutation depends on a misrepresentation of Torquatus' arguments. Here we are given one of these allegations made against Sulla: that he intended to recover his lost consulship by murdering his replacement, Torquatus' father (11.4n.), and then entering the forum (*descenderet*) attended by lictors on 1 January 65. This is the earliest of the sources to mention the Kalends of January, and the version of the plot given here reappears later, with accretions, at Suet. *Jul.* 9.1, Sal. *Cat.* 18.5, Liv. *epit.* 101 and Dio 36.44.3. In each of these accounts the consulships of 65 were to go to those who would most naturally be expected to have sought them, Sulla and Autronius (although in Sallust's confused account it is Catiline rather than Sulla who was to have been consul in 65 with Autronius (cf. 81.10n.); Sallust, persuaded by Hortensius' and Cicero's speeches as well as by Sulla's acquittal that the latter had had no part in the 'first conspiracy', has simply substituted Catiline's name for that of Sulla). It is therefore likely that Torquatus will have levelled a similar charge (which Cicero does not need to mention here) against Autronius, claiming that Sulla and Autronius were to have killed the two men elected in their stead, the elder Torquatus and L. Aurelius Cotta (11.2n.) respectively. The point of *descenderet ... cum lictoribus* is to emphasise the enormity of the crime alleged and so encourage disbelief that Sulla could have committed it: it is not 'a pointless rhetorical effect', as R. J. Seager suggests (*Historia* 13 (1964) 340). However, Seager is correct to infer (on E. L. Bowie's suggestion) that the murder was to have taken place in advance of 1 January, i.e. in 66, so as to allow Sulla's triumphant entry into the forum on that day. Seager (344) also rightly underlines the absurdity of Torquatus' allegation, pointing out that 'if the plan had succeeded ... Autronius and Sulla would have been lucky to escape with their lives. They could have had no hope of recovering the consulship even for a single day, much less for a whole year'. The factual basis which allowed Torquatus to make such a charge amounts to little: perhaps a display of violence such as is denied by Cicero below gave rise to a rumour that Sulla and Autronius intended to recover their consulships by force (cf. E. S. Gruen, *CP* 64 (1969) 20; Gruen 217, 219, 272, 442f.; J. T. Ramsey, *HSCP* 86 (1982) 131). For the other allegation made by Torquatus against Sulla, supposedly incompatible with this one, see 68.4n. The correction *consul* (for *consule* of the MSS) was first made by O. Müller at *Hermes* 12 (1877) 301.

68.4 sustulisti an indicative is natural in the apodosis of 'unreal' conditionals when the *si* clause grants a concession; cf. Woodcock 157.

hunc ... comparasse for *operas et manum* ('rowdies and a gang', i.e. a gang of rowdies) cf. *Vat.* 40 *cum Clodianas operas et facinerosorum hominum et perditorum manum videris.*

Here we are given a further allegation made by Torquatus, which Cicero maintains is incompatible with the charge that Sulla aimed to murder the elder Torquatus and seize for himself the consulship of 65 (68.2n.). Torquatus' allegation is this, that Sulla organized violence against the elder Torquatus with a view to securing Catiline's election to the consulship (cf. *cum Catilinae suffragaretur* below). The year in which Catiline was to have held this consulship is not stated, but Cicero's argument assumes it to have been 65 (correctly, as I shall argue). Cicero's contention, then, is that it is illogical for Torquatus to maintain that Sulla intended both to seize the consulship of 65 for himself and to attempt to secure it for Catiline (since both men were patricians, they could not have held the consulship together: one consulship would have been available for Sulla or Catiline, while Autronius could have taken the other).

Torquatus' apparent self-contradiction is traditionally accounted for by supposing that, according to Torquatus, Sulla's plan was to seize the consulship of 65 for himself by the murder of the elder Torquatus and then, when consul, to use his power to secure for Catiline the consulship of the following year, 64 (cf. W. Drumann, *Geschichte Roms* II (Königsberg 1835) 515 n.71; John 708–12; E. Meyer, *Caesars Monarchie und das Principat des Pompejus*[2] (Stuttgart and Berlin 1919) 20 n. 3; M.Gelzer, *RE* II A.1696.36ff.; R. J. Seager, *Historia* 13 (1964) 340). On this view, Cicero's argument would depend on the jury having forgotten the year in which, according to Torquatus, Catiline was to have had his consulship. But could Cicero really have relied so greatly upon the forgetfulness of his audience? The traditional explanation of Torquatus' position, in fact, suffers from fatal objections. Torquatus claimed that Sulla attempted to secure Catiline's election by organizing violence *contra patrem tuum*. One may note first that this is a plot which according to Torquatus did take place (cf. *cum Catilinae suffragaretur*): it is not a plot which might have taken place had his father been murdered. Secondly, if Sulla's support for Catiline's candidature is to be dated to 65, then it is unclear why violence against the elder Torquatus, who by then was consul, would have been necessary to achieve Catiline's election. Evidently, if the election of Catiline was to be effected by the use of violence against the elder Torquatus, then Catiline must have been standing against him in the same election. J. T. Ramsey (*HSCP* 86 (1982) 121–31) has therefore proposed an alternative explanation for Torquatus' apparent self-contradiction, viz. that the election at which Torquatus alleged that Sulla supported Catiline was the supplementary election of 66 (11.2n.; cf. 'he [Catiline] may have had reason to hope that the massive support given to Sulla in the first election... would be thrown to him', G. V. Sumner, *Phoenix* 19 (1965) 231). This is the only possible hypothesis which will make sense of *contra patrem tuum*: the election has to be an election in 66, when the elder Torquatus was a rival whom it would have been advantageous to oppose with violence, and the original election is ruled out because Sulla obviously would not have supported Catiline against himself. As Ramsey demonstrates, the evidence of Cicero therefore confirms Sallust's statement that it was at the supplementary election at which Catiline intended to stand before his candidature was disallowed (*Cat.* 18.3; cf. Asc. 89 C).

It is now possible to give an outline of the 'first conspiracy' as alleged by Torquatus. After Sulla and Autronius were convicted *de ambitu*, a date for a supplementary election was set. Catiline, newly returned from Africa, announced his intention of standing, and his candidature was supported, with violence, by Sulla. This is entirely plausible: Sulla's aim would have been to block his enemy's election by forcing the election of another patrician candidate. Catiline, however, was disqualified, and Torquatus elected. Sulla therefore, according to Torquatus, changed his plans: he determined to murder the elder Torquatus and seize his consulship on 1 January 65 (Autronius doing the same to Cotta). This is less plausible, for the reasons given above (68.2n.).

The argument may now be reviewed. Torquatus did indeed maintain both that Sulla supported Catiline for the consulship of 65 and that he plotted to seize it for himself; but these two accusations are not incompatible, because the second plot was alleged to have been resorted to only after the failure of the first. Cicero, on the other hand, has misrepresented Torquatus' allegations not by postdating the year in which Catiline was to have had his consulship (as is required by the traditional interpretation of this passage), but more simply by telescoping the events of the months following Sulla's conviction.

68.7 cum Catilinae suffragaretur 'when (as you assert) he was supporting Catiline's candidature', in the run-up to the supplementary election in 66, before Catiline's candidature was disallowed. See J. T. Ramsey, *HSCP* 86 (1982) 126.

68.9 neque enim ... suscipit transitional; Cicero quickly moves away from his argument. For *crimen suscipere* cf. *Ver.* 4.91, 5.105; *Rab. Perd.* 18. For persona, 'character', see 8.1n.

§§ 69–79 CONFIRMATIO I

Contrary to usual practice, Cicero will turn only now to a most important argument, that from Sulla's life and character. Character cannot suddenly be altered: witness the wicked lives of Catiline, Lentulus, Cethegus and Autronius. Sulla's life, by contrast, has always been exemplary: Cicero reviews his part in the proscriptions, his ambitus conviction and his self-imposed exile, together with his personal qualities. The Catilinarians, on the other hand, were monsters, who brought on themselves their own punishment: do not cast Sulla out among them! Evidence gained by torture and taken from witnesses is unreliable: instead, let the evidence of Sulla's life decide the verdict!

On Cicero's inversion of the *confirmatio* and *reprehensio* see pp. 46–8.

Cicero now at last begins his postponed *confirmatio*, the part of the speech in which the orator puts forward his own arguments, as opposed to the *reprehensio* in which he replies to those of the opposition. A simple definition is given at *Rhet. Her.* 1.4, *confirmatio est nostrorum argumentorum expositio cum adseveratione*; more illustrative of Cicero's method in *pro Sulla* (especially §§ 80–85), however, is the definition provided at *Inv.* 1.34, *confirmatio est per quam argumentando nostrae causae fidem et auctoritatem et firmamentum adiungit oratio.* According to Quintilian, the *confirmatio* is the only part of the speech which should under no circumstances be omitted (*Inst.* 5.*pr.*5).

The *confirmatio* begins, as was traditional, with *argumenta ex vita* (i.e. *confirmatio* I, §§ 69–79): *de vita hominis ac de moribus dicam* (§ 69). In the courts a man's past life was taken to have considerable bearing on the question of his innocence or guilt, and thus it was important that the orator take full account of this aspect of the case: *defensor autem primum, si poterit, debebit vitam eius qui insimulabitur quam honestissimam demonstrare (Inv.* 2.35); *defensor primum demonstrabit vitam integram, si poterit (Rhet. Her.* 2.5); *probi vero mores et ante actae vitae integritas numquam non plurimum profuerint* (Quint. *Inst.* 7.2.33). Sulla's character appears to have been quite difficult to present in a favourable light, and Cicero's letters show him to have been rapacious and disloyal. Nevertheless, in the passage which follows Cicero makes a good attempt at whitewashing his client; even Sulla's infamous part in his uncle's proscriptions (cf. *Off.* 2.29) is turned into a virtue (*misericordia*; cf. § 72), and the conviction for *ambitus* in 66 is presented as illustrative of his *modestia*. Cicero's method is to talk in general terms, thus skating over Sulla's faults while giving no direct evidence for his supposed virtues: Sulla's *constantia, dignitas, liberalitas, moderatio* and *pudor* are remarked upon but not substantiated (§§ 73–4). Likewise our attention is not allowed to focus on Sulla for too long: much of this section is taken up with invective against the Catilinarians, with whom Sulla is contrasted (cf. the σύγκρισις between Autronius and Sulla at §§ 15–20). It is also significant that most of the instances of *reticentia* and *occultatio* in the speech occur within this section. These, then, are the means by which Cicero creates a favourable picture, and it is surely here, rather than in the *partitio*, that his insincerity is most conspicuous. When he argues that he himself is a good man, we can believe him; but when he makes the same claim on his client's behalf it is more difficult.

On *argumenta ex vita* see further Arist. *Rh.* 3.17 (1418 b 24ff.); *Inv.* 1.35, 2.32–4 (prosecution), 35–7 (defence); *Rhet. Her.* 2.5; Quint. *Inst.* 7.2.28–35; Lausberg 204–6; Rohde 146–50; Strachan-Davidson, *Criminal Law* II.119–21; and on their use in *pro Sulla*, Michel 408f.; May 74–6. For *argumenta ex vita* in Cicero see the list given at J. M. May, *CJ* 74 (1978–9) 245 n. 13; also *Quinct.* 93; *S. Rosc.* 39, 84–91, 109; *Q. Rosc.* 17, 20; *Tul.* 3; *Caec.* 104; *Clu.* 70 (quoted at 69.1on.), 124; *Mur.* 11–14 (also quoted at 69.1on.); *Sul.* 45, 58 (*argumenta a persona*); *Flac.* 5; *Sest.* 5; *Vat.* 1; *Cael.* 3–22, 53; *Planc.* 3; *Mil.* 36; *Deiot.* 16; *Phil.* 1.27.

On the *confirmatio* in an ancient speech see Arist. *Rh.* 3.17; *Inv.* 1.34–77; *Rhet. Her.* 1.4, 2.3–12; *de Orat.* 2.331; *Part.* 33–43; *Orat.* 122; Quint. *Inst.* 3.9.5, 5.*pr*.5, 5.1.1–5.12.23. For modern accounts see Lausberg 190–236; Martin 95–137; Rohde 40–121.

69.1 criminibus...dissolutis *fere* is to be taken with *omnibus*; cf.

273

de Orat. 3.15; *Rep.* 6.18 (*TLL* vi.1.494.56ff.). For *dissolvere* as to 'refute' arguments, charges etc. cf. *S. Rosc.* 82; *Ver.* 2.68; Cic. (?) *Opt. Gen.* 15 (*TLL* v.1.1500.29ff.). The remaining charges were no doubt trivial. It may seem surprising that Cicero should admit that he has not answered all of the charges; but perhaps this is a means of keeping the jury in a state of expectation. In any case *fere* is more positive than the English 'almost': *omnibus fere* implies not so much that there are still charges remaining unanswered as that Cicero has indeed replied to virtually every single charge.

contra atque ... solet normally the *confirmatio* preceded the *reprehensio*, with the result that the *argumenta ex vita*, traditionally placed first within the *confirmatio* (cf. Quint. *Inst.* 7.1.12, 7.2.27), occurred near the beginning of the speech. The order found here is more in accord with Greek practice, in which the arguments from character were the last to be put forward; cf. Volkmann 373f.; Humbert 151f.; Stroh 253–5, with n. 56.

69.2 de vita ... ac de moribus a common phrase, denoting in rhetoric the *probabile ex vita* and in the *philosophica* the branch of philosophy concerned with ethics; see G. Landgraf on *S. Rosc.* 109.

69.3 de principio 'at the outset'. For *de* as 'immediately after' see *TLL* v.1.65.11ff.; K.-S.1.498. For an assessment of the reasons Cicero is about to give see pp. 47f.

69.5 qui Reid unnecessarily prints *quia* (cf. 4.9n.).

69.7 animos according to Zinzerling *E* read *animos vestros*, but this report is not to be trusted; see my note at *CQ* n.s. 39 (1989) 406.

XXV 69.10 admiserit 'perpetrated', as at §16. Sylvius remarks that the three verbs have been put in their logical order.

non ex crimine ... est ponderandum i.e. a man's past record is a surer indication of his innocence or guilt than the mere fact of someone's having brought an accusation against him (because, for instance, the accusation might be a false charge trumped up by an enemy). The argument is one recommended at *Inv.* 2.36: *iniquum esse et optimo cuique perniciosissimum non vitam honeste actam tali in tempore quam plurimum prodesse, sed subita ex criminatione, quae confingi quamvis false possit, non ex ante acta vita, quae neque ad tempus fingi neque ullo modo mutari possit, facere iudicium.* Cicero does not, however, claim that his *argumenta ex vita* should carry greater weight than his *reprehensio*: there is no implicit acknowledgement of the weakness of his reply to the charges. Cicero's reason for emphasising here the importance of *argumenta ex vita* is of course that he hopes to persuade the jury in advance that his arguments from Sulla's life and character will be strong ones. He is also perhaps ensuring that the jury do not stop listening to him now that he has finished his reply to the charges. The importance of *argumenta ex vita* as indicators of innocence or guilt is often stressed: cf. *Clu.* 70 *nam perinde ut opinio est de cuiusque moribus, ita quid ab eo factum aut non factum sit existimari potest*; *Mur.* 11 *intellego, iudices, tris totius accusationis partis fuisse, et earum unam in reprehensione vitae, alteram in contentione dignitatis, tertiam in criminibus ambitus esse versatam. atque harum trium partium prima illa quae gravissima debebat esse...* See also *S. Rosc.* 38, 53, 62, 68, 75, 118; *Q. Rosc.* 17; *Font.* 27.

69.12 neque enim...converti cf. §79 *valeat ad poenam et ad salutem vita plurimum, quam solam videtis ipsam ex sua natura facillime perspici, subito flecti fingique non posse.* The view that character is immutable was of great value to orators (allowing the use of *argumenta ex vita*), and is also regularly encountered among the biographers and historians. It is adopted by these authors to suit their immediate purposes, and should not be taken to represent either the individual author's personal perception of human psychology or a universally-held set belief (see my criticism of May: *JRS* 80 (1990) 204). At *Amic.* 32, for instance, the immutability of character (*natura mutari non potest*) is used to argue the permanence of true friendships; but at *Amic.* 33 and 54 men's characters are said to alter with advancing age (cf. Liv. 30.30.10). Here (*Sul.* 69, and at §79) Cicero asserts the impossibility of a sudden change of character because this is a necessary premise to his argument that Sulla's innocence is implied by his past record. His words, then, do not disclose his own view of character: they represent 'no more than the rhetorical overstatement of an argument...grouped under the heading of *probabile* and *coniectura*' (A. R. Hands, *CQ* n.s. 24 (1974) 314). In any case Cicero makes his contention more acceptable (even though he weakens his argument in so doing) by talking of a *sudden* change (*subito...repente*; Reid well compares Juv. 2.83 *nemo repente fuit turpissimus*): Cicero would, in theory, allow a gradual deterioration in Sulla's character. On Cicero's view of his own (consistent and unchanging) character see §8 (8.4n.). See further F. R. D. Goodyear on Tac. *Ann.* 1.1–54, pp. 37–40; A. R. Hands, *CQ* n.s. 24 (1974) 312–17; C. Gill, *CQ* n.s. 33 (1983) 469–87; C. B. R. Pelling (ed.), *Characterization and Individuality in Greek Literature* (Oxford 1990).

H. Kraffert proposed *refingi* for *fingi* (*Beiträge zur Kritik und Erklärung lateinischer Autoren* (Aurich 1881–3) III.118). *refingi* is more attractive rhythmically (double-trochee before *neque*); *fingi*, however, is supported by *fingique* at §79, while *refingere* does not occur in Cicero. For *fingere* as 'modify the character of (a person)', i.e. change what already exists, see *TLL* VI.1.773.25ff.

70.1 circumspicite...mentibus cf. *Font.* 25 *quae si iudex...non animo ac mente circumspiciet*; *Agr.* 2.45 *illud circumspicite vestris mentibus*. The play resembles *adeste omnes animis* at §33 (33.3n.).

70.2 ut alia omittamus an example of *reticentia* (22.10n.). *T* gives *mittamus*, but the closest parallels all point to *omittamus* (ω) as being the correct reading: cf. *Quinct.* 70, *de Orat.* 1.166, *Amic.* 9, *Phil.* 2.38 all *ut alia omittam*; *Luc.* 113 *ut omittam alia*; *Att.* 7.13.1 *ut enim alia omittam.*

70.3 huic adfines sceleri cf. § 17 *huius adfines suspicionis* (17.8n.).

Catilina the central argument of *confirmatio* I, that Sulla's past record implies his innocence (§§ 72–5), rests on the assumption that character cannot suddenly be altered (§§ 69, 79). The passage which follows (§§ 70–71), while also serving to provide a contrast between the Catilinarians and Sulla, aims to forestall a possible objection to Cicero's assumption, that the characters of the Catilinarians themselves were suddenly altered. Cicero therefore implicitly denies this possibility by emphasising that the criminality of the conspirators had always been notorious. In Catiline's case at least this was difficult to maintain given that on three previous occasions (§ 81) the *consulares*, and in 65 even the elder Torquatus, had lent him their support. At § 81 Cicero therefore accounts for the seeming contradiction by pointing to the consulars' duty to help an *amicus* in danger (81.5n.): *defendebant amicum . . . vitae eius turpitudinem in summis eius periculis non insequebantur.* So, Cicero implies, he is not overstating his case: Catiline's criminality was always apparent, but prior to 63 the *consulares*, who in any case were unaware of conspiratorial designs, had laudable motives for overlooking it. The truth of the matter is that, until he plotted against the state, Catiline's violent and disreputable past proved no obstacle to his social respectability. Thanks to his patrician birth he occupied a significantly higher social position than Cicero did, and it was quite natural for Cicero to consider speaking in his defence (*Att.* 1.2.1). Nevertheless, after the events of 63–62 the picture of Catiline found here became the orthodox view: Catiline was seen as a criminal from childhood (*a pueritia*), or even from birth (*ad civile latrocinium natum*). An interesting exception is *Cael.* 10–14, where, in order to excuse Caelius' connection with Catiline, Cicero attributes to the latter a paradoxical personality in which together with his vices were mixed *permulta maximarum non expressa signa sed adumbrata virtutum* (*Cael.* 12). This alternative characterisation was also influential, most notably on Sallust's portrait (*Cat.* 5.1–8, 60.7 etc.). See Hardy 8f.; Gruen 417f.

70.4 cuius aures . . . respuerunt another play involving parts of the body (*auribus respuere* must logically mean 'hear and then reject as untrue'); cf. *Pis.* 45 *nemo denique civis est . . . qui vos non oculis fugiat, auribus respuat, animo aspernetur; Planc.* 44 *respuerunt aures; Part.* 15 *auditorum aures moderantur oratori prudenti et provido; eae quod respuunt immutandum est.* See R. G. M. Nisbet and M. Hubbard on Hor. *Carm.* 2.13.32 *bibit aure*; A.

Gudeman on Tac. *Dial.* 9.2. *hoc* (ω) rather than *haec* (*T*) seems to accord better with what follows.

70.5 audacter see 16.4n.

a pueritia cf. Sal. *Cat.* 5.2 *huic ab adulescentia bella intestina caedes rapinae discordia civilis grata fuere, ibique iuventutem suam exercuit*; [Sal.] *Inv. in Cic.* 2.

70.7 flagitio stupro caede the crimes of Catiline's youth are amply, if somewhat confusedly, attested; cf. Syme, *Sallust* 84–6. Under *flagitia* one should class his *repetundae* acquittal in 65 (81.7n.); for the connection between *flagitium* and *flagitatio* (a vociferous demand for the return of property) see H. Usener, *RhM* 56 (1900) 1–28 (= *Kleine Schriften* IV (Leipzig and Berlin 1913) 356–82). General reports of *stupra* are plentiful: cf. *Tog. Cand.* ap. Asc. 86 C *stupris se omnibus ac flagitiis contaminavit; caede nefaria cruentavit*; *Cat.* 2.7, 2.9; Q. Cic. (?) *Pet.* 9–10; Sal. *Cat.* 14.6; *ibid. iam primum adulescens Catilina multa nefanda stupra fecerat*. Nevertheless, only three specific allegations emerge. First, Catiline was cited in 73 as the paramour in the trial *de incestu* of the Vestal Fabia, a half-sister (or cousin) of Cicero's wife Terentia; however, the charge seems to have been politically motivated (the prosecutor was P. Clodius, Catiline's prosecutor in 65), and was withdrawn upon the intervention of the young Cato (*Cat.* 3.9; *Sul.* 81; *Brut.* 236; Sal. *Cat.* 15.1, 35.1; Asc. 91 C; Plut. *Cat. Mi.* 19.3; *schol.* Gronov. 287 St.; Oros. 6.3.1; cf. E. S. Gruen, *Athenaeum* 49 (1971) 59–62; D. R. Shackleton Bailey on *Att.* 1.16.9; *TLRR* no. 167). The second allegation is still more scandalous: Catiline, it was alleged, married his own daughter, the issue of an adulterous union between an unidentified woman and himself (cf. *Tog. Cand.* ap. Asc. 91 C; Virg. *A.* 6.623–4, with my article at *CQ* n.s. 42 (1992) 416–20; Plut. *Cic.* 10.2, which mentions incest but not marriage). This daughter-wife is evidently Catiline's last wife (thus Syme, *Sallust* 85), the beautiful Aurelia Orestilla (cf. Sal. *Cat.* 15.2; on the date of their marriage see B. A. Marshall, *RFIC* 105 (1977) 151–4). Thirdly, Sallust alleges illicit sexual relations *cum virgine nobili* (*Cat.* 15.1), otherwise unknown. The *caedes* are better authenticated, and indeed date, for the most part, from Catiline's youth, when as a legate (82–80; cf. Sal. *Hist.* 1.46 M, with *MRR* II.72, III.192) under L. Sulla he participated in the proscriptions (from which, like Sulla (*Off.* 2.29), he profited greatly). He is alleged to have murdered (i) his wife's brother (?) M. Marius Gratidianus, a nephew of C. Marius and first cousin of Cicero's father (Q. Cic. (?) *Pet.* 10; Sal. *Hist.* 1.44 M; Asc. 84, 87, 90 C; V. Max. 9.2.1; Sen. *Dial.* 5.18.1–2; Plut. *Sull.* 32.2; *schol. Bern.* on Luc. 2.173, pp. 61–2 U; but cf. Hinard 46, 377–80; B. A. Marshall, *CQ* n.s. 35 (1985) 124–33; F. Hinard, *Kentron* 2 (1986) 118–22), (ii) his sister's husband Q. Caecilius (Q. Cic. (?) *Pet.* 9; Asc. 84 C; cf. Hinard 339f.), (iii) various others, M. Volumnius (Asc. 84 C; cf. Hinard

41of.), L. Tanusius (Asc. 84 C; Q. Cic. (?) *Pet.* 9; cf. Hinard 399f.), Titinius and Nannius (Q. Cic. (?) *Pet.* 9; cf. Hinard 380–85, 401f.), and (iv) his own brother, although this is less well attested (Plut. *Sull.* 32.2; *id. Cic.* 10.2; cf. Hinard 397). On these murders see C. Nicolet in *Mélanges d'histoire ancienne offerts à William Seston* (Paris 1974) 381–95. Catiline is further alleged to have killed his own wife (*Cat.* 1.14) or son (Sal. *Cat.* 15.2; V. Max. 9.1.9; App. *BC* 2.2; cf. Catul. 64.401–2) in order to secure his marriage to Orestilla. Generally speaking, 'the reliability of these stories does not stand high' (Gruen 417); nevertheless, Catiline's cruelty during the proscriptions is not in doubt.

versatum *grassatum* (*E*) is possible, although the word was archaic (cf. W. Kroll, *Glotta* 15 (1927) 302) and does not otherwise occur in Cicero (*grassator*, however, is found at *Fat.* 34). Nevertheless, in view of the frequency of *homo versatus in* (Merguet IV.864; cf. II.655f.), *versatum* (*Tω*) is more likely to be correct; cf. *S. Rosc.* 39 *homo audax et saepe in caede versatus*; *Pis.* 9 *homine in stupris . . . versato*.

70.8 perisse for Catiline's death see Sal. *Cat.* 61.4; Vell. 2.35.5; Plut. *Cic.* 22.5; Flor. 2.12.12; App. *BC* 2.7; Dio 37.40.1; Eutr. 6.15.

semper untrue (70.3n.). The forward position of the word gives it strong emphasis (8.1n.).

70.9 natum cf. *Cat.* 1.25 *ad hanc te amentiam natura peperit.*

70.10 societates cum indicibus cf. *Mur.* 49 *Catilinam . . . vallatum indicibus atque sicariis*; *Sest.* 95 [sc. *Clodius*] *qui stipatus semper sicariis, saeptus armatis, munitus indicibus fuit.* Lentulus' (16.3n.) associations with informers are not otherwise attested. However, Cicero has been alluding to crimes committed by Catiline under Sulla's dictatorship, and it is possible that he is now thinking of Lentulus' activities during the same period; this would accord with his aim of illustrating consistency of character throughout life. Lentulus held a quaestorship in 81 (*MRR* II.76), and it is likely that he was a supporter of Sulla's regime (cf. Gruen 125).

insaniam libidinum cf. Sal. *Cat.* 52.32 *verum parcite dignitati Lentuli, si ipse pudicitiae, si famae suae, si dis aut hominibus umquam ullis pepercit.* Cicero is perhaps thinking of Lentulus' expulsion from the senate in 70 (Plut. *Cic.* 17.1; Dio 37.30.4).

70.11 religionem an allusion to Lentulus' belief that he was destined to become the third of the Cornelii to rule Rome (16.3n.).

70.12 cogitasse . . . sperasse for the pairing cf. *Clu.* 177; *Leg.* 3.5. *stulte sperasse* refers again to Lentulus' foolish ambitions (previous n.).

70.13 quis . . . cogitat Cicero implies that Cethegus (53.3n.) had gone to Spain during the Sertorian war to murder Metellus Pius, but had succeeded only in wounding him; this may be the point of Sal. *Cat.*

52.33 *ignoscite Cethegi adulescentiae, nisi iterum patriae bellum fecit.* The attempted assassination is not otherwise attested (see Long's remarks on the speculations of his predecessors). Q. Caecilius Metellus Pius (*RE* III.1221.48ff., Caecilius 98; *MRR* II.33, 42, 78f., 83; III.41) was sent to Further Spain in 79, after his consulship (with L. Sulla) the previous year, and was joined by Pompey in 76; the war was not ended until 71. By the time of Sulla's trial Metellus Pius had died; Caesar took his place as *pontifex maximus* in 63 (*MRR* II.171).

70.15 carcer the prison in which Cethegus and the others were executed (30.10n.).

esse videatur see 3.9n.

71.1 omitto ceteros an example of *reticentia* (22.10n.).

71.2 tantum restrictive (21.12n.).

71.3 intellegetis for the parataxis see 5.9n. The future tense (β) gives better sense than the present (Tδ).

71.4 ab sua vita...damnatum the inclusion of *ab* offended Madvig (*Adv. Crit.* III.135), but Lebreton (409–13) has shown that, contrary to popular belief (e.g. Reid), the use of *ab* before 'things' after a passive verb is not unusual in Cicero. *ab* and *a* have equal MS authority; I accept *ab* as the *lectio difficilior* (*ab* is in any case much more common before *s-* than before some other consonants). β adds a further *a* after *quam* for the parallelism, but this is unlikely to be the reading of the archetype. The implication in this passage that the other Catilinarian trials all resulted in condemnation is supported by Dio 37.41.4.

71.5 Autronium the last conspirator to be treated before Cicero turns to Sulla (§72). Autronius is taken last for the sake of the contrast (cf. the σύγκρισις between the two at §§15–20).

eius nomen...crimini cf. §37 *Autroni commemoratio memoriam Sullae rettulisset.*

71.7 vita ac natura on this reading see p. 74.

audax...libidinosus see 16.4n.

71.8 deprensionibus *defensionibus* (ω) is unacceptable, as D. R. Shackleton Bailey wittily demonstrates (*HSCP* 83 (1979) 260). '(Legal) defences' and, more generally, 'justifications' do not fit: Cicero must be thinking of Autronius 'when caught in the act'. L. Håkanson's *depre(he)nsionibus*, which Shackleton Bailey cites, is exactly right; for the corruption cf. *defendis* in Florence, Laur. plut. 48.11 for *depre(he)ndis* at *Quinct.* 61. The word occurs once in Cicero, at *Clu.* 50 *manifesta veneni deprensione.*

71.9 esse scimus double-trochee. For the short final syllable of *esse* before *sc-* see M. Platnauer, *Latin Elegiac Verse* (Cambridge 1951) 62f.

pugnis et calcibus lit., 'with fists and heels' (πὺξ καὶ λάξ), proverbial for 'with extreme violence', as at *Ver.* 3.56; cf. *TLL* III.195.72ff.; Otto 66f. The ancients kicked with their heels, the toes being unprotected.

71.10   exturbare ... vicinorum violence was commonly resorted to in disputes over property (cf. *pro Tullio, pro Caecina*), and a large degree of self-help was tolerated in Roman law: see *RE* IX A.315.4ff.; Lintott 22–34. On rural violence see P. A. Brunt, *Italian Manpower, 225 BC–AD 14*[2] (Oxford 1987) 551–7.

71.11   spoliare fana sociorum perhaps when a legate in Greece, 73–72 (*SIG* 748; *MRR* II.112).

vi ... iudicia a reference to Autronius' attempts to halt his trial by violence in 66 (§ 15). There is little doubt that the archetype read *vi conatum et armis* etc.; *T* copied *et* too soon (after *vi*), but the scribe saw his mistake and deleted the word; β moved *conatum* to after *armis*; and *K* substituted *ornatum* for *conatum*. We have to decide whether to emend *conatum* (as *K* has done) or to delete the word (following Lambinus). Clark printed *comitatu*, without *vi*, but *vi* ought certainly to be retained in view of the frequency of the expression *vi et armis*. Pabón (11), pointing out that Autronius' attempts were not successful (§ 15 *ille ambitus iudicium tollere ac disturbare ... voluit*), proposed *vi conari*: i.e. it was Autronius' practice 'to *attempt* to break up courts'. This conjecture prompted Kasten (1966) to print *vi ⟨esse⟩ conatum*, which brings into play the deleted *et* in *T*; however, this gives the wrong tense, since *quem exturbare ... succumbere* is dependent on *solitum esse scimus* (if ⟨*esse*⟩ *conatum* were seen as replacing *solitum esse*, the following infinitives would have to be dependent on ⟨*esse*⟩ *conatum*). Other conjectures include *vi ornatum* by C. A. Lehmann (*Hermes* 15 (1880) 349; pre-empted by *K*) and Kasten's previous (1933, 1949) suggestion, ⟨*vidimus, quem*⟩ *vi conantem* (which spoils the *esse videatur* rhythm at *fana sociorum*; cf. R. G. M. Nisbet, *CR* n.s. 8 (1958) 285). Professor M. Winterbottom suggests to me *vi comitum*; although neat, this moves the blame away from Autronius. I also considered *vi comitia*, which would refer to Autronius' intended massacre at the consular *comitia* in 63 (§ 51); but this would create an undesirable, although not impossible, separation (in sense) between *vi ... et armis*. Ultimately the choice seems to be between Pabón's *vi conari* and deletion; not convinced that a reference to 'attempting' is desirable, I have opted for deletion. *conatum* is easily explained as a gloss intended to complete the sense.

71.12   in bonis rebus ... bonos cf. Pl. *Trin.* 446; *Amic.* 64 *aut si in bonis rebus contemnunt aut in malis deserunt*. For *boni* see 1.10n.

71.13   non ... cedere cf. *Cat.* 1.22 *ut temporibus rei publicae cedas non est postulandum.*

71.14   non ... succumbere *fortuna* (73.4n.) in Autronius' case is his conviction *de ambitu* in 66, to which his reaction was insufficiently submissive (§ 15). Curiously, *non fortunae succumbere* is elsewhere seen as a laudable course of action in that it exemplifies *fortitudo*; cf. *Deiot.* 36; *Tusc.* 3.36; *Off.* 1.66; *Fam.* 9.11.1. But here *ipsi* makes a difference: by personifying *fortunae*, *ipsi* brings out the futility of Autronius' resistance.

71.15   mores...ac vita see 69.2n.

XXVI 72.1   Agedum, conferte Cicero begins the argument for which he has been preparing since § 69, that Sulla's past record implies his innocence (§§ 72–5). *agedum*, used with reference to plural as well as singular addressees, is found elsewhere in Cicero only at *Scaur.* fr. (*m*) Clark (*agitedum*, used by Livy, does not occur in Cicero); cf. *TLL* 1.1405.67ff.; K.-S.1.59f., 201; Riemann 554 n. 2.

cum illius vita vitam cf. *quam posse debet civis civi dare* (below, § 72); *Sul.* 74 *conferte crimen cum vita, vitam...recognoscite*; *Phil.* 2.7 *tollere ex vita vitae societatem*. The polyptoton shows life being compared side by side with life. I assume that *Tω* between them give the reading of the archetype (already conjectured by Angelius): *T* has *cum illius vita*, and ω *cum illius vitam*. Alternatively, it is conceivable that ω is correct (with *vita* understood after *illius*). Madvig (*Adv. Crit.* 11.536 n.1) preferred the reading of *T*, with *vitam* understood, but this is ruled out by *notissimam*.

72.3   ante...proponite a common phrase; cf. *Ver.* 3.58; *Clu.* 11; *Dom.* 11; *Balb.* 65; *N.D.* 1.114; *Phil.* 11.13.

72.4   commissum 'undertaking' (*OLD* s.v. 1); the word is used as a substantive through the influence of *factum*.

audacius see 16.4n.

72.5   videretur the breaking of the sequence of tenses (*est* precedes) has often been commented on: see Lebreton 252f.; K.-S.11.185; Handford 38 (also commentators). The reason is that Cicero has mentally slipped from *est...factum* 'there is a deed' to *est ... factum* 'something has been done'. Kayser proposed *consideratum videatur*, giving a hexameter ending rhythm (cf. Zielinski 204); *consideratum esse videatur* would have produced a more satisfactory clausula.

factum quaero? another instance of *correctio* (51.10n.).

72.6   ex ore...excidit cf. *Dom.* 104 *ex isto ore religionis verbum excidere aut elabi potest?* See *TLL* v.2.1236.42ff.

72.7   in illa...victoria the language is characteristic of Cicero in his allusions (e.g. *Font.* 6 *turbulentissimo rei publicae tempore*) to L. Sulla's victory over the Marians in 82; cf. Achard 94f.; Diehl 167f. The *victoria* was *gravis* because it was won against Romans and followed by proscriptions. On Cicero's view of the dictator see R. T. Ridley, *WS* n.f. 9 (1975) 83–108; V. Buchheit, *Historia* 24 (1975) 570–91; Diehl.

72.8   quis P. Sulla...inventus est? this picture of Sulla is famously contradicted by *Off.* 2.29 *hastam illam cruentam ... quam P. Sulla cum vibrasset dictatore propinquo suo, idem sexto tricesimo anno post a sceleratiore hasta non recessit* (cf. Ross 77–9; Diehl 12). For Sulla's participation in Caesar's auctions (46) see also *Fam.* 15.17.2, 15.19.3, 9.10.3. Reid deleted *quis misericordior inventus est?* (*E*: om. *Τω*) as 'surely a gloss' (App. A); but the clausula (resolved molossus-cretic) is Ciceronian.

72.9 quam...deprecatus! *quam*, omitted by the MSS, is provided by Gel. 7.16.6 in a discussion of the verb *deprecari*, here 'try to obtain by prayer' (*TLL* v.1.600.4ff.), the opposite of 'beg off' (as in *Ver.* 5.125 *mortem...deprecaretur*). Hinard (58f.) affirms that no cases are known of the removal of a name from a list once it had been posted; probably, then, Cicero pictures Sulla merely as having asked his uncle not to include certain names. It is possible that Sulla acquired part of his wealth by exploiting his influence with the dictator: he could have taken bribes from those whom he claimed (whether truthfully or not) the dictator intended to proscribe, and he may even have threatened to have names entered in the lists unless those in question paid up (in which case his services would have resembled the *beneficium latronum* of *Phil.* 2.5). Cicero's refusal to give names certainly invites suspicion, and had Sulla declined to use his influence to his own advantage Cicero would surely not have let slip the opportunity of saying so. Nepos is more convincing when he asserts that during the proscriptions of 43 Atticus might have used his influence with Antony to increase his wealth, but refused to do so: *cuius gratia cum augere possessiones posset suas, tantum afuit a cupiditate pecuniae, ut nulla in re usus sit ea nisi in deprecandis amicorum aut periculis aut incommodis* (Nep. *Att.* 12.2).

72.11 equestris ordinis cf. *Clu.* 151 *pro illo odio quod habuit in equestrem ordinem.* The view that Sulla was motivated by a hatred of the equestrian order is no longer acceptable; cf. E. Gabba, *Athenaeum* 34 (1956) 124–38; P. A. Brunt, *Latomus* 15 (1956) 17–25; Nicolet 581–91; Hinard 61, 119.

72.12 quos ego nominarem Cicero says he has names but declines to give them: an example of *reticentia* (22.10n.).

72.13 sed quia...ipsi i.e. the saving of lives in this way is a greater favour than should be possible in a free state, therefore attribute to the evil of the times the fact that Sulla had such influence, but attribute to Sulla the fact that he used this influence as a force for good (for the topic cf. Sen. *Ben.* 2.20.3). A reason is expected after *quos ego nominarem* for Cicero's refusal to name those whom Sulla saved; at *sed quia...dare* the reason is hinted at, but Cicero then moves in a different direction and in the end fails to justify himself. As Hinard (59) remarks, 'on ne peut être plus évasif!'

73.1 quid...commemorem an instance of *occultatio*, where supposed omission is used as a means of covertly introducing arguments or assertions which will not stand up to more direct scrutiny (Cicero does not give evidence for the qualities he attributes to Sulla); cf. *Rhet. Her.* 4.37; S. Usher, *AJP* 86 (1965) 175–92 (lists Ciceronian instances). The technique resembles *praeteritio* (14.12n.) and *reticentia* (22.10n.). A further example occurs below at §75.

relicuam has to be taken in sense with *vitae*, which led Clark to adopt Richter's *relicuae*, citing §88 *quae solacia relicuae vitae* (the parallel is questionable, since at §88 the MSS are equally divided between *relicuae* and *relicua*, and in any case the order is different; cf. 88.6n.). Hypallage, however, is not unknown in Cicero, and is supported in this instance by *Cat.* 3.3 *relicuam coniuratorum manum*; cf. Müller's apparatus to *Agr.* 2.8; K.-S.I.221.

73.2 liberalitatem no instances are known, besides Sulla's bribery in 66 and his payment to Cicero for undertaking his defence (Gel. 12.12.2). It is possible that he had shown *liberalitas* towards the people of Pompeii.

73.3 moderationem...in publicis cf. *Mur.* 76 *odit populus Romanus privatam luxuriam, publicam magnificentiam diligit; Flac.* 28 *haec enim ratio ac magnitudo animorum in maioribus nostris fuit ut, cum in privatis rebus suisque sumptibus minimo contenti tenuissimo cultu viverent, in imperio atque in publica dignitate omnia ad gloriam splendoremque revocarent.* The topos also occurs at Dem. 3.25–6, 13.28–9, 23.206–8 (Weische 73–5); Sal. *Cat.* 9.2, 52.22; Muson. 19 (= 109 Hense); cf. R. G. M. Nisbet and M. Hubbard on Hor. *Carm.* 2.15.15. *splendor* occurs here in its common sense of 'magnificence' (contrast §1, 'spotlessness'): see T. E. Kinsey on *Quinct.* 72 (quoting *Planc.* 30); Hellegouarc'h 458–61. It was not an exclusively equestrian attribute (3.2n.): see *Clu.* 154 (quoted at 50.2n.); *Fam.* 1.7.7.

73.4 quae...compareant ω places *a fortuna* before, and *T* after, *deformata sunt.* The rhythm would favour ω (molossus-cretic, as against a series of long syllables), but to my mind the order of *T* better brings out the contrast between *fortuna* and *natura.* The metaphor concerns a visible object, now disfigured but still displaying the qualities it possessed before disfigurement. Reid takes the object to be a sketch, but *deformata...incohata* seems to suggest a statue or portrait bust which has been defaced (cf. *Mur.* 88 *eam imaginem clarissimi viri ... deformatam ignominia*: full quotation at 88.8n.); for the face as the mirror of character see 15.7n. (cf. §74 *aspicite ipsum, contuemini os*).

At this point *fortuna* becomes a more prominent theme of the speech, as Cicero looks back over Sulla's life (declining, however, to contrast his ill-fortune with the proverbial 'luck' of his uncle) and ahead to the outcome of the trial. Besides raising the emotional pitch, mention of *fortuna* serves to absolve Sulla of responsibility for his past misdemeanours by presenting him as a tragic victim of circumstances beyond his control. It also flatters the jury by reminding them that they are now the arbiters of Sulla's *fortuna*: they have been put in the position of the *deus ex machina*. This idea implicit in Cicero's references to *fortuna* is brought out more strongly at *Clu.* 195, where Cicero appeals to *vos, iudices, quos huic A. Cluentio quosdam alios deos...fortuna esse voluit*; cf. *Rab. Perd.* 5; *Mur.* 2; *Mil.* 44.

73.5   quae domus...cotidiana cf. *Mur.* 70; *Pis.* 64; *Att.* 2.22.3; *Q. fr.* 2.4.6. The more prominent a Roman senator was, the greater would be the number of clients and visitors at the early morning *salutatio*. See J. Marquardt, *Das Privatleben der Römer*² (Leipzig 1886) 259f.; J. P. V. D. Balsdon, *Life and Leisure in Ancient Rome* (London 1969) 21-4. *quae domus* is perhaps a little feeble in comparison with the following units, and it is tempting to accept Jordan's deletion of *quae* before *celebratio*, making *domus* genitive: a copyist may have taken *domus* as nominative and interpolated *quae*. But the objections to *quae* are not quite sufficient to justify deletion.

73.6   quae familiarium dignitas cf. §77 *ex hac familiarium dignitate*.

73.7   diu multumque quite a common phrase in Cicero (seven instances in this formulation).

73.8   multo labore quaesita cf. *Agr.* 2.95; *Fin.* 2.111; Lucr. 5.213 (U. Pizzani, *Ciceroniana* 5 (1984) 186). On *labor* see 5.4n.

una...hora throughout this section Cicero alludes to Sulla's conviction *de ambitu* in 66.

73.9   verum tamen he received a wound, but it was a wound of the type to which an ambitious man such as he seemed liable.

73.11   honestatis...cupiditatem euphemistic. *honestatis* means 'public honour', *dignitatis* 'office' (1.1n.). For the nominative and infinitive *habuisse...iudicatus est* see K.-S.1.708; H.-Sz.363-5.

73.12   quam si nemo Cicero presents the situation in the form of a *complexio* (10.3n.) in which Autronius is forgotten.

73.15   fortuna see 73.4n.

74.1   adflictumque in a series of three (or more) terms otherwise unconnected, *-que* is sometimes used to attach the last (*OLD* s.v. *-que*¹ 2b); cf. *S. Rosc.* 31; *Mur.* 1; *Rep.* 2.50; *Tusc.* 1.80.

74.3   lucemque vitare cf. *Ver.* 5.28; *Phil.* 3.24; also *Fin.* 1.61 *lucifugi*.

74.5   quae...restiterunt Sulla's friends remained loyal, unlike those of Autronius (§7, but see §19); Sylvius aptly compares Ennius, *amicus certus in re incerta cernitur* (*scen.* 351 Jocelyn (ap. *Amic.* 64)). Sauppe

moved *tamen* to after *afuit*, but *tamen* does make sense where it stands
('which were however the only things to remain ...'). For *quae...sola ...
restiterunt* cf. *S. Rosc.* 140 *quod solum prope in civitate sincerum sanctumque restat*;
O. Müller unnecessarily proposed *solida* (*Hermes* 12 (1877) 301).

74.6 afuit cf. *Luc.* 3 *afuit ab oculis et fori et curiae*; *Att.* 13.21A.2. *Ta* give
affuit; for similar confusions see §§ 7, 14 and 53.

cum lege retineretur the *lex Calpurnia* (67) under which Sulla was
convicted did not prescribe exile: this was added subsequently by Cicero's *lex Tullia* (63). See 17.8n.

XXVII 74.7 iudices the reading of *E*, previously unknown, hap-
pily confirms Angelius' emendation; see my note at *CQ* n.s. 39 (1989)
406.

74.8 creditis Clark accepts Zielinski's (204) *credatis*, which avoids
five consecutive *iambi* (cf. 5.4n.). But I am unwilling to alter the text for
this reason alone.

74.9 contuemini os for the face as revealing character see 15.7n.

cum vita, vitam cf. §72 *conferte nunc cum illius vita vitam P. Sullae*
(72.1n.).

75.1 mitto rem publicam an example of *occultatio* (73.1n.); cf. S.
Usher, *AJP* 86 (1965) 181.

75.2 cupidos sui *cupidus* + gen. may indicate political or personal
devotion to a person, and often both senses are felt. Here the personal
sense ('fond', Reid; 'devoted', Lord) rather than the political sense ('such
eager supporters', Macdonald) is appropriate; cf. *Sest.* 45; *de Orat.* 1.104;
Planc. 55.

75.3 ornatae cf. *Arch.* 16; *Fam.* 5.13.5 *ea quibus secundae res ornantur,
adversae adiuvantur*. The word is given as *ordinatae* in *Tω*: see 53.5n. on the
confusion.

75.4 Lentulo see 16.3n.

75.5 Cethego see 53.3n.

75.6 morte i.e. execution, when brought to justice.

non ... cadit in cf. *Cael.* 76 *sed ego non loquor de sapientia, quae non cadit
in hanc aetatem*. It is unnecessary to read, with Stephanus' MS, *non ⟨cadit
non⟩ inquam cadit in* (Stephanus 92); *inquam* is often used with repetitions,
but often also not (cf. Merguet II.713f.).

75.9 Nova ... exorta est Cicero has finished the central argument
of *confirmatio* I, that Sulla's past record implies his innocence (§§ 72–5).
Now for a contrast he turns to the characters of the Catilinarians (§§ 75–
6). These were treated individually at §§ 70–1; here they are attacked as
a group. On *immanitas* see 7.10n.; and on the metaphor (birth of monsters), 67.4n.

75.10 ex multis ... exarsit cf.§ 76 *ex magnis ... erupit*; *Brut.* 283

metuens... ne vitiosum colligeret, etiam verum sanguinem deperdebat. On *perditi* see 1.12n.

76.1 arbitrari *arbitrare* (*T*) may possibly be correct, as Kasten suggests. The active is found once between Plautus and ecclesiastical Latin, at *N.D.* 2.74: see A. S. Pease *ad loc.* It is also given by Paris lat. 7794 at *Prov.* 42.

76.2 neque... sit inventus cf. *Cat.* 3.25 *quale bellum nulla umquam barbaria cum sua gente gessit.* For *hostis patriae* see 15.7n.

76.4 beluae... exstiterunt stock terms of abuse in Cicero (cf. R. G. M. Nisbet on *Pis.*, p. 196); on *belua* see Opelt 143f.; A. Cossarini, *GFF* 4 (1981) 123–34; A. Traina, *RFIC* 112 (1984) 115–19. For the contrast between animals and men cf. *Cat.* 2.20; *Pis.* fr. xiv Nisbet *te tua... mater pecudem ex alvo, non hominem effuderit* (misquoted at Serv. *A.* 8.139); *Off.* 3.82 *quid enim interest utrum ex homine se convertat quis in beluam an hominis figura immanitatem gerat beluae?* (for further examples see Otto 55f.; Hofmann 158; C. Weyman, *ALL* 13 (1904) 266). D. R. Shackleton Bailey has indicated the possibility of corruption at *ex portentis* ('born of prodigies'): see *HSCP* 83 (1979) 260. However, his solution *et portenta* (cf. *Mil.* 63 *Catilinam atque illa portenta*) entails agreement of the adjectives with the remoter substantive. This is not of course impossible, but too unusual (I think) to introduce into the text; cf. Lebreton 23; K.-S.1.53. On the birth of monsters see again 67.4n.

76.8 Catilinae... Lentuli generalised accusations are now made against the same four conspirators as were treated individually at §§ 70–71. Catiline's *flagitia*, *stupra* and *caedes* are listed at 70.7n. For Autronius' crimes see §§ 15–20 and 71, with notes. For Cethegus see 53.3n.; 70.13n.; for Lentulus, 16.3n.; 70.10nn.

76.9 libidines... audacias see 16.4n.

76.11 facinorum... scelerum either *T* or ω has inverted these words; a decision is difficult, but perhaps *scelerum* is the more powerful of the two and should come later. If the words were a line apart in the exemplar of *T*ω that would be a reason for their inversion; cf. Pabón 8f., who compares §§ 3, 77. On *notas* (marks of disgrace) see 88.4n. For *parricidium* see 6.12n.; Cicero is thinking primarily of Catiline. On the metaphorical uses of *acervus* see *TLL* 1.376.28ff.; cf. *Scaur.* fr. (*g*) Clark *acervo quodam criminum*; V. Max. 1.8 *quorum* [sc. *miraculorum*] *e magno acervo.*

76.12 ex magnis... posset cf. § 75 *ex multis... exarsit.* The Catilinarian conspiracy was likened to a *morbus* at § 53, and here the image is developed: the plague was thought incurable (*desperatis* is used in a medical sense; cf. *TLL* v.1.742.29ff.), but the sudden discharge of its force enabled the state to recover (*convalescere*) and be healed (*sanari*). The MSS give *confecta et eiecta*, taken by Halm (who compares *Cat.* 2.2),

Reid and Macdonald as a reference to the digestion and expulsion of food; but this does not fit with the medical imagery. *confecta* would have to mean 'destroyed' (thus *TLL* iv.204.52f.), but this does not reflect the situation which Cicero describes: Rome did not recover once Catiline and his followers had been '*destroyed* and ejected' (this inverts the natural order) but when they had been '*collected* and ejected'. I have therefore written *collecta et eiecta*, essentially a change of one letter (*conlecta*). The image thus describes the force of the disease being concentrated together (*collecta*) and purged, a common means of treatment in the ancient world: once the suppuration (the Catilinarians) had been drawn off, the patient (the state) could return to health. For *colligere* used of diseases see *TLL* iii.1614.44ff.; cf. §75 *ex multis ab adulescentia collectis perditorum hominum vitiis* (also Larg. 229 *cum umoribus postea vitium veluti eiciebatur*, on the treatment of abscesses). Plutarch's description of the situation at Rome in January 49 should also be compared: ἤδη τῶν πραγμάτων ὥσπερ ὑπὸ φλεγμονῆς ἀφισταμένων ἐπὶ τὸν ἐμφύλιον πόλεμον (*Cic.* 36.6). The imagery of sickness and healing is frequently used by Cicero with reference to the state (e.g. *Div. Caec.* 70 *hoc remedium est aegrotae ac prope desperatae rei publicae*) and in connection with the Catilinarian conspiracy. A notable instance is *Cat.* 1.31 (Catiline's execution rejected as inexpedient because the relief from the *morbus qui est in re publica* which it would provide would be purely temporary); cf. *Cat.* 2.11 *quae sanari poterunt quacumque ratione sanabo, quae resecanda erunt non patiar ad perniciem civitatis manere*; *Cat.* 2.17, 2.25, 3.14, 4.2; *Sul.* 28. Sallust writes *tanta vis morbi atque uti tabes plerosque civium animos invaserat* (*Cat.* 36.5). Other metaphors worth noticing are *sin tu ... exieris, exhaurietur ex urbe tuorum comitum magna et perniciosa sentina rei publicae* (*Cat.* 1.12; cf. 2.7); *dicit* [sc. *Cato*] *enim tamquam in Platonis* πολιτείᾳ, *non tamquam in Romuli faece, sententiam* (*Att.* 2.1.8). See further Fantham 14–18; Pöschl 507f.; *TLL* viii.1482.18ff.; also 6.11n. on *contagio*. On *erumpere* see 67.4n.

76.17 haec stare cf. *Cat.* 4.16 *qui non haec stare cupiat*; *Pis.* 15 *his stantibus*; *Att.* 12.19.1 *si modo haec stabunt*. *haec* is 'Rome and her empire': see 32.7n.

76.18 Furiae conventionally the Furies are seen as avengers, and rationalised as the terrors of a guilty conscience; cf. *S. Rosc.* 66–7; *Ver.* 5.113; *Har.* 39; *Pis.* fr. iv Nisbet, 46–7; *Leg.* 1.40; *Parad.* 18; *N.D.* 3.46 (also E. Courtney on Juv. 13.192 sqq.). Cicero has been arguing that the conspirators were not ordinary criminals, they were madmen. This madness (*furor* (§75)), he now explains, did not drive them to carry out their intended destruction of Rome (*ad perficiendum scelus*); instead, it drove them to pay the price for their wickedness, by causing them to bring on themselves their own destruction. Truly the Furies must have been at work. In this passage Cicero is concerned as much to justify the execution of the conspirators as to contrast them with the innocent Sulla; mention of the Furies serves to transfer responsibility for the executions from Cicero to the conspirators themselves.

XXVIII 77.1 In ... gregem Cicero now gives a brief review of the implications of a guilty verdict; see C. J. Classen, Entretiens 163 n. 4 for a list of places where the jury are reminded of the consequences of their decision. Cicero often thus uses *grex* pejoratively (see Fantham 56; Achard 139); cf. *Cat.* 2.10 *desperatorum hominum flagitiosi greges*; *Cat.* 2.23 *in his gregibus omnes aleatores, omnes adulteri, omnes impuri impudicique versantur*; *Mur.* 74; *Sul.* 66; *Dom.* 24; *Pis.* 22 *tuis sordidissimis gregibus*; *Att.* 1.14.5 *totus ille grex Catilinae* (also *Dom.* 75 *Catilinae gregales*). But the word is also used in contexts where a pejorative sense would be out of place (e.g. *Fin.* 1.65 *amicorum greges*; *Amic.* 69 *in nostro ... grege*; *Att.* 1.18.1 *gregibus amicorum*; cf. V. Max. 4.7.7 *totumque beatae turbae gregem*), and this is clearly the situation at *ex his ... honestissimorum hominum gregibus* below. Cicero, then, is playing with the different ways in which the word may be used; alteration of *gregibus* (Reid suggested *coetibus*) is unwarranted.

77.2 atque vixerunt *aut* (*T*), as Richter points out, would imply that some of Sulla's friends no longer associated with him: either *ac* (β) or *atque* (δ) must be correct. The rhythm favours *atque*, giving a cretic-spondee in place of a series of long syllables; for *atque* before consonants see pp. 53f. *T* may also have written *aut* in error for *atque* at §46 (46.8n.).

hominum ... amicorum *T* inverts these two words, while ω gives *hominum* in both places. The inversion perhaps took place in the exemplar of *T*ω, where the words may have been a line apart; cf. Pabón 9, who compares §§3, 76. Pabón, however, goes too far in suggesting *hominum honestissimorum*, in order to separate *hominum* and *amicorum* further (although the collocation *hominum honestissimorum* is indeed more common; cf. Merguet II.501f.).

77.3 ex hac ... dignitate cf. §73 *quae familiarium dignitas*.

77.4 in impiorum partem cf. *Att.* 14.13.2 *haec pars perditorum*. For *pars* see 9.4n.

in parricidarum ... numerum cf. *Clu.* 171 *ut existimemus illum ad inferos impiorum supplicia perferre ... a liberum Poenis actum esse praecipitem in sceleratorum sedem atque regionem.* Halm suggests that our passage may also refer to the underworld, but Cicero probably now has in mind not so much the executed Catilinarians as those of them who upon conviction had gone into exile. For *parricidae* see 19.9n.

77.6 firmissimum ... pudoris cf. *Ver.* 5.34 *quot praesidia, quam munita pudoris et pudicitiae vi et audacia ceperit.* ω miscopies *firmissimum* as *fortissimum*; cf. §51 *praesidio firmo* (Merguet II.353).

loco 'occasion' (2.7n.).

77.7 existimationis...fructus cf. *Clu.* 39 *non ullum existimationis bonae fructum umquam cogitarat. existimationis* is used passively ('good reputation'), as are other verbal nouns formed from the participle in -*t*-, which normally have an active sense; cf. Nägelsbach 243-6.

77.8 si...deseret Richter and Kasten (1933) felt the want of an object: Richter inserted *nos* after *si* (a possibility given some support by *T*'s *si non* for *si in*), whereas Kasten read *deseruerit nos* (again supported by *T*, which after *deserit* continues *nsi* [sic] *non aderit*). *deserere* may however be used absolutely (cf. *Inv.* 2.112 *si tum, cum spes deseruisset*), especially in a military sense ('desert'): see *TLL* v.1.683.50ff.; *OLD* s.v. 2d. Here the image is military (*in ... discrimine ac dimicatione*) and there is no need to conjure an object out of the idiosyncrasies of *T*. Doubts are raised also over the tense of the verb, but it is fairly clear that a future is required to match the other verbs (all future) in the sentence: it is a small change from *deserit* of the archetype to *deseret* (*k*). The future perfect *deseruerit* (*q mg.*, Petrarch) is printed by some editors but this weakens the molossus-cretic rhythm. Halm (1856) attempted to resolve both problems simultaneously by reading *si non extremo* [as in *T*]...*deserviet*, but this is unsatisfactory (cf. Madvig, *Adv. Crit.* ii.210 n. 1; K.Nipperdey, *Opuscula* (Berlin 1877) 174f.), and further from *deserit*. On *fortuna* see 73.4n.

78.1 Quaestiones...minitatur in §§78-9 Cicero looks forward to the evidence to be extracted from Sulla's slaves (*Quaestiones ... servorum*) and taken from witnesses, comparing its reliability unfavourably with that of the evidence provided by Sulla's past record. In contrast to Athenian practice, evidence in a Roman trial was taken after the speeches (cf. *Ver.* 55 *cum omnia dicta sunt testes dantur*; Quint. *Inst.* 5.7.25), as is reflected by Cicero's occasional references forward to evidence not yet given (*S. Rosc.* 82, 84, 100-2; *Clu.* 18; *Cael.* 19-20, 63, 66-7; *Rab. Post.* 31; but note that in *repetundae* trials reference may be made in the *actio secunda* to evidence given at the end of the *actio prima*). As at Athens, slaves could be compelled to give evidence or confess their guilt only under torture; how frequently this practice was resorted to in Cicero's time is unclear, but a significant limitation on the use of slaves lay in the rule that, except in cases involving incest (*Mil.* 59; *Part.* 118), slaves were not permitted to testify against their master (*S. Rosc.* 120; *Deiot.* 3). However, an exception appears to have been made in the specific case of the Catilinarian trials (*Part.* 118); Sulla's slaves, therefore, could have been compelled to give evidence against him, if the prosecution wished, and it is this possibility which has led Cicero to argue the worthlessness of such evidence. The value of evidence gained by torture was a familiar *locus communis*, although it seems in fact to have been at least as common to argue in favour of the efficaciousness of torture as against it; cf. Arist. *Rh.* 1.15 (1376 b 31ff.); [Arist.] *Rh. Al.* 16; *Inv.* 2.50; *Rhet. Her.* 2.10; *Part.* 50, 117–8; *Top.* 74; Quint. *Inst.* 5.4.1–2; Anon. Seguer. 190 (=1.2.386 Spengel-Hammer); Volkmann 182f.; Martin 101. For the application see Antiph. 5.31–2, 6.25; Is. 8.12; Isoc. 17.54; Dem. 30.37; *Deiot.* 3; cf. *S. Rosc.* 77–8, 119–20; *Clu.* 176–7; *Cael.* 68; *Mil.* 57–60; Quint. (?) *Decl.* 269, 328, 338, 353; [Quint.] *Decl.* 7; cf. Rohde 152. See further *dig.* 48.18, *cod. Iust.* 9.41 (*de quaestionibus*); Greenidge 479f., 491–3; M. I. Finley, *Ancient Slavery and Modern Ideology* (London 1980) 94f. (citing the *lex locationis* of Puteoli (II.8–14), published by L. Bove in *Labeo* 13 (1967) 43–8); and on Athenian law, A. P. Dorjahn, *CJ* 47 (1951–2) 188; E. W. Bushala, *GRBS* 9 (1968) 61–8; C. Carey, *Historia* 37 (1988) 241–5.

For *accusator et tormenta* (*T*), ω reads *ac tormenta accusator*. The order of *T* is shown to be authentic by the rhythm. Cicero has chosen *minitatur* instead of *minatur* in order to finish the sentence with an *esse videatur* clausula rather than a hexameter ending; but if the order of ω is adopted, it is the hexameter ending after all which is produced. The dislocation of *accusator* in ω is presumably a normalisation. Kasten (1933 preface xvii; 1949, vii) infers from the mistake of ω that the archetype also read *ac*, but this does not follow. Either conjunction could be correct; I choose *et* on the grounds that *ac* is likely to have been conditioned by *accusator*.

78.3 gubernat dolor Cicero implies not that torture is inherently cruel, but that it produces unreliable evidence.

moderatur . . . corporis i.e. slaves will differ in their ability (mental and physical) to resist pain; cf. *Rhet. Her.* 2.10 *dolori credi non oportere, quod alius alio recentior sit in dolore*; *Part.* 50 *alii autem aut natura corporis aut consuetudine dolendi . . . vim tormentorum pertulerint*; Quint. *Inst.* 5.4.1 *quod aliis patientia facile mendacium faciat*. The *cum . . . tum* correlation (1.4n.) puts greater emphasis on *corporis*, appropriately, than on *animi*.

78.4 quaesitor the official in charge of the *quaestio servorum*, who supervised the activities of the *tortor* (Greenidge 492); cf. *Rhet. Her.* 2.10 *dolori credi non oportere . . . quod denique saepe scire aut suspicari possit quid quaesitor velit audire*; Quint. *Inst.* 5.4.2.

78.5 corrumpit . . . metus slaves will tell lies either in the hope of *praemia* (e.g. freedom) or from fear of further torture and execution; cf. *Clu.* 176 *cum essent animi servorum et spe et metu temptati ut aliquid in quaestione dicerent, tamen . . . in veritate manserunt*. The possibility that slaves might lie in the hope of being released from their torture is the most prominent of the arguments against torture offered by the rhetoricians; cf. Arist. *Rh.* 1.15 (1377 a 3–5) οὐδὲν γὰρ ἧττον ἀναγκαζόμενοι τὰ ψευδῆ λέγουσιν ἢ τἀληθῆ . . . ῥᾳδίως καταψευδόμενοι ὡς παυσόμενοι θᾶττον; [Arist.]

COMMENTARY: xxviii 78–79

*Rh.Al.*16 ἔπειθ' ὅτι πολλάκις τοῖς βασανίζουσιν ὁμολογοῦσιν οὐ τὰς ἀληθείας, ἵν' ὡς τάχιστα τῶν κακῶν παύσωνται; *Part.* 50 *saepe etiam quaestionibus resistendum est, quod et dolorem fugientes multi in tormentis ementiti persaepe sint morique maluerint falsum fatendo, quam verum dicendo dolere*; Quint. *Inst.* 5.4.1.

78.6 nihil... relinquatur a different view is given at *Deiot.* 3 *in qua quaestione dolor elicere veram vocem possit etiam ab invito.*

vita... torqueatur a return to the *probabile ex vita. torqueatur* surely alludes to the prosecutor's name (*q* actually miscopies the word as *torquate*, and *a* just avoids doing so). Holst 47–50 lists Ciceronian instances of play on proper names (cf. *Div.* 2.1 *cohortati sumus... Hortensius*); see also V. J. Matthews, *G&R* 20 (1973) 20–24.

78.7 libido i.e. the sort of passion which might have driven him to join the conspiracy.

78.8 crudelitas... audacia see 7.10n.; 16.4n.

erroris... obscuritatis cf. *Luc.* 147 ⟨*de*⟩ *obscuritate naturae, deque errore tot philosophorum*; *Fam.* 6.6.7.

78.10 verissima et gravissima *Pa* give *gravissima et verissima*, but the omission of *et verissima* in *Kq* implies that in ω *et verissima* was placed in the margin. *T* therefore presumably preserves the original order.

debet esse Cicero has chosen this order not to emphasise *esse* (thus Reid; it is difficult to see how emphasis on *esse* could affect the meaning), but to avoid seven consecutive trochees at the end of the sentence (cf. 5.4n.).

79.1 nullum... testem having compared the evidence to be extracted from slaves unfavourably with the evidence of Sulla's *vita*, Cicero now does the same to the testimony of the prosecution's witnesses, which will also be taken after the speeches (78.1n.).

79.3 fortuna see 73.4n.

vestra moveat Cicero returns to the consequences of the verdict, and appeals to the self-interest of the jurors: being honourable men themselves, it is not in their interest to lay down a precedent whereby honourable men may be ruined by dishonest witnesses. A similar point was made above at §77 *ubi erit... adiuvabit?*

79.4 vestra enim, qui an antecedent is not expressed, but has to be inferred from *vestra*; cf. *Cat.* 1.7; *Sul.* 80 *haec auctoritas nostra, qui... abstinuimus*; *Vat.* 29; *Planc.* 11; *Fam.* 2.11.1. See Ernout-Thomas 140f.; K.-S.1.30f.

elegantia 'discrimination', 'choosiness where associates are concerned'; cf. *Att.* 6.2.8 *ain tandem, Attice, laudator integritatis et elegantiae nostrae?*; *Planc.* 31; *Brut.* 295; *Senect.* 13; Liv. 35.31.14. See Nägelsbach 41 n. Cicero is flattering the jury.

291

79.5 ex libidine . . . testium Cicero employs the *locus communis contra testes*; cf. *Inv.* 2.50 *testibus credi oportere et non oportere*; *Rhet. Her.* 2.9 *contra testes . . . testimoniorum inconstantiam*; *Part.* 49 *nam et de toto genere testium quam id sit infirmum saepe dicendum est*; *Part.* 117; Quint. *Inst.* 5.7.3–7 (5.7.3 *in actionibus primum generaliter pro testibus atque in testis dici solet*); Volkmann 186–90; Martin 99f. Examples of its use in Cicero (e.g. *Cael.* 22, *Scaur.* 15, quoted at 79.13n. below) are listed at C. J. Classen, Entretiens 159 n. 2; Rohde 150–2.

79.7 disquisitionibus 'investigations', 'inquiries'; cf. *Rhet. Her.* 2.41 *vitiosum est pro argumento sumere quod in disquisitione positum est*; *Har.* 13 *quamquam ad facinoris disquisitionem interest adesse quam plurimos*; Liv. 8.23.14 *nec . . . comitia sunt habita, quia vitione creatus esset in disquisitionem venit*; Liv. 26.31.2; Tac. *Ann.* 3.60, 5.11 (*TLL* v.1.1450.79ff.). Madvig objected unnecessarily to the word, proposing *disceptationibus* (*Adv. Crit.* III.135); cf. E. Wölfflin, *ALL* 2 (1885) 144.

79.9 nolite . . . invidiae the imagery recalls that used at §50. *armis* represents the protection afforded by an exemplary *vita*, and therefore means defensive armour (such as would be stripped from a corpse), not 'weapons' (Lord, Macdonald). *arma* is often used metaphorically to refer to moral qualities: see J. G. F. Powell on *Senect.* 9 (*arma senectutis*).

79.10 munite . . . improborum! the military imagery continues; the *arx* (often metaphorical: 33.16n.) represents the same protection as did the *arma* above (previous n.), while the *perfugia* are the 'means of escape' (dishonest *testes* etc.) which will be resorted to by those (*improborum*, 1.12n.) whose *vitae* have been reprehensible.

79.11 valeat . . . plurimum on the importance of *argumenta ex vita* see 69.10n. Although preserved in β alone, *vita* must be correct; the word cannot be inferred from above because of the interposition of *munite . . . improborum!*, and its removal from this position (Jeep placed it before *valeat*) would impair the cretic-iambus rhythm. The omission of *vita* is easily explained after *salutē*: see Seyffert 24. The word was probably omitted by *Tδ* independently (thus Clark xiv). Kasten (1933 preface xii) attributed its occurrence in *P* to conjecture, and later (1949, v; 1966, vi), less plausibly, to contamination: see pp. 71f.

79.13 ipsam Mommsen's *per se* (adopted by Clark *et al.*) seems gratuitous; *ipsam* (ω) makes excellent sense.

subito . . . non posse cf. §69 *neque enim potest quisquam nostrum subito fingi neque cuiusquam repente vita mutari aut natura converti* (69.12n.). For the alliteration *flecti fingique* cf. *Cael.* 22 *in voluntate testium . . . quae facillime fingi, nullo negotio flecti ac detorqueri potest*; *Scaur.* 15 *testis . . . fingi, flecti potest*; *Brut.* 142.

§§80–85 CONFIRMATIO II

Is Cicero's auctoritas *to count for nothing, when he has refused to defend the others charged with conspiracy? This claim may seem offensive; but Cicero must defend his* dignitas. *The prosecution have criticised the consulars for their support of Catiline in earlier trials; Cicero defends their past conduct and praises their patriotism. He returns to himself: is it likely that he would defend a conspirator? He does not claim that Sulla should be acquitted simply because he is defending; nevertheless, he would not be defending Sulla if he thought him guilty, and when he was consul he heard nothing which indicated Sulla's involvement in the conspiracy.*

After making the best of Sulla's *ethos*, Cicero brings his own into play. He begins with an explicit appeal to his *auctoritas*, undermined by Torquatus (§§ 2, 35) but effectively reasserted by § 35. After a defence of the consulars (§§ 81–2), which reasserts their *auctoritas*, Cicero again centres the argument on himself: as consul in 63 he was pre-eminently in a position to know whether Sulla was guilty – and he would not knowingly defend a conspirator (§§ 83, 85). The conclusion is left to be inferred: that Sulla is innocent and should be acquitted. Throughout this argument Cicero's integrity is taken as proven, but when he defended his integrity at § 14 he did so by assuming Sulla's innocence. The main argument of the speech is therefore circular, and the question of Sulla's guilt ought instead to be assessed from Cicero's reply to the charges in the *reprehensio*.

Cicero's appeal to his own *auctoritas* is typically Roman: 'a Greek orator tends to argue his audience into believing something; a Roman by his authority convinces the audience that something should be believed because he says so' (Kennedy 42). Here, as earlier in the speech (§§ 10, 14), Cicero seems in effect to appoint himself as judge of Sulla's guilt. Orators who adopted such a stance ran a grave risk of appearing arrogant, as Quintilian observes: *adrogantes et illi qui se iudicasse de causa nec aliter adfuturos fuisse proponunt. Nam et inviti iudices audiunt praesumentem partes suas, nec hoc oratori contingere inter adversarios quod Pythagorae inter discipulos contigit potest: 'ipse dixit'* (*Inst.* 11.1.27). This fits the situation in *pro Sulla* exactly. However, Quintilian adds a qualification, *sed istud magis minusve vitiosum est pro personis dicentium: defenditur enim aliquatenus aetate dignitate auctoritate* (11.1.27–8); Cicero, then, would enjoy greater licence than lesser orators. Nevertheless: *quae tamen vix in ullo tanta fuerint ut non hoc adfirmationis genus temperandum sit aliqua moderatione* (11.1.28). It is interesting to learn from our passage that not even Cicero was exempt from the necessity of taking deliberate steps to prevent his assertions from giving the impression of arrogance (§ 80 *grave est hoc dictu fortasse, iudices, grave;*

§ 84; § 85 *grave esse videtur... non dico id quod grave est*). Cicero was well aware of the dangers of adopting an authoritative tone: he knew exactly how far to go.

On an orator's presentation of his own *ethos* (ἦθος τοῦ λέγοντος) see Arist. *Rh.* 1.2 (1356 a 5–13); *de Orat.* 2.182–4; Quint. *Inst.* 6.2.8–19, 9.2.58–63; W. Süss, *Ethos* (Leipzig and Berlin 1910); Lausberg 141f.; Martin 158–60; May, esp. 76f.

XXIX 80.1 haec auctoritas Cicero introduces the question of his own *auctoritas* (2.3n.), which will not in fact be treated fully until §§ 83–5.

semper ... dicetur as at § 10, Cicero explains that he must discuss his *auctoritas*, but will do so with moderation; cf. *Dom.* 96 *dicendum igitur est id, quod non dicerem nisi coactus*; *Planc.* 24 *timide dicam, sed tamen dicendum est.* It was expected that an orator should make some apology before talking about himself: see W. Allen, *TAPA* 85 (1954) 126–8. The hyperbole of *semper* is problematic: 'for my *auctoritas* must always be spoken of, although by me it shall be spoken of hesitantly and with moderation' (lit.; Macdonald's translation hides the problem). Clark boldly adopted Spengel's *saepe* in place of *semper*. Better in sense is the reading of *E* (recorded by Gulielmius, unknown to editors), *semper iam*, a solution which I formerly considered 'almost certainly correct' (*CQ* n.s. 39 (1989) 407). Professor W. S. Watt, however, has kindly drawn my attention to his article at *CQ* n.s. 30 (1980) 120–23, in which he shows that Cicero will allow *enim* to be displaced from its enclitic position only in certain specific circumstances (cf. 63.12n.): *semper iam enim* would be unparalleled (a similar situation arises at *Senect.* 31 *iam enim tertiam aetatem*, where Paris lat. 6332 and Zurich Rh. 127 give *tertiam iam enim aetatem*). It seems, then, that the reading of *Tω* should be tolerated. Perhaps the difficulty is reduced if *semper* is understood as 'throughout', or 'at every turn' (Reid). Certainly, *semper dicere* (cf. § 33) is a reasonably common idiom (Merguet IV.435), and by nature hyperbolic. See further May 188 n. 88.

80.3 haec auctoritas an example of *regressio* (20.8n.).

qui an antecedent (*nos*) has to be inferred (79.4n.).

80.4 P. Sullam adversative asyndeton.

80.5 grave ... grave ... grave 'offensive' (Long); Cicero returns to this theme in § 85. We miss much at this point through being unable to witness Cicero's delivery. The repetition is of a type known as κύκλος: see Volkmann 471. It is the repeated *grave* which has caused the omission of *grave est... iudices* in *Tω*; cf. Havet § 465. For *grave... dictu* cf. *Planc.* 16; *Phil.* 9.8 *grave dictu est sed dicendum tamen. dictum (E)* was corrected by Madvig (*Adv. Crit.* 1.69f.); cf. Havet § 1010.

80.8 **conceditis** a present tense is more natural in Latin than in English; Halm compares *Ver.* 4.3 *omnes hoc mihi ... facile concedunt.*

80.9 **libertatem** the nearest one-word Latin equivalent of παρρησία (25.12n.); cf. H. Kloesel in Oppermann, 137.

81.1 **accusati sunt ... consulares** the prosecution have stigmatised the consulars who have appeared in support of Sulla as unscrupulous men who will defend anyone: if they previously supported Catiline, their presence now can hardly prove Sulla's innocence. Cicero, therefore, before going on to speak of himself, defends the consulars and reasserts their *auctoritas* (§§ 81–2). Lambinus and Clark felt the want of *omnes*, the former adding it after *sunt*, the latter after *nomine*. It is easy to see how *omnes* could have dropped out after *nomine*; but the passage makes good sense as it stands. For *uno nomine*, 'under one head', see 21.7n.

81.2 **honoris ... nomen** i.e. the consulship; cf. *Red. Sen.* 10 *nomen ipsum consulatus, splendorem illius honoris*; *Phil.* 10.6 *amplissimi honoris nomen*; *Phil.* 14.25 *honoris nomen amplissimi.*

81.3 **'adfuerunt ... laudarunt'** the consulars, most notably Q. Catulus (cf. Sal. *Cat.* 35.1; Oros. 6.3.1), had supported Catiline and vouched for his good character (*laudarunt*; cf. 49.4n.) when in 73 he was cited as the paramour in the trial *de incestu* of the Vestal Fabia (70.7n.); this is the point of *vitae eius turpitudinem* below. On Cicero's use of ascribed *oratio recta* see 3.11n.; the argument in §§ 81–2 is set up in the manner of an *altercatio* (21.1n.).

81.5 **defendebant amicum** their behaviour was entirely in accord with Roman principles (6.8n.). Catiline was an *amicus* (48.4n.), and therefore deserved their support: only if he was known to have committed crimes *contra rem publicam* ought they to have deserted him. Cicero argued at § 70 that Catiline's criminality had always been notorious (70.3n.); here we learn that it was evidently not yet known to be so great as to preclude the support of *amici*. Catiline deceived the consulars; cf. *Cael.* 12 *optimis se viris deditum esse simulabat.*

81.7 **consul ... advocatus** the consulars can hardly be blamed for supporting Catiline in 73, given that in the summer of 65 he was assisted by the elder Torquatus (11.4n.) at his *repetundae* trial relating to his governorship (67–6) of Africa (*Cat.* 1.18; *Cael.* 10, 14; *Pis.* 95; *Att.* 1.16.9; Q. Cic. (?) *Pet.* 10; Sal. *Cat.* 18.3; Asc. 9, 85–92 C; cf. *TLRR* no. 212). Cicero thought Catiline unquestionably guilty (*Att.* 1.1.1), but nevertheless considered defending him (*Att.* 1.2.1); Catiline was acquitted, allegedly as a result of collusion with the prosecutor P. Clodius (*Att.* 1.2.1; *Har.* 42; *Pis.* 23; Asc. 87 C; but see E. S. Gruen, *Athenaeum* 49 (1971) 59–62, arguing against collusion). An *advocatus* is an influential 'supporter', or sometimes more specifically a 'legal adviser' to one of the parties; cf. Ps. Asc. 190 St. *qui defendit alterum in iudicio aut patronus dicitur, si orator est; aut advocatus, si aut ius suggerit aut praesentiam suam commodat amico.*

At *-tundis E* resumes. The MS has lost the folios which contained §§ 1–81: all readings given above are taken from sixteenth- and seventeenth-century collations, all readings given below are taken from the MS itself. See my article at *CQ* n.s. 39 (1989) 400–7.

81.8   improbo...audaci see 1.12n.; 16.4n.

81.10   ad eum written for *ad se* to express the situation not from the elder Torquatus' (the subject of *indicavit*) but from Cicero's own point of view; cf. Lebreton 126f.; K.-S.1.601. The usage is rare; Cicero perhaps adopts it here to aid the deception involved in *indicavit* (see next n.).

indicavit...non credidisse Cicero attempts to explain how the elder Torquatus could have supported Catiline at his trial in 65 if, as Cicero had asserted elsewhere, Catiline had planned to murder the consuls (including Torquatus himself) and the other leading men of the state on 29 December 66 (*Cat.* 1.15) and again (with Piso's assistance) on 5 February 65 (*Tog. Cand.* ap. Asc. 92 C; *Mur.* 81; the letter to Pompey (67.1n.); cf. 67.4n.). Cicero accounts for Torquatus' support of Catiline by ingeniously suggesting that he had heard rumours of a conspiracy but (wrongly) did not believe them. In reality, of course, Catiline's activities were not at this date seen as conspiratorial (even by Cicero, who himself considered undertaking Catiline's defence; cf. 70.3n.), and there was therefore no reason why Torquatus should not have supported him (Catiline's intention to stand against Torquatus at the supplementary election in 66 evidently did not damage their friendship: perhaps his readiness to abandon his candidature (Asc. 89 C) earned him Torquatus' gratitude; cf. G. V. Sumner, *Phoenix* 19 (1965) 231; J. T. Ramsey, *HSCP* 86 (1982) 131 n. 39). This situation is in fact tacitly acknowledged in the wording used here. As C. E. Stevens first pointed out, Cicero 'does not report Torquatus' words but invites an inference from his actions' (*Latomus* 22 (1963) 432): *indicavit* ('he showed'; cf. *TLL* VII.1.1153.27ff. (not 1156.4)) need not imply that Torquatus had actually made any reference at all to a conspiracy. R. J. Seager reinforces the point: 'his *indicium* consisted solely in his action in defending Catilina, not in anything that he said. Torquatus then may not have heard anything at all' (*Historia* 13 (1964) 340 n. 16). Stevens well describes this as 'a wonderfully misleading sentence', which, Stockton (75) adds, 'needs to be read with no less care than went into its composition'. It should be understood, however, that Cicero is not required to explain how Torquatus could have supported a Catiline who had conspired with Autronius to murder Torquatus and Cotta and seize their consulships on 1 January 65: the view that Catiline rather than Sulla had a part in that alleged plot does not appear until Sal. *Cat.* 18.5 (68.2n.) and on my interpretation is not implied at §68 (68.4n.). For the view which Cicero here attributes to Torquatus cf. *Cael.* 14 *me ipsum, me, inquam, quondam paene ille decepit* [an allusion to Cicero's near-defence of Catiline] ... *cuius ego facinora oculis prius quam opinione, manibus ante quam suspicione deprendi.*

81.11 'at idem ... ceteri' unlike the consulars, the elder Torquatus did not go on to support Catiline at his trial *de sicariis* in 64, when Catiline was prosecuted by L. Lucceius for the murders (70.7n.) which he committed during the Sullan proscriptions (*Att.* 1.16.9; *Pis.* 95; Asc. 91 C; Dio 37.10.3; cf. *TLRR* no. 217). The trial took place not long after the consular elections, at which Catiline stood unsuccessfully for the first time; thanks to the consulars' support, he was again acquitted. Torquatus went to Macedonia as governor during the year (11.4n.), but presumably not until after Catiline's trial, otherwise Cicero would have given this as the reason why Torquatus did not lend Catiline his support. On Cicero's use of ascribed *oratio recta* see 3.11n.

81.12 si postea why did the elder Torquatus support Catiline in 65, but not in 64? Cicero's answer is put in the form of a *complexio* (10.3n.): if it was because he had discovered something about Catiline in the interval (e.g. from the accusations made by Cicero in *Tog. Cand.*: ap. Asc. 92 C), the prosecution should not censure the consulars, who heard nothing; but if the 'first conspiracy' was the reason for his not supporting Catiline in 64, why should that have been considered a weightier factor when it had been known for a long time (64) than when it was fresh (65)? The archetype gave *sed* for *si*; *si* (*q mg.*) is Petrarch's correction (cf. S. Rizzo, *RFIC* 103 (1975) 10; at n. 2 it is in fact Clark who has reported *T* correctly).

81.14 iis the MSS give *his*, which is inappropriate since the word is merely a signpost to *qui*; the emendation of the Rome and Venice editions (both of 1471) was anticipated by *r*.

sin ... valuit *illa res prima* refers to *primam illam coniurationem* above. *valuit* is 'produced the effect' (Housman), i.e. deterred Torquatus from supporting Catiline ('effecit ne cum ceteris adesset', Manutius), not 'had any substance' (Macdonald). C. A. Lehmann proposed *patuit* for *valuit* (*Hermes* 15 (1880) 350f.); his argument is rejected by K. Busche (*Hermes* 46 (1911) 64f.), who reinforces the interpretation of Manutius, 'non debuit inveterata [*sc.* causa] eius animum movere quae recens non moverat'.

81.15 inveterata 'stale', 'old news'; cf. §24 *nos ... quorum iam et nomen et honos inveteravit.*

sed si Cicero returns to the trial of 65 (81.7n.), at which Torquatus lent Catiline his support.

81.16 suspicione cf. *indicavit se audisse aliquid, non credidisse* above.

81.17 advocationem in a collective sense, 'body of *advocati*'; cf. *TLL* 1.890.17ff.; Lebreton 50. The genitive which follows is objective (cf. *Dom.* 54); contrast *Caec.* 43 *advocationem togatorum*.

sella curuli . . . consulatus cf. §50 *ego vero quibus ornamentis adversor tuis . . ?* (50.2n.); §88 *quae habebit ornamenta . . ?*; §88 *honoris insignia atque ornamenta.* Torquatus appeared in court seated on his curule chair (a stool inlaid with ivory to which censors, consuls, praetors and the two 'curule' aediles were entitled), dressed in his *toga praetexta* and accompanied by lictors bearing *fasces*: full consular *insignia* were displayed (26.5n.). This was evidently normal; at Sulla's trial the younger Torquatus wore the *toga praetexta* won from Sulla in 66 (50.4n.). The significance of *et suis* is unclear; it may be that Torquatus had won a military decoration for his part in the battle of the Colline Gate (Plut. *Sull.* 29.4; for the numismatic evidence see M. Crawford, *Roman Republican Coinage* (Cambridge 1974) 1.386f.). If so, this would give added point to Torquatus' frequent designation in Cicero as *fortis* or *fortissimus* (11.4n.).

82.1 'at idem . . . non adfuerunt' the prosecution's last objection is that the consulars, who supported Catiline in 73, 65 and 64, did not support those accused of conspiracy in the early months of 62 (for their names see 6.6n.). This objection is intended to demonstrate the consulars' inconsistency (hence the references to *constantia* below); but in fact it neatly enables Cicero to conclude that they are honest and scrupulous men (81.1n.). On Cicero's use of ascribed *òratio recta* see 3.11n.

82.2 tanto scelere . . . oportere cf. §7 *statuerant tantum illud esse maleficium quod non modo non occultari per se sed etiam aperiri illustrarique deberet.* Again Cicero stresses that the consulars acted in accordance with Roman principles (81.5n.). For the pleonasm *adiumenti . . . opis . . . auxili* see 39.1n.

82.5 tacita . . . loquitur a favourite oxymoron; cf. *Div. Caec.* 21 *etiamsi taceant, satis dicunt*; *Cat.* 1.18 *patria . . . tecum, Catilina, . . . tacita loquitur*; *Cat.* 1.21 *de te autem, Catilina, cum quiescunt, probant . . . cum tacent, clamant*; *Sest.* 40 *hominibus omnia timentibus tacendo loqui . . . videbantur.*

82.6 cuiusquam . . . orationis cf. *Fin.* 1.14 *Platonis, Aristoteli, Theophrasti orationis ornamenta* (see J. N. Madvig *ad loc.*). For the construction with two or more genitives dependent on the same substantive see K.-S.1.416f.

82.7 quisquam dicere *E* reads *dicere quisquam*, but cf. *Orat.* 14 *potest quisquam dicere*; *Luc.* 21 *potestne igitur quisquam dicere . . ?* If an incision (with hiatus) is taken before *umquam*, *quisquam dicere* gives the more favoured rhythm (molossus-cretic rather than hexameter ending). Kasten's argument for *dicere quisquam* is flawed (1933 preface xv). The error perhaps arose as a result of the double *-quam*.

meliores...consulares contrast Sal. *Cat.* 53.5 *haud sane quisquam Romae virtute magnus fuit*.

82.10 optime *optime*, L. Spengel's conjecture for *apertissime* (ω), is demanded by concinnity; cf. *meliores fortiores constantiores consulares* above (*Philologus* 2 (1847) 297). The elder Torquatus was described at § 30 as *fortissimi consulis, constantissimi senatoris, semper optimi civis. optime*, followed by *fortissime* and *constantissime*, would very easily have been mistaken for *aptissime*.

82.11 sensit i.e. *sententiam dixit* (*OLD* s.v. *sentio* 7a); cf. § 25 *in senatu sentire libere*.

82.12 haec the extreme hyperbaton *haec... laus* places emphasis on *haec* (8.1n.).

82.13 praetores specifically in 63 (not generally, as taken by Bonnefond-Coudry 653). L. Valerius Flaccus and C. Pomptinus arrested the Allobroges' envoys and T. Volturcius at the Mulvian Bridge and captured the letters which incriminated the conspirators; cf. *Cat.* 3.5 *L. Flaccum et C. Pomptinum praetores, fortissimos atque amantissimos rei publicae viros ... qui omnia de re publica praeclara atque egregia sentirent; Cat.* 3.14 *L. Flaccus et C. Pomptinus praetores, quod eorum opera forti fidelique usus essem, merito ac iure laudantur.* Help was also received from the praetors Metellus Celer (65.4n.), C. Cosconius (one of the rapid writers: 42.4n.), Q. Pompeius Rufus (uncle of the Q. Pompeius mentioned at § 55) and C. Sulpicius: see *MRR* II.166f. On the order of precedence *consulares... qui praetores fuerunt... universus senatus* see Mommsen, *Staatsrecht* III.966–9.

universi senatus Cicero flatters the senators on the jury (cf. § 42), so as to identify their position with his own.

82.14 post hominum memoriam 'in the memory of mankind', as opposed to mythical times. The phrase is a common one (twenty-one occurrences in Cicero): see Merguet II.495.

82.16 descripti 'referred to (by description)', i.e. without naming names (*TLL* v.1.662.61ff.); cf. Nägelsbach 598. The consulars have been attacked *uno nomine* (§ 81).

82.17 tantum restrictive (21.12n.).

XXX 83.1 Sed quid ego? most editors punctuate *sed quid? ego*, but Reid's *sed quid ego?* (App. A) more neatly marks Cicero's return to the question of his own *auctoritas* (§ 80).

non laudavi unlike the other consulars; cf. § 81 *'adfuerunt' inquit 'Catilinae illumque laudarunt'* (81.3n.).

83.2 consul non adfui unlike Torquatus in 65 (81.7n.).

testimonium... dixi cf. § 21 *'quod, in quos testimonia dixisti,'* inquit *'damnati sunt ...'*; § 48 *'cur dixisti testimonium in alios?'* quia coactus sum.

83.3 alienus a sanitate Arusianus Messius had a different text: 'avius ab illa re, Cic. pro Sylla *et avi⟨us⟩ a sanitate'* (7.458 Keil; =78 della Casa). *et*, however, makes no sense, and *avius* does not otherwise occur in Cicero. For *alienus* as 'remote (from a state)' cf. *Ver.* 5.70 *homines a piratarum metu... alienissimos* (*TLL* 1.1574.57ff.).

83.6 in animum inducam Clark deletes *in*, as suggested by Reid; cf. J. N. Madvig, *Bemerkungen über verschiedene Puncte des Systems der lateinischen Sprachlehre* (Brunswick 1843–4) 11 n. 2. Elsewhere Cicero writes *animum inducere*, although *in animum inducere* may be the correct reading at *Clu.* 45 *neque enim legare quicquam eius modi matri poterat in animum inducere* (where *in* is omitted by the MSS but attested by Arusianus Messius); cf. *TLL* VII.1.1241.37ff.; K.-S.1.668, 671. In spite of Cicero's preference for *animum inducere*, I see no reason to delete; the phrase may be loosely translated '(do I appear so bereft of my wits ...) that I would take it into my head (to defend ...)'.

83.7 nuper see 89.9n.

ferrum... restinxerim cf. *Clu.* 123 *censorium stilum cuius mucronem multis remediis maiores nostri rettuderunt; Cat.* 3.2 *ignis ... restinximus, idemque gladios in rem publicam districtos rettudimus; Sul.* 28 *horum ego faces eripere de manibus et gladios extorquere potui; Dom.* 63 *in me omnia, quae ego quondam rettuderam, coniurationis nefaria tela adhaeserunt. ferrum* and *flamma* are both grandiose words, and commonly paired (see Wölfflin 259); cf. *Att.* 1.14.3 (quoted at 28.6n.).

83.8 si concessive; cf. Handford 129.

me dius fidius i.e. *ita me Dius Fidius iuvet*, a common oath used by Cicero only three times before *Dom.* (*S. Rosc.* 95; *Q. Rosc.* 50; here) but frequently thereafter; cf. *OLD* s.v. *Fidius*. Dius Fidius was the Italic god of good faith (cf. Ζεὺς Πίστιος). Ancient etymologies connect him with Hercules, son of Jupiter (*Diovis Filius*); this identification may have been encouraged by the existence of the oath *me hercule* (18.12n.). See R. Maltby, *A Lexicon of Ancient Latin Etymologies* (Leeds 1991) 233; P. McGushin on Sal. *Cat.* 35.2.

83.9 meis... periculis cf. § 5 *multis meis ac magnis laboribus et periculis.*

83.11 hoc... semper oderis recalling Dem. 1.7 ἐπειδὴ δ'ἐκ τῶν πρὸς αὐτοὺς ἐγκλημάτων μισοῦσι, βεβαίαν εἰκὸς τὴν ἔχθραν αὐτοὺς ὑπὲρ ὧν φοβοῦνται καὶ πεπόνθασιν ἔχειν; cf. Weische 76, 149.

83.13 sed... amplissimus cf. § 49 *at vero cum honos agebatur familiae vestrae amplissimus.*

83.14 gloria... singularis the similarity of *singularis* to *salutis*

COMMENTARY: xxx 83–85

(below) has caused the omission of *cum ... salutis* in *E*. Cicero's self-laudation is discussed at pp. 175f.

83.15 in hoc scelere Lambinus deleted *in*, but cf. *Inv.* 2.32 *si quo in pari ante peccato convictus sit*; *Ver.* 4.104 *omnibus in rebus ... convincitur*; Sen. *Ep.* 86.10 *convictum in aliquo scelere*; Tac. *Ann.* 15.44 *in crimine... convicti sunt*; *schol. ad Iuv.* 6.638 *convictum in crimine coniurationis* (*TLL* IV.877.46ff.; K.-S.1.465).

83.16 inventae 'won' (*TLL* VII.2.145.53ff.); cf. Pl. *Ps.* 45; *Tusc.* 4.49.

83.17 committam 'act in such a way that ...' (as at *Att.* 1.20.3, cited below).

quae ... gessi cf. § 26 *quae pro salute omnium gessi*; § 34 *quas ... pro salute rei publicae suscepi atque gessi*.

83.18 casu ... esse videantur Cicero was greatly concerned that his achievements should not appear the result of chance; cf. *Cat.* 3.29 *ita me... tractabo ut meminerim semper quae gesserim, curemque ut ea virtute non casu gesta esse videantur*; *Fam.* 5.2.8 *quis esset qui me in consulatu non casu potius existimaret quam consilio fortem fuisse?*; *Att.* 1.20.3 *relicua sic a me aguntur et agentur ut non committamus ut ea quae gessimus fortuito gessisse videamur*. See also Cato *Fam.* 15.5.2. On *esse videantur* see 3.9n.

84.2 dicet fortasse quispiam an objection, vividly expressed in ascribed *oratio recta* (3.11n.); on *dicet* used for *inquiet* see Wiesthaler 83.

84.3 ego vero *ego vero* sometimes carries the sense, 'my answer is that...'; cf. Nägelsbach 745f.

nihil adsumo having made good use of his *auctoritas* in §§ 80 and 83, Cicero is now careful in §§ 84–5 to avoid an impression of arrogance. He emphasises that he is not claiming that Sulla should be acquitted simply because he is defending (§ 84); nevertheless, he clearly feels that Sulla should be acquitted because he who is defending believes him to be innocent (§ 85). The distinction is a fine one.

84.5 reddo ac remitto cf. § 47 *remissum atque concessum. adsumere* and *remittere* are also contrasted at *Planc.* 56.

non ... versor i.e. the political situation and Cicero's own position are not such as to allow him to make this claim.

84.6 caput meum obtuli cf. *Cat.* 3.28 *eos... qui se pro salute vestra obtulerint invidiae periculisque omnibus*; *Pis.* 21 *unum me pro omnium salute obtuli*. I read *caput meum* (*Tω*) in preference to *meum caput* (*E*): given that emphasis is placed on both *ea* and *iis*, *meum* requires the less emphatic position, following its noun.

84.7 non ... quos vici Cicero enlarged upon this theme in § 28.

85.1 grave esse videtur for *grave* see 80.5n. Clark considered deleting *esse*, which would remove the hexameter ending (11.1n.); but the incision after *videtur* is slight, and in any case *esse videtur* is sometimes found before a pause (e.g. *S. Rosc.* 30; twice at *Har.* 6; *Tusc.* 1.100; *Senect.* 75; *Att.* 13.37A.1).

85.2 qui investigarit...patefecerit cf. §3 *'tu enim investigasti, tu patefecisti coniurationem'*.

85.3 cui...gratias egerit on 3 December 63; cf. *Cat.* 3.14 *primum mihi gratiae verbis amplissimis aguntur, quod virtute, consilio, providentia mea res publica maximis periculis sit liberata*; *Cat.* 4.5 *primum quod mihi gratias egistis singularibus verbis et mea virtute atque diligentia perditorum hominum coniurationem patefactam esse decrevistis*. In addition Cicero was hailed as *pater patriae* by Q. Catulus (*Sest.* 121; *Pis.* 6; Plin. *Nat.* 7.117; and later by Cato, Plut. *Cic.* 23.3; App. *BC* 2.7) and on the motion of L. Gellius Poplicola was voted the *corona civica*, a decoration awarded for saving a citizen's life in battle (*Pis.* 6; Gel. 5.6.15).

85.4 cui...decreverit also on 3 December, the first occasion on which a *supplicatio* (thanksgiving to the gods) had been decreed in honour of a citizen (*togatus*); cf. *Cat.* 3.15 *atque etiam supplicatio dis immortalibus pro singulari eorum merito meo nomine decreta est, quod mihi primum post hanc urbem conditam togato contigit, et his decreta verbis est: 'quod urbem incendiis, caede civis, Italiam bello liberassem'* (the wording is paraphrased at *Fam.* 5.2.8 (quoted at 33.13n.) and at *Sul.* 33); *Cat.* 3.23; *Cat.* 4.5 *maxime quod meo nomine supplicationem decrevistis, qui honos togato habitus ante me est nemini*; *Pis.* 6; *Phil.* 2.13, 14.24; *Fam.* 15.4.11; Quint. *Inst.* 2.16.7; Dio 37.36.3, 45.46.3. See L. E. Halkin, *La Supplication d'action de grâces chez les Romains* (Paris 1953) 39–41. Cicero laid great emphasis (*loci* listed at Buchheit, *op. cit. infra* n.11) on the fact that it was as a *togatus* (without recourse to military measures, §33) that he had saved the state (cf. *Cons.* fr. 6 Soubiran *cedant arma togae, concedat laurea laudi*); this was not best calculated to please Pompey. For Cicero's concept of the *consul togatus* see C. Nicolet, *REL* 38 (1960) 236–63; V. Buchheit, *Gymnasium* 76 (1969) 241–6. Cicero was granted a *supplicatio* again in 50, but not as a *togatus*; cf. Halkin, *op. cit.* 48–58.

85.5 'non...coniurasset' the argument of §83. Cicero's assertion may seem offensive (*grave*) because in making it he appears to be setting himself up as judge (10.3n.). Nevertheless, the indignant tone of *eum qui investigarit...decreverit* shows (within the context of the argument) that he does not himself regard such a claim as offensive: he considers his argument justified. He did not consider a similar argument justified at Murena's trial, however: *nam si quis hoc forte dicet, Catonem descensurum ad accusandum non fuisse, nisi prius de causa iudicasset, iniquam legem, iudices, et miseram condicionem instituet periculis hominum, si existimabit iudicium accusatoris in reum pro aliquo praeiudicio valere oportere* (*Mur.* 60). On the criminality of defending conspirators see 6.8n.

non dico...dico emphatic; but the repetition is of course unavoidable when the negative clause precedes the positive (3.5n.).

85.6 non auctoritati...meo but at §80 it had been presented very much as a matter of *auctoritas*. Halm takes *pudori* as 'Bescheidenheit', Reid as 'honour'. Neither interpretation seems quite right. I think that Cicero is referring to his 'self-respect' (i.e. his personal moral standards): he is horrified at the suggestion that he might knowingly defend a conspirator.

85.7 investigator atque ultor in that order. *investigator* is rare (*TLL* VII.2.168.4ff.); it occurs elsewhere in classical Latin only at *Brut.* 60; *Tim.* 1.

85.8 si...arbitrarer a concession, removing the arrogance of *si coniurasset* above.

85.9 ego, iudices this sentence is echoed in §86, and so could be taken as belonging to the *conclusio*. But it also looks back to the argument of §14 (the opening of *digressio* II) and signals the completion of the defence which was there begun; I therefore prefer to regard it as marking the end of the *confirmatio*. To some extent the structure of the speech is fluid (see p. 48): Cicero builds up to the *conclusio*, just as he slipped out of the *exordium*, in gradual stages.

85.10 cum...caverem omnia cf. *Mil.* 61 *praesertim omnia audienti, magna metuenti, multa suspicanti, non nulla credenti*. The four clauses are arranged in an A B B A pattern: on this order see 2.2n. *crederem non omnia* (*E*) is preferable to *non crederem omnia* (ω) because the main contrast in the second and third clauses is between *multa* and *non omnia. multa...caverem omnia* is omitted in *T* as a result of the double *-erem omnia*.

85.11 quod initio dixi at §14; cf. *nullus umquam de Sulla nuntius ad me, nullum indicium, nullae litterae pervenerunt, nulla suspicio*. The point was also made at §20 *nullum crimen, nullum indicium, nulla suspicio*.

85.12 nullius litteris see 14.7n.; cf. §17 *multorum litterae ac nuntii*.

§§86–93 CONCLVSIO

Cicero swears an oath that he is concealing no crime: when consul he heard nothing incriminating Sulla. He was severe when severity was required; now he can indulge his innate compassion. Sulla deserves pity: he has already been stripped of his position by his earlier conviction, and is now concerned only to avoid passing on further disgrace to his unlucky son. Torquatus should have been satisfied with ruining Sulla once; why does he now want to drive him into exile? Sulla's unanimous election to the consulship is contrasted with his present plight. Cicero makes a final appeal to the jury. They were selected by the prosecution for their supposed severity: instead let them protect innocence, and so rid both themselves and Cicero of an ill-deserved reputation for cruelty!

Once the orator has finished his argumentation, he should conclude his speech with an elevated finale, the *conclusio* (*peroratio*); cf. *Rhet. Her.* 1.4 *conclusio est artificiosus orationis terminus*; Quint. *Inst.* 6.1.51 *hic, si usquam, totos eloquentiae aperire fontes licet*; id. *Inst.* 6.2.1 *pars haec iudicialium causarum summe praecipueque constet adfectibus* ... *Quare adhuc opus superest* ... *movendi iudicum animos atque in eum quem volumus habitum formandi et velut trans-figurandi.* The *conclusio* was the part of the speech in which Cicero most conspicuously excelled, and it was for this reason that, whenever more than one *patronus* spoke for the defence, Cicero was always chosen to make the final speech: *Hortensius* ... *cum partiretur tecum causas* ... *perorandi locum, ubi plurimum pollet oratio, semper tibi relinquebat* (*Brut.* 190); *etiam si plures dicebamus, perorationem mihi tamen omnes relinquebant* (*Orat.* 130).

In Roman oratory the *conclusio*, broadly speaking, serves two func-tions: to recapitulate and to appeal to the emotions (with the emphasis usually on the latter). It is therefore different from the Greek ἐπίλογος, in which no emotional appeal is made (cf. Quint. *Inst.* 6.1.7); as Weische observes, 'In den demosthenischen Reden gibt es keine Partien, die in dieser Hinsicht etwa mit dem Schluß der Rede Pro Sulla ... verglichen werden könnten' (188; cf. V. Pöschl in Michel-Verdière, 213f., 225). The *conclusio* is divided into two basic parts reflecting its double function, the *enumeratio* and the *amplificatio* (*Part.* 52); alternatively, it may conform to one of two basic types (Quint. *Inst.* 6.1.1, 6.1.36). This scheme may be complicated by the subdivision of the emotional part (*amplificatio*) into two, thus giving a three-part arrangement consisting of *enumeratio* (*recapitulatio*, ἀνακεφαλαίωσις), *indignatio* (*amplificatio, exaggeratio*) and *con-questio* (*commiseratio, miseratio*). It is this tripartite scheme, outlined at *Inv.* 1.98 and *Rhet. Her.* 2.47, which is adopted, although with modifications, in *pro Sulla.*

The *enumeratio* ('recapitulation') is defined as follows: *enumeratio est per quam res disperse et diffuse dictae unum in locum coguntur et reminiscendi causa unum sub aspectum subiciuntur* (*Inv.* 1.98); *enumeratio est per quam colligi-mus et commonemus quibus de rebus verba fecerimus* (*Rhet. Her.* 2.47). It is not often used in Cicero's *conclusiones*, being more suited to accusation than defence (*Part.* 59–60). Reid (Introd. §38) and Rohde (134) deny that *pro Sulla* contains an *enumeratio*. It is true that Cicero nowhere in the *conclusio* recapitulates the points which he has made in defence of Sulla; never-theless, he does open the *conclusio* with a passage of recapitulation in which he reviews his own role in the case (§§ 86–7; § 85 also contains an element of recapitulation, but is best regarded as preparatory to the *conclusio* rather than part of it). Since this passage is firmly differentiated from the appeal to pity which follows, it should certainly be classed as *enumeratio*. It corresponds to the *enumeratio* prescribed by the rhetoricians, in fact, in exactly the same way as does the *partitio* to the *partitio* of the rhetoricians earlier in the speech (§§ 11–14).

After the *enumeratio*, the *indignatio* ought to follow, and finally the *conquestio*. In our *conclusio* Cicero blends these latter two parts together, including the *indignatio* (§ 90) within the body of the *conquestio*. This *indignatio* is not wholly conventional in that it does not consist of the amplification of emotional topics, but instead is used by Cicero as a vehicle through which to expostulate with Torquatus (cf. *digressio* IV, §§ 46–50). However, this difference may be explained by the fact that the *indignatio*, like the *enumeratio*, is more suited to accusation than to defence, and is treated by the rhetoricians from the accuser's point of view. But our *indignatio* does at least accord with the definition given at *Inv.* 1.100, *indignatio est oratio per quam conficitur ut in aliquem hominem magnum odium aut in rem gravis offensio concitetur.*

The *conquestio* ('appeal to pity'; cf. *Inv.* 1.106 *conquestio est oratio auditorum misericordiam captans*), on the other hand, is ideally suited to defence, and the *conquestio* of *pro Sulla* (§§ 88–9, 91) is one of Cicero's very finest. As recommended, it is not overlong, since, as Cicero was aware, 'nothing dries faster than a tear' (*Inv.* 1.109; *Rhet. Her.* 2.50; *Part.* 57; Quint. *Inst.* 6.1.27; cf. G. D. Kellogg, *AJP* 28 (1907) 301–10). In it Cicero conveys a powerful impression of the tragedy of a man whose life is already in ruins, who has already been punished enough, but who is now threatened by a still greater catastrophe. Cicero was famous for his heart-rending *conquestiones*, so much so that he was even accused of having added exile to the penalties for *ambitus* in his *lex Tullia* (63) simply to give himself opportunities for *miserabiliores epilogos* (*Planc.* 83). He attributed his conspicuous success in this field to his own genuine sympathy: *in quo ut viderer excellere non ingenio sed dolore adsequebar* (*Orat.* 130; cf. Antonius at *de Orat.* 2.189 *non me hercule umquam apud iudices aut dolorem aut misericordiam aut invidiam aut odium dicendo excitare volui, quin ipse in commovendis iudicibus his ipsis sensibus, ad quos illos adducere vellem, permoverer; ibid.* 190, 195; Hor. *Ars* 102–3 *si vis me flere, dolendum est / primum ipsi tibi*). It is easy to question Cicero's sincerity, especially in the present speech where his client is not a close friend and where his heavy emphasis on his own *misericordia* (§§ 1, 8, 18, 20, 47, 87) is so obviously politically motivated. Nevertheless, Cicero was a man who was easily moved (as the letters amply testify), and there is no reason to doubt that, when he spoke, Cicero was genuinely affected by the pathos of Sulla's plight. A *conquestio* which strikes the reader as calculated and false may well have been delivered with perfect sincerity. As Cicero recognised, *carent libri spiritu illo, propter quem maiora eadem illa cum aguntur quam cum leguntur videri solent* (*Orat.* 130). Imagination is needed, then, to enter into the spirit of the original performance.

On the *conclusio* in an ancient speech see Arist. *Rh.* 3.19; [Arist.] *Rh. Al.* 36 (1444 b 20ff., with 1443 b 14ff.); *Inv.* 1.98–109; *Rhet. Her.* 1.4, 2.47–50; *de Orat.* 2.332; *Part.* 52–60; *Orat.* 122; Quint. *Inst.* 4.1.28, 6.1.1–55. For modern accounts see Lausberg 236–40; Martin 147–66; Rohde 131–44; Laurand 327–31.

XXXI 86.1   Quam ob rem Cicero opens the *conclusio* with a passage which reviews those aspects of the case which concern himself (§§ 86–7). Structurally this corresponds to the *enumeratio*, for which see *Inv.* 1.98–100; *Rhet. Her* 2.47; *Part.* 52, 59–60; Quint. *Inst.* 6.1.1–8.

   di patrii ac penates cf. *Ver.* 4.17 *deos penatis te patrios reposcit*; *Dom.* 144 *patrii penates familiaresque, qui huic urbi et rei publicae praesidetis*; *Sest.* 45 *penates patriique dei*; *Har.* 37 *patrii penatesque di*. On the pairing see Wölfflin 270. Cicero swears an oath (§ 86) that he is concealing no crime on Sulla's part: in effect, the orator swears that his client is innocent. The appeal to the gods at this point in the speech is paralleled by the prayers at *Ver.* 5.184–9; *Man.* 70; *Dom.* 144–5; *Mil.* 85–6; on oaths (ὅρκοι) see Quint. *Inst.* 5.6.1–6; Volkmann 184–6; Martin 100. The expression *di patrii ac penates* is difficult to interpret precisely. Technically, *di patrii*, the national ancestral gods (not 'belonging to our country'), already include the *publici penates*; R. G. Nisbet (on *Dom.* 144f.) would therefore take *penates* as 'the private *penates* collectively of Rome'. But it is in my view more likely that the expression is tautologous, and that by *penates* Cicero means the *publici penates*. These were housed, appropriately, in the temple of Vesta (Tac. *Ann.* 15.41.1), at the south-east end of the forum. Sulla's trial took place in the forum (p. 16), and Cicero no doubt turned to the temple of Vesta as he addressed the *penates* (if he did not, it would have been an opportunity missed). There was another temple also containing *penates*, on the Velia (Richardson, *Rome* 289); but that was not so conveniently to hand. On the *penates* see *RE* xix.417.15ff.; G. Wissowa, *Religion und Kultus der Römer*[2] (Munich 1912) 161–6; S. Weinstock, *JRS* 50 (1960) 112–14. For Cicero's attitude towards religion see M. Van den Bruwaene, *La Théologie de Cicéron* (Louvain 1937); U. Heibges, *AJP* 90 (1969) 304–12; *id.*, *Latomus* 28 (1969) 833–49; R. J. Goar, *Cicero and the State Religion* (Amsterdam 1972) 36–129; J. Kroymann in Michel-Verdière, 116–28. Cicero used the gods to reinforce his own *auctoritas* also at § 40 above (40.3n.).

   qui...praesidetis cf. *Cat.* 4.3 *omnis deos qui huic urbi praesident*; *Dom.* 143 *ipsi di immortales qui hanc urbem atque hoc imperium tuentur*; *Dom.* 144 (quoted in previous n.); *Phil.* 13.20 *testor ... omnis deos qui huic urbi praesident*. On the formula see F. V. Hickson, *Roman Prayer Language: Livy and the A⟨e⟩neid of Vergil* (Stuttgart 1993) 38f.

86.3 hanc libertatem the freedom which Torquatus accused Cicero of having overthrown (21.1n.). On *libertas* see A. Dermience, *LEC* 25 (1957) 157–67; Wirszubski; Hellegouarc'h 542–65; H.Kloesel in Oppermann, 120–72; Brunt 50–52, 281–350.

haec tecta atque templa cf. §33 *his . . . templis atque tectis* (33.10n.).

86.5 testor *me* following *integro* may indicate a break after *testor* (2.7n.).

86.6 occultari cf. §7 *maleficium quod non modo non occultari per se sed etiam aperiri illustrarique deberet.*

86.7 nihil . . . comperi see 12.14n.

86.8 nihil audivi Havet (§225; cf. §1433) thought this third colon followed on feebly after the second, and suggested moving it in front of *nihil suspicatus sum*. But *nihil audivi* is the deliberate climax of a natural progression: 'I didn't discover anything, I didn't even suspect anything – and I didn't so much as hear the name mentioned'.

87.1 itaque resumptive, 'well, then'; cf. Nägelsbach 661; *TLL* VII.2.530.30ff. This section returns to the theme of Cicero's *misericordia* (1.10n.), repeating the argument of §8.

idem ego 'I (this same man) . . .' (20.1n.).

ille . . . visus sum Cicero seemed *vehemens* towards the conspirators executed on 5 December (*alios*) and *inexorabilis* towards the remaining conspirators (*ceteros*) in refusing to defend them. *inexorabilis* here means 'not capable of being moved by entreaty', not simply 'relentless' (as it is taken at *OLD* s.v. 1): we were shown Cicero refusing to yield to Autronius' entreaties at §§18–19 (cf. §§21, 83). Without this distinction *vehemens . . . inexorabilis* would be a pointless repetition of the same idea. *inexorabilis* occurs elsewhere in Cicero only at *Planc.* 40 and *Tusc.* 1.10 (in both cases the sense is literal). For the opposition *in alios . . . in ceteros* cf. §9 *quare necesse est, quod mihi consuli praecipuum fuit praeter alios, id iam privato cum ceteris esse commune.* There is no justification at all for Madvig's deletion of *in alios* (*Adv. Crit.* II.210).

87.2 persolvi . . . debui by crushing the conspiracy and then giving evidence against the conspirators who were put on trial. The metaphor is from finance; cf. *Red. Pop.* 23.

87.5 quam qui lenissimus 'as the mildest of men' (sc. *est*); cf. *Fam.* 5.2.6 *tam enim sum amicus rei publicae quam qui maxime*; *Fam.* 13.3 *tam gratum mihi id erit quam quod gratissimum.* See K.-S.II.479.

in quo . . . vobiscum *in quo*, as Reid points out, stands for *in ea re in qua*. *vobiscum*, picked up by *tum fuimus tam vehementes . . .* below, seems to be an attempt to pass off some of the responsibility for the executions onto the senate (21.3n.). C. A. Lehmann (*Hermes* 15 (1880) 351f.) objected to *vobiscum* (which does indeed impair the rhythm), but his solution *in quo vehemens fui, fui vobiscum* is unpersuasive.

nihil ... coactus cf. § 48 *'cur dixisti testimonium in alios?' quia coactus sum.* For *coactus* see 48.8n.

87.6 rei publicae ... subveni cf. § 1 *praecipitante re publica* (1.13n.). The state was collapsing, but Cicero came up underneath (*subveni*) to hold it in place.

patriam ... extuli cf. *Dom.* 137 *demerso populo Romano*; *Off.* 2.24 *demersae leges* (*TLL* v.1.479.63ff.; Nägelsbach 551f.). The image is that of the ship of state, a famous commonplace much used by Cicero (e.g. *Inv.* 1.4; *Mur.* 4, 81; *Dom.* 24, 129, 137; *Sest.* 20, 45–6, 73; *Prov.* 7; *Att.* 2.7.4; *Fam.* 1.9.21); cf. J. M. May, *Maia* 32 (1980) 259–64; R. G. M. Nisbet and M. Hubbard on Hor. *Carm.* 1.14 (p. 180); Pöschl 561f. For *efferre* as 'to rescue (from a shipwreck)' see *TLL* v.2.141.18ff.

87.7 tum in ω *tum* has been altered to *tunc*: see 9.8n.

87.8 tam vehementes 'only so strict'; cf. restrictive *tantum* (21.12n.).

87.9 una nocte Cicero refers to a critical night after his adoption of *severitas*, i.e. after the execution of the conspirators on 5 December; we are not, therefore, to think of the meeting at Laeca's house (6.6n.) on the night of 6–7 November (cf. § 52 *quae nox omnium temporum coniurationis acerrima fuit atque acerbissima*), or of the arrests at the Mulvian Bridge on the night of 2–3 December (cf. *Cat.* 4.19 *una nox*; *Flac.* 102 *o nox illa ..!*). The night immediately after the executions (*Flac.* 103 *o nox illa quam iste est dies consecutus ..!*) is one possibility; cf. Sal. *Cat.* 55.1 *consul optumum factu ratus noctem quae instabat antecapere, ne quid eo spatio novaretur, triumviros quae supplicium postulabat parare iubet.* Another, as Halm suggests, is the night of the Saturnalia (19 December), when the massacre and the burning of Rome were to have taken place (*Cat.* 3.10, 3.17; Plut. *Cic.* 18.1–2; D.S. 40 fr.5; cf. Sal. *Cat.* 43). But Cicero need not have any particular night in mind: *una nocte* achieves its effect not by bringing to mind one specific occasion but by suggesting, through association, darkness, rapidity, fear and surprise.

87.11 sum adductus ... deducor an elegant summing-up of Cicero's position. For the play cf. *Att.* 7.15.2 *si Caesar adductus sit ut praesidia deducat.* For play on different compounds of the same root see Holst 63–70.

88.1 Nihil video Cicero now moves to the *conquestio* (§§ 88–9, 91), the emotional appeal which was his special forte (see p. 305). On the *conquestio* see *Inv.* 1.98, 106–9; *Rhet. Her.* 2.47, 50; *Part.* 52–8; *Orat.* 130–33; *Top.* 98; Quint. *Inst.* 6.1.9–35; cf. Greenidge 472. For the rhetoricians on the *affectus* see F. Solmsen, *CP* 33 (1938) 390–404.

88.2 propulsandae ... causa even if he is acquitted, Sulla's *calamitas* (1.2n.) will still remain, owing to his *ambitus* conviction in 66.

88.3 confugit Reid takes this as perfect, but rhythm (double-cretic) implies a present tense.

88.4 generi ac nomini simply 'family and name'. Rohde (141) notes that Cicero here uses the fourth commonplace specified for the *conquestio*: *quartus, per quem res turpes et humiles et inliberales proferentur et indigna aetate, genere, fortuna pristina, honore, beneficiis, quae passi perpessurive sint* (*Inv.* 1.107).

nota . . . inuratur cf. *Clu.* 129 *is censoriae severitatis nota non inuretur?*; *Rab. Perd.* 24 *insignem notis turpitudinis*; *Cat.* 1.13 *quae nota domesticae turpitudinis non inusta vitae tuae est?*; *Sul.* 76 *quas turpitudines . . . .quas notas facinorum*; *Pis.* 41 *sempiternas foedissimae turpitudinis notas*; *Phil.* 13.40 *inustum verissimis maledictorum notis*. A *nota* was a mark placed by the censors against the names of citizens whom they degraded, hence a stigma or mark of disgrace. It is said to be branded (*inuratur*) so as to imply indelibility.

88.6 quae habebit ornamenta *habet* (ω) breaks the sequence, so I have adopted W. G. Pluygers' *habebit* (*Mnemosyne* 9 (1881) 138). The change is very slight, especially if *habebit* was abbreviated (*habeƀ*). On Sulla's forfeited *ornamenta* see 88.10n. below.

relicuae *E* reads *relicua* (spelt *reliqua*), but agreement would be more natural with *vitae* than with *solacia*; cf. *Quinct.* 98 *existimationem ac spem relicuae vitae*; *Ver.* 5.35 *meam voluntatem spemque relicuae vitae*; *Red. Sen.* 24 *exiguum relicuae vitae tempus*; *Dom.* 126 *dedecus et egestatem relicuae vitae*; *Fam.* 10.3.2 *relicuae vitae dignitatem*. Cicero wrote *relicuam constantiam vitae* at §73, but there *relicuam* (*relicuae* Richter) and *vitae* are separated (73.1n.). A further reason for preferring *relicuae* here is that it adds a pathetic allusion to Sulla's age.

88.7 credo ironic (11.7n.). Cicero begins the second commonplace specified for the *conquestio* (Rohde 140): *secundus, qui in tempora tribuitur, per quem, quibus in malis fuerint et sint et futuri sint, demonstratur* (*Inv.* 1.107).

88.8 aperientur . . . recuperabit as a consequence of his conviction in 66, Sulla will not display his ancestral *imagines* (27.3n.) or exchange the *sordes* which he is wearing in court (cf. Greenidge 472) for the *latus clavus* indicating senatorial rank (the *lex Calpurnia* (67) had prescribed permanent exclusion from the senate; cf. 17.8n.). The *imagines* were kept in cupboards (*armaria*) which were opened (*aperientur*) on special occasions: cf. Polyb. 6.53.6 ταύτας δὴ τὰς εἰκόνας ἔν τε ταῖς δημοτελέσι θυσίαις ἀνοίγοντες κοσμοῦσι φιλοτίμως; *Mur.* 88 *quo se miser vertet? domumne? ut eam imaginem clarissimi viri, parentis sui, quam paucis ante diebus laureatam in sua gratulatione conspexit, eandem deformatam ignominia lugentemque videat?*; Sen. *Con.* 7.6.10 *indicit festum diem, aperiri iubet maiorum imagines, cum maxime tegendae sunt*; Vopisc. *Tac.* 19.6 *senatores omnes ea esse laetitia elatos, ut in domibus suis omnes albas hostias caederent, imagines frequenter aperirent, albati sederent*. It is usually assumed that Cicero is here referring to Sulla's loss of the *ius imaginum*, a deprivation which seems to have applied to all convicted criminals; cf. Mommsen, *Staatsrecht* 1.442–7; *RE* ix.1103.61ff.; *OCD* s.v. *imagines*; Reid, Introd. §9. But the *ius imaginum* is elsewhere seen as the right to be represented oneself posthumously among the *imagines* (cf. *Ver.* 5.36 *ius imaginis ad memoriam posteritatemque prodendae*), not as the right to display one's ancestors' *imagines* on special occasions. It may be that convicted criminals (or perhaps, more specifically, those convicted under the *lex Calpurnia*), in addition to forfeiting the *ius imaginum*, were also forbidden any display of their *maiorum imagines* (Halm). But, as Reid admits, 'it is difficult to see how such a penalty could be enforced' (Introd. §9 n. 7), and on balance I think it more probable that Cicero is not referring to the loss of a right at all: I take *omnia... haec amissa sunt* as referring in a technical sense to the loss of the right to senatorial dress (*ornatum ac vestitum pristinum*) implied by Sulla's loss of senatorial rank, but in a non-technical sense to the decoration of his house and display of his *imagines* (*domus... imagines*). In other words, Cicero is saying simply that Sulla, even if acquitted, will have no cause for celebration: his house will not be decorated, he will not open up and wreathe with laurel his *maiorum imagines* and he will not (because he has lost his senatorial status) resume senatorial dress. This interpretation is essentially that of Long and Boulanger; cf. 'it does not seem probable ... that Sulla lost the privilege of taking his ancestors out of their boxes; ... it was the fashion for people in his condition to avoid any display of any kind' (Long); 'P. Sylla, exclu du consulat, s'était interdit toute manifestation de cette sorte' (Boulanger). *pristinum* is preserved only in *E*, and was doubtless omitted from *Tω* through similarity with *vestitum*.

88.10 honoris... ornamenta cf. §26 *praeclarae laudis insignia*; §50 *ego vero quibus ornamentis adversor tuis ..?* (50.2n.); §50 *insignia honoris ad te delata sunt*; §81 *sella curuli atque ornamentis*; *quae habebit ornamenta ..?*, above. In addition to his losses mentioned above (previous n.), Sulla had also had to forfeit his consular *insignia* (26.5n.) to his accuser, the younger Torquatus (50.4n.).

88.11 exstinctor patriae cf. *Dom.* 101; *Dom.* 141 *res ... publica quamquam erat exterminata mecum, tamen obversabatur ante oculos exstinctoris sui*; *Sest.* 144; *Har.* 49; *Pis.* 26.

88.12 hostis see 15.7n.

88.13 metuit the word recurs below, causing ω to omit *ne denique ... metuit*.

88.14 hic miser Sulla's son, to whom Cicero points. The use of a defendant's children (or other relatives) to move a jury to compassion was a familiar, and evidently effective, technique in Greek oratory, famously satirised by Aristophanes at *Vesp.* 975–84 (cf. 568–74), where the introduction of the dog Labes' puppies succeeds in moving the juror

Philocleon to tears; cf. Lys. 20.34–5; And. 1.148; Pl. *Ap.* 34 c–35 b; Dem. 21.99, 21.186, 21.188, 53.29; Hyp. 2.9, 4.41. The practice was widespread also at Rome (even in the second century BC; cf. *de Orat.* 1.228; *Brut.* 90; V. Max. 8.1 *abs.* 2; Quint. *Inst.* 2.15.8): the defendant's children should be referred to in the *conquestio* (*Inv.* 1.109, the fifteenth commonplace; *Rhet. Her.* 2.50; Quint. *Inst.* 6.1.24), and Quintilian recommends that they actually be produced in court (*Inst.* 4.1.28). The effect was not always carried off successfully (6.1.41, the boy replies that the *paedagogus* is pinching him), but even when things went wrong a good orator would be capable of rescuing the situation (as at 6.1.47). Cicero talks of his own use of children in court at *Orat.* 131: *miseratione... qua nos ita dolenter uti solemus ut puerum infantem in manibus perorantes tenuerimus, ut alia in causa excitato reo nobili, sublato etiam filio parvo, plangore et lamentatione compleremus forum.* The second case to which Cicero refers is usually (but probably wrongly) taken to be his defence of Flaccus (*Flac.* 106 *huic, huic misero puero vestro ac liberorum vestrorum supplici, iudices* etc.). A further example occurs at *Sest.* 144–6, while at *Font.* 46–9 similar use is made of Fonteius' sister (a Vestal, weeping over the fire) and at *Cael.* 79–80 of Caelius' father (80 *conservate parenti filium, parentem filio*). Cf. also *Clu.* 137. See V. Pöschl in Michel-Verdière, 206–26; K. J. Dover, *Greek Popular Morality* (Oxford 1974) 195–201.

Sulla's son, the *puer* to whom Cicero refers (he cannot have been more than twelve at the time of his father's trial, given that his parents married no earlier than 75; cf. 89.13n.), is not quite as unknown as Syme implies (*Sallust* 227). Also named P. Cornelius Sulla (*RE* IV.1521.38ff., Cornelius 387; *MRR* III.73), in 54 he acted as *subscriptor* to his father in his prosecution of Gabinius (*Q. fr.* 3.3.2). It is likely that it was he rather than his father who fought for Caesar and commanded his right wing at Pharsalia (*MRR* II.281, 290): see D. R. Shackleton Bailey on *Att.* 4.3.3. He outlived his father (*Fam.* 15.17.2, 15.19.3), whom he apparently resembled in character (*Fam.* 15.19.3; cf. 'the son was like the father, a greedy Roman', Long III.157), and was probably himself a senator and the father of the consul of 5 BC.

88.15 huic puero dependent on *metuit*; cf. Lebreton 154f.; K.-S.1.339.

88.16 honoris...fructus this presumably does refer to Sulla's loss of the *ius imaginum* (88.8n.): Sulla's son will never be able to keep his father's bust among the family *imagines*.

89.2 fortuna see 73.4n.

ut adflicta 'so far as his battered fortune permits' (Macdonald). *ut* is certainly limitative (as Reid suggested), rather than a repetition of the previous *ut*; cf. *de Orat.* 3.66 *orationis etiam genus habent fortasse subtile et certe* *acutum, sed, ut in oratore, exile; Brut.* 173 *erat etiam in primis, ut temporibus illis, Graecis doctrinis institutus.* See K.-S.11.452f.

89.4 campi et disciplinarum Sulla's son has already suffered on his father's account: he has had to neglect his exercises on the *campus Martius* and his education at the *disciplinae.* Neglect of the former would have been especially regrettable: exercises on the Campus Martius, partly on horseback, constituted a valuable military training (cf. *Cael.* 11; Hor. *Carm.* 1.8.3–4; *id. Ars* 161–2; Str. 5.3.8), which, incidentally, would have been useful to Sulla's son if it was indeed he who later fought under Caesar (88.14n.). The *disciplinae* were the elementary 'schools', where the boy, accompanied by his *paedagogus*, would have learned reading, writing and arithmetic (grammar and literature were taught from the age of twelve, but Sulla's son was twelve at most in 62). This use of *disciplina* is rare; cf. *de Orat.* 3.74 *cui disciplina fuerit forum, magister usus et leges...mosque maiorum*; Ulp. *dig.* 9.2.5.3 (see *TLL* v.i.1318.56ff.; Lebreton 71). The term *ludus* would have been more usual; perhaps *disciplina* sounded more rigorous and 'disciplinarian'.

89.5 non iam... contenditur i.e. Sulla's life has already been ruined by his *ambitus* conviction in 66 (*superiore iudicio*), so instead it is his burial which is in dispute in the present case. Cicero thus introduces a pathetic allusion to the fact that Sulla, if convicted and so driven into exile (see next n.), will not be buried in Italian soil (at Rome, even executed criminals were handed over to their families for burial). Cf. *Rab. Perd.* 37 *neque tam ut domo sua fruatur quam ne patrio sepulcro privetur laborat. Nihil aliud iam vos orat atque obsecrat nisi uti ne se legitimo funere et domestica morte privetis; Mil.* 104 *hicine vir patriae natus usquam nisi in patria morietur, aut, si forte, pro patria? huius vos animi monumenta retinebitis, corporis in Italia nullum sepulcrum esse patiemini?* On the method of Sulla's burial see p. 13.

89.6 ne corpus eiciatur sc. of Italy. Cicero enlarges below upon the prospect of Sulla's being cast out: *ut cum parente, cum liberis ... lugere suam calamitatem liceat, id sibi ne eripiatis vos, iudices, obtestatur* (§ 89); *quid est quod expetas amplius?... inimicum ut expellas?* (§ 90); cf. *Sest.* 146 *an ego in hac urbe esse possim, his pulsis...neque eae nationes...hunc exsulem propter me sine me videbunt.* Together these passages (with *Flac.* 96; *Att.* 3.2, 3.7.1 on the exile of the Catilinarian conspirators) show the penalty under the *lex Plautia de vi* to have been *aquae et ignis interdictio*, i.e. 'voluntary' exile (cf. *Rhet. Her.* 2.46 *quasi non omnes quibus aqua et igni interdictum est exsules appellentur; Caec.* 100). This was considerably more severe than the penalty paid by Sulla under the *lex Calpurnia de ambitu* (17.8n.). See Greenidge 507, 509–13; Strachan-Davidson, *Criminal Law* 11.23–50; W. E. Heitland on *Rab. Perd.*, App. C; Lintott 107–24.

89.8 quid est... videatur? cf. *de Orat.* 2.20; *Senect.* 7 *voluptati-*

bus ... sine quibus vitam nullam putarent (with J. G. F. Powell's note); *Amic.*
86 *sine amicitia vitam esse nullam*; *Fam.* 7.1.4 *tum vero hoc tempore vita nulla est.*
haec is written for *hoc* by attraction: see Lebreton 24–31.

XXXII 89.9 nuper i.e. in 66, between his election to the consulship and his conviction. *nuper*, like the French 'naguère', may look back
over a greater period of time (here four years) than the English 'recently', and therefore sometimes has to be translated 'earlier', 'previously', 'not all that long ago', depending on the context (cf. §63). I do
not think that Cicero here means 'only a short time ago' (Macdonald),
'noch vor kurzem' (Fuhrmann), 'hace poco tiempo' (Peña); the Latin for
that is *modo* (cf. H. A. Holden[3] on *Off.* 1.26). On words meaning 'recently'
used in moralistic contexts see D. A. Russell in E. M. Craik (ed.), *'Owls to
Athens': Essays on Classical Subjects Presented to Sir Kenneth Dover* (Oxford 1990)
293f. Rohde (139) notes that Cicero here uses the first commonplace
specified for the *conquestio: primus locus est misericordiae per quem quibus in bonis
fuerint et nunc quibus in malis sint ostenditur* (*Inv.* 1.107; cf. *Rhet. Her.* 2.50).

89.11 spoliatus for the image cf. §50.

89.12 quod ... fecit cf. *Ver.* 1.2, 2.101; Sal. *Cat.* 11.7. The genitive
relicui is better regarded as adverbial (H.-Sz.71f.) than partitive (Reid,
K.-S.1.432). On *fortuna* see 73.4n.

cum parente his mother: L. E. Reams (*CJ* 82 (1986–7) 301–5) has
demonstrated that Sulla's father (probably also named P. Sulla) is likely
to have died between 107 and 96. Cicero here uses the twelfth commonplace specifed for the *conquestio* (Rohde 143): *duodecimus, per quem dis-
iunctio deploratur ab aliquo, cum diducaris ab eo quicum libentissime vixeris, ut a
parente filio, a fratre familiari* (*Inv.* 1.109).

89.13 cum liberis his son P. Sulla (88.14n.) and his stepson Memmius are known; these two are mentioned with Caecilius (see next n.) at
Q. fr. 3.3.2 as being Sulla's *subscriptores* in his prosecution of Gabinius
in 54. Memmius was almost certainly the natural son of C. Memmius
(*RE* 7, a cousin of C. Memmius (55.3n.) the consular candidate for 53; cf.
T. P. Wiseman, *NC* 4 (1964) 157; *id. CQ* n.s. 17 (1967) 167) and Pompey's
sister Pompeia, who would therefore have married Sulla after her husband's death in Spain in 75 (*Balb.* 5; Plut. *Pomp.* 11.2; *id. Sert.* 21.1; Oros.
5.23.12): see p. 3 n. 11. F. Münzer (*RE*) has convincingly identified him
with C. Memmius (*RE* xv.616.35ff., Memmius 9; *MRR* 11.223; 111.141), the
tribune of 54 who prosecuted Gabinius successfully (cf. pp. 11f.) and
C. Rabirius Postumus with uncertain result; cf. E. Fantham, *Historia* 24
(1975) 436–8.

cum fratre Caecilius (62.7n.), present in court.

cum his necessariis including Hortensius, the Marcelli (19.9n.) and
Messalla 'Rufus' (20.4n.).

89.14   calamitatem see 1.2n.

90.1   Te ipsum Cicero now inserts into his *conquestio* a brief *indignatio* (§90) in which he repeats more forcefully the criticisms made of Torquatus at §§49–50. On the part of the *conclusio* known as the *indignatio* see *Inv.* 1.98, 1.100–5; *Rhet. Her.* 2.47, 2.47–9. This example is not typical: see p. 305.

90.2   par erat 'it is right'; on the tense (*erat* for *est*) see Lebreton 279–83; K.-S.1.171.

abstulissetis plural to include the father (11.4n.), since it was he who became consul in Sulla's place.

90.3   vos contentos *vos contentos* (*T*δ) rather than *contentos vos* (*E*β) is the more natural order, with *vos* in the unemphatic position (2.7n.). The inversion in *E*β will have been caused in each case by the endings in *-os* (cf. Pabón 12; although Pabón opts for *contentos vos*).

honoris . . . deduxerunt cf. §49 *honoris erat certamen*; *Off.* 1.38 (quoted at 49.8n.). Torquatus had a good motive for prosecuting Sulla in 66, his father's *honos*; but this time his motive is a poor one, simply *inimicitiae*, the continuation of a family feud (cf. 48.4n.).

90.5   cum honore i.e. 'along with his consulship'.

fortuna see 73.4n.

90.6   destitutus 'abandoned' (*TLL* v.1.762.22ff.); cf. *Caec.* 93 *hunc . . . nudum in causa destitutum videtis*. Seyffert (13f.) actually proposed the insertion of *nudus* before *destitutus*. The choice of the word *destitutus* implies that Cicero has acted honourably in coming to Sulla's aid.

quid . . . amplius? cf. §50 *quid est quod iam ab hoc expetas?*

90.7   lucisne . . . vis the question-and-answer sequence beginning here takes the form of a *complexio* (10.3n.); in contrast to the examples of *complexio* earlier in the speech, Cicero's purpose in this passage is to heighten the emotion rather than to press a logical point. *hanc* for *huius* (conjectured by Lambinus) is an instance of hypallage (73.1n.); at *Rab. Post.* 48 Cicero writes *usuram huius lucis*. Clark suggested *ei vis* for *vis* (the dative, rather than *a* + ablative, is usual after *eripere* in this sense), a conjecture doubtless prompted by *eius* in β; but this would produce a highly improbable word order.

90.9   reddiderit the future perfect is sometimes used for the future simple, especially in the comic poets, to express 'une nuance de facilité, de rapidité, de certitude' (P. Fabia, quoted by Lebreton); cf. Lebreton 200–3; K.-S.1.147–52. Here the sense is therefore 'he will surrender it on the spot' (Reid); cf. *Att.* 3.19.1 *nusquam facilius hanc miserrimam vitam vel sustentabo vel, quod multo est melius, abiecero*.

90.10   an . . . expellas? a further reference to exile (89.6n.). Within the context of the argument, *ut expellas* refers back to *expetas* above.

Grammatically, however, the construction is dependent on *vis*: *expetere* is followed by *ut* only very rarely in Latin (Liv. 10.7.12; Quint. *Decl.* 294 (p. 167.9); Tac. *Ann.* 6.8; cf. *TLL* v.2.1697.62ff.), and never in Cicero. Pabón, reporting *invitum* for *inimicum* in *m*, adds '*fort. recte*', a surprising judgement.

90.11 crudelissimus *retorsio argumenti* again (22.6n.). Torquatus had accused Cicero of *crudelitas* (7.10n.); now Cicero suggests that Torquatus may be a man of sadistic cruelty.

videndo . . . audiendo cf. *Off.* 1.105 *hominis autem mens . . . videndique et audiendi delectatione ducitur*. I follow Tω in reading *fructum caperes maiorem*; *fructum maiorem caperes* (*E*) looks like a normalisation.

91.1 O . . . diem Cicero reverts to the *conquestio* (88.1n.), beginning the sixth commonplace specified for it (Rohde 142): *sextus, per quem praeter spem in miseriis demonstratur esse, et, cum aliquid exspectaret, non modo id non adeptus esse, sed in summas miserias incidisse* (*Inv.* 1.108). The scholia omit *et* (cf. Seyffert 6, 47).

consul . . . renuntiatus est consuls were elected by the *comitia centuriata*, meeting usually in the Campus Martius (cf. §49 *ut victi in campo in foro vinceretis*, also referring to the election of 66). A candidate was declared elected (*renuntiatus est*) as soon as he had gained the votes of a simple majority of the 193 centuries into which Roman citizens were divided. It was therefore possible for a candidate to be elected by the votes of the first 97 centuries alone; when this happened (as, it appears, it frequently did), he was said to have been elected *omnibus centuriis* (cf. Cicero's election to the praetorship: *nam cum propter dilationem comitiorum ter praetor primus centuriis cunctis renuntiatus sum* (*Man.* 2)). That Sulla should have been so elected (Halm, Reid and E. W. Gray (*Antichthon* 13 (1979) 65) are not justified in doubting Cicero on this point) heightens the pathos of his subsequent conviction; Cicero may also mean to suggest that such was the feeling for Sulla that he would have won the election even without resorting to bribery. On electoral procedure see Taylor, *RVA*; E. S. Staveley, *Greek and Roman Voting and Elections* (London 1972) 121–216.

91.2 o falsam spem cf. *Mil.* 94 *o frustra . . . mei suscepti labores, o spes fallaces, o cogitationes inanes meae!*

91.3 fortunam see 73.4n.

caecam i.e. 'short-sighted' (Halm); cf. *Inv.* 1.2; *Dom.* 60; *Pis.* 57.

praeposteram 'premature' congratulations. Reid has needless difficulty with the word.

91.5 luctum et lacrimas for the alliteration see Wölfflin 265.

91.6 designatus for 65.

pristinae dignitatis see 1.1n. The words are postponed for the sake of the rhythm.

91.7 spoliato...fortunis cf. *Quinct.* 76 *spoliatum fama fortunisque omnibus*; for the image cf. §50. Sulla has been despoiled of his *fortunae* on account of the fine he was required to pay (17.8n.); but this hardly left him poor (Gel. 12.12.2).

91.8 calamitati see 1.2n.

91.9 relictus [esset] the archetype had *relictus esset*, as if *cui* were relative. The sense is as follows (lit.): 'Was there any misfortune which seemed (at the time of his conviction in 66) to be lacking to him ..? Or (to put it another way), for what new disaster did any room (at that time) (seem) to be left? (There seemed to be no room left for further disasters. Nevertheless...)'. To give the idea of 'seeming', which is necessary to the sense, an infinitive is required. *esse* (Stephanus' MS), with, as Halm notes, *videbatur* supplied from *videretur* (cf. Stephanus 94), would give exactly the right sense. However, this entails three consecutive trochees, which would be best avoided (5.4n.). It seems simplest, therefore, to accept Clark's deletion of *esset*, which gives the required sense and the best clausula (double-trochee).

fortuna see 73.4n.

XXXIII 92.1 Sed iam...dicam the *conquestio* over, Cicero ends with a final appeal to the jury's compassion (§§92–3). To be overcome by grief was a convenient way of bringing a speech to a close: *plura ne dicam tuae me etiam lacrimae impediunt vestraeque, iudices, non solum meae* (*Planc.* 104); *me dolor debilitat intercluditque vocem* (*Rab. Post.* 48); *sed finis sit; neque enim prae lacrimis iam loqui possumus* (*Mil.* 105). Cf. *Dom.* 97, *Cael.* 60 for the technique used in mid-speech. This is an example of *reticentia* (22.10n.).

92.2 vestrae...partes 'the part is now yours to play' (Macdonald), or 'it is now your turn to act' (Lord); cf. *Balb.* 1; *Ac.* 1.43; *Div.* 1.105; *Fam.* 11.14.3. On the image see 8.4n. (with *Mur.* 6 quotation).

92.4 vos...constituti *sensus quidem multae obscuritatis est*, the scholiast justly observes. Cicero touches upon two technical disadvantages faced by the defence, (i) the haste which, without warning, the prosecution introduced into the proceedings at the beginning of the trial (*vos...consedistis*), and (ii) the method of selection which has allowed a potentially unfavourable jury to be empanelled (*ab accusatoribus delecti*). The second point is clearer than the first, so let us begin with (ii).

The usual method of empanelling jurors was known as *sortitio* (cf. *schol. Gronov.* 335 St.; Mommsen, *Strafrecht* 214–16; Greenidge 437–41). A register (*album*) of jurors was drawn up each year and divided into *decuriae*; when a case came up for trial a *decuria* was assigned to it, and from this the *iudices* for the trial were selected by lot. Both prosecution and defence enjoyed the right to reject a number of these *iudices*; after this process (*reiectio*) the number of *iudices* was filled up once again by lot from the *decuria*.

Cicero, however, talks here of the *iudices* as having been *ab accusatoribus delecti*. From this it follows that under the *lex Plautia de vi* the *iudices* were selected not by *sortitio* (in spite of the scholia) but by an alternative means, *editio* (cf. Garatoni *ad loc.*; Mommsen, *Coll.* 63–7, esp. 65 n. 17; *id.*, *Strafrecht* 216f.; Greenidge 453f.). This was the method laid down in the *lex (Acilia?) repetundarum* (123 or 122) and the *lex Licinia de sodaliciis* (55), and also proposed by Ser. Sulpicius Rufus in 63, although not adopted in the *lex Tullia de ambitu* (17.8n.); cf. *lex rep.* (*CIL* 1².583) 24, ap. A. W. Lintott, *Judicial Reform and Land Reform in the Roman Republic* (Cambridge 1992) 94; *Mur.* 47; *Planc.* 36, 41. *Editio* was a procedure by which the accuser himself nominated the *iudices*, his selection then being modified by the defendant's *reiectio*; jurors empanelled by this method were known as *editicii iudices* (cf. Serv. *E.* 3.50 *editicius autem est iudex quem una pars eligit*). The *iudices* who tried Sulla had therefore been selected by the prosecution for their likely severity (*ad spem acerbitatis*; cf. *Planc.* 41 *ista editio per se... acerba est*), and it is this factor to which Cicero draws the jury's attention.

The other disadvantage ((i) above) to which Cicero refers concerns the use made by the prosecution of the procedure of *editio*: 'you, after the *reiectio* had been interposed (sc. between the prosecution's selection of *iudices* and the opening of the trial), without our suspecting anything, at once took your seats on this case, gentlemen' (Macdonald's translation is thoroughly misleading; he seems to be under the impression, here and at §93, that it was the prosecution who exercised the *reiectio* (which he translates as 'objections')). It is difficult to identify Cicero's grievance precisely, but his words seem to indicate that, after the defence had duly made their *reiectio*, the prosecution, without giving notice of their intention (*nihil suspicantibus nobis*), caused the procedure to be accelerated in some way unfavourable to their opponents (*repentini ... consedistis*). The traditional interpretation of this passage (first outlined by Mommsen in a letter to Halm, and later repeated by Reid, Introd. §26) is that the prosecution failed to give the customary notice of the names they intended to propose, thus giving the defence no time for consideration before being required to exercise their *reiectio*. This theory seems to have been accepted by Strachan-Davidson (*Criminal Law* II.99), who asserts that the jury 'was, for some reason, very hurriedly constituted' (Macdonald even translates *repentini* as 'you were hastily empanelled'!). However, an interpretation on these lines is at variance with *reiectione interposita*: by these words (repeated at §93) Cicero clearly indicates that the prosecution's acceleration of the proceedings occurred *after* the *reiectio* ('after the *reiectio* you took your seats at once'). So a better explanation of Cicero's grievance might be that the prosecution, without warning, began their accusation the moment the *reiectio* had been completed, without, say, waiting until the following day. If this conjecture is correct, the prosecution's motive may have been to deprive Sulla of the opportunity for bribery in the interval between the *reiectio* and the opening of the trial.

These, then, are the two disadvantages to which Cicero refers. The second of these ((ii) above), that the prescribed procedure was one which resulted in a jury biased in favour of the prosecution, was a delicate point to raise, and might easily have caused great offence to the jury at such a critical point. Cicero overcomes this difficulty by his reference to *fortuna* (73.4n.). Mommsen (*Strafrecht* 215 n. 5) characteristically sees this as evidence for an otherwise unattested system of selecting *iudices* by a combination of *editio* and *sortitio*, an unnecessary hypothesis which overlooks the tact which Cicero is called upon to display. The point, however, is well understood by Strachan-Davidson (*op. cit.*). In spite of a procedure (*editio*) weighted in the prosecution's favour, *fortuna*, Cicero argues, has nevertheless appointed *iudices* favourable to the defence – either because of the ignorance or incompetence of the prosecution in making their selection (cf. *Planc.* 41 *tu ita errasti ut eos ederes imprudens, ut nos invito te tamen ad iudices non ad carnifices veniremus*), or alternatively because of a lack of jurors available to the prosecution. Strachan-Davidson continues, 'Cicero wishes to complain of the method while at the same time congratulating himself... on "the men whom I see before me in the jury-box"; *fortuna* serves him conveniently to bridge over the inconsistency between the two insinuations'. One could add that it may also have been flattering for the jury to be made to feel in some way associated with the proverbial luck of the Cornelii Sullae.

Two minor textual points should be mentioned. The archetype read *ex reiectione*, but the preposition is rightly omitted by the scholia. Secondly, *E* gives *destituti* for *constituti*, less appropriately (Seyffert 13; *contra*, Zinzerling 123f.); *destituti* may have been influenced by *destitutus sit* at §90.

92.7 ut ego looking forward to *sic vos* below (the sentence is analysed by Nägelsbach 635). In what remains of the speech Cicero points out to the jury that their position is exactly the same as his own (cf. §93 *quoniam in re publica coniuncti sumus*). The action he took against the *improbi* (1.12n.) has made him appear *crudelis* (7.10n.) in the eyes of the Roman people, and the recent Catilinarian trials, all of which ended in convictions (71.4n.), have likewise given the jury a reputation for cruelty. It is therefore in the interest of both that Sulla be acquitted.

92.9 quae...suscepi cf. §5 *qui in hoc genere quaestionis defenderim neminem*. For the omission of *eam* see K.-S.ii.309–11; H.-Sz.564f.

92.11 **audacissimos** see 16.4n.

93.1 **cum...tum** greater emphasis is placed on the second reason, as would be expected in the *cum...tum* correlation (1.4n.).

93.2 **non esse...convenerit** lit., 'that you are not the men whom before all others it was advantageous (that the prosecution) should have come upon after the *reiectio*' (*accusatoribus* has to be understood after *convenerit*). Cicero refers again to disadvantage (ii) discussed at 92.4n. As at §92, *interposita reiectione* means simply 'after the *reiectio*'. The prosecution selected their jurors *ad spem acerbitatis* (§92), but 'after the *reiectio*' they were left with a different (reduced) body of men. Cicero now says, 'show by your votes that the *reiectio* has prevented the prosecution from obtaining the pitiless jury which they hoped they had managed to secure'.

93.5 **quoniam...coniuncti sumus** Cicero appeals explicitly to political considerations which in a modern court would be regarded as irrelevant. He reminds the jury of where, as *boni*, their duty lies (1.10n.).

93.6 **mansuetudine...vestra** for the alliteration see Wölfflin 266. The conjecture *nostra* (*Gdk*) for *vestra* is attractive, in view of the first-person emphasis in *ut communi studio...a nobis...repellamus. nostra*, however, could seem arrogant, implying that Sulla's acquittal would be due as much to Cicero's defence as to the jury's verdict, and this is not the moment for such self-praise. *vestra* is the safer choice: it gives exactly the right sort of compliment.

93.7 **famam repellamus** cretic-spondee. For analyses of the clausulae found at the ends of Cicero's speeches see Zielinski, *Constr. Rhyth.* 50f.; Laurand 180–2.

APPENDIX I

THE RELATIONSHIP OF P. SULLA TO L. SULLA

The relationship of Cicero's client to L. Sulla the dictator has been a subject of confusion for the last two centuries. Not that there is any confusion in the ancient sources. At *Off.* 2.29 (quoted on p. 1) Cicero describes P. Sulla as the dictator's *propinquus*. More specifically, Dio refers to him as the dictator's nephew: Πούπλιός τε γὰρ Παῖτος καὶ Κορνήλιος Σύλλας, ἀδελφιδοῦς ἐκείνου τοῦ πάνυ Σύλλου, ὕπατοί τε ἀποδειχθέντες καὶ δεκασμοῦ ἀλόντες ἐπεβούλευσαν τοὺς κατηγορήσαντάς σφων Κότταν τε καὶ Τορκουᾶτον Λουκίους...ἀποκτεῖναι (36.44.3). It is the purpose of this note to dispel the doubt surrounding the ancient evidence by briefly tracing the history of scholarly opinion on the question.

The doubt arises from the existence of a second P. Sulla mentioned together with his brother Ser. Sulla at §6 (6.6n.) and at Sal. *Cat.* 17.3 (*P. et Ser. Sullae Ser. filii*). This second P. Sulla was a senator who joined Catiline's conspiracy and was otherwise of no importance; he found no one to defend him when he was brought to trial in 62. In 1777 Garatoni, commenting on *Sul.* 6, raised the possibility that Dio may have confused the identities of the two P. Sullae. This would make Cicero's client a *propinquus* but not a nephew of the dictator, while the lesser-known P. Sulla and his brother would instead become the dictator's nephews. Garatoni's reasons for suspecting Dio to be guilty of error were entirely frivolous: 'Tamen vereor, ne sit error ex praenomine Dioni subortus. Nam Cicero non modo infra c. 26. L. Sullam Publii patruum non appellavit ...; verum etiam II. de Offic. 8. de hoc Publio loquens, *Dictatore*, ait, *propinquo suo*, ubi certe *patruo suo*, si verus esset Dion, videtur fuisse dicturus. Sic itaque P. & Serv. fratres conjurati patruum Dictatorem habuissent, noster autem Publius *propinquus* tantum Dictatoris fuisset'. The idea was taken up, however, by J. C. Orelli and J. G. Baiter (*Onomasticon Tullianum* II (Zurich 1838) 198) and was put forward, without any attribution, by F. Münzer in his *RE* article on the lesser-known P. Sulla (IV.1518.56ff.). Only in Drumann-Groebe were the sources correctly evaluated (II.436f. ('Dass aber Cicero jenen seinen "Verwandten",

320

nicht seinen "Oheim" nennt, kann nicht befremden, da er nur sagen will, Publius habe die Verwandtschaft benutzt', 437), 562f.). The authority of Münzer as the apparent originator of the theory has led most historians to play safe by referring to Cicero's client simply as the dictator's 'relative', as if Dio's testimony were genuinely in doubt. The commentators after Garatoni have each repeated the view of their predecessor (see 20.4n. for a similar case). Macdonald, unaware of the difficulties involved, even goes so far as to accept Dio by making our Sulla a nephew of the dictator (302), while simultaneously rejecting him by taking P. and Ser. Sulla to be nephews as well (305). On the other hand, H. C. Gotoff, commenting on a different speech (on *Marc.* 1), affirms that Cicero's client was the dictator's son.

In historical studies the evidence of the sources ought to be accepted unless there is a reason for rejecting it (this is not of course the same as maintaining that the sources should be believed unless they can be disproved). In this instance, despite Garatoni, the evidence of Dio is in no way contradicted by that of Cicero. Moreover, L. E. Reams in a recent examination of Münzer's view (*CJ* 82 (1986–7) 301–5: he is unaware of its earlier history) has demonstrated that there are no other, extraneous, grounds for questioning Dio's testimony. It should therefore be accepted as fact that the P. Sulla defended by Cicero was the nephew of the dictator.

APPENDIX 2

CODICVM *P* ET *K* LECTIONES AB APPARATV CRITICO EXCLVSAE

1 5 odio *om. K*   8 exsatiare β   14–15 conservatam misericordem ac mitem β   **2** 4 defensionis meae *K*   5 mei officii *K*   7–8 est facultas β   10 huius] eius β   11 ac *om. K*   12 P.] p. mei β   **3** 10 defendendus] defendendus sum quam illius (illius *om. P*) β   **4** 3 quod] quos *K*   antea fuisset] prius erat β   4 per] est per *P*   5 hoc] hic *K*   virtute auctoritate β   7 hortensio ad causam β   8 etiam illud β   9 putes β   **5** 1 an] ac β   2 atque lumina β   me *om. K*   4 magnis *om. K*   5 ac periculis β   6 accusas β   id] hoc *P*: hic *K*   **6** 8 affuitur (*sic*) *K*   quia] quis β   9 innocentes *P*   10 non *om.* β   11 contagio] contagio est β   **7** 1 nonne] num β   1–2 num veteres β   4 plurimique *P*   5 non occultari *bis K*   **8** 4 ipsam *om.* β   7 haec *om. K*   7–8 lenitatem et misericordiam β   **9** 1 quare *om. K*   5 enim *om. P*   7 causa illa β   11 ego *om.* β   **10** 3 ac *om. K*   6 retinendo *K*   8 laesam *K*   8–9 studium *om.* β   **11** 2 consulibus] consulibus si *K*   patre tuo consule *om.* β   3 esse facta *P*   4–5 viri atque optimi *om. K*   6 tecus *K*   6–7 expertem temporum illorum β   8 ad *om.* β   **12** 4 et dignitatem *P*   4–5 in re publica β   6 tum criminibus β   praecipue β   11 tamen] tum *K*   12 igitur] ergo *P*: *om. K*   13 ad nos β   14 sed vix] sinit *K*   **13** 6 coniurationis *bis K*   7 autem consulatus β   **14** 7 nuntius *om. K*   13 imitari *P*   **15** 3 noluit *K*   id *om.* β   6 quaesivit β   ita *om.* β   7 verum] sed β   8 infestis *K*   9 atque *om.* β   10 ex] e β   **16** 2 in *om. K*   3 quae tanta] quanta β   inter se *om.* β   5 cum autronio non β   6 admisit] non admisit β   7 non modo cum eisdem illis β   **17** 2 nuntii ac litterae β   3 simulavit β   5 relictus intus] relictis expectatus intus β   7 ad sanitatem numquam β   8 ita *om.* β   omni eo tempore β   12 tantam] hanc tantam *K*   **18** 11 oblivisceret *K*   **19** 1–2 cum vestrorum] tum vestrorum *P*   2 cum] tum *P*   cum] tum *P*   3 cum] tum *P*   cum] tum *P*   4 mentem] mentem discrimen β   5 universumque] immensumque β   9 illius] eius β   10 ac filio β   **20**

322

2 neque ego *P*   4 hominis] et hominis β   8 et] id est β   **21** 1
hic] hinc β   ille iudices se β   7 regnare] me regnare β   9 iri
om. β   **22** 1 suscepisses β   mihi] hic β   2 profulgisset *K*   3
hominem *om.* β   4 meo] in eo *K*   9 noluisti β   **23** 8 et quidem
β   9 tu *om.* β   10–11 civium partem β   11 conveniret] perti-
neret β   13 si] et si β   15 abs] ab *K*   **24** 1 peregrinos *P*   2
quarum *K*   3 quam tibi] quanti β   5 de omni honore et dignitate
β   8 tibi] vel β   9 se *om. P*   **25** 2 vos] nos *K*   2–3 oportet
β   4 a materno genere ipse *P*   8 dixeris] dixit is *P*   8–9 ne
derideare] nerideare *K*   9 tibi regnum β   10 serviatur *P*: serviar *ex*
servia..r *ut vid. K*   13 credere *P*   17 profer β   **26** 7 quid] quod
β   10 me *om.* β   12 vindicat] vendicatur β   15 quidquam
relinquatur *P*   16 qui *om. P*   16–17 invenire β   **27** 2 sunt β
conatis *K*   4 meae *om.* β   7 omnes β   **28** 7 vero *om.* β   8 sum
nescio *K*   **29** 1 illis meis praesidiis forte invides] me illis praesidiis
meis fortem vides β   3 suam] meam *K*   4 te *om.* β   mihi] modo
β   uni] viri *P*   **31** 3 nobis *K*   circa β   5 dicebat β   qui-
bus] de quibus β   vindicabat β   7 quaeque] quaecumque β   8
postularet β   9 videri] videro *K*: *om. P*   9–10 mortem poenamque
β   10 is] id *K*   **32** 1 tamen] tum *K*   3 qui] sed qui β   roma-
nae] romam *K*   5 tu horum] tuorum β   te] rem β   8 se] se ipsum β   9 ac nominis] et nominis auctorem β   **33** 11 capitis mei
K   14 internicione] interventione β   **34** 8 etiam *om.* β   13–14
auctoritate consilio β   **35** 4 te a se et] a te se et *P*: a te et se *K*   5
patiemur β   6 vos] vobis β   7 multa] stulta β   illo] ipso *P*   8
solum sillam β   10 esset in me *P*   13 a me orationem a me
K   **36** 1 sullam esse] est sillam *P*: esse sillam *K*   7 ac] ac qui β   9
responderet β   **37** 5 nobilita *K*   **38** 1 iam] at *K*   4 quaerendum
esse a cassio β   esset] eorum β   4–5 ne cum] necessarium
β   7–8 ne si argueret quidem] quidem si argueret β   **39** 3 num
arguatur] non arguatur β   etenim] et β   4 an] autem β   8 cassio β   10 in eo numero esse β   11–12 atque hoc] hic *K*   12
scierit] fuerit *K*   17 cassius sullam] cassium nec sillam β   **40** 2 aliter me β   3 nobis *K*   4 nostra *K*   10 insolentiae β   **41** 1 hoc
ego β   nisi] ut nisi β   4 id me multum] opimo multum me *P*:
opimo me multum *K*   **42** 4 facile β   cosconium] comum β   7–
8 putet aut ingenium] aut ingenium putet β   8 deinde] demum
K   9 ita *om.* β   15 nolui *K*   **43** 4 pervenerit] perscriptum
K   6 tantum *om.* β   8 umquam] aut β   9 ex] a β   12 putar-
etur] existimaretur β   **44** 2 iudicatus *K*   3 eius *om. K*   frequens
om. β   memoria recens β   4 iudicium *K*   6 non] et non
β   9–10 cum indicio] in indicio β   13 convictum tuo iudicio

β   **45** 1 mihi] nihil mihi β   4 ego denique *P*   crudeles β   6
iam] tam β   **46** 1–2 nonnumquam *om.* β   2 incitatum *post* tuam
β   ulciscendum β   7 me umquam β   8 sed] si *K*   **47** 1–2
dicendi consuetudinem β   3–4 arbitrari] putare β   6 tuae iniuriae
β   8 quo si *K*   **48** 14 inimicitiarum] inimicitiae tuae β   **49** 3
vir] nisi *P*: ñ *K*   4 et defenderent] defenderent *P*   hanc] enim
β   5 traditam esse β   7 tum] cum β   10 tum] cum ceteri tum
β   vos] nos β   12 nobis *K*   14 cuiusque faciebant] quique fave-
bant β   **50** 3 quid est quod iam ab hoc] quid quidem ab hoc iam *P*:
quod quidam ab hoc iam *K*   5 quem] quem ipse β   6 et reprendis]
reprehendis β   7 defenderim β   tibi non modo β   9 tibi] et tibi
β   **51** 3 quod praemi] quidquid praemi β   9 tum] tamen *P*   11
iudices tum β . suspicabimini *P*   12 firmo praesidio β   **52** 2 si
tum] se cum β   6 ipse *om.* β   7 iudicium adumbratum β   9
postremum β   15 confiteatur β   sibi *om.* β   17 et intromissus
β   meo] in eo *K*   **53** 4–5 praescriberet *P*   6 num romae] romae
β   longius β   7 conferebat β   10 enim *om. K*   ea *om.*
β   **54** 1 ergo] igitur *P*   3–4 prorsus] pro suis β   6 praebere]
praeparare β   7–8 aequorum] quorum β   8 exspectatione *K*   9
cum] tum β   10 dandi] audi *K*   propinquaret *K*   **55** 2 et *om.*
β   3 p. sillam β   4 et q. pompeium β   et c. nemmium (*sic*)
P   4–5 res gesta est tota β   5 familiae] familiae fausti β   iam si
om. β   6 est *om.* β   7–8 ad feras prospiciendas β   **56** 3 profectus
est l. iulio et c. figulo consulibus β   5 in *om.* β   11 aes] et
K   **57** 2 romae *om.* β   12 et *om. K*   **58** 3 ac] aut ea β   6 is]
suam β   8 aes] ex *K*   9 studio] gratia β   11 remissit *P*: remisit
K   11–12 quidquam β   **60** 1 esse *om. P*   2 ut *om. P*   4 tibi
pompeiani coniurasse] in pompeianum crimen coniurasse *P*: in pompeianum crimen *K*   videmur β   6 ac] atque *P*   10 res cognita]
recognita β   12–13 magis a silla β   13 sese] se *P*   **61** 2 homi-
num] horum non β   **62** 7 enim et] enim *P*   8 hoc in loco in *P*: hic
in loco *K*   **63** 2 qua re] qua β   5 in iudicatis β   12 iudicii
β   **64** 8 si] sed β   9 postulat] postulat si β   **65** 1 lex ante paucos
dies fuit proposita β   5 nolle illam rogationem de se fieri β   8 fore
om. β   obstitit β   10 honore β   **66** 1 in] etiam β   ne] ne
quid *P*: nequit *K*   2 quid ageretur] ageretur egit β   10 allevamento
atque remedio β   **68** 5 manum et operas β   10 persona sillae
β   **69** 5 de me aliquid] et de me β   6 dicere] aliquid dicere
β   vos] nos *K*   11 arguitur] accusatur β   12 nostrum quisquam
β   13 cuiquam β   vita repente *P*   **71** 6 maxime finitimum
β   huic β   9 improbissimis uti β   verum] quem β   10 quem
om. β   15 mores eum β   **72** 2 nobis β   10 nostri et] nostri

β   11 hic se *P*   12 neque enim] nisi quia β   14 civis] cui vis
β   **73** 2 commemorem *om.* β   2–3 dignitatem liberalitatem] liberalitatem dignitatem me commemorante recordemini β   5 compar-
eat *K*   7 quae] quaeque β   13 hic iudicatus est β   **74** 1–2
afflictum demissumque β   6 nostris β   non retineretur β   7
paene exilio β   **75** 9–10 incredibilis furor ac singularis fuit β   **76** 4
unus tam] nec unus β   patriae hostis β   5 formas β   7 causa
hac *K*   **77** 1 nunc *om.* β   2 qui cum] cum qui cum *K*   3 ex hoc]
et ex hoc β   4 in impiorum] impiorum *K*   5 erat *K*   6 in loco] in
loco in *K*   7 ad *om. K*   8–9 ac dimicatione] ad mutationem
β   **78** 1 servorum] severiores β   4 animi tum] animum β   5 ut
om. β   6 relinquitur β   9 nobis β   10 ea *om.* β   **79** 2 nihil
audisse nihil vidisse β   3 tamen] tum *K*   4 cum *om.* β   7 pon-
deretis β   7–8 repentinisque periculis et disquisitionibus β   8 esse
testem] testem ei esse sinatis β   9 nolite *bis* β   **80** 1 haec] haec
nostra β   2 a me *om. K*   3 qui a] quia β   5 hunc tandem] haec
inquam β   7 non *om.* β   tacemus] de nobis tacemus β   **81** 3–4
laudaverunt β   10 illam primam β   13 ignorasset] non nosset
β   14 si nulla res publica valuit β   16 tamen] tum *K*   19 quam
ob rem] quare β   adfuerunt] affuerunt et β   **82** 3 operis β   13–
14 laus est β   15 amores *K*   16 praescripti β   **83** 3 vobis] sum
β   3–4 adeo … adeo] a deo…a deo *K*   4 a me *om. P*   6
cupiam] culpam *P*: culpiam *K*   7 retruderim *P*   8 defendam
β   10 et periculis] periculis β   16 memoria *om.* β   inventae] in
mente β   **84** 2 quia *om. K*   3–4 in quo *om. K*   4 etiam *om.*
β   **85** 4 decrevit β   7 assumo β   11 quod hoc *K*   11–12 in-
dicio] iudicio β   **86** 2 publicae] publicae romam qui *K*   **87** 2 esse
om. β   5 quam qui] tam β   6 nisi coactus] incoactus β   7 adductus β   10 ut ad] ut *K*   11–12 ducor β   **88** 2 nunc *om.* β   4
nomini] numero β   12–13 tanti generis (*sic*) *post* familia β   **89** 2
aliquando si non] aliquem sine *P*: aliquem sum *K*   11 dignitate] virtute et dignitate *K*   12 repetit] reposcit β   quod] sed quod β   reliquiis β   13–14 suam calamitatem liceat] calamitatem suam possit
β   14 iudices vos β   14–15 obtestor *P*   **90** 7 vis] eius β   8–9
dolore et cruciatu *P*: dolore atque cruciatu *K*   11 esset *K*   **91** 1
omnibus] ab omnibus β   2–3 o volucrem] volucrem *P*   4 ex laetitia *post* voluptate β   6 fuisset] esset β   **92** 2 miseriis β   3–4 tu-
tam β   5 in nos] et vos *P*   7 ego ut β   8 existimaret] sentiret
β   10 sic vos] sicco β   11–12 lenitate ac misericordia mitigate]
levitate mea ac benignitate β   **93** 1 cum] autem β   6 con-
iunctissimi β   misericordia] mea et β   7 vobis *P*.

INDEX

Reference is made to sections (§§) of the Latin text and to pages of the rest of the book. Latin authors and Roman emperors appear under their familiar modern names; other Romans are listed by *gentilicium*.

INDEX

329

INDEX